HISTORY
OF
GALWAY RACES

HISTORY
OF
GALWAY RACES

FRANCIS P.M. HYLAND

Robert Hale · London

ISBN 978 0 7090 8215 6

Robert Hale Limited
Clerkenwell House
Clerkenwell Green
London EC1R 0HT

A catalogue record for this book is available from the British Library

2 4 6 8 10 9 7 5 3 1

Printed in Singapore by
Kyodo Printing Co (S'pore) Pte Ltd

CONTENTS

Acknowledgements

Grateful appreciate is expressed to Ray Dooley, Malachy Concannon and John Maloney for the help in providing and locating material for this book.

List of Illustrations

Illustration Credits

Galway Race Committee/Denis F. Moriarty: pages 12, 123, 175, 228, 234, 305, 333. Richard Brabazon Collection: pages 88, 238, 374. Healy Racing Photos: all other pictures.

Introduction

The Galway Racing Festival is officially recognized as the fourth largest race meeting in the world, according to figures released by the International Federation of Horseracing Authorities at its annual meeting in Paris, during the Prix de l'Arc de Triomphe weekend in October 2006. The Federation listed the official attendances at all the big race meetings throughout the world and the Galway Festival, in fourth position, is the only Irish meeting in the top ten. The top ten race meetings (with attendances) are:

 1: Melbourne Cup Carnival 404,500
 2: Royal Ascot 312,000
 3: Cheltenham Festival 312,000
 4: Galway 210,000
 5: Kentucky Derby 156,400
 6: Japan Cup 151,896
 7: Aintree Grand National 145,000
 8: Japanese Cup 140,100
 9: Epsom Derby 140,000
10: Japanese St Leger 136,700

This is the incredible story of a small provincial racecourse at Ballybrit, about 3 miles from the centre of the city, which has grown from humble origins to earn the right to be listed among the elite racecourses of the world. Beginning as a two-day meeting, Galway now extends to seven days, and its success has been achieved without the aid of group races on the flat or championship jumping events. Despite the lack of internationally renowned, richly endowed races, Galway has prospered by offering the public good, competitive horse racing, even if the prize money on offer is below that available at the other events that are in the top ten. Galway's traditional feature races, the Galway Plate and the Galway Hurdle, are handicaps

The modern Galway betting ring with the electronic boards, computerized ticket-machines and some parasols

and are barely known outside the British Isles, but it is the atmosphere of the occasion rather than internationally known races that makes the Galway Races special, and it fully deserves its place among the best attended courses in the world of horse racing. Galway's achievement is more remarkable bearing in mind Ireland's small population in comparison to Australia, Britain, the United States and Japan.

One of the reasons behind its continuing success is its policy of not segregating racegoers in the 'upstairs, downstairs' manner all too often seen on racecourses. At Galway ordinary people can mix freely with politicians and magnates, which makes going racing an uplifting experience. It is one of the reasons why crowds continue to flock to the meeting despite the strain put on the amenities by the sheer numbers. Another reason behind Galway's success is its management. The Galway Race Committee is dedicated to the Galway Races, devoting their time and effort without receiving payment of any kind, and maintains a policy of ensuring that the Galway Races are for all the people of Galway. That has always been the motive behind the races; all the profits are reinvested into the racecourse, enabling the facilities and the track itself to be ungraded and kept to the highest standards. Uppermost in the minds of the executive is to upgrade the facilities to cater for ever-increasing numbers, while keeping the traditional intimacy of Ballybrit. Galway produces competitive racing that the ordinary racegoer wants to see, owners love to win races there in front of all their friends, trainers need to have winners there to remind prospective owners of their presence, and it is now the biggest occasion in Irish racing, greater even than Irish Derby Day at the Curragh or the Punchestown Festival.

David Ashforth, the *Racing Post* journalist, has been touring all the racecourses in the British Isles, awarding marks out of five under ten different headings. On the betting issue, where he is not comparing like with like, Irish racecourses are at a disadvantage vis-à-vis the British courses, but in 2006 Galway received a respectable thirty-six points, failing on betting, getting there and toilets. As far as betting is concerned Ashforth's formula for judging value is flawed in an Irish context, where there is a betting shop, a large tote operation and a betting ring offering betting on a win, each way, without the favourite, without the favourite and the second favourite, without three and without four of the runners. Unlike in the British betting rings, each way is freely available, even in races where the bookmaker does not have a place margin, and fractions are available to all on request, not just to the trade. On public conveniences, particularly for ladies, he has a point, at least for the moment, but many more were available from 2007. The lavatory facilites have struggled to cope with the sudden increase in the numbers of women going racing and the more social nature of racegoing in general. The only way to make getting there easier is for fewer people to want to 'get there' and

The betting ring in 2004 looking towards the parade ring. The pagoda-type structure houses televisions showing pictures of the 'home' races plus the S.I.S. pictures of the 'away' meetings

nobody really wants that! As Ashforth puts it, the 'happy throng can't be wrong', but much of his complaint is that Galway is a racemeeting swamped by people. Come hell or high water, Galway is the place where people want to be during the last week of July, and long may that continue!

The Background

Galway

Galway, the principal town of the province of Connaught is situated near the north-east corner of Galway Bay, at the mouth of the short Galway River. The town, 132 miles west of Dublin and 64 miles north-west of Limerick, is a small seaport and an increasingly important manufacturing centre. A cathedral town, Galway is the gateway to Connemara and features the lovely seaside resort of Salthill and the popular holiday boating and fishing lake, Lough Corrib. The origins of the town lie in the seizure by Richard de Burgo of lands owned by the O'Flaherty and O'Halloran clans, the building of a castle beside the river to protect the conquest and the growth of a settlement around that castle in the late

Ballybrit Castle dates from the sixteenth century, has four floors and is 44½ feet high. It is a listed building and is maintained by the Galway Race Committee

thirteenth century. Over a hundred years later, in 1396, the English King Richard II granted Galway a charter, which freed it from the clutches of the de Burgo family, who were now known as Burke. Thereafter Galway town became a small English-speaking enclave in an Irish-speaking county.

The town prospered from its trade with Europe and effectively became a small, isolated city-state, run by the merchants. The ruling oligarchy consisted of fourteen families, who became known as the Tribes of Galway. Most were either of English or Norman extraction, and they bore the family names of Athy, Blake, Bodkin, Browne, Darcy, Deane, Font, French, Joyce, Kirwan, Lynch, Martin, Morris and Skerret. All had the gift of being able to make money. They were both staunch Catholics and loyal supporters of the English Crown. Their loyalty to the King endured despite the upheaval caused by the Reformation and the subsequent persecution of Catholics, but by 1642 they had had enough. Unfortunately their change of allegiance exposed Galway to the rampage of Oliver Cromwell. Under his direction, Sir Charles Coote laid siege to the town, enforcing a land and sea blockade for nine months before the town finally surrendered on 5 April 1652.

For many years the coat of arms of the town was prominently displayed on the front of the Galway racecard. It featured a wooden boat on a sea, with one mast and a big shield in the middle. The picture was surrounded by a circular inscription 'Inconaicia: de s:comvnitatis:wille:de:galve'. The coat of arms was recorded by Christopher Ussher and granted to the town in the last quarter of the sixteenth century. After the Second World War a simpler version, without the inscription, retained its place on the card, but in 1956 it was dropped altogether, never to return – not even on the centenary racecard of 1969.

Landlords and the Land Struggle

Flat racing was dominated by the nobility, the landlords and the wealthy professional and merchant class, virtually to the exclusion of ordinary people; it was the private pursuit of the privileged few. That changed, with the social changes that came about in the nineteenth century, with the invention of the train and the opening up of hunting to ordinary people. By ordinary people I mean Catholics, who were emancipated in 1829 to involve themselves in a society controlled by Protestants. The decline of the landlord class enabled Catholics to join hunts, which brought them into steeplechasing and ultimately into flat racing. The bitter battle between landlords and their tenants still simmered, but it only occasionally affected hunting and racing. Flat racing was very much under the control of the Turf Club, whose west of Ireland members included the Blakes, the Moores and the St Georges, all landlords, as was the Marquis of Drogheda, the supremo of the Club for many years. Another flat-racing man was Captain Boycott, whose horse Butte des Morts, trained by James Dunne, won on successive days at Galway in 1883. 'Sent to Coventry' by his tenants, he achieved notoriety, and his name became a new word in the English language. Lord Drogheda too ran into trouble with his disgrunted tenants, who 'boycotted' his stallion Philammon.

Christopher St George of Tyrone House, Oranmore, Co. Galway, was a particularly unpopular landlord, who was accused of evicting starving tenants at the height of the famine in the 1840s. The family are believed to descend from Baldwin St George, one of the companions of William the Conqueror, and settled in Ireland in the seventeenth century. Christopher St George was born in 1810 and was a significant owner of racehorses, notably Solon and Tom King. He also owned the Rathbride Stud on the Curragh. The leading owner in Ireland in 1865, he had been a member of the Turf Club since 1836 and twice served as the Senior Steward. A Conservative Member of Parliament for Galway from 1847 to 1852, he owned 23,989 acres of land, but his social standing was damaged by the accusations about his conduct towards his tenants. Brazenly denying any wrongdoing in the House of Commons, he organized a campaign to refute the allegations and to divert any criticism of him. The campaign was so successful that he came to be regarded, among his own class at least, as a resident and active landlord, even if his tenants did not agree. He died in 1877.

Christopher St George's mansion, Tyrone House, was an imposing structure built in 1779 on the top of a hill. It was was a remarkable sight from a distance because it was the only thing visible, with not a tree, a bush or a shed in sight. It is now in ruins, having been burnt down by the IRA in 1920. The story of its burning illustrates the local hatred of the St Georges, because the family had been gone from the area fifteen years, having abandoned the big house in 1905. Clearing out most of their possessions and boarding up the house, they left an old caretaker in charge. When the IRA band arrived that night they found the old caretaker in bed, infirm and incapable of rising, so they carried him, bed and all, downstairs and deposited him safely outside before torching the place. There was no point in burning the house down but it was a symbolic act and a popular one!

According to the 1841 Irish census, 7 per cent of land holdings were over 30 acres and 45 per cent less than 5 acres, but in the province of Connaught 64 per cent were smaller than 5 acres. However, landless labourers and the smallholders suffered the brunt of the potato famine of 1847, dying in their thousands from starvation and disease or fleeing their country to escape. After the famine the picture had changed dramatically; the smallholders were wiped out to such an extent that when it was over only 15 per cent of holdings were smaller than 5 acres! Nevertheless many of the Irish tenant farmers were trying to exist on holdings that were too small to provide an adequate living. They were protected somewhat by the old feudal system, which was defended by Sir Robert Peel's Tory government. Landlords were also encountering financial problems; many were living beyond their means, and in order to maintain their standard of living, including servants and houses in London, they put up rents to a level their tenants simply could not afford to pay.

The defeat of the Tories in the 1846 general election brought the Whigs (Liberals) to power, with Lord John Russell as Prime Minister. The Whig policy was that land should be brought under free-trade principles and in 1848 passed the Encumbered Estates Act, which made land easier to sell. The new Act did not work out as they had expected, however, because many of the traditional landlords felt that it was the beginning of the end of them and sold out. Unfortunately, most of the buyers were speculators, who lacked the traditional paternalism of the landlord class, and were absentees who continued to live in England. Their only interest was to extract as much income from rents on their land as they could and, being resident elsewhere, employed a steward to collect the money due. An employee with no discretion at all, the steward demanded that tenants pay up or face immediate eviction, which meant leaving the property, without any compensation for improvements that may have been done during their tenure. Evicted families were left penniless on the side of the road. These strong-arm tactics left the impoverished tenants bitter and led to a movement to secure tenants' rights.

A campaign was started by Gavin Duffy to demand the 'three Fs' – fixity of tenure, fair rent and freedom to sell one's holding – and he travelled the country trying to rally support. Matters became worse when, in 1860, Michael Deasy, the Attorney General for Ireland, introduced an Act proclaiming that land was based on contract, which was seen by the tenant farmers as a device to expel them from their holdings when their tenancy was up.

In 1879 Michael Davitt founded the Land League, appointing Charles Stuart Parnell as its President, and within two years he persuaded the Government led by William Gladstone to grant tenants the three Fs, creating a system of dual ownership of the land, with special courts fixing rents for fifteen years. Although this measure reduced rents by 15 per cent and met the tenants' demands, the Land League did not call off its agitation; its new aim was full ownership of the land. The so-called Land War inspired the killing of a few landlords and many more of their agents, creating an atmosphere of fear and uncertainty. Fearing an attack on their homes, landlords lived with loaded guns at the ready just in case; the women, however, were adamant that it was the arsenal itself that was the greatest danger to landlords and their families, not their Irish tenants. On several recorded occasions one of these weapons was discharged accidently, and there were many stories of bullets missing people by inches.

During this time Irish land had no value as collateral, so landlords were unable to raise capital and many became convinced that their days were numbered. The Land War finally came to an end with the Kilmainham Treaty, which released Davitt and Parnell from Kilmainham gaol and gave the traditional landlords an opportunity to sell out. The exit of the traditional landlord created a new class of Catholic Irish farmer, who had access to horses, fuelling the popularity of hunting and horse racing in Ireland.

Hunting in County Galway

Two hundred and fifty years ago the vast majority of the Irish people were miserably poor and could not afford to own a horse. Furthermore, those who could afford to do so were prohibited by the penal law from owning one worth more than £5, which meant that a Protestant was entitled to forcibly purchase any horse owned by a Catholic for that amount. Consequently, much of the Irish population was deprived of an important possession, because horse ownership brought access to both transport and relaxation. Unable to own a decent horse, the ordinary Irish people were virtually excluded from sports such as racing and hunting, so these sports were dominated by the nobility and gentry and their friends, many of whom were landlords.

The landlords were living beyond their means, enjoying the luxury of private packs of hounds, private stables full of horses, fully staffed private hunting lodges and of course residences in London. Faced with the realization that their tenants simply could not afford to pay higher rents, most were forced to prune their expenses. The passage of time had relaxed the strict enforcement of the Penal Law, horse ownership among the Irish was increasing and a new business class began to emerge, one that could afford to buy and to keep horses. One by one the private packs of hounds went public, seeking funds by broadening the membership, and many hunts were prepared to take on Catholic members. With hunting opening up to a new class of people, ordinary Irishmen acquired a taste for the thrill of the chase and ultimately this gave them an entrée to the glamorous world of horse racing – the Sport of Kings!

In the beginning all the early provincial racecourses in Ireland were run by the local hunt – Fairyhouse and Punchestown are examples – and Galway was no exception. Co. Galway is unique among Irish counties because on entering its confines it is obvious where you are – in stone-wall country. The fields are partitioned by stone-walls, the grey stones piled high and loosely without concrete, stretching for miles and strikingly similar throughout. First impressions might indicate that this type of country would not be suitable for hunting, but the opposite is true – Galway is superb hunting territory. Wide open and flat, with little or no shelter from the storms coming in from the Atlantic, growth is deterred, and overgrown ditches do not exist, offering clear runs and consistent fences, free from wire and briar. The wide, uniform stone-walls enable those following a hunt to ride and jump their horses up to thirty abreast, keeping all the followers close to the hounds throughout the chase. Animal lovers may wince at the thought of a horse jumping a stone-wall but Galway's are perfect because if a horse hits one of them it gives way and the stones tumble to the ground behind the horse, causing no injury to its legs.

Lough Corrib divides Co. Galway into east and west. The east stretches to Lough Derg and south to the border with Co. Clare and is bank and stone-wall country, while the west is desolate, mountainous and poorly inhabited. To the north lies Connemara, with the Twelve Pins mountain range on the horizon, a land of gorse and hazel scrub and beautiful, wild scenery. In 1869 the largest town was Galway, with a population of almost 20,000 souls, next came Tuam (4,500), Ballinasloe and Loughrea (3,500) and Gort (2,000). Athenry is the most central town in the county and it was near here that Galway's most famous hunting family, the Persses, lived at Moyode Castle, Craughwell.

Mr Persse of Moyode kept a private pack of hounds. He was famous throughout the land for his opulence; no expense was spared and his hunt servants were dressed in orange plush uniforms. He hunted deer, fox and hares all over the county, and paid top prices for the best hounds; his pleasure cost a lot of money. At first he could well afford this grandeur because he was the local distiller and Persse's Whiskey was a popular and profitable product. However, in time even he found the cost of keeping a large private pack of hounds prohibitive so in 1803 he economized. Dividing his hounds into two packs, he gave one to his nephew Parsons Persse, who established the Castleboy

Hunt, while he hunted the Athenry district with the other. Around 1840 John Dennis, known to all and sundry as 'Black Jack', founded the Galway Hounds but after a dozen years or so of independence it merged, in 1853, with the Moyode pack.

Twice a year the Galway Hunt held a joint meet with the Eyrecourt Foxhounds at Birr, where they would party all night in a local hotel. During one of those parties the hotel caught fire and from that day on the Galway Hunt became known as the 'Blazers'.

Burton Persse, son of Parsons Persse, was the Master of the Galway Blazers until he was killed in a fall on 27 May 1885, aged fifty-six. He had the reputation of being the best master of hounds of his generation and was famous in hunting circles in both Ireland and England. A subscriber to the Irish Racing Calendar, Burton Persse played a role in the revival of the Galway Races and supported the event. He owned the first-ever winner of a race at the new Galway course at Ballybrit in 1869, Tom Tit winning both heats of the Connaught Pony Race, to the delight of his hunting friends. Tom Tit was 14 hands 1 inch high, and was ridden by Mr Hubert Davis and trained by his brother, Joseph Davis, at French Furze House, Curragh. Thirty-five-year-old Joseph Davies was on the brink of giving up training, moving from the Curragh to farm at Clondalkin, where he died of tuberculosis in May 1874.

In 1871 Burton Persse purchased the mare Stella after she had won at Punchestown, with the intention of trying to win the 1871 Galway Plate. After she finished third in that race behind Aster and Venison, Burton transferred the mare to his brother, Henry Seymour Persse, who continued racing it.

The member of the family responsible for its distilling interests, Seymour Persse was also a member of the Race Committee set up by Lord St Lawrence for the purposes of reviving the Galway Races. Throwing his weight firmly behind the project, he put up the prize money for the Glenard Plate and worked tirelessly to get the meeting established. Seymour enjoyed immediate success with Stella, who won the valuable Grand Stand Steeplechase at Cork Park next time out, ridden by Mr Garry Moore. However, the Persses had no time for losers. It cost the same to keep a 'bad 'un' as it did a 'good 'un', and when Stella finished unplaced in the prestigious Prince of Wales's Steeplechase at Punchestown in 1872, Seymour Persse got rid of her.

Seymour Persse was the father of Atty Persse, who made a mark on the turf, first as an amateur rider and then as a leading racehorse trainer in England. Named Henry Seymour after his father, the boy was called Atty to distinguish them, and the name remained with him throughout his life. Earmarked for the family business, Atty hated the distillery and escaped when he came of age, deciding that the turf and the hunting field, rather than whiskey, was his calling. His career as a gentleman rider took him to America, and to Austria and Hungary, which had many big races for gentleman riders at the time. Shortly after returning from America, Atty Persse won the famous Conyngham Cup at Punchestown on Sweet Lavender in 1897, for Dick Dawson and his licence-holding groom, E. Woods. Dawson, who trained the Galway Plate winner Drogheda to win the 1898 Aintree Grand National, became one of the select few men to train both the winner of the biggest steeplechase of the time and the Derby, winning the latter race three times, with the filly Fifinella (1916), Trigo (1929) and Blenheim (1930). Mr Atty Persse was Champion Amateur Rider in Ireland in 1902 but he was already looking to the future, because that year he took stables at Castleknock, Co. Dublin, close by the Phoenix Park, and began to mix training and riding.

Having finished third in the 1906 Grand National on Aunt May, behind Ascetic's Silver and Red Lad, he more or less gave up race riding, moving to England to train jumpers. Instead he found himself training flat horses and made a mark as a very capable trainer of two-year-olds. Following a spell as private trainer to Colonel W. Hall-Walker (Lord Wavertree) and owner of the famous Tully Stud in Kildare, Atty Persse moved into a yard at Chattis Hill, Stockbridge, and in 1910 trained a very good horse named Bachelor's Double, winner of the previous year's Irish Derby, when trained on the Curragh by Michael Dawson (no relation to Dick Dawson). As a four-year-old, Bachelor's Double won the Royal Hunt Cup at Royal Ascot, finished third to Bayardo in the Gold Cup and won the Atlantic Stakes before running second in the Doncaster Cup, establishing Persse among the leading trainers in Britain. Three years later he won the Irish Derby with Bachelor's Wedding, an own-brother to Bachelor's Double, and followed up with Land of Song the following year, but these victories are now largely forgotten – although his best horse is not. Persse was the trainer of The Tetrarch, the 'spotted wonder' who blazed across the British turf in 1914.

Owned by his cousin, Dermot McCalmont, to whom Atty was related through the family of Lord Clanmorris, The Tetrarch was unbeaten on the racecourse as a two-year-old, its only season to race. In the autumn of 1913, he rapped himself on the fetlock joint in training and was retired for the year. Having seemed to recover from the injury, he did exactly the same thing again the following spring, but this time he did not recover and had to be retired to stud. Atty Persse described the horse as a freak and stated that he would never have been beaten, over any distance, had he remained sound.

Although Atty Persse trained four English and seven Irish classic winners, he never won the Epsom Derby, although he continued to train for The Tetrarch's owner throughout his life. He usually spent the winter months, during the close season for flat racing, hunting in Ireland, holding the mastership of the Limerick Hunt, but his world collapsed when his only son, John, was killed in action in Italy in 1944. In his grief Atty stopped training but was persuaded by his friends to resume his career. When Emily, his wife, died in 1953 he retired for good. He passed away in 1960.

The main hazard faced by hunts in the nineteenth century was rabies; infected foxes could wipe out an entire pack of hounds. The sport managed to survive the disruption caused by the Land League in 1881, and it was not unusual to see two hundred riders following a pack of hounds. Ladies, riding side-saddle, turned out in increasing numbers, which eventually led to the appointment of the first lady master, Miss Edith Somerville of the West Carberry Hunt in Cork, in 1903. At about this time Isaac Bell took took over as Master of the Galway Blazers. Hunting in Ireland was at its peak, but the best times lasted only until the outbreak of the Great War in 1914. Around this time wire began to appear in the countryside which, with the planting of trees on the banks, halted the runs, disrupting the hunt.

After the war another hazard began to encroach, the motor car, as well as tarmac roads. By this time many of the old masterships had come to an end, a generation of young men had been wiped out in the 'war to end all wars' and on top of this came the War of Independence in Ireland. On the other hand, women were now beginning to ride astride like the men and the arrival of the horsebox would make life a lot easier in the future. Hunting continued to be the schooling ground for young Irish steeplechase horses, where they learned how to jump before tackling point-to-points, then hunter chases and finally the big races under rules.

The Beginning of Steeplechasing

Steeplechasing, for long the backbone of what we now call National Hunt racing, was born in the hunting field. Its origins lie in the 'pounding races' and 'wild goose chases' enjoyed by the hunting community, which evolved into a 'chase the steeple' type of race, The celebrated 'first' steeplechase, run from steeple to steeple in Co. Cork in 1752, was not the first steeplechase at all; it was only the first recorded one. That race involved just two horses, ridden by Mr O'Callaghan and Edmund Blake, who raced each other from Buttevant church to St Leger church 4½ miles away. It was just another steeplechase; it had no particular significance at the time, except to the participants, and was quickly forgotten. However, a witness recorded the details of the event privately, and this account came to light many years later, when it was found among the papers of the O'Brien family of Dromoland, Newmarket-on-Fergus, Co. Clare. The day and the month are unknown, but this record is the earliest of its kind, hence its claim to be the first steeplechase.

Pounding races were particularly popular in the hunting field. This was a follow-the-leader type of race, in which the horse in front attempted to shake off its pursuers by following the toughest course it could take safely. The leading rider had to select the stiffest fences his mount could jump, hoping that those behind would fail to keep up. If the leader fell or could not keep up the pace, the next horse took over, and so on, a process that continued until there was only one horse still running, the field having been 'pounded' to a standstill. Steeplechasing was a variation of the pounding race, with the course being chosen at random, but it had the advantage that it was not as hard on riders and horses because the race ended when the leader reached the far-off steeple. When chasing steeples, riders could take any course they wished, the aim being to reach the steeple first; often the shortest route was not the wisest course to take. Local knowledge was important because there were no prizes for jumping the biggest and most difficult fences. It is likely that the first steeplechase was an impromptu race to a clearly visible church steeple somewhere in Ireland, but it quickly became a craze among the hunting community.

The popularity of this new sport among riders encouraged hunts to organize informal steeple races for their members. These also brought the local inhabitants out in force to watch the proceedings. They became annual local events and, spreading like wildfire, steeplechasing became an established feature of country life in Ireland. From there the sport spread into the hunting counties of England, notably Leicestershire, and began to evolve, just as flat racing had done many years before, from matches to multi-runner races, to the wearing of colours to distinguish the horses (recorded for the first time in 1804), and eventually to the running of big open steeplechase races.

While the Irish may have invented steeplechasing, it was the English who organized it along modern lines. The first valuable organized steeplechase race was run at Bedford in 1810 over a specially constructed 3-mile course, with eight fences. It was not an open race, being restricted to horses that had 'been in at the death of three foxes in Leicestershire' and had a certificate from the Master to prove it. Eight horses entered the race but only two turned out to run, much to the disappointment of the spectators, estimated at 40,000. The sheer size of the crowd indicated that steeplechasing had great potential as a spectator sport, encouraging hotels, inns and other promoters to organize similar races in order to bring business to their locality. The English system of organized steeplechasing spread back to Ireland, and in 1813 a big steeplechase race was held in Roscommon on St Patrick's Day, run over 6 miles.

These early steeplechases may have been organized to some extent but they certainly were not regulated, neither in England nor in Ireland. The races were run at 'catch weights', in other words no specific weight was allotted to a horse. There were no rules against foul riding and there were no stewards.

As early as 1819 steeplechasing was being noticed by a wider audience, one English commentator describing a steeplechase as 'a sort of race for which the Paddies are particularly famous'. Fearless the 'Paddies' certainly were, at least those who were brave enough to ride in a steeplechase held at Lismore. The course was so severe that the betting on the race was dominated by predicting the number of falls rather than the winner of the race. Six falls was the money favourite but that was well wide of the mark in what turned out to be a 'complete tumble-down race', with no fewer than twelve fallers. The winner, Brown Bess, actually fell four times in the race but her rider was fit enough to remount each time, and it was recorded that nobody was killed!

The first big organized open steeplechase – that is one that was open to any horse or any rider without restriction – was held in Hertfordshire in 1826. It was the brainchild of Thomas Coleman, the proprietor of the Turf Hotel in St Albans, a town some 20 miles north-west of London. He had been a training groom before going into the hostelry business, knew a lot about horse racing and organized the race as a publicity stunt to drum up business for his hotel. Confident that a big steeplechase would draw a crowd which would require both food and liquid refreshment, he invested a considerable sum in the venture, hoping to recoup his money from the business generated. The public was not charged an admission fee but the race was organized with the general public in mind and the day went off impeccably. A huge crowd was lured to the town and the spectacle included a parade of the runners, three abreast, through the streets to the start at the church at Hartlington. One of the attractions of this event from the spectators' point of view turned out to be Coleman's arrangement whereby the horses started and finished in the same place. The field ran 2 miles out into the country, rounded the obelisk in Wrest Park and raced back 2 miles to the starting point. This enabled the crowd to get a clear view of the start and the finish of the race. It proved so popular that the innovation was copied by the Aintree Grand National and became the blueprint for the big races of the future.

The first St Albans steeplechase produced an exciting finish, with Captain

McDowall, riding a grey horse named Wonder, narrowly beating the Irish chal-lenger, Nailer, ridden by Lord Clanrickarde. Ulick John De Burgh, the Marquis of Clanrickarde, was born in 1802 and succeeded to the title and family seat of Portumna Castle, Co. Galway, when only six years old. His marriage to Harriet Canning in 1825, the only daughter of Rt Hon. George Canning, led him to change his name to De Burgh Canning. Having acquired a handsome dowry, he was enabled to enjoy the life of a lord, travelling the country riding in the big open chases. An enthusiastic and talented rider over fences, Lord Clanrickarde won the first Corinthian race run in Ireland on a horse named Penguin in 1822, and won his first steeplechase over the stiff Roxburgh course in Co. Galway with its four stone-walls, all at least 5 feet high, and one reputed to be as high as 6 feet! He would later become Lieutenant and Custos Rotulorum of the county and town of Galway, Vice-Admiral of Connaught and Colonel of the Galway Militia.

The St Albans race was a great success and become an annual event, but rival promoters were climbing on the bandwagon, offering fierce competition for the best horses and riders by the offer of good prize money. In 1827 John Formby, a local landowner, held a race meeting at Maghull, near Liverpool, consisting of flat races only. Although cheaper to run than chases, provincial flat races could not deliver the big names, which made it difficult to draw a big crowd. But Formby did well enough to encourage William Lynn to hold a rival meeting in the area.

Lynn, the proprietor of the Waterloo Hotel in Liverpool, was eager to cash in on the big-spending racing community, and sank an enormous sum into his venture. Securing a lease from Lord Sefton, he set about building a new course at Aintree, erected a grandstand and held his first meeting on 7 July 1829. Having seen off Formby's venture in 1835 and jealous of the huge crowds that were flock-ing to St Albans, Lynn decided to run a big steeplechase to revive his flagging Aintree meeting. Copying the arrangements that had been so successful at St Albans, he arranged that the runners would start at Aintree, run off across the Melling road into the country before turning for home, back across the Melling Road to finish at the place from which they had started. The horses ran left-handed, and riders had to keep outside all flags and to complete two circuits of the course. Lynn called his race the Grand Liverpool Steeplechase, but made a dread-ful error by running it on the day after the big St Albans race, which meant that it was impossible for a horse or a rider to compete in both races.

The inaugural Grand National took place on a cold but sunny afternoon, perfect steeplechasing weather, and was won by an English runner, The Duke, ridden by Mr Henry Potts. Although described as 'a hunting cob', The Duke was good enough to pull away from the Irish challenger, The Disowned, ridden by Allen McDonough, to win easily. However, the Irishman got his revenge the following year (1838) when winning the second running of the famous steeple-chase on his own horse Sir William, beating Scamp and The Duke. Sir William, described as 'a handsome savage that nobody could do anything with except his owner', was a beautiful eight-year-old chestnut by Welcome, bred in Ireland by William Battersby.

Idolized in his native land, acclaimed the best horseman of his time both in Ireland and in England, Allen McDonough had a long career in racing, first as a rider, then as a trainer and finally as a starter. A native of Galway, having been born in Wellmont, a mile from Portumna, in either 1804 or 1808, his father was a keen hunting man but died when his son was only eight years of age. Thereafter, young Allen spent a lot of time with his uncle, Mr Doolan, who lived in Shinrone and was a racing man. Mr Doolan had a racehorse named Hugo de Lacy and he allowed the youngster to ride it in its races, giving the boy a winning ride in the Hunt Cup at Tipperary. A stylish rider, Allen McDonough was a firm believer in the 'Chifney Secret' of riding:

> Your head and your heart keep boldly up,
> Your hands and your heels keep down,
> Your legs close in to your horse's sides,
> And your elbows close to your own.

Sam Chifney was the leading jockey in England at the end of the eighteenth century until he was ruined by the Escape scandal, in which he was accused of organizing a betting coup on the horse owned by the heir to the throne. He was one of the first jockeys to use tactics during a race, perfecting the art of coming with a late run to win a race, which he called the 'Chifney Rush'. To raise badly needed funds, Chifney wrote one of the earliest racing autobiographies, *Genius Genuine*, in which he revealed his secret of succsss.

Allen and his brother, the ill-fated 'Willie The Blazer' – a reference to his hunting career with the Galway Blazers – travelled around the kingdom taking part in all the big steeplechases, riding hard and betting heavily, arousing a fierce rivalry with the local riders. Fearless in the saddle, Willie was said to have been the better rider of the two, but never won the Grand National. He was successful in the St Albans Steeplechase, winning that race in 1839 on Van Dyke, and must have had an iron constitution because he took a number of heavy falls during his career before one killed him. Both brothers had a huge public following in Ireland and in England but Allen had a longer career and rode into old age. He was also involved in the first Irish steeplechase to become the focus of virtually the whole nation, when he was booked to ride the top English steeplechaser, the grey Peter Simple, which came over to contest the 1843 Kilrue Cup.

Modern records indicate that a horse named Peter Simple won the Grand National twice, although the evidence is strong that the second Peter Simple was a different horse from the first. Incredible as it may seem, there were no less than eight horses named Peter Simple around between 1831 and 1859. The Peter Simples that won the Grand National were both chestnuts but the best-known one of the day was the grey horse by Arbutus, foaled in 1834. This horse failed to win the Grand National, although he was placed three times in it, but was one of the top English chasers of the time and was easily the best of all the Peter Simples.

The arrival of the grey Peter Simple in Ireland caused great excitement, particularly when it was discovered that Allen McDonough was down to ride. For days the Irish racing fraternity speculated on the chances of the raider being repelled. The betting was frantic; the main Irish hope of a victory was John J. Preston's brilliant mare Brunette, black as coal just like her sire Sir Hercules. The strong field for the race included the top Irish steeplechase horses and riders of the day, including Milo (Denny Wynne), Blueskin (Lord Waterford), Lady Longford (Captain Forrester), Paddy Whack (Mr Rutherford), Tee Totum (Charlie Lockwood) and Post Boy (Peter Alley of the Ward Union Hunt).

Confident of victory, but unwilling to trade at too short odds, Allen McDonough obtained 5 to 1 for his money by backing his mount to win the race without being headed after jumping the first fence, taking £100 to £20. Naturally, having had the bet, McDonough raced off in front on Peter Simple in an attempt to make all the running but his judgement had been impared by his wager, causing him to make far too much use of his mount. Running out of steam with three fences left to jump, the English crack dropped back beaten as Denny Wynne kicked for home on Milo and went clear. Refusing to panic, Mr Preston bided his time before launching his challenge on Brunette after jumping the last fence. Sweeping past Milo as if he were standing still, Brunette secured a memorable victory. Allen McDonough was widely blamed for his riding of Peter Simple. The reason for his error of judgement was not known at the time but, in his eagerness to land his bet, he made too much use of his mount – perfect proof, if proof is needed, that riding and betting do not mix! However, the defeat was only a temporary setback for the great rider, who joined John Preston's stable at Bellinter the following year and was associated with Brunette's victory in the next three renewals of the Kilrue Cup, one of which was secured despite the race being run in a blinding snowstorm.

Frigate, winner of the 1889 Grand National, was probably the best Irish steeplechasing mare of the nineteenth century, but Brunette was definitely the second best. Winner of four consecutive Kilrue Cups, one of the big Irish steeplechases of the day and worth £200, Brunette ran in the Aintree Grand National only once, in 1847, when past her prime at thirteen years of age. Ridden by her usual rider Allen McDonough, the veteran chaser had not the pace to go with the field in the early stages under the burden of 12 stones 6 pounds. She got left behind but stayed on well to finish sixth to Matthew, the second Irish-trained winner of the race, with another Irish-trained runner, St Leger, in second place. Both of these horses had been involved in the 1846 Kilrue Cup, when Brunette won the race for the fourth consecutive time – a race that would be talked about for years.

The Kilrue Cup was run on a course in Co. Meath about 12 miles from Dublin, between Fairyhouse and the Black Bull. The twelve-year-old mare won the race by a couple of lengths, from Matthew and St Leger, horses that were at the very top of the steeplechasing tree at the time. The following year Matthew and St Leger finished first and second in the Grand National and a month later St Leger went to France and won the Grand Steeplechase de Paris, with Jim Mason in the saddle, from John Elmore's Young Lottery, ridden by Allen McDonough.

Allen McDonough began training at Athgarvan Lodge, Curragh, in 1850 but continued to ride in races and did so until he was in his mid-sixties. His last mount was at the Punchestown meeting in 1872, when the veteran rode Humming Bird into third place, wearing a pair of white kid gloves of a previous generation. However, by this time Allen, who had been struggling to make ends meet for several years, was almost broke. Back in 1868, his friends had been unsuccessful in getting him the job of Deputy Ranger of the Curragh, so he had to soldier on in the only business he knew.

He owned and trained a winner at the 1870 Galway meeting, Master Garrett, winner of the Connaught Pony Race, and the future looked brighter than it had for some time. He had such high hopes for a yearling filly named Trickstress, which he had bought in England, that he parted with £15, a sum he could ill afford, to enter her in the Irish Derby. At two years, in 1871, Trickstress let him down by running unplaced in the big juvenile races, the Railway and the Beresford Stakes. Although she did finish second in a nursery, this was not enough to alleviate McDonough's dire financial position. Struggling on as best he could, he found himself so strapped for cash just before Christmas that he realized that he would not make it through the winter. Reluctantly he decided to sell up and asked his friend, the famous auctioneer Robert J. Goff, to conduct the sale of all his horses.

When Trickstress came into the ring, looking big and powerful with scope for improvement and holding an Irish Derby engagement, hopes must have been high for a good sale. Unfortunately for the hard-pressed vendor, the bidding stalled at 150 guineas, offered by a Mr Simpson, and Mr Goff, in his desperate attempt to get the bid up to 170 guineas, the reserve price, became confused. Under the mistaken impression that Mr Simpson had agreed to bid the 170 guineas, Goff knocked Trickstress down. It later transpired that Mr Simpson had only bid 150 and was unwilling to pay any more. The upshot of all this, fortunately as it turned out for Allen McDonough, was that Trickstress was not sold and remained in his ownership. However, the sale of his other horses gave him a respite from his creditors, enabling him to keep Trickstress.

In April 1872 Trickstress finished a close third to Maid of Athens, the previous year's Irish Derby winner, in a Queen's Plate at the Curragh, prompting Richard Bourne to make a bid for her there and then. Mr Bourne was new to racing but was spending heavily since leasing Rossmore Lodge from Denny Wynne, the former Irish Champion Jockey who won the 1847 Grand National on Matthew the previous year. Gambling was Mr Bourne's game and he treated the racing public with disdain. It was anyone's guess whether his runners were 'off' or being stopped until his money was on, but he was wealthy, and was ready to buy any horse that was likely to bring off a gamble. Aware of Allen McDonough's financial discomfort and sensing an opportunity, Mr Bourne bought Trickstress there and then and had the filly taken back to Rossmore Lodge. He had nothing to lose by declaring her, still a maiden having not yet won a race, for the Irish Derby, and the odds began to drift in the gambler's direction as the race cut up badly. The English-trained Shelmartin, deemed a certainty, was scratched on the eve of the race and Trickstress had only two horses to face, both owned by Paddy Keary and trained by Tom Connolly. On an untypically cold and wet June afternoon, Mr Bourne saw his opportunity and did not hesitate. Paddy Keary, a shrewd bookmaker, unexpectedly went for a touch on Speculation, a maiden like Trickstress, rather than Pleasure Seeker, who had winning form. As punters followed Paddy Keary's money, which was usually the right thing to do, Richard Bourne held his fire for a while before popping up to go for an audacious touch on his filly. Backing Trickstress to win a fortune and forcing the filly's price down to evens in the process, the unexpected move from the gambling stable caught everyone off guard, particularly the bookies. Leading from flagfall, Trickstress was never seriously troubled and won the race easily.

Although he had obtained a good price for Trickstress, it was heartbreaking for Allen McDonough to miss out on winning such a prestigious race. Disappointed and disillusioned, he quit racing there and then, closed down his stable and retired to live in Dublin. He rarely went racing again, except for the brief period when he acted as a starter for the Turf Club, a position his friends managed to secure for him. One of the great steeplechase riders of all time, he died in May 1888.

As the number of steeplechase meetings grew, the best riders from the hunting community were regularly racing against each other, with increasing rivalry. Betting, and the occasionally bitter Irish-English rivalry, drew patriotic support to these events, fuelling an interest in the sport to a wider public. Unfortunately this brought an unwanted by-product of drunkenness and fisticuffs to race meetings, and the disorder was not confined to the spectators. Accusations of cheating or a desire for retribution for some wrong committed during a race regularly led to riders assaulting each other with their whips, all too often leading to a mass brawl as the spectators joined in!

Those, both human and equine, who regularly competed in the great steeplechases of the time, became household names far beyond the hunting community, as the popularity of the sport soared. In Ireland the most famous were the McDonough brothers, Larry Byrne, Denny Wynne, Charlie Canavan, Chris Green, Tom Abbott, Alan Power and the Marquis of Waterford, and the horses they rode – Dan O'Connell, The Disowned, Sir William, The Nun, Rust, The Sea, Valentine, Matthew, Brunette and Abd-El-Kader. In England Captain Becher, Harry Potts, 'Black' Tom Olliver and Jem Mason were the heroes and Moonraker, Vivian, The Duke, Jerry and the outstanding Lottery their star steeplechasers.

Irish-bred horses proved to be particularly good steeplechasers, but many of them were 'half-bred' rather than thoroughbred and therefore not registered in the General Stud Book. Half-bred horses usually had a lot of thoroughbred blood in them; some were even fully thoroughbred but were not properly registered at one time or another. At one time a half-bred received a 7 pound allowance from a thoroughbred in a race, leading to some owners tearing up their horse's papers and pretending it was a half-bred.

In the late 1820s Lord Fitzwilliam brought a stallion named Humphrey Clinker from England to Co. Wicklow to cover the mares of his tenant farmers. A big, fast, beautiful golden-yellow bay foaled in 1822, Humphrey Clinker was at 17 hands described at the time as the biggest thoroughbred ever seen and, after a couple of seasons, returned to England, later siring a good, but by no means outstanding racehorse named Melbourne. However, Melbourne became a very successful stallion, was twice Champion Sire and sired the Triple Crown winner West Australian, Sir Tatton Sykes (Two Thousand Guineas and St Leger) and Blink Bonny (Derby and Oaks). Most of the foals sired by Humphrey Clinker in Ireland were out of mares that were never registered in the General Stud Book, consequently they could not be registered. However, this pool of half-bred horses and mares were closely related to some of the best racehorses in England and 'Melbourne blood' became a common factor in many of the top Irish chasers.

The Irish National Hunt Steeplechase Committee

The Turf Club claims to have been founded in 1790, but it is actually older than that, as Tony and Annie Sweeney have proved in *The Sweeney Guide to the Irish Turf*. Although the Sweeneys' assertion that its origins can be traced back to 1750, which would make it older than the Jockey Club (formed in 1751), is nebulous, they have produced unimpeachable evidence that it existed in 1784. Unlike its English counterpart, the Turf Club did recognize steeplechasing, although it did not have a set of jumping rules until the establishment of the National Hunt Steeplechase Committee in 1866. In Ireland steeplechasing was very much part and parcel of horse racing. Flat races and steeplechases were run on the same programme, the Racing Calendar returned the results of races under both codes and most of the trainers and jockeys and many of the horses were 'dual purpose', participating in both flat and jump racing.

Using the Jockey Club as its model, the Turf Club supervised racing only on courses that registered to race under their rules. Although registration was entirely voluntary, many courses found it necessary to do so because they could not enforce rules themselves and it was getting harder to attract owners and spectators when there were no rules. In addition, promotors of meetings were open to accusations of bias when disqualifying a visitor, and subject to vilification from locals if they disqualified one of their own. The public felt that they were being cheated at meetings that did not race under Turf Club rules and owners faced being banned from racing if they were discovered attending an unofficial meeting. Scams were rampant at unofficial meetings, with horses running under false names, fancied runners being wilfully stopped and deliberate foul riding commonplace. The Governing Body enforced the rules by supplying stewards to act at meetings; and they had the power to suspend offenders from participating at future meetings. While the suspension only applied to courses that raced under the Rules of Racing, this covered all those that offered decent prize money and also applied to races being run under the rules of another governing body. Consequently, a ban applied equally in Ireland, England and on the Continent, which meant missing out on almost all of the big races. This proved to be a real disincentive to getting caught. The meetings that signed up to race under rules prospered, while the others went into decline, destined to be dismissed as 'flapping meetings' run in rural outposts. As ponies were denied races under the Rules of Racing, unofficial meetings began to cater for the small horse and have survived to this day in that guise.

In Ireland flat and jump racing co-existed happily, and have continued to do so for nearly two hundred years, with jumpers regularly running on the flat and vice versa. However, the increasing power of the governing bodies began to threaten the local annual hunt race meetings, the modern point-to-points, called 'sportsman's' or 'red coat' races in those days, which were in danger of being designated as illegal meetings, with participants being disqualified from racing under Rules. Lord Drogheda, the most influential steward of the nineteenth century, recognized the problem and in 1890 defined this particular type of race meeting as follows:

> A red coat or sportsman's race meeting is one at which there are only four races, all of which are hunters' steeplechases to which not more than £20 is added (farmers' races excepted) and are confined to horses the property of members of, or subscribers to, a specified hunt; or of farmers residing within the limits of that hunt. The programme of the meeting must receive the sanction of the Stewards of the Irish National Hunt Steeplechasing Committee prior to the date of closing. Such sanction shall only be granted on payment of a fee of £1, and on satisfying the Stewards that such meeting is to be held under the management and control of some specified hunt club, and that a licensed clerk of the course and scales has been appointed.

This rule established point-to-points as a legitimate part of steeplechasing and a starting point for young jumpers at the beginning of their careers. Although point-to-points are still an integral part of steeplechasing, the jumping side of horse racing has been growing apart from the flat over the last thirty years. Irish racegoers prefer jumping, but the big money is in flat racing, which is being increasingly dominated by very wealthy owners, forcing the smaller flat owner and breeder to seek refuge in the jumping game. Flat racing has always involved the rich and the famous because blood horses, fast but frail, are expensive to buy, stud fees are enormous and only the very wealthy

The two closest fences in the world, only 70 yards apart

can expect to compete at the highest level. The flat is dominated by large owner/breeders, who never sell their best stock, so getting one's hands on top-class flat stock is next to impossible. Jumping on the other hand involves lots of small breeders, most of whom breed to sell, enabling a prospective owner to purchase top-class jumping horses at a reasonable price. The involvement of ordinary people in the sport has made jump racing very popular in Ireland; racegoers know each other and tend to be close to the connections of the leading National Hunt horses. The intimacy of the jumping community has a downside for flat racing, which appears aloof from ordinary people, many of whom resent the huge stakes and the big business that surrounds it.

The Park Courses

Until the middle of the nineteenth century, race meetings resembled the point-to-point meetings of today. A course was laid out using natural fences such as walls, banks, ditches and rails, and the runners had to race over whatever land was available, very often through ploughed fields and across roads. Only the fences were marked, with a flag flying at each side, one red, the other white or yellow, with riders directed to leave red flags to the left and the white/yellow flags to the right.

Once the runners had raced between all the flags they could take whatever route they wanted, consequently fields often spread out like snipe fleeing a gun, with riders seeking the most advantageous way to the next fence. Hills, pathways and better ground would be eagerly sought and riders spent hours before a race walking the course and considering the options. Horses were saddled anywhere and everywhere, the betting area seemed to be in the bleakest, remotest place, but then most backers did their racing on horseback, and the early bookmakers often did their business while sitting in a fly, a light horse-drawn cart. Tents were erected to accommodate the weighing room, the bar and the tearoom, and entry to the course was free, although a fee was charged to carriages. Outriders (mounted spectators) invariably accompanied the runners as the field raced round the course, sometimes causing interference and occasionally influencing the outcome of a race but constantly putting pedestrians at risk.

The hunting community was responsible for the growth in the number of race meetings being held in Ireland. Hunt members owned horses and wanted to race them against their friends and neighbours in a formal setting, which led to the establishment of the local hunt race. What started as one race developed into a number of races, as different types of horses began to compete, for example heavyweight hunters, lightweight hunters and ponies. Hunt committees soon got behind these events, using a race day as an opportunity to entertain the farmers over whose land they hunted, erecting a marquee especially for them. The feature race was usually a hunt challenge cup, put up by the local squire or a prominent businessman, which traditionally could be won outright if won three times by the same owner. Among the most famous examples of challenge cup races were the Kilrue Cup, the Barbour Cup and the Webster Cup. At first these meetings were purely local affairs, but the opening of the railways in the 1850s gave city dwellers the opportunity of going out into the country for the day in numbers. This gave rise to the idea of running a race meeting as a business and led to the formation of the Metropolitan Race Company.

This company laid out a racecourse at Baldoyle, near Sutton, beside the railway line on the northern coast of Dublin, designing it specifically for the collection of admission fees from the general public. Originally called gate money or enclosed meetings, latterly these courses have come to be known as park courses. The first in Ireland was Baldoyle. Offering an all-grass running track with specially built fences and hurdles, it was marked out with a white running rail, which replaced the old-fashioned ropes, chains and flags. In order to tempt the public to part with an admission fee, the park course provided everything that the spectator needed to enjoy a day out at the races. A paddock area was provided so that the public could view the horses before the race, a terraced stand enabled patrons to get a clear view of the race itself, and bookmakers were organized so that cash betting facilities would be available to racegoers. Previously unheard-of amenities such as lavatories and cloakrooms, a tearoom, a bar and a telegraph office were available and to keep its patrons informed as to what was going on (in those pre-loudspeaker days), the park course installed a number board. It listed the runners and riders before each race and afterwards displayed the full result, while a flag system provided additional information. For example, a blue flag signalled 'Winner all right', red meant that an objection had been lodged and white was used to signify that an objection had been overruled.

The park course had an immediate advantage over the old style because it could use some of the money generated by admissions to guarantee race values. Staging plates, races with a guaranteed value, meant that owners knew exactly how much money each race was worth and were not depending on how many horses were entered and then declared to run. The added money ensured that the big races run on park courses were more valuable than ones run on the natural or open courses, which depended on the stakes being put up by the owners themselves. The Curragh, the most important open or natural racecourse in Ireland, found itself at a distinct disadvantage and was forced to change quickly. In 1850 the top eight most valuable races run in Ireland were all held at the Curragh. Fifteen years later, the number had dropped to two and the most valuable Curragh race, the Railway Stakes, was only third in the list of most valuable races. The threat to the traditional Curragh races forced the Turf Club to make changes to the Rules of Racing in order to protect the integrity of racing and to attract the public. The Curragh copied Baldoyle, building enclosures and public facilities, but it had a particular problem – the viewing. No fewer than twenty-six different courses were used at the Curragh, with many races starting over the horizon, and the runners could not be seen until the race entered the closing stages. One by one it discarded the unsuitable courses, whittling the number down to seven. The Curragh is an example of the old open course enclosed.

Like the Curragh, all the open courses were forced to change or to die, but for many it resulted in a compromise. Natural features could not easily be changed, but sharp bends, narrow courses, public roads, ploughed fields, banks and stone-walls, features of many of the old racecourses, would gradually be eliminated from Irish racing. The most spectacular casualty among the open courses was the Heath Races, run on the Great Heath of Maryborough since 1752, which found itself unable to compete after 1871, and spent the next nineteen years trying to adjust to the changing times before it finally closed. New racing parks opened all over the country, usually on the railway system. The most prominent to come on stream after Baldoyle in 1853 were Jenkinstown Park (1854), Listowel (1858), Mullingar (1860), Cork Park (1869), Galway (1869), Rathkeale (1879), Leopardstown (1888), Dundalk (1889), Powerstown Park (1889), Limerick (1891) and Tralee (1896).

Early Racing in County Galway

Like all counties that had a prosperous hunting community, Galway had an abundance of racecourses down the years, most of which disappeared just as quickly as they came. The vast majority of the meetings were organized by the local hunt. However, with no income being generated because the public got in free of charge, they were costly affairs to run and were not held every year. Consequently, meetings came and went, with many being entirely dependent on the energies of the secretary of the hunt, the ability and willingness of the members to sustain the cost, and the availability of a suitable course. The first Racing Calendar was issued by John Cheny of Arundel in 1727 but it recorded only English racing, which has been chronicled every year since then. In 1741 Cheny began including Irish races, listing results from eleven Irish racecourses: Ballinasloe, Bellair (Co. Antrim), the Curragh, Carlow, Darlington (Queen's County), Downpatrick, Limerick, Shanes Castle (Co. Antrim), Tuam and Turloughmore. With two of the eleven venues situated in Co. Galway and one in Co. Mayo, it is obvious that Galway was a major racing centre, but unfortunately the record of Irish racing is not fully recorded until 1751. John Cheny was in declining health and in his last few years he stopped listing Irish results, so the continuous record of Irish racing only goes back to 1751, when Reginald Heber, who continued Cheny's work, reintroduced Irish meetings to his calendar.

Sixteen different meetings in Co. Galway held fixtures between 1751 and 1869, run on at least twenty different courses. The major fixtures were the Loughrea meeting, the Tuam meeting and of course the Galway races. The three meetings were independent of each other and were run by different committees and over different courses. The Galway fixture was in existence prior to 1829, when it was first recorded in a Racing Calendar, as evidenced by a magnificent silver salver, part of the collection of the National Museum of Ireland, which bears the inscription:

A FORTY POUND PLATE GIVEN BY YE GENTLEMEN OF YE COUNTY OF
GALWAY RUN FOR YE COURSE OF PARK YE 19TH SEPTEMBER 1741 BY
HORSES CARRYING TEN STONE.

The silver salver was won by a horse named Caesar, owned by Charles Lambert,
but the race was not run at the park course as intended, having been transferred
to the Gurranes course at Tuam because of an outbreak of plague in Galway
town.

Even this piece is not the earliest Irish horse-racing trophy extant, however. A
tazza, made by Joseph Walker of Dublin, survives from 7 May 1702, when it was
presented to the winner of a race at the Heath of Ballycolloe, Queen's County.

Not everyone in the locality approved of race meetings. The bishops spoke out
against the gambling, heavy drinking and immorality, the puritans also railed
against betting and alcohol and those who lived nearby were fearful for their own
safety. Rows fuelled by alcohol, faction fights and yobbish behaviour abounded at
certain meetings, giving the sport a bad name and forcing landlords to ban the
sport from their land. A shocking massacre took place during the week of the
Tuam races in September 1740, when eleven people and two dogs had their throats
slit during the night at Carrowbawn House. Oliver Bodkin, the owner of the property, his wife and son, a visitor from Galway who had come down for the races,
and seven servants were butchered in their beds. Although the murders had
nothing to do with the Tuam races, certain members of the community blamed
them for the crime, which was organized by a jealous son of Oliver Bodkin from
a previous marriage. Three men were later hanged.

The Galway Annual Races

The Galway Races held only fifteen annual fixtures in the 29-year period between
1829 and 1857, all of them being run over a course at Kiltulla, a common about
1½ miles north of the present course at Ballybrit. The races were run in 1829,
1830, 1836, 1840, 1844–6, 1849–51, 1854–5 and 1857. They were run under
Turf Club rules and became known as the Galway Annual Races, even though they
were not held annually. The 1840 meeting, a three-day affair due to be held on the
Monday, Tuesday and Wednesday of the first week of August, was put back a
week in order not to clash with the assizes taking place in the town. The stewards
of the meeting were Thomas N. Redington, Robert Bodkin, Thomas Appleyard
Joyce and John Francis Blake, the race ball was held at Kilroy's Hotel and the race

programme consisted of a Queen's Plate and six flat races, all run in heats over distances ranging from 1 to 2 miles. None of these gentlemen was around twenty-nine years later, when the meeting moved to Ballybrit, although the inclusion of Pierce Joyce and Captain Valentine Blake among the stewards indicates a clear connection with that old meeting.

The common at Kiltulla is still there today, but no trace of the racecourse remains, which is not surprising because the meeting would have been held without permanent buildings, posts or rails. Tents were erected for the necessary facilities and flags marked out the course, which was used from at least 1821. For some reason the commonage became increasingly prone to flooding, which was so bad that the meeting had to be abandoned in 1858, forcing a search for a more suitable location.

In 1859 the Galway Races were run over a course at Bushfield, beyond Oranmore, which had hastily been secured by the promoters, and most of its limitations were put down to inadequate preparation. The meeting did not appear in the Calendar in 1860 but a two-day Galway Flat and Steeplechase Races was run at Bushfield at the end of August 1861, after a lot of work had been done improving the course. All steeplechase races were over 4-foot-high stone-walls. The Midland Great Western Railway Company sponsored a race and £265 was added to the stake money for the seven races. Although this proved to be a successful meeting with good prize money, the course itself was most unsatisfactory and the Race Committee decided that continuing to race there would do more harm than good to the Galway Races in the long term. It therefore allowed the fixture to lapse until a more suitable venue in the locality could be found, and that took eight years.

County Galway's Nineteenth-century Racecourses

The rise and fall of courses was common in nineteenth-century Ireland, and Co. Galway was no exception. Galwegians had seen many of the county's fixtures lapse: Kilconnel (1805), Eyrecourt (1807), Brook Lodge, the Tuam estate of Martin J. Blake (1824), Rahassan (1828), Ballinasloe (1840), Ballymoe (1841), Dunmore (1849), Athenry (1859), Bermingham Hunt (run by John Dennis, Bermingham House, Tuam) (1861) and Carraroe Hunt (1862). With the closure of the latter and Tuam idle for a few years, the county only had two racecourses in use: Loughrea and Portumna. Even this pair did not race every year, however. Portumna did not race in 1864 or in 1867, so in those years Loughrea was the only

Co. Galway venue to hold a meeting. Although neither Loughrea nor Portumna held a fixture in 1866, the Tuam meeting went ahead over the modified Gurranes course, which consisted of four banks, two 4-foot stone-walls, two hurdles and a brook. The Turloughmore meeting was also revived, but it did not endure. Woodford came into the fixture list in 1868 but lasted only two years. However, the revival of the Galway Races in 1869 seemed to spark a new interest in racing in the county.

Ballinasloe was revived in 1871, unusually racing under Irish National Hunt Steeplechase Rules, except Rule 44, which was a controversial rule at the time that stated that the lowest weight carried in any race must be 10 stone. The revivals continued with Gort in 1873 and Dunmore in 1885, and new courses were also opened: Clare Tuam (1870), Newgrove (1873), Killimore (1879), Glennamaddy (1874), Moylough (1885) and Athenry (1887). However, it must be said that the Clare Tuam meeting was actually the Tuam meeting held at a different venue rather than on its traditional Gurranes course, and was a one-off event. These new fixtures found the going tough. Killimore lasted only one year, Newgrove managed a second meeting, Glennamaddy raced for five years and Athenry for eight before disappearing forever.

However it should be remembered that this list only includes meetings that were run under the Rules of Racing. Flapping meetings (those not registered with the Turf Club in Dublin) abounded, like the Ballygar meeting, run on a course beside a bog, the Kinvara Steeplechase meeting, run over a course of stone walls within a mile of the town, and the Mulpit course at Athenry. Despite the risk of being warned off all recognized racecourses if caught participating in a flap, many people were prepared to run the risk. Galway people such as Mr Hawkes of Briarfield, Mr Lynch of Loughrea, Mr Daly of Ballinlass and Mr Leary of Ballygar openly ran horses at Ballygar in July 1871, although those may not have been their real names. The unexpected was part of the fun of flapping, as was the opportunity to cheat with impunity because bookmakers were in attendance and horses could be backed for money. At that particular meeting at Ballygar all those years ago, the unexpected was the stopping of a favourite by a ruffian who flung a shillelagh at its rider, knocking him off!

The Major Racecourses in County Galway

Only seven Galway fixtures were still extant at the dawn of the twentieth century: Ballinasloe, Dunmore, Galway, Gort, Loughrea, Moylough and Tuam. By 1904 concerns were being aired by owners and trainers about the state of some of the Irish racecourses, in particular the dangerously sharp turns, poor racing surfaces and crowd encroachment interfering with the runners. Jumping trainers also pointed out that racecourses were running cheap flat races in preference to steeplechases, Captain Bob Dewhurst highlighting the fact that over a ten-year period the number of flat races being run had quadrupled but the average value had declined by a third. The Galway Races were just as guilty as the rest in this regard; the number of flat races increased from one to five and, leaving aside the Royal Plate, the top value, the Renmore Plate, declined from a high of £260 in 1873, down to £58 within a decade. Hurdle races were used as another cheap option as the number of steeplechases at Ballybrit tumbled from eight to only three at the turn of the century: the Galway Plate Handicap, the Galway Blazers Handicap and the Glenarde Plate, with penalties and allowances.

Demands for the appointment of an inspector of courses were growing but were being resisted by some members of the governing bodies. In an attempt to defuse the situation, the Turf Club refused to allot fixtures to seven racecourses in 1905 on the grounds that the racing surface was unsatisfactory. Two years later Percy La Touche spoke out about the dangerous condition of some of the flat courses in Ireland and was supported by Sir Henry Greer, which led to the appointment of Arthur Blennerhassett as the first Inspector of Courses in October 1907.

Blennerhassett visited every racecourse in the country to inspect the facilities, setting down minimum standards and advising the executive of what needed to be done. Although courses were not expected to make all the improvements immediately, the Inspector gave notice that the minimum standards would be upgraded over a number of years, and ultimately no course would be allotted a fixture unless it complied with this minimum standard. To bring many of the old courses up to the minimum standard required a capital investment, which in some cases could not be justified on economic grounds. The first casualty in Co. Galway was the Ballinasloe meeting, which was run for the last time in 1910. The Kilbegley course, over which the Ballinasloe meeting was run, was dreadfully narrow and uneven, the view of the racing from the stand was very poor and the straight was much too short. In addition to these drawbacks, the runners had to cross a public road several times during a race, which was far from ideal. One by one the Co. Galway courses closed down because the executives would not, or could not, spend the money necessary to bring the course up to the minimum standard. After Ballinasloe came Moylough (1911), Dunmore (1916), Gort (1916) and Loughrea (1920).

The Loughrea steeplechases had been run over the Knockbarron course since before 1752, the year from which records of the meeting are extant, and for many years it was by far the most important meeting in the county. The famous Irish steeplechase rider, Allen McDonough, from nearby Portumna, rode a winner there as a sixteen-year-old youth on a mare named Gulnare, and Major William Trocke, the well-known gentleman rider from Hillbrook, Birr, described seeing his mentor, John Hubert Moore, riding at Knockbarron in 1856, carrying 18 stone over a course consisting only of 4½-foot stone walls! The Knockbarron course also features in Charles Lever's novel *Jack Hinton the Guardsman* but the meeting had declined as the reputation of the Galway meeting at Ballybrit grew. The problem for Loughrea was that the Knockbarron course was generally inferior to Ballybrit, and efforts to improve it were hampered by the public road that went through it. This was not ideal in any age but became a major problem with the arrival of the motor car.

After the demise of the Loughrea meeting only Galway and Tuam were left. Tuam, first raced on the Friday after the Galway Races in 1923, retained that fixture, racing until it too closed down after the 1973 meeting. Now the Ballybrit course was 'the last green bottle standing on the wall'.

A public road also posed a problem for the Tuam meeting and was one of the reasons for the move to a new course at Parkmore in 1904. The old Gurranes course, situated 2 miles from the town, was much superior to the course at Knockbarron, but there had been a long-standing difficulty keeping the course clear during the races. Crowd encroachment became a hazard to both riders and spectators, forcing the Tuam stewards to resort to drastic measures to keep the course clear. They organized mounted men armed with big whips, wearing distinguishing green bands in their hats, to ensure that the public was kept off the course during the races. These men appeared wild to the genteel racegoers of that era, rough and ready Irish speakers with only broken English, but they carried out their orders to the letter. At the Tuam meeting all too often there were chaotic scenes of panic as people fled the flying hooves and the cracking whips, the course being kept clear by terror tactics, to the amazement of visitors to the course.

Most of these racecourses, Ballybrit included, were bleak places in the early days, with only basic facilities for the public and the riders. The famous jockey Steve Donoghue, in his book *Donoghue Up!*, describes the jockeys' room at pre-Great War Galway Races as 'just a little tent. Still it was shelter from the murderous rain outside.' That 'little tent' was a big improvement from the days Harry Sargent was riding. In his book *Thoughts Upon Sport*, published in 1895, he recalled dressing and undressing for a steeplechase using a fence for shelter from a storm of wind and rain, while a friend held an umbrella!

The survival of the Galway Races and its continued success down the years was entirely due to the efforts of the Race Committee to improve the course and the facilities for both public and riders.

The Revival of the Galway Races

The successful revival of the Galway Annual Races was the result of hard work by a group led by the perspicacious Viscount St Lawrence. Born William Ulick Tristram St Lawrence in June 1827, he was the Member of Parliament for Galway Borough from 1868 until 1874, when he had to resign his seat on succeeding to his father's title as the 4th Earl of Howth. Having given up on the Bushfield course after the 1861 meeting, Lord St Lawrence began to search for an alternative course. The years passed and, just when he was getting desperate, out of the blue Captain Wilson Lynch of Renmore came to the rescue with the offer of the use of his land at Ballybrit, rent free. An unofficial race committee, chaired by Viscount St Lawrence, was got together and included: the Marquis of Clanrickard, Portumna Castle; Lord Clanmorris, Cregclare, Ardrahan, Seamount, Galway; Captain Blake Forster; Henry S. Persse; Pierce Joyce, Merview, Galway; George Morris; and Valentine O'Connor Blake, Tower Hill, Ballyglass, and Bunowen Castle, Clifton. George Morris of Wellpark, Galway, a former Member of Parliament for the Galway constituency, was the great uncle of Lord Killanan, Chairman of the Galway Race Committee from 1970 until 1985.

The Galway Race Committee employed the well-known racecourse official and architect, Thomas G. Waters, to lay out the course at Ballybrit and to design the stand. Waters had been highly praised for his redesign of the Punchestown course and his work in Galway met with everyone's approval. The racing surface was praised as being perfect, with plenty of grass 'excelling any course in Ireland', and three different courses were available for the races: the flat course, capable of accommodating races of 6 furlongs upwards; the steeplechase course, consisting of six birch fences and two stone walls; and the hunt course, a type of cross-country course that included a double bank. A wooden grandstand was erected, 'offering a splendid view of the proceedings', and tents were used to provide other necessary facilities for riders and the public.

Viscount St Lawrence installed W.H. Halliday as Honorary Secretary, appointed Mr T. Flynn as Clerk of the Course and revived the old sponsorship deal with the Midland & Great Western Railway of Ireland and the Royal Canal Company. The railway did not sponsor a race but instead agreed to carry every horse to and from the meeting free of charge, provided that the horse's stable was more than 20 miles away and that it actually ran in one of the races. In those days two small steamers run by the Lough Corrib Steam Navigation Company shuttled between Cong in Co. Mayo and Galway town down the length of Lough Corrib. The MP arranged with the company that a 'race special' ferry be put on to make it easy for racegoers from Co. Mayo to get to Ballybrit.

Particular attention was given to the conditions of the races so that they would be attractive to a wide range of owner and rider and a number of innovations were introduced to make them more competitive. A special prize was awarded to the first four-year-old to finish in the Galway Plate. A 4-pound weight allowance per inch was given in pony races and smaller ponies were also given a head start. A system of penalties and allowances was drawn up to prevent certain half-breds – or so-called half-breds – which were sweeping up all the hunter races in the country dominating at Galway and making the racing uncompetitive. A 6-pound home training allowance was given in some races to private stables that had never run a horse in a race valued at £100 or more. Any jockey riding at the meeting who had never won a race to the value of £100 or more received a 6-pound allowance. Horses that had started in a race valued over £100 were excluded from the minor races and some races were restricted to horses trained in Co. Galway or the neighbouring counties. There was a race for every type of owner and horse. For instance, the Glanard Plate, worth £30 and presented by Henry S. Persse, was restricted to tenant farmers holding 50 statute acres of land or ratepayers (those engaged in trade or commerce) in the province of Connaught or in Co. Clare who had paid no income tax the previous year.

Gentlemen riders had to register with the committee if they wished to ride at the meeting, and had to produce a document, signed by two stewards, to the effect that they had never been in service, had never ridden for hire and were fit to ride at Galway. All jockeys were given notice that they would not be weighed out by the Clerk of the Scales unless they were dressed in proper racing costume. The Galway Race Committee gave prior notice that Aunt Sally was forbidden on the racecourse. This was a game in which participants tried to knock the nose off the face or the pipe out of the mouth of a wooden lady's head, using a special missile provided by the organizer. Clearly it was popular at the time but the executive considered it inappropriate to have dozens of games of Aunt Sally flourishing on the racecourse throughout the afternoon. Besides the obstruction that they would cause, and the danger to the public from a wayward missile, there was a real concern that these missiles would be used in the inevitable drunken brawls that accompanied race meetings at that time.

The First Meeting at Ballybrit

When the Galway Races reappeared in the Racing Calendar in 1869, the Liberals were in government and William Gladstone was Prime Minister of Great Britain and Ireland and his administration had just passed an Act to disestablish the Church of Ireland. President Ulysses S. Grant, the most distinguished Union general of the American Civil War, had recently been elected President of the United States, Queen Victoria was in the thirty-third year of her long reign and John Poyntz, 5th Earl Spencer, was Lord Lieutenant of Ireland. The previous year Irish horse racing had received a tremendous boost when the Prince of Wales, the heir to the throne, went racing at Punchestown during his state visit to Ireland. He and the Princess travelled to Sallins by train, taking a carriage from there to the course, and drew an enormous crowd, estimated at over 150,000, to the area for the occasion. The royal visit made racing fashionable, boosting attendances everywhere, and the Galway Executive hoped to benefit from the increased interest in the sport.

A relaxing perusal of form in the warmth of the sun

The first ever meeting on the Ballybrit course was held on Tuesday and Wednesday 17 and 18 August 1869, bringing chaos to Galway town as huge crowds flocked in, overrunning the facilities. Every available bed in the town was taken, not a stable could be found for a horse and, with demand far exceeding supply, prices soared as people battled for food and accommodation. Greed reigned, as landlords, innkeepers and livery stables reneged on their bookings and accepted inflated offers from the desperate, leaving those who had booked accommodation for themselves and their horses on the streets. Things were so bad that the Council was forced to allow the Eyre Square Park to be used as a camp site for the 'homeless' visitors. Food was in short supply and the only mercy was that the weather remained dry.

Just as the town had been swamped, so too was the racecourse. An enormous crowd, estimated at 40,000, arrived at Ballybrit, many of them hungry because of the difficulties of getting a meal in the town, and the racecourse simply could not cope. The caterers were strained to breaking point, people were everywhere and the Executive did really well to get all the races run off without disruption. It must be remembered that in those days the vast majority of people watched the races from the free area, with only the well-off being able to afford to pay for entry into the enclosure. The vast numbers of people roaming the infield made it difficult to keep the course clear for racing, and it was a miracle that nobody was killed. However, for many it was a case of 'never again' and the racecourse office was flooded with complaints about overcharging (or mulcting as it was called at the time). Owners and trainers, too, were up in arms, furious that they had been forced to stable their horses many miles from Ballybrit and had to pay exorbitant prices for substandard accommodation. However, the meeting was completed without a hitch and many people enjoyed the day despite the cramped conditions.

The first ever race run at Ballybrit was the Connaught Pony Race, a 1½-mile steeplechase run in heats, restricted to small horses or ponies under 15 hands that were not included in the General Stud Book (i.e. half-bred). An allowance of 4 pounds was given for every inch below 15 hands, and horses under 14 hands received a 16-pound allowance and in addition were given a 175-yard start! The race was won by Burton Persse's Tom Tit, ridden by the bearded Mr Hubert Davis and trained by Joseph Davis (1834–74) on the Curragh. A chestnut gelding by Woodpecker, 14.3 hands high, he was unquoted in the betting for the first heat but won it easily by ten lengths. That impressive win meant that he started an even-money favourite to win the final heat of the race, which he did easily, although the winning distance is not recorded. He turned out again on the second day of the meeting and was again unquoted in the betting. However, he ran a good third to

Snowdrift, ridden by Mr Robert Exshaw, the odds-on favourite, in the last race of the afternoon, the Visitors Plate, run over 1 mile on the flat. One of three horses all racing under the name Tom Tit in Ireland at the time, Mr Persse's Tom Tit never ran under Rules before Galway and appeared only once afterwards, finishing unplaced at the Woodford (Co. Galway) meeting a month later.

The Galway Plate

The Galway Race Committee agreed that the meeting needed a feature race to attract public interest. Steeplechases were popular among the public, particularly those that were open to all comers rather than being restricted to locals; the only problem was that a decent purse was needed in order to attract a competitive field. One hundred pounds was raised by subscriptions, and the race was an open handicap steeplechase, called the Galway Plate; the term does not refer to a trophy, but to the type of race.

A plate is a race of a definite value, guaranteed by the racecourse, not one dependent on payments by owners by way of entry fees, forfeits and subscriptions. On the other hand a sweepstakes, nowadays commonly called a stakes race, is a race funded by pooling the entry fees, forfeits and subscriptions paid by owners, for division between the winner and the placed horses. There is no connection between the Galway Plate and the Royal Plate (or King's/Queen's Plate) run at Galway between 1879 and 1958, other than that both were plate races rather than sweepstake races. The Irish Derby is an example of a sweepstakes, its final value dependent on how much money was paid into the pool.

Like most valuable open steeplechases at the time, the Galway Plate got plenty of publicity in the press in the weeks leading up to the meeting. An ante-post betting market developed and there was constant speculation about the probable runners. The inaugural race, run in 1869, was won by Absentee, trained by Newbridge trainer Dick Bell and ridden by William Bell, who beat off four challenges in a tight finish. Second was Quickstep, the 2 to 1 favourite on the strength of wins at Baldoyle and Punchestown, and third was the outsider Lady Clarendon, a recent winner at Roscommon. Among the unplaced horses were Christopher Ussher's Luckpenny, Burton Persse's Zuleika, who was subsequently sold and ran second in the 1872 Irish Grand National, and Henry Seymour Persse's four-year-old filly Alice Gray. Also unplaced in the race was Mr W. Joyce's mare A.M.B., whose rider Paddy Gavin was told on dismounting that he would be riding the horse again in the next race, the Members' Plate. It again finished unplaced, but was turned out again in the next event, the Ballybrit Plate, thus running unplaced in three consecutive races on the one afternoon. However, these were the only races that the mare competed in all year, the Galway meeting being used in a desperate attempt to get a beautifully bred mare a winning bracket.

One hundred and five years later Kevin Bell, a direct descendant of the trainer of the first Galway Plate winner, trained the winner Bunclody Tiger, which gave him particular pleasure at the time.

The Rest of the Card

The Members' Plate, a weight-for-age steeplechase over 2 miles with selling allowances, was the setting for a huge gamble on Ishmael. The opening price of 3 to 1, and higher in some places, was quickly snapped up; indeed every price seemed to be a good one and punters backed the horse at all prices. By the time the horses were at the post, Ishmael was the 5 to 4 favourite but he did not take part in the race; all bets were off and the punters had to be given their money back. What had happened was that Ishmael's rider, James Murphy, had weighed out as normal but somehow failed to get his mount to the start on time, leaving the starter no option but to start the race without the favourite. It was obviously a deliberate decision by owner John Ussher not to run the horse – almost certainly because his market was stolen and he wished to punish the guilty party. In the absence of Ishmael, Dick Bell's Annoyance (William Bell) started joint favourite and beat The Pilot (George Gray), giving the Bells a nice double. Third in the Forster Street Plate the following day, Annoyance was sold to Mr H. Blake and later won on the flat at Kilrush and Kilkee. The runner-up in the Members' Plate, The Pilot, owned by 'Mr H. Chester', otherwise H.S. Croker (1845–97), who later became the Senior Starter in Ireland, also ran in three races at the meeting but finished down the field in the other two.

The Ballybrit Plate, for half-bred horses and amateur riders, and run over 1 mile on the flat, was the last race on the card that day and Ishmael was declared to run, but with a change of rider. John Ussher might have expected to get a better price by putting up an amateur, in this case Mr William Coghlan from Claremorris, and because this was a flat race whereas the previous race was a 2-mile chase. However, the bookies were not fooled and cautiously priced Ishmael at 6 to 4. Punters who had previously helped themselves to odds in excess of 5 to 2 now had to be content with a lower price and were disgusted when The Pilot beat

Ishmael rather easily. However, relief was at hand when an objection was immediately lodged; The Pilot had gone inside a post, taking a short cut. The objection was sustained, The Pilot was disqualified, the race was awarded to Ishmael and the punters were paid. All's well that ends well!

The second day of the meeting began with the Glanard Plate, which was won by Black Bess, ridden by the ill-fated John Boylan. The jockey, who won the first two runnings of the Irish Grand National, on Sir Robert Peel, owned by 'Mr L. Dunne' (the assumed name of Charles Barrington), and on Tom Kirkwood's The Doe, was killed at the old Parkview course at Killarney on 30 August 1871. By that time he had ridden sixteen winners, a total that was not exceeded by any other rider that year, giving Boylan the title of Champion Irish Jockey posthumously.

Ishmael won his second race of the meeting in the Renmore Handicap Chase over 3 miles, beating Comet, and then the crowd settled down for the day's feature race, the Forster Street Plate. Sponsored by Captain Blake Forster, this was an open handicap steeplechase designed to be a Galway Plate consolation race, with owners being permitted to enter horses on the evening before the race, well after the Plate had been run. For the convenience of owners, entries were being received by Robert Hunter Jr, Adelaide Road, Dublin, by W.H. Halliday, Bushey Park, Galway, and in Blake's Hotel, Galway. Some of the race names used at the meeting were taken from local townlands, such as Ballybrit, Glenard and Renmore, but the Forster Street race was named after the street in the town, not after Captain Blake Forster, who probably agreed to sponsor it after it had been named. The Galway Race Committee had an office in Forster Street, which in later years, from 1879, became the terminus for the Galway to Salthill tram service, a 2-mile journey in which the trams were pulled by horses.

Quickstep (second), Erin (fourth) and Luckpenny (unplaced) were the Galway Plate runners that contested this consolation, as well as Annoyance and Lady Gladstone, the joint favourites which finished first and third in the Members' Plate, and Ace-of-Hearts, which finished behind them. It looked a competitive race, Erin starting favourite, but with 2 of the 28 furlongs remaining only Erin and Luckpenny counted. The duo battled it out to the line, with Christopher Ussher's Luckpenny eventually getting the better of Erin and Annoyance, Lady Gladstone and Ace-of-Hearts a long way behind, finishing in that order.

With no race run in heats that day, the fourth and last race was the Visitors' Plate, over 1 mile on the flat. The odds-on Snowflake duly became the sixth winning favourite at the meeting, beating Allen-a-Dale and Tom Tit, with Erin, The Pilot and Lady Gladstone all finishing unplaced.

A Victim of Its Own Success

The inaugural Galway meeting was an outstanding success, as far as attendances, the number of runners and the quality of the racing was concerned. However, there was general dissatisfaction from all quarters with the arrangements and facilities available on the racecourse and in the town. Many problems had surfaced during the two-day meeting, mainly concerning accommodation for both people and horses and the prices charged for it. With demand far outstripping supply, prices soared, finding accommodation was difficult, and it was impossible to get a meal in the town. As far as every visitor to Galway was concerned, the meeting had been a fiasco.

Accepting that owners, trainers and members of the public had genuine complaints, Lord St Lawrence acted immediately, knowing that his hopes of establishing the Galway fixture would be wrecked unless the problems that surfaced at the first meeting were addressed. He used his influence with the business people of the town to put pressure on the hotels and inns to address the issue of overcharging. They agreed on a fixed price for accommodation during the 1870 race week for private rooms, inns and hotels. In return for agreeing to charge a standard, guaranteed price for accommodation, the Galway Race Committee compiled a list of these official establishments and circulated them to every owner in the country, as well as to anybody who requested it, saving them the expense of having to advertise for business. In addition, Lord St Lawrence sought out people willing to let rooms at this fixed price, expanding the amount of accommodation available in Galway during the races. In order to reduce the demand on the limited facilities in the town, Lord St Lawrence then approached the railway company with a proposal to start the races later than usual, at 1.45 p.m., to facilitate the running of race special-day return trains from Dublin, enabling racegoers to return home in the evening. The Midland & Great Western Railway agreed to run two special trains to Galway from its headquarters at the Broadstone Terminus in Dublin, one at 7 a.m. and a first-class only express train at 8 a.m. St Lawrence then got permission from the Borough Council to erect a large marquee in Eyre Square, from which the racecourse caterers, Messrs Byrne & Sheridan of 19 South Great Georges' Street, Dublin, would serve dinner on the evening before the races and on each evening of the meeting, at a fixed price.

These measures worked reasonably well in 1870. Most of the hotels and private houses honoured their agreements but demand continued to outstrip supply, with the race week being completely booked out two months before the meeting. With every house on the list booked out, Mr Halliday, the Secretary, was besieged with requests for help with accommodation, but could only suggest Ballinasloe, about 40 miles from the course, as the best place to start looking! The train took the strain, however, and Mr J.E. Ward, the railway official in charge, was widely praised for his work ensuring that the 10,000 racegoers who came from Dublin got to the races on time.

While the profiteering was brought under control as far as humans were concerned, it still remained a big problem for prospective Galway runners. Livery stables convenient to the railway station and to Ballybrit were charging sky-high prices and still turning horses away. Much of their business involved carriage horses and hacks, and they had no interest in talking to Lord St Lawrence at all. It was essential that this problem be addressed in time for the 1871 meeting if the races were to attract decent fields. Without the support of the livery stables, Lord St Lawrence announced that Galway would guarantee suitable accommodation for horses running at the meeting at an agreed fixed price. He further declared that if any owner was forced to pay more, then the Race Committee would reimburse the difference between the price charged and the agreed rate. In addition, he acquired 20 acres of land at Oranmore, which was within ½ mile of Galway railway station and a similar distance from Ballybrit, upon which eleven roomy loose boxes were erected, reserved for runners, which would be permitted to exercise on the adjacent grass field.

These measures worked to the extent that the meeting attracted healthy fields but the situation was far from ideal and, with the livery stables still refusing to cooperate, Lord St Lawrence decided to wage war on the local profiteers. The Galway Race Committee introduced a rule for the 1872 meeting: 'Any horse standing at a stable where an excess of livery was charged will only receive one-half the added money in the event of his winning a race: the other half will go to the fund.' (Added money is the sum added by the racecourse (or a sponsor) to the fund. The fund is the money contributed by the owners by way of entry fees and is paid out to the winner, less the portion reserved for the placed horses.)

The Galway Races were proving an important source of income for the town and many businesses relied on race week for their profits, but local pressure was having little effect on the livery stables. However, the policy of the Race Committee of renting private stables for the week and making them available to horses running at the meeting was working and enabled the livery stables to be by-passed althogether.

With the war against mulcting finally won, the Race Committee could concentrate on improving the facilities on offer. These were being constantly upgraded and, with good PR and local support, the Galway races developed an exciting charm as well as a course that was superior to most in Ireland at the time. Locals backed the meeting through subscriptions and their new motto was 'Racing is the sport of kings and everybody in Galway during the races is a king'. A respectable level of prize money helped draw fields of good quality, upgrading the sport on offer and attracting more and more racegoers. The annual influx, together with the rise of Salthill's popularity as a seaside resort, expanded the amount of accommodation available in the town, which helped alleviate the chronic shortage of available rooms.

The following is an extract from the *Irish Sportsman & Farmer* of 5 August 1871:

Racing Rhymes No. 1 – The Galway Plate

'I feel it when I sorrow most, I hold it true whate'er befall,
'Tis better to have won and lost, than never to have won at all.'

Tennyson

'Home Rule' is the cry of the day,
Let England make laws for her own:
Its success on the turf, in a marvellous way,
By the entry above is well shown.

To adopt English weights the Committee agreed,
Lord St Lawrence's scale they suppress:
Perhaps to his views they'll now give more heed,
For 'there's nothing succeeds like success.'

An entry unequalled attests to his skill,
While proving his judgment the best:
What Lord Howth has achieved at his own famous Hill,
His son has outdone in the west.

So I'll try by this effort in verse,
To give backers a turn if I can:
But though we may be on the wrong horse,
Doubtless Galway has got the 'right man'.
If wise men are quite puzzled to choose,
When the question is only a 'match',

The work seems cut out for my muse,
When in scores they come up to the scratch.
'How happy could I be with either,
Were t'other sweet charmer away.'
But instead, when you find ninety-three there,
You see – 'tis the devil to pay.
Yet I'll not write whole columns of stuff,
Explaining what horses can't win:
But come straight to some form 'good enough'
For backers to put down their 'tin'.
Smoker, June Wine and Miss Susan and Aster,
With McDonough's, read very well-in,
And the four year old 'un that goes faster
Than Helen McGregor will win.
But since Comet last year pulled me through,
I confess to some faith in the stars,
So this time I'll stick to them too,
And stand Stella (late Lady of Kars).

Sir Oracle

Key to the Runners in 1871 Plate:

	Trainer:
1: H.S. Chester's ASTER (Mr R. Exshaw) aged 11st 1b 9/1	Robert Exshaw
2: Captain Poynter's VENISON (M. Murphy) aged 10st 10lb 8/1	James Murphy
3: B.R.P. Persse's STELLA [late Lady of Kars] 5yo 10st 10lb 10/1	Thomas Connolly
8: T. Dodd's SMOKER 5yo 10st 11lb 5/1f	Richard Bell

Non-Runners:

F. Wallace's June Wine (trained Allen McDonough)
Mr Malone's Miss Susan
Lord Howth's Helen McGregor
Mr Moffat's Comet (Winner of the race 1870)

The rhyming tipster who called himself 'Sir Oracle' plumped for Stella, who was formerly known as Lady of Kars, and was listed in the racecard and newspapers as Stella (late Lady of Kars). Fifth in the inaugural Irish Grand National in 1870 as Lady of Kars, her name was changed by Mr Power after he purchased the mare from the northern sportsman Captain J.F. Montgomery. It is hard to fathom why he wanted to call her Stella, because there were three other mares named Stella racing in Ireland at that time. It is doubtful that the name was changed to confuse people, as the mare was well known and afterwards was always known as Stella (late Lady of Kars), to avoid confusion with the others. One of the other 'Stellas', a mare of unknown parentage, won at Listowel but Stella (late Lady of Kars) was easily the best of the four. Bought by Burton Persse after she won the Railway Open Handicap Chase over 2½ miles at Punchestown, she ran a very respectable third of twenty-nine runners in the Galway Plate, the biggest field in the history of the race. Next time out she won the Grand Stand Handicap (Autumn) at Cork Park, the joint most valuable steeplechase (with its sister race run in the spring) run in Ireland that year, with only the two big Curragh two-year-old events, the Railway and the Anglesey Stakes, being worth more. Eventually Stella (late Lady of Kars) was bought back by Captain Montgomery and for him ran third to The Torrent and Scots Grey in the 1873 Irish Grand National.

At this time there was a special prize for the first four-year-old to finish but Sir Oracle's selection, Lord Howth's Helen McGregor, did not run. Five four-year-olds ran in the Plate that year and the prize was won by the only horse of that age to complete the course, Mr W.E. Murphy's Wild Vixen, who finished fourth. Smoker, ridden by William Bell and trained by Dick Bell, started favourite at 5 to 1 but could only finish eighth. Allen McDonough's French Horn finished in the rear but was a winning favourite in the Forster Street Handicap the following day, ridden by 'Honest Paddy' Gavin. French Horn had also won that Galway Plate consolation race the previous year and raced under McDonough's assumed name of 'Captain Williams', probably because he did not train the horse himself but put it in the care of James Monaghan. Mr F. Wallace's June Wine, winner of the Bellewstown Cup the previous year, came from the powerful yard of J.H. Moore but did not appear at Galway and neither did Miss Susan, who was narrowly held on form by Stella (late Lady of Kars) anyway. However, by mentioning the winner, Aster, and mentioning only four horses from the field of twenty-nine that actually ran in the race, Sir Oracle was entitled to be pleased with his work!

The Development of the Races

The First Race over Hurdles at Ballybrit

King George IV (1820–30) made an indelible mark on the 'sport of kings', both directly and indirectly – directly, by his ownership of a Derby winner and his patronage of the sport, and indirectly, by his boycott of Newmarket and his enjoyment of jumping sheep hurdles, which ultimately led to hurdle racing. He was a prominent owner of racehorses when he was the Prince of Wales, giving the sport respectability and making it fashionable among the wealthy gentry. His numerous horses were stabled at Newmarket and that small town profited greatly from his influence and patronage and it flourished as a racing and training centre. His racing activities cost him a fortune, with Parliament having to bail him out several times, but he did enjoy success on the turf, notably with Sir Thomas, the first Royal winner of the Derby in 1788. Three years later he abandoned Newmarket following a row with the Jockey Club, the body that owned the Heath, ran the racing there and controlled the training gallops. Sam Chifney, the leading jockey of the day and the Prince's retained jockey, was accused by the Jockey Club of pulling Escape, one of his horses, in a race at Newmarket. Forced into action by the raucous protests of the crowd after the race, the stewards found Chifney guilty but, in deference to their royal patron, decided to leave the punishment of the jockey to the Prince. To the dismay of the Jockey Club, the heir to the throne refused to accept that Chifney had pulled Escape and immediately issued a public statement that he was standing by his jockey and had complete faith in him. When the stewards insisted that if the Prince continued to employ Sam Chifney no gentleman would race against him, George took this as a slur on his integrity and decided to pull out of Newmarket altogether.

The scandal damaged racing at Newmarket initially, revealing the seedy characters lurking in the betting side of the sport, associating the racing of horses with excessive gambling and exposing it to the fury of the strong, anti-gambling religious lobby. But while the loss of the Prince's horses badly affected the economy of the town in the short term, the incident was the making of the Jockey Club, whose stewards were seen by the public to have stood up to one of the most important figures in the land despite the threat of losing the extensive royal patronage. With owners' confidence in Newmarket Rules soaring, more and more racecourses were forced race under them, extending the influence of the Jockey Club far beyond their own property of Newmarket Heath. The Prince's stand rebounded on him because he excluded himself from any course racing under Jockey Club Rules, which effectively excluded his horses from all the valuable races. Sam Chifney's career was also finished for the same reason but he had no choice in the matter, having been 'warned off' any racecourse where Jockey Club Rules were in force.

However, despite his anger over the Escape matter, the Prince of Wales never lost his love of horse racing and continued in the sport as best he could. Shortly after being crowned King George IV, he came to Ireland in August 1821 on a celebrated visit, which began with his arrival by boat at Dun Leary, an event that was commemorated by renaming the town Kingstown in his honour. During his visit he attended the Curragh races, where a three-tier stand was hastily erected to accommodate the royal party and the large attendance, and marquees were set up to provide refreshments for ordinary local people who turned out for the occasion. His Majesty presented the Royal Whip, for the owner of the best horse in Ireland weight for age, and provided an annual purse of 100 guineas for the race. His declared motive was to encourage the breeding of strong Irish horses, and royal plates would continue to benefit Irish racing for many years to come.

Although he did not realize it at the time, the Prince's lasting contribution to horse racing came about as a result of his visits to the Royal Pavilion at Brighton, which was built in 1787. For recreation he and his companions would ride out to hunt on the Sussex Downs above the town, where they began to jump in and out of the sheep pens for amusement, until they were stopped by complaints from the shepherds that the sheep were being disturbed. Sheep pens consisted of hurdles, small wooden rails that were light and portable so, in response to these complaints, the royal party instead borrowed some of them, lining them up to be jumped on the Downs well away from the sheep. Thereafter the jumping of sheep hurdles became popular with equestrians, who were able to enjoy the thrill of jumping without having to venture on to a neighbour's property or to be a member of a hunt. Easy to move, sheep hurdles could be erected in a field without any hidden risks such as barbed wire, and were generally a lot safer, for both horse and rider, than the fences traditionally encountered in the hunting field.

Once riders got used to jumping hurdles it was only a matter of time before they wanted to race 'over the sticks'. The first recorded hurdle races were held in 1821, near Bristol, the races being run in heats over 1 mile, with five hurdles to be jumped. Despite receiving the boost of being recognized by the flat-race authority, the Jockey Club, hurdle racing failed to attract much support from a public addicted to steeplechasing. Lost in the shadows of flat racing for many years, hurdle racing in Ireland only began to grow in popularity after being assid-uously promoted by the new park racecourses. Unlike steeplechasing, hurdle racing was very much an English sport and comparatively few hurdle races were run in Ireland during the first half of the nineteenth century. The traditional jumping meetings, such as Punchestown and Fairyhouse, did not run such events and the Curragh, not surprisingly because of all the sheep, was the centre of hurdle racing in Ireland until the establishment of the Irish National Hunt Steeplechase Committee in 1870.

The arrival of the park courses was a big boost for hurdle racing, with Baldoyle, Down Royal and Cork Park putting on valuable hurdle races. Executives found that hurdles could easily be erected on the flat course, which gave the exec-utive a flexibility that was impossible with steeplechase fences. This encouraged the park courses to promote hurdle racing, which they did by putting up good prize money in order to attract a better class of horse, and to arouse public inter-est. When Galway decided to run its first hurdle race in 1877, the richest hurdle race in Ireland was the Malborough Hurdle, run at the Maze and worth £365 to the winner, making it the third most valuable race run in Ireland that year. Cork Park, Curragh and Baldoyle all featured valuable hurdle events, with the Baldoyle race, the May Plate (£200), being run over both hurdles and steeplechase fences. This was not that unusual at the time, as some of the big steeplechases, including the Aintree Grand National, included a preliminary hurdle before the first fence. Hurdle races were also proving popular with the strand meetings, which could not run steeplechases, with Laytown, Termonfeckin and Annagassan including hurdle races in their programmes, while the Dungarvan strand meeting consisted only of hurdle races. The only other Irish racecourses to run a hurdle race back in 1877 were Cappoquin, Cloyne, Fermoy and Kilkennny. This branch of horse racing was still very much in its infancy.

Galway's Bushy Park Handicap Hurdle was run over a 1½ miles, over six flights of gorsed hurdles, and was put in as the first race of the meeting. Worth £99 to the winner, it was the sixth most valuable hurdle race to be run in Ireland that year and attracted plenty of interest. Seven runners went to the post and Thirsk and Ilderim started joint favourites at 5 to 2. Thirsk represented the powerful stable of John Hubert Moore and its owner, Moses Taylor, did not keep a bad horse for long. Competing in the top steeplechases all year, Thirsk had some form over the smaller obstacles, having won the May Plate at Baldoyle, a 2-mile race over fences and hurdles, and was the obvious favourite. However, there was strong public support for Ilderim, possibly because he had previously won at Galway. By Selim, the inaugural winner of the Irish Derby, Ilderim was successful in two flat races at Galway three years earlier but his owner, Willie Long, had died the previous year. Now the property of the bookie Michael Sage and trained by William Bell beside the Curragh grandstand, Ilderim had good form over fences, having won a steeplechase at the Wexford meeting in May and dead heating with Thiggin Thue, when the pair were beaten by a neck by Negress at the Bandon and Cashelmore Hunt Races. Thiggin Thue had beaten Thirsk out of sight in the Irish Grand National, which may have lulled some backers into dismissing the latter's impressive form.

An entire horse by the Derby winner Thormanby, Thirsk skipped over the six hurdles to win the race effortlessly by five lengths, while Ilderim (William Bell) had to battle for second place, holding off Richard the First (Paddy Gavin) by a neck. Third of three in the 1871 Irish Derby, Richard the First was now a chaser and had won at Bellewstown on its previous start. Thirsk was owned by Moses Taylor, the owner of a fine property on the banks of the River Liffey at Morristown-Biller, near Newbridge, whose red, white and blue colours were prominent on the turf. Taylor bred a horse called, appropriately as it turned out, Grand National, sent him to Pat Doocie, who trained him to win one of Ireland's most valuable two-year-old races, the National Produce Stakes at the Curragh in 1873. Transferred to the maestro Henry Eyre Linde for his jumping career, Grand National carried off the Irish Grand National in 1876. Despite this success Taylor was regarded as an unlucky owner, failing to get much return for the enormous sum he spent on the sport. He tended to use a number of trainers; The Prophet, a useful half-brother to Grand National, was trained by Tom Connolly and of course Thirsk, named after the Yorkshire racecourse, was sent to J.H. Moore at Jockey Hall. Taylor came into racing in 1864, winning two races with a useful three-year-old unnamed colt by Newton-le-Willows out of Daphne; and his final winner came on 6 September 1882 when Arizona, a half-sister to Grand National and The Prophet, won a nursery at the Curragh. A fortnight later he was dead, at the age of sixty-two.

At the time of his death Taylor had an unraced two-year-old in Connolly's stable named Bendigo, after a brand of tobacco. Home-bred, Bendigo was by the Irish Derby winner Ben Battle, which Taylor also owned, and was sneakily bought by Tom Connolly at the dispersal sale of the Taylor horses, auctioneer Robert J. Goff knocking the colt down to him at only 72 guineas. Passed on to English owner Major Hedworth T. 'Buck' Barclay, Bendigo turned out to be a champion, winning the Cambridgeshire, Lincolnshire, Hardwicke Stakes, Jubilee Stakes, Champion Stakes and the inaugural running of the Eclipse Stakes in 1886, beating St Gatien, winner of the Derby two years earlier. Captain Boycott bought well at the sale, securing Butte des Morts for 80 guineas and more than recouping his outlay when the filly won twice at the following year's Galway meeting.

John Hubert Moore, the trainer of Thirsk, was one of the leading jumping trainers in Ireland and, at the time, was based at Jockey Hall on the Curragh. Born in Shannon Grove, Co. Galway, in 1819, the son of Captain Garrett Moore, who claimed to be a descendant of the O'Moores of Leix, he was educated in Carlow and at Trinity College. He joined the hunting fraternity, first with a pack of hounds in King's County and later with John Dennis, Master of the Galway Blazers. Moore's attempt to sell off his family's estates after the famine greatly angered the local population and, having survived two assassination attempts, he was forced to flee to Moatfield in Co. Tipperary in 1853, where he started a stable. During the winter months, when there was little or no racing at home, he moved his string to Cherry Hall, Malpas, Cheshire, where he decided to remain, raiding the top Irish races with horses such as Joey Ladle and Tom Thumb.

Racked with rheumatism and tired of Cheshire, he returned to Ireland in 1872, settling at Jockey Hall, where he prospered due in no small part to the riding abilities of his son Garrett (Garry). Soon a fierce rivalry grew up between himself and his neighbour Henry Linde, the other famous Irish trainer of jumpers, whose horses were ridden by the talented Tommy Beasley. Moore won the Irish Grand National in 1872 and again in 1875 with Scots Grey; Linde responded with victories by Grand National and Thiggin Thue. Moore hit back with the 1878 winner Juggler and trumped his neighbour by winning the Aintree Grand National with The Liberator the following year; but after that it was all Linde. In 1880 he won both the Irish and English Grand Nationals with Controller and Empress; the following year he and Tommy Beasley won the Aintree race again, this time with Woodbook, and in addition he won the big French jumping races at Auteuil, the Grand Course de Haies with Seaman (1881) and the Grand Steeplechase de Paris with Whisper Low (1882) and Too Good (1883).

The Moores first descended on Ballybrit in 1870, winning the Members' 2-mile Steeplechase with Stronghold, the first leg of a four-timer by young Garry, who finished the meeting as the leading jockey. Garry was never as successful at Ballybrit thereafter, winning only six more races there. He never won the Plate and was placed only once in it, on Ishmael, beaten by six lengths by Belle in 1872. Garrett Moore was one of a number of brilliant Corinthians riding in Ireland in the latter half of the nineteenth century. Born in 1851 when his father was training in England, his career in the saddle was short due to his love of the high life and his distaste for starvation. On his retirement from the saddle, he took over the Jockey Hall stable, won two Irish Derbies with Theologian (1884) and Theodemir (1886), before moving to England, where he was to remain for the rest of his life. His father, John Hubert Moore, was the top trainer at Galway with thirteen winners until his record was surpassed by James Dunne in 1888. Moore did not train a winner at Galway in the eighteen years after 1877 but got his fourteenth and final success with Capricious, successful in the Renmore Chase in 1896. He did train two winners of the Galway Plate, Revoke (1874) and The Liberator (1875), but this record was eclipsed by his rival Henry Linde, who trained six winners of the race: Martha (1876), Nightfall (1881), Sugar Plum (1882), Ventriloquist (1883), Alexander (1889) and Double Primrose (1896). He kept the record until it was equalled by Fred Cullen in 1902 and passed by Harry Ussher in 1940. Ussher's final tally of nine Galway Plates was a race record until it was equalled by Paddy Sleator in 1975, when O'Leary was successful.

Hurdling at Galway

The Galway Race Committee was delighted with the first hurdle race, run in 1877, deeming it such a success that two were advertised the following year. The Bushy Park Handicap opened the meeting again, and the Moyode Handicap Hurdle opened proceedings on the second day, but the two races were too similar for the good of either. Although the new race was 4 furlongs longer, it was £30 less well endowed, and basically catered for the same type of horse; moreover, hurdlers were not plentiful in Ireland at the time. There should have been no surprise at the lack of runners but it appears that there was great disappointment when only six horses turned out between the two races, four running in each with two horses contesting both events.

The Bushy Park Handicap Hurdle produced an odds-on favourite, Captain Stamer Gubbins's four-year-old half-bred filly May Day, a winner over hurdles at Cork Park, but she could only finish a close third behind Mestiza and Richard the First. Trained by Tom Connolly at Curragh View, Mestiza was owned by 'W. Holland', otherwise William Bourke of Roscrea, who had owned Madeira, winner of the Irish Derby a decade previously. A filly by Marksman out of Tawney, Mestiza was bred by Lord Mayo, owner of the mighty Palmerstown Stud, and was closely related to two Irish Derby winners. Her grand-dam, Caprice, was also the dam of Frailty, dam of Billy Pitt, successful for trainer Tom Connolly in 1870; his half-brother, Soulouque, also trained by Tom Connolly, won the Irish Derby in 1879.

Both Mestiza and Richard the First turned out again the following day in the Moyode Handicap Hurdle, opposed by Lord Fermoy's Lottery, the favourite, and Captain Rochfort's no-hoper Fairwind. Neither Lottery (by Master Bagot) nor Fairwind had won a race that year, but both had competed in the Galway Plate, with Lottery finishing a poor third behind The Inny (subsequently disqualified) and Jupiter Tonans. Richard the First, a half-brother to Fairwind, had won a minor handicap chase at Wexford and represented a good jumping yard, that of Matt Maher at Ballinkeele. Punters must have been bemused when Lottery fell over these smaller obstacles, leaving Richard the First to win comfortably by four lengths.

Stung by the disappointing response to their hurdle races, Galway reverted to running only one in 1879, introducing a conditions race instead of a handicap. The Claddagh Hurdle, weight-for-age, with penalties and a selling allowance, drew nine moderate runners and was won by Eurasian, ridden by Mr John Beasley and owned by Captain P. Butler of Geraldine, Athy, whose son Piery rode the winner of the 1907 Galway Plate. Eurasian was also out of the mare Tawney, making him a half-brother to Mestiza, the winner of one of the hurdle races the previous year. He claimed a selling allowance but there was no bid for the horse at the auction held after the race. Eurasian reappeared in a handicap chase the following day, was unquoted in the betting and finished down the field.

After the 1880 race, won by Granuaile, Galway abandoned hurdle racing, turning the Claddagh Hurdle into the Claddagh Plate, a 5-furlong sprint. That turned out to be a fiasco because Matt Maher's Purple walked over. The Claddagh race was dropped in 1882 but hurdle racing was not brought back. In 1883 the Claddagh Plate, now a 6-furlong sprint, was run, being won by Garry Moore's Barbarian, after which the race name was dropped.

After a ten-year gap, hurdle racing returned to Ballybrit in 1890, when no less than three hurdle races were featured, the Moyode, County and Express Hurdles.

The Stewards Disqualify The Inny

The 1878 Galway Plate, worth £220 to the winner, attracted a strong field, which included that year's Irish Grand National winner, Juggler. An outstanding four-year-old chaser in 1874, Juggler had been plagued by injury since then but had come good at Fairyhouse, pegging back the huge lead established by Bob Ridley to justify favouritism. Trained by John Hubert Moore, Juggler was ridden at Fairyhouse by Mr John Beasley because Garry Moore was unable to do the weight; he kept the ride at Galway. Juggler was easy to back in the market, however, as punters preferred Jupiter Tonans, a headstrong, five-year-old stallion trained by Captain George Joy and ridden by his owner, 'The Shaver' – Mr J.F.S. Lee-Barber, a lieutenant with the 3rd Dragoon Guards. His recent form was not inspiring but he had won the Grand Military Steeplechase at Punchestown the previous year. The price dropped down to 2 to 1 as Juggler eased in the market from 3 to 1 to 5 to 1. The Inny was priced at 6 to 1. She was an eight-year-old mare owned by Sir Walter Nugent, a member of the Turf Club, and trained by Michael Dennehy, and had been running in the top chases, wining three times, two of which were at the recent Bellewstown meeting.

The race became a farce when The Inny's rider, a professional jockey named Byrne, mistook the course, went inside a post and emerged with a handsome lead, which he never surrendered. Jupiter Tonans tried hard to reduce the gap, going right away from the remaining runners, but was still three lengths in arrears at the line. The stewards had no option but to disqualify The Inny but Sir Walter Nugent got a decent consolation prize of £130 the following day when she easily won the Forster Street Plate.

The headstrong Jupiter Tonans developed into a very good chaser, winning the 1879 Irish Grand National and finishing fourth in the 1880 Aintree Grand

National. Starting a 50 to 1 chance at Aintree and watched by the Prince of Wales, Jupiter Tonans was running very nicely until the field reached Valentine's Brook on the first circuit. Now that he was facing home, he seemed intent on getting back to the paddock area as quickly as possible, and pulled hard to get away. His owner/rider, 'The Shaver', struggled gallantly to restrain his mount and managed to do so reasonably well, although he could not prevent him from racing into the lead, until Downpatrick, ridden by Paddy Gavin, took him on passing the stands, at which point Jupiter Tonans took off 'at flat race speed'. Powerless to stop him, Mr Lee Barber could do nothing but sit tight as he raced clear, building up a huge lead. At one point the horse was over a furlong ahead, and everybody, including the other jockeys, expected the runaway to run out of steam at any moment. However, he raced on, showing no sign of stopping, until it began to look as if he could not be caught and even Paddy Gavin, Tommy Beasley, Garry Moore and Harry Beasley were anxiously urging their mounts to try and reduce the lead. As the leader began to slow, Downpatrick, Empress and The Liberator were closing fast, and in the end all three passed the exhausted Jupiter Tonans. Empress and Tommy Beasley went on, chased by The Liberator and settled the outcome with a magnificent leap at the last hurdle, winning by two lengths. The Liberator just managed to hold on to second position by a head from Downpatrick, who was staying on strongly, with Jupiter Tonans fourth, two lengths further back, having got a second wind.

The Inny won two valuable steeplechases at Baldoyle the following year but was beaten out of sight in the Galway Plate by Rocksavage (Mr J.F. Lee-Barber up). The next day she ran again, finishing second in the Forster Street Plate, but she failed to win a race in 1880 and would never win again. The mare had completely lost her form for some reason, although her connections persevered despite two defeats early in 1881. Surprisingly, The Inny was backed to beat favourite Victor II, who had finished seventh behind Empress in the dramatic Grand National featuring Jupiter Tonans, in a race at Kells. She failed to cope with the experienced entire but did finish a good second. Shortly afterwards she dropped down dead, indicating that her loss of form may have been due to something being wrong.

The Royal Plate

Royal plates, usually called His/Her Majesty's Plate or King's/Queen's Plate, depending whether a king or a queen was on the throne at the time, were a series of races endowed by the monarch for the improvement of the breed and run under special articles. First set down in 1717, these articles were updated every so often but in 1879 they stipulated that such races be run between 25 March and 15 November of each year, on the flat, over a distance of not less than 2 miles. The weights were set out according to the age of the horse, the month of the year and the distance of the race. These races were to be run no later than 3 p.m. and could not be run at a fixture where added money to the other flat races did not amount to £150. Geldings were barred from running and a number of the races excluded horses that had not been trained in Ireland for the previous six months. In 1879 twelve royal plates were to be run at the Curragh, two at the Maze and one each at Bellewstown, Cork Park and Londonderry.

In 1878 the Londonderry meeting was run over the Ballyarnet course on 8 and 9 August and Mr S.G. Barry's Valour, ridden by Frank Wynne, won the Queen's Plate. Although the results are recorded in the Irish Racing Calendar, the official return of the meeting was not made to the Turf Club as required, which was probably an attempt by the executive to hide its breach of the Queen's Plate Articles – added money to the other flat races at Londonderry did not amount to £150 and had not done so for a number of years, which disqualified the meeting from running a Queen's plate. When the breach of the articles was confirmed, the prestigious race was taken away from Londonderry and switched to Galway, which raced around the same time of the year. It was run at Galway for seventy-nine years, until the fund was consolidated and the race dropped after the 1958 race. The loss of the Queen's Plate proved to be the beginning of the end for the Londonderry meeting, for which folded in 1881. Briefly revived as the Derry and Stabane, then Londonderry and Strabane, in 1890, it finally gave up the ghost after the 1905 meeting.

The first Queen's Plate was run at Galway on Thursday, 7 August, attracting the classy Shinglass. One of the leading juveniles the previous year, Shinglass had won the Baldoyle Derby but was beaten in the Irish Derby by the Tom Connolly-trained Soulouque. Made favourite at Galway, he was again thwarted by a Connolly-trained runner, this time Tom Thumb, a 100 to 8 outsider, who beat him by a length. Tom Thumb's victory was the second of the afternoon, the second and last horse to win two races on the same day at the Galway Races. A beaten favourite on the first day of the meeting when it came second in the Renmore Plate over 1 mile, Tom Thumb was turned out the following day for the Members' Plate over 6 furlongs and duly won. Although he won another Queen's Plate, at the Curragh the following month, he never won another race after that.

Only four horses won Galway's Royal Plate more than once: Baron Farney (1880 and 1881), Yellow Vixen (1900 and 1902), Royal Hackle II (1912 and 1914) and Italassu (1954 and 1955). The winners in the early years, when 100 guineas was a very good purse, were of good quality, including Charles J. Blake's two Irish Derby winners, Sylph (1883) and St Kevin (1885), and Garry Moore's Irish Derby runner-up, Theorist (1882), whose remarkable dam Miss Theo bred three Irish Derby winners but the quality declined with the years. The last horse that had been placed in the Irish Derby to go on to win the Galway Royal Plate was Charles Blake's Goldminer, winner in 1892, while the last Irish Derby winner to contest it was Eustace Loder's Gallinaria, who, as a four-year-old in 1901, was beaten by Glenmalur, a good horse owned by F. Frame and trained by Denis Shanahan.

The decline of the Royal Plate continued down the years and the last winner of the race that was considered good enough to run in the Irish Derby was Golden Lancer (1936) – and he finished last! The final winner of the race By-Passed, trained by George Robinson and ridden by his son Willie, was a low-class handicapper that won at minor courses such as Laytown, Ballinrobe and Bellewstown. George Robinson and his jockey son enjoyed an exciting but frustrating season with Paddy's Point, runner-up in both the English and Irish Derbies. Third to Hard Ridden in the Irish 2,000 Guineas, Paddy's Point was a 100 to 1 outsider at Epsom but ran the race of his life to finish second, again to Hard Ridden, despite hanging left in the straight. George Robinson's charge was undone by a combination of a steady early pace and an inspired Charlie Smirke but, in Hard Ridden's absence, looked sure to win at the Curragh. Again he was to be undone by a non-stayer, and a maiden to boot, Anne Biddle's Sindon, who got first run, while interference forced Paddy's Point wide. Willie Robinson's late charge just failed, and Paddy's Point was beaten by a short head. They say tight finishes shorten lives and poor George Robinson died the following November. However, Willie prospered as a jump jockey, being best remembered for his partnership with Arkle's great rival Mill House.

Champion Irish jockey in 1958, Willie Robinson won the Grand National on Team Spirit, the Cheltenham Gold Cup on Mill House and the Champion Hurdle on Anzio and Kirriemuir before his retirement in 1970. He was also successful at Galway, winning the Plate on Terossian (1968) and the Hurdle on Tymon Castle (1957) and Commutering (1960), as well as being placed in the latter race five times. Willie trained at Stepaside, Curragh, until 1984, winning the Irish 2,000 Guineas with Bert Firestone's Kings Company in his first season. That horse also won the Cork and Orrery Stakes at Royal Ascot, a feat Willie repeated nine years later with Kearney. His mother later owned Pheopotstown, winner of the McDonogh Handicap in 1988, trained by Paddy Mullins.

The Queen's Plate was run for the last time at Galway on Thursday, 31 July 1958. The crown had sponsored the race to the tune of 100 guineas and continued to do so after Irish independence in 1922. When this was raised in the House of Commons the Financial Secretary to the Treasury replied that the money involved was small, £1,563. It had been voted annually to Irish racing by the House for over a hundred years and in view of the special nature of the payment it was decided to continue the payment after the establishment of the Irish Free State. However, the value of the sponsorship was never increased and while 100 guineas was a decent sum in 1879, when the Queen's Plate was the second most valuable race on the card, its value was seriously eroded by inflation down the years. Eighty years later it was still worth £105, but it was now the least valuable race on the Galway twelve-race programme, being worth £30 less than minimum value at the time. Consolidation was necessary but there was the fear that if the matter was brought to the attention of the crown, the endowment might be discontinued altogether, so nothing was said. Eventually the nettle was grasped in 1958. The crown agreed to a reduction in the number of royal plates, with the prize fund for the remaining races being increased to £208. The Galway race was one of those to be abandoned, being replaced by the Barna Handicap in 1959, the year the meeting was extended to three days for the first time.

Charles Blake was the leading owner of Galway royal plate winners, with five, all at a time when the race was valuable both in prize money and prestige. This was also true of the leading trainer, James Dunne, whose nine wins were achieved between 1880 and 1914, including four of Charles Blake's five winners. The leading rider was Jim Parkinson's ill-fated stable jockey, John Thompson, with five winners between 1903 and 1909. Herbet Holmes rode four winners and Morny Wing rode three in succession. Aubrey Brabazon's only win came in 1951, on Ollerton Hills, the first of trainer Paddy Prendergast's four winners, and this horse never got a mention in Brabazon's autobiography!

Galway's royal plate was a good race for punters because in its seventy-nine renewals, minus the seven walkovers, no fewer than forty-one of the races were won by the favourite – a 57 per cent strike rate! It may have been a difficult race for bookies to bet on but two racecourse bookmakers enjoyed success in the race as owners, John James with Tranby Croft (1894) and Dick Power with Striped Silk (1928).

John James, the leading bookie in the ring at the time, took what is probably the largest bet ever struck on an Irish racecourse, on the favourite for a race and having it beaten! It happened at the Curragh Derby meeting in 1895, where Prince Francis of Teck, the future King George V's brother-in-law, was having a bad day and found himself owing John James £1,000. Almost penniless at the time, Prince Francis attempted to clear his account with James by wagering £10,000 on the two-year-old Bellevin at odds of 10 to 1 on, risking that enormous sum to win nothing! Bellevin, the horse on which he invested so heavily, was trained at Heath House by Shem Jeffrey and raced in the maize and red hoops and light blue cap of T.L. Plunkett, a Portmarnock businessman who raced horses in partnership with Charles J. Blake. Bellevin came to the Curragh as a juvenile with a big home reputation, easily winning the valuable Waterford Testimonial Stakes on the first day of the three-day meeting. Reappearing on the third day over the same course and distance, Bellevin looked a certainty, with two of his four opponents having no earthly chance of winning. The only danger was Winkfield's Pride, trained and ridden by Michael Dawson, the winner of the valuable Lee Plate at Cork Park on his debut. However, he ran in a nursery at the Curragh the previous afternoon, getting well and truly hammered by Fred Cullen's The Mute by no less than ten lengths.

Bellevin may have looked a certainty but he was not and the Prince was about to learn that there is no such thing as a certainty in horse racing. Winkfield's Pride won by a length and a half, which meant that Prince Francis now owed John James £11,000 and did not have the wherewithal to pay. He knew that when he struck the bet, but at that time he thought he could not lose. John James, on the other hand, definitely could not lose because, even if Bellevin won, the Prince would get no money from James, merely the cancelling of a debt. Although the bookie may have feared that the Prince could not pay up, he could be reasonably sure that the royal family would be forced to settle the account to avoid a scandal. And so it proved: Prince Francis of Teck had not a bean, and it was left to the future king, then the Duke of York, to pay John James.

Bellevin had come up against a really good horse, because Winkfield's Pride won the Cambridgeshire, one of the bigges handicaps in England, the following year, while Bellevin never won another race.

Fred Cullen Trains All Five Winners

Thursday, 8 August 1889 was red-letter day for trainer Frederick F. Cullen of Rossmore Lodge, Curragh – he trained all five winners at his home meeting, in front of all his friends, setting a training record that has not been equalled since. Born in Galway in 1853, Fred's parents sent him to study medicine in Dublin. Young Fred loved everything about life as a student – except study. University in those days was full of young men with a love of racing, Fred got in with this set and the sport dominated his life more and more. During the summer holidays in 1875, Fred rode his first winner, Retort, a grey pony of unknown parentage owned by P.J. Bodkin, in a 2-mile steeplechase worth £15 at the Glenamaddy Steeplechases on 21 July.

Never among the elite of the amateurs in an age when standards were high, Fred rode a lot of winners and in 1879 won his first race at Galway, riding Mr J. Lloyd's unnamed stallion by Draco to victory in the Mervue Chase. By this time his brother Willie, eight years younger, had also caught the bug. He was showing promise as a rider and Fred was in a position to give him rides, because by this time he was training a number of horses for himself. Willie Cullen rode his first winner, an old chaser named The Colonel, an entire horse trained by Fred, in the Consolation Plate, a 2-mile handicap chase, at Ennis in September 1879. However, Fred's university life was at an end and he decided to try a new life in New Zealand, departing shortly after riding that old stalwart The Colonel to victory in the Commercial Handicap Chase at the Curry (Co. Sligo) meeting at the end of October.

Desperately homesick, Fred barely lasted three years in the Antipodes, returning to Ireland in 1882. While he was away, brother Willie set up a private stable at Cloonheen, Ballinasloe, combining riding and training, mainly for Mr J.W. Furlong and Mr Francis R. Fawcett. The best horse in his care was Erin's Hope, which provided him with his first Galway winner in 1881, the valuable Forster Street Handicap Chase. Although Mr W.P. Cullen was Champion Irish Jockey twice, in 1886 and again in 1889, his riding career was slow to get started and he did not ride his first Galway winner until 1884.

When Fred returned home the two brothers reversed roles, with Fred now riding horses trained by Willie, with considerable success. In 1883 Willie trained Lady Pauline to win the County Handicap Chase at Galway, with Fred riding. However, pickings were slim for a provincial trainer based in Ballinasloe. Most of the fixtures and the valuable races were run in the Dublin metropolitan area and the brothers realized that they would have to move. Deciding to go into partnership, they rented a stableyard at Islandbridge, Dublin, and were so successful that they were forced to move to larger premises, at Montpelier Hill, and take on a professional jockey to assist them. They chose John Gourley, who would later ride Drogheda, the second and last Galway Plate winner to win the Grand National, to victory at Aintree in 1898.

The premature death of Frank Wynne, the three-times Irish Champion Jockey, who had been training at Rossmore Lodge only three seasons, had left that famous training establishment on the Curragh vacant. During the summer of 1886 it was reported that the Cullen brothers were moving there, but it transpired that only Fred came because the brothers had decided to go their separate ways. Willie moved into Jockey Hall, recently vacated by Garry Moore, who departed to Hampshire, and began training on his own account once again.

Once settled on the Curragh, Fred Cullen enlisted the experienced Robert Exshaw, who had ridden Aster to victory in the 1871 Galway Plate, as his assistant, and began what turned out to be a very successful training career. The Cullen brothers had trained Erin's Star when it won the 1885 Galway Plate, but Fred added to this with victories by Victrix (Mr W.P. Cullen) in 1885, Queen of the May (Mr W. Beasley) in 1891 and Tipperary Boy, the three-times winner of the race in 1899, 1901 and 1902. Willie Cullen was easily the better jockey of the pair but Fred had the better record as a trainer, sending out a host of winners on the flat and over jumps, including Noble Howard, winner of the 1898 Irish Derby, Royal Meath, the last Irish-trained winner of the Grand Steeplechase de Paris in 1890, Lady Vic (Drogheda Memorial) and Tipperary Boy, winner of the Irish Grand National and the only horse to win the Galway Plate three times. However, it is hard to get away from the fact that Fred Cullen's training career went into decline after the death of Robert Exshaw in August 1898.

One of the leading riders in the pre-Beasley era, Exshaw was Irish Champion Amateur in 1868 and 1872, and maintained a stable at Hybla House, Monasterevan. His retirement from race riding in the mid-1870s left him isolated and without enough owners to support a training yard, forcing him to accept a position as private trainer to Mr P. George of Beachfield House, Clontarf. After a few years with Mr George's moderate horses, Exshaw was delighted to receive the offer from Fred Cullen; it was the beginning of a successful association. Although Fred controlled the stable, Exshaw was an important figure in the operation and was responsible for the actual training of the horses. Aged sixty when he died, his name was always written as 'Exshaw', throughout his racing career but it seems that it actually may have been 'Eglshaw', the surname that appears on his death certificate.

There is no doubt that his death was a terrible loss to the Rossmore Lodge stable. It must be said that Fred Cullen completely lost heart after the death of his ten-year-old son, Henry Pitt Cullen, in an accident with a gun in November 1902, but signs that all was not well at Rossmore Lodge were plain to see before that tragedy. In July 1902, Fred Cullen had to be forced by a court to release the horse Well Fort, which the owner wanted to transfer to the stable of M.J. Harty at Croom. Well Fort, owned by J.R. D'Arcy, the clerk to the Rural District Council of Galway and named after his residence in Kilkerrin, Ballinasloe, had won the Mervue Handicap at Galway in 1899 but had been without a win since September 1900, when he was successful at Wexford. In fairness to Fred Cullen, 'The Boss' failed to get much good out of Well Fort, his only victory being a lowly steeple-chase, worth less than £12, at Newcastle West, and he walked over for that! Fred Cullen trained his last winner in 1907 and vacated Rossmore Lodge the following year (John Smith moved in), returning home to Ballinasloe. He had to suffer another tragedy in 1920, when his jockey son Frank died as a result of a fall at Hurst Park.

Frederick F. Cullen was nine times leading trainer at Galway (if you include the two in partnership with Willie), and won thirty and a half races at the meeting between 1883 and 1902, which was the highest total until passed by Michael Dawson in 1924. His training career, though very successful, was short – it only spanned twenty-five years – and he retired at the age of fifty-five. He outlived his younger brother, who died in 1937. He died at home in Cloonkeen, Kilkerrin, Ballinasloe, on 9 October 1938, after a long illness. His great feat at Galway on Thursday, 8 August 1889, when he trained the winners of all five races on the card, will probably never be equalled. Three of his horses started outright favourite, one was joint favourite and the other, the first winner, was a 3 to 1 chance, making it a memorable day for punters and one to forget for the bookmakers.

The sequence began in the Express Plate, a flat race for hunters, when Ambition, owned by Colonel R. Thomson, a member of the Turf Club, and ridden by Willie Cullen, upset the odds-on favourite Podophyllon, who had won his last two races. A moderate mare, Ambition was an own sister to Queen of the May, who won the Galway Plate for Colonel Thomson and Fred Cullen in 1891. Their sire, Xenophon, was an unraced half-brother to Solon who got few opportunities at stud in Co. Roscommon but bred some nice winners including Seaman (1882 Grand National), Peace (the top Irish two-year-old of 1882), May Boy (Beresford Stakes 1883) and Little May, dam of Noble Howard.

Cullen's second winner of the afternoon was Zulu II, a ten-year-old entire horse, in the County Handicap Steeplechase over 2 miles. Already a prolific winner, he had won the Galway Plate three years previously, when owned by Captain K. St Lawrence and trained by Dan Broderick, beating Lord Chatham, trained and ridden by Fred Cullen, and Eva, trained by Willie Cullen. Most unfashionably bred, Zulu II was bought by Fred Cullen the following year, finished third to Fethard in the 1888 Galway Plate and was only beaten a length by Alexander in that same race the previous afternoon. Expected to win, Zulu II duly did so, coming home alone as its three opponents all fell, winning its sixth race in Fred Cullen's blue and scarlet stripes.

The Queen's Plate was the feature race and Fred Cullen had high hopes of winning this valuable prize with Gawsworth, winner of the Baldoyle Derby and

Madrid Handicap and fourth in the Irish Derby. Owned by Mr C.W. Bagge of Summerville, Mallow, for whom Fred won the Galway Plate with Victrix in 1887, Gawsworth had only two moderate opponents to beat, Annagor and Pythias – and Fred Cullen knew all about the latter, having trained it until a month previously. Now a four-year-old, Pythias had run in Ireland thirty-six times, winning only three races, the last being in a handicap at the Curragh the previous year. That victory ended on a sour note when his jockey, John Gourley, was warned-off for nine months for wilful disobedience to the starter. A year later, at the Curragh Derby meeting in June, Pythias ran really well to be beaten only by half a length by Annagor, who was getting 19 pounds! The pair beat John Gubbins's filly Queen May out of sight, which probably inspired the latter's trainer, H.E. Linde, to buy Pythias. His form had not really improved since he had joined the maestro of Eyrefield Lodge. The previous day he had started as odds-on favourite for the Renmore Handicap but was well and truly beaten by Andrew Tiernan's Little Widow, trained by Fred Cullen. Dick Dawson's Annagor had won two hurdle races prior to scoring at the Curragh and had subsequently won two flat races at the Maze, but seemed to have little chance of beating Pythias at level weights. Ridden by Joseph Foster, Gawsworth did not have things all his own way, however. Pythias and Tommy Beasley put up a spirited challenge before going under by a length and a half.

The fourth race cut up badly with only two runners going to the post for the Trader's Handicap, a flat race over 6 furlongs. Fred was represented by Andrew Tiernan's Little Widow, seeking a second win at the meeting, and her sole opponent was Black Witch, owned and trained by 'Hooky' Gisbourne Gordon. Fresh from his success with Tragedy in the Irish Derby, 'Hooky' had lost an arm in a shooting accident and had a wooden arm with a hook in place of a hand. By Xenophon and as black as coal, Black Witch's value increased dramatically when her half-sister Tragedy won the Irish Derby.

Keen to win this race, 'Hooky' took a gamble by putting up an unknown apprentice jockey named Greenshields, who had not ridden three winners so was entitled to claim a 5 pound allowance. Black Witch was a sprinter, albeit a moderate one, and although Little Widow had won over 7 furlongs the previous day, the mare had been successful in the Irish Cesarewitch, run over 14 furlongs! 'Hooky's' ploy did not work; Little Widow had too much speed for the well-bred sprinter and won the race easily by two lengths giving jockey Joseph Foster a double.

Owner Andrew Tiernan of New Grange, Drogheda, who died in October 1893, had been fortunate to unload Pythias the previous month but he was not a lucky owner. Racing on a large scale, Mr Tiernan spent a small fortune on horses with relatively little success, bearing in mind the number of horses that ran in his violet jacket. He had high hopes for Slane, an own-brother to the champion Bendigo, which he picked up cheaply at the disposal sale of Moses Taylor's horses, but the horse turned out to be worse than useless.

With four winners in the bag, Fred Cullen's hopes of a clean sweep of the races depended on Colonel Thomson's Bailsman in the Glenarde Hunters' Chase and once again 'Hooky' stood in the way. Bailsman was an inexperienced four-year-old that had finished second at the Maze the previous month, while 'Hooky' had trained the experienced mare, Amazon, winner of three races already that year. Amazon had easily beaten Mr G. Tyson's Shylock at the Maze in July, only to lose the race on a technicality, and the question was whether he would be able to concede nearly 2½ stone to Bailsman. For some reason Willie McAuliffe replaced Willie Cullen aboard Bailsman, while 'Hooky' got the professional Terry Kavanagh to ride Amazon instead of the usual amateur. The excitement was intense, and punters could not make up their minds about the pair, both starting joint favourites at 5 to 4. The other two runners, Joy Bells and Crescent, were ignored, which in the latter's case was fair enough because he was a maiden, but Joy Bells had won six of her last seven races as well as seven times the previous year. The race did not live up to the hype: the two outsiders fell and Amazon never looked likely to win; in the end she was beaten by miles.

Selling Races

Another innovation of the park courses was the 'seller', a race run specifically to enable owners to sell horses from it. All selling races ended with the winner being auctioned in public after the race, and anybody was free to bid. The horse would be sold to the highest bidder and there was nothing the owner could do about it except to buy it himself, or 'buy it in'. In order to ensure that there would be bids, the inventor of selling races devised a number of elaborate rules. To keep out good horses, every selling race had an advertised price, which was intended to confine the race to horses at or around that value. Any runner that ran in a seller without winning could be claimed by any person at the advertised selling price, which warned owners not to enter horses worth more than this value in the race. Although the winning horse was auctioned after the race, the owner did not get the auction price but the advertised price, any surplus being divided equally between the owner of the runner-up and the racecourse. This gave an incentive to the owner of the second horse to bid up the price of the winner.

Owners frequently entered horses more valuable than the advertised price of the race in order to land a gamble, which led to abuses in the system as they tried to retain the winner after the race. Intimidation, persuasion and influence were regularly employed by owners and trainers to stop others from bidding at the auction or from claiming the beaten horses. This became so prevalent that a convention grew up that it was not the 'done thing' to bid for another man's horse in this manner. This eventually proved the downfall of the 'seller' in Ireland, where there is a small, intimate racing industry. The modern version, the claiming race, is a popular method of selling horses in America, but in Ireland they are dogged by the old-fashioned convention that racing people do not claim.

Although Galway ran a selling chase in 1875, the course usually framed races that included an allowance if the horse was to be sold. This 'voluntary seller', with the winner being sold only if it had claimed a selling allowance, was designed to attract horses that were genuinely for sale and to eliminate unpleasantness after the race. Unfortunately, the races did not work out that way because people began to claim the selling allowance in order to obtain an edge, but were most unwilling sellers when their horse won. So it was at Galway on Thursday, 2 August 1894, when John Murnane entered his horse, Lizzy Hermit, in the Glenarde Chase and claimed 8 pounds because the horse was to be sold at £75. Lizzy Hermit was trained at bookmaker Bryan O'Donnell's private stable at Ballyclough House in Limerick and took on Mrs Wilson-Slator's useful mare The Brown Princess, which became the first horse owned by a woman to run in the Irish Grand National when she finished fourth in 1895. She was not for sale, however, and did not claim a selling allowance at Galway. Starting joint favourites at 3 to 1, Lizzy Hermit and The Brown Princess dominated the race, the former eventually winning by three lengths.

There were disorderly scenes after the race as the auctioneer attempted to sell Lizzy Hermit in the face of Mr Murnane's objections. His problem was that he had entered a four-year-old filly that had won chases at Tipperary, Gort and Tuam that summer to be sold for only £75, simply in order to claim the 8-pounds allowance, while believing that she was worth more than that. Completely ignoring the fact that the allowance enabled Lizzy Hermit to defeat The Brown Princess, who claimed no selling allowance, and to land some substantial winning bets in the process, John Murnane would not accept that people were bidding for his horse. Amid disorderly scenes, he verbally abused bidders. Lizzy Hermit was eventually knocked down for £245 to James Phelan, the three-times Champion Irish Amateur Jockey, who ran a private stable at Lisfuncheon, Clogheen, Co. Tipperary, with Larry Ryan in charge.

Leaving his winning bets aside, John Murnane had won the £48 10s prize money for winning the race, plus the £75 advertised value of the horse, which meant that he had actually sold Lizzy Hermit for £123 10s. James Phelan had paid £245 for a horse that was supposed to be worth only £75, while Mrs Wilson-Slator, owner of the second placed horse, received prize money of £1 10s. for second place, plus half the surplus over the selling price, i.e. £85. Irate and agitated, Mr Murnane refused to give up Lizzy Hermit to James Phelan after the auction and the matter was referred to the Irish National Hunt Committee. The Stewards severely cautioned Mr Murnane, ordering him to release the filly to James Phelan, if the latter still wanted it. The exact outcome is in some doubt because Lizzy Hermit never raced afterwards.

The Early Twentieth Century

The first hundred years of the Galway Races produced just one English-trained winner, and that was from an Irish string based in England. Ireland and England were one country until 1922 and several Irish-based trainers took horses to England during the winter months, when there was so little racing at home. The length of the trainer's stay depended on the success of his horses, but it could be weeks, months or even years. John Hubert Moore used to travel to Cheshire and back, but on one occasion did not return for a couple of years. Willie McAuliffe spent one season, 1897, training in England and Willie Cullen and Harry Ussher also trained in England for extended periods.

The connections of English-trained Amlah celebrate their Galway Plate victory in 1998

After the establishment of the Irish Free State, extended stays in England became more difficult and trainers tended to send horses over to a 'friendly' trainer there, rather than come over themselves with a string. Frank Morgan did this with Ballinode, the first Irish-trained winner of the Cheltenham Gold Cup, sending the mare to English trainers for a campaign before bringing her back home again. English-trained runners in Ireland were occasionally despatched without their trainers, being sent over to an Irish stable for the race. In some case these horses are recorded as being trained by the Irish trainer, who might only have had the horse for a week! And then there were trainers who put the licence in the name of the head lad. Modern travel facilities have changed all that. Dermot Weld has trained winners on four of the five continents, and it is a simple matter for English trainers to send a horse to Galway. Winning races is another matter; the racing is competitive and the standard high, which is the only deterrent nowadays.

By my reckoning, twenty-one races at Galway have been won by English-trained horses, including two Galway Plates and two Galway Hurdles.

English-trained Winners at Galway

1904 C.E. Byrne's STRATEGY (A. Magee) – Galway Plate £166 (W.P. Cullen)

1971 J.E. Bigg's SEA ROBBER (J.B. Brogan) – Corrib Hurdle £467 (W. Wharton)

1979 G.J. Freyne's MAJESTIC NURSE (C. Roche) –Thomas McDonogh Handicap £6,103 (C.R. Nelson)

1986 Jim Ennis's RUSHMOOR (P. Scudamore) – Galway Hurdle £16,900 (R.E.Peacock)

1991 David L'Estrange's TRI FOLENE (P. Scudamore) – Albatross Chase £5,177 (M.C. Pipe)

1991 M. Dooley's SAGAMAN (Mr P. Fenton) – Galway Hurdle £19,045 (L.J. Codd)

1994 Risk Factor Partnership's BOBBY SOCKS (P.J. McLoughlin) – Galway Blazers Handicap Chase £4,110 (R. Lee)

1998 Salvo Giannini's AMLAH (B.G. Powell) – Galway Plate £40,162 (P.J. Hobbs)

1999 P. Byrne's MYSTIC RIDGE (J.P. Spencer) – Albatross Handicap flat £5,500 (B.J. Curley)

1999 Mrs B.J. Curley's MAGIC COMBINATION (J.P. Spencer) – Smithwicks Handicap flat £5,672 (B.J. Curley)

2001 Mrs B.J. Curley's KALINGALINGA (J.P. Spencer) – Compaq Handicap flat £8,280 (B.J. Curley)

2002 Mrs B.J. Curley's MALAKAL (S.W. Kelly) – H.P. Handicap flat €10,695 (B.J. Curley)

2003 Dwyer, Finn & O'Rourke's LOVE TRIANGLE (M.J. Kinane) – Smithwicks 2yo Maiden €10,350 (D.R.C. Elsworth)

2003 Patrick Kelly's THE PRINCE (J.P. Murtagh) – Frederick's Claimer flat €13,000 (Ian Williams)

2004 So Long Partnership's GENERAL FEELING (P.B. Beggy) – H.P. Handicap flat €9,328 (S. Kirk)

2005 J. Duddy & T. Fawcett's UHOOMAGOO (N. Callan) – Michael McNamara Handicap flat €65,100 (K.A. Ryan)

2006 Enda Hunston's BOLODENKA (K. Fallon) – Arthur Guinness Handicap flat €11,747 (R.A. Fahey)

2006 Cheveley Park Stud's ELUSIVE DREAM (D.P. McDonogh) – St James's Gate flat €14,322 (Sir Mark Prescott)

2006 Enda Hunston's BOLODENKA (D.P. McDonogh) – Michael McNamara Handicap flat €65,100 (R.A. Fahey)

2007 Liam Mulryan's HOVERING (P. Carberry) – GPT Sligo Novice Hurdle €17,577 (M.G. Quinlan)

2007 J.J. Staunton's SADLER'S KINGDOM (M.C. Hussey) – GPT Van & Truck 3yo Handicap €12,092 (R.A. Fahey)

Barney Curley trained four Galway winners from Newmarket, making him the most successful foreign-based handler. A gambler all his life, Barney did not change his spots when he turned to training horses, becoming a scourge of bookmakers. He is one of those gamblers the bookies fear most, one that ensures the head rules the heart. Needless to say, when Barney brought horses to Galway he returned east afterwards with his pockets full of bookies' money.

Declaration to Win

Until October 1927, when the rule was deleted by the Turf Club and the Irish National Hunt Steeplechase Committee, the Rules of Racing (141) and the Steeplechase Rules (138) read as follows:

> Any owner intending to run two or more horses in any race may declare to win with one of them, and such declaration must be made at scale. The rider of a horse with which the owner has not declared to win, must on no account stop such horse except in favour of the stable companion on whose behalf declaration to win has been made.

The last owner to register a declaration to win with the Clerk of the Scales at Galway was Baron de Tuyll, before the Renmore Corinthian Plate in 1910. He ran two horses, Love in a Mist (Mr R.H. Walker) and Denis Simple (Mr C. Brabazon), both trained by Maxie Arnott, and declared to win with the former. This entitled Cecil Brabazon to pull his mount if he had to, without having to face the displeasure of the stewards, but only to let Love in a Mist win. The declaration allowed punters who thought that Love in a Mist would win to ignore the stable companion Denis Simple. This race had a happy ending for punters because Love in a Mist, one of the joint favourites, ran out an easy winner, with Denis Simple back in third place.

In Ireland both rules were changed to read: 'Every horse which runs in a race shall be run on its merits whether its owner runs another horse in the race or not.' There is nothing more frustrating for punters than to see their selection beaten by its stable companion. A few stables had a knack of doing this down the years, pulling off a quiet little coup in the process, but the rule states that both horses must be ridden to win. In France, the Pari Mutuel couples all horses in the same ownership for betting purposes, punters being on a winner if any of them win the race.

Galway Races 1913

This anonymous rhyming tipster's verse on the prospects for the 1913 Galway Plate was not as successful as Sir Oracle had been forty-two years earlier. Four of the horses tipped actually ran in the 1913 races, the best of those being the third-placed Prince Abercorn. However, the rhymer plumped for Dear Sonny, the winner two years previously, who was unplaced, and the winner, George B, was never mentioned. George B, the winner of minor steeplechases at Downpatrick and Cashel, was trained by Jack Ruttle, who sent out Workman to win the Grand National a quarter of a century later, and was owned by Sir Thomas James Dixon (1868–1950), a Belfast timber merchant and ship owner, who held the office of High Sheriff of Antrim and whose racing colours were peach, with a primrose cap.

> There is a Race in the West
> That is made for the Best
> And only the best ever win;
> And the Handicap's grand,
> If you once understand
> How some of the best have got in.
>
> Now there's 'Cortigan's Pride'
> Is one I have spied,
> She ought to be 'Caught again Bob';

And that grand Horse of War,
If he's not gone before,
Will fairly be out on the job.

And that Noble from Greece,
Whose weight don't increase,
Must surely be in the first flight,
And that high-weighted Mount
I think we must count,
If wee Reggie can only sit tight.

We were not aware
Harry U would be there,
Or ever would be in such form,
Though a worse one we see
In that double L.B. –
It's a bad combination to storm.

And there's one 'Shaun-na-Scaub'
That has worried poor Bob,
As oft do the ones in that Stable,
And Dick Power, he'll say,
Gave a fortune away
If he has to pay over 'Blue Label'.

And 'Prince Abercorn',
If he's there on that morn,
And 'Sonny', the pride of the West,
And Lowry's 'L.B.'
Are the best I can see,
So now you can work out the rest.

The Course is too hard
For the most on the card,
Though they're all pretty good if they're there,
But the one I like best
Is the 'Son' from the West,
And I think Bob has treated him fair.

Key to the 1913 Galway Plate Entries:

'Bob'   = Robert McK. Waters (Handicapper)

'Reggie' = Mr Reginald Walker (Amateur Rider)

L.B.   = the horse named L.B. and Leslie Brabazon (Amateur Rider)

Result of Race:	*Trainer*
1: Sir T. Dixon's GEORGE B (Mr G. Harty) 6yo 10/1	John Ruttle
2: P. Cullinan's RAIDA (Mr J.C. Kelly) aged 10/1	L. Hope
3: H.L. Fitzpatrick's PRINCE ABERCORN (T. Dowdall) aged 10/1	Owner
0: H.L. Fitzpatrick's DEAR SONNY (E. Lawn) aged 5/1jf	Owner
0: Mrs Croft's PICCANINNY II (Mr H. Ussher) aged 5/1jf	W.A. Ussher
0: T. Killian's SHAUN-NA-SCAUB (Mr J. Murphy) aged 6/1	R.G. Cleary

Non-Runners:

T. Sheehan's CORTIGAN'S PRIDE [late Thingmebob]	T.J. Hartigan
Sir G. Abercromby's NOBLE GRECIAN	M. Arnott
Albert Lowry's L.B.	C. Brabazon
Bryan O'Donnell's BLUE LABEL	R. Moss

Dear Sonny (1911) and Noble Grecian (1912) were previous winners of the race.

Tax, Duty, a Slump and Betting Shops

With the Great War dragging on and the Government resigned to a long conflict, a ministry was established to ensure that valuable resources were used properly and not wasted. This led to an instruction being given to the Turf Club that transport must be considered when allocating fixtures. This meant that racing would have to be centralized, as it was in Britain, and that racing would only be permitted at the Curragh, Baldoyle, Leopardstown, Fairyhouse and Punchestown, courses close to the main training centres of Clonsilla and the Curragh. Galway would not be allowed to race. Alarmed at this prospect, the traders of Galway rallied behind Martin McDonogh, who began a campaign to get the Galway Festival exempted from the order. In his capacity as Chairman of the Race Committee, he wrote a passionate letter to the Fixtures Committee pointing out that Galway town depended on race week; without it many business would not be viable and the cancellation of the races would damage the whole economy of the area. After several meetings with the ministry, he got his exemption and the Galway fixture continued throughout the war years.

The fifteen years from 1915 were extremely difficult for Ireland's racecourses. The outbreak of the World War had hit attendances and on top of that came the introduction of an entertainments tax in 1916. It applied to racecourse admission prices and was an imposition that would severely weaken the financial structure of Irish racing. Admission prices were not low, ranging from 10s to £1, so the courses had no option but to absorb the tax. This was achieved by cutting back their contribution to stakes. Prize money was falling and the political outlook was troubled. The uncertainty of the War of Independence and the chaos of the Civil War led to an exodus of Irish owners to Britain. Racecourses stopped paying dividends and the provincial courses were particularly hard hit. Although the Civil War caused the cancellation of the 1922 meeting at Galway, it was the strongest of the provincial courses financially and was not looking for more fixtures. Nevertheless, it supported the other provincial racecourses, which were suffering badly from the recession and were particularly aggrieved that the metropolitan (Dublin) courses appeared to be receiving favourable treatment with regard to fixtures. Their grievance led to the establishment of the Provincial Racecourse Executives' Association in 1924, which Galway joined, and which was soon to become embroiled in a row with the Turf Club over the fixture list.

When Cork Park closed down after its Easter Monday meeting in 1917, the fixture was allotted to Tramore the following year. The Fairyhouse meeting was not held in 1919, so Tramore clashed with Down Royal that Easter, but it was back to normal in 1920, when Fairyhouse and Tramore raced and the status quo continued until 1925. However, three Irish fixtures were held on Easter Monday 1926, with the Turf Club allotting the date to Fairyhouse, Tramore and Mallow. When the Mallow fixture was abruptly dropped from the list the following year, Fred MacCabe, famous as the trainer of Orby but now the manager of Mallow racecourses was furious and accused Fairyhouse, a metropolitan course, of influencing the stewards in their decision. He struck a chord when he complained about an invisible circle drawn 30 miles around Dublin. The Turf Club refused point blank to meet him or the Provincial Racecourse Executives' Association, and during the battle of words that followed the issue spread to the fees the Turf Club charged the racecourses, which they claimed were excessive, and then into a row over who would control the tote, which was soon to be legislated for by the Government.

While this war of words raged, racing continued to decline. The 1926 Betting Act, which legalized off-course betting shops, had passed into law and that year's

Budget, by Minister of Finance Ernest Blythe, imposed a new betting tax. Initially fixed at 5 per cent both on and off course, intense lobbying had forced the minister to back down and he agreed to reduce the rate of on-course bets to 2½ per cent. However, the combination of off-course betting shops (instead of the illegal street bookies) and betting tax resulted in a further collapse in the numbers going racing. Attendances halved, driving many Irish racecourses into the red. The crisis was so serious that the Government decided to establish an interdepartmental committee to examine Irish racing. It found that the majority of Irish racecourses were in a precarious financial state and that owners were putting up 50 per cent of the prize money by way of entry fees. It blamed, among other things, the entertainments tax, and recommended that a tote be established. Broadly accepting the recommendations, the Government exempted racecourse admissions from the entertainments tax in 1928 and introduced the Totalisator Act the following year.

During this time the Provincial Racecourse Executives' Association lobbied the Government not to give control of the tote to the Turf Club, on the grounds that it was too sympathetic to the Dublin racecourses and charged the provincial meetings excessive fees. With the Government committed to the introduction of a tote, which was seen as a lifeline for racing, accusations of 'rocking the boat' were hurled at the new association as the internecine war waged on. It had developed into a public battle as the various vested interests jockeyed for control of the tote, which was expected to bring substantial revenues into racing. The row became more complicated when the provincial racecourses began fighting among themselves. In a blaze of publicity, Listowel resigned from the association over its policy on the tote.

By this time the initial cause of the row, Mallow's Easter Monday fixture, had been completely forgotten as the parties fought over the tote, but the Turf Club concentrated minds unexpectedly by restoring the fixture in 1928. Clearly there was a need for a united front pending the introduction of the tote and the action by the Turf Club calmed the situation and led to constructive discussions. Eventually a compromise was reached whereby the Turf Club and the Irish National Hunt Steeplechase Committee were jointly given a fifteen-year licence to operate a tote. A condition of the licence was that its management be delegated to a board of control consisting of six members from the governing bodies, two representing owners and breeders and one each for the metropolitan and provincial racecourses. The war finally ended when the Provincial Racecourse Executives' Association nominated Martin McDonogh of Galway as its representative on the new Tote Board of Control.

The Decade of Disappointment and the Economic War

The 1930s promised better times for Irish racing; expectations were high that the tote would deliver the riches that it had in other countries. Prize money in Ireland in 1921 was £145,151, but this had dropped to a low of £85,440 in 1929 before increasing slightly over the following three years. Sir Walter Nugent, Senior Steward of the Irish National Hunt Steeeplechase Committee, stressed the importance of maintaining the closest cooperation with the Totalisator Board, which had demanded – and been granted – the overnight declaration of runners. At the same time the stewards advised the general use of crash helmets by all riders in steeplechases and hurdle races. The lifting of the entertainments tax had helped racecourses, which faced the future with optimism, confident that better times lay ahead.

Galway racecourse had been able to weather the depression better than most. It was not a limited company and it did not have shareholders, so it did not have to worry about paying out a dividend. All profits were ploughed back into the racecourse and an annual subscription from local benefactors enabled it to survive those difficult years. The 1929 Totalisator Act empowered racecourses to charge bookmakers a pitch fee, equal to five times that paid by the general public for admission, and this was a new source of income for racecourses, which were committed to a policy of reducing the price of admission.

In 1931 A.D. (Dan) Comyn, a solicitor from Loughrea, became Senior Steward of the National Hunt Steeplechase Committee for the first time – he would later serve two more terms in 1936 and 1941. A former Irish international cricketer, he was becoming an influential figure in Irish jump racing and would soon be invited to join the Galway Race Committee. He was also one of the select band of Committee members, no more than half a dozen, who had a winner at the Festival, with Brown Admiral, trained by Maxie Arnott, winner of the Corrib Hurdle in

1930 – Far left: The new buildings are ready and the Tote is open for business at Galway for the first time. Left: The second Galway grandstand, built in 1898 and replaced in 1952

1941, and Majestic Star, trained by Dick O'Connell/Dan Moore, successful in a bumper in 1944. He was a brother-in-law of Brigadier Mahony, who was elected to the Galway Race Committee in 1952. He was a member of the Board of Control that ran the tote, alongside Martin McDonogh, but resigned when he became Senior Steward.

The introduction of the tote had gone smoothly, the buildings had been built on time and the business had been established. Unfortunately, when trying to unite the racing industry behind their proposal that the governing bodies should have control of it, the promoters had raised unrealistic expectations of revenue. The expected windfall never materialized, prize money began to decline again, dropping dramatically in 1932 to £79,667 and continuing its decline to £73,455 two years later.

Fianna Fail won the 1932 General Election, sweeping the Cosgrave government out of office; Eamon de Valera was elected President of the Executive Council. The new Government was most unwelcome in the world of horse racing. Despite the troubles over the introduction of the betting tax, W.T. Cosgrave was regarded as a friend of racing, while President de Valera had no interest in the sport at all. Racing's fears appeared to be well founded when the new Government became embroiled in an economic war with Britain that led to a duty being imposed on all Irish imports of livestock and bloodstock to the United Kingdom. Irish farmers and bloodstock breeders were badly hit, which inevitably had a knock-on effect on racing, which was in still in crisis, notwithstanding the introduction of the tote. The financial situation had not improved much since the late 1920s, exports of horses were falling, jobs were being lost and prize money was so poor that it was threatening the viability of racing. Concerned about the state of the horse industry, the Government set up a commission of enquiry, chaired by Judge W.E. Wylie, which reported in 1935. Its recommendations, to vest all racecourses in the Turf Club so that the metropolitan courses could subsidize the provincial ones and to introduce an off-course tote monopoly, did not find favour within the cabinet and were not implemented.

The Second World War and Beyond

The Racing Board

The outbreak of the Second World War in September 1939 led to a state of emergency in Ireland. Blacking-out of artificial light at night, rationing, double summer time and an efficient use of resources were introduced. And, as the war dragged on, the restrictions became more severe.

In 1940 the Government gave a £100,000 grant towards the prize money of one race per programme, which would be confined to horses trained in Ireland before 1 September 1939. Galway, as a Class 3 course, was given £100, and the Committee selected the Galway Blazers Handicap Chase as the beneficiary of the government grant. This grant continued for the next four years. In 1942, with the country critically short of petrol, the Government established the Central Racing Advisory Committee, to work with the Turf Club in compiling the fixture list to ensure that it restricted unnecessary travelling and the efficient transport of both people and horses. Chaired by former Government minister Paddy Ruttledge, with Joe McGrath and Judge Wylie as members, its task was to centralize racing during the war.

All this time the Government was keenly aware of racing's problems and the need to do something, although it was not prepared to fund it. The tote had failed to deliver what its promoters had promised and its licence was coming up for renewal in 1945. The prize money situation was desperate. It was put up by owners in entry fees and topped up by the racecourses by way of added money, but new money was essential. Although the tote was making a contribution, its costs proved to be a lot higher, the competition from the bookmakers more fierce and the profits much lower, than expected. The racecourses were struggling to survive, with attendances static and costs rising, and there seemed to be no way out of this vicious circle. Although the Turf Club and the trainers were

The emergency restrictions imposed during the Second World War banned the sale of petrol so other means of transport had to be utilized. Lelia Brabazon gives friends and jockey Eddie Newman a lift to the Galway Races in 1942

lobbying strongly for a tote monopoly, the Government was reluctant to abolish the bookmaker and was not prepared to let racing continue to run the tote. Impressed by just how well the Central Racing Advisory Committee had worked, it was interested in a proposal from Joe McGrath. He believed that bookmakers were an essential part of the Irish racing scene and recommended that a new body be established to run the tote and put up added prize money, to be funded by a levy (limited by law to a maximum of 5 per cent) on the turnover of the course bookmakers. This was the basis of the Racing Board and Racecourses Act, 1945.

The Racing Board consisted of eleven members, six of whom had to be members of the Turf Club or the Irish National Hunt Steeplechase Committee. It took charge of the tote, regulated bookmakers and revolutionized Irish horse racing by increasing stakes, reducing entry fees, imposing a standard admission charge for racegoers and introducing grants for racecourse improvements. The bookmakers' levy was introduced from the Curragh meeting on 6 October 1945, at the maximum rate of 5 per cent, but was reduced to 2½ per cent from 1 July 1946. The Racing Board was replaced by the Irish Horseracing Authority in 1994.

A King of the Jungle Foiled by The King of the Jungle

Itsajungleoutthere was the name of a horse running in Ireland some years ago. The real jungle of Irish racing is the betting ring, the only market left in the world where insider trading is not a criminal offence and 'dogs eat dogs' on a regular basis. One king of this particular 'jungle' was bookmaker John O'Keeffe. He went for a 'big touch' on his wife's horse Desdichado in the Galway Hurdle in 1945, the meeting being run on the Tuesday and Wednesday that year. King of the Jungle, owned by Dick McIlhagga, trained by Barney Nugent and ridden by Danny Morgan, was a good horse and had been laid out for the race. He was expected to start favourite, which indeed he did. The main danger appeared to be Belted Monarch, owned and ridden by Bunny Cox. Second on the flat the previous day, the versatile Belted Monarch had previously won the valuable Mickey Macardle Memorial Steeplechase at Dundalk. However, the springer in the market was Desdichado, on whom there was a massive gamble.

Although a winner on the flat when owned by Mrs Percy Reynolds, Desdichado was a maiden over hurdles and was coming up against the more than useful King of the Jungle, who had nine wins under his girth! It was a tall order for an inexperienced horse, but punters concluded that the Form Book did not mean very much when John O'Keeffe was putting his money down. Originally from Kerry, O'Keeffe moved to Dublin and lived in Sandycove, between Dun Leary and Dalkey, in a house that later became famous as the Mirabeau Restaurant. Run by Sean Kilsella, the Mirabeau was the most expensive restaurant in Ireland in the 1970s and had an international clientele. 'Big John' O'Keeffe was a substantial bookmaker in his day, had good pitches on the rails and became acquainted with trainer Tim O'Sullivan. Based at St Marnock's, Portmarnock, O'Sullivan began training in Ireland in 1938 and did well with moderate horses until his death in 1955. Aubrey Brabazon described the gamble on Desdichado as 'ambitious', but there was always a question mark over O'Sullivan, who was said to have a 'magic bottle'.

King of the Jungle was by Sir Walter Raleigh, an own-brother of the dual Irish Classic winner Smokeless. Although placed in the Irish Derby, Sir Walter Raleigh turned out to be a good handicap sprinter before retiring to the Brownstown Stud, Curragh, in 1934. King of the Jungle was bred by George Ainscough of Blarney, who raced the horse at two and three years. His grand-dam, Bushey Belle, won the first running of the famous Phoenix 1500, beating Hackler's Pride, who went on to win two Cambridgeshire Handicaps. Put into training with Bob Fetherstonhaugh, King of the Jungle failed to win at two but won four races on the flat as a three-year-old in 1943, at Mallow, Baldoyle, Listowel and Clonmel, before being sold out of the stable for jumping. Now owned by Dick McIlhagga and trained by Barney Nugent, he won his maiden hurdle at Leopardstown in February 1944, and ran second in three successive hurdle races, including the important Rank Hurdle at the Phoenix Park, before being campaigned on the flat because of the lack of opportunities over jumps. His rider, Danny Morgan, was going for a big race double, having won the Plate on Grecian Victory the day before.

The betting market on the Galway Hurdle set Galway alight. The sight of bookmakers' dusters rubbing furiously, sprinting runners knocking over punters and tic-tacs gesticulating with all their might, backed up with loud whistles, shouts of 'aye aye' and curses from disrupted bystanders got everyone interested. A 'springer' was setting the market alight, inciting inquisitive punters to pop up, as if from nowhere, to follow the money and back Desdichado. With ordinary punters joining in, his price crashed to 4 to 1, while King of the Jungle eased in the market, although the latter still started favourite at 3 to 1. The stylish and talented horseman Aubrey Brabazon was booked to ride, and into the Galway Parade Ring he sauntered, completely unaware of the commotion going on in the betting ring. He was taken aback when John O'Keeffe told him that the stake of £444 was his if he won the race; it was the last thing he wanted to hear. As the jockey wrote in his autobiography, *Racing Through My Mind*: 'Telling a jockey that the stake is his means only one thing – "We've had a fortune on the horse."'

Brabazon was among the best jockeys riding in a generation of exceptionally talented riders but he was never a 'stick jockey'. His mount won if it was good enough but it was never Aubrey's style to beat a horse past the post and he disliked abusing them. Unfortunately, when connections went for a big gamble they tended to put pressure on a jockey to win at all costs, with complete disregard for the welfare of the horse. The easiest way for a jockey to show that he had tried hard and to deflect criticism if defeated was to employ the whip liber-

The betting area, as it was in 1946. It is in the same position today but the number board, once the focus of attention, is obsolete on a modern racecourse

ally; to be seen doing one's best. The gamble failed by a head. Aubrey put the defeat down to the inexperience of his mount, a bad mistake at the last hurdle and a brilliant finishing performance from Danny Morgan on King of the Jungle. As the old adage goes, it is one thing to catch the bookie but the horse still has to win.

Grecian Victory, the first leg of Danny Morgan's big Galway double, was trainer Harry Ussher's ninth and final winner of the Plate, a race record jointly held with Paddy Sleator. Every year Harry Ussher came back home for Galway Race Week, rented a house for the occasion and liked to bring a few guests down with him. Among the guests staying with him in 1945 was Mrs Sweeney, a daughter of trainer Jim Parkinson, and her son Tony, now the highly respected racing journalist and historian. Tony told me himself of the celebration afterwards in the Great Southern Hotel, during which a drunk Barney Nugent came up to Harry Ussher seeking some advice – he was prone to drinking too much, so nobody was surprised to see him in that state. A forthcoming decision was preying on his mind and he needed good advice. He was in a quandary about an improving two-year-old called Momentum and sought the advice of an experienced and wily trainer.

Momentum was entered in two races at the forthcoming Phoenix Park meeting, now only ten days away, and Barney could not make up his mind whether to run him in the Nobber Plate, for maidens at entry and worth £178, or to let him take his chance in the 1500, a high-class race worth over £1,000. Barney reckoned that Momentum was a certainty to win the minor race, but should he take the risk and go for the jackpot? Mischievously, Harry insisted that of course he should go for the big pot. So Momentum lined up for the 1500, one of the most important two-year-old races in the calendar. Everyone was surprised, including Harry Ussher, when Momentum scorched home a shock 20 to 1 winner, beating the Aga Khan's talented colt Claro and Joe McGrath's hot favourite Imaal. Unintentionally Harry Ussher had convinced Barney Nugent to take the gamble with Dick McIlhagga's Momentum and it had paid off, enabling the connections to pull off an unusual double of winning the Galway Hurdle and the Phoenix 1500 in the same year.

Fair Pearl Loses the Galway Hurdle But the Punters Are Paid

Dick McIlhagga's six-year-old stallion, King of the Jungle, came back to Galway in 1946 to defend his Hurdle title. With the ending of the Second World War and the establishment of the Racing Board, the future looked bright for Irish racing; it now had an income from a levy on the turnover of the racecourse bookmakers. During the war, when National Hunt racing was suspended in England, there was a glut of good-quality hurdlers running in Ireland. Owing to the Government's refusal to sanction enough jumping meetings, and with no prospect of selling a horse to England, there was a lack of opportunity at home and, therefore, no incentive for owners to send their horses chasing. All that was now in the past, the English market had opened again and life was getting back to normal.

King of the Jungle had thrived on racing and was improving with age, but he had been campaigning on the flat during the summer of 1946, without winning. His last victory came in a hurdle race at Aintree, having previously finished fourth in the County Hurdle at Cheltenham. This form was good enough for punters, who made him favourite for the big Galway race. Locals followed their hearts rather than the form, and many ordinary people put their money on Fair Pearl, trained and ridden by Mickey Tully, whose colours were those of the Corinthians Rugby Club. Runner-up at Thurles and Ballinrobe, Fair Pearl had finished in front of King of the Jungle at Leopardstown the previous February. Since he came only eighth, this form probably did not mean very much but it was some source of encouragement, particularly since he had not won since Naas, the previous November. He was trained at that time by Captain Cyril Harty, a professional trainer, but now Mickey was training him himself at home.

Michael J.P. Tully of Rockmount, St Mary's Road, Galway, was known to everyone as Mickey. He was involved in racing as a breeder, owner and rider. The family had been in racing for years, and had its share of winners at Galway. The famous jockey Martin Molony started with Tully before moving to Captain Harty at Chapalizod. Tully's decision to train Fair Pearl himself rather than leave him with Captain Harty proved to be a costly one and ultimately cost him the Galway Hurdle. On a memorable day for the locals, Fair Pearl, ridden by his enthusiastic owner, lowered the colours of the mighty King of the Jungle by two and a half lengths to record a very popular local victory and send his supporters joyfully back to their bookies to collect. In what was an unusual celebration gesture at the time, Mickey stood up in the saddle on reaching the winning post in front, took off his jockey's cap and waved it at the crowd, who responded with a mighty cheer.

After Mickey had weighed in, punters who had backed Fair Pearl collected their winnings as normal. However, the stewards refused to pay Mickey Tully the winner's purse of £444 because it transpired that he was on the Forfeit List, meaning that he had not paid entry fees incurred on his account. However, the Turf Club mistakenly continued to accept entries from him. Mickey was quite open in his defence, admitting that he had unpaid entry fees on his account and accepting that Fair Pearl's entry for the Galway Plate should have been refused. However, he maintained that, having accepted the entry, the result should stand, particularly as the winning stake more than covered the outstanding arrears. However, the stewards of the Irish National Hunt Steeplechase Committee disqualified Fair Pearl and placed him last, awarding the race to King of the Jungle. Nevertheless, the punters were allowed to keep their winnings. The stewards also disqualified Magic Memory, owned by D. Mahon and trained by Michael Connolly, who was ridden to victory in a bumper at the Tuam meeting by Mickey Tully, on the grounds that the rider was on the forfeit list.

Once Mickey had paid up his account, Fair Pearl's entries were accepted and he ran prominently in the Irish Cesarewitch and Naas November Handicap, although unplaced in both races. However, Mickey Tully's joy knew no bounds when he rode him to victory in the valuable Independent Hurdle at Naas in December 1946.

Unnoticed Changes

With hindsight everything is clear but very few of us are perspicacious enough to identify changes that are happening around us at any given time. It is now quite clear that by the late 1950s the railway system was beginning to lose out heavily to road transport, but the Irish people, including the Galway Executive, were not aware of the silent revolution that was taking place right under their noses. For a hundred years the railway was the backbone of the world's transport system but it was now disintegrating and would lose virtually all its freight business within a decade. The collapse of the large railway network was due to a combination of changes in society which crept up on business unnoticed, such as a more affluent population, technical advances in motor transport and a lack of forward planning and proper investment by the railway sector. Intransigent and militant trade unions insisted on keeping old work practices that had been made redundant through modern technology, confident in their limited minds that the revolution started by the train could not continue without it. As the stoker who fuelled the fires of the old steam engines sat idly in the cab of the diesel train, being paid to do nothing, new technology was boosting unseen competitors. A weak management, cocooned in the state sector, could not envisage freight moving on to the roads – it was unthinkable in a country of narrow, winding roads, with not a motorway of any description in sight or even proposed.

In the years after the Great War the railway companies began losing money. Costs were rising, fares were increasing as business was being lost, and within a decade the railway system was on the brink of collapse. The loss of the railway system was unacceptable, prompting Eamon de Valera's government to nationalize all transport of people and freight in Ireland, giving a monopoly to the new state company, CIE. All buses, trains and lorries were owned by that company and all movement of goods, animals and people had to go through it. The newly formed Racing Board introduced a free carriage scheme and entered into a contract with CIE to bring the runners to and from the various race meetings. One of the reasons for the outstanding success of the park course had been the railway, which enabled both horses and people to get to the races in ease and comfort. Railway companies were among the first sponsors of races in Ireland, one example being the Railway Stakes at the Curragh, first run in 1851; they also sponsored the carriage of horses to the races. Originally all horses were walked to the various racecourses, the exercise being part of their training programme. However, this practice was both expensive and time consuming and was largely abandoned after Lord George Bentinck sent his horse Elis to Doncaster in a horse-drawn van in 1836 and the horse won the St Leger. However, the train was faster and considerably cheaper than a horse van and before long the railway carried all the runners to the various racecourses.

For many years the Race Committee rented stables wherever they could, including Irwin's Yard in Eyre Street, a premises that now houses an undertaking business. As the meeting prospered, and with stabling in short supply, the racecourse decided to build its own stable yard to increase capacity. For this purpose, land adjacent to the sports ground in College Road was purchased in 1930, beside the rugby ground, about ½ mile from the railway station. College Road was a continuation of Forster Street and the horses would be walked to and from the station through the streets of the town. On the morning of the races, the runners would be walked the 3 miles to Ballybrit, coming up the old Mass Path, past Mary Burke's house (approximately where the Digital factory now stands), on to the racecourse in the dip (where the Moneen fences are) and from there they were walked up the track to the paddock area. After the race the horses would make the return journey to College Road to await a train home.

An extra day was introduced in 1959, which meant that more boxes had to be built at College Road to accommodate the horses arriving by rail. Aware also that a number of runners, mostly locals, would arrive directly at the racecourse, the Race Committee decided to build a proper stableyard at Ballybrit as well, and arranged for seventy boxes to be constructed there. Mick Connolly, a local building contractor who did a lot of work for the racecourse, was given the contract and commenced building racecourse stables in two different locations, 3 miles apart, around the same time. With hindsight it does not make sense, but nobody thought it at all odd at the time. A world without the train was unthinkable fifty years ago; yet within a couple of years, the College Road stables were redundant as the railway lost its entire horse transport business to the lorry virtually overnight. By the end of the decade the city stables had been abandoned and the site was sold off.

Not long after the horses stopped using the Mass Path so too did the people, with the exception of youths taking a short cut to the outside enclosure on race days. The path led from the church at Castlegar down to the six cottages that are situated beside the main gate to the racecourse, with a connecting path leading to the old main road opposite the stands. The increasing availability of motor transport, coupled with a decline in attendance at mass, meant that it ceased to be used by churchgoers. Forgotten and overgrown, the path has long since disappeared under the concrete of an expanding Galway city. Although the College Road site was sold for a song, compared with its value today, the money was used to buy land at Ballybrit, which would be worth millions of euros if put on the market today. All the horses and the vast majority of racegoers arrive at the Galway Races by road nowadays, the railway being an irrevelance.

The Modern Era

The Closure of Tuam Racecourse

There was organized horse racing in Tuam before 1754, the date from which there is an unbroken record of Irish race meetings. Racing first on the Gurranes course, the Tuam meeting moved to the more modern Parkmore course on the Dublin Road in 1904, and continued, with brief interruptions during the War of Independence and the emergency years of the Second World War, until it closed in 1973. Those who are old enough to remember the Tuam Races will associate the meeting with the Friday of Galway Race Week, the only day of the year it raced, but actually it only moved to that date in 1923. The Galway Executive often accused Tuam of cashing in on their meeting and doing little to help itself, with some justification because the Tuam made no real progress while the Galway meeting went from strength to strength. Tuam offered paltry prize money but in 1967 it did manage to attact a potentially good sponsor, United Breweries of Ireland. That company contributed £200, 10 per cent of what Guinness was putting into the Galway Hurdle, towards the Carling Black Label Lager, a maiden race for two-year-olds. After four years United Breweries withdrew, and the local firm of John Egan & Sons stepped in to fill the breach. The race was renamed the Parkmore Plate.

The Mr What Cup, a 2½ mile handicap steeplechase was worth only £218 to the winner in 1960, only £16 more than the minimum value offered at Galway, so describing it as a feature race definitely would have infringed the trades description act, if it had been in force at the time. The Galway Plate, a similar type of race, was worth £1,160 to the winner and creamed off all the good summer chasers and those that were left had the option of the Galway Blazers Handicap Chase. The Cup was named after the Irish-trained winner of the 1958 Grand National, owned by David Coughlan, a director of Tuam Races. Trained by Thomas J. Taaffe in Rathcoole, he won the Troytown Chase at Navan before winning the Grand

National, beating Tiberetta by thirty lengths. Toss Taaffe, the trainer's jockey son, usually partnered Mr What but he had an agreement with Vincent O'Brien to ride his steeplechasers and did not expect to be free to ride the horse in the Grand National. By the time he discovered that O'Brien would not have a runner, Arthur Freeman had already been booked and old Mr Taaffe was not inclined to drop him. Toss Taaffe then switched to Brookling, trained by Georgie Wells, only for Freeman to declare that he would have to put up 6 pounds overweight. By this time it was too late to do anything, Freeman took the mount on Mr What and won the race easily by thirty lengths.

Mr What never won another race from thirty-three attempts, although he finished third twice in future Grand Nationals, behind Oxo and Wyndburgh in 1959 and Kilmore and Wyndburgh three years later. Transferred to Danny Morgan's yard in 1960, Mr What continued to carry David Coughlan's distinctive colours, maroon jacket with yellow hooped sleeves, which had previously been carried by Carey's Cottage, successful in the Kerry National and third behind Quare Times (Pat Taaffe) and Tudor Line (G. Slack) in the 1955 Grand National, with Toss Taaffe up.

Born in 1898, David Joseph Coughlan lived at Inniskel, King Edward Road, Bray, and was in business as a manufacturing chemist. His companies were David Coughlan Ltd, The Harbour, Bray, and Stafford Miller Ltd, Hatfield, Herts, England. He served in the Royal Navy throughout the Great War and was a keen golfer. David Coughlan died in 1961.

Winners of the Mr What Perpetual Challenge Cup Handicap Steeplechase

1959 Captain E.A. Gargan's CULLEENROI (G.W. Robinson) 7/1 Private £149

1960 D. Boyd's HAPPY STRANGER (C. Kinane) 7/1 Private £218

1961 Mrs R.W. McKeever's PRINCE APPROACH (M.J. Kennedy) 6/1 C. Magnier £218

1962 Mrs G.A.J. Wilson's SAN MARCO (R. Coonan) 7/1 G.H. Wells £261

1963 Mrs G.A.J. Wilson's SAN MARCO (R. Coonan) 5/1 G.H. Wells £219

1964 Skeets Martin's QUINTIN BAY (John J. Rafferty) 9/2 A. Brabazon £219

1965 William Murdoch's GREEK LAD (B. Hannon) 9/4f W. Murdoch £303

1966 Mrs C.P. Bellairs's GOSLEY (T. Carberry) 11/10f D.L. Moore £303

1967 R. McIlhagga's PECCARD (John Crowley) 5/2 G.H. Wells £302

1968 R. McIlhagga's PECCARD (G.W. Robinson) G.H. Wells £412

Walked Over

1969   D. Fisher's THE WIND II (D.T. Hughes) 1/1 M.A. O'Toole £302
1970   D. Fisher's THE WIND II (D.T. Hughes) 7/2 M.A. O'Toole £302
1971   Mrs Gabriel Mulholland's ALASKA FORT (H.R. Beasley) 4/5f M.A. O'Toole £301

Amateur Handicap Hurdle

1972   Mrs M.A. O'Toole's HIGH RULER (Mr T.M. Walsh) 11/8f M.A. O'Toole £286
1973   P.A. Cummins's MARTIN (Mr M.J. Grassick) 9/2 K. Bell £276

The last race run at a Tuam race meeting was the Grange Bumper on Friday, 3 August 1973, won by an odds-on favourite, Lord Edward, trained by Adrian Maxwell and ridden by Mr Michael 'Mouse' Morris. That was the end; the Parkmore course was sold and is gone forever, most of it now being covered with houses. Visitors will recognize some familiar buildings that are incorporated into the development, but other than that it is hard to imagine that racing ever took place there. Fading memories of Parkmore can be revived by a taking a close look at a railing situated on top of the Galway weighing room, adorned with horses' heads. These railings were purchased at the Tuam closing-down sale and brought to Galway, where they were erected and remained until the weighing room area was redeveloped. These railings were made by a Belfast company, which hoped to sell them to several racecourses, but only got two orders, one from the Curragh and one from Tuam.

The weighing room is a busy place at Galway; 772 horses ran at the 2007 Festival

In 1974 Galway took over the old Tuam date, running for five days for the first time, but none of the Tuam races survived, not even the 'feature' Mr What Cup. Galway did take on the sponsored two-year-old race, naming it the Tuam Two-Year-Old Race and retained the Parkmore name for a flat maiden. Galway had no intention of inheriting Tuam's mediocrity, but its old neighbour did not go into oblivion without a brief fight. Appalling weather hit the Galway Festival in 1974, the like of which had not been seen for years. Torrential rain caused the opening day to be abandoned after three races had been run; the Tuesday went ahead as usual but Wednesday's card, Plate day, had to be called off. Anxious not to lose the Plate, Galway decided to run the Wednesday card on the Friday, causing the programme allotted to the old Tuam date to be abandoned. The Parkmore name was dropped from the Galway programme in 1988 and the Tuam race was renamed in 1990.

Women's Galway Record

Although women had been prominent as owners at Galway since the start of the twentieth century, female trainers and riders only began to be seen in the 1980s. These are the pioneers.

First Woman Owners:

1:	Bertha Dewhurst	1900 ASHSTICK [Captain R. Dewhurst] Flat
2:	Mrs Joseph Widger	1901 SUNNY SHOWER [J.J. Parkinson] Chase
3:	Lady Clancarty	1901 BLACK SATIN [F.F. Cullen] Flat
4:	Miss Mansergh	1902 BAYLEAF [M. Dawson] Hurdle
5:	Mrs M.J. Harty	1904 OLD TIM [M.J. Harty] Hurdle
6:	Mrs N.J. Kelly	1906 RYE VALE [N.J. Kelly] Chase
7:	Pansy Croft	1911 SHOEBLACK [M. Arnott] Chase
8:	Mrs L. Hope	1914 LADY ELIZABETH [L. Hope] Hurdle
9:	Mrs P. Sheehan	1917 THE FLY III [P. Sheehan] Chase
10:	Mrs O. Toole	1920 CLONREE [F. Morgan] Chase
11:	Mrs D. Moloney	1921 ROCKDAILE [D. Moloney] Hurdle
12:	Mrs A.E. O'Reilly	1923 MIRATHORN [R. Fetherstonhaugh] Hurdle
13:	Miss E.L.M. Barbour	1925 BLANCONA [C. Brabazon] Chase
14:	Miss M.D. Barbour	1925 ALROI [C. Brabazon] Hurdle
15:	Mrs R. Adams	1926 SILVER RIVER [H.S. Kenny] Flat

First Woman Trainers:

1:	Gillian O'Brien	1982 ASKAMORE [Mrs Miles Valentine] Chase
2:	Ursula Ryan	1984 RIVER VENTURE [Michael F. Cunningham] Hurdle
3:	Janet Morgan	1984 FOXTROT TANGO [Father Sean Breen] Flat

4: Mrs B.W. McKeever	1986 SWAP FASHIONS [Owner] Hurdle
5: Anne Collen	1987 RANDOSS [S.W.N. Collen] Chase
6: Emer Purcell	1990 THE MUSICAL PRIEST [Mrs Seamus Purcell] Chase
7: Anne Marie Crowley	1991 SKY RANGE [Joseph Crowley] Hurdle
8: Jessica Harrington	1991 BLACK MONEY [Jessica Harrington] Chase
9: Diane Coleman	1992 MERRY JOHN [Diane Coleman] Hurdle
10: Joanna Morgan	1997 ONE WON ONE [Heavenly Syndicate] Flat
11: Frances M. Crowley	1998 GO FOR GRACE [P. Evans] Flat
12: Susan Bramall	2001 HEEMANELA [Winning Post Syndicate] Flat
13: Margaret Mullins	2006 ACES OR BETTER [Mrs John Magnier] Bumper

First Woman Riders:

1: Joanna Morgan	1977 MOVE ON WAG [P. Canty] Flat
2: Sarah Collen	1989 BOLD FLYER [J.T.R. Draper] Chase
3: Margaret Mullins	1989 ARAPAWAY [A. Mullins] Bumper
4: Lulu Olivefalk	1989 LORD DE-MONTFORT [Captain D.G. Swan] Hurdle
5: Anne Marie Crowley	1990 FOREST WILDLIFE [James Shanahan] Bumper
6: Chanelle Burke	1995 BAMAPOUR [M. Cunningham] Bumper
7: Jayne Mulqueen	1998 GO FOR GRACE [Frances M. Crowley] Flat
8: Rachel Costello	2001 CLASS SOCIETY [M. Halford] Flat
9: Helen Keohane	2002 AVENA SATIVA [R. Donohoe] Flat
10: Nina Carberry	2005 DASHER REILLY [D.K. Weld] Bumper
11: Katie Walsh	2006 DRUMDERRY [W.P. Mullins] Bumper
12: Jessica Harrington	2007 DREAMY GENT [A.D. Leigh] Hurdle

Women's Winning Totals at the Galway Festival

Owners:

17 Mrs John Magnier (plus 1 with Michael Tabor)

14 Pansy Croft

12 Dorothy Paget

Trainers:

9 Jessica Harrington and Frances Crowley

4 Anne Marie Crowley

3 Susan Bramall and Joanna Morgan

Riders:

5 Joanna Morgan

5 Nina Carberry

3 Anne Marie Crowley

Nina Carberry, once the star of the pony racing circuit, now the Champion Irish Amateur Rider

Joanna Morgan, successful on Move on Wag in 1977, became the first woman to ride a winner at Galway

Sarah and Anne Collen were daughters of Standish Collen, a building contractor who lived at Kinsealy, Malahide, Co. Dublin. Anne was born on the same day as Jim Draper, 30 January 1951, and took out an amateur rider's licence and a permit to train in 1974, converting to a fully licensed trainer in 1980. Training for her father and friends at Streamstown, she trained Kilkilowen and Randoss, the latter winning the 1987 Galway Plate ridden by Ken Morgan.

Two years later her sister, Sarah, riding as an amateur, led from start to finish on Bold Flyer to win the Galway Plate by eight lengths. Bold Flyer, trained by Jim Draper for Standish Collen, was completing a three-timer at Galway, having previously won at Gowran Park and Roscommon, Sarah Collen up on both occasions. She rode a winner at Galway in 1990 on Robert Sangster's Boadicea's Chariot in a qualified riders' flatrace. Married to Ray Jennings, Sarah and her husband went to Japan but returned to Ireland to a stud near Naas.

Anne Collen was the fifth woman to train a winner at the Festival and the first to send out the winner of the Galway Plate. Sarah Collen was only the second lady rider to win at the meeting, although Margaret Mullins and Lulu Olivefalk would also ride winers at that Galway meeting in 1989. Sarah was the first lady rider to win the Plate and also the first to win a steeplechase at the famous festival. It was a clear sign of the increasing participation of women in jump racing, following Anne Ferris's win in the 1984 Irish Grand National.

A Betting Shop at Ballybrit

In 1989 Leopardstown became the first Irish racecourse to open a betting shop when it accepted a tender from Paddy Power Bookmakers. Situated in an old tote building at the back of the stand between the racecourse entrance and the parade ring, it was actually a kiosk rather than a conventional betting shop. The counter area was in the building but the punters' area was outside in the open air – just as the tote windows operate. The passing of the Irish Horseracing Authority Act enabled the body that replaced the old Racing Board to operate betting shops, which it decided to do under the banner of Tote Arena. The siting and services offered by the new Leopardstown betting shop brought the Irish Horseracing Authority into conflict with the race-course bookmakers over the Pitch Rules and Regulations, which the Authority claimed were not binding on it. (Bookmakers betting on racecourses have to comply with the 'Racecourse Executives' Pitch Rules and Regulations', which set out their rights and responsibilities.) The result was a 'stand down' by the Leopardstown bookmakers on Saturday, 28 October 1995 and on two other days before a truce was agreed in time for the Christmas meeting. This involved a trial period of a year, all of 1996, that would monitor the impact of the betting shop. Leopardstown and the Curragh would be part of the trial and no betting shops would be allowed to open on other Irish courses until the data from the trial had been assessed.

In the early summer of 1996, John Moloney, the Galway Manager, approached the Irish National Bookmakers' Association, seeking its cooperation in allowing Galway to open a betting shop at the Festival. He assured the bookmakers that Galway fully recognized the Pitch Rules and Regulations and would not use the shop to undermine the seniority of the racecourse bookmakers. The outcome was that Galway had a betting shop at the 1996 Festival, with the full support of the bookmakers.

Modern Developments

Galway went through the invisible barrier that divides one century from another as a building site. Down came the old and up went the Millennium Stand, with its standing terrace, balcony of reserved seats and panoramic views out across the course to Galway Bay. To accommodate the increasing numbers of vehicles coming to Ballybrit on race days, an underpass from the dual carriageway in front of the stands to the centre of the course was opened in 2001, enabling vehicles to enter and exit the racecourse without having to cross the course. The underpass eliminated the need to halt all traffic while the horses were on the course, speeding up the entry and exit times. The following year an underpass for pedestrians was opened, which allowed users of the infield car park to enter the enclosures without having to cross the track, allowing people the freedom to come and go as they pleased. In that same year, 2002, Galway became the first Irish racecourse to open a website, www.galwayraces.com, with full details of the runners and riders and up-to-date information about the facilites on offer. Galway's Chairman, John Coyle, commented that it was fitting that Galway led the field in computer technology

The magnificent Millennium Stand as viewed from the infield

because the city was 'in at the very birth of Ireland's technology boom with the establishment of the Digital plant here in 1973'. Digital became part of the Compaq group in 1998, which in turn became Hewlett Packard in 2002, and the new company sponsored the Galway Racecourse website. Having sponsored the Galway Plate for twenty-one years, under the Digital/Compaq/Hewlett Packard banner, the company withdrew from the sponsorship after the 2005 race and was replaced by the British bookmaking firm William Hill.

After the 2006 Festival, the old West Stand was pulled down and a replacement went up, along with a new Mayor's Garden complex, extending the enclosures by 2 acres and was ready for 2007. This relieved the crush a little but, be warned, better facilities may bring even more people, drawn by the unique atmosphere of a large crowd all doing the same thing, enjoying a day out at the Galway Races.

The Galway Race Committee

Ballybrit racecourse is owned by a trust, which owns the freehold to the 150 acres and the stands and buildings. The trustees run the racecourse through the Galway Race Committee, a self-appointed group of local sportspeople, which can consist of up to twelve members. New members are appointed by invitation, with a balance to be kept between the town business people and the country hunting fraternity. Committee members are unpaid and all profits made by the race company, after taxes are paid, are used to improve the course and its amenities.

When the Ballybrit course was first opened in 1869, an informal Race Committee was set up to run the meeting and was given use of the land, rent-free, by the Wilson Lynch family. The main function of the Race Committee was to collect subscriptions from local businesses and from friends and benefactors, which were used to guarantee the prize money for each race. This casual arrangement was fine at a time when overheads were tiny and there was sufficient income to maintain the course to a high standard. The grandstand consisted of a set of stone steps, covered by a galvanized hay-shed type roof, which provided a good view of the racing and gave shelter from the elements. Although it cost money to erect and was subject to rates, the stand required virtually no maintenance and there were no other buildings, tents being erected annually to accommodate the stewards, the jockeys and the catering. However, the increasing demands for improvements by owners, trainers and riders, and the appointment by the Turf Club of an inspector of courses, required investment and a proper management committee.

Blennerhassett was appointed first Inspector of Courses in October 1907. He visited every racecourse in the country to inspect the facilities, setting down minimum standards and agreeing a timescale for the executives to do remedial work. He also gave notice that the minimum standards would be upgraded over a number of years and ultimately no course would be allotted a fixture unless it complied with the standard. Aware that a financial investment would be required to bring the Ballybrit course up to the standard required, Martin McDonogh and Joe Young set about making the necessary improvements. Before sinking money into the course, they put the lease to the racecourse lands on a proper legal footing instead of the loose arrangement that existed at the time. Working as an informal two-man committee, Messrs McDonogh and Young set down the principles that they would not receive any payment for their efforts on behalf of the Galway Races and that all the lands used for racing would be held in trust for the people of Galway. The pair began the delicate task of getting Captain Thomas Wilson Lynch to put his casual agreement with the Race Committee on to a proper legal footing.

Lynch had been a good friend and great supporter of the Galway races down the years and he was happy with the existing arrangements, so care had to be taken not to offend him. McDonogh and Young convinced him that a formal legal agreement was in the best interests of the Galway Races and on 12 July 1912 he gave the Committee a 999-year lease on the lands at Ballybrit at an annual rent of £100. Meanwhile, the Race Committee invested heavily to ensure that the course itself was brought up to a stardard above the minimum set by the Inspector of Courses. This investment not only enabled Galway to satisfy the Inspector, it offered better conditions for horses and riders and considerably enhanced the reputation of the meeting. The positive response of Michael McDonogh and Joe Young helped the Galway Races to prosper while other courses in the county were closing down: Ballinasloe (1910), Moylough (1911), Dunmor (1916), Gort (1916) and Loughrea (1920).

The informal arrangement whereby Martin McDonogh and Joe Young acted as trustees had been transformed into a two-man Management Committee, with George Mack acting as Secretary/Manager. When Mack retired in 1918, Martin Thomas Donnellan, a shopkeeper in Ship Street and a member of Galway Urban Council for many years, replaced him. Although in his early sixties when appointed, Donnellan was an energetic racing manager, with plenty of experience and contacts, and he oversaw substantial improvements to the stands, the track and the paddock area during his twenty years in the position.

Having successfully complied with the new regulations, the Galway Races then had to meet the successive challenges of the Great War, the Easter Rising, the War of Independence and the Civil War. The Great War affected racing: tens of thousands of men volunteered for military service and the army needed all the food, fodder and petrol it could get, which led to a shortage and a need to preserve vital stocks. The Government put the Turf Club under severe pressure to drastically cut back on the number of meetings run in Ireland and to central-ize those that were run. The Galway Races, being remote form the main training centre on the Curragh, was in severe danger of being dropped from the fixture list, and was only saved by some fierce lobbying. Martin McDonogh worked on the Turf Club, while Joe Young, who was working for the army getting volun-teers to enlist, used his contacts in the military to persuade the Government to keep the Galway Races going. They were fully backed by the traders of the town, who depended on the two-day meeting for their very survival, and it was this economic argument that convinced the authorities to allow the meeting to continue. Having overcome that threat, another came out of the blue – the Easter Rising, on 24 April 1916. This caused the complete shut-down of Irish racing for about six weeks, but fixtures resumed on 9 June and the 1916 Galway meeting went ahead without incident.

The end of the 'war to end all wars' briefly offered hope of stability. Christy Kerrin, an agent for Guinness, was invited on to the Race Committee, increas-ing its number to three. However, having come through the terrible Great War, the Easter Rising and the War of Independence virtually unscathed, Galway suffered a setback in 1922, when the Civil War forced the cancellation of the meeting. The upheaval that led to the foundation of the Irish Free State, together with Martin McDonogh's political connections with President Cosgrave's government, produced an opportunity to buy the freehold to Ballybrit. The Land Commission was set up by the new government to redis-tribute land and a deal was done whereby it acquired the extensive acreage of Captain Wilson Lynch but sold the freehold of the racecourse land at Ballybrit back to the Race Committee.

In 1925 the Committee doubled in size, when Martin J. Hynes of Blackrock House, Thomas C. McDonogh of Flood Street and Michael J. Crowley of Shop Street joined. All the papers from the time make it clear that the members of the Race Committee could have no beneficial interest in the lands of the Galway Race Committee. They were trustees on behalf of the people of Galway, and none of them could personally benefit in the event of a sale of racecourse lands or receive any payment for their services. About this time it was agreed that the Chairman of the Race Committee would be appointed on seniority and that future Committees would be balanced between the hunting people of the country and urban business people. Galway also became a member of the Provincial Racecourse Executives' Association.

At this time the most senior member of the Committee was elected Chairman for life, enabling Martin McDonogh to serve twenty-seven years and Joe Young for twenty-three. The longevity of Joe Young, who was a member of the Committee for fifty-one years, deprived Christy Kerrin, who died in the mid-1950s, of the chance to become Chairman and limited Joe Costello's term to just one year. It was during Paddy Ryan's term (1986–91) that the rules were changed and it was agreed that in future the Chairman would serve a three-year term and be limited to two terms only. The current rules, set out in 1998, state that the most senior member of the Committee will assume the position of Chairman, but can only serve one four-year term.

The rules limit the number of Committee members to twelve, with a compulsory retirement age of seventy-five and include a commitment to maintain the balance between town and country members. However, this is proving difficult because the balance has swung very much to the town members since the death of Jerome 'Min' Mahony on 25 January 2001. Associated with the Blarney Woollen Mills business, his mother came from the Spanish nobility and he was one of the hunting members of the Race Committee.

Not all members of the Race Committee are racing people. Gerald I. Corbett for example had no interest at all in the sport; he was a Chamber of Commerce man and was appointed in 1952 because of his contacts in the town's business community.

Chairmen and Other Prominent Members

Martin McDonogh (1855–1934)
Chairman 1907–34

Owner: 1913 DOUBLE MAC (R. Trudgill) – Galway Blazers Chase £59 10s (W.A. Ussher); and 1931 KYLECLARE (C. O'Connors) – Galway Hurdle £220 (J.J. Parkinson)

Martin McDonogh was a son of Thomas Redmond McDonogh (1800–70), founder of the well-known Galway firm that bears his name. Thomas McDonogh was born into a Connemara fishing family but came to Galway to find work, which he did in Gunning's Sawmills in Merchants Road. His wife ran a grocery shop and when the ailing Gunning's business was sold off in 1825, Thomas bought it. However, it was his son Martin who expanded the business, moving into fertilizers, and he began the family's long association with the Galway races. Big in stature, Martin was known locally as 'Martin Mor' or 'Morty Mor' or 'Big Martin' and was an enthusiastic supporter of the Galway Races.

The McDonogh family connection with the Galway Races goes back over one hundred years and the McDonogh Handicap has been sponsored since 1971. The runners take the final turn in this 8½ furlong race

Big in stature, big in business and big in politics, Martin McDonogh was a member of Galway County Council for many years and was firmly behind President William T. Cosgrave as the country slid into civil war. A member of the ruling Cumann na Gaedheal party, McDonogh entered the Dail Eireann in the June 1927 election, when elected to represent the Galway constituency. He retained his seat with an increased majority in the second general election of 1927, only to lose it in the 1932 election that swept Eamon de Valera's Fianna Fail party into power. Although in his late seventies, Martin stood again in the general election of 1933, regaining his seat in the Dail, but he died the following year. Bearing in mind his strong political opinions and the bitter divisions left by the Civil War, it was natural that he preferred his horses to be trained by one of a similar mind, which was basically a hatred of de Valera. Although Jim Parkinson was elected to the Senate as an independent, non-party candidate, he too was a great friend of

President Cosgrave and was pro-Treaty. Another of like mind was the writer Oliver
St John Gogarty, also a senator and a great friend of Martin McDonogh. Gogarty
describes his friend in his poem 'The Dublin–Galway Train':

> The Station Master opens a door
> And clears a passage for Morty Mor,
> For Morty Mor is known to own
> The principal works of Galway town.
> He is not one of the county set
> (Though he helps them out when they lose a bet).
> His saw-mills hum and he sells cement,
> Potash and lime to his heart's content.
> The workers he sacks on Saturday night
> Are back on Monday morn contrite;
> In spite of his temper, deep at the core
> The heart's all right in Morty Mor.

Residing in Belmore, Salthill, Martin McDonogh was a member of the governing body of University College Galway and a member of the Tote Board, representing the provincial racecourse companies. He died in December 1934 and was
succeeded as Chairman of the Galway Race Committee by Joe Young.

Martin kept a couple of broodmares and had horses in training, and his
proudest moment on the Turf was winning the Galway Hurdle in 1931 with
Kyleclare, a horse he had bred himself. He had also raced Kyleclare's dam, a
mare named Acclida, which won him a handicap flat race at Miltown Malbay
back in 1916, when trained by Ronnie Moss. Kyleclare impressively won two
bumpers, at the Curragh and Leopardstown, in 1930, and looked an exceptional jumping prospect when winning his maiden hurdle at Naas early the
following year. Unfortunately the bubble burst when Kyleclare was beaten at
2 to 1 on at Baldoyle. Despite this setback, Jim Parkinson prepared the horse
for the Galway Hurdle. It is probable that Kyleclare only ran in the big Galway
race because his owner was the Chairman of the racecourse, because he did not
appear to be at all fancied. However, Kyleclare rose magnificently to the occasion, winning the Galway Hurdle in some style, beating Gus Mangan on
Sahabelle by five lengths. Although the horse had not been backed, the public
loudly cheered Martin McDonogh, who had done so much for Galway, as an
employer and a politician.

Although Kyleclare finished fourth in the Cotswold Chase at the 1932

Cheltenham meeting, he never won another race but Martin McDonogh's disappointment was tempered by his half-brother, Irish Fun, which was just embarking on a glittering career. Also trained by Jim Parkinson, Irish Fun won twice at two years, at the Phoenix Park and the Curragh, won the Irish Cambridgeshire Handicap at the Curragh at three years and won four races in 1934. That year he started second favourite to hat-trick-seeking Knuckleduster for the Galway Hurdle, but both horses finished unplaced behind Red Hillman. Inexperience over hurdles cost Irish Fun the race and he could not cope with the fluent jumping of the experienced hurdlers.

After Martin McDonogh's death, Irish Fun became the property of his brother, Thomas McDonogh, who also inherited the yellow, red sleeves and black cap colours. Irish Fun swept all before him on the racecourse in 1935, when he was the unbeaten winner of seven races, three on the flat and four over hurdles. Unfortunately, his career was cut short when he died in training.

Another horse inherited by Thomas was Corofin, winner of the Mervue flat race at the 1935 Galway Festival, but his new owner died in the autumn of 1936, shortly before his victory in the Irish Cesarewitch. The horse passed to Martin's son, Michael, who was a medical doctor before retiring to take control of the family firm, and he was invited to fill the 'McDonogh seat' on the Race Committee. He too enjoyed success with Corofin, whose victory in the 1937 Grand Metropolitan Handicap at Epsom, at that time one of the big English handicap races, was trainer Jim Parkinson's last big winner in England. Dr Michael preferred to spell his name 'McDonough', while his wife apparently opted for 'McDonagh' but their son, Thomas, reverted to the traditional 'McDonogh'. Dr Michael died in 1949 and his son, Tom, joined the Race Committee in 1959.

Joseph S. Young OBE (c. 1867–1958)
Chairman 1935–58

Martin McDonogh, Joe Young and Lord Killanin are the major players in the Galway Races success story. Young and McDonogh put together the leases, the money, the facilities and the management structure that secured the future of the Galway Races for the people of Galway, while Lord Killanin took the meeting on to a higher level. Joe Young became Chairman when McDonogh died in 1935, being the most senior member, and held the position for twenty-three years. Usually seen in a broad-brimmed hat, Joe Young was the proprietor of a mineral water company based in Eglinton Street, Galway. A committed Unionist, during the Great War he recruited soldiers for the British Army and was awarded an OBE for his services to the crown. He was proud of this honour, although it was frowned upon by Republicans, and it was always attached to his name thereafter, including on the plaque that commemorated the opening of one of the new stands. This later caused some anxiety at Ballybrit because at one stage the IRA threatened to blow the stand up, apparently affronted by those three letters. Fortunately, the voice of reason, or perhaps the force of local opinion, prevailed and the threat was never carried out. An active Chairman to the end, at ninety years of age he was there to welcome Sean T. O'Kelly, the first president of Ireland to pay an official visit to the Galway Races, when he arrived in the 1950s and led the inspection of the course during the traditional walkabout on the Sunday before the Festival in 1958, the year of Young's death.

Joseph F. Costello (died 1959)
Chairman 1959

A chemist by profession, Joe Costello was an independent councillor on the County Council who found himself elected the Lord Mayor of Galway year after year. The make-up of the Council was such that neither of the big parties had enough votes to elect its own candidate, but each was determined to prevent the other side getting the prize. Consequently Joe Costello found himself the perennial Lord Mayor of the city. Traditionally the Lord Mayor of Galway comes to Ballybrit on the Wednesday (Plate day) and nobody can remember a time when he failed to turn up.

Elected every June/July, the outing to the Galway Races is usually the first for the new mayor and in days gone by he would be driven to the races in a carriage, which would be parked in the garden at the end of the grandstand, adjacent to the final turn. On the lawn in the garden, he would host a picnic or tea party during the races, away from the dedicated racegoers – an early example of the corporate area now common on Irish courses. Although that ritual has been discontinued long since, the area is still known as the Mayor's Garden and is now undergoing development as an enclosure in its own right. Initially there was a refreshment room there called the Mayor's Parlour but since then bars, tote betting and a line of bookmakers have been provided in order to ease the pressure on the facilities in the parade ring area of the course by spreading the crowd during the Festival meeting. With Joe Young as active as ever at ninety, Joe Costello must have wondered if he would ever become Chairman but he eventually made it – just! He became Chairman in 1959, serving just one year before he too passed away.

In 1969 The Mayor's Parlour snack bar was a retreat for the locals as most racegoers were unaware of its existence

Thomas McDermott Kelly
Chairman 1960–69

Owner: 1942 MOUNT BROWN (D.L. Moore) – Salthill Handicap Hurdle £49 (Owner); and 1943
MOUNT BROWN (H. Harty Jr) – Renmore Chase £84 (Owner)

The vet from Athenry, Thomas Kelly, was from the hunting faction on the Committee, rather than the city business set. One of the founders of the Connemara Pony Society along with Christy Kerrin, Tommy Kelly was close to Lord Killanin, who was also a member of the hunting fraternity, and prevailed on him, busy as he was, to become Chairman of 1970. Tommy Kelly was the racecourse vet at Ballybrit for many years and owned and trained Mount Brown, winner of two races at Galway. He was the first Chairman of the Race Committee to step down rather than keep the job for life, and did so after ten years in the position.

Gerald D. Naughton
Elected to the Race Committee 1945
First Vice Chairman of the Race Committee 1970–80

Gerald Naughton, a hardware merchant in Galway, should have succeeded Tommy Kelly as Chairman, having been a member of the Committee since 1945. However, in an admirable demonstration of unselfish devotion to the Galway Races, he decided to stand aside in favour of Lord Killanin, an influential and powerful personality in Ireland at this time. Gerald Naughton believed that Lord Killanin's appointment would give the racecourse considerable prestige and would help attract sponsors. In recognition of his gesture, and also because Lord Killanin would be away a lot because of his position with the Olympic Games, Gerald Naughton became the first Vice Chairman of the Race Committee, a position he held until his retirement in 1980. His son Tim was elected to the Committee in his place.

Lord Killanin (1914–99)
Chairman 1970–85

Chairman of the International Olympic Committee from 1972 to 1980, member of the Turf Club, Chairman of the Connemara Pony Society from 1952 to 1970 and Chairman of the Galway Races, Lord Killanin was an influential figure with international contacts. Descended from one of the twelve tribes of Galway, his grand-father was the first Catholic Attorney-General and his great uncle was Sir George Morris of Wellpark, Galway, once the member of parliament for the Galway constituency. Lord Killanin began his career as a journalist, took holidays to attend the Galway Races every year, and hunted with the Galway Blazers. It was through the hunting set that he became a member of the Galway Race Committee in June 1947. It was during his chairmanship that the Galway Races really began to expand, sponsors were signed up for the races and the increased prize money improved the quality of all the races. During his term Galway started breaking records and rose to become the fourth most popular race meeting in the world. It was because of Lord Killanin's insistence that the Racecourse Manager should live on the spot that the Committee built a manager's house, which was first occupied by Captain Luke Mullins.

Lord Killanin's son, Michael Morris, was a leading jockey in the 1970s when riding for Edward O'Grady, but his only win at the Galway Festival was as an amateur in 1971, winning the Dangan Amateur Handicap Hurdle on Wild Buck, trained by Peter McCreery. Nicknamed 'Mouse', Michael turned to training on his retirement, displaying a sense of humour by having a picture of a little mouse on his horses' rugs. His small stable has enjoyed success down the years with jumpers such as Cahervillahow, Foxchapel King, His Song, Mixed Blends and New Co. The best horse he trained is undoubtedly War of Attrition, winner of Cheltenham Gold Cup, owned by Ryanair boss Michael O'Leary.

Patrick D. Ryan (died 2004)
Committee Member 1959–99
Chairman 1986–91

Paddy Ryan was the proprietor of the Anthony Ryan ladies' and gents' drapery shop in Shop Street, a business founded by his father. A former Mayor of Galway,

Paddy was also the owner of the Ardilaun Hotel in the city, which is crammed with influential racing people during race week. He was elected to the Committee on 31 December 1958, along with Lord Hemphill, Thomas McDonogh and Dr Michael O'Malley, but for reasons of clarity I have dated the appointment from 1959, on the basis that during the 1958 meeting none of these men was a member of the Race Committee. The dates I use for all appointments to, and retirements from, the Race Committee relate to the position at start of each festival meeting.

Paddy Ryan was not a racing man as such but he was appointed to the Committee for his promotional flair. Committed to the principle that the Races are for the people of Galway, he continued the policy of improving the facilities and raising the profile of the meeting. It was during his term as Chairman that a rule was introduced that the Chairman's term of office be limited to three years and that he could only be re-elected once. Paddy and Breda Ryan liked to take a share in the odd horse or two owned by their family or friends down the years, but without much success. However, one of these, Ballybrit Boy, trained by Paddy Osborne, gave them a wonderful thrill when he won at the Galway October meeting in 1992.

Lord Hemphill (1928–)

Committee Member 1959–2004
Chairman 1992–96

Peter Patrick Martin is a member of an old West of Ireland family, one of the twelve tribes of Galway according to lore. One member of the family, Edward Martin, was a leading figure in the literary revival at the turn of the twentieth century. President of the Gaelic League, Edward Martin, along with W.B. Yeats and Lady Gregory, was one of a group of people who founded the Abbey Theatre in Dublin, and he wrote plays for it.

Peter Patrick inherited the title Lord Hemphill when his father died in 1957. His father, always known as 'The Baron', had a small stud and liked to keep a few horses in training, the best of whom was probably the useful mare Cillie Dolly, trained by Harry Ussher, twice a winner at the Galway Races. Lady Hemphill owned Sound Track, winner of the King's Stand Stakes at Royal Ascot, trained by Phonsie O'Brien, as well as Peggy West, the grand-dam of Ksar, winter favourite for the 1973 Derby and runner-up in the Eclipse Stakes. Lord Hemphill was a poultry farmer and marketed Tulira Farm Eggs in association with the Galway Milk Company – the first graded eggs in the West of Ireland. For twenty years he was the Master of the famous Galway Blazers Hunt and he continued his father's small stud, being frequently among the leading vendors at Goff's Bloodstock Sales. A prominent figure in Irish racing for many years, he was a steward of the Turf Club and the Irish National Hunt Steeplechase Committee, and served as Senior Steward between 1985 and 1987.

Had the old rules concerning the Chairmanship of Galway remained in force, Lord Hemphill would not have become Chairman until 2004, when Paddy Ryan died. Still hale and hearty in his mid-seventies, as it was Lord Hemphill passed the retirement age that year and had to step down from the Race Committee. In an age obsessed with youth, public relations dictate that a thoroughly modern racecourse must have a young chairman, but the 'old boys' did not do so badly! During Lord Hemphill's term Galway racecourse sponsored a race at Uttoxeter.

Thomas 'Tom' McDonogh
Committee Member 1959–2004
Chairman 1997–2000

The son of Doctor Michael and a nephew of the influential Martin 'Mor' McDonogh, Tom ascended to the family seat in 1958 and served as Chairman from 1997 to 2000. Now an honorary member, having passed the retirement age, his son Thomas junior continues the family's long association with the Galway Races. During his term as Chairman the new Millennium Stand was opened, as was the underpass from the main road to the infield.

John D. Coyle
Elected to Committee 1975
Chairman 2001–05

John Coyle is the Chairman and major shareholder of Hygeia Chemicals Ltd of Oranmore, the first sponsors of the Galway Plate (1979–81). Founded by his father, Dr Donny Coyle, in 1939, Hygeia manufactures agrochemicals, sprays to protect crops and control weeds. John Coyle was elected to the Race Committee for his business skills rather than his knowledge of racing, being one of the leading businessmen in Galway. A director of Galway Airport and a member of the Harbour Board, he is the owner of the famous Renvyle House Hotel in Connemara and a prominent member of the Royal National Lifeboat Institution, the charity that provides a sea rescue service. During his term as Chairman of Galway, the pedestrian underpass was constructed, the new weighing room and offices were built and there was a substantial amount of improvement work done to the actual course. John Coyle has had shares in many horses down the years but none has been successful and he is still awaiting his first winner at Galway.

(Left to right) *Galway built new tea rooms, restaurant, water tower and weighing room in 1946*

Raymond J. Rooney

Elected to Committee 1975

Chairman 2005–

Owner: 1992 ARABIC TREASURE (M.J. Kinane) – GPT 2yo Maiden £5,522 (D.K. Weld); 1993
GARBONI (M.J. Kinane) – Guinness Handicap flat £6,902 (D.K. Weld)

At time of writing, Ray Rooney, erstwhile Senior Steward of the Turf Club and well-known Galway auctioneer, is Chairman of the Galway Race Committee; his term of office lasts until 2008. Like many Irishmen Ray Rooney has loved horses all his life and often went racing as a boy. Born and reared in Nun's Island, Ray went into the insurance business on leaving school, before setting up his own business, Rooney Insurances, in Eyre Square, Galway, in 1964. Branching out into auctioneering, he decided to separate the two businesses and it is the Rooney Life and Pensions business, managed by Niall, his eldest son, that has sponsored the Leading Rider Award at Galway for over a quarter of a century. A director of the Galway Harbour Board, Ray is a keen tennis player and tries to fit in a few games every week. He has less time nowadays for his other loves, fishing and golf, with his business interests, his membership of state boards and his grandchildren.

In 1975 Ray Rooney was invited to become a member of the Galway Race Committee and the new rules, limiting the term of the Chairman, have fast-tracked him to that position. Appointed Chairman on seniority, Ray's fixed term is from 2005 until 2008. Elected a member of the Turf Club in 1984, he became Senior Steward in 1998, which involved him with the complicated business of bringing about the Government's desire to have one Irish governing body, Horse Racing Ireland, instead of three: the Irish Horseracing Authority, the Turf Club and the Irish National Hunt Steeplechase Committee. A grant to racing of almost 50 million euros depended on progress in establishing a new body, which had to be done in a hurry and required considerable goodwill on all sides to bring about. It has taken nearly seven years to sort everything out but now Horse Racing Ireland is responsible for the running of racing, with the Turf Club and Irish National Hunt Steeplechase Committee looking after the stewarding and integrity of racing. These bodies have five seats on the board of Horse Racing Ireland, and Ray served on it during his stint as Steward, and then Senior Steward, of the Turf Club, before he completed his stint in 2003. He was made an honorary steward of the Australian Jockey Club, the first member of the Turf Club to receive such an honour.

Most racegoers think of Golden Cygnet when Rooney's name is mentioned because time has not dimmed the memory of that brilliant but ill-fated hurdler. Golden Cygnet won the Waterford Crystal Supreme Novice Hurdle at Cheltenham in 1978 by seventeen lengths from Western Rose, to the dismay of the latter's trainer, Fred Rimell. Having backed his horse to win a fortune, he could not believe that there was another horse in the land that could beat her so decisively. Sent to Ayr to contest the Scottish Champion Hurdle the following month, Golden Cygnet was taking on Sea Pigeon, Night Nurse and Beacon Light, second, third and fourth in the Champion Hurdle. Ridden by Mr Niall Madden, who had partnered the horse in all his races, including an unbeaten six-race winning sequence that season, Golden Cygnet started 7 to 4 joint favourite with Sea Pigeon, a really good horse over hurdles and on the flat. Challenging at the last, with every chance of winning, Golden Cygnet took a crashing fall but got up afterwards and appeared to be all right. Unfortunately, it transpired that the horse had been seriously injured, having broken vertebrae in his neck, and he died two days later. The death of Golden Cygnet was a tragic loss for Irish racing but a particularly bitter one for Ray Rooney, trainer Edward O'Grady and 'Boots' Madden.

Ray's first venture into horses was the purchase of Princess Ken for £200 in 1960, in partnership with three friends. The horse broke her leg during a race at Clonmel but was insured for £300. This money was used to buy another horse and Ray has been involved in racehorse ownership ever since. He has owned two Galway Festival winners, Arabic Treasure and Garboni, both trained by Dermot Weld and ridden by Michael Kinane.

John Moloney

From Knocklong, Co. Limerick, John Moloney was a farmer and bloodstock breeder who got the job of Assistant Manager at the Limerick Junction racecourse on a part-time basis but was snapped up by Galway as a replacement for the retiring Captain Luke Mullins in 1989. A brother of the trainer Paddy, Luke Mullins had been in charge since 1971 and during his time the meeting had grown rapidly and was creating new attendance and betting records almost every year. It was a hard act to follow but John has succeeded in continuing the trend, to such an extent that the Galway Festival is one of the biggest events in the Irish Racing Calendar. It is inevitable that this record-breaking run will stall at some point in the future but there is no sign of it doing so yet; meanwhile the course makes some major improvement to its facilities every year. Under John Moloney the corporate hospitality side of the business has really taken off and is second only to the Punchestown Festival.

The Racecourse

Galway racecourse employs three office staff and three ground staff on a full-time basis throughout the year. The racing surface is maintained to the highest standards and the course may be watered in mid-summer, but only to prevent the grass from burning and to ensure a good growth to protect the racing horses. The racecourse is particularly well laid out, being able to cater for really big crowds while managing to retain some intimacy and atmosphere at its minor meetings. The Grand Stand faces south, and standing on its terrace one has a panoramic view of the course. On one's left, east of the Grand Stand, is the weighing room, the parade ring and the betting ring. The latter is situated between the parade ring and the Grand Stand, enabling the public to view the horses before placing their bets on the way back to watch the race. The stand complex consists of the Grand Stand, the West Stand and the Mayor's Garden, in that order down the course from the winning post, all affording a fine view of the racing.

Standing on the steps of the Grand Stand and looking southwards across the course, one will see the ruins of Ballybrit Castle straight ahead. Dating from the first half of the sixteenth century, the ruined castle, maintained by the Race Committee, consists of four floors. It is 44 foot 6 inches high and is a listed building. To the left of the castle is the Lisheen part of the course, named after the small graveyard situated adjacent to the second fence past the stands. To the right is the part of the course known as the Moneen, the Irish for a marsh. As its name implies, the Moneen is boggy land, liable to get very heavy in the winter months, which is why Galway does not race later than October. A January meeting was tried on a Monday in 1971 and was successful, among the winners being Dermot Weld, who rode Brass Coin to win the bumper for trainer Brian Lusk. However, the going did get very heavy and the following year, 1972, the executive decided to abandon the January fixture and to extend the October meeting to two days instead.

The course is 10 furlongs round and is much the same for flat and jump racing. After passing the Ballybrit Castle landmark the runners briefly leave the townland of Ballybrit, running over a strip of ground at the top of the hill which is part of Parkmore, the adjoining townland. Then they run downhill into the Moneen, which gives the runners a nice breather before tackling the stiff, uphill finish to the winning post. However, in flat races it is easy to be hampered at this point, when beaten horses begin to drop back as the pace quickens, so jockeys have to be alert.

The steeplechase course has seven fences per circuit. The first fence past the stands is the widest on the course – it has to be because being just before the bend the riders are all jockeying for position. The second fence past the stands is the Lisheen fence, named after the adjacent graveyard, the third the Pen fence, so-called because a sheep pen was situated nearby, and the fourth is the Regulation fence, which is opposite the remains of Ballybrit Castle.

The Regulation fence was introduced in 1889, when the stewards of the Irish National Hunt Committee added a rule that every course had to have at least one fence conforming to the following specifications: a ditch 6 feet wide and 3 feet deep on the take-off side, which could be open or guarded by a single rail; either a bank not less than 3 feet high or a hedge not less than 4 feet 6 inches high, and, if it was of dead brushwood or gorse, 2 feet in width. The introduction of this rule was very controversial at the time, dividing the jumping community, but the stewards were adamant that the tendency of racecourses to lower the fences and shorten the length of their races was having a detrimental affect on steeplechasing. They further decreed that no steeplechase could be run over a distance of less than 2 miles and every jumping programme must include a steeplechase of 3 miles or over. *Sport* and *The Irish Sportsman and Farmer*, the two weekly newspapers that gave full coverage of racing in Ireland, were inundated with letters from owners and trainers about the merits or otherwise of the Regulation fence. The stewards refused to budge: every course had to build a fence to the specifications laid down and this fence became known on all Irish racecourses as the Regulation. This rule is still in force and the specifications of the Regulation fence remain exactly as they were when introduced nearly 120 years ago.

After the Regulation is Paddy's Jump, the fence at the top of the hill. It was named after Paddy McDermott, who lived in a house beside the fence, long since demolished, on a site now occupied by the Digital premises. After this obstacle there is a downhill run into the two remaining fences on the circuit, known as the Moneen fences. About 70 yards apart, they are the closest two fences in the world, closer than the celebrated Railway fences at Sandown Park. Having safely negotiated these, or raced past them in flat races, the horses sweep past the Mayor's Garden as they turn

The perfect race-course layout, Galway's parade ring is separated from the grandstand by the betting area

into the straight (there are no fences in the straight), race past the West Stand and most of the Grand Stand before reaching the finishing line. The uphill finish is deceptively stiff, and it is a good test of a horse's courage in the closing stages of a race.

A new 1 mile course was opened in 1872 and used for sprint races until 1906. The distance of the sprint races tended to vary each year but 5-furlong races were run until 1887 and 6- and 7-furlong races until 1906. There used to be a shoot joining the course just before the second fence past the stand to facilitate the running of 9-furlong flat races. This enabled the sharp turn after the Grand Stand to be omitted. It seems to have been opened in 1909, replacing the 1 mile course used between 1872 and 1906. In 1909 the Mervue Plate was reduced in distance from 10 to 9 furlongs and was won by Lady Geraldine trained by Michael Dawson. The race distance was dropped to 1 mile the following year and Lady Geraldine remains the only horse to have won a race over 9 furlongs in Galway. The modern distance for this type of race is 8½ furlongs and dates from 1958. It appears that this shoot was used only once, in 1909, before being abandoned, although it still appears on the map of the course printed in the 1916 race card.

The original wooden stand was replaced by a new structure in 1898, which was basically a set of concrete steps with a hayshed erected over it. This basic stand provided good, if cramped, viewing until it too was demolished to make way for

The West Stand was completed in 1972 and survived until after the 2006 meeting, when it was demolished

a big new stand, which was opened in 1952. The new Grand Stand, the third in the history of the course, featured an open top tier, offering a marvellous view of the races and of the country and city stretching out as far as Galway Bay. Among the facilities contained in this stand was the famous Long Bar, stretching a world record 210 feet. In 1972 the West Stand was built below the Grand Stand, greatly expanding the viewing and the facilities available at Ballybrit.

The Grand Stand lasted until 1998, when it was pulled down and replaced by the lovely modern structure which was opened the following year. During the winter of 2006/07 the old West Stand was demolished and was replaced by another new stand, full of all the modern conveniences to cater for the customary enormous crowds.

Everyone will be familiar with the sight of long queues of cars travelling on the roads leading to Ballybrit, but in bygone times there were similar queues of horse-drawn carriages. There were fewer of them of course, but in those days the roads were narrower and cursed with dust. People may complain about the pollution caused by motor cars, but in the past, travellers to the races, even on the short journey from the town to Ballybrit, would arrive with their hair and clothes grey from the swirling dust. Nor did pedestrians enjoy a carefree stroll along carless roads. The walk was continually interrupted as pedestrians had to seek protection in the ditch from speeding horses and carriages, which swept past them as if they did not exist. It is said that the first motor car turned up at the Galway Races in 1904 – in fact two arrived – and the numbers have been increasing ever since, except during the Second World War, when the absence of petrol put virtually every car off the road. This temporarily revived the dying business of the jarveys, who hastily re-established themselves to run a shuttle horse and cart service to Ballybrit. Unable to keep up with the demand, the inexperienced jarveys worked their horses too hard; several dropped down dead from exhaustion before the day was over.

The celebrated poet William Butler Yeats was inspired to write a poem about the Galway Races, which appeared in a collection of poems published in 1914. Yeats may have been one of the great poets of the twentieth century but unfortunately 'At the Galway Races' is not one of his better poems. However, the fact that he wrote about the Galway Races at all indicated just how important the fixture had become in ordinary Irish life. People travelled from miles around to attend at least one of the days' racing and an uncle of mine vividly described his first trip to the Galway Races. It was in the 1930s, when he was ten or twelve years old, and he travelled with his parents by car to Galway via Portumna, Loughrea and Oranmore. He remembered the intense excitement setting out that morning and his shock and surprise when they met a car coming towards them. It was driving *away* from the Galway Races! This was something he could not understand because he thought that everyone went to the Galway Races.

The first radio broadcast of the Galway Races took place in 1929, television coverage began in 1963 and a couple of years later Raymond Guest, the American Ambassador to Ireland, arrived in a helicopter, the first to land on the course. When Lord Killanin became Chairman, the races got wide publicity; people wanted to go there, owners wanted their horse to win there and politicians wanted

1969 was the centenary of racing at Ballybrit and the crowd was so large that the stands could not cope. Racegoers left on the ground had a good view of the Galway Hurdle start. Bonne, ridden by Pat Taaffe, was the victor

to be seen there. Once this bandwagon started to roll, the meeting forged ahead, setting record after record year in, year out. It cannot go on breaking records forever but that was being said a decade ago and Galway has not stopped yet. Bearing in mind Ireland's relatively small population, over 210,000 people attend the seven-day Galway Festival meeting – an average of over 30,000 per day. This is almost double the average attendance at the Irish Derby three-day meeting at the Curragh, the Listowel Festival and the four-day Leopardstown Christmas meeting. A course record attendance, over 52,000, turned out on Galway Guinness Hurdle day and witnessed More Rainbows's shock victory in 2005, a figure that was dwarfed by the record attendance of 53,820 on Hurdle Day in 2006.

Everybody who is anybody must be seen on at least one day of the Galway Races. Horse Racing Ireland, the body that runs the sport, holds a board meeting in Galway during race week, knowing that every member of the Board will be at the races and it is a case of 'killing two birds with one stone'. Fianna Fail, the biggest political party in Ireland, hires a tent at the Galway races for the purposes of fund raising, hosting some of the biggest names and the richest people in the country, many of whom have no direct connection with racing. This tent is now part of the folklore of the Galway Races, provoking so much comment in the press and broadcast media that ordinary people often wonder what goes on in there and who is allowed in. Actually entry is open to anyone who is prepared to rent a table for the day; a premium price is charged for the food and facilities and the surplus cash goes directly to the Fianna Fail party. Local Fianna Failers are not enormously keen on this tent, believing that it is seen as elitist, but they realize that it generates badly needed funds and keep quiet. Almost 32.5 million euros is bet at Galway, accounting for over 14 per cent of total Irish on-course betting – figures that speak for themselves. Naturally, every race is sponsored.

The new Killanin Stand, named after the late influential Chairman of the Galway Race Committee, was officially opened by Taoiseach Bertie Ahern on Monday, 9 July 2007. Built at a cost of 22 million euros, the four-storey glass-fronted stand can accommodate 7,000 racegoers and provides free seating for 700 on the first-floor balcony. Ray Rooney, Chairman of the Galway Race Committee, said:

> In providing this facility Galway has a two-fold objective. The first was to continue with the policy of providing a standard of excellence in all facilities on the race-course, and the second was to reward and pay tribute to the many thousands of loyal supporters who continually come to the Galway races. The completion of the Killanin Stand completes a massive seven-year development, which provided the new Millennium Stand, the underground car and pedestrian pass, the new weighing room complex, which includes offices and a state of art media centre.

The town of Galway had suffered all year from a contaminated water supply, which left the tap water unfit to drink. This inconvenient and unpleasant situation affected all those living in the Galway area and was caused by pollution, possibly by building contractors. The locals took it all as just another trial sent by God to test their Faith and certainly did not blame it on the politicians – all of whom retained their seats in the 2007 General Election. To ensure that polluted water would not spoil the Galway Races for the thousands who would flock to Ballybrit, the Galway Race Committee invested in a water filtration and UV light system, which tests proved deliver a water supply completely free of Cryptosporidium, the problem germ, and ensured that all the water used at the races was safe to drink.

The 2007 meeting took place in the middle of 'monsoon-type' weather conditions, which persisted during race week but mercifully refrained from dousing racegoers during the actual event. It rained before the meeting, it rained after the meeting and it rained all night and the bad weather, together with a slight downturn in the Irish economy, contributed to a slight fall in attendances compared with 2006.

The social story of Irish Racing in 2007 was the knock-on effect of the blitz on drinking and driving through the random breath test on motorists. Racegoers at the Punchestown Festival were targeted on all four days of the meeting, with a number being asked to blow into the bag more than once even though they were stone cold sober. If the police did not catch the toper then, they had another go the following morning by randomly testing drivers on their way to work. While the policy appears to be having the desired effect (road deaths are falling) it has impacted on rural life, causing drink sales in pubs and in racecourse bars to collapse.

Just as the police targeted drinking drivers, the Turf Club have gone after drinking jockeys by introducing a random breath test for riders in May 2007. The first jockey to be 'bagged' by the new regulations was Paul Carberry, who 'huffed, puffed and failed' when tested by Al Guy at Galway on the Friday evening. Having failed the test, Carberry was hauled before the stewards, who stood him down for the day for his own safety, causing him to miss the winning ride on Zum See, trained by Noel Meade. In addition they banned Carberry from riding for three days for exceeding the limits allowed. All jockeys that evening were randomly tested a half an hour before they went out to ride in a race and the limits are similar to those allowed to motorists. People of my generation will probably disagree that Paul was any danger to himself. On the contrary, many jockeys down the years used to take a 'reviver' before a race for one reason or another. Fred Archer, the famous English Champion jockey, virtually lived only on champagne, the wily Joe Canty's potion consisted of black coffee and brandy, and there is a painting that depicts the dread of jockeys riding into Becher's Brook with the whiskey dying inside them.

Galway 2007 featured the usual non-racing sideshows including the Sunderland AFC tent, where racegoers were invited to meet the Chairman Niall Quinn, the football legend Charlie Hurley and the manager Roy Keane. The team were over to play the local football team on the Wednesday night and the togged-out girls from Sunderland were an attractive diversion as they distributed invitations to the tent to meet the heroes. 'A €50m Orgy of Extravagance' was the headline in the *Daily Mail* as it reported that €8,000 was bet every minute amid an array of Bentleys, helicopters and Dom Perignon champagne. Galway racegoers are well used to traffic tailbacks but those taking to the skies now have to deal with jams in the air. One racegoer who travelled down from Dublin for the day by 'chopper' told me that they had to queue behind fourteen other helicopters as they waited to land. With no fewer than eighty-four helicopters requiring landing facilities at Ballybrit, the course had to open an air traffic control system so that the machines could land and take off safely. John Moloney, the Galway Manager, will not allow helicopters to fly over the stands or enclosures at any time during the meeting, just in case an accident leads to heavy casualties on the ground.

Although helicopter space was increasing in demand, attendances at the 2007 meeting declined by 3 per cent despite the increased capacity. More than 900 runners competed in the fifty-one races but the quality of the racing, particularly the maidens, looked to be below the quality of previous years. This may have been due to the ground, which was wetter than usual because of the appalling weather, but it is obvious that the meeting is too important to be lumbered with races catering for some of the worst horses in training. Galway Plate day, for instance, includes five moderate flat races, three low-class handicaps and two races for maidens at starting in its eight-race programme.

As Galway city spread out to Ballybrit with amazing rapidity, one can clearly see the inadequacy of Ireland's planning laws. The Galway Races bring so much business to the area yet the planners see no need to protect the racecourse from the urbanization which will eventually kill it. Getting in and out of Ballybrit gets more difficult with each passing year and by next year the road that runs behind the stands will effectively be a main street. The two large fields at the back of the stands, adjacent to the weigh room complex, are being developed and will be occupied by several new business premises next year. With Galway fast becoming an inner city racecourse, John Moloney and the race committee will face some complex challenges in the future if, as is sure to happen, the wonderful new facilities attract record numbers of patrons.

The Galway Festival Horse Heroes

ABSENTEE

(Brown mare 1864 Artillery – Swallow by Lanercost)

Breeder: William Disney, Lark Lodge, Curragh
Winner of the 1869 Galway Plate
Won 3 races (1 flat and 2 chases)

Owner and trainer: Richard Bell
Curragh 16 October 1867 (T. Miller) Won Selling Stakes 6f Flat £45 Bar
Newbridge 15 February 1869 (Walshe) Won Open Handicap Chase 3m £64 Bar
Galway 17 August 1869 (W. Bell) Won Galway Plate Handicap Chase 2½m £100 3/1

Absentee, the first ever winner of the Galway Plate, was bred by William Disney and foaled at his Lark Lodge Stud, Curragh, in 1864. A brown filly, she was by the resident stallion Artillery and was an own-sister to Bird of Passage and Emigrant. Artillery was a very good racehorse, winning the Prince of Wales Stakes (York), Criterion Stakes (Newmarket), North Derby (Newcastle), Ebor St Leger (York) and Dun Stakes (York) as well as dead-heating for second place behind Warlock (by Birdcatcher) in the 1856 St Leger, with the odds-on Derby winner Ellington behind. William Disney snapped him up as a replacement for his brilliant but ageing stallion Birdcatcher, eight times Irish and twice British Champion Sire.

Foaled in 1833 and the winner of six races, all at the Curragh, Birdcatcher turned out to be a sensationally successful stallion, elevating Irish flat racehorse breeding considerably. The quality of his stock helped eradicate a prejudice against non-English thoroughbreds and greatly improved the quality of the Irish-bred horse. Artillery's dam, Jeannette, was by Birdcatcher, and Mr Disney was supremely confident that a horse as sound as a bell and free from blemish, with top-class racing form, would be an instant hit with breeders. He was very put out when initial support for Artillery was poor, particularly when every breeder wanted Birdcatcher, notwithstanding his age. With Birdcatcher having difficulty covering his mares, many breeders went elsewhere rather than using Artillery. Legend has it that when Birdcatcher failed to cover the mare Queen Bee, whose produce of the previous year turned out to be Roman Bee, in March 1860, a disgusted William Disney ordered that the 27-year-old stallion be taken to the edge of a disused sand pit nearby and shot. He was unceremoniously dumped in this unmarked and now unknown grave. Birdcatcher got only two juvenile winners in Ireland in 1862 – and these were actually described as being by Birdcatcher or Artillery – Breda and Roman Bee. Both were cracking good juveniles: the filly, Breda, won the North of Ireland Produce Stakes and a valuable race at the Curragh, and the colt, Roman Bee, won three races, including the prestigious Anglesey Stakes.

With Birdcatcher out of the way, Artillery got more support but he did not cover Queen Bee, who was despatched to the nearby Brownstown Lodge Stud of Michael Clancy to be covered by Claret, a good handicapper that had finished fourth in the 2,000 Guineas. Artillery's detractors could put the feats of Roman Bee and Breda down to Birdcatcher, but there was no doubt about the parentage of Spring Daisy, winner of four good races in 1863, It's Curious and Owen Roe, successive winners of the Anglesey Stakes. William Disney walked around with an 'I told you so' look now that his judgement had been vindicated but, unfortunately for him, Artillery died young, posthumously siring the 1873 Irish Derby winner Kyrle Daly.

William Disney loved all field sports. A cock-fighting enthusiast who continued his participation in that sport long after it had been banned, in the mid-1830s he owned a brilliant coursing greyhound named Puss and, besides Birdcatcher, he owned Skylark (winner of the Royal Whip three years in succession, 1830–2), Justice to Ireland (Anglesey Stakes) and Indian Warrior (Railway and Anglesey Stakes). He died on 29 July 1875 aged seventy-seven years.

Absentee was obviously highly thought of because she made her racing debut in the valuable Waterford Testimonial Stakes for two-year-olds at the Curragh, sporting the all-pink silks of William Disney. Well supported at 6 to 1 she failed to make the first four. She was also backed for the Anglesey Stakes three months later but finished unplaced; she subsequently ran a good second in a Curragh nursery, however. In 1867 she ran second over 6 furlongs at the Curragh but failed when stepped to longer distances, being beaten twice at the Heath races, on the great Heath of Maryborough. Brought back to the Curragh and to sprinting, she was made the 5 to 4 favourite but was beaten by a length over ½ mile by Porto Rico, the mount of 'Lucky' Charles Maidment. She was disappointing and expensive to follow, so Mr Disney sold her off to Dick Bell, who trained her for himself at Loughbrown, Newbridge.

Bell dropped Absentee in class, running her in a seller over 6 furlongs at the Curragh, and she caused an upset by winning the race by a head. Bell succeeded in keeping her by buying her in, but she failed to win in her next eight races on the flat, over distances ranging from 4 to 8 furlongs, although she was placed twice. However, it was a different story when she was tried over fences; she won on her steeplechase debut at Newbridge in February 1869. She suffered a temporary setback when she fell in her second race of that afternoon, which affected her confidence when jumping and also her form. However, after patient schooling Dick Bell got her right on the day of the Galway Plate, where she beat the favourite Quickstep rather cleverly by a length and a half. However, she never won another race. Retired to stud, she only had three foals that lived, all colts, before dying in 1882.

ISHMAAL (late Nannie's Son)

(Brown gelding 1864 Newton-le-Willows – Nannie by Thunderbolt)

Breeder: Unknown
First horse to win twice at the Festival

Owner: J. Ussher. (Trained privately)
Galway 17 August 1869 (Mr W. Coghlan) Won Ballybrit Plate 8f flat £40 6/4f
Galway 18 August 1869 (Mr Williams) Won Renmore Handicap Chase 3m £50 1/1f
Carrickmacross 27 October 1869 (P. Gavin) Won Handicap Chase 2m £30 4/1

Owner: Captain F. Wallace
Baldoyle 14 September 1872 (G. Gray) Won Grand Metropolitan Chase 3¼m £250 4/1

Ishmaal was a half-bred horse by Newton-le-Willows, a decent horse in Ireland at two and three years and good enough to be sent over to Epsom to contest the Derby, where it finished unplaced behind Blink Bonny. Despite being by the champion sire Melbourne, Newton-le-Willows did not get many chances at stud, first in Co. Roscommon and then in Limerick. However, he was the sire of Olympia, winner of the 1868 Conyngham Cup. Ishmaal was originally called Nannie's Son, his owner, Martin D. Colahan of Ballinasloe, naming the horse after his dam, a mare named Nannie. Nannie's Son turned up at the Loughrea Steeplechases, in June 1869 and finished second, with Hubert Davies in the saddle, to Christopher

Ussher's Luckpenny. Obviously on the lookout for a horse likely to win at the soon-to-be-revived Galway Races, the brothers Christopher and John Ussher bought him on the spot.

The first thing John Ussher did was to change his name to Ishmaal. Perhaps he named it after the banished son of Abraham, founder of the Arabs, from whom Mohammed claimed descendency; but more likely the name was copied from a famous Irish stallion of the past. That Ishmaal was the sire of the Irish-bred and trained pony Abd-el-Kader, 'Little Ab' as he was known, winner of the Grand National in successive years. It was certainly a ploy to confuse the bookmakers, as the name would not be recognized and therefore might not be associated with Nannie's Son. While John Ussher may have fooled the bookmakers, however, the local people knew that Ishmaal was Nannie's Son and could not wait to back him, piling their money on as if he were a certainty to win the Members' Plate. However, they ignored the old betting adage to ensure that the connections are on first; when the Usshers went to back Ishmaal all the fancy prices were long gone, so they refused to allow the horse to start.

A combination of things encouraged these outsiders to back Ishmaal. The horse was obviously bought because of his second place to Luckpenny at Loughrea. It was known that Luckpenny was highly thought of by the Usshers and had run well in the Galway Plate, and it was deduced that the strange decision to change Nannie's Son's name to Ishmaal was suspiciously like the action of a man going for a coup. The public had guessed correctly – Luckpenny had ability and, although he finished unplaced in the Galway Plate, he won the consolation race, the Forster Street Handicap, the following day, and the Usshers had a line of form to go on. I have previously related how John Ussher cynically withdrew Ishmaal from the Members' Plate in a fit of pique when his price was taken, but he was quite prepared to take the same short price for the next race now that the bookmakers' cards had been marked. He was simply not prepared to allow members of the public who had backed Ishmaal at odds in excess of 3 to 1, to collect, so everybody had to be content with 6 to 4. Clearly a certainty, Ishmaal duly obliged in the Ballybrit Chase, the last race of that day, and won again the following afternoon.

He won at the Carrickmacross meeting later in the season but ran a cracking race to finish second in the valuable Old Rock Handicap Chase at the Old Rock, Chichester and Route Hunt Meeting, run in Antrim the following November. Passed on to Captain F. Wallace of the Scots Greys, Ishmaal reappeared at Galway in 1872, ridden by Garry Moore, and was runner-up to Belle, trained and ridden by the Bells, in the Plate. The field for that year's big race confusingly included two mares named Quickstep, one a thoroughbred by Rapid Rhone owned by 'Mr

Chester', which finished third, the other a talented half-bred by General, owned by Thomas Jackson. Being "in the know' was essential if punters were to survive in those days. Gallant Ishmaal fell and was killed during the running of the 1873 Old Rock Handicap Chase, won by Scots Grey, the two-time Irish Grand National winner.

ASTER

(Brown horse 1864 Planet – Tidy by Birdcatcher)

Breeder: Captain J. Croker, Ballinagard, Limerick
Winner of the 1871 Galway Plate
Winner of 23 races in Ireland

Owner: 'H.S. Chester'. (Trained privately)
Curragh 5 September 1867 (James Miller) Won Stewards' Plate 8f flat £70 4/1
Curragh 15 October 1867 (James Miller) Won Kildare Handicap 10f flat £90 5/2
Curragh 23 April 1868 (T. Miller) Won Stewards' Plate 8f flat £94 7/1
Curragh 3 September 1868 (T. Miller) Won Stewards' Plate 8f flat £62 6/4f
Carlow 15 September 1868 (T. Miller) Won Carlow Handicap 12f flat £82 6/4
Carlow 16 September 1868 (T. Miller) Won Bagnalstown 5f flat £40 6/4jf
Curragh 30 September 1868 (T. Miller) Won Lord Lieutenant's Plate 12f flat £104 6/4f
Limerick 13 October 1868 (T. Miller) Won Her Majesty's Plate 2m flat £104 6/4f
Curragh 23 June 1869 (T. Miller) Won Stewards' Plate 8f flat £66 4/5f
Curragh 24 June 1869 (T. Miller) Won Handicap 8f flat £62 7/4f
Down Royal 15 July 1869 (T. Miller) Won Belfast Handicap 15f flat £150 5/2
Londonderry 5 August 1869 (T. Miller) Won Open Handicap 16f flat £55 No SP
Londonderry 5 August 1869 (T. Miller) Won Tradesman's Plate 12f flat £37 No SP
Londonderry 6 August 1869 (T. Miller) Won Railway Handicap 12f flat £33 No SP
Londonderry 6 August 1869 (T. Miller) Walk Over Her Majesty's Plate 2m flat £104
Cork Park 2 September 1869 (T. Miller) Won Her Majesty's Plate 2m flat £104 1/3f
Maryborough Heath 27 July 1870 (T. Miller) Won Heath Scurry 6f flat £51 2/1jf
Curragh Military 9 September 1870 (Mr W. I'Anson) Won Open Stakes 8f flat £47½ 4/1
Curragh 18 October 1870 (S. Fleming) Won Scurry Stakes 6f flat £60 Bar
Galway 16 August 1871 (Mr R.L. Exshaw) Won Galway Plate 2½m chase £300 9/1
Ennis 22 August 1871 (Mr R.L. Exshaw) Won Ennis Handicap Chase 3m £100 1/1f
Fethard 28 May 1872 (Mr R.L. Exshaw) Won Consolation Chase 3m £20 No SP
Cappoquin 30 September 1872 (W. Bell) Won Cappoquin Handicap Chase 3m £99 No SP

Aster was conceived at George A. Harris's stud in Kilmallock, Co. Limerick, when his dam, Tidy, was covered by Planet, one of the stallions resident there. A rich bay with no white whatever, Planet was by a Derby winner, Bay Middleton, out of the sister to Plenipotentiary, also a Derby winner, and was bred by Lord George Bentinck. The winner of the Molecomb Stakes at Goodwood and runner-up in the 2,000 Guineas, he won the Croker Challenge Cup for best weight-carrying thoroughbred stallion at the Cork Grand National Show.

Aster ran in the 1867 Irish Derby, apparently fancied although still a maiden, having run once unplaced at two. Making his three-year-old debut with jockey Pat Conolly putting up 2 pounds overweight, the race was lost at the start when Aster whipped round as the flag dropped, losing many lengths which he never looked likely to recover, and in the end finished a poor last of the four runners behind Golden Plover. Although he later narrowly reversed the form with Golden Plover at Down Royal, the pair were beaten by six lengths by Honestish. Athough he took some time to win his first race, Aster was a sound, consistent handicapper on the flat, winning nineteen races, including three royal plates, before being sent over fences. The biggest prize he won on the flat was the Belfast Handicap at Down Royal, worth £150, but he won twice that sum when winning his first steeplechase, the Galway Plate in 1871. Having won three more steeplechases, Aster, an entire horse, was retired to Captain Croker's stud in 1874 at Ballinagarde, Limerick.

'I doubt it said Croker' is a Limerick expression that was once commonly used. It came from a story of old Captain Croker, who lamented on his deathbed that he would be leaving his lovely Ballinagarde. The parson, who was at his bedside, comforted him by reminding the dying man that he was going to a better place. To which old Croker replied, 'I doubt it!'

THE KITTEN

(Bay mare 1870 Ward Union – North Kerry's dam)

Breeder: Unknown
The only horse to win twice on the same day at Galway

Owner and trainer: Mr John Griffin, Ballyheigue, Tralee
Killarney 12 August 1874 (P. Gavin) Won Herbert Chase 2½m £30 No SP

Owner: Mr J. Apleton
Trainer: John Hubert Moore
Galway 11 August 1875 (Joseph Doyle) Won Provincial Handicap Chase 2½m £100 3/1

Galway 11 August 1875 (T. Ryan) Won Wellpark Chase 2m £100 1/1f
Killarney 1 September 1875 (Mr J. Apleton) Won Selling Chase 2½m £35 1/3f
Old Rock and Chichester 28 October 1875 (W. Canavan) Won Smoking Room Chase 2m £90 2/1f

With two The Kittens and two North Kerrys racing in Ireland in the early 1870s, the pedigree of this particular horse is vague, but being a half-bred that did not matter much. She originated in Kerry, winning a race for Kerry Farmers at Killarney when owned by John Griffin of Ballyheigue, Tralee. Sold to Mr Apleton and sent to John Hubert Moore, she won £325 in prize money in the space of eleven weeks in the late summer and autumn of 1875, including four chases. Kicking off the sequence by winning twice on the first day of the Galway meeting, the only horse ever to have done so, she finished unplaced in Forster Street Chase, won by Pride of Kildare, the following day but went on to win at Killarney and in the North of Ireland. The Kitten is a good example of the glorious uncertainty of horse racing, even in those olden times when money was in short supply; a cheap horse could win a fortune and still be little better than a selling plater. On these dreams the sport of horse racing was built.

THE LIBERATOR

(Bay gelding 1869 Dan O'Connell – Mary O'Toole by Annandale)

Breeder: George D. Stokes
Winner of the 1875 Galway Plate
Winner of the 1879 Grand National

Owner: G.D. Stokes. (Trained privately)
Cork Park 20 May 1874 (J. Connolly) Won Lee Handicap 12f flat £130 Bar
Cork Park 5 May 1875 (Lynch) Won Park Open Handicap Chase 2½m £250 10/1

Owner: C. Hawkes
Trainer: J.H. Moore
Galway 11 August 1875 (T. Ryan) Won Galway Plate Handicap Chase 2½m £365 7/1
Aintree 28 March 1879 (Mr G. Moore) Won Grand National Handicap 4½m £1,665 5/1

Owner: E. Woodland
Manchester 1 January 1883 (H. Davis) Won Manchester Handicap Chase 3m £237
Cheltenham 1 May 1884 (Mr L. Goodwin) Won Grand Annual Handicap Chase 3½m £122 5/1

John Hubert Moore of Jockey Hall, the Curragh, probably expected to win the 1875 Galway with the joint-favourite Pride of Kildare, ridden by George Gray, but it was his second string, The Liberator, that did the honours. An enormous horse, standing 17 hands and one of the few good horses to have been bred in Co. Kerry, The Liberator had been well supported in an open betting market. After he won on his chasing debut, easily defeating the classy flat horse Grand National at Cork, Charles Hawkes, of The Grange, Tulsk, Co. Roscommon, bought The Liberator from his breeder, George Stokes. The Galway Plate was his first race in Mr Hawkes's black and white silks and he won the race more easily than the judge's verdict implied. With only a couple of lengths separating the first three horses home, Mimalus (Paddy Gavin) finished second and John Hubert Moore's other runner, Pride of Kildare, third. Few present could have suspected that they had seen a future Grand National winner and another who would be placed in that great race. Having won the Galway Plate, The Liberator went over to Aintree to contest the Grand National, but was a rank outsider at 50 to 1. Tom Ryan, who had ridden him to victory at Galway, was again aboard, but he fell.

The horse had proved difficult to train and Mr Hawkes wanted to get out. Fearful that he might leave his stable, the wily J.H. Moore was determined to buy him, even though he could not afford to, and sought financial support from Plunkett Taaffe, another Roscommon man, to complete the deal. The terms were agreed orally and would later lead to a serious dispute between the two men. However, now running in the name of his trainer, The Liberator lined up for the 1877 Grand National a 25 to 1 shot but with the brilliant 'Mr Thomas' aboard. 'Mr Thomas' was actually Tommy Pickernell, who was having his seventeenth and what turned out to be his final mount in the great race, which he had already won three times. Austerlitz, ridden by Fred Hobson having his one and only ride in the race, attempted to lead from start to finish, one by one repulsing all challenges until The Liberator loomed up, looking the likely winner. Having headed Austerlitz, The Liberator struggled to get clear of the long-time leader, who got a second wind, enabling him to sail past the Irish horse and race on to victory. The Liberator was not even runner-up, being caught on the line by Congress and losing second place by a neck.

In 1878 The Liberator was heavily backed to win the Grand National on the strength of his performance the previous year. Disgracefully, he was wilfully prevented from running by Moore, who made the decision to withdraw him on the eve of the race on the pretext of a leg injury. However, it was well known that someone had pinched the market and he was about to exact revenge. Racked with rheumatism, he was cantankerous at the best of times, but armed with a grievance he was a loose cannon. Initially surprised at the rush of money for The Liberator, who had been well beaten by Pride of Kildare in a secret trial, Moore soon suspected that he had been misled. Squealing like a pig, he threatened that if he could not back the horse to win a reasonable sum at a fair price he would not run him, in an effort to induce those who had taken the price to share their bets with Moore, so that they were not lost on a non-runner. However, they could not do so without their identity being exposed and they decided that a financial loss was infinitely more desirable than having to face Moore, who would be incandescent with rage and bristling with aggression. When nobody came forward to let the trainer have some of the bets struck at long prices, Moore spitefully scratched The Liberator. Those who had 'stolen his price' had lost their money but so too had the racing public, and there was a lot of bad feeling about the withdrawal. The press went to town, describing the scratching as a 'dirty business', 'a cause for revulsion', and 'unsportsmanlike'. Feeling the heat, Moore leaped to his own defence, defiantly asserting that he had every right to withdraw the horse. The Liberator had cost him more that he could afford and had been backed by people who had never paid a penny towards the cost and the keep of the horse, and that he had no obligation to them whatsoever.

Years later the news of a secret trial between The Liberator and another inmate of his stable, Pride of Kildare, emerged. Moore wanted to gauge which of the two horses had the best chance of carrying off the big race. The trial was to be held at first light on a replica Aintree course at Eyrefield Lodge, belonging to his neighbour Henry Linde. Linde's stable jockey, Tommy Beasley, rode The Liberator, while John Moore's son, Garry, partnered Pride of Kildare. Garry was known to be fond of a drink and the Beasley brothers inveigled him into joining them for a night on the town on the eve of the trial. Well inebriated when he finally retired, Garry had hardly been in his bed an hour when he was roused by his father and arrived in the field 'under the weather', and a most reluctant participant. When the trial got under way, the 28-year-old realized that he was not fit to ride the horse, so he took the easy way out and missed out all the fences except the one by which his father was standing watching that dark, misty morning. With The Liberator jumping all the fences and Garry Moore taking a shorter route inside the jumps on Pride of Kildare, the trial was a charade and naturally Pride of Kildare won easily. Garry was afraid to admit the facts to his father, who had seen Pride of Kildare win the trial and believed that this was the horse to be on. Of course, the Beasley brothers and their cronies all knew different but were afraid to come forward and admit what they had done, preferring to lose their cash than to face an angry Moore.

In the absence of The Liberator, Pride of Kildare, ridden by Garry Moore, finished third to Shifnal and Martha at Aintree, which clearly indicated that The Liberator would probably have won the race had he been allowed to run. Although the Beasleys still had the information revealed by that trial a year later, only Moore knew for certain whether The Liberator would run in the Grand National in 1879. Having had their fingers burnt the previous year, the Beasleys had to hold off backing The Liberator until they were certain that Moore's bets were on, which enabled the trainer to get his money on at the right price. When he had done so, supporters of The Liberator knew that horse would go to Aintree as fit as a flea and could back him with the confidence of getting a run at the very least.

However, once again his participation was put in doubt, this time by Plunkett Taaffe, the man who had supplied the trainer with the funds to buy the horse from Mr Hawkes. Relations between the pair had deteriorated to the point where Taaffe applied to the courts in Dublin for an injunction to stop Moore from running the horse in the Grand National. Although the injunction was not granted, significantly The Liberator ran in the big race as the property of Garrett Moore instead of John Hubert Moore. This scare having passed, a rumour surfaced that the horse had pulled up lame after a gallop but the public did not care; they followed the canny Moore and backed The Liberator for all they were worth. The surprise favourite for the race was the former winner Regal, owned by Captain James Machell who had won three recent Grand Nationals with Disturbance (1873), Reugny (1874) and Regal (1876). He had sold the latter to Lord Lonsdale after his victory three years before but had now bought him back, which some people considered significant. There was a substantial gamble on Regal, who had fallen in the race two years previously when The Liberator finished third, and the price tumbled to an unattractive 5 to 2. This made the market for the backers of The Liberator, supporting its price at 5 to 1, which was infinitely better value than the bookmakers realized.

Four Beasley brothers rode in the race. One of them, Tommy, had blazed a trail on Martha the previous year, only to be caught in the closing stages by Shifnal. He gave that mare a more restrained ride on this occasion but still could not quicken when The Liberator challenged in the closing stages. The Liberator, ridden by Garry Moore, raced to an effortless ten-length victory, while Jackal and Martha battled it out for the minor placings, finishing in that order.

The handicapper hit the lightly raced The Liberator with a 17-pound rise in his weight in the 1880 race, burdening him with 12 stones 7 pounds. Regal again started favourite; he had fallen the previous year but his jockey had remounted and they had finished sixth. The Liberator was priced at 11 to 2. The first five horses to finish were all Irish-trained: first Empress, ridden by Tommy Beasley and trained by Henry Linde; second The Liberator, Garry Moore up; third Downpatrick, ridden and trained by Paddy Gavin of French Furze, Curragh, the only pro in the bunch; fourth was the Irish Grand National winner Jupiter Tonans, trained by Captain George Joy and ridden by Mr 'The Shaver' Lee Barber; and fifth was Mr Linde's second string, Woodbrook, ridden by Harry Beasley, which his brother Tommy would ride to victory to following year.

The Liberator never ran in Ireland after he had finished third at Aintree in 1877, which was not unusual at a time when Irish stables often moved to England for the winter months. He ran twice more in the Grand National, finishing unplaced on each occasion. In seven attempts, from seven to thirteen years, he had won, finished second and third, been unplaced once and fallen on two occasions. A horse named The Liberator ran unplaced in 1886 but this was an eleven-year-old and definitely not the former winner of the race, who would have been a geriatric seventeen-year-old!

Garry Moore described The Liberator as 'a cunning old horse', his problem being the easier fences of the park courses, which he tended to take too casually. This led to falls and, unfortunately for his owner, when The Liberator fell he tended to get hurt, which was the reason why he ran in so few races during a long career and only won three in his life. Just to confuse things a bit there was another Liberator racing in Ireland at this time. The second Liberator, by East Lancashire out of Madam O'Donoghue, was owned by J.E. O'Connell, and won a number of races but was not in the same class as the Grand National winner.

MARTHA

(Bay mare 1871 The Coroner – Martha by Windfall)

Breeder: Thomas N. Wade
Winner of the 1876 Galway Plate

Owner: Thomas N. Wade
Trainer: Henry Eyre Linde
Longwood 5 April 1875 (T. Burke) Won Longwood Chase 2m 19gns Bar
Killarney 1 September 1875 (Mr T. Beasley) Won Standhouse Chase 2½m £50 7/4
Killarney 2 September 1875 (Mr T. Beasley) Won Handicap Chase 2½m £80 2/1
Attanah 21 March 1876 (T. Burke) Won Stradbally Handicap Chase 3m £100 5/1
Galway 2 August 1876 (Mr T. Beasley) Won Galway Plate Handicap 2½m £245 8/1
Sandown Park 27 February 1878 (Mr T. Beasley) Won Prince of Wales Handicap Chase 3m £480 2/1f

Martha may have been only five years old when she contested the 1876 Galway Plate but she had plenty of experience over fences, having won four steeplechases and been placed several times. Not that she needed experience because she was trained by Henry Linde, a brilliant trainer of jumpers, who had his own miniature course of Aintree-type fences at Eyrefield Lodge. Having won a 3-mile handicap steeplechase over the old Orchard course in Co. Leix, she contested the Irish Grand National, but as a second-string to Moses Taylor's horse Grand National, which duly won the race after which he was named. Deserted by the stable jockey Tommy Beasley, Martha ran well enough to finish third, ahead of Scots Grey, twice winner of that race. In view of this form, it is surprising that Martha was not particularly fancied to win the Galway Plate, but she did so, beating Ilderim easily by three lengths. Sold to Captain A. Crofton, another patron of the Linde stable, Martha won a valuable race at Sandown Park and was narrowly beaten into second place at Croydon *en route* to a crack at the 1878 Grand National.

Despite representing one of the most powerful stables in Ireland and having the services of Mr Tommy Beasley, Martha was a 20 to 1 outsider for the twelve-runner race, reflecting the fact that an Irish-trained horse had not won the Grand National since Wanderer in 1855. She made most of the running, setting a fast pace which saw fellow Irish challenger Pride of Kildare, ridden by Mr Garrett Moore, struggling to keep in touch. However, Martha could not shake off Shifnal, who raced along with the mare throughout the first circuit. After passing the stands, Martha kicked, established a clear lead and coming to the last fence looked a certainty. Unfortunately for the Irish, she stopped to nothing on the run-in and was passed by Shifnal, who won by two lengths, with Pride of Kildare staying on well to finish third, a further ten lengths in arrears. To the annoyance of the connections of Shifnal, who felt that it was not the 'done thing', Tommy Beasley lodged an objection to the winner on the grounds of foul riding. It was the first time an objection had been lodged against the winner of the Grand National but the stewards dismissed it.

Returning to Aintree the following year, having been sold to a Mr Oeschlaeger, Martha was ignored in the market, starting at 50 to 1 despite her prominent run the previous year. The reason for this was The Liberator, backed to a man by the Irish, to the exclusion of the other Irish runners. The four Beasley brothers had rides in this race, Tommy on Martha, Harry on Turco, Willie on Lord Marcus and John on Victor II. Tommy Beasley attempted to ride Martha with more restraint, so that he might have something in reserve for the finish, but she pulled hard and made the running as she had done the previous year, attended by Lord Marcus and Bob Ridley. The Irish-trained Bob Ridley, ridden by English amateur Ted Wilson, forged into a three-length lead but the roar of the Irish in the crowd indicated that

The Liberator was closing up fast. Passing Bob Ridley as if that horse was standing still, The Liberator drew away to a famous victory, chased home by Jackal, with Martha finishing a weary third. Bob Ridley was also exhausted by his exertions and dropped right away to finish only fifth in the end.

JUPITER TONANS

(Bay horse 1873 Thunderbolt – Beatrice Gray by Buccaneer)

Breeder: Mr Alexander
Winner of the 1878 Galway Plate
Winner of the 1879 Irish Grand National

Owner: J.F.S. Lee Barber
Trainer: George Joy
Kildare Hunt 13 February 1877 (W. Behan) Won Schooling Handicap Chase 2m £5 1/1f
Punchestown 17 April 1877 (J.F. Lee Barber) Won Irish Grand Military Chase 3m £345 4/1
Sandown Park 9 March 1878 (Mr J.F. Lee Barber) Won Lightweight Grand Military Chase 3m £215 2/1
Galway 31 July 1878 (Mr J.F. Lee Barber) Won Galway Plate 2½m £220 2/1f
Fairyhouse 14 April 1879 (Mr J.F. Lee Barber) Won Irish Grand National 3m £320 7/1
Aintree 10 November 1880 (Mr H. Beasley) Won Grand Sefton Chase 3m £327 3/1f
Aintree 23 March 1882 (Mr J.F. Lee Barber) Won Second Liverpool Hunt Chase 4½m £140 7/4

The cherry jacket and black cap colours of Mr Lee Barber were carried prominently in Ireland between 1875 and 1881, when 'the Shaver', as he was nicknamed, was stationed at Cahir. A lieutenant with the 3rd Dragoon Guards, 'the Shaver' joined the army in 1874 and, falling in with the racing set, took up steeplechasing the following year. A keen and talented rider, he came to Ireland with his regiment, riding his first winners there in September 1975 at the Curragh Garrison meeting. He was the fourth amateur rider to become Champion Jockey in Ireland when he headed the list in 1879. His big, headstrong stallion Jupiter Tonans was the only thoroughbred foal out of Beatrice Gray, who died young early in 1874. He was bought with military steeplechases in mind but proved to be a high-class chaser. An entire horse, he won valuable military steeplechases at Punchestown and Sandown Park before winning the Galway Plate on the disqualification of The Inny. After being successful in the Irish Grand National at Fairyhouse in 1879, he and Captain Lee Barber lined up for the 1880 Aintree Grand National as a 50 to 1 outsider, in a field that included Regal and The Liberator, previous winners of the race, as well as Woodbrook, a future winner, and a French challenger, Wild Monarch. Having passed the stands for the first time and just about to start the second circuit, Jupiter Tonans suddenly 'ran away at flat-race speed' and opened up a lead of about a furlong. Nobody was quite sure if 'the Shaver' was in full control or not, but the bookies gave Jupiter Tonans no chance of staying there, howling their willingness to lay the leader at 50 to 1 as loudly as their lungs would let them. Sure enough, the pace was too hot and Jupiter Tonans came back to the field, although he did stay on well again to finish a respectable fourth behind Empress.

Onlookers wondered what might have been if Jupiter Tonans could have been ridden with more restraint. Many blamed the rider, not realizing that he was one of the tops in Ireland, but the horse was a hard puller and just bolted. He was a decent horse when he could be restrained and went on to win the Grand Sefton Chase at Aintree the following November, but Mr Lee Barber never ran him in the Grand National again. Moving with his regiment to Scotland, he continued his successful riding career there, twice winning the Scottish Grand National, then run at Bogside, on The Peer (1884) and Ireland (1888).

BARON FARNEY

(Brown colt 1877 Cambuslang – XL by Polish)

Breeder: P. Kenney
Winner of Her Majesty's Plate in 1880 and 1881

Owner: Charles J. Blake
Trainer: James Dunne
Galway 4 August 1880 (C. Whelan) Won Renmore Handicap 1m £100 2/1
Galway 5 August 1880 (F. Wynne) Won H.M. Plate 2m 100gns 6/4f
Curragh 8 September 1880 (F. Wynne) Won H.M. Plate 2½m 100gns 4/5f
Curragh 20 October 1880 (J. Callaghan) Won Cesarewitch Handicap 1¾m £153 8/1
Galway 3 August 1881 (J. Callaghan) Won Renmore Handicap 1m £58 5/2
Galway 4 August 1881 (J. Callaghan) Won H.M. Plate 2m 100gns 5/2

Charles J. Blake moved into Heath House, on the Great Heath of Maryborough, in 1880, and installed James 'Fairy' Dunne as his private trainer. Baron Farney, by the Northumberland Plate winner Cambuslang, had been entered up in all the important Irish two-year-old races but did not appear on the racecourse in 1879. Obviously highly thought of, he was quietly fancied for the following year's Irish

Derby, although he would be making his racing debut. A gallant second to King of the Bees, he ran a fine race to be beaten by a length, and again ran really well the following day when beaten by a head by the four-year-old Shinglass.

Brought to Galway, Baron Farney won the Renmore Handicap over 1 mile on the first day, and then landed the 2-mile Queen's Plate on the second afternoon. The horse obviously liked the Ballybrit course because he carried off the same double the following year (1881). Winner of the Irish Cesarewitch at the Curragh, he contested some of the big handicaps in England later in his career, which ended after a defeat in the 1882 Grand International Hurdle at Croydon. He retired to stud the winner of six races, four of which were at Galway, but his racing career was somewhat disappointing in view of his home reputation and the promising run in the Irish Derby. Perhaps he was flattered in that race because Frank Wynne, who rode the winner, King of the Bees, later described that horse as 'moderate, delicate and a whistler'.

Baron Farney retired to stud but got few opportunities and died young, on 16 November 1891. His first winner in Ireland was the four-year-old Miss Georgie, on whom 'Mr Wildman' won an open hunters' hurdle race at the Curragh Military meeting in September 1890. 'Mr Wildman', otherwise Graham Wildman 'Tommy' Lushington, was one of the best amateur riders of the day and well able to compete on the flat against the professionals, as was proved by his win on Gallinaria in the Irish Derby of 1900. No doubt he had forgotten Miss Georgie long since and had never visualized her breeding a Derby winner, but she did just that when Lord Rossmore won the 1903 Irish Derby. Miss Georgie was not the best racehorse sired by Baron Farney; that honour must go to Miss Baron, winner of nine races on the flat, over hurdles and over fences in 1894–5.

James Grew of Portadown acquired Miss Georgie and sent her to the stallion Cherry Ripe and was so impressed by the offspring that he kept sending her back again. For the next four years Miss Georgie was covered by Cherry Ripe but the sequence was broken by the death of the stallion in August 1902. Nobody mourned the loss of Cherry Ripe more than James Grew because Miss Georgie bred three high-class Cherry Ripe colts: Lord Rossmore, Cherry Pip and Silver Wedding. All three were good enough to take their chances in the Irish Derby. Lord Rossmore was a winning favourite, Cherry Pip finished a disappointing seventh and Silver Wedding, who was purchased by the real Lord Rossmore, owner of the now deceased Cherry Ripe, briefly flattered before fading to finish a close-up fourth. Cherry Ripe was a big, handsome chestnut horse with a prominent blaze who, owing to an injury, was never trained. An own-brother to Enthusiast, winner of the 2,000 Guineas, he got very few opportunities at stud but did sire the brilliant two-year-old Red Heart and the Grand National winner Drogheda.

Starting stalls were introduced at the Curragh in September 1966, used for the Classics and all races below a mile in 1968 and a couple of years later extended to all races on the flat

ST KEVIN

(Chestnut colt 1882 Arbitrator – Lady of the Lake by Lord of the Isles)

Breeder: Charles J. Blake
Winner of Her Majesty's Plate in 1885

Owner: Charles J. Blake
Trainer: James Dunne
Curragh 24 June 1885 (H. Saunders) Won Irish Derby 1½m £460 Bar
Galway 30 June 1885 (H. Saunders) Won Renmore Handicap 1m £59 4/7f
Galway 1 July 1885 (H. Saunders) Walked Over H.M. Plate 2m 100gns
Curragh 28 April 1886 (H. Saunders) Won Wellington Handicap 1¼m £133 7/4

St Kevin, Charles Blake's unfancied maiden second string, sprang a surprise when winning the Irish Derby at the Curragh. Ridden by the English-born lightweight Henry Saunders, he poached a lead over the favourite, Madcap, in the straight and held off the latter's desperate late challenge to win Ireland's premier race. Clearly a fortunate winner, Madcap's jockey having been caught napping, St Kevin was not the best of the moderate lot that contested that particular race but he was a Derby winner and the first of that ilk to come to the Galway races. Trainer 'Fairy' Dunne sent him on the 'Baron Farney route', contesting the Renmore Handicap over 1 mile and the Queen's Plate over a distance twice as long. Starting 7 to 4 on, he just about managed to win the handicap – all out to beat Salami by a short head – and even this unconvincing performance failed to encourage other owners to take him on in the Royal Plate, allowing Mr Blake's horse to walk over for the 100 guinea prize.

Asked to race on all three days of the Curragh October meeting, St Kevin finished second over 6 furlongs to Salami, was third to Tice in the Curragh Cesarewitch over 14 furlongs and was beaten out of sight by Wavelet and The Chicken in the Lord Lieutenant's Plate over 12 furlongs. The following year he was beaten by fifteen lengths in the Wellington Stakes at the Curragh but successfully objected to the winner, Alcester, who was owned by Lord Drogheda, the Senior Steward of the Turf Club, and the next day finished last of four in a Queen's Plate.

VICTRIX

(Brown mare 1880 Ben Battle – Ada by Massinissa)

Breeder: John Nolan
Winner of the 1887 Galway Plate

Owner: T.J. Dixon
Trainer: James Gannon, Straw Hall, Curragh
Down Royal 25 July 1883 (M. Dawson) Won Lurgan Handicap 5f flat £39 4/5f
Curragh 4 September 1883 (W. Miller) Won Flying Handicap 5f flat £38 2/1f
Ballybar 2 October 1883 (W. Miller) Won Ballybar Handicap 5f flat £38 5/1

Owner: Frederick F. Cullen
Trainer: F.F. and W.P. Cullen, Islandbridge, Dublin
Redcross 19 May 1884 (Mr F.F. Cullen) Won Redcross Handicap Hurdle 2½m £33½ 3/1
Swinford 29 May 1884 (Mr F.F. Cullen) Won Commercial Handicap Chase 2m £28 1/1f
Tuam 13 August 1884 (Mr F.F. Cullen) Won Commercial Selling Chase 2m £24 1/1
Limerick 9 September 1884 (Mr F.F. Cullen) Won Tradesman's Handicap Chase 3m £136 2/1f

Owner and trainer: Frederick F. Cullen, Rossmore Lodge, Curragh
Down Royal 20 July 1886 (Mr F.F. Cullen) Won Marlborough Handicap Chase 2¼m £64 7/4f

Owner: C.W. Bagge
Trainer: Frederick F. Cullen, Rossmore Lodge, Curragh

Galway 3 August 1887 (Mr W.P. Cullen) Won Galway Plate Handicap 2½m £132 9/4

Bellewstown 10 August 1887 (Mr F.F. Cullen) Walked Over Drogheda Tradesmen's Handicap
   Chase 3m £48

Punchestown 25 April 1888 (Mr W.P. Cullen) Won Railway Selling Chase 2½m £97 1/2f

Athenry 23 August 1888 (L. Ryan) Won Athenry Handicap Chase 2m £54 5/1

Ben Battle was the first of the really good Irish Derby winners and also the first to make a significant mark at stud. Sire of the outstanding Bendigo, winner of the Cambridgeshire, Lincolnshire, Hardwick Stakes, Eclipse Stakes, Jubilee Stakes and Champion Stakes, he also sired Theodemir and Tragedy, both winners of the Irish Derby, as well as the Grand National hero Ambush II. He had a big head and a Roman nose, very like his grandsire The Baron, but was back at the knees and raised his forefeet high when galloping. For over one hundred years Ben Battle was the only Irish Derby winner to sire a winner of the Galway Plate, until Ansar's win in 2004 enabled Kahyasi to join the club. Kahyasi also won the Epsom Derby, the third winner of that race to sire a Galway Plate winner, the previous pair being Kingcraft (Springfield Maid) and Larkspur (Persian Lark).

Victrix, bred by John Nolan, went into training with James Gannon but proved disappointing, running three times unplaced at two. Unsure of her best distance, Gannon tried her over 10 furlongs before deciding she was a sprinter, which is the reason why she ran second six times before finding a winning bracket. However, by the end of the season she had won three minor races over 5 furlongs. Bought by Fred Cullen for jumping, she won a hurdle race at the long-forgotten Redcross meeting in Co. Wicklow, before going on the win eight steeplechases, including the Galway Plate. It should have been nine because she won a handicap chase at Tralee in August 1886 and survived a technical objection by Bryan O'Donnell, the owner of Lady Ronald. The objection concerned Fred Cullen's suspension, incurred on Victrix's previous run at Tuam. There the stewards were not satisfied that he had tried to win the race and he was suspended from riding for a year, beginning 3 August 1886. Mr O'Donnell contended that this barred Mr Cullen from owning, or indeed part-owning, any runner under Rules and asked the Tralee stewards to award the race to Lady Ronald. They refused, declaring that Mr Cullen was suspended from riding, not from ownership, but on appeal the stewards of the Irish National Hunt Steeplechase Committee disagreed and took the race off Victrix.

Forced to sell, Fred Cullen passed Victrix on to his patron, C.W. Bagge of Summerville, Mallow, and she dead heated with John Gubbins's Sweetness in a 2½-mile steeplechase at Baldoyle. Both owners agreed to a run-off. The second time Sweetness ran out an easy winner. That was the form line that encouraged punters to make Sweetness, now ridden by Harry Beasley, the 6 to 4 favourite for the Galway Plate, but Victrix reversed the placings by four lengths, holding off the challenge of Mr A.E. McCracken's Lord Chatham, ridden by Willie McAuliffe, by a head.

Victrix was known to bolt and to run out but she only fell once in her life, in a race in Limerick. Although only a moderate handicapper, she won twelve races in her career and later did well at stud. Retired in 1889 and retained by C.W. Bagge for her entire stud career, she bred the useful Lady Vic, winner of the Drogheda Memorial Plate at the Curragh at two years and Easterling, placed third in the 1903 Irish Derby.

SPRINGFIELD MAID

(Bay mare 1886 Kingcraft – dam by Prince)

Breeder: Unknown
Winner of the 1892 Irish Grand National
Winner of the 1892 Galway Plate

Owner and trainer: S.A. Leonard
Punchestown 22 April 1891 (W. Hoysted) Won Farmers' Challenge Cup 3m Chase £100 10/1
    (Race declared void)
Bellewstown 9 July 1891 (T. Kavanagh) Won Corporation Cup Hunt Chase 3m £39 4/6f
Fairyhouse 18 April 1892 (Mr L. Hope) Won Irish Grand National 3m £245 6/1
Galway 3 August 1892 (E. Reilly) Won Galway Plate Handicap Chase 2½m £137 4/1

The prestige of the Epsom Derby may have declined somewhat in recent years but 120 years ago it was undisputedly the greatest horse race in the world. Such was its reputation, that Derby winners were sought as stallions by eager breeders from all over the world, in a business where the maxim was to breed the best with the best, in order to get the best. The Derby was first run in 1780 and only five winners of the race spent some time at stud in Ireland before Orby, who became the first Irish-trained winner of the race when successful in 1907. Neither of the two Irish-bred winners, Galtee More (1897) and half-brother Ard Patrick (1902), bred in Co. Limerick by John Gubbins, retired to stud in Ireland. The former was sold to Russia, later moving to Germany, while Ard Patrick was exported directly to Germany.

The first Derby winner to come to an Irish stud was Serjeant, winner of the fifth renewal of the race in 1784, the year the distance was increased from 1 mile to 12 furlongs. Serjeant was owned by Denis O'Kelly, who came to England from Ireland as a penniless, illiterate teenager, to live a life working and gambling every penny he had in between his incarcerations in prison for debt. One day this fearless and reckless gambler, who had nothing to lose, got lucky. For the umpteenth time in his life, he bet all the money he had in the world on the brilliant horse Eclipse to win a race by a distance. Having landed his 'Eclipse first – the rest nowhere' bet he bought the champion racehorse and eventually retired him to stud, the unbeaten winner of eighteen races. He put his windfall to good use, purchasing an army commission and establishing a large stud at Epsom, where Eclipse held court, and his luck held because his champion racehorse become one of the most successful stallions in the history of the turf. The owner of two of Eclipse's three Derby winning sons, Young Eclipse and Serjeant, Colonel O'Kelly sold the latter to Thomas Conolly of the Castletown House Stud in Leixlip, Co. Dublin. Known as Squire Conolly and married to money, he was one of the biggest owners of race-horses in Ireland, lived in the biggest house in the country and was a member of parliament for Londonderry.

While Serjeant did not leave a permanent mark on the Irish turf, the second import was more successful. This was Champion, owned by a Yorkshireman named Christopher Wilson, who was successful in the Derby of 1800 and became the first Derby winner to go on to win the St Leger. Mr Wilson sold Champion to Colonel Charles Lumm for 1,000 guineas in May 1802. Lumm took him back to his residence, Lumm Lodge on the Curragh. Sired by Eclipse's most successful son, Pot-8-os, Champion became the sire of Colonel Lumm's Norfolk, Irish horse of the year in 1811.

The third Derby winner imported to Ireland was far more successful than any of the others, becoming champion sire and siring five Irish champions. Pope, always known in Ireland as Waxy Pope, won the Derby in 1809, pipping the favourite Wizard, owned by Christopher Wilson, on the post. Owned by the Duke of Grafton, a former Tory prime minister, he won eleven races before being sold to the Marquis of Sligo in 1810. He won three more times for him before retiring to his Irish stud at Westport. A Derby winner by a Derby winner – his sire, Waxy, a son of Pot-8-os, was victorious in 1793 – Waxy Pope became Champion Sire in Ireland on nine occasions, beating the eight set by Master Bagot, a record which still stands today. The championship is based on prize money, all of which might have been won by one very good horse, so the list of leading sires of winners may be a better guide to the success of a stallion. According to this list Waxy Pope was also a phenomenal success, heading it on a record ten occasions, a feat that has only been equalled since by the sensational Birdcatcher and the remarkable Vulgan. In his long career (he survived until 1831) Waxy Pope sired five champion racehorses. The Dandy, Starch, Sligo, Skylark and Mounteagle. His best offspring, Skylark, won forty races, including twenty-three King's Plates, was champion racehorse in Ireland in 1829, 1830 and 1831 and later became a champion sire, in 1840.

The fourth Derby winner to go to stud in Ireland during the nineteenth century was Kingcraft, winner of the 1870 Derby and placed in both the 2,000 Guineas and the St Leger. Like the other three, he traced back to Eclipse, through Harkaway, the best horse ever bred in Ulster, and Waxy, the sire of Pope. A fine, sound horse and the winner of ten races, he had been raced until he was seven, despite repeatedly failing to reproduce his three-year-old form. Consequently, memories of his failures rather that his Derby victory were foremost in breeders' minds by the time he retired to stud in England. Having disappointed there, he was imported by William Pallin of the Athgarvan Lodge Stud on the Curragh in 1884 to stand alongside his big-name stallions. Ben Battle, winner of the Irish Derby, Favo, destined to be Champion Sire, and Lurgan, a half-brother to the Champion Sire Uncas. Athgarvan Lodge was a house with a history. King George VI visited there when he was in Ireland in 1821; the famous Irish Corinthian rider Allen McDonough lived and trained there; and it was now a model stud farm run by William Pallin, a veterinary surgeon and an anti-Catholic bigot. There he stood the Epsom Derby winner at 10 guineas per mare, with half-bred mares accepted at half price, for three seasons before selling the horse off for export to the United States. Kingcraft never made it to the New World, however, dying during the voyage in December 1886.

Among the mares covered by Kingcraft in 1885 was a half-bred mare by Prince, which duly threw a filly foal. Named Springfield Maid, this turned out to be the best of the Derby winner's Irish offspring, albeit as a steeplechaser. Although she only won three races in her life, all over fences, these included the Irish Grand National and the Galway Plate in 1892, the same year she finished second in the Conyngham Cup to Lady Helen.

The last of the five Derby winners to cover mares at an Irish stud was Sir Hugo, successful in 1892. This horse had a weak pedigree, his sire Wisdom having failed to win a race of any description, but he was a Derby winner, beating the champion two-year-old filly and 1,000 Guineas winner, La Fleche, by three-parts of a length. However, the 40 to 1 outsider was a lucky winner on two counts. First, Orme, the outstanding juvenile of the previous year and hot favourite for the 2,000 Guineas, took ill shortly before that race – said to have been poisoned – and was not fit enough to run in the Derby. And secondly, Orme's stable companion, La Fleche, got a deplorable ride from her jockey George Barrett, who in retrospect was beginning to show signs of the mental illness that led to his early death in 1898. Sir Hugo retired to the Shropshire stud of his owner/breeder Lord Bradford in 1894 but turned out to be a very poor sire and was sold off. William Pallin took a chance with the horse, buying him for his Athgarvan Stud on the Curragh in 1904. On Pallin's death, Sir Hugo moved to the Jockey Hall Stud, where John Hubert and Garry Moore used to train; he dropped dead there in February 1910. Useless as a sire in England, Sir Hugo was worse than useless at stud in Ireland, his five crops of Irish foals yielding only five moderate winners.

DROGHEDA

(Brown gelding 1892 Cherry Ripe – Eglantine by Hollywood)

Breeder: George F. Gradwell
Winner of the 1897 Galway Plate
Winner of the 1898 Grand National

Owner and trainer: G.F. Gradwell
Fairyhouse 6 April 1896 (J.J. Doyle) Won Dunboyne Chase 2¼m £88 4/1
Baldoyle 8 June 1897 (T. Dowdall) Won Dublin Open Chase 3¼m £132
Bellewstown 8 July 1897 (T. Dowdall) Won Grand Stand Handicap Chase 2½m £58½ 6/4f
Galway 4 August 1897 (T. Dowdall) Won Galway Plate Handicap 2½m £166 4/1

Owner: C.G.M. Adams
Trainer: Richard C. Dawson (E. Woods licence holder)
Aintree 25 March 1898 (J. Gourley) Won Grand National Handicap 4½m £1,975 25/1
Trainer: R. Collins
Kempton Park 2 February 1900 (G. Williamson) Won Kempton Handicap Hurdle 2m £175 8/1
Kempton Park 9 March 1900 (G. Williamson) Won Stewards' Chase 2m £140 8/13f

George F. Gradwell of Knockbrack, Drogheda, Co. Louth, was a talented Corinthian rider, winning races in Ireland and England and on the Continent. An owner and a breeder, he also acted as the Clerk of the Course at the Galway Races and later, from 1910 to 1931, was the Secretary of the Ward Union Hunt.

There is a prejudice in racing against black horses, to the extent that breeders usually register a black horse as brown, unless it is as black as coal. Eglantine was one of the latter. She ran second in the Conyngham Cup of 1887 – one of the rare occasions when the Punchestown meeting was held before Easter – and went on to win the Irish Grand National on Easter Monday. A mare by a good middle-distance handicapper named Hollywood, she was not registered in the General Stud Book and thus classed as a half-bred, but she could gallop and jump. She was one of the winners at the Dundalk Inauguration meeting on 28 May 1889.

She was mated with the unraced stallion Cherry Ripe, who spent his entire stud career in Co. Monaghan and was destined to sire the 1903 Irish Derby winner Lord Rossmore. The result was Drogheda, a plain colt but forward enough to race as a juvenile. Sporting Mr Gradwell's scarlet with French grey cross belts, Drogheda ran three times at two – at Bellewstown, Down Royal and Baldoyle – without reaching a place, and was taken out of training for a year. Returning to the racecourse in February 1896, he fell in a steeplechase at Leopardstown but next time out won the Dunboyne Steeplechase Plate at Fairyhouse. Having been unfancied and unplaced in a Dundalk bumper, he headed for the Galway Plate, although he was only four years old and an inexperienced chaser. After finishing unplaced behind Richard Dawson's Castle Warden, ridden by Willie Cullen, he was put away until the following year.

After a quiet run in a Dundalk bumper in May 1897, he won chases at Baldoyle and at Bellewstown before returning to Galway to contest the Plate again. Renewing hostilities with Castle Warden, he jumped brilliantly and won easily by three lengths. Dick Dawson, who had expected Castle Warden to become the first horse to win the race twice, was so impressed that he bought Drogheda there and then. In addition to the price, Mr Gradwell extracted a contingency of £300 if the horse won the Grand National. He only had to wait just over six months for his extra bonus. Defying appalling conditions – the course had been battered by heavy rain all morning and the race itself was run in a snowstorm – Drogheda powered to victory at Aintree, his rider John Gourley looking like a snowman, gamely repulsing the sustained challenge of Cathal.

Manifesto is, quite rightly, acclaimed as being one of the really great Grand National winners. Winner in 1897, an injury forced him out of the race the following year, leaving the way clear for Drogheda. It has been implied that Manifesto would have won the 1898 Grand National had he been fit to race but Drogheda was a really good chaser; injury prevented him from showing just how good he was. An injured hock prevented him from running against Manifesto in 1899, and the younger horse, in his prime, might have made a race of it. Unplaced in the Great Lancashire Handicap Chase at Manchester a month after his Aintree victory, he only ran once the following season, finishing fourth to Ambush II in a valuable handicap steeplechase at Sandown Park in February. A strained hock caused his withdrawal from the 1899 Grand National and kept him off the course for nearly a year, during which he changed stables, having been moved to John Collins at Weyhill, Hampshire. Collins was the licence holder for Willie Moore, younger brother of Garry Moore, who trained Grand National winners Why Not (1894) and The Soarer (1896), and had charge of Manifesto when he won in 1899.

Drogheda made a comeback in the Great Midland Handicap Chase at Nottingham in December, and finished second. The horse, still only an eight-year-old, got back to winning ways by successive victories at Kempton Park, a hurdle race and a steeplechase. Plans to run him in the 1900 Grand National had to be abandoned when he suffered a recurrence of the leg trouble which had dogged him for over a year. Deciding that only a complete rest would solve the problem, it was decided to put him out of training; it was two years before he would race again. Returning at Kempton Park in February 1902, he finished a bad third of three to Ambush II, but the leg again gave trouble and the merry-go-round started all over again. Another year's rest, another comeback and yet another breakdown. Drogheda's career was over – another great steeplechase career ruined by injury.

SWEET CHARLOTTE

(Chestnut mare 1891 Baliol – Mill Pond by Lord Gough)

Breeder: D.R. Callaghan
Winner of 1897 H.M. Plate

Owner: James Phelan
Trained privately at Lisfunchton, Co. Tipperary
Limerick 9 April 1896 (Mr J. Scully) Won Spring Bumper 2½m £33¾ 5/2f
Kilkenny 5 May 1896 (C. Hogan) Won Citizens' Handicap Chase 2m £68 4/6f
Tramore 1 July 1896 (Mr W. McAuliffe) Won Tyrone Handicap 2m flat £26 7/2
Galway 6 August 1896 (J. O'Brien) Won County Handicap Chase 2m £67½ 5/1
Cork Park 30 September 1896 (J. O'Brien) Won Park Handicap Chase 2m £132 5/2f
Limerick 14 October 1896 (J. O'Brien) Won Tradesman's Handicap Chase 2m £88 2/1f
Trainer: Richard C. Dawson (E. Woods), Cloghran, Co. Dublin (James Phelan)
Leopardstown 26 December 1896 (J. O'Brien) Won St Stephen's Handicap Chase 2m £64 5/2f
Baldoyle 18 March 1897 (J. O'Brien) Won Paddock Handicap Chase 2m £45 5/4f
Cork Park 18 May 1897 (J. O'Brien) Won Grand Stand Handicap Chase 3m £225 6/4f
Tramore 23 June 1897 (J. O'Brien) Won Cadogan Handicap Chase 2m £36 6/4f
Baldoyle 2 August 1897 (J. O'Brien) Won August Handicap Chase 2m £63 4/1jf

Galway 5 August 1897 (J. O'Brien) Won H.M. Plate 2m flat £104 7/4

Baldoyle 14 September 1897 (J. O'Brien) Won Metropolitan Handicap Chase 2½m £194 10/1

Trainer: Richard C. Dawson (E. Woods), Whatcombe, Berkshire (James Phelan)

Kempton Park 2 December 1897 (J. O'Brien) Won Stewards' Handicap Chase 2m £262 7/2jf

Windsor 13 January 1898 (J. O'Brien) Won Castle Handicap Chase 2m £142 4/5f

Punchestown 26 April 1898 (J. O'Brien) Won Prince of Wales Handicap Chase 3m £370 4/1

Sandown Park 3 December 1898 (J. O'Brien) Won Pond Handicap Chase 2m £92 4/1

Gatwick 31 January 1899 (J. O'Brien) Won Holmwood Handicap Chase 2m £176 7/2f

Kempton Park 3 February 1899 (J. O'Brien) Won Littleton Chase 2m £147 8/100f

Kempton Park 1 March 1899 (J. O'Brien) Won March Handicap Chase 2m £175 7/2

Punchestown 24 April 1900 (J. O'Brien) Won Prince of Wales Handicap Chase 3m £370 8/1

Sandown Park 20 October 1900 (J. O'Brien) Won Handicap Chase 2m £183 2/1

Owner: Mr Leybuck

Trained privately

Baldoyle 19 March 1901 (T. Kavanagh) Won Regulation Chase 3m £50 5/2

Owner: Abel Buckley Jr

Trainer: F. Moran, Galtee Castle, Mitchelstown

Manchester 31 March 1902 (M. Walsh) Won Swinton Chase 2m £98 7/4f

Limerick 15 May 1902 (E. Malone) Won Greenpark Handicap Chase 2m £45½ 2/1f

Baldoyle 20 May 1902 (M. Walsh) Won Qualifying Chase 2¼m £49 1/2f

In the nineteenth century the Queen's Plate run at Galway was a valuable race and was usually won by a quality flat-race horse. Seeing an opportunity that nobody else saw, Dick Dawson entered Sweet Charlotte, an accomplished steeplechaser, in this race although the mare had had only one flat race in her life and that a very modest event at Tramore. Royal plates never attracted big fields, but the 1897 renewal of the Galway race was a particularly weak affair, Turkish Bath having scared off everything except Sweet Charlotte. A winner twice over hurdles during the winter, Turkish Bath had won queen's plates at the Curragh and Down Royal as well as a flat handicap at Leopardstown, but the four-year-old was an undistinguished filly among an undistinguished crop of four-year-olds. Remembering Sweet Charlotte's win in the County Handicap Chase the previous year, punters preferred the chances of the younger horse but there were few takers at 2 to 1 on. The race became a game of 'cat and mouse' between Algy Anthony aboard the favourite and James O'Brien on Sweet Charlotte but the 'cat' was never going to win on this occasion. Turkish Bath ran way below herself, much to 'Fairy' Dunne's disappointment.

Turkish Bath reversed the form in no uncertain manner in the Queen's Plate at the Curragh the following September, but still could only finished second, beaten by Lady Vic, owned by C.W. Bagge and out of his broodmare Victrix. It does seem that Sweet Charlotte's victory in the Queen's Plate was a fluke; the mare was a good, although not a top-class, handicap chaser and never won another flat race afterwards. She was a hard puller, which made her difficult to settle in a slow race, but she won the valuable Prince of Wales Handicap Steeplechase at Punchestown twice and finished runner-up to Castle Warden in the 1896 Galway Plate. An odds-on favourite when beaten in the Irish Grand National and when sent to Auteuil, France, she moved with Dick Dawson from Cloghran to Whatcombe in 1897. She came back regularly, however, for raids on the big Irish chases.

After a couple of changes in ownership, she became the property of Abel Buckley Jr, who ran a private stable at his home in Galtee Castle. He sent her on a raid to England on Easter Monday 1902, the inaugural meeting on the new Castle Irwell racecourse; she won the very first race run on that course. There were celebrations afterwards with lots of champagne, and the management of Manchester racecourse presented the winning jockey, M. Walsh, with a gold-mounted riding whip to commemorate the occasion.

Sweet Charlotte's breeder, Denis Richard O'Callaghan, intended to breed rather than race her and she was covered by a stallion at three years and again when she was four, but she was barren to both coverings. Denis O'Callaghan passed her on to James Phelan and she went into training. When she was retired from racing in 1902, she went back to Mr O'Callaghan and immediately went into foal to General Peace.

Born in Cork in 1827, Denis O'Callaghan had a stud at Brackenstown and owned the broodmare Moira, dam of Oppressor, winner of the Irish Derby, and General Peace, winner of the Lincolnshire Handicap and the Auteuil Hurdle. When he died in May 1904, Sweet Charlotte became the property of his wife.

YELLOW VIXEN

(Chestnut filly 1894 Gallinule – Miss Vixen by Hillingdon)

Breeder: William Jackson
Winner of 1900 and 1902 H.M. Plate, Galway

Owner: William Jackson
Trainer: Michael Dawson, Rathbride Manor, Curragh

Curragh 14 April 1896 (M. Dawson) Won Juvenile Plate 5f flat £116 7/1

Leopardstown 5 November 1897 (J. Waterson) Won Autumn Handicap Hurdle 1½m £87 10/1

Tullamore 19 May 1898 (J. Behan Jr) Won Province Chase 2m £21 7/4f

Galway 3 August 1898 (M. Dawson) Won Mervue Handicap 7f flat £29¼ 1/1f

Galway 4 August 1898 (J. Behan Jr) Won County Handicap Hurdle 1½m £73 4/6f

Curragh 31 August 1898 (T. Archer) Won Stewards' Handicap 10f flat £49 6/1

Curragh 18 October 1898 (J. Behan Jr) Won Zetland Handicap Hurdle 1½m £127 6/1

Galway 10 August 1899 (J. Behan Jr) Won County Handicap Hurdle 1½m £58½ 3/1

Cork Park 31 August 1899 (J. Behan Jr) Won Embankment Handicap Hurdle 1½m £93 2/1jf

Leopardstown 28 April 1900 (T. Farrell) Won April Plate 7f flat £101 6/1

Galway 2 August 1900 (J. Behan Jr) Won H.M. Plate 2m flat £104 8/11f

Leopardstown 26 April 1901 (Mr W.P. Cullen) Won Paget Handicap Hurdle 1½m £169 4/1

Leopardstown 8 June 1901 (Mr W.P. Cullen) Won Park Handicap Hurdle 1½m £92 3/1

Bellewstown 4 July 1901 (T. Harris) Won H.M. Plate 2¼m flat £104 5/4

Down Royal 10 July 1901 (Mr W.P. Cullen) Won Tradesman's Handicap Hurdle 1½m £92 4/6f

Leopardstown 26 August 1901 (Mr J.J. Parkinson) Won Dublin National Hunt Flat 2m £184 6/1

Galway 7 August 1902 (D. Condon) Won H.M. Plate 2m flat £104 5/2

The horse with the most wins at Galway up to this time began her career with a win in the first two-year-old race of the Irish season in 1896. She won five times at Galway, winning the second day's feature race, the Royal Plate, on two occasions. The filly also won the County Handicap Hurdle two years in succession, and won the Mervue Handicap over 7 furlongs on the flat once, as well as finishing second in the Stewards' Handicap in 1899. Carrying the green with cream sleeves and black cap of William Jackson, she won seventeen races in all, including eight over hurdles and one steeplechase.

Her last season on the racecourse was in 1902 when, in foal to Bushey Park, the Liverpool Cup winner, she was successful in Galway's Royal Plate. Unfortunately, her career ended on a sour note when she was beaten at 1 to 6 by Driftwood in a match for the Royal Whip over 4 miles on the Curragh. Her stud career was a fiasco; she lost the foal by Bushey Park, a colt that died at birth, and then stubbornly refused to go into foal until she produced a filly, Golden Vixen, by Bushey Park or Enthusiast in 1905, which turned out to be her only produce. Mr Jackson wisely parted with her after that because there were five more wasted seasons of barrenness, during which Yellow Vixen was sold and resold. William Jackson put Golden Vixen into training in due course but the filly was useless and was sent to South Africa in 1910.

TIPPERARY BOY

(Bay/brown horse 1894 Royal Meath – The Tart by Geologist)

Breeder: T.B. Holmes
Winner of the 1899, 1901 and 1902 Galway Plate
Winner of the 1901 Irish Grand National

Owner: T.B. Holmes
Trainer: Frederick F. Cullen at Rossmore Lodge
Tramore 10 August 1898 (C. Hogan) Won Summerville Chase 3m £52½ 5/2
Baldoyle 17 March 1899 (T. Moran) Won St Patrick's Handicap Chase 2½m £87 5/2
Fairyhouse 3 April 1899 (T. Moran) Won Fairyhouse Handicap Chase 2½m £166 7/2f
Cork Park 10 May 1899 (T. Moran) Won Park Handicap Chase 3m £92 7/2f
Galway 9 August 1899 (T. Moran) Won Galway Plate Handicap Chase 2½m £166 8/1
Baldoyle 19 March 1901 (T. Moran) Won Qualifying Chase 2¼m £39 6/4f
Fairyhouse 8 April 1901 (T. Moran) Won Irish Grand National 3m £166 4/6f
Leopardstown 26 April 1901 (T. Moran) Won Castle Open Chase 2m £170 7/4jf
Leopardstown 27 April 1901 (T. Moran) Won Irish International Handicap Chase 3m £261 3/1f
Galway 7 August 1901 (T. Moran) Won Galway Plate Handicap Chase 2½m £166 5/2f
Baldoyle 19 May 1902 (T. Moran) Won Dublin Chase 3m £87 4/5f
Galway 6 August 1902 (T. Kavanagh) Won Galway Plate Handicap Chase 2½m £166 6/1

Rarely does one see an entire horse racing over fences today. Canards such as that stallions risk injury to their delicate parts while clearing the jumps abound but, while it never was commonplace, many more stallions raced over fences a hundred years ago. Indeed, the entire horse Fortina won the Cheltenham Gold Cup as recently as 1947 but remains the only stallion to have done so. Stallions successful in the Galway Plate were Tattoo (1877), Jupiter Tonans (1878), Zulu II (1886), Star One (1894), Tipperary Boy (1899, 1901 and 1902) and Tony Lad (1927). Ascetic's Silver was winner of the Aintree and Irish Grand Nationals.

Tipperary Boy, the only horse to win the Galway Plate three times, was an entire horse by Royal Meath out of The Tart by Geologist. Royal Meath had also been a steeplechaser, winning the Conyngham Cup at Punchestown, a very big betting race at the time, and the Grand Steeplechase de Paris. Bred by T.B. Holmes of St David's, Nenagh, he was sent to the Curragh to be trained by Fred Cullen at Rossmore Lodge, who also had trained Royal Meath. While Mr

Holmes retained Tipperary Boy he disposed of the dam, The Tart, to Mr J. Gleason, for whom she bred four foals before dying at the age of fourteen in 1901.

Having finished third on his debut in a steeplechase at Punchestown in 1898, Tipperary Boy was made odds-on favourite to win in Mr Holmes's black and white hoops at his local meeting, over the Lisbony course. He took a crashing fall in a chase sponsored by the Grand Canal Company, which affected his confidence to such an extent that he failed to win any of his next six races, including the Clonard Chase at Galway. After winning easily at the Tramore meeting, Tipperary Boy had three poor runs before displaying the first signs of top-class form at the Leopardstown Christmas meeting. Although the outsider of the field, he finished second to the Prince of Wales's Ambush II, future winner of the Grand National, beaten by only three lengths. The following year, 1899, he won at Baldoyle on St Patrick's Day, won the Fairyhouse Plate on Easter Monday and was fancied to complete a three-timer in the Conyngham Cup. Ridden by Captain E. Peel, member of the Turf Club and owner of Irish Ivy, winner of the 1899 Irish Oaks, he nevertheless made no show behind Covert Hack. Reunited with his professional rider Tommy Moran, he won at Cork Park before coming to Galway and lifting the Plate, beating two 33 to 1 outsiders, Carline and Blue Guts, by six lengths and three lengths.

Tipperary Boy ran only once in 1900, but the following year won both the Irish Grand National and the Galway Plate. While Jupiter Tonans, Golden Jack and Feathered Gale have won both races, only Red Park, Alberoni and Umm have managed to emulate Springfield Maid and Tipperary Boy by doing the double in the same year. In 1902 Tipperary Boy won the Plate for a third time. That remains a race record, although by only the three and a half lengths that Far From Trouble had in hand over the treble-seeking Ansar in the 2006 Plate.

Retired to stud after that third win in the Galway Plate, Tipperary Boy took up residence at the Springfort Stud, Nenagh, in 1903, the winner of twelve steeplechases. Available to breeders at 9 guineas for thoroughbred mares, 4 guineas for half-bred mares, with winners or dams of winners half price, he found it almost impossible to get thoroughbred mares because he was a half-bred; his sire, Royal Meath, was not in the General Stud Book. There were more horses named 'Tipperary Boy' racing at this time than winners by him. The only ones I can trace in Ireland are For Ever, Giacomo and Royal Irish, winners of eleven chases and one hurdle race between them.

APOLLO BELVEDERE

(Bay/brown gelding 1901 Apollo – Pella by Buckshot)

Breeder: T.Y.L. Kirkwood
Winner of the Galway Plate 1907

Owner: Colonel Thomas Y.L. Kirkwood
Trainer: Maxwell Arnott
Listowel 10 October 1905 (John Doyle) Won Railway Handicap 9f flat £44 2/1f
Listowel 11 October 1905 (John Doyle) Won Visitors' Handicap 1½m flat £44 2/1
Longford 10 May 1906 (Mr J.W. Widger) Won Midland Counties Hunt Flat 2m £49 2/7f
Leopardstown 26 May 1906 (H. Buxton) Won Country Plate 1m flat £49 5/1
Galway 1 August 1906 (P. Cowley) Won Express Hurdle 1½m £34 4/6f

Owner: Colonel Thomas Y.L. Kirkwood
Trainer: J. Currid
Baldoyle 16 March 1907 (Mr P. O'Brien Butler) Won St Patrick's Day Chase 2¼m £131½ 2/1f
Bellewstown 3 July 1907 (Mr R.H. Walker) Won Drogheda Tradesmen's Handicap Chase 2m £93 7/2
Galway 7 August 1907 (Mr P. O'Brien Butler) Won Galway Plate Handicap Chase 2½m £182 6/1
Baldoyle 17 September 1907 (Mr R.H. Walker) Won Dublin Handicap Chase 2¼m £88 6/1
Cork Park 23 September 1908 (Mr P. O'Brien Butler) Won Corporation Hurdle 2m £146 7/2

Tom Kirkwood of Woodbrook, Carrick-on-Shannon, was a well-known racing figure, his blue with white sleeves and cap having been carried to victory in both the Irish and Aintree Grand Nationals. By buying The Doe for 5 shillings, he saved the mare from the knacker's yard and was rewarded when she beat Lysander by a head in the 1871 Irish Grand National at Fairyhouse. Put to stud, she further rewarded her owner when she bred Woodbrook, winner of the Grand National in 1881 to complete a third successive win for Irish stables. Following in the footsteps of The Liberator and Empress, Woodbrook, trained like Empress by Henry Eyre Linde, galloped through ground that had become as heavy as a bog because of incessant rain, to beat Capain Machell's Regal, a former winner of the race, by an effortless four lengths. A decade later Tom Kirkwood acquired a young mare named Pella, from which he bred a top-class flat horse and two very useful steeplechasers: Paddy Maher, foaled in 1900, Apollo Belvedere, in 1901, and The White Knight in 1903.

The White Knight was an outstanding stayer on the flat, winning two Ascot Gold Cups, one of the most prestigious races for older horses in the world at the time, two Coronation Cups (Epsom) and the Goodwood Cup. In 1907 The White Knight dead heated with the French raider Eider at Royal Ascot but the latter's jockey, George Stern, had deliberately fouled his rival in the straight and the Stewards disqualified him and awarded the race to The White Knight. While they were deliberating, the Gold Cup itself was sitting on a table, awaiting presentation to the winning owner and, distracted by the controversy, those who should have been keeping an eye on the valuable trophy did not do so. One moment it was there, the next it was gone; the Ascot Gold Cup had been stolen from under the noses of everyone, including the King, and neither the Cup nor the thief was ever recovered.

The own-brothers Paddy Maher and Apollo Belvedere were both by Apollo, the sire of the Irish Grand National winner Small Polly, who stood at George Walker's stud at Rathvale, Athboy. Both horses were sent to be trained by Captain Bob Dewhurst at just about the time that trainer was setting up his stable in England and Maxie Arnott was taking over at Clonsilla. After three seasons Tom Kirkwood decided to take both Paddy Maher and Apollo Belvedere back home to Co. Roscommon, to be prepared for their races privately by a man named J. Currid. Both took some time to find some form but the younger, Apollo Belvedere, won two flat races at four years (trained by Dewhurst/Arnott) and won two flat races and a hurdle at five. In that year, 1906, he won the Express Hurdle Plate, the first race on the first day of the Galway meeting, and the following day finished second to High Wind in the County Plate, a handicap chase. Mr Paget O'Brien Butler rode him in the chase, when he finished second, but professional jockey Patrick Cowley rode him to victory in the hurdle race. Cowley, who was the Champion Jump Jockey in England the following year, was fated to be killed in a racing fall during a hurdle race at Hooton Park, near Liverpool, in August 1911.

Apollo Belvedere came to the 1907 Galway meeting to compete in the Plate with 'Piery' O'Brien Butler in the saddle, fighting out the finish with the 5 to 1 favourite, Cowboy (Reggie Walker up), with the two amateurs ten lengths in front of the third horse, Prospect II, ridden by Algy Anthony. Apollo Belvedere prevailed by a neck at odds of 6 to 1 but after winning three valuable races within seven weeks, his career abruptly waned while that of his own-brother Paddy Mahar was taking off. Winner of the Conyingham Cup in 1908 and the Prince of Wales's Plate the following year, Paddy Maher was the Kirkwood representative in the 1908, 1909 and 1910 Aintree Grand Nationals. Unfortunately, the horse could not cope with the big fences and fell on each occasion.

DEAR SONNY

(Bay gelding 1904 Son of a Gun – Cherry Blossom by Cherry Stone)

Breeder: Miss A.M. Purcell
Winner of the 1910 Galway Blazers Plate
Winner of the 1911 Galway Plate

Owner: H. Lindsay Fitzpatrick
Trainer: Mr Butler of Thornton Lodge
Slane 1 August 1907 (E. Charters) Won Committee Handicap 10f flat £37½ 5/1
Carnew 20 August 1907 (E. Charters) Won Coollattin Handicap 1m flat £47 2/1
Dunmore 24 July 1908 (M. Kelly) Won Maiden Chase 2m £20½ 3/1
Trainer: George L. Walker
Bellewstown 8 July 1909 (Mr R.H. Walker) Won Tally-Ho Handicap 2m flat £27¼ 4/1
Ballinrobe 9 September 1909 (Mr H.I. Ussher) Won Connaught Handicap Chase 2m £22½ 2/1jf

Owner and trainer: H. Lindsay Fitzpatrick
Galway 3 August 1910 (A. Anthony) Won Galway Blazers Chase 3m £52½ 1/1f
Boyle 7 June 1911 (G. Brown) D-Htd Visitors' Handicap Hurdle 1½m £10¼ 3/1
Ballinrobe 4 July 1911 (E. Lawn) Won Committee Handicap Hurdle 1½m £22½ 3/1f
Ballinrobe 4 July 1911 (Mr C. Brabazon) Won Connaught Handicap Chase 2m £22½ 2/1jf
Tuam 12 July 1911 (E. Lawn) Won Directors' Handicap Chase 3m £45½ 7/4f
Galway 9 August 1911 (E. Lawn) Won Galway Plate Handicap Chase 2½m £216 5/2
Tramore 14 August 1911 (E. Lawn) Won Summer Handicap Chase 2¼m £39 2/1jf
Tuam 29 August 1911 (E. Lawn) Won September Handicap Chase 2¼m £32 7/2
Ballaghadereen 5 September 1911 (E. Lawn) Won Commercial Handicap Chase 2m £24½ 1/4f
Sligo 30 April 1912 (Mr C. Brabazon) Won Lakeside Handicap Hurdle 1½m £23½ 7/1
Kells 13 June 1912 (Mr L. Firth) Won County Handicap Hurdle 1½m £36¼ 10/1
Limerick 26 July 1912 (Mr L. Brabazon) Won Munster Handicap Chase 3m £29¼ 5/1
Ballinrobe 30 July 1912 (Mr L. Brabazon) Won Hollymount Open Chase 2m £24½ 2/7f
Kells 12 June 1913 (W. Watkinson) Won Smith Cup 3m chase £31¼ 4/5f
Tuam 8 July 1913 (W. Watkinson) Won Ladies' Handicap Chase 2¼m £45½ 4/1
Roscommon 24 July 1913 (E. Lawn) Won Hayden Handicap Chase 3m £27½ 2/1jf
Baldoyle 30 September 1913 (E. Lawn) Won 3 Miles Chase 3m £50 10/11f
Ballaghadereen 30 June 1914 (H. Harty) Won Ladies' Handicap Chase 2m £22½ 3/1

Starting out racing in sellers at two years when owned by his breeder Miss A.M. *Flat racing at Galway*
Purcell, Dear Sonny was passed on to Lindsay Fitzpatrick of Hollymount, Co.
Mayo, for whom he raced for the rest of his career. Having won a couple of small
handicaps and running second to the odds-on Lady Geraldine in the Mervue Plate
at Galway during a three-year-old campaign on the flat, he was sent jumping.
Having looked way out of his class on two visits to Galway in 1908 and 1909, he
showed distinct improvement the following year, winning the Galway Blazers
Steeplechase, although that was the only race he won that year. He went on to win
seventeen races over the next three seasons, however. During the summer of 1911
he won four races off the reel, including the Galway Plate, by far the most valuable race that he won during his career. His record in subsequent Galway Plates
was disappointing. He started second-favourite and joint-favourite in successive
years only to finish unplaced on each occasion. His twenty-second, and what
proved to be his penultimate, victory came at Baldoyle at the end of September

1913, when he started a slight odds-on favourite in a match over fences. Although he refused at one stage during this match, his rider Edward Lawn, the leading professional jump jockey at the time, eventually got him over the fence and he raced to victory because his only opponent, Frank Barbour's Bachelor's Gift, fell.

RED DAMSEL

(Chestnut mare 1908 Red Prince II – Gay Lass by Gay Reveller)

Breeder: R. Bell
Winner of the 1913 Galway Hurdle

Owner: Baron F. de Tuyll
Trainer: Maxwell Arnott
Down Royal 2 October 1912 (Mr R.H. Walker) Won Ulster Plate 14f Flat £39 4/5f
Mullingar 14 April 1913 (G. Brown) Won Newbrook Maiden Chase 2m £175 5/2
Leopardstown 25 April 1913 (G. Brown) Won Maiden Chase 2m £165 2/1
Phoenix Park 7 June 1913 (F. Hunter) Won Welter Handicap 10f flat £92 2/1
Galway 7 August 1913 (F. Morgan) Won Galway Handicap Hurdle 1½m £166 10/1
Tramore 14 August 1913 (F. Hunter) Won Guillamene Handicap 1½m flat £46½

Owner: Thomas Widger
Trainer: Robert Gore
Gatwick 6 January 1914 (P. Woodland) Won Reigate Handicap Hurdle 2m £82 10/1

Owner and trainer: Thomas Widger
Tramore 21 September 1914 (F. Morgan) Dead-Heat Curraghmore Handicap 1m flat £18 6/1

Sired by the Derby winner Bend Or, Kendal was a very talented two-year-old trained by John Porter at Kingsclere, winning five races before irreparably breaking down. In Porter's stable at the same time was the brilliant Triple Crown winner Ormonde, unbeaten on the racecourse and only ever beaten once in a trial at home on the gallops. The horse that beat him in that trial was Kendal. Retired to stud, Kendal was sold to John Gubbins, for whom he sired Galtee More, the first Irish-bred winner of the Epsom Derby. In 1888, Kendal covered Empress, winner of the 1880 Grand National, who was now breeding for her erstwhile trainer Henry Eyre Linde at his Eyrefield Lodge stud. The union produced Red Prince II. Inheriting precocious speed from his sire, Red Prince II won the National Produce Stakes at the Curragh at two, beginning a sensational sequence of five successive winners for owner/trainer Linde and his jockey William Hoysted, the others being First Flower, Ball Coote, Burnett and Chit Chat. A genius with steeplechasers, Linde expected every horse under his care to be able to jump, even if it was a flat racer. The popular trainer Sam Darling wrote of a visit he paid to Eyrefield Lodge in 1892 when Ball Coote was led out for his inspection, the asking price being a stiff 1,000 guineas. While the lad walked and trotted Ball Coote up and down, Linde suddenly lost patience, gave the horse a belt of his walking stick and got the year-ling to jump down a drop fence into the field below. Amazed that such a valuable young horse was expected to be able to jump a fence, and mindful of the risk of injury, Darling asked why on earth Linde had done it. The Irish trainer quite seri-ously replied, 'They must walk before they trot.'

With such schooling it was no wonder that Linde's horses could jump and Red Prince II was no exception, producing some brilliant jumping performances at four years, including a sensational eight-length victory over the previous year's Irish Grand National winner Greek Girl in the Lancashire Handicap Chase at Manchester. Worth £2,170 to the winner, more than Cloister got for winning the Grand National, it was the richest steeplechase run that year and was held on the New Barns course, later swallowed up to make way for docks for the newly opened Manchester Ship Canal. Red Prince II, an imposing chestnut thoroughbred, retired to the Athgarvan Stud, where he became very successful as a sire of jumpers. He won the prestigious Croker Challenge Cup at the Royal Dublin Society Horse Show four times and his handsome stock won many prizes in the show ring. Among the best of his offspring was Red Lad, winner of the Irish Grand National and second to Ascetic's Silver in the Grand National, and Famous, winner of the Conyngham Cup ridden by Mr Jack Widger. He was third in the list of leading National Hunt sires in Britain when the studmaster, William Pallin, died suddenly in June 1907. Dubbed the father of the modern Irish stud in his obituar-ies, his model stud farm passed to his son, Cyril, and began its dramatic decline. The following year a German offer for Red Prince II was accepted and the stallion departed for the Continent, leaving behind a yearling filly, subsequently named Red Damsel, the winner of the inaugural Galway Handicap Hurdle race five years later. A month before Red Damsel's historic win at Galway, Red Prince II had to be destroyed for humane reasons at his German stud.

Second on the flat over 2 miles at Kilbeggan, ridden by her owner, Mr R. Bell, Red Damsel was sold to Baron de Tuyll before winning a race. A winner on the flat, over hurdles and over fences, she was a half-bred and was the dam of Eureka II, winner of 12 chases.

GOLDEN FLEECE

(Chestnut gelding 1911 The Raft – Golden Quid by Quidnunc)

Breeder: L.S. Ward
Winner of the 1918 Galway Plate

Owner and trainer: L.S. Ward
Bellewstown 5 July 1916 (Mr L.S. Ward) Won Hill Chase 2m £44 100/8
Bellewstown 6 July 1916 (Mr L.S. Ward) Won Stewards' Handicap Chase 3m £50 2/1f
Limerick 4 October 1916 (Mr L.S. Ward) Won Tradesman's Handicap Chase 2m £116 2/1
Dundalk 15 May 1917 (Mr L.S. Ward) Won Mountain Handicap Chase 2½m £93 3/1f
Leopardstown 2 March 1918 (Mr L.S. Ward) Won March Handicap Chase 2m £88 2/1f

Owner: William Parrish
Trainer: John T. Rogers
Galway 7 August 1918 (A. Stubbs) Won Galway Plate Handicap Chase 2½m £422 7/1jf
Leopardstown 23 August 1918 (H.H. Beasley) Won Provincial Handicap 2m flat £132 5/1jf
Baldoyle 14 September 1918 (H.H. Beasley) Won Raheny Handicap 15f flat £93 5/2f
Curragh 22 April 1919 (H.H. Beasley) Won Scurry Handicap 6f flat £93 2/1f
Leopardstown 2 May 1919 (H.H. Beasley) Won Leopardstown Handicap Chase 2m £540 6/4f
Haydock Park 23 May 1919 (Mr H.A. Brown) Won Match 1m flat £500 1/7f
Haydock Park 24 May 1919 (C. Hamshaw) Won Copeland Plate 12f flat £147 11/10f
Phoenix Park 14 June 1919 (H.H. Beasley) Won Weight for Age Plate 10f flat £185 2/5f
Curragh 22 October 1919 (H.H. Beasley) Won Equinox Plate 1m flat £420 4/5f
Trainer: Captain Darby Rogers
Kempton Park 28 December 1920 (W. Smith) Won Twickenham Hurdle 2m £269 1/2f
Uttoxeter 10 May 1921 (W. Smith) Won Wood Lawn Hurdle 2m £249 7/2
Worcester 27 May 1921 (W. Smith) Won Grand Annual Handicap Chase 2m £167 6/4f
Worcester 30 June 1921 (H.H. Beasley) Won Gheluvelt Welter Stakes 12f flat £221 10/11f
Trainer: John T. Rogers
Curragh 18 October 1921 (H.H. Beasley) Won Scurry Handicap 6f flat £166 6/1
Trainer: H.S. Harrison, Bangor-on-Dee
Cheltenham 16 May 1923 (J. Goswell) Won Seven Springs Selling Chase 2m £103 2/1f
Wolverhampton 5 November 1923 (J. Goswell) Won Shifnal Selling Chase 2m £132 5/2jf
Wolverhampton 26 December 1923 (G. Goswell) Won Shifnal Selling Chase 2m £132 4/5f
Birmingham 8 January 1924 (G. Goswell) Won Ward End Selling Chase 2m £143 3/1f
Ludlow 7 February 1924 (F.B. Rees) Won Knighton Handicap Selling Chase 2m £93 2/1f
Leicester 19 February 1924 (J. Hogan) Won Worksop Handicap Selling Chase 2m £186 4/1

Wolverhampton 17 March 1924 (F.B. Rees) Won Shifnal Selling Chase 2m £83 8/13f

Cheltenham 23 April 1924 (J. Goswell) Won Seven Springs Selling Chase 2m £103 2/5f

Shirley Hunt 8 September 1924 (J. Goswell) Won Shirley Handicap Selling Chase 2m £92 1/1f

Wolverhampton 16 March 1925 (F.B. Rees) Won Shifnal Selling Chase 2m £82 5/4f

Cheltenham 15 April 1925 (F.B. Rees) Won Seven Springs Selling Chase 2m £103 2/5f

Worcester 30 April 1925 (T.E. Leader) Won Kempsey Selling Chase 2m £93 5/2f

Trainer: Benjamin Roberts, Cheltenham

Newport 1 June 1925 (C. Johnson) Won Abertillery Handicap Chase 2m £87 8/1

There have been three very good Irish-trained horses named Golden Fleece. The best-known of the trio is the most recent, the American-bred Derby winner of 1982, owned by Robert Sangster and trained by Vincent O'Brien. That Golden Fleece started favourite for the Derby but Pat Eddery gave his backers a terrible fright, lying way out of his ground before coming with a breathtaking run, from a seemingly impossible position, to sweep past Touching Wood and win the race quite comfortably in the end. The son of Nijinsky never ran again, being retired to the Coolmore Stud in 1983, only to die the following year, after which there was a public wrangle with the insurance companies, which refused to pay out on the policy because of a technicality.

The least well-known Golden Fleece was a filly by the 1807 Derby winner Election out of Moll Roe, who won an early attempt at establishing an Irish Oaks at the Curragh in June 1817, but does not appear to have made it to stud.

The third was a useful steeplechaser, miler and sprinter, foaled in 1911 and a gelding, sired by the Sussex Stakes winner, The Raft, out of Golden Quid, a half-bred mare by Quidnunc. This particular Golden Fleece was the bane of the bookies' lives during his long career, with Dick Duggan, the leading Irish book-maker of the time, stating publically that the horse had cost him more money than any other during his entire bookmaking career. Claiming to have lost a big fortune on him between 1916 and 1919, when he won fourteen races and started favourite for twelve of them, Duggan reflected that it would have paid him to buy the horse for £30,000, when he was a foal, and to have had him shot there and then.

Golden Fleece began his career in bumpers as a four-year-old in 1915 but failed to make an impression. Sent chasing the following year, he fell in his first chase, at Baldoyle but came good at Bellewstown in July 1916 when, ridden by his owner, Mr L.S. Ward, he comprehensively beat Maxie Arnott's 1-to-3 hot-pot Roman General, who had demolished a good field at Cork Park. Never again would Golden Fleece do the bookies a turn. Sent to Galway for the Plate, he finished a good third behind Never Fear and Alice Rockthorn, returning the following year to finish second to Privit, owned by Major Dermot McCalmont and trained by Maxie Arnott. However, that was very competitive race because behind Golden Fleece that day was the future Grand National winner, Shaun Spadah, as well as Picture Saint, who would win the Galway Plate two years later. In March 1918 Golden Fleece impressed all present when romping home in a handicap chase at Leopardstown, his owner/trainer/rider literally being showered with bids for him as he made his way back to scale. Yielding to the temptation, Mr Ward accepted the offer made by trainer Jack Rogers, acting on behalf of William Parrish, a wealthy English colliery owner.

Born in 1866, J.T. Rogers rode as an amateur jockey for many years and was over forty when he got his only ride in the Grand National, finishing sixth on the fancied Leinster in 1909. He began training at Cheltenham but moved his stable to Ireland in 1915, when racing in Britain was cut back owing to the war. Nowadays remembered as a flat trainer, he had a successful career, being the Champion Irish Trainer three times in succession (1935–7), winning eleven Irish classic races, three of them with Museum, the Irish Triple Crown winner of 1935. He also trained the subsequent Derby winner Trigo during his two-year-old career, when he was trained in Ireland. He was the father of the trainers Bryan, killed in the Second World War, and Captain Darby Rogers, and the grandfather of Mickey Rogers, trainer of Hard Ridden and Santa Claus. When he decided to move to Ireland, his principal patron, William Parrish, allowed him take some of his horses with him. So successful were these horses, that Mr Parrish authorized the purchase of more, the additions to his string continuing until he had over fifty horses in training with Rogers on the Curragh. However, with the ending of hostilities, Parrish lost his enthusiasm for racing in Ireland and decided to bring his string back to England, sending his horses to Stanley Harrison, who trained at Bangor-on-Dee.

Having purchased Golden Fleece, Jack Rogers gave the horse a break before bringing him to Galway, where he lined up for the 1918 Galway Plate in the millionaire's old gold, with black hooped sleeves and a quartered cap. Previously he had finished third and second in the race in Mr Ward's maroon jacket, but was now assisted by professional jockey Arthur Stubbs. He started 7-to-1 joint-favourite with Semper Idem, Michael Dawson's sensational four-year-old steeplechasing prospect, who had hacked up in his three unbeaten starts by an aggregate distance of fifty-eight lengths. The joint-favourites had the race to themselves, going right away from a field of top chasers, such as Ballyboggan, Privit, Hill of Camas, Picture Saint and Happy Moments. Arthur Stubbs on Golden Fleece and Joe Canty on Semper Idem gave their best in a thrilling finish that lasted all the way to the line, with Golden Fleece eventually winning the race by a neck.

Semper Idem went to the Tramore meeting and won two races, albeit one of them as a walkover, and Golden Fleece also won his next two races, a steeplechase at Leopardstown and a flat race of 15 furlongs at Baldoyle. This decided Jack Rogers to try and win important flat races with his steeplechaser, selecting the Irish Cesarewitch at the Curragh. Harry H. Beasley, son of the famous amateur of the same name and later father of Paddy Sleator's jockey Bobby, was given the mount. For many years first jockey to Atty Persse, H.H. Beasley had the reputation of being coolness personified, as well as being a talented rider, but Golden Fleece was not quite good enough, finishing second, five lengths behind the easy winner Krooboy, trained by Shem Jeffrey and ridden by Martin Quirke.

It transpired that Golden Fleece had the speed to win over 6 furlongs and 1 mile at the Curragh, encouraging Jack Rogers to send him over to his son Darby, then training Sparsholt, for a flat campaign in the big English handicap races. Running in the likes of the Lincolnshire and the Royal Hunt Cup, the Galway Plate winner was out of his depth and finished the 1920 flat season with no wins and only one placed effort to his name, but he did win a hurdle race, his first ever, at the Kempton Christmas meeting. Alternating between Jack and Darby Rogers during 1921, he won flat races at Worcester (12 furlongs) and the Curragh (6 furlongs), a hurdle race at Uttoxeter and a steeplechase at Worcester. However, in the autumn of that year all the Parrish horses, including Golden Fleece, joined Stanley Harrison.

Born in Liverpool in 1880, Mr H.S. Harrison was a well-known amateur rider in Austria, Hungary, Germany and Ireland, where he was the leading amateur rider in 1918. The Galway Hurdle was a lucky race for him – he rode two winners, Elgon and Jenny Jones, both for Reggie Walker, but the latter victory prompted his sudden retirement from the saddle. After beating Pansy Croft's Maroc, trained by Harry Ussher, who had won the race the previous year, the eight-year-old Jenny Jones and her veteran 39-year-old rider came in to a warm reception from the big Galway crowd. As the horse made its way through the throng to the winner's enclosure, Harrison heard a racegoer remark, 'A great old mare and a great old man', and decided that it was time to retire. He fulfilled his obligation to Reggie Walker and rode Lord Ednam in the last race, the Traders' Plate, a 2-mile flat race, finishing third behind the dead-heaters Wingate and My Rath, who ran off to decide the winner, with the former winning the extra race by one and a half lengths.

This was the last time that a dead heat was rerun at the Galway Races. In bygone times, if a race ended in a dead heat the owners had the option of either splitting the prize money or having a run-off between the two horses, over the same course and distance. A run-off was exciting for the spectators and was not considered unduly arduous on the horses, bearing in mind that some regularly contested two races on the same day and it was common for horses to race on successive days. Run-offs took place in big races too: the 1828 Epsom Derby ended in a dead heat between Cadland and The Colonel, with the former winning the run-off; and the St Leger was twice settled by a run-off, the most famous being between the Derby winner Voltigeur, owned by the leading Freemason Lord Zetland, and the Irish-bred Russborough in 1850. Since the inception of racing at Ballybrit in 1869, there had been five dead heats, two of which were divided and the other three run off. John Nally and Mr Coghlan agreed to divide in 1871 after Queen Scotia and Banshee dead-heated for the Western Hunt Chase, which was not surprising because the race was run over 3 miles, including a double fence and a 4½-foot-high stone wall. Again in 1890 owners Mr Bernard and P.A. Kirk agreed to share the £46, when BA and Lady of the Glen dead-heated in a 2-mile hurdle race, the Express Plate. However, it is interesting that the three races that were run off at Galway prior to 1919 were all the last race on the card that day. In 1878, F.C. Osborne's Jollification II (Mr J.F. Lee Barber) beat H.E. Linde's Bijou (Mr T. Beasley) in the run-off for the Glenard Handicap Chase over 2½ miles; in 1885 Captain Chetwynd's Wellington, ridden by Willie Cullen, won the run-off of the Farewell Hunt Chase, over 2 miles, beating Ringlet; and in 1898 Red Ray, trained and ridden by Willie Cullen, beat Trueno.

Golden Fleece won twelve selling chases for William Parrish and his trainer Stanley Harrison between May 1923, when he was twelve, and April 1925. After a seller, the winner was sold by public auction but his owner was allowed to buy him in. Mr Parrish had to do this nine times at prices between 1,500 and 65 guineas. As we have seen, under the rules that applied to 'sellers' at the time, if the winner was advertised to be sold for, say £50, then the owner would be given that sum, plus the prize money if the winning horse was sold. The price actually paid for the horse, even if it was bought in by the owner, went in equal proportions to the owner of the horse that had finished second and the racecourse executive. This was to encourage the owner of the runner-up to bid up the winner if the connections were attempting to buy it in, and there is always plenty of drama at those post-race sales. However, after Golden Fleece won at Worcester in April 1925, there was some misunderstanding at the subsequent auction and the horse was not bought-in on behalf of Mr Parrish; the fourteen-year-old was knocked down instead to a Mr Allen for 150 guineas. Sent to former jockey Benjamin Roberts, who trained at Cheltenham, he won his last race, a handicap chase at Newport, and four races later ran for the last time, finishing third in a handicap chase at

Monmouth on 18 May 1927. At this point William Parrish repurchased his Galway Plate winner and put the sixteen-year-old out to grass for a well-earned retirement. A winning favourite twenty-six times in his racing career, Golden Fleece can truly be described as a punters' friend.

CLONREE (late Kruiscik)

(Bay/brown gelding 1914 Atlas – Miss Eger by Egerton)

Breeder: J. Fox
Winner of the 1920 Galway Plate
Winner of the 1923 Welsh Grand National

Owner: Owen Toole
Trainer: Francis Morgan
Limerick Junction 12 June 1919 (F. Morgan) Won Maiden Chase 2m £176 6/1
Curragh 23 October 1919 (F. Morgan) Won New Abbey Hurdle 1½m £186 5/2
Aintree 6 November 1919 (F. Dainty) Won Grand Sefton Handicap Chase 3m £805 100/8
Leopardstown 27 December 1919 (F. Morgan) Won St Stephen's Handicap Chase 3m £176 5/2jf
Croom 26 February 1920 (F. Morgan) Won Adare Cup 2m Chase £22½ 4/9f
Galway 4 August 1920 (F. Morgan) Won Galway Plate 2m 5f Handicap Chase £592 3/1f
Trainer: Captain Percival A.O. Whitaker, St Giles, Salisbury
Lingfield Park 21 January 1921 (P. Whitaker) Won Newchapel Bumper 2m £191 8/11f
Trainer: G. Spittle, Wantage
Cardiff 3 April 1923 (J. Hogan Jr) Won Welsh Grand National 3½m Handicap Chase £785 5/2f

Bred by Captain J. Fox, Clonree was originally named Kruiscik by his breeder and raced, without winning, under that name until being bought by Owen Toole. His new owner immediately changed his name to Clonree and was rewarded with a victory in a steeplechase at Limerick Junction. A faller in the 1919 Galway Plate, Clonree finished second at the Tramore meeting, won over hurdles at the Curragh and ended the year with a victory in the valuable Grand Sefton Handicap Chase at the Aintree winter meeting. Although he only won two races in 1920, one of them was the Galway Plate, which he won by twenty lengths. He had previously fallen at Cheltenham and in the Grand National, but finished third in the Lancashire Handicap Chase at Manchester. He never managed to win a flat race but was only beaten by a short head by Riverside Fairy in the 1920 Irish Cesarewitch at the Curragh, the third horse being Athasi, later to become the dam of the Derby winner Trigo.

Sold to England, Clonree joined the stable of Captain Percy Whitaker, a Boer War veteran and former master of foxhounds, who was still riding in races despite being in his early fifties. He was Champion Amateur Rider in Britain in 1908, the year he finished third in the Grand National on his own horse The Lawyer III, only to lose the horse when he dropped down dead on pulling up. Captain Whitaker proved to be a versatile trainer, later moving to Newmarket from Salisbury, sending Silvo over to France to win the Paris Grand Steeplechase in 1925 and winning the Lincolnshire Handicap, the first big flat race of the season, with Knight Error in 1931. A director of Bournemouth (Ensbury Park) Racecourse, where Atty Persse was also on the Board, Percy Whitaker won a handicap hurdle race there on April Fools' Day 1926 with Hamlet, ridden by James Hogan Jr. Although this was only another winning favourite at the time, it was the first British winner for H.J. 'Jim' Joel, who became one of the great owner/breeders on the turf, winning the Derby with Royal Palace in 1967.

Shrewd as far as horses were concerned, Captain Whitaker won a bumper on Clonree at Lingfield Park before deciding to sell him with a Grand National engagement, which always tempted buyers. Now trained by G. Spittle, Clonree refused at one of the big Aintree fences but he later finished second behind Mythical in the Welsh Grand National, a race he won two years later. First run in 1895, the Welsh Grand National was more valuable than the Galway Plate and the Irish Grand National and was run on the Ely course at Cardiff until that course closed down in 1939, when it was transferred to Chepstow. Clonree never won another race, dying in training early in 1924.

CLONSHEEVER

(Bay gelding 1915 Avidity – Wise Gull by The Gull)

Breeder: P. Cleary
Winner of the 1923 and 1924 Galway Plate

Owner: J.E. Tyrrell
Trainer: F.F. McDonogh
Down Royal 1 April 1921 (M. Colbert) Won Barbour Handicap Chase 2m £260 4/1
Navan 13 December 1921 (M. Colbert) Won Rathcairne Handicap Chase 3m £65 4/1

Owner and trainer: J.E. Tyrrell
Leopardstown 28 April 1922 (M. Colbert) Won Leopardstown Handicap Chase 2m £422 100/8

Owner: J.E. Tyrrell

Trainer: H.I. Ussher

Galway 1 August 1923 (J. Hogan Jr) Won Galway Plate Handicap Chase 2½m £392 10/1

Limerick Junction 17 October 1923 (J. Hogan Jr) Won Junction Handicap Chase 2½m £93 6/4f

Leopardstown 1 March 1924 (J. Hogan Jr) Won Stewards' Handicap Chase 3m £83 5/4f

Mallow 30 May 1924 (J. Hogan Jr) Won Rakes of Mallow Handicap Chase 3m £116 5/4f

Galway 30 July 1924 (F.B. Rees) Won Galway Plate Handicap Chase 2½m £442 8/1

Navan 16 August 1924 (J. Hogan Jr) Won Bective Handicap Chase 3m £51 1/1f

Baldoyle 2 June 1925 (J. Hogan Jr) Won Malahide Chase 2¼m £83 6/4

Naas 1 September 1925 (J. Hogan Jr) Won Naas Handicap Chase 3m £83 4/6f

Leopardstown 31 October 1925 (J. Hogan Jr) Won Stewards' Handicap Chase 3m £83 11/10f

Bred by P. Cleary, Clonsheever was the only living foal out of Wise Gull, who died at the age of seven. By the handicapper Avidity, the winner of eleven races between the ages of two and five years, he won twelve steeplechases in his career to a value of £2,173, before dying in training early in 1926 at the age of eleven. Having failed to win for his breeder, he was sold to J.E. Tyrrell, who retained him for the rest of his career.

Sent initially to F.F. McDonogh, who had the useful Dog Fox and Riverside Fairy in his yard at the time, Clonsheever's first win came in the valuable Barbour Handicap Chase at Down Royal. When McDonogh gave up training, Tyrrell trained the horse for a brief period before sending him to Harry Ussher, who had just moved from Galway to Brackenstown. The Galway maestro won two Galway Plates with him, in 1923 and 1924, and he made a gallant attempt at winning a record three-in-a-row. Starting the 2-to-1 favourite, despite having to carry 13 stones 1 pound, he finished third to Blancona and Ingomar in 1925. He was dead before the next Galway meeting, dying shortly after finishing second in a handicap chase at Baldoyle on New Year's Day 1926.

KING MICHAEL

(Brown gelding 1914 Fariman – Diavolezza by Robert le Diable)

Breeder: J.J. Maher
Winner of the 1921 Galway Hurdle

Owner: J.J. Moore
Trainer: Michael Dawson, Rathbride Manor, Curragh

Phoenix Park 7 July 1917 (Joseph Harty) Won Duffers' Plate 10f flat £92 2/1

Curragh 27 July 1917 (Joseph Harty) Won Loughbrown 3yo Maiden (entry) £187 1/2f

Leopardstown 2 March 1918 (J. Fagan) Won Maiden Hurdle 1½m £88 5/1

Mullingar 9 December 1918 (Joseph Canty) Won Lough Ennel Handicap Chase 2½m £37 6/1

Trainer: Cecil Brabazon, Kilcumney House, Kildare

Mullingar 15 February 1921 (Mr C. Brabazon) Won Newbrook Handicap Hurdle 2m £64 4/1

Leopardstown 5 March 1921 (John Burns) Won Newtown Handicap Hurdle 1½m £118 6/1

Curragh 26 May 1921 (Mr C. Brabazon) Won Ballysax Handicap Hurdle 1½m £167 7/2

Leopardstown 3 June 1921 (Mr C. Brabazon) Won Bray Handicap Hurdle 1½m £88 7/1

Leopardstown 4 June 1921 (Mr C. Brabazon) Won County Handicap 12f flat £88 2/1f

Curragh 22 June 1921 (Joseph Canty) Won Summer Plate 10f flat £166 5/1

Limerick Junction 29 June 1921 (Joseph Canty) Won Milltown Plate 12f flat £68½ 8/11f

Galway 4 August 1921 (Joseph Canty) Won Galway Hurdle Handicap 2m £246 2/1f

Phoenix Park 12 August 1921 (Joseph Canty) Won Greenmount Plate 8f flat £176 1/1f

Curragh 23 August 1921 (E.M. Quirke) Won Friarstown Plate 10f flat £83 1/2f

Trainer: E.P.M. Barthropp, Cheshire

Haydock Park 9 December 1921 (Joseph Canty) Won Garswood Handicap Hurdle 2m £264
    100/8

Trainer: Cecil Brabazon

Baldoyle 6 May 1922 (Joseph Canty) Won Swords Handicap 15f flat £88 100/30

It was an open secret at the time that King Michael was owned by the jockey Joe Canty. The Rules of Racing prohibited a professional jockey from owning horses so he ran in the name of J.J. Moore of Maddenstown, Curragh. Bred by James J. Maher, the very successful Irish breeder and horse dealer, he began his career with Michael Dawson and was placed thrice at two years. Having won two flat races and a hurdle, he fell in the Galway Hurdle, won by Maroc, and was then sent over fences, winning a minor race at Mullingar in December 1918. At Mullingar that afternoon Picture Saint and Jenny Jones both won races and the pair went on to win the big races at Galway in 1919, Picture Saint capturing the Plate and Jenny Jones the Hurdle.

Transferred to Cecil Brabazon, King Michael was lightly raced and failed to win in 1920, which enabled him to drop down the handicap. This enabled him to make hay in 1921, when he won eleven races, six handicap hurdles and five races on the flat, including the Galway Hurdle. A public favourite during this winning run, he was written up as a future champion but failed to live up to that billing, being simply a good, well-handicapped handicapper. Campaigned

in England from Max Barthropp's Cheshire stable, King Michael won at Haydock Park but failed in a number of the better English Handicap Hurdle races, although he did finish third to Winter King in the Salford Handicap at Manchester.

Nowadays riders do not have to worry about persons picnicking in the shelter of the fences!

ALROI

(Bay gelding 1920 Santoi – Cascatel by Marcovil)

Breeder: W.C. Carr
Winner of the 1925 Galway Hurdle

Owner: Miss M.D. Barbour
Trainer: Cecil Brabazon
Down Royal 17 April 1925 (C. Donnelly) Won Down Royal Maiden Hurdle 1½m £73½ 4/7f
Down Royal 18 April 1925 (Mr P. Nugent) Won Antrim Plate 2m flat £44 2/1f
Galway 30 July 1925 (C. Donnelly) Won Galway Hurdle Handicap 2m £196 2/1f

Trainer: G.P. Bracebridge
Dundalk 10 September 1925 (C. Donnelly) Won Ballymascanian Chase 2½m £68½ 2/5f
Nottingham 2 February 1926 (C. Donnelly) Won Tollerton Handicap Chase 2m £137 4/1

The theatre producer George Edwardes bought a yearling in 1898 and named him Santoi, after a musical he was involved with at the time. Bad tempered he may have been, but Santoi was a versatile racehorse, winning the Jubilee Handicap over 10 furlongs at Kempton and the Gold Cup over 2½ miles at Royal Ascot – a much more prestigious race then than it is now. The famous American jockey, Tod Sloan, who brought the modern riding style to England, loved Santoi and listed him as among the best horses he ever rode.

Tod had a brother named Cash, who in 1900 came to England to try to establish himself as a jockey, riding on the coat tails of his famous brother. Cash Sloan got his break when Tod persuaded Santoi's trainer, Walter Davis, to let him ride the horse at Royal Ascot; Tod was committed to ride Crestfallen for George Lambton, a great supporter of his, but he thought that Santoi was a certainty and told Cash so. With Tod aboard Crestfallen, he naturally started favourite, but Tod did not expect to win and spent the race 'minding' his brother as best he could because Santoi was not the easiest of rides. During the race he began to hang and Tod instructed his brother to drop the horse in behind and let him settle. Cash failed to accomplish this simple task and 'rode the worst race that a jockey could ride', as Tod later described it. Coming with a late surge when it was all too late, Santoi finished second, beaten a length by Crestfallen. Everyone blamed the jockey; the occasion and the big crowd had made him nervous, he had given Santoi a terrible ride and lost a race he should have won. In the harsh world of flat racing he would not be given a second chance – that was the end for him in England and he departed to Russia to ply his trade there. Santoi had a long stud career at the Ballykisteen Stud, Limerick Junction, Co. Tipperary, where he got lots of winners without producing a champion racehorse.

In 1919 Mr W.C. Carr sent his well-bred mare Cascatel to Santoi; the resulting foal was named Alroi. In retrospect it was not perhaps the best choice of stallion because Cascatel was a stayer and probably needed a stallion with a bit of speed rather than another stayer. When she was subsequently mated with a miler, Cascatel produced the stayer Sol de Terre, winner of the Irish St Leger.

Bearing in mind his stout breeding, it is not surprising, at least not in hindsight, that Alroi was run off his feet in the big two-year-old races he contested in 1922, the Anglesey Stakes and the National Produce Stakes. He did finish second in the Madrid Handicap at the Curragh on his three-year-old debut, after which he was taken out of training, gelded and sold to Frank Barbour, who was buying as many prospective jumping horses as he could get his hands on at the time. From Belfast, Barbour had made a fortune in the linen trade and came into racing via hunting, having been Master of the County Down Staghounds from 1896 to 1903 and the Westmeath Foxhounds from 1908 until 1912. He regularly rode in point-to-points and instituted the Barbour Cup, a trophy run for at the Westmeath Hunt point-to-point for many years. Owner of a fine estate at Trimblestown, Co. Meath, his vermilion, steel belt and arm bands, and quartered cap were becoming a formidable force in jumping races, as graphically illustrated at the Sligo races, over the old Hazelwood course, on Tuesday, 30 May 1922. There Frank Barbour's horses, all trained by Reggie Walker and ridden by Clyde Aylin, won five of the six races on the programme, four of them starting favourite.

The Barbour horses ran in the names of several members of the family. Frank himself owned Punch (Irish Grand National), Elgon (Galway Hurdle) Koko (Cheltenham Gold Cup) and Easter Hero (Becher Chase); his daughter Miss E.L.M. Barbour, owned Blancona (Galway Plate and Hurdle); his niece Miss M.D. Barbour had Alroi (Galway Hurdle) and his nephew J.M. Barbour Jr Jerpoint

The connections of Blancona and Alroi, winners of the Plate and the Hurdle in 1925: Charley Donnelly (jockey) Cecil Brabazon (trainer), Frank Barbour and the Misses Barbour

(Irish Grand National). In the beginning Frank Barbour's horses were trained by Reggie Walker at Rathvale, Athboy, Co. Meath, but the association ended in 1923, presumably because of the decision to lay out a private training establishment, with its own miniature racecourse, at Trimblestown. Sam Armstrong was the first trainer at Trimblestown but in 1924 was succeeded by Cecil Brabazon, who remained until the autumn of 1925, when G.P. Bracebridge took over. Bracebridge lasted less than a year before he, in turn, gave way to Alfred Bickley. The turnover of trainers continued when the Trimblestown training centre was closed down in 1927, with all the horses going to a yard at Bishops Cannings, in Wiltshire, where they were to be trained by Thomas Pardy. Two years later, when Frank Barbour's health broke down, the whole operation was shut down and the horses were sold off in January 1930.

Cecil Brabazon gave Alroi plenty of time to settle into the new routine; the horse was showing considerable promise and great things were expected from him. He chose a Baldoyle bumper in January 1925 for the first race of his jumping career and the trainer rode him himself. Alroi's reputation at home was reflected in the betting market, when he started 3-to-1 second-favourite to the eventual winner, Kitty Lightfoot, but ran unplaced. For his next run Cecil chose Mallow, taking both Alroi and Blancona there. Both horses finished second, Alroy in a 12-furlong hurdle race and Blancona, ridden by the trainer, in a bumper, but neither horse would be beaten again that year.

Charlie Donnelly, from Tuam, was chosen to ride both horses and he teamed up with Alroi for the first time at Down Royal a couple of weeks later. Supported to 7 to 4 on in the betting, he sauntered home by six lengths to record his first victory. Turned out again the following day, he won a bumper, with Paddy Nugent in the saddle; the 2-to-1 favourite demolished the field to win by ten lengths. With the Galway Hurdle fourteen weeks away and firmly in his sights, Cecil Brabazon decided to give the horse a break and to go to Galway without a preparatory race. On the first day of the Festival, he won the Plate with Blancona, ridden by Charlie Donnelly. The following afternoon, Brabazon and Donnolly won the Hurdle, when Alroi, the 2-to-1 favourite, just got the better of Pansy Croft's Bolshevist by half a length, with Holy Fooks four lengths further back in third place.

After this win, Alroi was sent chasing. Making his debut over fences at Dundalk, he scared everything away except Newtown Park, who had won a steeplechase. He started 5 to 2 on and won the race by a distance. The horse's big home reputation was now being reproduced on the racecourse and he was looking an outstanding steeplechase prospect and a future champion. Cecil Brabazon moved on and was replaced by Alfred Bickley, who sent Alroi over to Nottingham in February 1926 for a handicap chase, which he duly won. But he would never win another race; a fall at Manchester temporarily halted his steeplechase career and caused him to be put back to hurdling. Having finished third in the County Hurdle at Cheltenham and fourth in a hurdle race at Aintree, he was put back over fences, his comeback race being the important Great Lancashire Handicap at Manchester. Again he had difficulty coping with the fences, eventually crashing out of the race and receiving fatal injuries.

Frank Barbour often lamented that Alroi was one of the best horses that he had ever owned and would have gone to the very top had he survived. Unfortunately, his career was a brief one, lasting only one year after he won the first of his five races, and the undoubted potential of this Galway Hurdle winner was never realized.

BLANCONA

(Chestnut gelding 1920 Great Sport – Benedictine by Lemberg)

Breeder: William Ashe
Winner of the 1925 Galway Plate
Winner of the 1926 Galway Hurdle

Owner: Frank Barbour
Trainer: Cecil Brabazon
Bellewstown 1 July 1925 (C. Donnelly) Won Hill Chase 2m £44 5/1

Owner: Miss E.L.M. Barbour
Down Royal 15 July 1925 (C. Donnelly) Won Stormount Chase 3m £51 No SP
Galway 29 July 1925 (C. Donnelly) Won Galway Plate Handicap Chase 2½m £442 6/1
Trainer: G.P. Bracebridge
Curragh 21 October 1925 (G. Archibald) Won Irish Cesarewitch Handicap 14f flat £560 7/1
Trainer: Alfred Bickley
Galway 29 July 1926 (E. Foster) Won Galway Hurdle Handicap 2m £196 4/7f
Limerick Junction 25 August 1926 (E. Foster) Junction Handicap 1½m flat £215 4/1
Aintree 10 November 1926 (E. Foster) Won Becher Chase 2¼m £335 7/4
Trainer: G.H. Blackwell, Newmarket
Newmarket 28 June 1927 (B. Carslake) Won Hare Park Handicap 12f flat £709 9/1
Trainer: Thomas R. Leader, Newmarket

Doncaster 12 September 1928 (J. Childs) Won Rufford Abbey Handicap 2¼m flat £325 2/1f

Sandown Park 20 March 1930 (Major H. Misa) Deat Heat Littleworth NH Flat 2m £127 13/8f

Manchester 22 April 1930 (T.E. Leader) Won Jubilee Handicap Hurdle 2m £265 100/30

Worcester 16 May 1930 (T.E. Leader) Won Seven Stoke Hurdle 2m £92 1/3f

Southwell 9 May 1931 (T.E. Leader) Won Southwell Handicap Hurdle 2m £82 7/4f

Southwell 26 October 1931 (T.E. Leader) Won Lowdham Handicap Hurdle 2m £58 1/1f

Cecil Brabazon knew how to train horses and proved it during his long career. His brief spell in charge of the Barbour horses at Trimblestown was particularly impressive, getting the best out of two talented five-year-olds in the yard, Alroi and Blancona. Alroi always showed a bit of class on the gallops, raising his owner's hopes, but Blancona's tremendous year took everybody except perhaps the trainer by surprise. Bred by Willie Ashe, who also bred the Grand National winner Ambush II, Blancona was by Great Sport, erroneously placed fourth by the judge in the controversial Derby of 1913. Photographs clearly show that he actually finished fifth; the judge completely missed Day Comet. He was then promoted to third place when the winner, Craganour, was subsequently disqualified. By the sensationally successful Irish sire Gallinule, Great Sport stood at the National Stud, Tully, Co. Kildare, until he was exported to Belgium in 1922 and, as so often is the case, his best offspring surfaced after he had gone.

Blancona made his debut in a bumper at the 1924 Leopardstown Christmas meeting, ridden by Cecil Brabazon. He was completely unfancied and made no show. On his next run, in a flat race at Mallow the following March, he finished second, beaten by only a neck, and was then sent chasing. Following wins at Bellewstown and Down Royal, he lined up for the Galway Plate unbeaten over fences, but Clonsheever was the horse to beat. Winner of the Plate in 1923 and again the following year, Harry Ussher's charge was the 2-to-1 favourite to emulate Tipperary Boy and win the race a third time. On a form line through Reggie Walker's Black Toi, Clonsheever appeared to have a stone in hand over Blancona at the weights. However, the latter was likely to be on the upgrade, and so it proved. Blancona put up a brilliant performance to race away to an eight-length success over Ingomar, with the favourite a gallant third, three lengths further behind. It was the first leg of a famous double for Cecil Brabazon and jockey Charlie Donnelly, winning the two big Galway races. Trainer Reggie Walker had done exactly the same with Never Fear and Elgon in 1916, but Charlie Donnelly had ridden a double that no jockey had done before him.

The next race chosen for Blancona was the Irish Cesarewitch, run over 14 furlongs at the Curragh the following October. Brabazon booked the good but short-lived American jockey George Archibald to ride. Archibald who was attached to P.P. Gilpin's stable at Newmarket but had often ridden at the Curragh, was second in that year's Irish Derby, a race he had won on two occasions. The opposition in a high-class field of eighteen included the favourite Hidennis, a really good three-year-old making a belated seasonal debut, East Galway, winner of three handicaps and a future dual Galway Plate winner, as well as Striped Silk, owned by the bookmaker Dick Power and trained by Harry Ussher to win eight races that year. Racegoers watched in disbelief as the 'steeplechaser' hacked up by twelve lengths from Flying Dinah, who had finished third in the Irish St Leger last time out.

Blancona's career suffered a similar hiccup to Alroi's early the following year when he fell in a chase at Nottingham. He stayed on his feet at Cheltenham, where he ran third to the future Grand National winner Sprig, but then was second at Baldoyle, when an odds-on favourite. Although he had never run over hurdles, a decision was made to try him over the smaller obstacles. Thrown in at the deep end, his first ever race over hurdles was the Galway Hurdle, a competitive handicap contested by experienced, fast-jumping hurdlers, but that did not deter the punters. A well-backed 7 to 4 on favourite, Blancona showed the class that had won a Galway Plate and an Irish Cesarewitch, winning the race easily by three lengths. The winning jockey was Eric Foster, who began life as a butcher's boy, then was a coalman and finally a milkman before getting into racing to become English Champion National Hunt Jockey in 1923. The trainer who supervised the switch from fences to hurdles was G.P. Bracebridge, now in his last days as the trainer at Trimblestown, and when Blancona reappeared at Limerick Junction less than a month later, Alfred Bickley was his trainer. Runner-up on the flat at Haydock Park, Blancona then won the important Becher Chase at Aintree in November but, after falling in the Champion Chase at Aintree in March 1927, was never asked to run in a steeplechase again.

Sold off by the Barbours, Blancona joined the stable of George Blackwell, later moving to another Newmarket trainer, Tom Leader, one of a family that had been in racing for generations. His father, also called Tom, had trained George Frederick, winner of the 1874 Derby, but Tom Leader junior specialized in training jumpers, notably Sprig and Gregalach, both Grand National winners. His son Thomas Edward 'Ted' Leader became Champion National Hunt Jockey, and won the Grand National on Sprig, the Cheltenham Gold Cup on Golden Miller and the Champion Hurdle on Insurance. During his time with Leader, Blancona dead-heated in a flat race for amateurs at Sandown Park in 1930 when ridden by Major H. Misa, a keen hunting man who established his own personal record on the turf.

In October 1928 Major Misa travelled down, for one ride only, to Wye race-course, a tight track in East Kent that was effectively closed down in 1974 by the Jockey Club's Inspector of Courses. During the second race, a two-horse affair, one of the runners, Golden Duke, ridden by a claiming rider named McMullen, fell and the horse ran loose. Major Misa, who happened to be watching nearby, caught him, jumped into the saddle and rode him home to collect second prize. That would not be allowed today but in those days a substitute rider was acceptable provided that the horse completed the full course and the substitute rider did not weigh in light. Major Misa also claimed to have done the same on Don Sancho at Cheltenham the following year, but I can find no record of this.

Substitute riders were banned in England after a similar incident occurred at Sandown Park in April 1930. They were not banned in Ireland until many years later and there was a case there as recently as 31 March 1960 at Ballinrobe. During the running of the Western Hunters' Chase, Mr H. Kerrigan created some kind of record, managing to fall twice in the same race, off two different horses. He was riding Bridge Echo and Mr R.E. Snow was on Glenmore Girl, when the two horses fell at the same fence. Mr Kerrigan mistakenly remounted the wrong horse and rode off in a quest for third place, only two horses having been left standing, but he crashed at the last fence. Had she successfully negotiated the fence, Glenmore Girl would have been entitled to third place under Rule 180, provided of course that Mr Kerrigan did not weigh in under the allotted weight. Those were the days! Things are different now, as budding Major Misas should note – Rule 180 has been abolished.

Blancona came back to Ireland for a hurdle race at Leopardstown in April 1931, his first appearance on an Irish racecourse for five years, but finished down the field behind Arctic Star. A fortnight later he was a winning favourite in a hurdle race at Southwell, his penultimate victory, and was retired later that year after winning again at the same venue.

EAST GALWAY

(Bay gelding 1919 William Rufus – Little Shower by Aquascutum)

Breeder: J.A.B. Trench
Winner of the 1928 and 1930 Galway Plate

Winner of the 1930 Lancashire Handicap Chase

Won 34 Races including 16 steeplechases

Owner and trainer: J.A.B. Trench.

Thurles 23 June 1924 (Mr J.H. Wallace) Won Corinthian Plate 2m flat £41½ 4/6f

Dundalk 9 July 1924 (Mr J.H. Wallace) Won Mount Pleasant Plate 2m flat £46 1/1f

Owner: J.S. Shepherd

Trainer: Maxwell Arnott

Leopardstown 1 May 1925 (Mr J.T. Widger) Won Foxrock Handicap 2m flat £83 6/4f

Baldoyle 9 May 1925 (D. Ward) Won Stewards' Handicap 15f flat £162 3/1f

Mullingar 19 October 1925 (Mr J.T. Widger) Won October Handicap 2m flat £44 2/1jf

Leopardstown 28 December 1925 (D. Ward) Won Stillorgan Chase 2m £83 4/6f

Naas 6 January 1926 (D. Ward) Won Mail Chase 2m £44 2/5f

Naas 6 March 1926 (D. Ward) Won Naas Maiden Chase 2m £166 5/4f

Baldoyle 18 March 1926 (Mr T.B. Cullinan) Won Marino Plate 17f flat £83 5/4

Leopardstown 7 May 1926 (Mr J.T. Widger) Won Newtown Handicap 2m flat £83 3/1jf

Naas 11 May 1926 (Mr S.H. Dennis) Won Punchestown Handicap Chase 2m £166 5/2jf

Mullingar 7 June 1926 (D. Ward) Won Clonhugh Plate 11f flat £73½ 5/4f

Mallow 16 June 1926 (D. Ward) Won Cahirmee Plate 12f flat £76 1/8f

Limerick 29 September 1926 (Mr J.T. Widger) Won Stewards' Plate 2m flat £83 1/1f

Navan 23 October 1926 (D. Ward) Won Sallypark Plate 10f flat £46 4/6f

Leopardstown 27 December 1926 (Mr J.T. Widger) Won Amateur Riders' Chase 3m £78 1/3f

Leopardstown 1 August 1927 (D. Ward) Won Sugar Loaf Handicap 12f flat £78 4/5f

Baldoyle 10 September 1927 (D. Ward) Won Portmarnock Plate 12f flat £68½ 1/1f

Limerick 28 September 1927 (Mr J.T. Widger) Won Stewards' Plate 2m flat £46 4/6f

Naas 1 November 1927 (D. Ward) Won Farewell Handicap Chase 3m £46 2/1f

Kempton Park 2 March 1928 (Mr J.T. Widger) Won Ashford National Hunt Flat 2m £107 4/5f

Trainer: Thomas Pardy, Bishops Cannings

Sandown Park 22 March 1928 (Mr J.T. Widger) Dead Heat Littleworth NF Flat 2m £81 4/6f

Trainer: Maxwell Arnott, Clonsilla

Galway 1 August 1928 (D. Ward) Won Galway Plate Handicap Chase 2½m £442 1/1f

Limerick 26 September 1928 (Mr J.T. Widger) Won Stewards' Plate 2m flat £46 8/100f

Naas 11 September 1929 (D. Ward) Won Harristown Handicap Chase 3m £63½ 1/1f

Limerick 26 December 1929 (Mr J.T. Widger) Won Dunraven Cup 2m flat £83 1/4f

Leopardstown 12 April 1930 (D. Ward) Won Stillorgan Handicap Chase 3m £73 5/4f

Manchester 21 April 1930 (J. McNeill) Won Lancashire Handicap Chase 3½m £1,725 100/8

Galway 30 July 1930 (J. McNeill) Won Galway Plate Handicap Chase 2½m £442 5/4f

Mallow 27 August 1931 (J. McNeill) Won Mallow Handicap Chase 3m £97½ 7/4

Listowel 29 September 1931 (J. McNeill) Won Listowel Chase 3m £53½ 1/7f

Down Royal 6 May 1932 (S. Magee) Won Governor of Northern Ireland's Perpetual Challenge
Cup Chase 3m £83½ 3/1

Ballinrobe 14 June 1932 (S. Magee) Won Irish National Hunt Handicap Chase 3m £46½ 4/5f

Owner and trainer: Maxwell Arnott

Claremorris 30 May 1933 (J. McNeill) Won Claremorris Handicap Chase 3m £44½ 1/1f

For whatever reason, some horses fire the imagination of the ordinary racegoer and become public favourites. One such horse was East Galway. The public loved him, wanted to see him win and tended to back him every time he ran, whether or not his odds offered value. In a career that lasted ten seasons, East Galway won thirty-four times, although his official tally is only thirty-two and a half because two were dead-heats, with one being run off. East Galway did not show up for the run off, allowing his opponent to walk over. Amazingly, he was the winning favourite on thirty occasions and actually started favourite forty-four times in his long career, positive proof of his enduring popularity.

Foaled in 1919, East Galway was by a horse named William Rufus, runner-up in the St Leger and the Sussex Stakes at three years. Exported to Hungary after only two seasons at stud, he was brought back to Ireland in 1910 to stand at Jim Parkinson's Maddenstown Lodge stud. His Irish career got off to a flying start when his first crop included several winners for Parkinson, including King's Common, winner of the prestigious Railway Stakes, and his stock won fifty-two races that year. Full each year, his fee increased from 150 to 250 guineas in 1916, only to crash down to a mere 9 guineas in 1918 as the winners dried up. That is what 'Crasher' Trench paid to have his Aquascutum mare covered. Unnamed at the time, East Galway's dam was given the name Little Shower late in life, in 1926 at the age of fourteen, which was unusual for a mare at stud and not racing. She also bred Stormproof, a useful filly on the flat in 1928.

East Galway's breeder, Mr J.A.B. Trench, a farmer from Eyrecourt, Co. Galway, who was well known in racing, hunting and polo circles, rode as an amateur and won the 1911 Irish Grand National on Repeater II. It was his association with Captain Bacon, trainer of Repeater II, which provided him with the opportunity to train Stone Chase, a half-sister to the Grand National winner Troytown, who won a 5-furlong sprint at Leopardstown at three years and four 2-mile chases for Captain Bacon at four. When the latter retired at the end of 1914, 'Crasher' Trench took charge of the mare and trained her to win six more

2-mile chases over the next two years. Unfortunately, 2 miles was an unfashionable distance for steeplechases at that time; there were no big races in Ireland to run in and England was closed because of the war. That was how it came to pass that Stone Chase was sold to an American stud. Mr Trench, who had land at Clonfert and in Co. Dublin, held a licence for only six years before drifting out of racing under Rules. His wife Dolly was a well-known point-to-point rider – women were allowed to compete against men 'between the flags' – and it was this branch of the sport that occupied him in later years. For many years Master of the East Galway Hunt, he worked tirelessly to promote their point-to-point meeting. He died suddenly in December 1945, while supervising improvement work on the course.

The year following East Galway's first win, in a bumper at Thurles, Mr Trench accepted a bid for the horse from J.S. Shepherd, a patron of Maxie Arnott's stable. East Galway really came good in 1926, winning ten races, which does not include the 2-mile handicap steeplechase at Mallow that ended in a dead-heat. It is said that given enough weight a donkey should be able to beat a Derby winner, and East Galway just failed to concede 3 stone to Simonstown, the judge declaring a dead-heat. As the Rules then stood, the owners could agree to divide the stakes or to re-run the race. Mr O'Driscoll, the owner of Simonstown, unsportingly insisted on re-running the race. Naturally, Mr Shepherd and Maxie Arnott were reluctant to ask their horse to run another race over 2 miles, conceding 3 stone to a horse that had nearly beaten him first time round, and allowed Simonstown to walk over and collect the full prize.

In 1928 East Galway came to the Galway Races after a four-month break from racing since running really well to finish third at Manchester. In a field of eleven, he was made an even-money favourite to win the race and did so by three lengths from Willie Ashe's Tiranogue. Arnott tried similar tactics the following year, running in a big race in England, and giving East Galway a four-month rest before a tilt at the Plate. The big race on this occasion was the Welsh Grand National, then run on the old Cardiff course at Ely, but East Galway finished down the field. Twelve opponents were waiting for him at Galway, including Guiding Light from Joe Dawson's Curragh stable. Punters were not in the least put off by East Galway's burden of 12 stones 7 pounds, making it a firm 6-to-4 favourite. Guiding Light had not raced in Ireland all year, having been sent over to Frank Morgan for an English campaign, returning specifically for this race and getting 30 pounds from the previous year's winner. The pair went clean away from the field in the closing stages, but Guiding Light was always travelling that little bit better than East Galway, whose big weight took its toll in the closing stages. Although Guiding Light won the race, Dinny Ward immediately objected, claiming that Paddy Powell, a jockey who was often fortified by alcohol, had caused him interference by foul riding. The stewards were not sympathetic and overruled the objection.

In 1930 it was the same ritual, a crack at the Great Lancashire Steeplechase at Manchester, a three-month break, and then off to Galway for the Plate. Things had gone exceedingly well that year for East Galway, who won at Leopardstown and at Manchester. It had not been so good for Arnott's stable because his longtime stable jockey, Dinny Ward, died at the end of May. Forty-year-old Ward had been with Arnott twenty years and was among the leading jockeys in Ireland every year, although had never been Champion. He was riding Tony Boy for his retaining stable in the Railway Plate at Limerick Junction, a long odds-on favourite to beat its only opponent, when he suffered a simple fall. He got to his feet and limped back to the jockeys' room. He did not appear to be seriously hurt but he had actually fractured his leg. Gangrene set in, and suddenly Ward was seriously ill. Doctors had to amputate his leg, but to no avail, and he died eleven days after the fall. Born in Rathkeele, Co Limerick, Denis Ward had ridden eleven winners at Galway, including Plates on Fair Richard and East Galway.

The twelve-year-old East Galway lined up for the 1930 Plate the hot 5-to-4 favourite, despite his burden of 12 stones 7 pounds and a new jockey, John McNeill, clad in Mr Shepherd's dark blue jacket with crimson sleeves. McNeill had ridden the horse only once previously, winning the big race at Manchester. Once again the Galway Plate had attracted a high-class field, including the Irish Grand National winner Fanmond. On this occasion East Galway made no mistake, winning by three lengths, to the raucous cheers of the Galway crowd, who were on it to a man.

East Galway was unplaced in the Plate in 1931 and with the years and the mileage clocking up, Maxie Arnott decided to give Galway a miss the following year but brought East Galway back in 1933, by-passing the Plate for the easier option of the Galway Blazers Handicap Chase, but he finished unplaced. Retired after the Listowel meeting the following September, his final win came at Claremorris on 30 May 1933, where he won a 3-mile handicap chase, his fifteenth win over fences. Strange as it may seem East Galway never ran in a hurdle race during his long career.

RED PARK

(Bay gelding 1926 Redmond – Lady Alwine by Benvenuto)

Breeder: E. Hogan
Winner of the 1933 Galway Plate
Winner of the 1933 Irish Grand National

Owner and trainer: John McEnery
Punchestown 21 April 1931 (J. Lenehan) Won Drogheda Chase 2m £146 6/1
Leopardstown 7 November 1931 (Mr T. McCarthy) Won Leopardstown Handicap Chase 2m
      £58½ 10/1

Owner: Lady Helen McCalmont
Trainer: J.J. Barry
Mallow 25 August 1932 (Mr M. Barry) Won Buttevant Chase 2m £44 1/2f
Fairyhouse 17 April 1933 (D. Kirwan) Won Irish Grand National Handicap Chase 3½m £740 4/1
Galway 2 August 1933 (D. Kirwan) Won Galway Plate Handicap Chase 2m 5f £442 3/1
Leopardstown 11 November 1933 (D. Kirwan) Won Bray Handicap Chase 3m £58½ 7/2
Trainer: James Russell, Mablethorpe, Lincolnshire
Wolverhampton 11 November 1935 (E. Brown) Won Oteley Chase 3m £117 7/2
Kempton Park 30 January 1936 (E. Brown) Won Cranford Handicap Chase 2½m £244 100/7
1936–7 Trainer: Walter Nightingall

Owner: A.F. Jacks
Trainer: W. Madden
Towcester 18 April 1938 (H. Haley) Won Towcester Handicap Chase 2m £195 7/1

Red Park won the Irish Grand National and the Galway Plate in the same year, emulating Springfield Maid and Tipperary Boy, a double that has only been done twice since, by Alberoni (1952) and Umm (1955). Bred by E. Hogan, Red Park began his racing career on the flat at four years, when owned by John McEnery and trained by Captain Darby Rogers. On his second start he ran second to Martin McDonogh's Kyleclare over 12 furlongs at the Curragh. Mr McEnery trained the horse himself the following year, when he won two chases, but sold him to Lady Helen McCalmont after he had fallen in the Prince of Wales Chase at Punchestown. Although unplaced in the Galway Plate in 1932, he returned to win the race the following year but proved a big disappointment subsequently. Sold off to race in England, the highlight of Red Park's career there was when he won the

Cranford Handicap Chase at Kempton Park, beating the Cheltenham Gold Cup winner Morse Code, the only horse to beat Golden Miller at Cheltenham.

KNUCKLEDUSTER

(Bay gelding 1926 Iron Hand – Lake Lass by Morena)

Breeder: M. O'Brien
Winner of the 1932 and 1933 Galway Hurdle

Owner and trainer: Major H.D. Beamish
Bellewstown 3 July 1930 (Mr F.E. McKeever) Won Shallon Handicap 13f flat £44 7/2
Baldoyle 25 May 1931 (Mr F.E. McKeever) Won Corinthian Handicap 17f flat £58½ 5/2
Bellewstown 1 July 1931 (Mr F.E. McKeever) Won Meath Hurdle 13f £44 4/5f
Galway 28 July 1932 (Mr F.E. McKeever) Won Galway Hurdle Handicap 2m £220 7/2
Down Royal 6 May 1933 (T. Burns) Won Whinny Hill Handicap 9f flat £46 5/4f
Galway 3 August 1933 (Mr F.E. McKeever) Won Galway Hurdle 2m £220 6/4f

Owner: R. Strutt
Trainer: Peter R.A. Thrale, West Horsley, Surrey
Hawthorn Hill 9 November 1937 (G. Wilson) Won Taplow Selling Handicap Chase 2m £65
    100/30
Privately trained by R. Strutt
Towcester 16 April 1938 (W. Redmond) Won Heathencote Selling Handicap Chase 3m £92 3/1
Woodland Pytchley 21 April 1938 (Mr R. Strutt) Won Open Nomination Chase 3m £- 2/5f
Buckfastleigh 6 June 1938 (W. Redmond) Won Licensed Victuallers Selling Handicap Chase
    2m £63 6/4f

Iron Hand, an own-brother to the Irish Derby winner He Goes, won the Ebor Handicap and three hurdle races before retiring to stud in Fermoy, Co. Cork. The best horse he sired was Knuckleduster, the double Galway Hurdle winner, whose career might have been more glorious had he been under the care of a more experienced trainer. As far as Major Beamish was concerned Knuckleduster was a steeplechaser and, having won a bumper at four, contested his first chase early the following year. Ridden by the talented but ill-fated amateur Eric McKeever, he was an odds-on favourite to win a modest Downpatrick three-horse chase, with one of the runners not having any chance of winning. Knuckleduster first refused to jump the fences and, when coaxed to

Taking off at Galway

do so, promptly fell, leaving Drumara to saunter home, beating the no-hoper by a distance.

The bucolic surroundings of Fairyhouse and the firm hand of Major Scott, an experienced hunting man, appeared to be an ideal environment for the horse to redeem himself but again Knuckleduster fell. A poor run followed at Leopardstown, so to help restore his confidence Knuckleduster was given a run over hurdles at the Maze. To the surprise of his trainer Knuckleduster ran an excellent race, finishing second. He was kept hurdling until he won, which he duly did on the first day of the Bellewstown meeting. Major Beamish decided that it was now time to put him back over fences, and did so the following day. Once again Knuckleduster fell but still Major Beamish would not give up, running the horse in the Galway Plate, despite it being a competitive handicap race contested by experienced chasers. Few people could have been surprised when the horse crashed out of the Plate yet the connections persevered over fences until the whole country was convinced that Knuckleduster would never make a steeplechaser.

Besides winning two Galway Hurdles, Knuckleduster finished second to Loch Leven in the 1932 Irish Cesarewitch. His career was interrupted by the death of Major Beamish in 1934, and the 1933 Galway Hurdle was the last of the six races he won in Ireland. Sold to England, Knuckleduster finished his career running in selling chases.

HONOR'S CHOICE

(Black horse 1935 Embargo – Thistle Lass by Thistleton)

Breeder: Executors of the late Martin McDonogh
Winner of the 1939 Galway Hurdle

Owner: Dr Michael McDono(u)gh
Trainer: James J. Parkinson, Maddenstown Lodge
Baldoyle 6 June 1938 (O. Moran) Won Summer Maiden 9f flat £41 100/8
Tramore 17 August 1938 (M. Wing) Won Annstown Handicap 10f flat £41 11/10f
Curragh 21 September 1938 (M. Barrett) Won H.M. Plate 2½m flat £208 20/1
Clonmel 13 July 1939 (J. Barrett) Won Thurles Hurdle 13f £44¼ 1/4f
Galway 3 August 1939 (J. Barrett) Won Galway Hurdle Handicap 2m £369 2/1f
Tramore 14 August 1942 (Mr P.J. Lenehan) Won Lismore Plate 12f flat £41 2/7f

Honor's Choice was bred by the executors of the late Martin McDonogh, later passing to his son Dr Michael McDono(u)gh. Unlike his father, Dr Michael liked to spell his name with a 'u'. He worked as a dispensary doctor until he retired to take over the family firm, Thomas McDonogh, a private company of merchants based in Galway.

Trained by the family's preferred trainer, Jim Parkinson, Honor's Choice ran five times unplaced at two years and, after winning a maiden at Baldoyle the following summer, was optimistically allowed to take his chance in the Irish Derby. Way out of his class, he finished last behind Rosewell. However, he won the Galway Hurdle as a four-year-old in 1939, having been beaten in the Stewards' Plate the previous afternoon, enabling the handicapper to get his measure. He never won over jumps again. Retired to stud at Kilmore, Clonmel, he sired Kerstin, one of only four mares to have won the Cheltenham Gold Cup.

ST MARTIN

(Bay gelding 1933 Tommy Atkins – Dorcas by Chosroes)

Breeder: Lady Beatty
Winner of the 1941 Galway Plate

Owner: Miss M.O. Mathieson
Trainer: Cecil Brabazon
Limerick Junction 29 June 1940 (A. Brabazon) Won Cashel Maiden Hurdle 2m £83 5/4f
Limerick Junction 21 August 1940 (A. Brabazon) Won Waterford Chase 2m £44 1/2f
Claremorris 29 August 1940 (A. Brabazon) Walked Over Mayo Chase 2m £49
Listowel 24 September 1940 (A. Brabazon) Won Limerick Plate 2m flat £44 4/5f
Limerick 7 November 1940 (A. Brabazon) Won Garryowen Handicap Chase 3m £85 6/4f
Leopardstown 15 February 1941 (A. Brabazon) Won Ranelagh Handicap Chase 3m £83 5/2jf
Leopardstown 8 March 1941 (A. Brabazon) Won Red Cross Handicap Chase 4m £742 5/2f
Leopardstown 12 July 1941 (A. Brabazon) Won Rathlin Handicap Chase 2½m £83 4/5f
Galway 30 July 1941 (A. Brabazon) Won Galway Plate Handicap 2m 5f £740 6/4f
Leopardstown 26 December 1941 (A. Brabazon) Won Carrickmines Handicap Chase 2½m £88 1/6f
Leopardstown 22 August 1942 (A. Brabazon) Won Foxrock Handicap Chase 2½m £260¼ 3/1
Leopardstown 7 November 1942 (A. Brabazon) Won Clifden Handicap Chase 3m £83 1/2f

When asked what was the best horse he had ever ridden, Aubrey Brabazon invariably replied St Martin, although he reluctantly conceded in his autobiography that
Cottage Rake probably deserved the top spot. On a visit to Aubrey's father Cecil
at Rangers Lodge in 1938, the recently retired Champion Jockey Steve Donoghue
was admiring St Martin, who was unraced at the time. Having discovered his
breeding Donoghue revealed that he had ridden both Tommy Atkins and Dorcas,
the sire and dam. He depressed Cecil Brabazon by informing him that Tommy
Atkins had plenty of speed and Dorcas did not stay 4 furlongs! Brabazon had high
hopes that St Martin would make a chaser but that insight into his pedigree
suggested that he might have difficulty staying the minimum distance of 2 miles.
However, any such fears proved quite groundless because he turned out to be a top
staying steeplechaser, winning the Red Cross, Galway Plate and Foxrock Handicap
Chases and twelve races in all. The abandonment of the 1941 Irish Grand National
due to an outbreak of foot-and-mouth disease denied him his obvious chance of
winning that race, but he still enjoyed a fine season, winning two big chases, the
Red Cross and the Galway Plate. The Red Cross Steeplechase, worth just £2 more
than the Galway Plate, was the richest steeplechase of that year in Ireland, yet

neither St Martin's owner nor his trainer was present to witness the victory. Miss Mathieson was stuck at home in Scotland, marooned by wartime travel restrictions and delays, while Cecil Brabazon was in his sickbed at home in Rangers Lodge.

In 1940 Tom Dreaper had sounded Aubrey Brabazon out about riding for him and St Martin was one of the reasons the jockey declined the offer. It was soon clear that Aubrey was missing out on the rising star Prince Regent, but he was confident that St Martin would give the Dreaper horse a run for his money. The day of reckoning came on Easter Monday 1942 when St Martin took on Prince Regent in the Irish Grand National. With a 7-pound pull at the weights, Aubrey was confident that St Martin would win but a minor injury disrupted his preparation and put his participation in doubt until the very last moment. Although he did not stride out well in the early stages of the race, he ran the injury off and stayed on really well to finish third to Prince Regent and Golden Jack, beaten by two and a half lengths. Aubrey was convinced that the injury had cost him the race. In his heyday St Martin might well have given Prince Regent a run for his money but his career was effectively ended by injury in 1942 and he never won afterwards. Off the course for two years, he returned to racing in 1945, at the age of twelve and way past his best, and never recovered his former form.

GOLDEN JACK

(Bay gelding 1935 Goldcourt – Jacaru by Jackdaw)

Breeder: T. Brady
Winner of the 1942 Galway Plate
Winner of the 1943 Irish Grand National

Owner: Miss Dorothy Paget
Trainer: Charles A. Rogers
Baldoyle 6 July 1940 (Mr P.P. Hogan) Won Coolock Plate 14f flat £78 10/1
Leopardstown 8 March 1941 (W.T. O'Grady) Won Dundrum Maiden Chase 2m £78 4/5f
Mullingar 22 March 1941 (D.L. Moore) Won Mullingar Chase 2m £83 1/1f
Galway 31 July 1941 (D.L. Moore) Won Galway Blazers Handicap Chase 2m 5f £101¾ 5/1
Naas 3 September 1941 (D.L. Moore) Won Meath Handicap Chase 3m £83 4/6f
Limerick 2 October 1941 (D.L. Moore) Won Munster National Handicap Chase 3m £249 11/10jf
Baldoyle 18 October 1941 (D.L. Moore) Won Troytown Handicap Chase 3m £249 1/2f
Leopardstown 8 November 1941 (D.L. Moore) Won Clifden Handicap Chase 3m £88 No SP
Leopardstown 22 November 1941 (D.L. Moore) Won Avonmore Handicap Chase 3m £83 6/4

Baldoyle 4 July 1942 (D.L. Moore) Won Sutton Hurdle 2m £41 8/1

Galway 29 July 1942 (D.L. Moore) Won Galway Plate Handicap 2m 5f £444 7/4f

Fairyhouse 26 April 1943 (D.L. Moore) Won Irish Grand National Handicap 3½m £745 5/2

Dorothy Paget, the eccentric millionaire who owned Golden Jack, never saw the horse in her life, except in photographs. The younger daughter of Lord Queenborough, she was the dominant owner in National Hunt racing at this time and Charlie Rogers was her Irish trainer and manager of her two studs, Killeen and Ballymacoll. In the years leading up to the Second World War, her brilliant Golden Miller won five Cheltenham Gold Cups and the Grand National, while Insurance won two Champion Hurdles. She was less successful in Ireland, winning the Irish Grand National and the Galway Plate only once, with Golden Jack, winner of the Plate in 1942 and the Irish Grand National the following year, and she never owned the winner of the Galway Hurdle. Her horses won 1,532 races before her death in 1960, including Straight Deal in the Derby in 1943.

Golden Jack finished second to Prince Regent in the 1942 Irish Grand National, beaten by a length in receipt of 12 pounds, with the below-par St Martin a gallant third. A hot favourite to win that year's Galway Plate, Golden Jack duly obliged at odds of 7 to 4, beating The Gripper and Drumlargin rather cleverly. Returning to Fairyhouse to take Prince Regent on again in the Irish Grand National of 1943, the handicapper for some reason allotted Golden Jack only 10 stones 3 pounds. Unbelievably having dropped 20 pounds since his second the previous year, having won the Galway Plate in the meantime, Golden Jack was now getting 33 pounds from Prince Regent. However, the champion was held in such high regard that punters reckoned that he would still beat Golden Jack, sending Tom Dreaper's charge off the favourite at 5 to 4.

Dan Moore elected to make the running on Golden Jack, setting a fast pace in an attempt to weary Prince Regent, burdened with 12 stones 7 pounds. The tactic worked like a dream; Prince Regent made a serious jumping error as the pressure mounted and when Tim Hype drove the champion up to Golden Jack, the latter just sprinted away to win by four lengths. On returning to the paddock, Golden Jack and Charlie Rogers were jeered by an angry crowd, disappointed that their champion was beaten and suspicious of the methods employed. The stewards were also suspicious, immediately calling Rogers before them to explain Golden Jack's improvement in form compared with his previous running at Leopardstown. Only after hearing from one of the stewards who officiated at Leopardstown did the Fairyhouse stewards accept Charlie Rogers's explanation. The all-clear from the officials did not placate racegoers, and there were sustained mutterings of foul play, which forced the

Irish National Hunt Steeplechase Committee to investigate. It broke with precedent by reopening the inquiry, after which it issued the following statement:

> The Stewards of the INHS Committee met at the Curragh on Saturday, May 1 1943 to enquire into the running of Golden Jack in the Irish Grand National as compared with the horse's previous running. Having interviewed Mr C.A. Rogers (trainer) and D.L. Moore (rider), they considered Mr Rogers's explanation most unsatisfactory and although not entirely satisfied with his explanation they gave him the benefit of the doubt and severely cautioned him and warned him as to his future conduct. The Stewards considered the Handicapper was also greatly to blame as he appears not to have taken into consideration the horse's previous form.

Golden Jack never won another race. Withdrawn from the 1944 Irish Grand National because Dan Moore was not fit to ride, he was beaten at odds-on in the Galway Blazers Handicap Chase at Galway, finishing a six-length second to Callaly, trained by Willie O'Grady. Golden Jack won twelve races during his career, one on the flat, one over hurdles and ten over fences, and he was one of eight horses to have won both the Galway Plate and the Irish Grand National. Five of those eight won both races in the same year, but Jupiter Tonans, Golden Jack and Feathered Gale won in different years.

SWINDON GLORY

(Bay gelding 1934 Swindon – Rosemint by Orpiment)

Breeder: J.A. Mangan
Winner of the 1943 and 1944 Galway Plate

Owner and trainer J.A. Mangan
Leopardstown 19 February 1938 (Mr J.A. Mangan) Won Corinthian Bumper 2m £44 4/1
Baldoyle 18 March 1938 (Mr J.A. Mangan) Won Raheny Bumper 2m £41 6/4f
Naas 6 January 1940 (D.L. Moore) Won Press Handicap Chase 3m £83 3/1jf
Navan 13 April 1940 (Mr T. Molony) Won Tara Handicap Chase 3m £98 7/2
Leopardstown 12 October 1940 (Mr P.P. Hogan) Won Laragh Handicap Chase 3m £88 1/1
Naas 1 November 1940 (Mr P.P. Hogan) Won Grand National Qualifying Handicap Chase 3m
    £262½ 4/1
Galway 28 July 1943 (A. Brabazon) Won Galway Plate Handicap 2m 5f £444 5/1

Leopardstown 22 July 1944 (W.T. O'Grady) Won Rathlin Handicap Chase 2½m £74 7/2

Galway 1 August 1944 (A. Brabazon) Won Galway Plate Handicap 2m 5f £444 7/2f

Navan 2 November 1946 (A. Brabazon) Won Webster Cup Handicap Chase 3m £222 6/1

Gus Mangan of Castlebagot, Newcastle, Co. Dublin, enjoyed great success at Galway as an owner, trainer and rider. He rode Pucka Ranee to victory in the 1930 Galway Hurdle and Pucka Shikhari to win the Plate the following year. Aubrey Brabazon partnered Swindon Glory, his dual Galway Plate winner in 1943 and 1944. Only the third horse to win the Plate two years running, Swindon Glory's achievement has only been repeated three times in the intervening years, by Ross Sea, Life of a Lord and Ansar. He showed ability as a four-year-old, winning two bumpers and running a respectable third in the Irish Cambridgeshire at the Curragh behind Solford.

Although failing to win in 1939, Swindon Glory won four good chases the following year, including a valuable Grand National qualifier at Naas, before being hit by an injury that kept him off the course for over two years. Aubrey Brabazon described him as a 'good, genuine handicapper that excelled at Galway', but then he never rode the horse before he was injured. Apparently, Gus Mangan trained his horses up and down hills, which Brabazon believed helped the horse to handle the Galway track. Unplaced in the 1945 Galway Plate and runner-up to the highly-rated Keep Faith the following year, Swindon Glory's last victory was in the Webster Cup at Navan. Although sold to England, he was by then incapable of winning even the lowly chases in which he was competing there.

POINT D'ATOUT

(Brown gelding 1936 Vatout – Point Pleasant by Teddy)

Breeder: Bred in France
Winner of the 1942 and 1947 Galway Hurdle

Owner: James V. Rank
Trainer: Noel Cannon
Haydock Park 20 April 1940 (D. Smith) Won Gamekeepers' Handicap 12f flat £333
Trainer: Robert Fetherstonhaugh
Baldoyle 8 February 1941 (Pierce J. Murphy) Won Killester Maiden Hurdle 1½m £78 10/1
Naas 6 January 1942 (J. Costello) Won Leinster Leader Selling Handicap Hurdle 1½m £41 2/1jf

Owner: Miss A.E. Hall

Trainer: Barney Nugent

Navan 21 February 1942 (A. Brabazon) Won Meath Handicap Hurdle 2½m £41 6/1

Navan 18 April 1942 (Mr John Lenehan) Won Harristown Bumper 2m £41 4/1jf

Galway 30 July 1942 (J. Lenehan) Won Galway Hurdle Handicap 2m £220 9/2

Curragh 30 October 1943 (John Power) Dead Heat Irish Cesarewitch Handicap 2m flat £217 10/1

Naas 13 November 1943 (K. Gilsenan) Won Park Handicap Hurdle 2m £74 5/1

Leopardstown 28 December 1943 (K. Gilsenan) Won Shankill Hurdle 2m £74 4/5f

Mullingar 11 January 1947 (J. Brogan) Won Athlone Handicap Hurdle 2¼m £148½ 4/6f

Phoenix Park 7 May 1947 (M. Molony) Won Farmleigh Handicap Hurdle 2m £222 7/1

Galway 31 July 1947 (Mr A.O. Scannell) Won Galway Hurdle Handicap 2m £740 10/1

Roscommon 13 September 1949 (B. Cooper) Won Castle Handicap Hurdle 2m £100 7/1

Selling races may be the lowest standard of race but the occasional good horse was bought out of them down the years. One such fortunate purchase was Point D'Atout, winner of two Galway Hurdles five years apart. Bred in France, he was owned by Prince Regent's owner Jimmy Rank until bought by the famous bloodstock agent Bertie Kerr for £50 after winning a selling hurdle race at Naas. Kerr was acting on behalf of trainer Barney Nugent and would in future race in the green, with a white V back and front and red cap colours of Miss A.E. Hall. Point D'Atout proved an outstanding investment, winning three races including the Galway Hurdle within seven months. Although unplaced in the 1943 Galway Hurdle, he dead-heated with Dorothy Paget's Astrometer for the Irish Cesarewitch later that year. Both dead-heaters headed the market for the 1944 Galway Hurdle and both finished out of the money. Point d'Atout raced on for three years without winning a race of any kind. A change of stables failed to refresh him in 1945 and he returned to Barney Nugent the following year. After three years in the doldrums, he dramatically recovered his form, winning three good hurdle races including a second Galway Hurdle.

ROMAN HACKLE

(Bay gelding 1933 Yutoi – Wanoya by Wavelet's Pride)

Breeder: Captain and Mrs G.W. Hastings
Winner of the 1940 Cheltenham Gold Cup

Owner: A.S. Bellville
Trainer: Captain A. Bankier

Nottingham 15 February 1938 (B. Hobbs) Won Stayers Handicap Hurdle 2¾m £122 9/2

Birmingham 29 November 1938 (F. Walwyn) Won Burton Handicap Hurdle 2m 5f £122 5/2

Owner: Miss Dorothy Paget

Trainer: Owen Anthony, Letcombe Bassett

Newbury 22 February 1939 (G.W. Archibald) Won Spring Chase 3m £332 9/4f

Cheltenham 8 March 1939 (G.W. Archibald) Won Broadway Novice Chase 3m £405 5/2f

Windsor 16 March 1940 (E. Williams) Won Wargrave Chase 2m £112 9/2

Cheltenham 20 March 1940 (E. Williams) Won Gold Cup 3m Chase £495 1/1f

Plumpton 8 March 1941 (E. Williams) Won Ardingly Chase 2m £82 7/2

Trainer: Charles A. Rogers, Balfstown, Mulhuddart, Co. Dublin

Leopardstown 17 February 1945 (D.L. Moore) Won Sandyford Handicap Chase 3m £74 3/1

Galway 1 August 1945 (D.L. Moore) Won Galway Blazers Handicap Chase 2m 5f £178 2/1

Clonmel 4 October 1945 (D.L. Moore) Won Shannon Handicap Chase 3m £89 1/1f

Leopardstown 10 November 1945 (R.J. O'Ryan) Won Leopardstown Handicap Chase 3m
        £178 7/2

George Edwards, a famous theatrical producer, purchased the Ballykisteen Stud, Limerick Junction, Co. Tipperary, in 1901 as a base for his Ascot Gold Cup winner Santoi. Over twenty years later Yutoi, Santoi's Cesarewitch-winning son, was installed there in 1923 and this horse became the sire of Roman Hackle. His dam, Wanoya, had been covered on a number of occasions by Yutoi, but the stud culled the mare, following a reorganization, selling her to Captain and Mrs G.W. Hastings, who had the credit of breeding Roman Hackle. Breeders do not usually name their stock, but the Hastings named this colt Samurai, only to find that his new owner renamed him Roman Hackle.

A big, plain gelding, Roman Hackle was bought out of the stable of Captain A. Bankier, formerly assistant trainer to Jack Anthony, by Dorothy Paget, after he won two handicap hurdles in 1938. The gelding impressed over fences for his new trainer, Owen Anthony, and was strongly fancied for the 1940 Cheltenham Gold Cup. War regulations required land to be ploughed to grow crops, which meant that fields that had been left in grass for generations had to be cut up and part of Cheltenham racecourse had to be set aside for that purpose. This forced the big race to be reduced in distance to 3 miles and the meeting reduced to two days, but along came the snow to cause the second (Gold Cup) day to be postponed for a week. Dorothy Paget and Owen Anthony enjoyed a good first day, winning the two big races, the Champion Hurdle with Solford and the National Hunt Handicap Chase with Kilstar, but their attempt to bring off the big treble had to wait for a week. Meanwhile, Roman Hackle was re-routed to Windsor, to run in a 2-mile chase, a distance really too short for him, but he won impressively before coming back to Cheltenham four days later. Supported to even money for the Gold Cup, he won the race in style, with fans optimistically predicting that he would be another multi-Gold Cup winner like Golden Miller.

The horse never lived up to his reputation even accepting that steeplechasing was severely restricted by the war, and he was the beaten favourite in the 1941 Gold Cup. When steeplechasing was suspended in Britain, he was sent over to Charlie Rogers, Miss Paget's Irish trainer, to race in Ireand. Although he raced for two years there without winning, he finally hit form in 1945, winning four races including a sensational defeat of the Irish hero Prince Regent at Leopardstown. Ridden by Bobby O'Ryan, he won by a short head, but the champion was conceding no less than 3 stones to the in-form former Gold Cup winner. This is only one of many lines of form that prove the ability of Prince Regent and explains Tom Dreaper's reluctance to proclaim Arkle as the best horse he ever trained.

KING OF THE JUNGLE

(Bay horse 1940 Sir Walter Raleigh – Sonninia by Happy Warrior or Sonning)

Breeder: G. Ainscough
Winner of the 1945 and 1946 Galway Hurdle
Winner of the 1946 Liverpool Handicap Hurdle

Owner: G. Ainscough
Trainer: William T. O'Grady
Mallow 26 April 1943 (Herbert Holmes) Won Mount Ruby Plate 9f flat £74 2/1jf
Baldoyle 11 September 1943 (Joseph Canty) Won Howth Plate 9f flat £74 10/1
Listowel 22 September 1943 (G. Cooney) Won County Handicap 12f flat £74 4/6f
Clonmel 28 October 1943 (G. Cooney) Won Slieve Bloom Handicap 13f flat £74 2/1jf

Owner: Richard McIlhagga
Trainer: Barney Nugent
Leopardstown 19 February 1944 (D. Morgan) Won Stand Maiden Hurdle 2m £74 4/1jf
Leopardstown 10 March 1945 (K. Gilsenan) Won Dalkey Handicap Hurdle 2m £148 5/1
Baldoyle 17 March 1945 (K. Gilsenan) Won Sutton Handicap Hurdle 2m £149 4/1
Phoenix Park 2 May 1945 (D. Morgan) Won Eglinton Handicap Hurdle 2m £74 4/1
Naas 26 May 1945 (D. Morgan) Won Killiney Handicap Hurdle 2m £370 4/1
Galway 1 August 1945 (D. Morgan) Won Galway Hurdle Handicap 2m £444 3/1f

Aintree 3 April 1946 (D. Morgan) Won Liverpool Handicap Hurdle 2m 1f £1,020 7/1
Galway 1 August 1946 (D. Morgan) Won Galway Hurdle Handicap 2m £444 5/2f (awarded race)

Bred by Mr G. Ainscough, King of the Jungle had a flat pedigree and was put into training with Bob Featherstonhaugh at Loughbrown Cottage, Curragh. After he had run nine times at two without winning, Mr Ainscough realized that his horse's future was probably 'over the sticks', and with this in mind he transferred King of the Jungle to Willie O'Grady's stable. Having won four races, albeit minor ones, on the flat for Mr Ainscough, he was purchased by the northern sportsman Dick McIlhagga, a wealthy toy importer who later enjoyed considerable success on the turf with Princess Trudy (Irish 1,000 Guineas) and Impeccable (winner of fifteen races including the City and Suburban). He transferred King of the Jungle to Barney Nugent at the Ward, which was much nearer his northern home, and the horse won eight races for him, including two Galway Hurdles. It must be said that he was probably fortunate to have won a Galway Hurdle at all because in 1945 the gambled-on Desdichado made a terrible blunder at the last and was only beaten by a head: The following year King of the Jungle was beaten fair and square by Fair Pearl, only to be subsequently awarded the race on a technicality. King of the Jungle, an entire horse, was retired to stud in Co. Meath, where he sired Royal Day, twice winner of the Galway Plate.

ALBERONI

(Chestnut gelding 1943 His Reverence – Lady Pamela by McKinley)

Breeder: A.D. Wingfield
Winner of the 1952 Galway Plate
Winner of the 1952 Irish Grand National

Owner: Lt-Col. A.D. Wingfield
Trainer: M.V. O'Brien
Limerick Junction 28 October 1948 (A. Brabazon) Won Greenpark Maiden Hurdle 1½m £100 7/4f
Clonmel 4 November 1948 (A. Brabazon) Won Cahir Handicap Hurdle 2m £133½ 4/6f

Owner: W.A. Smith
Trainer: M.V. O'Brien
Baldoyle 2 July 1949 (A. Brabazon) Won Marino Handicap Hurdle 2m £202 1/1f
Tramore 15 August 1949 (A. Brabazon) Won Holiday Maiden 12f flat £133½ 2/7f
Worcester 20 September 1949 (T. Molony) Won Hagley Handicap Hurdle 2m £204 8/11f

Naas 4 February 1950 (A. Brabazon) Won Rathcoole Handicap Hurdle 2m £133½ 1/1f

Leopardstown 15 July 1950 (A. Brabazon) Won Leopardstown Handicap Hurdle 2m £478¾ 5/4f

Leopardstown 17 February 1951 (M. Molony) Won Milltown Novice Chase 2m £202 13/8f

Owner: H.H.M. Stanley

Trainer: M.V. O'Brien

Limerick Junction 3 April 1952 (L. Stephens) Won Limerick Junction Handicap Chase 3m £100 4/7f

Fairyhouse 14 April 1952 (L. Stephens) Won Irish Grand National Handicap 3¼m £1,485 6/1

Galway 30 July 1952 (L. Stephens) Won Galway Plate Handicap 2m 5f £1,110 3/1jf

Phoenix Park 6 August 1952 (W.P. Riley) Won Monkstown Handicap 2m flat £286 7/2

Naas 1 November 1952 (L. Stephens) Won Blessington Handicap Chase 3m £202 9/4f

Limerick 28 December 1953 (D.O'Sullivan) Won Mid-Winter Chase 2m 1f £100 7/4f

Bred by Tony Wingfield, who put him into training with Vincent O'Brien, Alberoni won valuable races over hurdles and over fences, including the Galway Plate and the Irish Grand National – one of five horses to win both races in the same year. Having won one flat and six hurdle races, he was sent chasing and ran really well in the 1951 Galway Plate, finishing second, three lengths behind St Kathleen II. After this he was sold to 'Horrible Hugh' Stanley, the younger brother of the 18th Earl of Derby.

Vincent O'Brien had been 'messing around' with Alberoni early in his career. The stewards noticed, and when he won at Baldoyle in July 1949 they pounced. Demanding an explanation for the horse's improved form, they accepted O'Brien's explanation most reluctantly, making it quite clear that they had 'grave doubts' about the matter. Three years later he was in hot water again over the running and riding of Alberoni. Suspicious that the horse was winning over fences and running poorly on the flat, the stewards were watching him closely. After being unplaced at the Phoenix Park on 5 July 1952 when unfancied and ridden by O'Brien's little-known apprenctice John Relihan, he then proceeded to win over fences in Killarney before returning to the Phoenix Park a month later. Ridden by the English apprentice William Reily, he landed a huge gamble and Vincent O'Brien naturally proffered the excuse that Reily was much more capable than Relihan. This was obvious, leaving the stewards with little option but to caution Vincent about his use of jockeys. Still not satisfied, however, they began to monitor the running and riding of O'Brien's horses, gathering sufficient evidence to suspend him for three months in April 1954 for their inconsistent running.

Hugh Stanley, Alberoni's new owner, insisted that Len Stephens, second jockey to Arthur Thompson at Neville Crump's English stable, should ride the horse in his races. When Alberoni was running, Stanley's friends, including Fred Pontin, the holiday camp owner, came over from England in force to see the race, to feast on good food and to bring home decent supplies, which were denied to them at home because of the wartime austerity measures still in force.

Alberoni came back to Galway in 1952 to contest the Plate, having won the Irish Grand National in the meantime, and was made joint-favourite, but had to pull out all the stops to beat his stable companion, Lucky Dome, by a short head. Alberoni was Vincent O'Brien's only winner of the Galway Plate.

AMBER POINT

(Bay gelding 1948 Steel-point – Amber Castle by Gilling Castle)

Breeder: E. Cunningham
Winner of the 1954 and 1956 Galway Plate

Owner: N. Galway-Greer
Trainer: Patrick Sleator, Grange Con
Down Royal 9 May 1953 (Mr F. Flood) Won Stand House Hunt Chase 3m £100 11/10f

Owner: John Crow
Trainer: Patrick Sleator, Grange Con
Down Royal 24 Mar 1954 (Mr F. Flood) Won March Hunt Chase 3m £100 6/4f
Dundalk 15 May 1954 (Mr F. Flood) Won Sweet Afton Cup Hunt Chase 3m £286 4/6f

Owner: Anne M.B. Biddle/Mrs R. More O'Ferrall
Trainer: Patrick Sleator, Grange Con
Galway 28 July 1954 (C. Sleator) Won Galway Plate Handicap Chase 2m 5f £1,110 6/1f
Navan 21 January 1956 (C. Sleator) Won Bective Novice Hurdle 3m £133 5/2
Galway 1 August 1956 (P.A. Farrell) Won Galway Plate Handicap 2m 5f £1,160 2/1f
Phoenix Park 11 August 1956 (L. Ward) Won Naul Maiden 2m flat £202 4/6f
Curragh 5 October 1957 (L. Ward) Won J.T. Rogers Memorial Gold Cup 2m £286 1/2f

Amber Point, bred by E. Cunningham, was initially owned by Nat Galway-Greer, the famous horse dealer from Dunboyne, Co. Meath, and began his career in Hunter Chases. After winning the Sweet Afton Cup, he was purchased by Mrs Biddle and proved more than capable at a higher level, winning five races: two Galway Plates, two flat races and one over hurdles. Winner of the Plate in 1954, when wearing down the flattering Dovetail, Amber Point was sidelined by a leg injury that kept him off the course for all of 1955, but made a triumphant return to

Galway in 1956 to win the Plate a second time. A winning favourite, beating New Hope and Brookling easily, he became the fifth horse to win the Galway feature race more than once. Mrs Biddle also owned his own-brother Knight Errant, winner of the Galway Plate, the Galway Hurdle and the Punchestown Cup.

NAS NA RIOGH

(Brown mare 1947 Cariff – Breviary by His Reverence)

Breeder: Peter Keely
Dam of Mill House

Owner: Mrs B. M. Lawlor
Trainer: Thomas J. Taaffe, Rathcoole, Co. Dublin
Punchestown 29 April 1952 (P. Taaffe) Won Blessington Hunt Cup 2m £205 11/10f (Winner Cool
        Fellow subsequently disqualified on a technicality)
Fairyhouse 6 April 1953 (P. Taaffe) Won Dunboyne Handicap Chase 2¼m £202 10/1
Bellewstown 1 July 1953 (P. Taaffe) Won Drogheda Tradesmen's Handicap Chase 2m £202 9/4f
Killarney 21 July 1953 (P. Taaffe) Won Crafty Prince Cup Handicap Chase 2m £133 7/4f
Galway 29 July 1953 (P. Taaffe) Won Ballybrit Chase 2¼m £133 2/7f
Galway 30 July 1953 (P. Taaffe) Won Corrib Hurdle 2m £133 6/4f
Punchestown 27 April 1954 (P. Taaffe) Won Drogheda Chase 2m £202 4/9f
Naas 17 June 1954 (P. Taaffe) Won Grangecon Hurdle 2m 1f £202 2/1f
Limerick Junction 19 August 1954 (P. Taaffe) Won Mangerton Handicap Chase 2m £202 7/2

Nas na Riogh was owned by Mrs Lawlor, a well-known hotelier from Naas who did the catering on many Irish racecourses at the time. By the Irish 2,000 Guineas winner Cariff, she went chasing at four years but, like so many chasers, her confidence was shaken by a couple of falls. Transferred from J. Burke's stable to that of Thomas J. Taaffe, she benefited from the sympathetic handling of the trainer's son Pat Taaffe, to develop into a useful handicap chaser. She also had the speed to win over hurdles, being allowed to take her chance in the 1954 Galway Hurdle although she finished unplaced, before retiring to Mrs Lawlor's stud. Mated with King Hal in 1956, she produced the giant Mill House, destined to be one of the best chasers of all time until bumping into Arkle.

Mill House joined the Thomas Taaffe's stable and was hunted regularly by Pat Taaffe, ironically destined to be Arkle's jockey. Having impressively won a Maiden Hurdle at Naas with Pat Taaffe in the saddle, Mill House fell in the

Champion Novice Hurdle at Punchestown, crashing out of the race at the third last hurdle when going really well. He was ridden on that occasion by the English jockey Dave Dick, later to take advantage of Devon Loch's dramatic fall on the flat to win the Grand National on ESB, who confirmed Pat Taaffe's opinion that this was a high-class horse. Then bloodstock agent Jack Doyle stepped in, buying Mill House for an English client. Initially trained by Syd Dale (who liked to call himself LSD – pounds, shillings and pence) at Epsom, he was later transferred to Fulke Walwyn at Lambourn. For him he won the 1963 Cheltenham Gold Cup before beating Arkle to win the Hennessy Gold Cup. Proclaimed a true champion, Mill House never beat Arkle again and it was the latter that turned out to be the true champion. It is often said that the brilliant Irish champion broke Mill House's heart because at his prime he was a horse of the highest class, although clearly inferior to Arkle.

UMM

(Brown gelding 1947 Birikan – Ecilace by Interlace)

Breeder: Peter Doyle
Winner of the 1955 Galway Plate
Winner of the 1955 Irish Grand National

Owner: Mrs P.G. Gray
Trainer: William T. O'Grady
Mallow 11 June 1952 (Mr B. Whelan) Won Ballyclough Bumper 2m £99½ 1/2f
Tramore 12 August 1952 (Mr J.R. Cox) Won Suir Maiden Hurdle 2m £99½ 5/4f
Limerick 9 October 1952 (P.J. Doyle) Won Adare Handicap Hurdle 2m £133 9/4
Clonmel 16 October 1952 (P.J. Doyle) Won Suir Handicap Hurdle 2m £133 6/4f
Limerick Junction 23 October 1952 (P.J. Doyle) Won Fethard Handicap Hurdle 1½m £100 6/4f

Owner: J.G. de Pret Roose
Trainer: Daniel L. Moore
Roscommon 25 August 1953 (C. Grassick) Won Castle Handicap Hurdle 2m £100 4/6f

Owner: Mrs H.B. Brassey
Trainer: Daniel L. Moore
Baldoyle 26 September 1953 (C. Grassick) Won Sutton Handicap Hurdle 2m £202 7/4f
Cheltenham 14 October 1953 (B. Marshall) Won Tewkesbury Chase 3m £259 7/4f
Trainer: Captain C.T.A. Carlos-Clarke

Chepstow 24 October 1953 (J. Dowdeswell) Won Novice Chase 2m £102 10/11f
Leicester 23 November 1953 (B. Marshall) Won Belvoir Chase 2m £204 5/2

Owner: C. Rooney
Trainer: George H. Wells
Fairyhouse 11 April 1955 (P. Taaffe) Won Irish Grand National Handicap 3¼m £1,485 100/7
Tramore 30 May 1955 (A. Power) Won County Handicap Hurdle 2m £202 6/1
Galway 27 July 1955 (P. Taaffe) Won Galway Plate Handicap 2m 5f £1,110 11/4jf
Tramore 17 August 1955 (A.P. Thompson) Won Tramore Handicap Hurdle 2m £286 5/4f

Bred by Peter Doyle, Umm was sold as a yearling for 400 guineas to Pat Grey of
Coole Abbey, Clonmel, who gave him to his wife as a present. Pat and Anne Gray
were patrons of Willie O'Grady's stable at Ballynonty, near Thurles, where Icy
Calm, their winner of the 1951 Irish Grand National, was trained. The Grays
tended to be sellers if offered a decent price, parting with Icy Calm, Umm and
Sundew all within a four-year period. Icy Calm was sold with a Grand National
engagement and so too was Sundew, winner of the big race in 1957, and when Dan
Moore put in a bid for Umm it was accepted.

After winning over hurdles at Roscommon, the first of a winning sequence of
five, Umm was sold again, to Mrs Brassey, and transferred to Sandy Carlos-Clarke,

Steeplechasing at Galway

the forty-year-old ex-film actor, professional boxer, cowboy and Second World War commando, now training at Hill House, Lambourn. Having won twice for his new trainer, Umm lost his form, falling and pulling up in his races, and Mrs Brassey decided to send him back to Dan Moore. The former jockey George Wells, at the time starting up as a trainer, picked him out as a possible Irish Grand National winner, convincing two of his patrons, Con Rooney and Tom Griffin, to buy him.

Lining up at Fairyhouse on Easter Monday 1955, having had only one race in over a year when second in a hurdle race at Mullingar a fortnight previously, Umm scored a surprise victory; his jockey, Pat Taaffe, who had just won the Aintree Grand National on Quare Times, became the first jockey to win both the English and the Irish Grand Nationals in the same year. Umm went on to win the Galway Plate later that summer, becoming only the fifth horse, to win the Irish Grand National and the Galway Plate in the same year, joining Springfield Maid, Tipperary Boy, Red Park and Alberoni. Again ridden by Pat Taaffe, he survived a mistake at the second last to get up on the line to beat Athenian by a head.

Arthur Thompson, a former Irish Champion Apprentice and winner of two Grand Nationals, on Sheila's Cottage and Teal, rode Umm to victory in a hurdle at Tramore next time out. Unfortunately, it was Umm's final victory because he broke a leg in the Marino Handicap Hurdle at Baldoyle, on 10 September 1955, when ridden by Paddy Powell, and was destroyed. He had plenty of speed, and talent in abundance, but for some reason had more than his fair share of falls, many of them over hurdles. Mr C.B. 'Buster' Harty, who rode Umm when he fell in the Mullingar Cup, reported that the horse galloped straight into the fence, never appearing to have seen it at all. Umm's dam, Ecilace subsequently bred Foinavon (by Vulgan), winner of the shambolic Grand National of 1967, and his third dam, Miss Eger, bred Clonree, winner of Galway Plate in 1920.

KNIGHT ERRANT

(Bay gelding 1950 Steel-point – Amber Castle by Gilling Castle)

Breeder: E. Cunningham
Winner of the 1957 Galway Plate
Winner of the 1958 Galway Hurdle

Owner: Mrs A.B. Biddle
Trainer: Patrick Sleator, Grange Con

Mullingar 21 March 1956 (Mr F. Flood) Won Greville Cup Hunt Chase 3m £100 5/2

Naas 19 May 1956 (Mr F. Flood) Won Wicklow Hunt Chase 3m £202 11/10f

Gowran Park 24 May 1956 (Mr F. Flood) Won Tetratema Cup Hunt Chase 3m 1f £202 4/6f

Galway 2 August 1956 (P.A. Farrell) Won Corrib Hurdle 2m £133 4/6f

Kilbeggan 27 August 1956 (C. Sleator) Won Ballinagore Maiden 13f flat £100 1/3f

Dundalk 12 July 1957 (H.R. Beasley) Won Dundalk Handicap Hurdle 2m £202 7/4f

Galway 31 July 1957 (H.R. Beasley) Won Galway Plate Handicap 2m 5f £1,160 4/1f

Galway 31 July 1958 (H.R. Beasley) Won Galway Hurdle Handicap 2m £748 5/2f

Punchestown 25 April 1961 (T.E. Hyde) Won Punchestown Cup Handicap Chase 3m £893¾
      100/7

Nowadays most racehorses begin their careers in bumpers, flat races specially designed for jumping horses, before going hurdling and finally going on to race over fences. In the past, even in living memory, jumping horses raced regularly over both hurdles and fences, as well as contesting races on the flat. The normal route for a modern horse is to win the Galway Hurdle and then try for the Galway Plate, just as Ansar and More Rainbows did. However, that was not always the case and of the three horses to have won both races, only Ansar won the Hurdle first. Blancona and Knight Errant both did the double backwards, winning the Plate the first year and the Hurdle the next.

Knight Errant was an own-brother to, and stable companion of, Amber Point, twice winner of the Plate and third to Biddy Meehan's Tymon Castle and John McShain's Ballybrittas in the 1957 Galway Hurdle. Coming to racing via the hunting field, point-to-points and hunter chases, he beat Mr What, the 1958 Grand National winner, in the Corrib Hurdle in 1956. What Amber Point narrowly failed to do in 1957, Knight Errant achieved in style in 1958, winning the Galway Hurdle easily, with Bobby Beasley up. Unbelievably, it took him nearly three years to win again, and he would only win once more. Placed seventh, fourth and ninth in successive Irish Grand Nationals, he finally came good again at Punchestown but failed to win another race, despite being one of the Sleator horses selected to run in England under the Arthur Thomas banner. When that failed, Mrs Biddle took him back home to see if Tommy Shaw could do anything with him. If a maestro could not do it, Shaw had no chance and Knight Errant ran for the last time in March 1963, finishing last of four finishers in a handicap chase at Leopardstown.

ROSS SEA

(Brown gelding 1956 Arctic Star – Chloris II by Chateau Bouscaut)

Breeder: Lt-Col. and Mrs James Silcock
Winner of the 1964 and 1965 Galway Plate

Owner: C. Mahlon Kline
Trainer: M.V. O'Brien, Ballydoyle, Cashel
Phoenix Park 19 March 60 (G. Bougoure) Won Athlumney Handicap 10f flat £202 4/5f

Owner: John A. Wood
Trainer: A.S. O'Brien, South Lodge, Carrick-on-Suir
Leopardstown 17 February 1962 (G.W. Robinson) Won Stillorgan Maiden Hurdle 2m £202 4/7f
Fairyhouse 24 April 1962 (G.W. Robinson) Won Fingall Hurdle 2m £612¾ 5/2
Leopardstown 26 December 1962 (Mr W.A. McLernon) Won Glencairn Handicap Hurdle 1m 5f
     £372 2/1jf
Naas 2 March 1963 (S. Mellor) Won Robertstown Handicap Hurdle 2m 1f £370 5/1

Owner: Mrs Gillian Buchanan
Trainer: A.S. O'Brien, South Lodge, Carrick-on-Suir
Sligo 17 June 1964 (H.R. Beasley) Won Yeats County Handicap Chase 2½m £158½ 5/1
Galway 29 July 1964 (S. Mellor) Won Galway Plate Handicap Chase 2m 5f £1,530 9/2f
Mallow 17 April 65 (T. Carberry) Won Holiday Chase 2m £203 7/4
Galway 28 July 1965 (S. Mellor) Won Galway Plate Handicap Chase 2m 5f £1,900 8/1

The success of Ballymoss had hastened Vincent O'Brien's move from a jumping to a flat-race trainer, bringing a new breed of owner into Ballydoyle. One of these was Mahlon Kline, a wealthy pharmaceutical manufacturer, who bought Ross Sea on looks and the small, unattractive El Toro on his racecourse form. A half-brother to Trouville, third in the Irish 2,000 Guineas, and an own-brother to Arctic Sea, destined to win the 1959 Anglesey Stakes, Ross Sea was bred in Co. Tipperary by Lt-Colonel and Mrs James Silcock. He ran twice unplaced at two but it was in the highest class, the Anglesey and the National Stakes, and his three-year-old career got off to a flying start with a win over 10 furlongs at the Curragh, providing Garnie Bougure, Vincent's new Australian stable jockey, with his first Irish winner.

Brought back to 7 furlongs at the next Curragh meeting, Ross Sea was the O'Brien second string but ran a 'blinder' to be narrowly beaten by Sovereign Path, trained by Cecil Brabazon, the pair being eight lengths clear of the field. Suitably impressed, Bougoure elected to ride Ross Sea in the Irish 2,000 Guineas rather than eventual winner, El Toro – yet another jockey to pick the wrong horse. Reverting to 10 furlongs, Ross Sea won at the Curragh on Irish Derby Day but was well beaten in the Warren Stakes at Goodwood. Having won the Royal Whip at the Curragh, he was sent to Manchester to contest the famous November Handicap. Forty-nine horses lined up for the race. John Benstead's Operatic Society caused mayhem at the start, charging the tapes, unseating Ken Gethin and bolting up the course, delaying the start by fifteen minutes. Despite these antics, Operatic Society got off to a flying start and was always amongst the leaders, kicking clear at the distance. Geoff Lewis on Ross Sea gradually threaded his way through the pack to get into a challenging position only to find that the leader had flown. Getting the first run, Operatic Society won the race by two lengths from Ross Sea, who finished a clear, and possibly unlucky, second.

Ross Sea began his four-year-old career with a narrow win in a handicap at the Phoenix Park in March 1960 but a combination of events kept him off the course for nearly six months. First he was proving difficult to train; secondly he got caught up in the 'Chamour Affair', which led to Vincent O'Brien being warned off the turf in May; and thirdly he was gelded. Chamour had won the Ballysax Maiden Plate at the Curragh on 20 April but the routine post-race dope test turned out to be positive. Nobody had any idea how the prohibited substance was administered to the colt or by whom. His owner Walter Burmann offered a £5,000 reward for information, but none was forthcoming. However, according to the rules in force at the time the trainer was responsible if a horse was doped, whether or not he had anything to do with the actual act. Although the stewards never intended to suggest that Vincent O'Brien had actually doped Chamour, he was the trainer and as such was responsible for ensuring his horses were not doped by anyone. A warning-off sentence was much more severe than a suspension because it meant that the person was not allowed to attend a race meeting or to enter a licensed training stable. That meant that Vincent O'Brien could not enter his own stable yard or live in his own house unless he closed down his training stable, which he did not want to do. The only way out of this quandary was for him to exchange houses with his brother Phonsie. Overnight Ross Sea had a new trainer, A.S. O'Brien rather than M.V. O'Brien.

Phonsie O'Brien was closely involved with Vincent during his riding career being the stable's amateur jockey. With the most powerful jumping stable behind him, he was Champion Amateur Rider in Ireland twice and had ridden Royal Tan into second place behind Nickle Coin in the 1951 Grand National. However, he only rode one winner at Galway during his career, Kilballyowen in a bumper in

1953, who was also trained by Vincent. When Vincent began his move into flat racing, Phonsie had to look to the future and in 1956 began training a small string of jumpers at South Lodge, Carrick-on-Suir. He was the perfect man to 'hold the fort' at Ballydoyle and did more than just keep the stable intact; he managed to keep the winners flowing to such an extent that he finished the season as the Champion Trainer in Ireland. Chamour, the horse that had caused all the trouble, came out and won the Irish Derby, successfully passing the post-race dope test and drawing a spontaneous roar of 'We want Vincent!' from the spectators. Most racegoers could not believe that a leading trainer would dope a Derby winner in order to win a modest maiden race. In recognition of the public disquiet over the affair, the stewards reduced Vincent's bad to one year, and he took charge of Ballydoyle again in May 1961.

Phonsie moved out, followed shortly afterwards by Ross Sea. Difficult to train and obviously not good enough for the flat, the horse's future was over jumps and not in Ballydoyle, which was now an exclusively flat-racing stable. At this point Mahlon Kline sold him to John A. Wood, a prosperous Cork builder who loved a tilt at the ring. After unplaced runs in the Irish Cambridgeshire and the Naas November Handicap, he made his hurdling debut at Leopardstown on St Stephen's Day 1961. Ridden by Phonsie's jockey Willie Robinson, he was made an odds-on favourite but could only finish second to the more experienced Moonsun, trained by Aubrey Brabazon. A fortnight later he returned to Leopardstown for a hurdle race; once again was the odds-on favourite and just as before found another horse too good, being beaten by a neck by Winning Fair, the subsequent Champion Hurdler.

Despite these two setbacks, Ross Sea had solid hurdling form and when he reappeared at Leopardstown in February 1962 for the Stillorgan Maiden Hurdle he was considered a good thing and duly obliged. Sent over to Cheltenham for the Gloucestershire Hurdle (Division 1), he led over the last but was caught on the run-in, finishing third to Tripacer and Trelawny. Having won the Fingal Hurdle at Fairyhouse, he was a well-beaten favourite in the Champion Novice Hurdle at Punchestown but later won handicaps at Leopardstown and Naas, when Stan Mellor was up.

Unplaced in Winning Fair's Champion Hurdle at Cheltenham in March 1962, Ross Sea had ability but looked to be ungenuine and consequently often raced in a hood. That apparatus failed to do the trick in the Galway Hurdle, in which he finished down the field behind Snow Trix. It was therefore decided to send him chasing. It took a long time for him to get going over fences despite an encouraging first run in the Independent Cup at Leopardstown in November 1963, when he was runner-up to the useful Rainlough. He was still a maiden over fences when starting favourite for the Prince of Wales Handicap Chase at Punchestown, and again was beaten, a moderate third to Devenish Artist, after which John Wood sold him to Gillian Buchanan. Then he did what he had never done before: fell in his next two chases. Appearing to have learned a lesson, Ross Sea was foot perfect next time out, winning his first steeplechase at Sligo in June 1964. Although beaten by a short head at Killarney, Ross Sea was obviously coming into form and with Stan Mellor, the former English Champion Jockey, aboard was a winning favourite in the Galway Plate, beating the veteran Highfield Lad by one and a half lengths. Decent chasers like Height O'Fashion, Loving Record and Baxier finished behind Ross Sea that day, and Mrs Buchanan's prize of £1,530 was an unbelievable turn, since she had bought the horse only three months previously.

Ross Sea returned to contest the Galway Plate again the following year, having won only once, at Mallow, in the interim. On this occasion the horse had 11 pounds more to carry, and although Stan Mellor was again taking the mount punters did not fancy his chances of emulating Tipperary Boy, Clonsheever and Swindon Glory by winning the top summer handicap chase twice in succession. Arkloin, winner at Bellewstown, from Tom Dreaper's powerful jumping stable and ridden by Pat Taaffe, started favourite at 3 to 1, with Ross Sea an 8-to-1 chance, supported by the once-a-year racegoers who had seen him win the previous year. Also in the race was Mahlon Kline's Arctic Sea, an own-brother to Ross Sea, who was also trained by Phonsie O'Brien but a 20-to-1 outsider. Arctic Sea crashed out of the race at the second fence, but a cool ride from Stan Mellor brought Ross Sea with a late run that took him past Greek Lad and Ben Hannon on the run-in, drawing away to win easily by three lengths. That was the last of Ross Sea's twelve victories. Mrs Buchanan did not persevere with the horse long afterwards, passing him on to Mrs J. Jones, in whose name and colours he ran in the 1966 Plate. He never looked likely to emulate Tipperary Boy, eventually finishing last of the eleven runners behind Cappawhite, Splash and Arctic Sea.

When Ross Sea lined up for the 1967 Galway Plate it was for new connections yet again, now carrying the white with royal blue collar, cuffs and cap of Mrs M.F. Cunningham, a patron of the Francis Flood stable, and ridden by the reigning English Champion Jockey Josh Gifford. The top English riders were available to ride at Galway because the meeting took place during the jumping close season across the Irish Sea. Josh's brother, Macer, was also at Galway that year, riding Rock Venture for Willie Rooney and Stan Mellor rode Arctic Sea for Phonsie. The Gifford brothers played a prominent part in the race but Irishman Bobby Coonan beat them all on Royal Day, by a neck, from Rock Venture, with Ross Sea six lengths further back in third place. Afterwards Ross Sea was unplaced in three top handicap chases before being sent to England, where he was killed in his first race, being brought down, and breaking his neck in a handicap chase at Windsor in January 1968.

TICONDEROGA

(Bay gelding 1959 Talgo – Marjorie Castle by Windsor Slipper)

Breeder: Mrs B. Yorke-Reid
Winner of the 1964 Players Navy Cut Amateur Handicap
Winner of the 1965 Galway Hurdle

Owner: Col. James Reid
Trainer: John Oxx, Currabeg, Curragh
Phoenix Park 26 May 1962 (J. Larkin) Won Harcourt Handicap 9f flat £414¾ 9/4
Leopardstown 21 July 1962 (J. Larkin) Won Hennessy Handicap 12f flat £1,081¼ 8/1
Curragh 20 October 1962 (P. Sullivan) Won October Handicap 12f flat £601¾ 8/1
Trainer: Charles L. Weld, Rosewell House, Curragh
Galway 28 July 64 (Mr D.K. Weld) Won Amateur Handicap 2m £1,077¼ 100/7
Baldoyle 20 February 1965 (J. Malone) Won Balgriffin Handicap Hurdle 1¾m £287 3/1
Leopardstown 10 May 1965 (Mr D.K. Weld) Won Kingsway QR Handicap Hurdle 2m £1,066 2/1f
Galway 29 July 1965 (P. Powell Jr) Won Guinness Hurdle Handicap 2m £1,975¾ 15/2

Ticonderoga was one of the twenty-four runners in the inaugural Irish Sweeps Derby in 1962, the richest race ever run in Europe up to that time. A 200-to-1 rank outsider and John Oxx's second string, Ticonderoga was a no-hoper but his stable companion Arctic Storm was fancied and ultimately finished second, beaten by a short head by Tambourine II. Bred by Mrs B. Yorke-Reid, Ticonderoga raced in her husband's name and was by Talgo, winner of the 1956 Irish Derby and runner-up to the great Ribot in the Prix de l'Arc de Triomphe. He was an own-brother to Biscayne, winner of the Irish St Leger. Colonel and Mrs Reid lived in New York and had horses in training with John Oxx and Charlie Weld in Ireland and in England with Ryan Jarvis, who won an Irish 1,000 Guineas with Front Row. Ticonderoga won three good handicaps at three years, after which Colonel Reid sent him to Charlie Weld, to be gelded and trained to race over hurdles.

He won the Players Navy Cut Amateur Handicap at Galway in 1964, ridden by the trainer's son Dermot Weld on the eve of his sixteenth birthday. The following year, ridden by Paddy Powell Jr, he won the Galway Hurdle, beating the rank outsider Tinker's Hill and the fast-finishing Hunch. At the Listowel meeting in September 1966, ridden by Mr Dermot Weld, he ran in the Double Diamond Handicap Hurdle and was involved in a pile-up when a horse named Easy Money slipped up on the flat, bringing down Ticonderoga, which in turn brought down KO. Dermot Weld was injured, although not seriously, but his gallant mount received fatal injuries in the fall.

ROYAL DAY

(Bay/brown gelding 1957 King of the Jungle – Sunny Birthday)

Breeder: Patrick Dunne Cullinan
Winner of the 1967 and 1969 Galway Plate

Owner: Patrick Dunne Cullinan
Trainer: Patrick Sleator, Grange Con
Gowran Park 26 July 62 (Mr F. Flood) Won Brichfield NH flat 2m £168 2/1
Leopardstown 29 September 1962 (Mr F. Flood) Won Johnstown NH flat 2m £203 5/2
Naas 30 March 63 (C. Finnegan) Won Clane Maiden Hurdle 2m 1f £203 4/5f
Bangor-on-Dee 6 April 63 (H.R Beasley) Won Dee Novice Hurdle 3m £204 4/5f
Leopardstown 19 November 1966 (R. Coonan) Won Lehaunstown Handicap Hurdle 2m 3f £592 7/1
Punchestown 15 December 1966 (R. Coonan) Won Ballycahan Handicap Hurdle 2½m £287 1/1f
Mullingar 11 February 1967 (R. Coonan) Won Rathluirc Cup Chase 2m 1f £203 4/5f
Fairyhouse 27 March 1967 (W.T. Bourke) Won Grange Chase 2½m £432¼ 11/8f
Mullingar 13 June 1967 (R. Coonan) Won Tullamore Novice Chase 2½m £287 1/2f
Galway 2 August 1967 (R. Coonan) Won Galway Plate Handicap 2m 5f £1,900 19/2
Punchestown 11 October 1967 (F. Shortt) Won Double Diamond Handicap Chase 2½m £751 11/4
Limerick 8 May 1969 (R. Coonan) Won Sarsfield Handicap Chase 2½m £372 6/1
Galway 30 July 1969 (R. Coonan) Won Galway Centenary Plate Handicap Chase 2m 5f £2,380 7/1
Punchestown 15 October 1969 (R. Coonan) Won Naas Handicap Chase 2½m £923 3/1
Trainer: J.P. Leigh, Willoughton, Lincolnshire
Market Rasen 29 August 1970 (Mr A. Kavanagh) Won York Bar 3m Chase £340 9/4

Royal Day, sired by King of the Jungle, is the only Galway Plate winner to have been sired by a Galway Hurdle winner. Bred by Paddy Dunne Cullinan, he started in bumpers, ridden by Francis Flood, Sleator's long-standing amateur jockey, won his maiden hurdle with Cathal Finnegan in the saddle, and a novice hurdle in the hands of Bobby Beasley, before injury kept him off the course for two years. When he returned to racing in 1966, Bobby Coonan was stable jockey at Grange Con and had eight races on Royal Day: six chases and two hurdles, which included both Galway Plate successes.

A bizarre accident further interrupted Royal Day's career, causing him to miss the 1968 Galway meeting and putting him out of action for a year. A rabbit hunter, armed with a .22 rifle, shot him in the shoulder by mistake. However, he recovered and returned to Ballybrit in 1969 to win the Plate a second time. A twelve-year-old in 1969, joining Gallant Wolf as the oldest winner of the Plate, Royal Day finished his career racing in England, when still in the ownership of Mr Dunne Cullinan.

ALLANGRANGE

(Chestnut Colt 1967 Le Levanstell – Silken Princess by Arctic Prince)

Breeder: Joseph McGrath
Winner of the 1970 Spiddal Handicap

Owner: Joseph McGrath
Trainer: Seamus McGrath, Sandyford, Co. Dublin
Limerick Junction 9 July 1970 (G. McGrath) Won Junction Maiden 12f flat £372 3/1
Galway 28 July 1970 (G. McGrath) Won Spiddal Handicap 12f flat £610 5/1
Curragh 15 August 1970 (G. McGrath) Won Flat Rath Handicap 12f flat £372¾ 5/1
Tralee 2 September 1970 (G. McGrath) Won Carling Black Label Lager Handicap 13f flat
       £1,240½ 3/1f
Curragh 26 September 1970 (G. McGrath) Won Irish St Leger 14f flat £13,550 9/1

Allangrange was a typical product of the McGrath bloodstock empire, built by Joe McGrath on his purchase of Smokeless, bookmaker Dick Duggan's dual Irish classic heroine, back in 1935. By this time Duggan, one of McGrath's partners in the Irish Hospital Sweepstakes venture, was terminally ill, and he offered Smokeless to his friend as a present. Refusing to accept the gift, McGrath promised to buy her instead at public auction, getting Harry Ussher to buy her on his behalf for 4,000 guineas. McGrath invested heavily in good bloodlines when the outbreak of the war forced English owners to dump their horses, paying 14,000 guineas for Carpet Slipper, a half-sister to the Derby third Charles O'Malley and the dam of Godiva, winner of the 1,000 Guineas and the Oaks in 1940. Joe had previously purchased her foal, named Windsor Slipper, from the executors of his breeder, the late Lord Furness, and his ability encouraged him to buy the dam also. In 1942 Windsor Slipper won all three Irish classic races open to colts to become the second – and the last – winner of the Irish Triple Crown. Prevented by the Second World War from running in England, Windsor Slipper retired to stud the unbeaten winner of six races, one of the best horses to race in Ireland in the twentieth century. His dam, Carpet Slipper, would later become the great-grandam of Allangrange.

Joe McGrath was Champion owner in Ireland eight times, including five years in succession – 1941 to 1946 – and again in 1955, 1957 and 1959. He was the leading owner in Ireland in the number of races won (nine times) and owned Windsor Slipper, Arctic Sun and Panaslipper, all Champion Racehorses of their year in Ireland. Michael C. Collins, father of Con, was Joe McGrath's first trainer. During the war years, when a blackout was enforced, Joe McGrath's limousine would eerily arrive at Conyngham Lodge in the black of the night, unlit and unseen, bringing the owner for one of his conferences with his trainer. After the war, Joe McGrath established a large private training stable at Glencairn, behind Leopardstown racecourse, installing his son Seamus as trainer. His breeding operation was at the Brownstown Stud on the Curragh, and all of the stock bred there went into training, mostly at Glencairn. One that did not was Arctic Prince, out of the top-class filly Arctic Sun, who was sent to Willie Stephenson at Royston, Herts. Stephenson ran a mixed yard and later trained a winner of the Grand National, Oxo, but Arctic Prince was a surprise winner of the 1951 Epsom Derby, winning by six lengths at odds of 28 to 1.

The huge McGrath bloodstock empire remained in one piece after Joe's death in 1966, being run by his sons Patrick, Joseph and Seamus. Joseph ran the stud side of the business, Seamus did the training and Paddy ran the business empire, which included Waterford Glass. Paddy was also Chairman of the Racing Board and did tremendous work for Irish racing, much of it at his own expense.

Allangrange took a long time to show any ability, having been unplaced nine times before trotting up in a weak Limerick Junction maiden in July 1970. Having finally won a race, he was transformed into a winning machine by scoring in his remaining five races before being retired to stud. He lowered the colours of Mighty Quin in a handicap at Galway, beat another hot-pot, Rosemartin, at the Curragh and was a convincing winning favourite in the valuable Carling Black Label Lager Handicap at Tralee, before lining up for the Irish St Leger. Meadowville, second in the St Leger at Doncaster to the great Triple Crown winner Nijinsky, was odds-on to win the Irish equivalent, having previously been placed second in the Irish

Derby. Trained at Newmarket by Michael Jarvis, Meadowville now had the services of Lester Piggott, the best big-race jockey in the world, and had form in top-class races, which made him look a certainty to win the weakest Irish classic. However, George McGrath elected to make the running on Allangrange, building up a nice lead, before staying on strongly to hold off the persistent challenge of the English horse by a length and a half.

Having made enormous improvement in a three-month period, which may have been due to easier ground conditions, Allangrange was retired to the stud. Phil Bull of *Timeform* expressed his disappointment: 'Had Allangrange remained in training, it might have been that his winning the Irish St Leger on his final outing marked not the summit of his career as a stayer but a notable milestone on the way. He could have made a good Cup horse in 1971 but instead he will stand as a stallion at the Waterloo House Stud, Cork.'

When Allangrange's first crop of foals only produced two minor winners, the stallion was despatched to Japan. However, one member of that first crop that flopped at two was Miralla, Sir Hugh Nugent's Irish 1,000 Guineas winner of 1975, who may have gone on to even better things had not the going remained firm all season. The export of Allangrange was premature because the stallion left behind some useful handicappers such as Abednego (a half-brother to Deep Run, who was just below top-class), Stetchworth Lad, Bedford Lodge, Irish Poet and Chokwaco.

CAPTAIN CHRISTY

(Bay gelding 1967 Mon Capitaine – Christy's Bow by Bowsprit)

Breeder: George Williams
Winner of 1971 Lough Atalia Bumper

Owner: Mrs T. W. Nicholson
Privately trained
Galway 26 July 1971 (Mr Thomas Ryan) Won Lough Atalia Bumper 2m £428 6/4f
Listowel 29 September 1971 (Mr Thomas Ryan) Won Newcastle West Bumper 2m £202 4/5f

Owner: Major Joseph Pidcock
Privately trained
Baldoyle 1 January 1972 (Major J. Pidcock) Won Sutton Maiden Hurdle 2m £733¾ 4/1

Owner: Mrs Jane M.A. Samuel
Trainer: Patrick Taaffe

Naas 11 November 1972 (H.R. Beasley) Won Rossmore Hurdle 2m 1f £953 2/1f

Leopardstown 18 November 1972 (H.R. Beasley) Won Sandymount Hurdle 2m £974¾ 6/4f

Leopardstown 27 December 1972 (H.R. Beasley) Won Sweeps Hurdle 2m £11,045 15/2

Leopardstown 17 February 1973 (H.R. Beasley) Won Scalp Hurdle 2m £1,272¾ 1/2f

Ayr 14 April 1973 (H.R. Beasley) Won Scottish Champion Hurdle 2m £1,438½ 2/1

Clonmel 1 November 1973 (H.R. Beasley) Won Magner, O'Brien & Moynihan Novice Chase 2¼m £690 1/2f

Punchestown 7 November 1973 (H.R. Beasley) Won Wills Premier Chase 2½m £1,170 1/2f

Punchestown 9 February 1974 (H.R. Beasley) Won Poulaphouca Novice Chase 2½m £690 1/2f

Thurles 28 February 1974 (H.R. Beasley) Won P.Z. Mower Chase 2½m £690 1/2f

Cheltenham 14 March 1974 (H.R. Beasley) Won Gold Cup Chase 3¼m £14,572½ 7/1

Fairyhouse 16 April 1974 (H.R. Beasley) Won Power Gold Cup Chase 2¼m £1,783½ 4/5f

Kempton Park 26 December 1974 (R. Coonan) Won King George VI Chase 3m £6,963½ 5/1

Thurles 27 February 1975 (R. Coonan) Dead Heat P.Z. Mower Chase 2½m £445 1/2f

Naas 22 March 1975 (R. Coonan) Won Kildare Handicap Chase 3m £861½ 2/1

Enghien 10 June 1975 (R. Coonan) Won Prix de Velay Handicap Chase 2m 3f £2,880

Punchestown 13 December 1975 (R. Coonan) Won Punchestown Chase 2½m £1,499 1/2f

Kempton Park 26 December 1975 (G. Newman) Won King George VI Chase 3m £6,963½ 11/10jf

Owned and trained by Tom Nicholson, Captain Christy finished fourth to Grantstown Victor in a Limerick bumper on his racing debut. On the strength of this run, Galway racegoers made Captain Christy a firm 6-to-4 favourite to win the Lough Atalia Bumper, the last race on the Monday, the first day of the 1971 Festival meeting. The day had been good for the punters, the five previous races having been won by three favourites and two second-favourites, and they played up their money, severely scalding the bookies when 'the Captain' hacked up by eight lengths.

Having stepped up in class to finish third in the Havasnack Plate at Tralee, Captain Christy reappeared in a bumper at Listowel on the third day of the meeting, which extended to four days at that time. In contrast to Galway, all five favourites had been beaten that day at Listowel and punters turned to Captain Christy to bail them out. As they plunged, the Captain's price went odds-on but in these circumstances, with money chasing money, any price was a good one. In this instance the punters got it right; Captain Christy impressed all with an emphatic twelve-length success and was already being talked of as a future champion.

Obviously impressed, Major Joe Pidcock bid £10,000 for the horse, which would now have to go hurdling; it was an offer that Tom Nicholson could not refuse. Choosing a maiden hurdle at Limerick's Christmas meeting on the old Greenpark course, Major Pidcock took the mount himself on Captain Christy. Despite his inexperience as a rider, backers were not deterred, but unfortunately for the major and those that backed Captain Christy that day, four horses took the wrong course and he followed them out of the race. This was the first of a number of frustrating lapses, which so irritated his backers during the next few years and prompted the jockey Bobby Beasley to describe the horse as 'the most brilliant jumper in training, but a little bit crazy'. Pulled out again on New Year's Day at Baldoyle, this time the punters shied away from the 'crazy Captain' and the 'sporting major'. They backed Barney Moss's The Met, trained by Paddy Mullins, down to odds-on, only to kick themselves after the race when Captain Christy won. Having ridden the horse in four subsequent races, the best position being third in the Scalp Hurdle at Leopardstown, Major Pidcock sold him to Jane Samuel, who transferred him to the stable of Pat Taaffe.

After finishing third in a hurdle at Naas and running unplaced in the Irish Cesarewitch on the flat, Captain Christy teamed up with the former Irish Champion Jockey Bobby Beasley, now a reformed alcoholic, winning three races in succession culminating in a sensational six-length victory in the Sweeps Hurdle. Having beaten top-class hurdlers such as Comedy of Errors, Brendan's Road, Bula and Inkslinger, his next target was the 1973 Champion Hurdle at Cheltenham. Given a preparatory race in the Scalp Hurdle at Leopardstown, in which he beat Brendan's Road effortlessly by fifteen lengths, Irish hopes were high that he could dethrone Bula, who had won the last two runnings of the race and was an odds-on favourite to emulate Hatton's Grace, Sir Ken and Persian War. But Captain Christy had his measure approaching the last hurdle. Tracking the leader, Easby Abbey, he looked the likely winner until he was mowed down by the blistering finish of Comedy of Errors. In the end his connections had to be satisfied with third place, Easby Abbey staying on stoutly under a magnificent ride from Ron Barry to secure the runner-up spot. Easby Abbey was made favourite to win the Scottish Grand National at Ayr the following month but was well beaten by Captain Christy, who stayed on well to hold off the fast-finishing Indianapolis, ridden by Bill Smith.

With so many talented hurdlers competing at the top level, Captain Christy's connections decided to send him chasing, despite his success at Ayr, because his jumping at speed was too erratic for a top-class hurdler; the lengths lost after hitting a hurdle just could not be regained at this level. On Thursday, 1 November 1973, he made his chasing debut at Clonmel with his usual jockey, Bobby Beasley, in the saddle. Starting an odds-on favourite, Captain Christy won the race by a distance and followed up with another easy victory in a Wills Premier Chase qualifier at Punchestown. The valuable Black & White Gold Cup at Ascot was the next step on the steeplechasing ladder. Captain Christy was made favourite to beat his three opponents, which included the former champion hurdler Bula. Dashing off in front, he made the running until challenged by Bula three fences from home, the pair quickening clear. The two former hurdlers raced into the penultimate fence together but while Bula sailed over it, Captain Christy made a mistake that sent his jockey Bobby Beasley flying out over his head.

The fall brought Captain Christy back to hurdle racing. An honourable second to Maddentown, who was getting almost 3 stones in weight, at Fairyhouse encouraged Pat Taaffe to keep him hurdling and he contested the 1973 Sweeps Hurdle at Leopardstown, a race he had won so convincingly the previous year. However, on this occasion he could not cope with Comedy of Errors, who stormed clear to win the race by eight lengths, from Brendan's Road, with Captain Christy a well-beaten third. It was obvious to Pat Taaffe that his charge had little chance of reversing the form with Comedy of Errors in the Champion Hurdle, so it was decided to send him to Haydock Park to contest the Wills Premier Chase Final and resume his steeplechasing career. Backed from even money to odds-on, he raced into a clear lead and it was 'bar a fall' from a long way out. Unfortunately the second to last fence proved a bogey, and just as at Ascot the horse made a jumping error and Bobby Beasley was unseated. At Ascot there was the excuse that he blundered when under pressure from Bula but at Haydock Park there was no such excuse. A weak-looking novice chase at Punchestown was chosen as a rehabilitation, which he won without being extended. He also won a more competitive PZ Mower Chase at Thurles and the next stop was the Cheltenham Gold Cup.

English racegoers thought that Pendil, trained by Fred Winter, was a certainty, despite the presence of The Dikler, who had beaten him by a short head the previous year. However, the fall of High Ken, who was leading the field at the time, had a significant bearing on the race because he fell in the path of Pendil, bringing the favourite down. Pendil's jockey Richard Pitman was widely condemned, the 'after dinner speakers' being adamant that Pendil ought not to have been tracking High Ken because that horse was a dodgy jumper and might fall. Understandably Pitman saw it differently, stating that High Ken fell into Pendal's path, giving the horse no chance of staying on his feet. The incident left The Dikler, ridden by Ron Barry, in front, with Bobby Beasley, having held up Captain Christy as long as he could, closing steadily. At the second to last the race only concerned those two horses, and the Irish, watching from the stands or on television, held their breath, heaving a sigh of relief now that the horse's bogey fence was out of the way. However, only moments later a thousand hearts were in their owners' mouths, as the Captain blundered the last, but Bobby sat tight and stayed aboard. With the fences out of the way, the veteran jockey rode his mount out and Captain Christy quickened past The Dikler to win, and to return to the usual raucous welcome afforded by the Irish to their winners, backed and unbacked. He was led in amid a particularly enthusiastic and heartfelt chorus of cheers from the multitude that would be collecting winnings in just a few minutes' time.

The Irish Grand National was the next target for the champion and a record crowd turned up at Fairyhouse to see the race. Burdened with 12 stones 2 pounds, he would have to give a stone or more to experienced steeplechasers such as Highway View and Colebridge, who started favourite. The race was run at a fast pace, with Bobby Beasley settling his mount at the rear of the field. At a time least expected by the spectators, Captain Christy made an unforced error, dumping his jockey on the firm turf, his exit bringing a loud groan from the stands. He continued riderless with the field for the duration of the race, which was eventually won by Colebridge by a short head from the double Cheltenham Gold Cup winner, L'Escargot.

Pulled out again the following day for the Power Gold Cup, a novice chase with only three opponents, Captain Christy looked an absolute certainty bar a fall but there were few brave enough to back him at odds-on. However, even money could not be resisted and the bookies had to offer these generous odds in order to lay a bet. This proved to be one of Captain Christy's good days; he gave a spectacular exhibition of jumping, sauntering home an easy fifteen-length winner.

Although an enigma, on his day Captain Christy was a brilliant chaser. Few of those present will forget his spectacular victories in the King George VI Chase at Kempton Park on Boxing Day. In 1974 he beat Pendil by eight lengths, suggesting that Pendil might not have won the Gold Cup, had he not been brought down. In that race the following year Captain Christy put up one of the most brilliant performances seen in a steeplechase in recent times, routing the talented Bula by thirty lengths. With Gerry Newman deputizing for the injured Bobby Beasley, he gave an unforgettable exhibition of jumping at speed. Second in the Grand Steeplechase de Paris at Auteuil and fourth in the Colonial Cup at Carolina in 1975, he sustained a tendon injury in February 1976. The winner of two bumpers, six hurdle races and twelve steeplechases, he had given his jockey a 'second start', which is what Bobby Beasley called his autobiography.

SPANNER

(Bay gelding 1967 Orchardist – Prairie Fire by Mustang)

Breeder: Moore Hill Estates
Winner of the 1972, 1973 and 1975 Amateur Handicap
Winner of the 1974 Galway Hurdle

Owner: Mrs M.T. Jackson
Trainer: Charles L. Weld, Rosewell House, Curragh
Limerick Junction 13 May 1971 (Mr D.K. Weld) Won Carron Bumper 2m £202 5/4f
Mallow 22 June 1971 (Mr D.K. Weld) Won Glantane Bumper 2m £202 11/10f
Trained: Dermot K. Weld, Rosewell House, Curragh
Baldoyle 1 January 1972 (P. Russell) Won Sutton Maiden Hurdle 2m £734 8/11f
Galway 1 August 1972 (Mr D.K. Weld) Won Amateur Handicap 2m flat £1,480 7/4f
Limerick 14 September 1972 (P. Russell) Won Greenpark Hurdle 2m 1f £370 2/5f
Dundalk 1 November 1972 (P. Russell) Won Dunany Hurdle 2m 1f £370 1/1f
Mallow 23 April 1973 (P. Russell) Won Mallow Novice Chase 2m £370 1/1f
Galway 31 July 1973 (Mr D.K. Weld) Won Amateur Handicap 2m flat £1,380 7/1
Ballinrobe 4 April 1974 (P. Russell) Won Connaught Handicap Chase 2m 2f £202 4/5f
Down Royal 27 April 1974 (Mr T.M. Walsh) Won McMurray Hurdle 2m £552 1/4f
Gowran Park 29 May 1975 (P. Russell) Won Jack Duggan Handicap Hurdle 2m £691 20/1
Galway 29 July 1975 (Mr D.K. Weld) Won Amateur Handicap 2m flat £1,381 2/1f
Galway 31 July 1975 (P. Russell) Won Galway Hurdle Handicap 2m £2,203 10/1
Clonmel 29 October 1977 (R. Shortt) Won Barrow Handicap 2m flat £483 10/1

Spanner was easily the best offspring of the game and consistent staying handi-capper Orchardist, the disqualified winner of the Cesarewitch in 1962. Although also a winner over hurdles, Orchardist was a poor sire but Spanner was a good winner on the flat, over hurdles and over fences. A three-time winner of the Amateur Handicap (a race record), winner of the Galway Hurdle and beaten favourite for the Galway Plate, according to Dermot Weld he was 'an ideal 2-mile horse'. Owned by Molly Jackson, who lived in Ryegate, Surrey, Spanner won his first Amateur Handicap, sponsored by the cigarette firm Players Wills, in 1972, beating Mighty Quin (Mr M.F. Morris) and Clondra Boy (Mr T.M. Walsh). The aftermath of the race was marred when Mighty Quin, owned by Joseph Lewis and trained by Mick O'Toole, broke a leg on pulling up and had to be destroyed.

Although Spanner went chasing the following year, he returned to Galway to win a second Amateur Handicap before resuming his steeplechasing career. In

1974 he started the 7-to-2 favourite, with Peter Russell riding, to win the Plate but could only finish fourth to Bunclody Tiger, the race having been postponed until the Friday because bad weather had caused the Wednesday card to be cancelled. It was then decided that Spanner was a better horse over hurdles and his chasing career was abandoned. Returning to Galway in 1975, he beat Double Default by a length to win his third Amateur Handicap, with both horses going on to win the Galway Hurdle that year. That came about because of a stupid decision to divide the Hurdle and run it in two divisions. This was often done in minor races but important races were never divided, and it is the only time the Galway Hurdle was downgraded in this manner. Spanner won the first division and Double Default, ridden by Colin Magnier, the second. Double Default eventually won the Amateur Handicap in 1978. Spanner lived in retirement until he had to be put down in 1993, on the very day that Vintage Crop won the Melbourne Cup.

PINCH HITTER

(Grey gelding 1978 Auction Ring – Centennial Rose by Runnymede)

Breeder: Ballykisteen Stud
Winner of the 1982 and 1983 Galway Hurdle

Owner: F.J. Quinn
Trainer: Noel Meade
Gowran Park 24 July 1980 (S. Craine) Won Greenvale 2yo Maiden 7½f £1,037 9/4f

Owner: Brendan Carolan and Finbar Cahill
Trainer: Noel Meade
Naas 13 June 1981 (S. Craine) Won Harristown Handicap 9f flat £5,708 3/1jf
Galway 27 July 81 (S. Craine) Won McDonogh Handicap (Listed) 8½f flat £8,028 20/1
Fairyhouse 31 December 1981 (J.P. Byrne) Won Hogmanay Maiden Hurdle 2m £828 8/11f
Punchestown 7 January 1982 (J.P. Byrne) Won Dunmurray Hurdle 2m £1,104 4/5f
Leopardstown 10 July 1982 (B. Coogan) Won Hennessy Handicap (Listed) 9f flat £8,738 25/1
Galway 26 July 1982 (S. Craine) Won McDonogh Handicap (Listed) 8½f flat £10,110 6/1
Galway 29 July 1982 (J.J. O'Neill) Won Guinness Galway Hurdle Handicap 2m £15,249 6/1
Tralee 31 August 1982 (T. Carmody) Won Ballybeggan Racegoers' Handicap Hurdle 2m £7,200 2/1f
Galway 28 July 1983 (J.J. O'Neill) Won Guinness Galway Hurdle Handicap 2m £14,646 7/2f
Bellewstown 3 July 1985 (P. Leech) Won Meath Hurdle 2m 1f £968 2/5f

A tough, versatile racehorse, Pinch Hitter was a good handicapper on the flat and over hurdles, winning eleven races despite having a leg problem that made him difficult to train. Owned by Brendan Carolan, a London-based builder, and Finbar Cahill, a Dublin solicitor, he won two McDonogh Handicaps and was beaten by a neck in a third. Besides being the only horse to win that listed flat handicap over 8½ furlongs more than once, Pinch Hitter remains the only horse to win both that race and the Galway Hurdle, winning both at the 1982 Galway meeting. He also became the third, and last to date, to win two successive Galway Hurdles. A fast-ground specialist, he was a summer horse but ran well enough in the Sweeps Hurdle, run in January 1984, finishing seventh of eighteen to Fredcoteri. Out for over a year after this with leg trouble, he made a comeback in a flat race at Naas, finishing last but returning sound, and a month later won a weak hurdle at Bellewstown. It was not a comeback; he had permanently broken down and never raced again.

In 1982 Jonjo O'Neill rode Pinch Hitter to victory at the Galway Hurdle, beating Hi Harry and The Centaur, and Noel Meade booked the former British Champion Jockey to ride the horse at the Tralee meeting in late August. He booked a small plane to take him to Farranfore, the nearest airstrip to Ballybeggan Park racecourse, and was scheduled to take off from his Cumbrian base at 9 a.m. Bad flying weather is not usually expected in August, but on this particular morning fog and dense mist enveloped all of the British Isles, visibility was poor and the pilot was nervous. Jonjo was keen to get to Tralee because Meade had told him that he thought that Pinch Hitter was a certainty, but the journey had to be done in three legs. The first stop was to refuel at Douglas, Isle of Man, the second at Shannon Airport, to refuel and clear customs, before the final leg of the journey to Farranfore. The small plane took off into the gloom and soon the pilot was battling with the elements. He found it impossible to keep the plane steady in the wind and map read at the same time, so Jonjo had to hold the controls as the pilot tried to work out where they were. Beads of sweat on his forehead betrayed the pilot's nervousness but once they got near Douglas the visibility had improved sufficiently to enable them find the airport and land safely. However, the pilot was not going any further until the weather cleared and Jonjo was marooned on the Isle of Man.

Not content to kick his heels in Douglas when he could be in Tralee, Jonjo eventually found a local pilot willing to have a go and set off for Shannon airport, arriving safely without too much trouble. The weather reports from Co. Kerry were not encouraging but the pilot was advised to fly down the Tralee to the Killarney railway line that passed through Farranfore. Taking off again, they soon found themselves in dense mist, the pilot having to take the aircraft lower and lower as

Pinch Hitter, brilliant winner of the McDonogh Handicap in 1981 and 1982 and the Galway Hurdle in 1982 and 1983

both men peered into the gloom looking for the railway line. His wristwatch was the only distraction for Jonjo – the time was ticking by – while the aviator battled to fly the plane in a gale, read a map and at the same time peer into the mist to try to make visual contact with some landmark. Jonjo put his face to the Perspex and gazed out into the gloom searching for those elusive tracks, which were down there somewhere but could not be seen. The pilot descended down so low that the plane was skimming trees and missing telegraph poles by inches, but still could see no sign of the railway. They were lost in the skies above County Kerry and the pilot advised Jonjo to go back to Shannon – it was too dangerous to keep flying low without being certain where they were exactly. So near and yet so far, a disappointed Jonjo agreed that it was not worth dying for the ride and the plane headed back to Shannon, its first leg of a journey back to the Isle of Man. It was a wise decision because many years later a helicopter pilot, due to collect a party from Tralee racecourse after racing, crashed into a mountain attempting an approach in bad visibility.

Meanwhile, at Tralee, Noel Meade awaited Jonjo's arrival but aware of the difficult flying conditions he told Tommy Carmody to stand by to deputize on Pinch Hitter if Jonjo failed to make it on time. When he did not come, Tommy weighed out for the chance ride, which turned out to be a winning one, just as the trainer had predicted.

TRY A BRANDY

(Chestnut gelding 1982 Apollo Eight – All Purpose)

Breeder: Nicholas Allen

Winner of the Amateur Handicap and the Galway Hurdle in 1988

Owner and trainer: Martin Dunne

Thurles 13 November 1986 (Mr J.P. Dempsey) Won Paulstown Bumper 2m 1f £828 7/2

Curragh 11 October 1987 (Thomas J. Manning) Won Irish Cesarewitch Handicap 2m flat
    £16,450 20/1

Gowran Park 1 May 1988 (P. Gill) Won Avonmore Cheddar Handicap Hurdle 2m £5,920 6/1

Galway 25 July 1988 (Mr F.J. Flood) Won Amateur Handicap 2m flat £10,052 8/1

Galway 28 July 1988 (H. Rogers) Won Galway Hurdle Handicap 2m £15,225 4/1jf

Clonmel 20 September 1990 (H. Rogers) Won Silverspring Handicap Hurdle 2m £1,735 5/1

Tramore 15 August 1992 (C. O'Dwyer) Won Gain Novice Chase 2m £2,760 4/1jf

Naas 14 November 1992 (C. O'Dwyer) Won Quinns of Baltinglass Chase 2m £4,140 12/1

A permit holder from Co. Wicklow began relieving bookies of their money in a five-year period from 1984. It began at Leopardstown with a horse named Gala's Image landing a huge gamble in a bumper, continued with a couple of gambles on his half-brother Silent Jet, and culminated in a blitz of gambles with Try A Brandy. The inflicter of this pain was Martin Dunne, an ordinary dry stock farmer, who was a neighbour of Francis Flood, Paddy Sleator's old amateur, now training at Grange Con.

Try A Brandy won a Gowran Park bumper run at Thurles in 1986 and the following year was sensationally awarded the Irish Cesarewitch under bizarre circumstances. The easy winner, Excellenza, was disqualified for not wearing blinkers, which had been declared, and the outsider was awarded the race. Armed with this purse, Martin Dunne backed Try A Brandy from fancy prices all the way down to 6 to 1 at Gowran Park, duly collecting when the horse won a handicap hurdle. On to Galway they went, landing a big race double by winning the Amateur Handicap and the Galway Hurdle, backing the horse freely on both occasions. A small gelding, Try A Brandy was not a weight carrier so Martin Dunne's neighbour's son, Francis Flood Jr, was given the ride in the amateur race because he could claim a 7-pound allowance. Having won the first leg on the flat, there would be no penalty for the hurdle, for which Try A Brandy had been allotted the minimum weight of 9 stones 7 pounds. Believing the horse to be a certainty, another big gamble was organized and collected as Harry Rogers just had to steer him home.

Being unable to carry big weights forced Try A Brandy to go chasing, winning twice before losing his way somewhat. Racing at Killarney in May 1994, he led until he made a bad mistake at the penultimate fence but was still a close third when he crashed at the last, receiving fatal injuries.

DAWN RUN

(Bay filly 1978 Deep Run – Twilight Slave by Arctic Slave)

Breeder: John J. Riordan
Winner of 13 races in Ireland value £81,243, 6 races in England value £135,157, 2 races
     in France
Winner of the 1984 Champion Hurdle
Winner of the 1986 Cheltenham Gold Cup

Owner: Charmian Hill
Trainer: Patrick Mullins, Goresbridge, Co. Kilkenny
Tralee 23 June 1982 (Mrs C.D. Hill) Won Castlemaine Bumper 2m £692 5/1
Galway 31 July 1982 (Mr T. Mullins) Won Tonroe Bumper 2m £1,380 10/11f
Tralee 2 September 1982 (Mr T. Mullins) Won Havasnack Flat Race 2m £1,725 8/1
Navan 20 December 1982 (A. Mullins) Won Blackhills Maiden Hurdle 2m £966 4/6f
Leopardstown 28 December 1982 (A. Mullins) Won Findus Hurdle 2m 2f £1,520 12/1
Punchestown 5 February 1983 (A. Mullins) Won Fournoughts Hurdle 2m 4f £2,070 3/1
Aintree 8 April 1983 (A. Mullins) Won Page Three Handicap Hurdle 2m 5f £4,097 stg 7/2jf
Punchestown 26 April 1983 (A. Mullins) Won B.M.W. Champion Hurdle 2m £8,038 5/2f
Down Royal 5 November 1983 (A. Mullins) Won A.R. Soudaver Hurdle 2m £1,104 2/5f
Ascot 18 November 1983 (J.J. O'Neill) Won Vat Watkins Hurdle 2m 4f £10,524 stg 1/3f
Kempton Park 26 December 1983 (J.J. O'Neill) Won Christmas Hurdle 2m £15,776 stg 9/4
Leopardstown 18 February 1984 (J.J. O'Neill) Won Wessel Champion Hurdle 2m £21,754 4/5f
Cheltenham 13 March 1984 (J.J. O'Neill) Won Champion Hurdle 2m £36,680 stg 4/5f
Aintree 31 March 1984 (A. Mullins) Won Sandeman Hurdle 2m 5f £13,180 stg 4/6f
Auteuil 28 May 1984 (A. Mullins) Won Prix la Barka Hurdle 2m 3f £12,376 stg
Auteuil 22 June 1984 (A. Mullins) Won Grande Course de Hales Hurdle 3m 1f FF500,000
Navan 1 November 1984 (A. Mullins) Won Nobber Chase 2m £3,450 4/5f
Punchestown 14 December 1985 (A. Mullins) Won Durkan Brothers Chase 2m 4f £9,404 5/4f
Leopardstown 30 December 1985 (A. Mullins) Won Sean P. Graham Chase 2m 2f £4,140 4/9f
Cheltenham 13 March 1986 (J.J. O'Neill) Won Gold Cup Chase 3m 2f £54,900 stg 15/8f
Punchestown 23 April 1986 (A. Mullins) Won A Match (Chase) 2m £25,000 4/6f

Dawn Run, the only horse to win both the Champion Hurdle and the Cheltenham Gold Cup, was owned by Charmian Hill, the wife of a Waterford doctor. Mrs Hill was the first woman to ride against men under National Hunt Rules and the first in Ireland to ride winners on the flat, over hurdles and over fences. When Mrs Hill had recovered sufficiently from a terrible fall from Yes Man in a hurdle race at Thurles in November 1980, which killed her horse and left her seriously injured, she went about finding a replacement. At the 1981 November Sales she purchased Dawn Run for 5,800 guineas and sent her to trainer Paddy Mullins.

Determined to start race riding again, Mrs Hill declared herself fit to ride Dawn Run on her racing debut, at Clonmel the following May, although the stewards were uneasy, being aware of general concerns about her safety. Dawn Run ran prominently although unplaced at Clonmel but she really caught the eye on her next appearance, in a bumper at Thurles. On that occasion Mrs Hill rode an atrocious race, getting tailed off early on and running on really well, despite running wide on the bends, to finish fourth in the end, only twenty-five lengths behind the winner, Determined Angel. However, excuses could be made for the veteran rider because the race was run at a false pace, with the odds-on favourite, Ballyline Dancer, racing off into a clear lead at breakneck speed. Soon after the halfway point in the race Ballyline Dancer weakened, dropping away so dramatically that the stewards ordered a dope test, but by that time Dawn Run had been left with too much to do.

Unfortunately for Mrs Hill, the stewards of the Turf Club decided that she was too old to continue riding in races and served her notice that her licence to ride would be withdrawn at the end of June 1982. Bitterly disappointed, Mrs Hill knew that she was riding in her last race when she partnered Dawn Run in a Tralee bumper on 23 June. Punters had more faith in Mrs Hill than did the stewards because there was a massive gamble on Dawn Run, 14 to 1 to 5 to 1 in a very strong market in which five other horses were backed for money: Espeut, ridden and trained by Jonjo Walsh, Chick Way, Paka Lolo, the unraced Willya What and Instanter. Dawn Run and Espeut raced together at the head of affairs and dominated the race. Espeut, on the outside of Dawn Run, was carried wide entering the straight but had every chance and was beaten fair and square by a length. Although overjoyed by her final victory, the fearless grandmother was angry and bitter over the decision and now had to be content riding Dawn Run at exercise only.

Dawn Run's next race was at Galway, in the Tonroe Bumper. Ridden by the trainer's son Tom, she decisively beat Ramble Home, ridden by Mr Anthony Powell, who had been successful in the Lough Atalia Bumper on the first day of the meeting. When Dawn Run won her maiden hurdle, at Navan in December 1982, she was ridden by 20-year-old Tony Mullins, son of the trainer, who had been riding as a professional since January 1980 and became her regular jockey. However, when the big occasion arrived and Dawn Run was going to Cheltenham for the 1983 Sun Alliance Hurdle, Mrs Hill insisted that a 'more experienced' jockey be engaged. This put Paddy Mullins in a difficult position because he was being asked to 'jock-off' his own son, who he believed got on well with the horse and had done nothing wrong. Nevertheless, Paddy accepted that the owner paid the piper and therefore called the tune and engaged the English-based Irishman Ron Barry. Dawn Run and Ron Barry finished second, beaten three lengths by Sabin du Loir, after which Tony Mullins was reinstated on Dawn Run, finishing first and then second, on successive days at Aintree before winning the Punchestown Champion Hurdle. The jockey issue arose again when Dawn Run was being sent to Ascot the following November; Mrs Hill wanted a top jockey and Paddy selected Jonjo O'Neill.

Jonjo O'Neill won four top-class hurdle races on Dawn Run, culminating in a win in the Champion Hurdle, despite making a bad mistake at the final flight. However, an injury to Jonjo enabled Tony Mullins to regain the ride on Dawn Run and he went on to score six successive victories on her. Having won twice over hurdles in France including their Champion Hurdle, Dawn Run was sent chasing and it was Tony who rode her to victory on her debut in the Nobber Chase at Navan. In the latter race Dawn Run jumped well and easily defeated Dark Ivy and Buck House by ten lengths and the same but it transpired that in doing so she had been injured. Off the course for a year, Dawn Run returned to score decisive victories at Punchestown and Leopardstown and Tony's place as her jockey seemed secure. Unfortunately, he was unseated in the Holsten Chase at Cheltenham in January 1986 and rashly remounted to finish a distant fourth. The incident annoyed Mrs Hill, who wanted Jonjo O'Neill to ride Dawn Run in the forthcoming Cheltenham Gold Cup and again got her way. Having looked unlikely to win, Dawn Run battled on gamely and got up to win the race by a length and make history, inspiring chaotic scenes in the winner's enclosure after the race. Less than three weeks later Jonjo rode Dawn Run for the last time, crashing out of the Whitbread Gold Label Cup at Aintree at the first fence.

Now a national heroine in Ireland, Dawn Run's connections were sounded out about Dawn Run taking on Buck House, the Irish-trained 2-mile champion chaser. When they agreed to do so, the Coolmore Stud, Seamus Purcell and Gowran Park racecourse put up £5,000 each for a race to be run at the local racecourse, which enabled the challenge to take place. Due to be run on 4 May, the sponsors were shocked when Dawn Run did not appear among the entries but so too was Mrs Hill, who made no attempt to hide her annoyance. It transpired that Paddy

Mullins, through an oversight, missed the entry date. It was Vincent O'Brien, the famous trainer, who suggested a match and, having been assured that Dawn Run would compete, arranged one to be run at Punchestown. Set down for the third day of the Punchestown Festival, Seamus Purcell, the Coolmore Stud and Punchestown racecourse put up £5,000 each, with the Racing Board contributing a further £10,000, with the winner taking all. The match was run over Buck House's distance and Dawn Run did not receive the normal sex allowance but still the Gold Cup winner started favourite and won the race decisively. Unbelievably both horses were dead within a couple of months.

The following month Dawn Run returned to France, the plan being to contest the two races she had won two years previously, the Prix la Barka and the Grande Course de Haies, the French equivalent of the Champion Hurdle. Reverting to the smaller obstacles and ridden by Tony Mullins, Dawn Run could not cope with the finishing speed of Le Rheusois and was beaten into second place. Tony and Paddy thought it pointless to take on Le Rheusois again in the big race but Mrs Hill insisted and the experienced French jockey, Michel Chirol, was booked to ride. On a scorching hot Friday afternoon in Paris, Dawn Run lined up alongside Le Rheusois, the English-trained Gaye Brief, ridden by Peter Scudamore, and the American-trainer Flatterer, ridden by Richard Dunwoody. Gaye Brief had fallen at the practice hurdle before the race and again during it, but Dawn Run was going well until taking off too soon at the fifth hurdle from the finish. She took a crashing fall, broke her neck and died instantly. Dawn Run had won twenty-one of her thirty-five races.

Charmian Hill and Paddy Mullins were distraught at the loss of Dawn Run but got some consolation when Boro Quarter won the Galway Plate a month later. It was Paddy's first win in the famous summer handicap, which had proved his bogey race down the years with Height o'Fashion, Herring Gull, Andy Pandy and Doubtful Venture, all exceptional horses, just missing out and finishing second. However, having broken the ice Paddy won the race twice more, when The Gooser hacked up in 1992 and Nearly a Moose sprang a surprise nine years later. Paddy retired from training in 2005, when his son Tom took over the stable. Mrs Hill later broke her leg in a fall from Boro Quarter at exercise, spending many weeks in hospital. She never fully recovered and died from a stroke in 1990. Tony Mullins, who was jointly with Frank Berry the leading National Hunt jockey in Ireland in 1984, gave up riding over fences when he took out a trainer's licence. He trained Afford the King, ridden by Padge Gill, to win the 1988 Galway Plate and in 1990 rode Grabel, trained by his father, to victory in the richest hurdle race in the world, worth $300,000 to the winner, at the Dueling Grounds, Franklin, Kentucky.

KIICHI USA

(Bay gelding 1985 Perrault – Kahaila)

Breeder: Allen E. Paulson and J. Loya (USA)
Winner of the 1990 Galway Plate

Owner: Allen E. Paulson
Trainer: Dermot K. Weld, Rosewell House, Curragh
Galway 27 July 1987 (M.J. Kinane) Won GPT Dublin Maiden 7f flat £3,452 1/1f
Listowel 21 September 1987 (M.J. Kinane) Won Lartigue Nursery 10f flat £2,760 7/1
Fairyhouse 6 April 1988 (M.J. Kinane) Won Tattersalls Sales 9f flat £5,920 9/4

Owner: Michael W.J. Smurfit
Trainer: Dermot K. Weld, Rosewell House, Curragh
Fairyhouse 19 October 1988 (B. Sheridan) Won Birch Hurdle 2m £1,380 7/4f
Leopardstown 20 November 1988 (B. Sheridan) Won Smurfit 3yo Hurdle 2m £16,250 4/6f
Naas 3 March 1990 (B. Sheridan) Won Irish Life Nas na Ri Chase 2m £6,900 9/4f
Galway 1 August 1990 (B. Sheridan) Won Digital Galway Plate Handicap Chase 2m 5f £22,100 2/1f
Naas 2 March 1991 (B. Sheridan) Won Newlands Handicap Chase 2m 3f £3,450 100/30

Kiichi was the first two-year-old winner at Galway to come back later and win the Galway Plate. Trained thoughout his short career by Dermot Weld, Kiichi was the property of Allen Paulson when winning at Galway in 1987, being sold off to Michael Smurfit as a jumper in 1988. Although he won a valuable three-year-old hurdle at Leopardstown, sponsored by his owner, he failed to establish himself as a hurdler before being sent over fences. Winner of the Galway Plate in 1990, he quickly made a mark over the bigger obstacles and was on odds-on favourite to win the Cathcart Challenge Cup Chase at the 1991 Cheltenham Festival. Disaster struck the promising six-year-old, when he injured himself during the race, and went lame; Brendan Sheridan had to pull up. Disaster turned to tragedy when he later had to be put down.

GO AND GO

(Chestnut colt 1987 Be My Guest USA – Irish Edition USA by Alleged USA)

Breeder: Moyglare Stud Farm
Winner of the GPT Dublin 2yo Maiden 1989
Winner of the Belmont Stakes 1990

Owner: Moyglare Stud Farm

Trainer: Dermot K. Weld

Galway 31 July 1989 (M.J. Kinane) Won GPT Dublin 2yo Maiden 7f £3,452 1/1f

Curragh 19 August 1989 (M.J. Kinane) Won Tyros Stakes (Listed) 2yo 7f £11,520 2/1jf

Laurel Park USA 21 October 1989 (C. Perret) Won Futurity (Grade 2) 2yo 8½f £100,000 Dirt

Phoenix Park 2 May 1990 (M.J. Kinane) Won Minstrel Stakes (Listed) 1m £12,332 2/7f

Belmont Park USA 9 June 1990 (M.J. Kinane) Won Belmont Stakes (Group 1) 12f £255,652 Dirt

During the years when Lord Killanin was Chairman of the Race Committee, the Galway Races greatly improved the quality of its flat-racing programme. The meeting began to attract a higher class of runner than it had in the past and trainer Dermot Weld can take all of the credit for this. Ever since he took over his father's stable on the Curragh in 1972, he has supported the Galway Races but he did not send his 'duds'; he was prepared to allow the most promising horses in his yard to run there. This raised the quality, and consequently the profile, of the flat races, encouraging the bigger stables to follow suit; owners of flat horses caught the bug and desired a winner at Galway.

The jockeys emerge from their modern rooms, a far cry from the 'little tent' of 100 years ago!

The first two-year-old race was run on the Ballybrit course in 1971, the Athenry Stakes over 7 furlongs. Run on the Monday, the first winner of the race was Master Albert, trained by Charlie Weld, Dermot's father, who retired at the end of that year. The following year Dermot trained the winner in his first season, with the useful juvenile Klairvimy, who beat the favourite Riverstown, a filly trained by Stephen Quirke, with the subsequent Prix de l'Arc de Triomphe winner Star Appeal back in third place. The following evening Dermot won the prestigious Amateur Handicap with Spanner. These were the first two Galway Festival winners for the trainer, who in the next thirty-five years amassed a total of 192. Dermot Weld has won the Athenry Stakes, renamed GPT after its sponsor from 1987, no less than seventeen times, far more than any other trainer, and the race has attracted horses from the top stables in the country, with winners down the years being trained by Michael Kauntze, the late Paul Doyle, Jim Bolger, Liam Browne, Patrick Prendergast, John Oxx, Aidan O'Brien and Kevin Prendergast. Weld trained six winners of the race in succession between 1987, when Kiichi won, and 1992, when Arabic Treasure, owned by Galway Race Committee member Ray Rooney, was successful. The third winner of the sequence was Go and Go, one of the best horses ever to have won at Galway.

Go and Go was by the top-class miler Be My Guest, who had previously sired Assert, winner of the 1982 Irish and French Derbies. Making his racecourse debut at the Curragh on 2 July, he showed good early speed before fading to finish a respectable sixth behind Wedding Bouquet, trained by Vincent O'Brien and ridden by John Reid. Ripe for Galway, the bookmakers marked Go and Go up at a cautious 2 to 1 but were besieged by punters desperate to get on. Despite the strong betting market, the sheer volume of money produced by the oversized rugby scrums that were pushing and shoving outside every bookmaker's pitch, dropped the price steadily, a quarter of a point at a time, until it rested at even money at the off. The bookmakers were always in trouble. Go and Go tracked the leader, Galway Star, down the hill before sweeping past on swinging into the straight, going away to win in a canter by two and a half lengths, from Welsh Blend and Arowvale. Owned and bred by the Moyglare Stud Farm, he won in the manner of a high-class colt and confirmed this promise by stepping up to win in listed class at the Curragh next time out. Having run disappointingly badly in the Group 1 National Stakes (Curragh) in September, behind the English raider Dashing Blade, trained by Ian Balding, he was sent to America to contest the Laurel Futurity.

The race was supposed to have been run on the turf course at Laurel Park but was switched to the dirt track after heavy rain left the grass course waterlogged. Go and Go had never raced on dirt in his life but seemed to enjoy the conditions, going clear with Robyn Dancer, who he eventually defeated by a head. That Grade

2 race was worth £100,000 sterling; only eight races in Ireland were worth more than this, and was a good example of Dermot Weld's ability to discover valuable foreign races for inmates of his Curragh stable.

Go and Go ran poorly in his final race that season, the Grade 1 Breeders' Cup Juvenile at Gulfstream Park in November, behind Rhythm. Nevertheless, the international handicappers rated him at 110 in the two-year-old ratings, fifth place in the Irish classification, 5 pounds behind the top-rated horse, The Caretaker.

Dermot Weld decided that Go and Go was his Derby horse in 1990. Waiting until early May before giving him a run, he chose a soft listed race at the Phoenix Park, which he duly won at the prohibitive price of 7 to 2 on. Although he won, he did so by only a half a length, and when he was beaten in the Derrinstown Stud Derby Trial at Leopardstown, plans to go to Epsom were scrapped and Go and Go was rerouted to America. Following the modern practice of arriving as late as possible, he arrived in Belmont Park three days before the race. Putting up an impressive performance, he tracked the leaders before quickening clear to win by eight and a quarter lengths. Wearing a visor for the first time, he trounced the short-priced favourite and Kentucky Derby winner, Unbridled, who finished a disappointing fourth. That horse had run on the anti-bleeding drug Latex in his previous races but medication is not allowed in New York, and that was given as the reason for his poor run. However, this was disproved when Unbridled, not running on Latex, reversed the form with Go and Go in the Breeders' Cup Classic, run at Belmont later that season. Although Go and Go finished last of the fourteen runners, he had been struck into during the race. He remained in America, with trainer D. Wayne Lucas, for the remainder of his career.

LIFE OF A LORD

(Brown gelding 1986 Strong Gale – Ruby Girl)

Breeder: John Costello
Winner of the 1995 and 1996 Galway Plate

Owner: M.J. Clancy
Trainer: Thomas Costello, Newmarket-on-Fergus, Co. Clare
Dundalk 22 May 1992 (Mr T.S. Costello) Won Tallanstown Hunt Chase 3m £2,245 2/1f
Tipperary 10 July 1992 (S.H. O'Donovan) Won Power Solicitors' Handicap Chase 2½m £3,452 5/2jf
Sligo 20 August 1992 (S.H. O'Donovan) Won Heineken Handicap Chase 2½m £4,140 4/7f
Roscommon 30 August 1993 (G.M. O'Neill) Won Percy French Handicap Chase 3m £3,452 10/1
Galway 8 September 1993 (G.M. O'Neill) Won Northern Telecom Handicap Chase 2¾m £5,820 8/1

Limerick 27 December 1993 (M. Flynn) Won James McMahon Handicap Chase 2½m £3,700 5/2

Trainer: Aidan P. O'Brien

Gowran Park 28 June 1995 (A.J. O'Brien) Won Evergreen Handicap Chase 2¾m £2,740 10/1

Tipperary 23 July 1995 (C.F. Swan) Won Aer Rianta Handicap Chase 2½m £6,850 3/1f

Galway 2 August 1995 (T. Horgan) Won Galway Plate Handicap 2¾m £31,125 12/1

Listowel 27 September 1995 (C.F. Swan) Won Kerry National Handicap Chase 3m £24,800 9/2

Sandown Park 27 April 1996 (C.F. Swan) Won Whitbread Gold Cup Handicap Chase 3m 5f
    £57,806 12/1

Galway 31 July 1996 (C.F. Swan) Won Galway Plate Handicap 2¾m £31,125 9/2

Starting out in point-to-points, Life of a Lord was a product of Tom Costello's famous academy in Co. Clare. Graduating from points to hunter chases, Life of a Lord was good enough to hold his own in handicap chases, winning five before being moved to the stable of Aidan O'Brien after a barren year in 1994. The young up-and-coming training genius got six more handicap chases out of the horse in a period of eighteen

Life of a Lord won three steeplechases at the Galway Festival including the Plate twice

months. Having won the Galway Plate/Kerry National double in 1995, which only Spittin' Image, trained by John Bryce-Smith, had done before, Life of the Lord won the Whitbread Gold Cup in 1996 and went on to collect a second Galway Plate. Starting the 5-to-2 favourite to win a second successive Kerry National, a feat only achieved once before, by Packed Home in the 'sixties, he broke a leg in running, had to be pulled up and the vet called to put him out of his misery.

FEATHERED GALE

(Bay gelding 1987 Strong Gale – Farm Approach)

Breeder: N.J. Connors
Winner of the 1994 Galway Plate
Winner of the 1996 Irish Grand National

Owner: E.P. King
Trainer: Arthur L.T. Moore, Naas
Fairyhouse 18 November 1992 (T.J. Taaffe) Won Curragh 5yo Maiden Hurdle 2½m £3,105 7/2
Clonmel 19 May 1994 (J. Shortt) Won Holycross Novice Chase 2½m £2,228½ 2/1f
Tipperary 3 July 1994 (F. Woods) Won Galway Plate Trial Handicap Chase 2¾m £9,675 7/1
Galway 27 July 1994 (F. Woods) Won Galway Plate Handicap Chase 2¾m £27,375 8/1
Limerick 15 October 1995 (P. Carberry) Won Munster National Handicap Chase 3m £12,900 9/1

Owner: M.D. O'Connor
Trainer: Arthur L.T. Moore, Naas
Fairyhouse 9 April 1996 (F. Woods) Won Irish Grand National Handicap Chase 3m 5f £62,700 8/1
Killarney 16 July 1997 (P. Carberry) Won Doyle Brothers Chase 2½m £3,767½ 7/1

Since the inauguration of the Irish Grand National, a year after the Galway Plate, in 1870, eight horses have been successful in both races. Springfield Maid (1892), Tipperary Boy (1901), Red Park (1933), Alberoni (1952) and Umm (1955) managed to win both races in the same year, while Jupiter Tonans, Golden Jack and Feathered Gale won both races but in different years. Feathered Gale, the last horse to win both races, was a good summer chaser, winning the Galway Plate and the Munster National in 1994, and two years later added the Irish Grand National.

Bred by N.J. Connors, he was owned by Eamonn King, the well-known owner and breeder of National Hunt horses, but he parted with the horse to M.D. O'Connor before he was successful in the Irish Grand National. He remained with Arthur Moore throughout his career, which ended after he had to be pulled up in a race in Cork in

October 1997. Although he only won six steeplechases and one hurdle race, Feathered Gale did amass over £120,000 in win prize money, and he was placed in a number of leading steeplechases during his career. Runner-up to Into the Red in the Becher Chase (Aintree) and also in the Munster National to Audrey Healy's Monkey Ago, he also finished second to Eugene M. O'Sullivan's Another Excuse in the Midlands Grand National (Uttoxeter) in March 1996 and was third behind Charles J. Haughey's Flashing Steel and Rust Never Sleeps in the 1995 Irish Grand National.

The 1994 Galway Plate produced an exciting finish, with the first three home separated only by a head and a neck. Minister for Fun, the second-favourite for the race, trained by Edward O'Grady and ridden by Charlie Swan, looked the certain winner when kicking clear early in the straight, with his nearest rivals Feathered Gale and Mubadir (Paul Carberry) under pressure. The latter had lost his chance through a jumping error when challenging for the lead, but Minister for Fun flagged as he approached the finish, enabling Franny Woods to force his mount up to nick the verdict by a head, with Mubadir only a neck away in third. The heavily backed favourite, Will Phone, trained by Michael O'Brien and ridden by Richard Dunwoody, dropped away quickly in the closing stages, having been prominent, eventually trailing in towards the tail of the field.

ANSAR

(Bay gelding 1996 Kahyasi – Anaza by Darshaan)

Owner: Aga Khan
Trainer: John M. Oxx, Currabeg, Curragh
Dundalk 12 July 1999 (J.P. Murtagh) Won Drumcar Maiden 12f £2,600
Breeder: Aga Khan Studs
Winner of the 2001 Galway Hurdle
Winner of the 2004 and 2005 Galway Plate

Owner: Michael Watt
Trainer: Dermot K. Weld, Rosewell House, Curragh
Galway, 1 August 2000 (N. Williamson) Won Albatross Maiden Hurdle £5,520 9/10f
Galway 4 August 2000 (P.J. Smullen) Won Guinness Race £5,865 4/6f
Tralee 24 August 2000 (K.R. O'Ryan) Won Denny Havasnack 17f £8,300

Owner: Mrs K. Devlin
Galway 30 July 2001 (B.J. Geraghty) Won GPT Dublin Handicap Hurdle £9,750 7/2
Galway 2 August 2001 (P. Carberry) Won Guinness Galway Hurdle Handicap 2m £66,875 6/1

Tipperary 7 October 2001 (P. Carberry) Won John J. McManus Hurdle 2m £42,750

Galway 1 August 2002 (P. Carberry) Won Guinness Novice Chase 2m 1f €13,000

Tralee 1 September 2002 (P. Carberry) Won Brogue Inn Trophy Novice Chase 2m 4f €11,550

Galway 28 July 2004 (D.J. Casey) Won Galway Plate Handicap Chase 2m 6f €103,725

Galway 27 July 2005 (D.F. O'Regan) Won Galway Plate Handicap Chase 2m 6f €121,800

Wexford 27 August 2005 (P.J. Smullen) Won Tote Handicap 16f €7,000

Ansar, winner of the Galway Hurdle in 2001 and the Plate in 2004 and 2005

Ansar is only third horse, after Blancona and Knight Errant, to win both the Plate and the Hurdle and the only one to win the Hurdle before winning the Plate. Bred by the Aga Khan and by his double Derby winner Kahyasi, Ansar went into training with John Oxx, ran twice unplaced at two years and won once and was placed four times in his five races at three. He won a maiden race at Dundalk before coming to the 1999 Galway Festival, where he started favourite but only finished third in the GPT three-year-old Handicap to Ciel D'Or. After finishing third to Miltonfield in the Irish Cesarewitch, he was sold to Michael Watt and transferred

Nearly A Moose (right), winner of the 2003 Galway Plate and the last big winner at the meeting trained by Paddy Mullins

to Dermot Weld. Runner-up in the Chester Cup, he won twice at Galway in 2000, a maiden hurdle and a flat race, before going on to the Tralee meeting, where he lifted the Havasnack. On his next visit to Galway, in 2001, he again won twice: two handicap hurdles including the feature Galway Hurdle.

Sent chasing, Ansar won a novice chase at Galway 2002. He did not win in 2003, however, finishing fifth in the Galway Plate behind Nearly A Moose. He then won the Galway Plate in successive years before his gallant attempt to equal Tipperary Boy's record of three Galway Plates in 2006, which he failed by three and a half lengths. The winner was John P. McManus's Far From Trouble, trained by the former Champion Flat Jockey Christy Roche, and ridden by Roger Loughran, who was deputizing for Tony McCoy, who broke a wrist in a fall from Sporting Limerick in the second race.

A fast-ground horse and a natural jumper, Ansar loves Galway and the big crowds, and has run at every Festival since 1999, winning seven races from nine attempts. A real money-spinner, he has won nearly half a million euros in prize money and may not be finished yet. After he finished second in 2006, a huge roar greeted him and Ruby Walsh as he took his mount into the enclosure. Dermot Weld was delighted with the run, commenting: 'It was as big a cheer for a horse finishing second as I've heard anywhere.' He continued: 'Ansar has run a great race and I'm very proud of him. All being well, he'll come back next year and try to win the race for the third time.' Ansar finished fourth in the Galway Plate in 2007.

GREY SWALLOW

(Grey colt 2001 Daylami –Style of Life by The Minstrel)

Breeder: Marguerite Weld
Winner of the 2004 Irish Derby

Owner: Mrs Rochelle Quinn
Trainer: Dermot K. Weld, Rosewell House, Curragh
Galway 28 July 2003 (P.J. Smullen) Won GPT 2yo Maiden 7f €13,455. 11/8
Leopardstown 27 October 2003 (P.J. Smullen) Won Killavullan (Group 3) 7f €45,550 4/9f
Leopardstown 18 April 2004 (P.J. Smullen) Won 2,000 Guineas Trial 8f €32,550 4/9f
Curragh 27 June 2004 (P.J. Smullen) Won Irish Derby (Group 1) 12f €736,600 10/1
Curragh 22 May 2005 (P.J. Smullen) Won Tattersalls Gold Cup (Group 1) 10f €155,000 13/2

Owner: Vega Fze
Trainer: Dermot K. Weld, Rosewell House, Curragh
Hollywood Park 13 May 2006 (A. Solis) Won Jim Murray Handicap 12f €126,390

Grey Swallow looked a colt out of the ordinary when trouncing Rock of Gibraltar's brother, Rock of Cashel, by ten lengths at Galway. He went on to win the Killavullan Stakes and was officially rated the top Irish two-year-old of 2003, with only the French-trained Bago being rated higher in the European Classification. Working like a good horse at home, Grey Swallow was aimed at the Classics and was heavily backed to win the 2,000 Guineas after winning a preparatory race at Leopardstown. Having finished a disappointing fourth to Haafhd at Newmarket, Grey Swallow looked to have a better chance in the Irish 2,000 Guineas. Haafhd was not in the field and the race looked a match between Azamour and Grey Swallow, third and fourth at Newmarket, separated by only a length. Again Azamour, trained by John Oxx, confirmed the placings with Grey Swallow, but only by half a length, but both were beaten by a horse that had finished way behind them at Newmarket. Bachelor Duke, an English-trained maiden, stormed up the centre of the track to win the race by a length.

Dermot Weld was of the opinion that the best of Grey Swallow had yet to be seen so he boldly took on North Light, the Epsom Derby winner, in the Irish Derby. Because Grey Swallow was running over 12 furlongs for the first time fears were expressed that he might not stay the trip, which caused many punters to desert him. His pedigree was that of a middle distance horse; Daylami, his sire, won over 12 furlongs, and while his dam did not win beyond a mile, she was by

The Minstrel. Like Grey Swallow, The Minstrel failed in both Guineas but won the English and the Irish Derbies before beating six classic winners in the King George VI and the Queen Elizabeth Stakes at Ascot. Weld clearly stated that he believed Grey Swallow worked like a horse that would stay further than a mile but North Light started the odds-on favourite, while Grey Swallow drifted out to 10 to 1.

North Light hit the front 2 furlongs out and kicked for home, but Grey Swallow responded when Pat Smullen asked and quickened to track the leader. Pouncing inside the final furlong, he stayed on well to defeat the Epsom Derby winner by half a length. Sir Michael Stoute, trainer of North Light, commented, 'He was second best on the day.' Mark Weld, the trainer's son, proudly called Grey Swallow 'The family horse' – which he was, having been bred by his grandmother, who still retained a share in him. As the Welds dreamed of races to come, experts rubbished the form because Tycoon, Aiden O'Brien's fifth-string, a 150-to-1 rank outsider making his seasonal debut, finished third, right on the heels of the leaders.

Grey Swallow's North American racing career was disappointing although the horse did win the Grade 2 Jim Murray Memorial Handicap over 12 furlongs on turf. Having finished third in the Grade 1 Manhattan Handicap at Belmont Park in July 2006, Grey Swallow was sold to the Australian Wadham Park Syndicate for about AUS $5 million. Taken to Australia to continue his racing career, Grey Swallow was injured at Moonee Valley in October 2006 when he managed to get a leg entangled in the starting stalls. He suffered bone damage to his leg and, although the horse has made a full recovery, his owners have decided to retire him from racing. With his sire Daylami sold to stand in South Africa, Grey Swallow's owners are keen to stand him at a European stud in 2008 before bringing him back to their Australian stud.

MORE RAINBOWS

(Bay gelding 2000 Rainbows For Life Canada – Musical Myth USA by Crafty Prospector)

Breeder: Sir Anthony O'Reilly
Winner of the 2005 Galway Hurdle

Tramore 16 August 2003 (R. Walsh) Won Nolan Ryan 3yo Maiden Hurdle 2m €7,700
Tralee 27 August 2003 (P. Carberry) Won Val's Bar 3yo Hurdle 2m €9,100
Navan 16 May 2004 (P. Carberry) Won Scanlons of Kilberry Hurdle 2¼m €9,800
Limerick 18 June 2004 (F.M. Berry) Won Irwin Bros Handicap 12f €9,100
Down Royal 10 July 2004 (P.J. Smullen) Won Summer Handicap 12f €10,500

Navan 10 June 2005 (N.P. Madden) Won Ladbrokes Hurdle 2½m €15,510
Galway 28 July 2005 (N.P. Madden) Won Guinness Galway Handicap Hurdle 2m €115,900
Roscommon 11 June 2006 (D.F. O'Regan) Won George McCourt Novice Chase 2m €10,150
Navan 16 June 2006 (D.F. O'Regan) Won Generali Novice Chase 2½m €12,600

In the 1970s changes were made to the Rules of Racing to allow for multiple ownership of racehorses. Syndicates and companies were permitted to enter horses in
races, opening up an expensive pastime to ordinary people by spreading the costs.
The Neighbours' Syndicate consisted of a group of neighbours and their friends
from Dunshaughlin, Co. Meath. It was established because of some of its members
knew Eamon Reilly, a bloodstock agent, who suggested that it purchase flat horses
out of a training stable as prospective jumpers. One of the horses he suggested was
More Rainbows, bred by Sir Anthony O'Reilly and owned by Lady O'Reilly, which
was being sold off. He had run once on the flat at two years, when trained by
Declan Gillespie, but was too backward to make a mark on the flat at three.
Purchased by Eamon Reilly for the Neighbours' Syndicate, he was transferred to the

*Ruby Walsh, the top Irish jump
jockey of his generation*

stable of Noel Meade, near Dunshaughlin, who usually trains the syndicate's horses, much to the disappointment of Gillespie, who was particularly anxious to keep him.

Although he won a flat race at Down Royal at three, hurdling proved to be his forte, with him winning three three-year-old hurdles in 2003. A summer horse, better on a fast surface than on soft ground, he was put out in a field for the winter months with another horse named Tiger Cry. Strange as it may seem, these two horses, who would fight out the finish of the 2005 Guinness Galway Hurdle, spent the winter together grazing peacefully side by side. More Rainbows sprang a 33-to-1 surprise victory in the big Galway race, giving untold pleasure to his large band of owners. However, he was a handicapper; the big championship hurdle races were beyond his ability, and he had risen markedly in the weights, which limited his prospects of further big wins. Therefore, the decision was made to send him steeplechasing.

Everything was going to plan; More Rainbows had been well schooled over fences, and was working well, and hopes were high for the future. He made his chasing debut at Punchestown in June 2006, and was made odds-on favourite, but he did not jump well and was beaten. While his jumping had been disappointing, Noel Meade felt that he had straightened it out when More Rainbows turned out again a fortnight later at Roscommon. This time it was a very different story; with Denis O'Regan in the saddle, More Rainbows jumped much better and defeated the favourite, Kit Carson, ridden by Ruby Walsh. Not bothered by the prevailing firm ground, the horse reappeared five days later at Navan, again winning convincingly, despite a number of jumping errors. Two days afterwards he ran at Killarney. He started favourite but did not jump fluently and finished a well-beaten fourth. Initially very disappointed, the trainer was relieved when it transpired that one of his shoes had been pulled off in running, which would account for the poor performance and indifferent jumping. It was then decided that he should be allowed to take his chance in the Galway Plate, in which he was set to carry only 9 stones 10 pounds.

Denis O'Regan could not do that weight so he switched to More Rainbows's stable companion Carlesimo, and Tom Ryan took the mount on More Rainbows. One year to the very day since his victory in the Galway Hurdle, he fell in the closing stages of the race. Although at first he appeared all right, he proved to have internal injuries, his condition deteriorated gradually and he died the following day.

The People

Hon Reginald J.M. Greville-Nugent (1848–78)

Rode as 'Mr St James'

Owner, green and white bars:

1872 BRUNETTE (Mr St James) – Members' Chase £49 (J.H. Moore)

1874 REVOKE (T. Miller) – Galway Plate Handicap Chase £365 (J.H. Moore)

Rider:

1872 Mr St James's BRUNETTE – Members' Chase (J.H. Moore)

1872 Mr O'C. Morris's CALL – Curragh 6f flat

1877 P.N. Fitzgerald's SWEET MEADOW – Forster Street Handicap Chase (C. Heavy)

It was not the done thing at the time for members of the nobility to ride in races and, in order to save his family from social embarrassment, Reginald Greville-Nugent did not use his own name when racing. Racegoers knew him as 'Mr St James'. He rode under that name and his horses ran in that name; outsiders believed that that was his real name. Born in Brighton, he was the fourth son of Lord Greville, 1st Baron, Clonyn Castle, Delvin, Clonhugh, Mullingar, Colonel of the Westmeath Militia and a former member of parliament for Co. Longford.

A former Coldstream Guardsman, The Honourable Greville-Nugent was known to his friends as 'The Limb'. Married in 1871, he was based at Miletta Lodge on the Curragh and rode extensively in Ireland and England. A brilliant rider, he became the second amateur, after Joseph D. Whyte, to become Irish Champion Jockey when winning the title in 1874. Sadly, his career came to a premature end when he was killed in a fall at Sandown Park on 26 February 1878.

Charles J. Blake (d. 1917)

Owner, French grey, scarlet hoop and cap:

1873 WATERWITCH (Behan) – Renmore 6f flat £260 (J. Dunne)

1880 BARON FARNEY (C. Whelan) – Renmore Handicap 8f flat £100 (J. Dunne)

1880 BARON FARNEY (F. Wynne) – Her Majesty's Plate 2m flat £104 (J. Dunne)

1880 GAY LADY (P. Lynch) – Farewell Handicap Chase £40 (J. Dunne)

1881 BARON FARNEY (J. Callaghan) – Renmore Handicap 8f flat £58 (J. Dunne)

1881 BARON FARNEY (J. Callaghan) – Her Majesty's Plate 2m flat £104 (J. Dunne)

1883 SYLPH (T. Harris) – Her Majesty's Plate 2m flat £100 (J. Dunne)

1885 ST KEVIN (H. Saunders) – Renmore Handicap 8f flat £59 (J. Dunne)

1892 KILLOWEN (T. Harris) – County Handicap Hurdle £67½ (T. Harris)

1892 GOLDMINER (T. Harris) – Her Majesty's Plate 2m flat £104 (T. Harris)

The Blakes came to Ireland with King John in 1185 and settled in the west. They were one of the tribes of Galway of lore. The younger son of Valentine O'Connor Blake of Towerhill, Co. Mayo, and a member of the Galway Race Committee, Charles Blake was educated at Stonyhurst and Trinity College, Dublin and, although he qualified as a barrister, never practised, going into business instead. He made his fortune supplying wool to the British Army for its uniforms and came into racing through his friendship with his neighbour, George H. Moore.

In 1865 he registered his French grey, scarlet hoop colours and bought his first thoroughbred, Lady of the Lake, who ran once unplaced for him at the Maze as a two-year-old. With three horses called Lady of the Lake racing in Ireland at this time, it was perhaps understandable that the Irish Racing Calendar initially got the breeding of his horse wrong. His filly was by the 2,000 Guineas winner Lord of the Isles out of Lady Olympia by Vatican and was bred by George H. Moore of Moore Hall, Co. Mayo. She won a steeplechase at Westport, a 2-mile race over 4-foot walls, ridden by James 'Fairy' Dunne, before being retired to stud. There she bred St Kevin, the second of Charles Blake's three winners of the Irish Derby. His first Irish Derby winner was Sylph in 1883, whose dam, Dryad, Blake bought personally at Newmarket in October 1869 after she had finished third in Great Eastern Handicap. On the death of his father, Charles Blake purchased Heath House, on the Great Heath of Maryborough. There he established his stud and private training stable towards the end of 1880, which was put under the care of the former jockey 'Fairy' Dunne, who had ridden Roman Bee to victory in the Anglesey Stakes of 1862.

Although Heath House was a private stable, it did have a professional trainer in charge, rather than a head groom, and Charles Blake's close friends were free to send horses there if they wished. Captain Machell, Edmund Smithwick, Joseph Lyons, T.L. Plunkett and Sebastian Nolan were some of those who did so. Captain James Machell, who trained at Newmarket, always had a couple of Blake horses among his string, notably Arbitrator and Sibyl, and reciprocated by having a horse or two in the Blake stable, notably Portmarnock, winner of the 1895 Irish Derby.

Arbitrator, winner of four races at two years, including a nursery at Warwick by twenty lengths with Fred Archer in the saddle, was the best horse to carry Charles Blake's colours but his three-year-old career was cut short by an illness. Despite the setback, Arbitrator won the Liverpool Autumn Cup and Great Lancashire Handicap on successive days and finished fourth in the big Cambridgeshire Handicap behind Jongleur. He became a successful sire, being Champion in Ireland in 1886 and 1888, and his stock included Kilwarlin, winner of the 1887 St Leger. Unfortunately for Charles Blake, he died just as he was becoming established as a top stallion, in 1888 at the early age of fourteen.

After eight years in charge, during which time he trained two winners and five placed horses in the Irish Derby, 'Fairy' Dunne moved on and was replaced in 1889 by the veteran trainer Pat Doucie. An ailing Doucie had to retire after two years in charge, and died in June 1891. The stable jockey Thomas Harris filled the void while Blake looked for a suitable trainer. This process took a frustrating two years and was only resolved when Captain Machell suggested 'Shem' Jeffrey, a competent and loyal stableman in Captain Machell's stable at Newmarket for twenty years. Jeffrey undertook the long train and boat journey to Heath House alone, but Blake arranged for a hackney driver, a man named Fogarty, to meet his new trainer from the boat at the North Wall. Mr Fogarty regularly ferried racing people around Dublin, and got in with the racing crowd and ultimately the bookmakers – indeed he became one himself. Successful in his new calling, he gave up driving his horse and carriage to go racing full time and he founded a Fogarty dynasty of bookmakers.

A member of the Turf Club since 1866, Charles J. Blake was elected a steward in 1874 for a three-year term but he was continually re-elected until 1906 because of his outstanding abilities as an administrator. A confirmed bachelor, he died in 1917, leaving his property to his nephew, another bachelor, Isidore Blake, with the stipulation that Jeffrey should have a job for life. That was not a problem because he had been there for years but he found it difficult to adjust to the new generation. When Colonel Arthur J. Blake, Isidore's brother, returned from the war suffering from shell shock he was given a home at Heath House, taking an active interest in the stable as he slowly recovered from his ordeal. Arthur's interest did not suit Jeffrey one little bit; he felt that he was no longer in sole charge and resented any changes being made. A difficult relationship further deteriorated when Jeffrey effectively found himself in the position of assistant trainer in 1925, Arthur Blake having taken out a trainer's licence. Jeffrey retained his licence but was no longer in charge and Arthur Blake became the official trainer at Heath House.

In his first season, the stable produced a very fast two-year-old named Fohanaun, who won four of his five races, including the prestigious National Produce Stakes. His only defeat occurred at Ayr, where he was second in a nursery, and his target was the 1926 Irish 2,000 Guineas, run over a mile. Colonel Blake had doubts about Fohanaun's ability to go the distance so he gave him a very tough preliminary race against older horses in the Victoria Cup Handicap at Hurst Park, over a distance of 7 furlongs. Set a daunting task for a three-year-old, even for one with classic aspirations, Fahanaun was unquoted in the betting, despite his top-class form, but ran a great race in the circumstances to finish fifth. He lined up a 9-to-2 third-favourite in the Irish 2,000 Guineas but Embargo, ridden by Steve Donoghue, ran away with the race, with Fohanaun finishing unplaced. During the inquest after the race, Jeffrey apparently told Arthur Blake, who owned the colt in partnership with Isidore, that Fohanaun was a sprinter and would not stay the stiff Curragh mile. Although Jeffrey denied this later, it was reasonable to assume that this was the case because the colt had plenty of speed and had not won beyond 6 furlongs.

Whether or not Jeffrey asserted that Fohanaun was a sprinter, the colt did return to racing in sprints. Sent over to Aintree to contest a 5-furlong handicap, he faced a difficult task against older horses, and was not in the least fancied in the betting market; he made no show. Having been well beaten, it was strange that he was despatched to contest a similar event at the Ebor meeting at York, where he faced another impossible task. Once again he was the rank outsider in the betting, and once again he was well beaten. On returning home to Heath House he was given a break.

Reappearing at the Curragh in November in the Irish Cambridgeshire, run over 1 mile, on paper he was hard to fancy, having failed to win with 34 pounds less to carry over distances that appeared to suit him better. Now burdened with 9 stones 4 pounds and giving weight to everything except the hot favourite, the six-year-old English raider, Polish Patriot, Fohanaun looked a forlorn hope but someone fancied him. Well supported in the market, he started at 10 to 1, second-favourite, and stormed to victory by an effortless six lengths. It was not the performance of a mere sprinter and Arthur Blake furiously accused Jeffrey of misleading him and running the horse to land bets for himself. Months of pent-up frustration flooded Jeffrey's mind and he abruptly walked out on his job for life, ending an association that had lasted over thirty years. Poor Shem did not prosper during the six years left to him on this earth but Arthur Blake did. The departure of Jeffrey left him in sole charge and he went on to enjoy a very successful career, training no less than seventeen Irish classic winners, which was a record that stood until it was beaten by Vincent O'Brien.

Francis Wynne (1857–85)

Rider:

1873 Mr Sanford's CRUST – Flying Plate 5f flat (T. Kelly)
1880 C.J. Blake's BARON FARNEY – Her Majesty's Plate 2m flat (J. Dunne)
1882 P. Wall's DANSEUSE – Members' Handicap 6f flat (M. Dennehy)

Francis Wynne was born in 1857, the younger son of Denis Wynne, a former jockey who had won the Grand National on Matthew in 1847. Fifteen years later his elder brother, Joe, was killed in the same race following a fall off a horse named O'Connell right in front of the grandstand. Frank Wynne began his career with his father, who was training for Christopher and William St George at Rathbride Cottage on the Curragh, a yard that would later be occupied by Willie Cullen. He was given his first mount in public at the age of thirteen, when weighing just 4 stones, on William St George's unnamed filly by Outcast, unplaced over 6 furlongs at the Curragh September meeting 1870. Dick Bell, trainer of Absentee the first winner of the Galway Plate, provided young Frank with his first winner, Conciliation at Baldoyle in March 1871. Two years later he won the first 5-furlong race run at Ballybrit, on Crust, trained by Thomas Kelly.

Like his father and brother Joe before him, Frank Wynne became Irish Champion Jockey, heading the list three times in succession in 1880, 1881 and 1882. He rode three Irish Derby winners in four years – Redskin, Madame Dubarry and King of the Bees – but with his opportunities on the flat limited by rising weight he began taking mounts over fences. With an eye to the future, although he was only twenty-five years old, he started training, while continuing to ride on the flat and over fences, succeeding Joseph French at Rossmore Lodge in 1883. The following year he trained and rode Mallow to win the Waterford Testimonial Stakes at the Curragh, as well as the Patriotic Stakes at Baldoyle, and trained the winners of successive Royal Whips, Xema and Sylvan Queen in 1884 and 1885, both for Andrew Tiernan. Struck down by an illness early in 1885, he recovered briefly only to finally succumb on 3 December 1885.

Only seven races over the minimum flat distance of 5 furlongs have run at Galway:

Fr Breen gives communion to the faithful during the traditional Sunday mass

1873 Mr Sanford's CRUST (F. Wynne) – Flying Plate 5f flat £60 Bar (T. Kelly)

1876 Mr J.W. Nuttall's BIRDS-EYE (M. Miley) – Renmore Plate 5f flat £80 5/1 (J.W. Nuttall)

1877 R. Webb's CLYDA (M. Miley) – Members' Handicap 5f flat £50 6/4f (T. Connolly)

1881 Mr M.A. Maher's PURPLE (Patrick Behan) – Claddagh 5f flat Walk Over £20 (Private)

1884 Captain L.H. Jones's RAPPAREE (Rowan) – Mervue Plate 5f flat £48 4/6f (G. Moore)

1887 Mr Maple Leaf's QUEEN OF THE ROSES (P. Lynch) – Renmore Handicap 5f flat £79 6/4f (D. Broderick)

1887 A.E. McCracken's BELGRAVE (J. Gourley) – Traders' Handicap 5f flat £49 4/5f (F.F. Cullen)

Henry Eyre Linde (1835–97)

Trainer, Eyrefield Lodge, Curragh:

1874 H.E. Linde's TINKLING SOUND (Mr T. Beasley) – Ballroom Handicap 16f flat £150

1876 Captain Aubertin's THE ADMIRAL (Mr T. Beasley) – Merview Chase £100

1876 T.N. Wade's MARTHA (Mr T. Beasley) – Galway Plate Handicap Chase £245

1876 A. Croften's SULTANA (Mr T. Beasley) – Forster Street Handicap Chase £150

1878 H.E. Linde's BIJOU (Mr T. Beasley) – Forster Street Handicap Chase £70

1881 H.E. Linde's FUNNY EYES (Mr T. Beasley) – Mervue Hunt Chase £28

1881 H.E. Linde's NIGHTFALL (Mr T. Beasley) – Galway Plate Handicap £148

1882 Captain T.Y.L. Kirkwood's SUGAR PLUM (Mr H. Beasley) – Galway Plate £178

1883 Captain Walker's VENTRILOQUIST (Mr H. Beasley) – Galway Plate £138

1888 John Gubbins's ILENE (T. Kavanagh) – Committee Hunt Chase £29¼

1888 John Gubbins's ILENE (T. Kavanagh) – Glenarde Hunt Chase £49

1889 E. Frazer's ALEXANDER (T. Kavanagh) – Galway Plate Handicap Chase £132

1895 H.E. Linde's DOUBLE PRIMROSE (W. Hoysted) – Galway Plate Handicap Chase £132

The outstanding Irish trainer of the nineteenth century, Henry Linde was the first to target the big steeplechase prizes in England and France rather than move his stable to England. He took over Eyrefield Lodge, the house in which he was born, on the death of his father in 1862, and established a powerful public training stable by the early 1870s. His incredible run of big winners began in 1873, when Gamebird and Highland Mary won valuable races for the stable. Every year from 1873 until 1894, except 1874, a Linde-trained runner was successful in one of the major races in Ireland and England. Linde trained two winners of the Grand National – Empress (1880) and Woodbrook (1881) – but Too Good, Cyrus and Martha finished second in that important steeplechase; Martha also finished third. He owned Seaman himself, winner of the Conyngham Cup and the 1882 Grand Hurdle de Auteuil, a race won by Dawn Run 103 years later, but sold him to Lord Manners because he had a doubtful leg.

The great trainer was humbled the following year when Seaman beat his charge, Cyrus, by a head to win the 1882 Grand National. However, Linde gained some consolation by winning the big French race, the Grand Steeplechase de Paris with Whisper Low. In 1883 he won the race again, this time with Too Good, named by the Empress of Austria during a visit to Eyrefield Lodge in 1879. Invited to name three horses, the Empress named the first Valerie, after her daughter, the second Empress after herself, but commented that the third was 'too good for a name'. Having won the Irish Grand National with Grand National, Thiggin Thue and Controller, Linde had built up a formidable stud of flat-race horses and, just like Vincent O'Brien about seventy years later, began to concentrate on the flat from 1883 onwards. He still won some important jumping races, like the Conyngham Cup with Cork (1886) and Small Talk (1887), and the Galway Plate with Alexander (1889), as well as big chases with his former flat racer Red Prince II.

The dominant trainer of his era, Harry Linde won the Galway Plate six times, a record which was equalled by Fred Cullen in 1902 and beaten by Harry Ussher thirty-five years later. Linde trained three Plate winners in succession, from 1881 to 1883. Galway maestro Harry Ussher did likewise but Phonsie O'Brien surpassed them with four in a row between 1962 and 1965. On the flat Linde enjoyed great success as a breeder, owner and trainer, winning the Irish Derby with Pet Fox, the Irish Cesarewitch with Whisper Low (1881) and big two-year-old events with Mayboy, Donnycarney, Grecian Bend, Ash Plant, May Moon, The Rhymer, Red Prince II, Swanshot, First Flower, Starlight III, Ball Coote, Burnett, Chit Chat and Rinvanny. He trained Little John (1888 and 1889), Chatterbox, Red Prince II and Starlight III to win the Royal Whip at the Curragh and besides had three seconds and a third in the Irish Derby.

Henry Eyre Linde fell into bad health and decided to retire during 1895, beginning the process by selling off some of his horses at Eyrefield Lodge on 24 June. The following month he sold Buttonhole, Dan Mack and Night Disturber to Germany and began the process of handing over control of the stable to his head lad Dan McNally, who had been with him for many years. Linde died on March 18 1897. He was married twice (his first wife died in 1883) but he had no children and on his death Eyrefield Lodge was sold to Captain Eustace Loder. Dan McNally continued to train at Eyrefield Lodge and he was the trainer of Ambush II, the property of the future King Edward VII, winner of the Grand National in the Royal colours and ridden by Algy Anthony. Ambush II was the last big winner to be trained at Eyrefield Lodge, which Captain Loder turned into a stud farm. The dramatic collapse of Devon Loch only yards from the winning post in 1956 ensured that Ambush II remains the only Royal winner of the famous Aintree race.

Mr Thomas Beasley (1848–1905)

Champion Irish Jockey 1875 and 1878

Rider:

1871 John Nally's QUEEN SCOTIA – Western Hunt Chase (A. McDonough)

1874 R.H. Long's ILDERIM – Renmore Handicap 8f flat (H. Bell)

1874 R.H. Long's ILDERIM – Corinthian Handicap 6f flat (H. Bell)

1874 H.E. Linde's TINKLING SOUND – Ballroom Handicap 2m flat (H.E. Linde)

1875 Captain Bates's PRIDE OF KILDARE – Forster Street Handicap Chase (J.H. Moore)

1876 Captain Aubertin's THE ADMIRAL – Mervue Chase (H.E. Linde)

1876 T.N. Wade's MARTHA – Galway Plate Handicap Chase (H.E. Linde)

1876 A. Crofton's SULTANA – Forster Street Handicap Chase (H.E. Linde)

1878 W. Holland's MESTIZA – Bushey Park Handicap Hurdle (T. Connolly)

1878 H.E. Linde's BIJOU – Forster Street Handicap Chase (2nd Class) (H.E. Linde)

1881 H.E. Linde's FUNNY EYES – Mervue Hunt Chase (H.E. Linde)

1881 H.E. Linde's NIGHTFALL – Galway Plate Handicap Chase (H.E. Linde)

Aintree Grand National

1878 2nd MARTHA (H.E. Linde)

1879 3rd MARTHA (H.E. Linde)

1880 1st EMPRESS (H.E. Linde)

1881 1st WOODBROOK (H.E. Linde)

1882 2nd CYRUS (H.E. Linde)

1889 1st FRIGATE (M.A. Maher)

Irish Grand National

1876 1st GRAND NATIONAL (H.E. Linde)

1877 1st THIGGIN THUE (H.E. Linde)

1887 2nd BLUE STOCKINGS (H.E. Linde)

The eldest of the five Beasley brothers, Tommy was the best jockey of the quintet and could more than hold his own with the professionals, both on the flat and over fences. His outstanding achievement, which is unlikely ever to be equalled, is his Grand National/Irish Derby double in 1889 on Frigate and Tragedy. A son of Joseph L. Beasley of Salisbury House, Athy, Tommy went to school in Carlow and rode his first winner on a pony named Blazes, owned by his uncle, Tom Pope of Popesfield, at a local sports event at Athy. When he rode Mr Brett's True Blue to victory in the Scurry Steeplechase at the long defunct Queen's County Hunt meeting over the Orchard course on 7 April 1870, his first official winner, Allen McDonough was impressed. The former crack steeplechase rider was training at Athgarvan Lodge at the time and he invited the 22-year-old to join his stable. When McDonough dramatically retired in September 1972, Tommy moved to Henry Linde at Eyrefield Lodge, with whom he remained until 1892, when he virtually retired from race riding. The Linde–Beasley partnership became one of the most formidable in racing in Ireland, England and in France, winning two Grand Nationals, two Irish Grand Nationals, the Grand Steeplechase de Paris (on Whisper Low) and a Galway Plate. In addition Mr Tommy rode a third Grand National winner, Frigate, for Matt Maher, and won two Irish Derbies, on Tragedy (1889) and Narraghmore (1891).

Light enough to ride at 8 stones 7 pounds, he won his second Irish Derby on Narraghmore, trained at Newmarket by Charles Archer, the younger brother of Fred, one of the greatest jockeys to ride on the English turf. Tommy Beasley rode against Fred Archer, at the Curragh in October 1886, the English crack's only appearance in Ireland, having been invited over by Charles Blake. Taking three mounts, Archer rode the first two to win but was beaten into third place on Black Rose by Tommy Beasley on Spahi and Willie Cullen on Lord Chatham, to the delight of the enormous crowd. It was one of the most memorable moments of Tommy Beasley's career and a poignant one as Archer shot himself a couple of weeks later during an illness brought on by excessive wasting.

Although Tommy Beasley cut back on his riding commitments from 1892, he actually retired after riding Percy La Touche's Killougher to victory in a match at the Curragh April Meeting 1899. The death of his wife, an English lady named Miss Fisher, shook Tommy badly and he never really recovered, dying after a long illness in August 1905 at his residence, Cryhelp Lodge, Dunlavin. His ability over fences is reflected by the few falls he suffered during his riding career, which was virtually free of serious injury.

Mr John Beasley (c.1854–98)

Rider:

1878   J.D. Whyte's UNCLE – Farewell Handicap Chase (H. Grattan)

1879   Captain P. Butler's EURASIAN – Claddagh Hurdle

1879   Mr Hartigan's ADVOCATE – Forster Street Handicap Chase

Irish Grand National

1878   1st JUGGLER (J.H. Moore)

1880   2nd VICTORIA (G. Moore)

1881   2nd LOBELIA (G. Moore)

The best placing Mr Jack Beasley achieved in the Aintree Grand National was eighth place on Victoria, behind Empress, in 1880. He was attached to John Hubert Moore's Jockey Hall stable on the Curragh, riding his first winner in February 1876 at Newbridge on Shock. The race, the Newbridge Harrier Hunt Cup, presented by Moses Taylor, a 3-mile steeplechase, was actually won by New Purchase but J.H. Moore lodged a successful objection for crossing and the winner was disqualified. Mr Jack had a short riding career, which effectively ended when old J.H. Moore handed his stable over to his son Garry, who began to drift into the flat. Jack Beasley joined his brothers Harry and Willie at Eyrefield House, remaining there until his death in October 1898.

Mr Henry Beasley (1852–1939)

Champion Irish Jockey 1883 and 1885

Rider:

1880 W.G. Jameson's MARCHIONESS – Forster Street Handicap Chase (H. Beasley)

1882 Captain T.Y.L. Kirkwood's SUGAR PLUM – Galway Plate (H.E. Linde)

1883 Captain Walker's VENTRILOQUIST – Galway Plate (H.E. Linde)

1888 Henry Beasley's ROSCOE – Moyode Hunt Chase (H. Beasley)

Aintree Grand National

1883 3rd MOHICAN

1884 2nd FRIGATE (M.A. Maher)

1885 2nd FRIGATE (M.A. Maher)

1886 2nd TOO GOOD (H.E. Linde)

Irish Grand National

1880 1st CONTROLLER (H.E. Linde)

1889 1st CITADEL (H. Beasley)

1891 1st COME-AWAY (H. Beasley)

Trainer, Eyrefield House, Curragh:

1880 W.G. Jameson's MARCHIONESS (Mr H. Beasley) – Forster Street Handicap Chase £100

1886 G. Tyson's SAFETY (Mr W. Beasley) – Glenarde Hunt Chase £49

1888 Henry Beasley's ROSCOE (Mr H. Beasley) – Moyode Hunt Chase £49

1888 Hugh Gore's GREEK GIRL (Mr W. Beasley) – Express Hunt Flat 2m £49½

Mr Harry Beasley started riding in races a bit later than usual and retired much later than usual, on 10 June 1935 after he felt that he had given his mount, Mollie, a bad ride. His career in the saddle lasted fifty-nine years. One of the four brothers who had such a good record in the Grand National, Mr Harry rode his first winner when C.E. Livesay's Straffan won a Hunters' Chase at Baldoyle in April 1876 and had his first mount at Aintree in 1879, on Turco in the Liverpool Hurdle. He won the Grand National on Come-away in 1891, was placed third on Mohican (1883) and finished runner-up on each of the next three years, on Frigate (1884 and 1885) and Too Good (1886). Champion Irish Jockey in 1883 and 1885, he established a record by winning the prestigious Prince of Wales's Plate at Punchestown five times in a row (1883–7). He also won two Irish Grand Nationals, on Controller (1880) and Citadel (1889), and had his last ride in that race in 1924, when finishing tenth on Pride of Arras, who started joint-second-favourite at 7 to 1. Riding into old age, Mr Henry Beasley won a steeplechase at Punchestown in 1923 when he was seventy-one and rode against two of his sons, Henry H. and Rufus, in a flat race at Naas in February 1927. He eventually retired after riding Mollie in a handicap flat race at Baldoyle in 1935.

He established a training stable at Eyrefield House, not far from Linde's Eyrefield Lodge, and remained there until his death in 1939. Assisted by brothers Willie and Jack, he trained the Conyngham Cup and Aintree Grand National winner Come-away and the Irish Grand National winners, Citadel and Greek Girl, as well as good winners on the flat, notably the two-year-olds Shillelagh (Beresford Stakes), Baccarat (Railway Stakes) and Instability (Anglesey Stakes), and the older horses Athel (Leopardstown Grand Prize) and Gauntlet (Drogheda Memorial). The stable had a sensational Punchestown meeting in 1892, winning the four most valuable races, but the celebrations were brought to an abrupt halt by the serious injury sustained by Willie Beasley in a fall on the second day, from which he later died. His death was a big blow to the Eyrefield House stable, which went into rapid decline thereafter and would never be a force again.

His three sons, Henry Herbert, William and Patrick (Rufus) all rode as professional jockeys, William winning three chases at Galway in the 1920s, including the 1921 Ballybrit Plate on the Irish Grand National winner and Aintree Grand National runner-up, Ballyboggan. Six years later he won the Ballybrit Plate again, this time on Pansy Croft's Golden Rebel, who walked over for the Galway Blazers Steeplechase the following afternoon. Rufus never won a race at Galway but Henry H. won three, all for Harry Ussher, including a double on Plate Day 1921.

Mr William Beasley (1859–92)

Champion Irish Amateur Jockey 1881 and 1882

Rider:
1882 R. Stacpoole's SCAMP II – Mervue Hunt Chase (Private)
1886 G. Tyson's SAFETY – Glenarde Hunt Chase (H. Beasley)
1888 Hugh Gore's GREEK GIRL – Express Hunt Flat 2m (H. Beasley)
1891 Col R. Thomson's QUEEN OF THE MAY – Galway Plate (F.F. Cullen)
1891 Mr Cahill's THE LAMB – Mervue Handicap 8f flat (J. Phelan)

Aintree Grand National
1888 2nd FRIGATE (M.A. Maher)

Irish Grand National
1891 3rd FAIR FIGHT (Private)

The youngest of the four brothers, William Beasley started out with John H. Moore at Jockey Hall and rode his first winner when Lord Marcus won a steeplechase at a meeting in Kinnegad, Co. Westmeath, on 4 March 1878. He went to England with Garry Moore but returned after a short time, joining his brother Harry at Eyrefield House. Unmarried, he was an important member of that training establishment and his early death was a tragic loss from which the stable never recovered. He died in 1892 from a fractured skull, sustained in a fall from All's Well in the Kildare Hunt Handicap Chase at Punchestown, when he received a kick in the head from a horse following behind. Twice Champion Irish Amateur, Willie rode his last winner on Flying Column at the Newbridge meeting on 1 March 1892.

Michael Sage (d. 1889)

Owner, maize and brown:

1877 ILDERIM (W. Bell) – Glenard Handicap Chase £70 (R. Bell)
1880 LADY NEWMAN (D. Meany) – Galway Plate £175 (J. Monahan) (ran in James Monahan's name)

Racecourse bookie Michael Sage had many horses in training but ran them in a variety of assumed names. 'G. Cranna' and 'Mr Salmon' are among those we know he used, but Lady Newman, his Galway Plate winner, actually ran in her trainer's name. The subterfuge was suspicious because Mr Sage had colours registered and ran horses in his own name, like Foxhound, runner-up to Tattoo in the 1877 Galway Plate. The use of other names was clearly intended to disguise the owner-ship of his horses, which reflected poorly on him and the betting ring. For a number of reasons, but mainly owing to infiltration by undesirable characters, bookmaking was getting a bad name, and the activities of Mr Sage were making matters worse. A patron of trainers James Monahan, who died in February 1883, and 'Honest' Paddy Gavin at French Furze, Michael Sage liked to give the Albert Club, Dublin, as his contact address. He died in December 1889.

Captain Edward Roderick Owen (1856–96)

Rider:

1882 William Hilliard's ADARE – Moyode Hunt Chase (W. Hilliard)

Roddy Owen, a famous military rider, described by George Lambton, a top amateur rider and later the trainer of the great little horse Hyperion, as 'as good a steeplechase rider as I ever saw', was born on the English/Welsh border. A career soldier, he spent several years abroad, but whenever he could get leave he travelled the country chasing mounts. He served in far-off lands such as Canada, Cyprus, Malta and India before coming briefly to Ireland, where he acted as ADC to the Lord-Lieutenant.

Roddy Owen came into racing with a burning desire to win the Grand National, but at the time he rode at Galway in 1882 he was virtually unknown and had never even ridden in that great race. Apparently he rode 254 winners between his win in Galway and the fulfilment of his ambition to win the Grand National in 1892, to become a household name, even among those only casually interested in racing. He won the first running of the Leopardstown Chase, in 1889, on Kilworth, trained in England by Captain Harding, and won the race again two years later on Roman Oak. His success in seeking out mounts and his 'win at all cost' mentality made him unpopular with the professional jockeys but he was respected because of his charm and his willingness to take a beating if it came – not that he came off second best very often; he was very capable of taking care of himself during a race, even when the other jockeys ganged up against him.

During the 1880s his soldiering career was put on hold, and he did as little army work as he could get away with, now that race riding was his main concern. As the winners flowed, he always maintained that he would retire and go back to soldiering full time if he won the Grand National. Nobody believed him, of course. He had six rides in that race: Kilworth fell in 1885, Ballot Box fell in 1887, Gamecock, the winner the previous year, was seventh in 1888, and Kilworth refused in 1889. He appeared to have blown his chance of ever winning the big race when, in 1891, he loomed up on Cloister (winner of the race in 1893) to challenge Why Not and the Irish-trained favourite Come-away. Why Not was not given much room by Come-away at the last fence, and took a crashing fall, leaving the two crack amateurs, Roddy Owen and Harry Beasley, fighting out an exciting battle all the way to the line. Cloister looked the more likely winner but Beasley was riding his mount tenderly because of fears about his dodgy leg. The Owen made a tactical error. He went for a small gap between Come-away and the rails and, after he had committed himself, the wily Beasley closed the gap, squeezing Owen to such an extent that he could not get through or get out. Beaten by half a length at the finish, Owen immediately lodged an objection (to the fury of the Irish contingent who had backed Come-away heavily) but the stewards rejected it and the result stood.

The following year, 1892, he lost the Grand National ride on Cloister because the horse was sold in the interim, but he still had six, albeit lesser, mounts to choose from. He decided to ride the one that most people considered the least likely to win, Father O'Flynn, owned and trained by an Australian named Gordon Wilson, another army man. Cloister started favourite because he had the best form, but his rider was an unknown amateur, which was a disadvantage in so tough a race. Slipping the field at Valentines, Cloister raced into a clear lead, but his inexperienced rider had gone for home too soon. As the horse tired, his burden of 12 stones 3 pounds took its toll, and Cloister had nothing left to respond to the challenge of Father O'Flynn, in receipt of 26 pounds. The disappointment of the previous year was forgotten as the dashing Captain Owen fulfilled his life's ambition by winning the Grand National. True to his word, he retired from race riding, bid goodbye to his friends and volunteered for service abroad in India and later in Egypt. He died from cholera at Dongola, in the Sudan, in July 1896. The Irish-trained winner of the 1958 Cheltenham Gold Cup, owned by Lord Fingal and trained by Danny Morgan, was named after him.

Captain Charles Boycott (1832–97)

Owner, green, rose sleeves and black cap:
1883 BUTTE DES MORTS (H. Saunders) – Renmore Handicap 8f flat £58 (J. Dunne)
1883 BUTTE DES MORTS (T. Harris) – Kylemore Handicap 7f flat £48 (J. Dunne)

Captain Boycott was just another ex-army man who liked to ride in races until he found himself in the middle of a bitter political campaign. He became the unwitting victim of the Land War, which left him fearing for his life and about to give a new word to the English language. Captain Charles Boycott of Loughmask House, Ballinrobe, was the land agent of the Earl of Erne, responsible for the collection of rents. In 1880 he refused to accept rents at the figures set by the tenants and was 'sent to Coventry' by the locals, who ensured that nobody would have anything to do with him. His servants were compelled to leave him, his property was damaged and he was cut off from society and left to fend for himself as best he could. It was another chapter in a Land War that had simmered for years. Locals called this new weapon in their land reform campaign a 'boycott'. The campaign turned bitter when a number of Orangemen from Ulster volunteered to help Captain Boycott to save his crops, but it took a force of 900 soldiers to protect them. The boycott weapon spread to other parts of Ireland and not only humans were affected. Lord Drogheda's stallion Philammon, runner-up in the 1877 Irish Derby, at stud in Monasterevan was boycotted because of his ownership, which resulted in his transfer to an English stud.

Captain Boycott was an amateur rider in Ireland, riding a number of winners, including at a steeplechase at the Glennamaddy, Co. Galway, meeting in 1875. His three-year-old filly Butte des Morts won four races and £209 in 1883, including two at Galway, at distances from 6 furlongs to 1 mile, including a win on Derby day at the Curragh. Butte de Morts literally means 'the mount of the dead', but she was named by her breeder, P.J. Russell, not Boycott. Captain Boycott's horse Martinet finished third in the 1877 Galway Plate, ridden by Paddy Gavin.

Mr Robert Brabazon (1858–91)

Rider:
1883 T. Jackson's CHARITY – Glenard Handicap Chase
1884 P.N. Fitzgerald's NEW MEADOW – Galway Plate (G.L. Walker)
1887 J.F. Brabazon's GENTLE ANNIE – Moyode Handicap Chase (R.H. Brabazon)
1887 J.F. Brabazon's GENTLE ANNIE – Express Bumper (R.H. Brabazon)
1887 W. Meredith's DAINTY – Glenard Hunt Chase (W.J. Hilliard)

Talented amateur riders abounded in nineteenth-century racing, but were particularly dominant in steeplechasing – understabably because the weights carried were substantially higher than on the flat. Twenty-four years of the Galway Annual Races were to pass before the professional jockeys won every race at the meeting, and this rare event was repeated only three times afterwards, in 1920, 1921 and 1925. However, it must be said that it is impossible for the professionals to win all the races nowadays because a number of races are confined to qualified riders. There has always been friction between the professional and the gentlemen riders, as those struggling to make a living found themselves competing for rides against well-to-do gentleman riding for fun. There was no problem when the amateur was riding his own horse, but professionals objected when mounts were taken from them. Their problem was that many of the amateurs riding in the nineteenth century were better than them and were being sought out by owners. Resentful, bitter and sometimes committing fouls, the professionals often ganged up against the amateurs, who had to be good enough to take care of themselves if they were to succeed. These tactics did not work against the good amateurs, but for the sake of peace a convention grew up that an amateur would pay a professional jockey to stand down. This enabled the amateur rider to ride in as many races as he liked, without affecting the livelihood of the professional jockey.

Robert Brabazon was one of those full-time amateur riders. Although he was not considered to be the best amateur at the time, he did win the Irish Jockeys' Championship, sharing the honour with another amateur, Mr R.B. Norcott, in 1884, the pair beating all the professionals, both flat and National Hunt.

Born on 1 April 1858, Robert Brabazon was a brother of William Thomas Brabazon, the father of Cecil (Champion Irish Amateur in 1920 and a leading trainer) and Leslie (Irish Champion Jockey 1913). Unmarried, he lived in the family home at New Meadow House, Mullingar, and rode his first Galway winner in 1883, Charity in the Glenard Handicap Chase. Two horses that would feature in his life afterwards were winners at Galway that year: J.F. Brabazon's Gentle Annie and P.N. Fitzgerald's New Meadow. The latter won two chases as a seven-year-old in 1883, including the prestigious Meath Hunt Cup, which earned him a tilt at the following year's Irish Grand National. Third-favourite at 3 to 1 in a four-horse race, and ridden by professional jockey William Behan, New Meadow made all the running and, although slipping the field, was caught in the dying strides and beaten by a neck by The Gift, who was winning the race for the second time in a row.

The view from the grandstand in 2005

Robert Brabazon got his first ride on New Meadow a fortnight later in the Navan Cup, scoring a bloodless victory when his only rival fell. Although deserting the horse to ride Heather Bell, in receipt of 29 pounds, at the Athboy meeting (a correct decision as it turned out) he was reunited with New Meadow for the Galway Plate. Jumping like a buck, New Meadow gave him a thrilling ride, jumping the field into the ground and winning easily in the end by ten lengths. A win and a good second at Bellewstown established Brabazon as the gelding's regular rider, the pair eventually going to Liverpool for the Aintree meeting in November 1884. Contesting the Grand Sefton Chase, New Meadow was the first English ride for the young amateur and, although he managed to win the race by a neck, his riding was universally criticized by the English press. Worse was to follow when the connections of the runner-up objected on the grounds that New Meadow was insufficiently described at entry; the objection was sustained and the Irish raider was disqualified and placed last.

Racing journalists in the past usually filed weekly reports of the events, so they did not have to write in the heat of the moment. Consequently, their copy was written after some reflection, which tempered some of the criticism that might have rushed to the mind immediately after the race. However, when those journalists did go into a critical mode they went to town and, once they had started on the unfortunate Robert Brabazon, they continued to lambast the rider, even when he was winning. The Irish weekly sports newspaper, *Sport*, condemned him for being beaten on New Meadow at Limerick, where admittedly he had been outridden by Fred Cullen, one of the top amateurs of his day. Although the same correspondent praised him to the skies for his ride on Gentle Annie at the same venue a couple of weeks later, it was the first article that was remembered, and it became fashionable to criticize Brabazon. The English press did not know him and may have assumed that he must be a bad jockey; if that was the case they were wrong. That very same year, he rode twenty-two winners in Ireland, to head the list of winning jockeys both amateur and professional.

New Meadow was sent over to Epsom to be trained for the Grand National but in March 1885, only three weeks before the big race, he broke a fetlock on the gallops and had to be put down. Robert Brabazon continued to ride winners and won the 1887 Irish Grand National on Eglantine, later the dam of the Galway Plate and Grand National winner Drogheda. Eglantine was owned and trained by George F. Gradwell, himself a useful amateur rider, who later acted as the Clerk of the Course at Ballybrit. That same year Brabazon rode a treble at Galway, including two wins on Gentle Annie and one on Dainty, trained by William Hilliard at Deer Park, Castleknock.

In 1889 he ran into trouble with the Galway stewards, who reported him to the Irish National Hunt Steeplechase Committee following an incident in the

Committee Plate. Viscount won the race from Merry Maid, with Mr Brabazon's mount The Wanderer back in third place, but the owner of the second horse objected to the winner on the grounds of crossing at the last fence. During the inquiry, the stewards discovered that Robert Brabazon had missed out two fences but rejoined the race instead of pulling up as the rules required, and banned him from riding for six months. Jockey Patrick Fiely, who rode one of the unplaced runners, gave evidence to the stewards in relation to the objections, which turned out to be false. Satisfied that he had deliberately tried to mislead them, the stewards slapped a six-month ban on him also.

Robert Brabazon died young, riding his last winner at the Blackrock Strand meeting on 2 July 1891, on The Admiral in a hurdle race. Dubbed 'Mr Mitchell's slave' by the press, this winner of the 1894 Irish Grand National ran 162 times in Ireland, winning fifty-three races, being placed fifty-six times and being disqualified after winning once. The Admiral's tally of forty-seven jumping races is an Irish record.

Although Robert Brabazon was first past the post aboard Utah at Roscommon at the end of that month, Utah was objected to on the grounds that having won a race worth more than £15 it was not qualified to run. The stewards upheld the objection, placing Utah last and awarding the race to Stour Glen, ridden by 'Mr Wildman', the riding name of Mr G.W. Lushington. That was Brabazon's last mount. He caught pneumonia and died after a short illness on 15 September 1891 at the age of thirty-four. He shares an anniversary with Selim, the first winner of the Irish Derby, who died the same day at his stud in Co. Carlow.

Gentle Annie (1879), a half-bred mare by Lothario out of Little Annie by Hospodar, was a prolific winner just like her dam, who won eighteen steeplechases in Ireland between 1871 and 1874. Gentle Annie ran second in the Marble Hill Stakes at the Curragh at two years and went on to win twenty-one steeplechases and two Hunter Flat races. She later bred six winners at stud.

Frederick F. Cullen (1853–1938)

Rider:

1879 J. Lloyd's Unnamed colt (Draco II, photograph) – Mervue Chase (F.F. Cullen)
1883 P.H. Bourke's LADY PAULINE – County Handicap Chase (W.P. Cullen)

Trainer, jointly with William P. Cullen, Islandbridge, Co. Dublin:

1884 J.A. Burke's EVA (P. Coghlan) – Glenard Handicap Chase £48
1884 F.R. Fawcett's ERIN'S STAR (Mr W.P. Cullen) – Farewell Hunt Chase £27

Trainer, jointly with William P. Cullen, Montpelier Hill, Dublin:

1885 F.R. Fawcett's ERIN'S STAR (Mr W.P. Cullen) – Galway Handicap Chase £137

1885 J.A. Burke's EVA (P. Coghlan) – County Handicap Chase £74

Trainer:

1879 J. Lloyd's Unnamed colt (Draco II, photograph) – Mervue Chase £65

1887 C.W. Bagge's VICTRIX (Mr W.P. Cullen) – Galway Plate Handicap Chase £132

1887 A.E. McCracken's BELGRAVE (J. Gourley) – Traders' Handicap 5f flat £49

1888 A. Tiernan's PREFECT (J. Waterson) – Traders' Handicap 6f flat £49

1889 A. Tiernan's LITTLE WIDOW (J. Foster) – Renmore Handicap 7f flat £79

1889 Colonel R. Thomson's AMBITION (Mr W.P. Cullen) – Express Hunt Flat 18f £49½

1889 F.F. Cullen's ZULU II (Mr W.P. Cullen) – County Handicap Chase £78

1889 C.W. Bagge's GAWSWORTH (J. Foster) – Her Majesty's Plate 2m flat £104

1889 A. Tiernan's LITTLE WIDOW (J. Foster) – Traders' Handicap 6f flat £32½

1889 Colonel R. Thomson's BAILSMAN (Mr W. McAuliffe) – Glenarde Hunt Chase £48

1890 E.M. Bernard's B.A. (L. Ryan) – Committee Hunt Chase £43½

1890 E.M. Bernard's B.A. (L. Ryan) – Express Hunt Hurdle £25 (Dead Heat)

1890 A.E. McCracken's MERVYN (J. Foster) – Her Majesty's Plate 2m flat £104

1890 F.F. Cullen's LETTERS (James Murphy) – Traders' Handicap 7f flat £48

1891 Colonel R. Thomson's QUEEN OF THE MAY (Mr W. Beasley) – Galway Plate £137

1891 A. Tiernan's LITTLE WIDOW (J. Doyle) – Traders' Handicap 7f flat £43½

1891 R.N. Talbot's GOLDEN CRESCENT (J. Doyle) – Her Majesty's Plate 2m flat £104

1892 F.F. Cullen's LITTLE WIDOW (J. Dunne) – Traders' Handicap 8f flat £49

1893 F.F. Cullen's CARDCUTTER (P. Hegarty) – Traders' Handicap 6f flat £48½

1894 F.F. Cullen's CARDCUTTER (J. Bambrick) – Renmore Chase £43½

1897 J. Dunbar's MISS NOEL (W. Horton) – Mervue Handicap 6f flat £29¼

1898 F.F. Cullen's GOLDEN RIDGE (C. Hogan) – Express Hurdle £34

1898 F.F. Cullen's GAY GIRL (C. Hogan) – Galway Blazers Chase £51½

1899 F.F. Cullen's TRUENO (T. Moran) – Stewards' Handicap 10f flat £73

1899 T.B. Holmes's TIPPERARY BOY (T. Moran) – Galway Plate £166

1899 J.R. Darcy's WELL FORT (T. Moran) – Mervue Handicap 7f flat £29¼

1901 R.N. Talbot's GOLDEN KNOT (J. McQuillan) – Stewards' Handicap 10f flat £73

1901 T.B. Holmes's TIPPERARY BOY (T. Moran) – Galway Plate £166

1901 Lady Clancarty's BLACK SATIN (Mr H. Nuttall) – Renmore Handicap 20f flat £29½

1902 T.B. Holmes's TIPPERARY BOY (T. Kavanagh) – Galway Plate £166

As we have seen, Fred Cullen had a clean sweep of all five races on the second day of the Galway Races in 1889. It is worth mentioning that he also dominated the

Traders' Handicap flat race, training the winner of the race seven times in succession between 1887 and 1894. During this period the distance of the race seemed to change every year and Fred Cullen's wins varied between 5 furlongs and a mile. One of his charges, Little Widow, won the race three times, over three different distances, and was also successful once in the Renmore Handicap, a similar type of race. Indeed the Galway Executive were following an undesirable trend, prevalent at the time, running poorly endowed flat races in preference to steeplechases. Although Fred Cullen did not train a winner of the Traders' Handicap after 1894, where he left off his brother Willie stepped in, sending out four winners of the race in the six years between 1895 and 1900.

Mr William P. Cullen (1861–1937)

Rider:

1884 F.R. Fawcett's ERIN'S STAR – Farewell Hunt Chase (Cullen Brothers)

1885 F.R. Fawcett's ERIN'S STAR – Galway Plate Handicap Chase (Cullen Brothers)

1885 W. Coghlan's Unnamed gelding (Bar One-Helen) – Express Hunt Chase (Private)

1885 Captain Chetwynd's WELLINGTON – Farewell Hunt Chase (W. Hilliard)

1886 T. Jackson's SEAHORSE – Express Hunt Flat 16f (W.P. Cullen)

1887 C.W. Bagge's VICTRIX – Galway Plate Handicap Chase (F.F. Cullen)

1889 Colonel R. Thomson's AMBITION – Express Hunt Flat 18f (F.F. Cullen)

1889 F.F. Cullen's ZULU II – County Handicap Chase (F.F. Cullen)

1896 R.C. Dawson's CASTLE WARDEN – Galway Plate (W.P. Cullen)

1899 W.P. Cullen's DAINTY DISH – Express Hurdle (W.P. Cullen)

1900 W.P. Cullen's LILLIAN NOEL – County Handicap Hurdle (W.P. Cullen)

1902 J.H. Locke's RANUNCULUS – County Handicap Hurdle (W.P. Cullen)

1902 E.S. Jackson's SPANISH QUEEN – Renmore Handicap 20f flat (D. Shanahan)

1906 Mrs N.J. Kelly's RYE VALE – Galway Blazers Handicap Chase (N.J. Kelly)

Trainer, Ballinasloe, Co. Galway:

1881 F.R. Fawcett's ERIN'S HOPE (M. Ryan) – Forster Street Handicap Chase £96

1882 F.R. Fawcett's ERIN'S HOPE (D. Canavan) – Farewell Handicap Chase £39

1883 P.H. Bourke's LADY PAULINE (Mr F.F. Cullen) – County Handicap Chase £88

Trainer, Jockey Hall, Curragh:

1886 T. Jackson's SEAHORSE (Mr W.P. Cullen) – Express Hunt Flat 16f £50

Trainer, Rathbride Cottage, Curragh:

1891 Major McFarlane's LOTUS (T. Kavanagh) – Renmore Hunt Chase £25½

1892 R.N. Talbot's GOLDEN RING (J. Dunne) – Zetland Handicap 8f flat £73

1893 W.P. Cullen's CLOGHRAN (A. Magee) – Her Majesty's Plate 2m flat £104

1895 R. Richard's CALCHAS (J. Bresname) – Her Majesty's Plate 2m flat £104

1895 R. Richard's IDALUS (A. Magee) – Traders' Handicap 6f flat £43½

1896 R.C. Dawson's CASTLE WARDEN (Mr W.P. Cullen) – Galway Plate £132

1896 R.J. Love's CATCH THE WIND (J. Bresname) – Her Majesty's Plate 2m flat £104

1897 J.H. Locke's HAMPTON VINE (T. Fiely) – Stewards' Handicap 8f flat £63

1897 W.P. Cullen's MISS DRUMMOND (T. Fiely) – Traders' Handicap 6f flat £43½

1898 O. Mosley's RED RAY (Mr O. Mosley) – Stewards' Handicap 8f flat £63

1898 O. Mosley's RED RAY (Mr O. Mosley) – Traders' Handicap 8f flat £43½

1899 W.P. Cullen's DAINTY DISH (Mr W.P. Cullen) – Express Hurdle £34

1899 W.P. Cullen's LILLIAN NOEL (J. Westlake) – Her Majesty's Plate 2m flat £104

1900 W.P. Cullen's LILLIAN NOEL (Mr W.P. Cullen) – County Handicap Hurdle £63

1900 W.P. Cullen's CLAN GRAHAM (J. Murphy) – Traders' Handicap 8f flat £54

1902 J.H. Locke's RANUNCULUS (Mr W.P. Cullen) – County Handicap Hurdle £63

Trainer, Rothestone House, Shrewton, Wiltshire:

1904 C.E. Byrne's STRATEGY (A. Magee) – Galway Plate Handicap Chase £166

Trainer, jointly with Frederick F. Cullen, Islandbridge, Co. Dublin:

1884 J.A. Burke's EVA (P. Coghlan) – Glenard Handicap Chase £48

1884 F.R. Fawcett's ERIN'S STAR (Mr W.P. Cullen) – Farewell Hunt Chase £27

Trainer, jointly with Frederick F. Cullen, Montpelier Hill, Dublin:

1885 F.R. Fawcett's ERIN'S STAR (Mr W.P. Cullen) – Galway Handicap Chase £137

1885 J.A. Burke's EVA (P. Coghlan) – County Handicap Chase £74

The younger of the two brothers from Co. Galway, William Parke Cullen rode his first winner at Ennis in 1879, on Fred Cullen's The Colonel in a 2-mile chase. An amateur rider for thirty-three years, he mixed riding and training throughout his career. Like many Irish trainers at the time, he liked to take his horses to England during the winter months, when there was so little racing at home. The duration of his stay there depended on his luck and the ability of his lesser lights picking up prize money at the small country courses. Willie decided to stay in England for the 1903 season rather than return to Ireland, but returned on a foray to his native Galway the following year, winning the Plate with Strategy. He was a probably a better rider than his brother Fred (he was Irish Champion Jockey in 1886 and again in 1889), but then he rode a lot more. Among the big races he won were the Conyngham Cup on Royal Meath and three Galway Plates, on Erin's Star, Victrix and Castle Warden. Like all jockeys, his ambition was to win the Grand National but he was never even placed in that race. In 1897 he was booked by Willie McAuliffe to ride the favourite, Manifesto, but at the eleventh hour owner Harry Dyas intervened, and Willie Cullen was replaced by Terry Kavanagh. It was the biggest disappointment of his career and he did not know his fate until Kavanagh turned up wearing Mr Dyas's colours.

Willie Cullen began training at Ballinasloe but when his brother returned from Australia the pair trained together until 1886, when they went their separate ways: Fred moved into Rossmore Lodge, while Willie trained first at Jockey Hall, then at Conyngham Lodge and later at Rathbride Cottage. Willie trained two Irish classic winners – Kosmos (Irish Oaks 1896) and Wales (Irish Derby 1897) – and was Champion Irish Trainer in 1898 and 1899. Hired by octogenarian James Lonsdale, who had recently won an Irish Oaks with Topstone, to be his private trainer at Waterford Lodge, Willie Cullen had charge of the future Irish Derby winner Aviator when he was a two-year-old but resigned before the year was out, in September 1909. He then moved into French House, with Jack Behan replacing him at Waterford Lodge, but retired from training in April 1912. Moving to England, Willie Cullen was employed by Captain Dewhurst and then Atty Persse until the outbreak of the Great War, when he returned home to manage Sir William Nelson's new stud in County Westmeath. He retired to Clonkeen, County Galway, where he died in June 1937.

Michael Dawson (d. 1926)

Rider:

1884 T. Andrews's DEEPDALE – Kylemore Handicap 6f flat (P. Conolly)

1886 G. Weir's CORYBAS – Mervue Plate 6f flat (P. Conolly)

1890 Rice Meredith's INA – Mervue Handicap 8f flat (R. Meredith)

1891 Mr Donovan's LOPPY – Zetland Handicap 7f flat (R. Meredith)

1894 E. Shaw's FLORIDA – Mervue Handicap 8f flat (M. Dawson)

1898 W. Jackson's YELLOW VIXEN – Mervue Handicap 7f flat (M. Dawson)

Trainer:

1894 E. Shaw's FLORIDA (M. Dawson) – Mervue Handicap 8f flat £29¼

1894 E. Shaw's FLORIDA (John Doyle) – Traders' Handicap 6f flat £44

1898 W. Jackson's YELLOW VIXEN (M. Dawson) – Mervue Handicap 7f flat £29¼

1898 W. Jackson's YELLOW VIXEN (J. Behan Jr) – County Handicap Hurdle £73

1899 W. Jackson's YELLOW VIXEN (J. Behan Jr) – County Handicap Hurdle £58½

1900 W. Jackson's YELLOW VIXEN (J. Behan Jr) – Her Majesty's Plate 2m flat £104

1902 Miss Mansergh's BAYLEAF (C. Graham) – Express Hurdle £34

1902 W. Jackson's YELLOW VIXEN (D. Condon) – His Majesty's Plate 2m flat £104

1903 M. Dawson's LITTLE TOM (Mr T. Price) – Express Hurdle £34

1903 T. McMahon's HAMPTON BOY (A. Anthony) – Galway Plate £166

1904 W. Jackson's LITTLE VIXEN (Mr T. Price) – County Handicap Hurdle £63

1904 M. Dawson's SLEEP (F. Morgan) – His Majesty's Plate 2m flat £104

1905 M. Dawson's SLEEP (Mr T. Price) – Express Hurdle £34

1905 Joseph Whelan's LAUREL VALE (A. Anthony) – Galway Blazers Chase £51½

1907 J. O'Neill's MRS LYONS (S. Donoghue) – Stewards' Handicap 12f flat £54

1908 Joseph Whelan's GAME FOWLER (S. Donoghue) – Mervue Plate 10f flat £32

1909 W. Jackson's NO CLASS (Mr T. Price) – Salthill Handicap Hurdle £46

1909 M. Farrell's SCHWARMER (A. Anthony) – Galway Plate £181

1909 T. O'K. White's LADY GERALDINE (John Doyle) – Mervue Plate 9f flat £32

1910 M. Dawson's NELL BRENDAN (A. Sharples) – Mervue Plate 8f flat £46

1911 W. Jackson's DEAR BOY (Mr L. Firth) – Moyode Bumper 2m flat £49

1913 Captain F. Blacker's NILE VALLEY (Joseph Canty) – Stewards' Handicap 12f flat £73

1913 T. O'K. White's TULLYLOST (Joseph Canty) – Traders' Handicap 8f flat £54

1913 T. Leonard's LAOGHAIRE (James Canty) – His Majesty's Plate 2m flat £104

1914 T.M. Carew's NELLA'S FAVOR (Joseph Canty) Stewards' Handicap 12f flat £74

1914 W. Jackson's ROSA VISTA (Joseph Canty) – Traders' Handicap 8f flat £54

1915 G.H. Dennehy's NAUGHTY EARL (C.O. Hawkins) – Galway Handicap Hurdle £166

1917 J. O'Neill's NAVAN LASS (Joseph Dawson) – Stewards' Handicap 12f flat £74

1919 A. McMahon's WALTZAWAY (Joseph Canty) – Express Hurdle £90

1919 Joseph Whelan's ALWAYS (Joseph Canty) – Maiden Chase £176

1924 F. Burke's HOLY FOOKS (Joseph Canty) – Galway Handicap Hurdle £196

The best Irish jockey never to have been Champion, Michael Dawson's father was a hackney driver who knew Pat Conolly and asked the trainer to look after his son. Joining the staff at Curragh View, Michael rode his first winner in 1882 and, being able to ride comfortably at 5 stones 9 pounds, his services were soon in demand. He was a first-class jockey and rode exclusively on the flat, modelling himself on the stylish stable jockey, John Conolly. When the Conollys left Curragh View and Rice Meredith moved in, Michael Dawson became stable jockey, winning the first of his three Irish Derbys in 1890 on Kentish Fire. Having moved with Meredith to Rathbride Manor in 1891 and ridden two more Irish Derby winners for the stable – Roy Neil (1892) and Bowline (1893) – Dawson suddenly found himself in charge when Rice Meredith was warned off in June 1893. Landing into the hot seat, he first combined riding and training, notably with Winkfield's Pride, before his retirement from the saddle in 1898.

Dawson's timing was impeccable because almost immediately a brilliant apprentice emerged from his yard, David Condon. The trainer's faith in the youngster can be judged by his decision to install Condon as the stable jockey and give him a mount on St Brendan, the best horse Dawson would ever train. The pair scored a memorable victory over John Gubbins's English-trained favourite, Port Blair, to win the 1902 Irish Derby but tragically the eighteen-year-old was killed the following year. On one terrible day in May 1903, he was unexpectedly asked to stay back after riding work to school a horse over hurdles at Rathbride Manor. During the school he had a fall and died later from his injuries.

Michael Dawson was Champion Irish Trainer thirteen times, won six Irish classic races, an Irish Grand National and two winners of the Galway Hurdle. Besides training horses, he farmed on a large scale. Joe Canty, another of his apprentices, developed into a Champion Jockey. Having caught a chill at Manchester Races, Michael Dawson developed pneumonia and died just before Christmas in 1926.

Terence Kavanagh (d. 1908)

Rider:

1886 Captain St Lawrence's ZULU II – Galway Plate (D. Broderick)

1887 J.W. Nuttall's CLAN CHATTAN – Her Majesty's Plate 2m flat (J.W. Nuttall)

1888 John Gubbins's ILENE – Committee Hunt Chase (H.E. Linde)

1888 C. Tormey's NELLY BOY – Mervue Handicap 12f flat (H. Beasley)

1888 John Gubbins's ILENE – Glenarde Hunt Chase (H.E. Linde)

1889 E. Frazer's ALEXANDER – Galway Plate (H.E. Linde)

1891 Major McFarlane's LOTUS – Renmore Hunt Chase (W.P. Cullen)

1894 John James's TRANBY CROFT – Her Majesty's Plate 2m flat (C. Ellison)

1897 B. Gill's SPRINGFIELD – County Handicap Chase (Private)

1902 T.B. Holmes's TIPPERARY BOY – Galway Plate (F.F. Cullen)

Born near the Curragh, Terry Kavanagh served his time with Henry Linde at Eyrefield Lodge before leaving to join Dan Broderick. His stay at Mountjoy Lodge was brief and he returned to Linde and for many years was his professional jockey. He rode mainly on the flat for ten years but later became better known as a jump jockey. A tough customer rather than a finished horseman, he was a good jockey and achieved a rare double when he won the Irish Derby and the Aintree Grand National. Strong and brave, he won the 1887 Irish Derby on Pet Fox, trained by H.E. Linde. His victory at Aintree on Manifesto in 1897 came a week after Linde's death. The last of his three Galway Plate winners was in 1902, when he stood in for Tommy Moran on Tipperary Boy, but by that time he was coming to the end of his career. Although he held a licence until 1904, he rode very little after 1902 and died in January 1908.

Algernon Anthony (1872–1923)

Rider:

1894 Mr Williams's DUCK WING – Express Hurdle (C. Perkins)

1895 Hugh Gore's HELEN – Glenarde Chase (L. Sheil)

1897 E.S. Jackson's SPITFIRE – Galway Blazers Chase (D. Shanahan)

1898 H. Walker's FRIARY – Her Majesty's Plate 2m flat (D. Shanahan)

1899 H. Walker's FRIARY – Traders' Handicap 8f flat (D. Shanahan)

1900 Captain Campbell's PARMA VIOLET – Glenarde Chase (D. Shanahan)

1901 G. Hurley's ESME LEE – Express Hurdle (D. Shanahan)

1902 G. Hurley's ESME LEE – Ballyglunin Chase (D. Shanahan)

1903 T. McMahon's HAMPTON BOY – Galway Plate (M. Dawson)

1905 Joseph Whelan's LAUREL VALE – Galway Blazers Chase (M. Dawson)

1906 D.J. Cogan's HIGH WIND – County Handicap Chase (D. Shanahan)

1907 M.J. Swaine's GOLDEN JUBILEE – Express Hurdle (L. Hope)

1909 M. Farrell's SCHWARMER – Galway Plate Handicap Chase (M. Dawson)

1910 H.L. Fitzpatrick's DEAR SONNY – Galway Blazers Chase (Private)

Trainer:

1914 J. Nugent's ALICE ROCKTHORN (Mr P. Nugent) – Galway Plate £246

One of a select band of seven men to have both ridden and trained winners of the Galway Plate and the Grand National, Algy Anthony rode on the flat and over jumps. Born at Oxendon, near Cheltenham, and apprenticed to Sam Darling at Beckhampton, he came to Ireland towards the end of 1892 to ride for Charles Perkins, the licence holder at Conyngham Lodge for Noble Johnson and Mr G.W. 'Tommy' Lushington. It was through Lushington that Anthony became associated with Ambush II, winner of the 1900 Grand National in the colours of the Prince of Wales, a connection which has confused racing historians considerably.

When Henry Eyre Linde died in March 1897, Eyrefield Lodge was sold to Captain Eustace Loder for £8,500, and the new owner put Noble Johnson in charge of affairs, with Dan McNally, Linde's long-serving head lad, holding the trainer's licence. Johnson dismantled his Conyngham Lodge stable, and Perkins moved to Clifton Lodge for the 1898 season, while S. Doyle took a lease on Conyngham Lodge. This unheaval took Ambush II from Conyngham Lodge to Eyrefield Lodge, so it was Dan McNally who trained the horse to win the Grand National, and contemporary sources clearly confirm this fact. The confusion is compounded because different sources list both Algy Anthony and Joseph Hunter as the trainer of Ambush II. Joe Hunter is erroneously credited because when Johnson and Lushington moved out of the Eyrefield Lodge stable and went back to Conyngham Lodge in 1904, Joe Hunter became the licence holder there. Although Hunter was apprenticed to the Eyrefield Lodge stable and worked there during Ambush II's time, he was never the trainer at that establishment.

One of the best amateur riders of his time, Mr G.W. Lushington bought Ambush II on behalf of the Prince of Wales, supervised its training, rode it in races and was the contact between the royal owner and the stable. If proof is needed that Lushington, who was still riding at the time, moved to Eyrefield Lodge with Noble Johnson, one only has to look at the 1900 Irish Derby. That race was won by Captain Loder's Gallinaria, ridden by Mr Lushington, and trained at Eyrefield Lodge by Dan McNally. Lushington was the second, and the last, amateur rider to win the Irish Derby, Mr Tommy Beasley having won it in 1889. At the turn of the twentieth century is was common to put the licence in the name of the head lad, in this case Dan McNally, and there is a case for crediting the training of Ambush II to Messrs Noble Johnson and Lushington.

Irish Champion Jockey three times in a row from 1896 until 1898, Algy Anthony won the Irish Derby on Oppressor (1899) and Carrigavalla (1901), the Irish Oaks on May Race (1900) and Juliet II (1906), and Galway Plates on Hampton Boy (1903) and Schwarmer (1909). On his retirement in 1912, he began training at Westenra, Curragh, training a number of big winners including Alice Rockthorn (Galway Plate), Double Dew (Curragh Grand Prize) and Troytown, the best horse he trained. Owned by Major T.G. Collins Gerrard, one of the founders of Proudstown Park racecourse in Navan, Troytown won the Grand Steeplechase de Paris and the Grand National and is rated as one of the greatest winners of the big Aintree race. After winning the 1920 Grand National, Troytown went back to Auteuil for the Grand Steeplechase de Paris, in which he finished third. Pulled out again the following week for another race there, Troytown broke a leg and had to be destroyed. The Troytown Chase, run at Navan in November each year, is named after that great horse. Poor Algy Anthony did not long survive the best horse he trained, dying at Westerna after a long illness in November 1923.

James Joseph Parkinson (1870–1948)

Trainer:

1900 Mrs Joseph Widger's SUNNY SHOWER (Mr H.S. Persse)–Galway Blazers Chase £51½

1900 P.W. Connolly's BALAUSTA (J. Thompson) – Mervue Handicap 7f flat £39¼

1900 Mrs Joseph Widger's SUNNY SHOWER (J. Behan Jr) – Glenarde Chase £50½

1903 Captain Harding's STRELMA (J. Thompson) – His Majesty's Plate 2m flat £104

1904 W.A Byrne's STAGE DUKE (J. Thompson) – Mervue Handicap 7f flat £29½

1904 W.A. Byrne's STAGE DUKE (J. Thompson) – Traders' Handicap 7f flat £54

1905 P.J. Brophy's FAMOUS FANCY (J. Thompson) – Mervue Handicap 7f flat £29½

1906 Richard Croker's INDIANA (J. Thompson) – Ballybrit Handicap 10f flat £54

1906 J.J. Parkinson's LADY DAINTY (J. Thompson) – Renmore Handicap 12f flat £26½

1906 John Widger's INVESTOR (M. Widger) – Traders' Handicap 7f flat £44

1907 P.J. Brophy's JIGGINSTOWN (J. Thompson) – His Majesty's Plate 2m flat £104

1907 J.J. Parkinson's AVOCA (J. Thompson) – Traders' Handicap 10f flat £46

1911 J. Nugent's KILLEAVY (J. Thompson) – Mervue Plate 8f flat £46

1915 H.M. Hartigan's LAVECO (Mr W.J. Parkinson) – Stewards' Handicap 12f flat £74

1916 A.H. Ledlie's SPRIG OF MINT (Joseph Harty) – Mervue Plate 8f flat £44

1919 E. Desmond's STOLEN OATS (M. Connors) – Salthill Handicap Hurdle £90

1923 E. Bellaney's DESMOND DALE (T. Burns) – Salthill Handicap Hurdle £83

1923 Lt-Col O'Malley-Keyes's SMOKE CLOUD (T. Burns) – Galway Hurdle £196

1924 J.J. Parkinson's TEMPLEXYON (T. Burns) – Salthill Handicap Hurdle £83

1925 J. Musker's GROSVENOR'S PRIDE (E.M. Quirke) – Mervue Plate 8f flat £83

1925 J.J. Parkinson's FATHER TOM (P. Beasley) – His Majesty's Plate 2m flat £104

1926 T.P. O'Neill's LOUVIXEN (E.M. Quirke) – His Majesty's Plate 2m flat £104

1927 A. Willis's O MAY (E.M. Quirke) – His Majesty's Plate 2m flat £104

1929 J.J. Parkinson's PRINCE PRINCIPLE (E.M. Quirke) – Mervue Plate 12f flat £44

1929 Sir T. Dixon's CRAFTY CAPTAIN (E.M. Quirke) – His Majesty's Plate 2m flat £104

1930 J.J. Parkinson's BLACK MONDAY (Mr H.G. Wellesley)– Oranmore Handicap 12f flat £83

1931 Martin McDonogh's KYLECLARE (C. O'Connor) – Galway Hurdle £220

1935 Thomas McDonogh's COROFIN (W. Howard) – Mervue Plate 12f flat £49

1937 J.J. Parkinson's JOBURG (Mr P.J. Lenehan) – Oranmore Handicap 12f flat £83

1938 Michael McDono(u)gh's PETER'S WELL (T.V. Ryan) – Ballybrit Chase £49

1938 Michael McDono(u)gh's COROFIN (M. Wing) – His Majesty's Plate 2m flat £104

1939   Mrs E.M. McGrath's DURBAR (M. Wing) – Mervue Plate 12f flat £49

1939   Mrs E.M. McGrath's ERADICATE (Mr E. Parkinson) – Moyode Bumper £49

1939   J.J. Parkinson's DUNMANWAY (J. Barrett) – Corrib Hurdle £49

1939   Michael McDono(u)gh's HONOR'S CHOICE (J. Barrett) – Galway Hurdle £369

1939   Michael McDono(u)gh's COROFIN (M. Wing) – His Majesty's Plate 2m flat £104

1940   Michael McDono(u)gh's CLONBERN (M. Wing) – Mervue Plate 12f flat £49

1940   Mrs E.M. McGrath's ALLANWOOD (Mr P.J. Lenehan) – Moyode Bumper £49

1940   Mrs E.M. McGrath's BAMBOLA (M. Wing) – Stewards' Handicap 8f flat £49

1940   Mrs E.M. McGrath's ERADICATE (Mr P.J. Lenehan) – Oranmore Handicap 12f flat £83

E. Parkinson, trainer:

1941   Mrs P.J. Fleming's BIG BLAZE (W. Barrett) – Mervue Plate 12f flat £49

Born in Tramore, Co. Waterford, James J. Parkinson used to spend holidays with Michael Dennehy, who trained at French House, Curragh, and took mounts as an amateur, riding his first winner on 25 July 1893 at Roscommon: Noiseless. After he had qualified as a veterinary surgeon, Parkinson began a practice from Brownstown Lodge, later setting up as a trainer at Maddenstown Lodge. Early in his career he ran into trouble with the stewards, which cost him an Irish Derby and forced him out of his home. At Leopardstown in 1902, he ran two juveniles, Fame and Fortune and Lord Rossmore, in the Cadogan Plate, taking the mount on the former himself. Having been boxed in, Parkinson forced his way out of the pocket and then won the race. He then had to face an objection for bumping and foul riding, which was sustained, and he was reported to the stewards of the Turf Club. Warned off for a year for foul riding, he did not want to shut down his stable entirely and let all the staff go so he had to move out of Maddenstown Lodge and sell off all his horses, including Fame and Fortune. Captain Harding moved in to hold the fort on his behalf, while Parkinson took the opportunity to go on a work experience holiday to America. Several horses were taken out of the yard, including Lord Rossmore, the winner of the Irish Derby the following year.

Reinstated in July 1903, Jim Parkinson quickly got back to business with a double at the Phoenix Park and winners at the Curragh and Baldoyle before going to Galway to pick up the King's Plate with Captain Harding's Strelma, the 100-to-8 on favourite. In 1926 he won the same race with Louvixen, a 20-to-1 on shot, but this was not a record for that race because in 1914 Patrick Cullinan's Royal Hackle II, trained by James Dunne, won at odds of 25-to-1 on.

Having lost one Derby winner, within five years Parkinson somehow managed to lose another, Orby, the first Irish-trained winner of the Epsom Derby and the

first horse to win both the English and Irish Derbies. The corrupt American politician Richard 'Boss' Croker brought his string of American-bred horses to England
but the Jockey Club refused permission for them to be trained at Newmarket.
Incensed, Croker headed for Ireland, selected Jim Parkinson as his trainer and sent
his horses to the Curragh. The death of Lord Clifford early in 1906, left a number
of the inmates of Maddenstown Lodge without an owner and one of these, Electric
Rose, was recommended to Croker. As part of the deal, it was agreed that all prize
money won by Electric Rose that year would go to the trainer and not to Croker,
which was acceptable until Electric Rose defeated Orby in the Railway Stakes.
Already showing promise, Orby was given a tender ride by John Thompson and
finished third, two lengths behind Electric Rose. Furious that the stake of £633
was going to Parkinson rather than to him and disappointed that Orby had been
beaten, an emotional Croker lost his cool in the winner's enclosure, accusing the
trainer of stopping Orby to let Electric Rose win so that he could collect the stake.
Outraged at the accusation, Parkinson ordered Croker to remove his horses from
Maddenstown Lodge and in that moment of madness out of his stable went
another Derby winner.

The magnificent Killanin Stand, opened for the first time in 2007, serves the Mayor's Garden area

Parkinson sent out winners in great numbers, winning 2,577 races in his career, a record that stood until the year 2000, when it was surpassed by Dermot Weld. Most of these winners were minor ones but he won two Irish Derbies, four Irish Oaks, all the major two-year-old races and three Galway Hurdles. Nine times leading trainer at Galway, Jim Parkinson trained a vast string of horses, located in three separate yards, while serving as a senator from 1925, as well as being a director of Tramore and Limerick Junction racecourses, Goffs Bloodstock Sales and Tote Investors Ltd. Champion Trainer in Ireland on eight occasions, he was the leading trainer (based on number of winners rather than prize money) no less than twenty-four times. His son Billy, who had never sat on a horse until he was seventeen, immediately displayed ability in the saddle, and became Champion Jockey three times in succession: 1914, 1915 and 1916. His career was interrupted when he volunteered to join the forces fighting for their lives in France. Although he returned safe and sound, his weight had gone out of control and he was unable to get it down again. His career had ended before he was twenty-one. His younger brother Emanuel was Irish Champion Amateur in 1939 and eventually took over the reins at Maddenstown Lodge.

John Thompson (1881–1913)

Rider:

1901 P.W. Connolly's BALAUSTA – Mervue Handicap 7f flat (J.J. Parkinson)

1902 J. Brankin's AMPORT – Mervue Handicap 7f flat (R. Orton)

1903 Captain Harding's STRELMA – His Majesty's Plate 2m flat (J.J. Parkinson)

1904 W.A. Byrne's STAGE DUKE – Mervue Handicap 7f flat (J.J. Parkinson)

1904 W.A. Byrne's STAGE DUKE – Traders' Handicap 7f flat (J.J. Parkinson)

1905 P.J. Brophy's FAMOUS FANCY – Mervue Handicap 7f flat (J.J. Parkinson)

1905 Captain W. Scott's YOUNG ABERCORN – His Majesty's Plate 2m flat (T. McGuire)

1906 Richard Croker's INDIANA – Ballybrit Handicap 10f flat (J.J. Parkinson)

1906 James J. Parkinson's LADY DAINTY – Renmore Handicap 12f flat (J.J. Parkinson)

1907 M. McCann's PRINCE CHARLIE – Mervue Plate 10f flat (Private)

1907 P.J. Brophy's JIGGINSTOWN – His Majesty's Plate 2m flat (J.J. Parkinson)

1907 James J. Parkinson's AVOCA – Traders' Handicap 10f flat (J.J. Parkinson)

1908 W.W. Bailey's BOUNCING BESS – His Majesty's Plate 2m flat (M. Arnott)

1909 R.A. Wilson's WARLOCK – Traders' Handicap 9f flat (R.E. Harrison)

1909 R.A. Wilson's OCTOCIDE – His Majesty's Plate 2m flat (R.E. Harrison)

1911 J. Nugent's KILLEAVY – Mervue Plate 8f flat (J.J. Parkinson)

Jim Parkinson came back from America with the firm conviction that the forward riding seat, used with devastating results in England by Tod Sloan, enabled horses to run faster. At his master's insistence, John Thompson sat up the horse's neck and in no time had perfected the forward seat. The first jockey to ride regularly in that fashion in Ireland, he was immediately successful, being Champion Jockey ten times between 1901 and 1912, including a record seven titles in succession. Like most jockeys when they ride too short to use their knees, Thompson relied on his whip to keep his mounts going but was an honest, loyal jockey, who could always be trusted. He became the number one at Maddenstown.

A native of Enniscorthy, he rode his first winner in 1898 at Tralee and came to prominence when riding Berrill to victory in the Cambridgeshire Handicap at Newmarket in 1900. Berrill, trained on the Curragh by Phillie Behan, was owned by J.C. Sullivan, who had backed his horse heavily but was concerned by persistent rumours that Tod Sloan was fixing the race. He instructed Behan to find the best young jockey he could and to keep his identity a secret for as long as he could. Behan selected nineteen-year-old Thompson, who did not let him down despite the threats hurled at him by Sloan.

Thompson hunted regularly with the Kildare Hounds and for many years Parkinson banned him from riding over jumps, fearing that he might be injured. However, with his weight creeping up, and unable to ride at weights under 8 stones 7 pounds the jockey began taking mounts over hurdles. On 15 May 1913, two days after finishing second in the Baldoyle Derby on Sleipner, he had a bad fall while schooling Willie Wagtail over hurdles. Removed to hospital with bad concussion, he never really regained consciousness. Having momentarily rallied, he took a turn for the worse and died exactly a fortnight later. He rode over 500 winners in his brief career and his five winners in Galway's Royal Plate is a race record.

Francis Morgan (1887-1970)

Rider:

1904 M. Dawson's SLEEP – His Majesty's Plate 2m flat (M. Dawson)

1913 D.J. Higgins's GLENPATRICK – Ballybrit Chase (T.J. Widger)

1913 Baron F. de Tuyll's RED DAMSEL – Galway Handicap Hurdle (M. Arnott)

1914 S. Grehan's CLONMEEN – Galway Handicap Hurdle (M. Arnott)

1914 T. Nolan's NEVER FEAR – County Handicap Chase (R.H. Walker)

1916 T. Nolan's NEVER FEAR – Galway Plate Handicap Chase (R.H. Walker)

1918 Lord Saville's BEE FAST – Stewards' Handicap 12f flat (M. Arnott)

1918   Lord Saville's GOLCAR – Ballybrit Chase (M. Arnott)

1920   Mrs Owen Toole's CLONREE – Galway Plate Handicap Chase (F. Morgan)

1920   Frank Barbour's SIR HUON – Ballybrit Chase (R.H. Walker)

1923   Charles A. Rogers's HARRY HART – Galway Blazers Handicap Chase (M. Arnott)

Trainer, Curragh:

1920   Mrs Owen Toole's CLONREE (F. Morgan) – Galway Plate £592

'Frank' Morgan was born in Waterford in July 1887. His mother was a daughter of Tom Widger, a horse dealer who supplied horses to clients all over Europe and was said to have traded 3,000 animals every year. He farmed at Drough and had nine children, six boys and three girls. All the boys, with the exception of William, who became a Franciscan priest, were involved in horses and racing. The boys were fascinated by the stories they had heard about the Grand National and, with the confidence of youth, decided to try and win the race. With this in mind, John, Mick and Joseph set out to buy a National Hunt horse with a limited 'tank'. They were drawn to The Wild Man from Borneo, owned by another famous horse dealer, trainer and breeder, James J. Maher. In early November 1893, The Wild Man from Borneo ran third to Bird's Eye at Leopardstown and was then dispatched on a mini-campaign in England, a practice that was pioneered by Mr Maher. This time he put his brother-in-law, Leonard Sheil, in charge of the raiding party, which headed to Liverpool and the Aintree November meeting. Sheil, a qualified Dublin solicitor, had caught the racing bug and the Maher stable was providing him with plenty of winners. He was the Irish Champion Amateur Rider-elect at the time, a title that he was to retain until his untimely death in a fall at the old Boyerstown meeting at Navan in March 1899.

The Wild Man from Borneo did not win during this foray but he did finish second twice over the Grand National fences and the following week finished second again, this time at Kempton Park. Two of these seconds were to former Grand National winners, Father O'Flynn and Gamecock, which inspired the Widger boys to snap The Wild Man from Borneo up for £600.

They decided to leave the horse in England, sending it to James Gatland, who provided his friend Roddy Owen with many winners, at Somerset House, Alfreston, Sussex, to be specifically trained for the Grand National. The brothers recouped almost all the purchase price when The Wild Man from Borneo, ridden by Joe, won twice in four days just before Christmas, at Leicester and Nottingham. In the 1894 Grand National, he ran in John Widger's all-scarlet colours (his Irish colours included a blue birds'-eye cap). Although an unconsidered 40-to-1 shot, he ran a blinder to finish third behind Why Not and Lady Ellen II, beaten by one and a half lengths and a head. A bitterly disappointed Joe Widger blamed himself for the defeat, believing that he ought to have ridden the horse with more restraint, but he had underestimated his mount. Their father reminded the boys that the race would be run again the following year, but he did not live to see it, dying suddenly two months later. However, The Wild Man from Borneo did come back and win the Grand National in 1895, this time as a well-supported third-favourite, and the Widgers were famous in England and public heroes at home.

Frank Morgan was initially apprenticed to his uncle, Tom Widger, who was probably a better jockey than his brother Joe but not as successful. When he reached fourteen years of age, Frank was sent to Jim Parkinson at Maddenstown Lodge, riding his first winner for his new master, William Brophy's Sweet Ulva, on 16 April 1902 at the Curragh. Six weeks later Parkinson was 'warned off' for foul riding at Leopardstown and had to leave Maddenstown Lodge. The upheaval led to the indentures of young Frank being transferred to another Curragh trainer, Michael Dawson at Rathbride Manor. This move proved to be fruitful because Dawson put the young apprentice up on Royal Arch in the 1904 Irish Derby and it proved to be a winning ride. Frank was barely out of his teens when he began to have trouble with his weight and became too heavy for the flat. After that he rode mainly over hurdles and fences, equalling Frederick 'Titch' Mason's achievement of riding every winner on a card; Mason won all five races at Cavan on 8 September 1900 and Frank did the same at Downpatrick on 12 March 1914, four for George Walker and one for trainer Larry Hope. By a morbid coincidence both trainers died shortly afterwards, Walker the following July, upon which his stable was continued by his son Reggie, and Hope in November 1915. Frank Morgan won the Galway Plate on Never Fear (1916) and the first two runnings of the Galway Hurdle on Red Damsel (1913) and Clonmeen (1914). He was Irish Champion Jockey in 1917 and in 1918 began to combine training with riding, which was permitted at the time, based on the Curragh. In 1920 he rode and trained Clonree to win the Galway Plate but he handed in his jockey's licence the following year.

Nowadays Frank Morgan is remembered, if at all, as a trainer rather than a former champion and Irish Derby winning jockey. That is because he was the trainer of J.C. Bentley's Ballinode, often called the 'Sligo mare', who became the second winner of the Cheltenham Gold Cup and one of the few mares to do so. She was a difficult mare to ride and inclined to take chances with the fences, but Frank Morgan knew her well and contemplated coming out of retirement to ride her in the 1925 Cheltenham Gold Cup. In the end he settled for the strong and stylish English jockey, T.E. 'Ted' Leader, who rode her to victory and became her regular rider. The success of Ballinode opened opportunities in England for Frank and he moved to Cheshire later that year and never returned.

Five Morgan brothers rode as professional jockeys around this time: Richard (Dick), William (Billy), Frank, Issac and E.R. (Rees), while the other brother, John, was a successful trainer and horse dealer. John had the honour of owning LAP, the first winner on the modern Tramore racecourse, and was the father of jockeys Tommy and Danny, as well as the well-known shipping agent Dick. Danny Morgan rode Morse Code to victory in the Cheltenham Gold Cup and later trained Roddy Owen to win the race and rode Grecian Victory to win the Galway Plate for Harry Ussher.

Apart from Frank, the only brother successful at Galway was Richard, who rode Royal Tara to win the 1906 Galway Plate for trainer Denis Shanahan. He later trained in England, at Wantage, and died in 1944. Billy Morgan rode Matthew, owned by his uncle, John Widger, into second place in the 1902 Grand National but was killed in February 1915 in a schooling accident. Issac, who died in 1933, and (Edward) Rees Morgan were good, honest pros.

Maxwell Arnott (1882–1954)

Trainer, Clonsilla:

1904 Lord Dudley's DELPHIE (John Doyle) – Stewards' Handicap 10f flat £73

1904 Sir W. Nugent's SINCERITY (P. Cowley) – Ballyglunin Chase £51½

1906 Colonel T.Y.L. Kirkwood's APOLLO BELVEDERE (P. Cowley) – Express Hurdle £34

1907 Mr Tim's CLEAR CASE (G. Brown) – Ballyglunin Chase £50

1908 M. Arnott's SHADY GIRL (G. Brown) – Galway Plate Handicap Chase £181

1908 W.W. Bailey's BOUNCING BESS (J. Thompson) – Plate 2m flat £104

1910 Mr Silver's BLAIR HAMPTON (G. Brown) – Moyode Hurdle £46

1910 Baron F. de Tuyll's DESMOND O'NEILL (G. Brown) – Express Hurdle £73

1910 P. Fox's ANOTHER DELIGHT (G. Brown) – Irish National Hunt Chase £198

1910 Baron F. de Tuyll's LOVE IN A MIST (Mr R.H. Walker) – Renmore 2m flat £44

1911 Baron F. de Tuyll's DESMOND O'NEILL (G. Brown) – Salthill Handicap Hurdle £46

1911 Mrs R.P. Croft's SHOEBLACK (G. Brown) – County Handicap Chase £74

1912 H.M. Hartigan's ADDINSTOWN'S PRIZE (Mr H.M. Hartigan) – Moyode 2m flat £49

1912 Sir G. Abercrombie's NOBLE GRECIAN (G. Brown) –Galway Plate Handicap Chase £291

1913 M. Arnott's KOUBA (John Doyle) – Mervue Plate 8f flat £44

1913 Baron F. de Tuyll's RED DAMSEL (F. Morgan) – Galway Hurdle £166

1914 S. Grehan's CLONMEEN (F. Morgan) – Galway Hurdle Handicap £166

1915 S. Grehan's LADY ALDBOROUGH (M. Farragher) – Ballybrit Chase £83

1917 Major D. McCalmont's PRIVIT (W. Smith) – Galway Plate £422

1917 Lord Savile's BEE FAST (Mr L.L. Firth) – Amateurs' 2m flat £34

1918 Lord Savile's BEE FAST (F. Morgan) – Stewards' Handicap 12f flat £74

1918 Lord Savile's GOLCAR (F. Morgan) – Ballybrit Chase £69

1919 B.W. Parr's ROI ALLIE (M. Beary) – Moyode 20f flat £90

1920 Lord Lascelles's KING EBER (T. Burns) – Galway Hurdle Handicap £201

1921 P. Rogers's DRINMOND (H.H. Beasley) – Moyode 20f flat £103

1923 C.A. Rogers's HARRY HART (F. Morgan) – Galway Blazers Handicap Chase £84

1923 P. Rogers's DOUBLE FIRST (D. Ward) – H.M. Plate 2m flat £104

1924 Richard Power's LARRY THE FLAIL (D. Ward) – Stewards' Handicap 8f flat £83

1924 E.W. Hope Johnstone's ISCHEVAHA (D. Ward) – Ballybrit Chase £83

1924 P. Rogers's BLUE FISH (D. Ward) – H.M. Plate 2m flat £104

1925 M. Arnott's PRIVIT'S PRIDE (Joseph Canty) – Stewards' Handicap 8f flat £83

1926 M. Arnott's FAIR RICHARD (D. Ward) – Galway Plate Handicap Chase £442

1926 M. Arnott's MATADOR (Mr S.H. Dennis) – Moyode 20f flat £83

1927 Lord Lascelles's BULGARIAN (D. Ward) – Stewards' Handicap 8f flat £83

1927 J.S. Shepherd's KILCASKIN (D. Ward) – Mervue 8f flat £83

1928 J.S. Shepherd's PRIORY WOOD (D. Ward) – Stewards' Handicap 8f flat £73½

1928 J.S. Shepherd's EAST GALWAY (D. Ward) – Galway Plate £442

1928 M. Macabe's BALLY YARN (Mr T. Nugent) – Galway Blazers Handicap Chase £59

1929 M. Macabe's BALLY WEAVER (D. Ward) – Ballybrit Chase £44

1929 M. Macabe's BALLY WEAVER (Mr T. Nugent) – Traders' 2m flat £44

1930 M. Arnott's SUN FLAME (Mr T. Nugent) – Salthill Handicap Hurdle £66

1930 J.S. Shepherd's EAST GALWAY (J. McNeill) – Galway Plate Handicap £442

1930 J.A.B. Trench's SERGEANT GRISCHA (Mr T. Nugent) – Moyode 16f flat £44

1930 J.E. Ryan's SEA FISHER (J. McNeill) – Ballybrit Chase £44

1930 C. Odlum's LAGONDA (J. Moylan) – H.M. Plate 2m flat £104

1931 J.P. Maher's CLEAR NOTE (Mr T. Nugent) – Ballybrit Chase £49

1935 T.N. Atkinson's TOCSIN (W. Howard) – Stewards' Handicap 8f flat £49

1937 Mrs V.H. Parr's GOG (E.M. Quirke) – Mervue 12f flat £49

1938 P. Dunne Cullinan's WEST POINT (D.L. Moore) – Galway Blazers Handicap Chase £49

1940 F. Rogers's ROYAL GOLD (S. Magee) – Renmore Chase £49

1941 A.D. Comyn's BROWN ADMIRAL (J. Brogan) – Corrib Hurdle £49

1942 P.D. Daly's PETER'S GIFT (Mr P.J. Lenehan) – Moyode 16f flat £49

1948 C. Dowdall's COUNT GABRIEL (M. Gordon) – Salthill Handicap Hurdle £133½

1948 Mrs M. Ferns's LADY QAIM (M. Gordon) – H.M. Plate 2m flat £104

Clonsilla used to be a major training centre, being handy for the big metropolitan racecourses and the railway. The Greenmont stables, by the railway bridge, lay opposite the place of the Shackletons, a family related to the famous explorer.

Local legend declares that the Irish crown jewels are buried there somewhere, having been stolen by one of the Shackletons, who worked in Dublin Castle. He was caught but the jewels were never recovered and, being too hot to sell, must be hidden somewhere; Clonsilla is as likely as spot as any. Nowadays visitors to the area are drawn by the prospect of treasure trove because Clonsilla's racing heritage has died out, the only trace being on the stone slabs in the graveyard.

Cecil John Maxwell Fitzgerald Arnott was a leading Irish owner and trainer for fifty years until his retirement in 1952. Succeeding Bob Dewhurst at the Greenmont Stables, he was Champion Irish Trainer only once, in 1911, but as a predominantly jumping trainer he was at a big disadvantage because that honour is based on the amount of prize money won. However, in terms of the number of races won, Arnott was top on six occasions in an era dominated by Jim Parkinson. At Galway he and Harry Ussher were supreme, battling it out every year. Arnott was leading trainer at Galway twelve times against Ussher's eleven, but in total number of wins Ussher finally got the edge, fifty-eight to fifty-four. Both trainers loved to win at Galway and laid out horses especially for the Festival. Harry Ussher won a record nine Galway Plates to Arnott's five, but the latter won the Galway Hurdle count by four to one. 'Maxie' Arnott also trained Distel to win the 1946 Champion Hurdle at Cheltenham.

He began his career assisting Captain Bob Dewhurst, who originally trained at Greenmont. He rode as an amateur in flat races without much success, but when Dewhurst decided to open a training stable at Bedford House, Newmarket, he put Maxie in charge of the Irish side of the business. Dewhurst, who was as mad as a hatter, originally intended to train both in Ireland and in England but discovered that it was difficult to be in both places. Aware that Captain Dewhurst was miles away in Newmarket, journalists began attributing winners trained at Greenmont to Arnott. Irritated, Bob Dewhurst made a particular point of correcting the error, reiterating that he was the trainer at Clonsilla. Nobody believed him but the newspapers went along with him for a while – until the end of September 1904 to be precise, when it seems a decision was made to credit all winners from the Greenmont stable as being trained by Maxwell Arnott. Consequently, I have decided to credit Maxwell Arnott with the two Galway winners of 1904, credited to Bob Dewhurst in the press, because the latter had little or nothing to do with their training and he never trained in Ireland again.

Jockeys George Brown, the Irish Champion Jockey in 1909, and Dinny Ward were associated with the Arnott stable throughout their careers.

Arnott was educated at Clifton College. He was a decent polo player and a director of the *Irish Times*. In the summer of 1915, he volunteered to go to the

Front and arranged for Joseph Maher to take control of the stable, but he was rejected for service and returned to training. He died at his home, The Cottage, Clonsilla, on 31 August 1954.

Stephen Donoghue (1884–1945)

Rider:

1907 J. O'Neill's MRS LYONS – Stewards' Handicap 12f flat (M. Dawson)

1908 Joseph Whelan's GAME FOWLER – Mervue Plate 10f flat (M. Dawson)

1915 J. Meleady's CHRISTINA II – Traders' Handicap 8f flat (Private)

Born in Warrington of Irish immigrant parents, Steve Donoghue wanted to be a jockey from the moment he looked down on the Roodee from the walls of Chester to watch the Chester Cup. Running away from home, he joined the stable of John Porter at Kingsclere but ran away after being given a thrashing, having been blamed for upsetting the stable star, Flying Fox, on the gallops. Using the alias Steve Smith, he drifted from stable to stable working as a lad before ending up in France, where he stayed in one yard long enough for his undoubted riding talent to be noticed. The upshot of all this was that he was much older than the average jockey when he had his first ride in public. In 1905 he rode his first winner, at a small country racecourse called Hyères, halfway between Toulon and St Tropez. Having signed a retainer to ride for the Italian owner Prince Doria, he went home on holiday with a bright future ahead of him for the first time in his life.

During this break he went to Ireland to visit his brother George, who was working for Michael Dawson on the Curragh. George Donoghue was a good rider but he was work-shy and flitted from stable to stable. He was now complaining that he was not being paid his wages. On hearing this, Steve confronted the Irish trainer, who said that he was holding the money on George's behalf for his own good and the problem was settled. Afterwards Steve rode for Dawson, one of the best flat jockeys in his day, who was so impressed that he immediately offered him the position of second jockey to Clyde Aylin. Steve was adamant that he would never ride as second jockey to anyone. Why should he? He had secured a valuable retainer to ride in Italy as first jockey and that was where he was going. Dawson strongly advised him not to go to Italy but to stay in Ireland, and introduced him to Phillie Behan, another Curragh trainer. On Dawson's recommendation Behan offered Donoghue the job of first jockey there and then. Just as he would later do to other people many times in his career, Steve let the Italian down, ignored his agreement and signed up to ride for Behan in Ireland. The result was the he became Champion Jockey and later married the trainer's daughter, Bridget Behan.

He was a class act; many informed judges proclaim him to be the best Champion Jockey of the twentieth century. He had everything – good hands, a natural riding seat and an instinctive feel for a horse – and he dominated the Irish flat-racing scene. However, in May 1908 he had a terrible fall at the Phoenix Park when his mount, a mare named Dalness, dropped dead during a 5-furlong sprint. Although injured internally, he rode on but as the months went by he became weaker and weaker. Eventually he consulted a doctor, who immediately sent him into hospital for an emergency operation. Although it was a success, Steve contracted typhoid during his recovery and was out of the saddle for over a year.

His first winner in England came at Aintree on Grand National day 1909, when he rode Golden Rod, trained by Phillie Behan, to victory in a 5-furlong handicap. Before long he was travelling back and forth to England for rides. Tired of all this toing and froing, he jumped at the opportunity when Atty Persse offered him a retainer to ride for his stable in 1911. This led to his association with The Tetrarch, 'the spotted wonder' whose unbeaten run as a two-year-old in 1913 was so impressive that he was made winter favourite for the Derby and was being hailed as a certain champion. As history relates, injury floored the wonder horse, but Steve Donoghue was heading to the top of his profession, roared on by the 'Come on Steve' shouts of encouragement from adoring racegoers. He was Champion Jockey for ten consecutive seasons, 1914–23.

In his autobiography, he relates an interesting story about a visit to the Galway Races in 1915. He had ridden a winner at the meeting in 1907 and another the following year, when he was based at the Curragh, but came as a visitor on this occasion and had no intention of taking a mount. His friend, Fred Hunt, who trained jumpers at Winchester, was running his Aintree Champion Chase winner Couvrefeu II in the Galway Plate. He expected the horse to win and was bringing over a party that included his rider Mr Jack Anthony, his brother Ivor and the well-known billiards player Tom Reece; would Steve like to join them? Of course he would. The party rented a house that was about a mile away from Ballybrit. All bet on the invader and lost their money, as Couvrefeu II could only finish a very bad seventh to the outsider Hill of Camas, owned and trained by Captain Molony, the father of the top jump jockeys Tim and Martin. The party was due to return to England the following day, Galway Hurdle day, but Joe Canty told Steve that he was riding a certainty that day called Tickler. It was a good thing and Canty urged him to help himself. Hunt and the jockeys had to return to England but they left £200 with Steve to have on Tickler, and Tom Reece decided to stay the extra day with him. For some reason the cab that was to take the pair to the racecourse did not turn up, forcing them to set out on foot in the heavy rain. Soaked to the skin on reaching the course, Steve headed straight for the jockey's tent to dry himself and ran into J. Meleady, a horse dealer and trainer, who begged him to ride his mare Christina II. He was most reluctant to do so but Mr Meleady thrust his black jacket with its rose sleeves into his hands and disappeared.

On meeting up with Tom Reece again Steve told him the story and it turned out that Christina II was running against Tickler. Having made enquiries, he discovered that Christina II had run the previous day, finished a field behind the winner and had no chance at all on the book. Giving the £200 plus his own bet to Reece, Steve donned the colours and headed for the parade ring to ride the no-hoper. The incessant rain had left the course like a bog. Tickler was backed down to odds-on favourite, while Christina II, despite having the services of the reigning English Champion Jockey, was only lightly backed at 10 to 1. Jumping off last in the mile-long race, Steve pulled his mount wide in the straight in order to avoid the flying mud and felt his mount quicken. Almost blinded by the driving rain, he pushed the mare out racing up the hill and, on the better ground, she began overtaking the horses that struggled through the mud on the inside rail. Steve had no idea whether Tickler was in front of him or behind him – he was not even sure who had won the race – but it transpired that he had, by a length, having caught and passed Tickler close to home. Joe Canty was furious, and Tom Reece was shocked, but all Steve Donoghue could do was laugh.

Fred Hunt provided him with his one and only winner over hurdles, and it came about in a strange way. Albert 'Snowy' Whalley had finished third in the jockeys' list in 1912 on ninety-nine winners, and in order to reach the century decided to ride over hurdles during the winter. On being teased by Donoghue, 'Snowy' retorted that Steve did not have the nerve to ride over jumps. An experienced rider to hounds, Donoghue was indignant and the pair decided to have a bet – £50 to the first man that rode a winner over jumps. Determined to win the bet, Steve immediately contacted his friend Fred Hunt about setting up a suitable winning ride. It happened that he could – the following week at Birmingham. Fred had two horses entered in the Sutton Handicap Hurdle over 2 miles, Bachelor's Charm, which would be ridden by Ivor Anthony, and Lady Diane, Steve's mount.

However, an unexpected problem arose when Sir William Nelson, who retained Steve, voiced his objections, which, true to form, his jockey totally ignored. Obviously concerned, Sir William turned up on the day, 26 November, to put a stop to the nonsense but succumbed to Steve's charm, eventually hastening off to back Lady Diane. The hostility of the jump jockeys took Steve by surprise; they

The huge crowd gets a close-up of the action on the big screen, which was first used at Galway in 1994

resented a leading flat jockey taking their rides as they saw it. They were eventually placated, but not without some difficulty, by Dick Morgan. One of the famous jockey brothers from Waterford, he was a respected professional jump jockey and he spoke personally to all the jockeys and reassured them that Steve's mount was a one-off over hurdles. Starting 11-to-8 favourite, Lady Diane duly won the race, giving Steve his jumping winner and landing his £50 bet.

The dominant flat jockey of his era, the gullible Donoghue had perennial money problems and his disloyalty to owners would have made him many enemies but for his riding ability and his personal charm. While he welcomed the money offered by retainers – lucrative contracts to give an owner or trainer first claim on his services – Steve was not prepared to stick by his agreement when something better was offered. In a series of public wrangles over Epsom Derby mounts, he wriggled his way out of his obligations, much to the annoyance of his owners, the exasperation of trainers and the fury of the affected jockeys.

Even today many large owners and stables offer a fee to a good jockey to ride exclusively for them. The advantage of this arrangement is twofold: firstly the stable has a top jockey to ride its horses, and secondly it stops a top jockey from riding against them. Steve was quite happy to accept the retainer at the start of the season but wanted none of the disadvantages, being keen to operate as a freelance jockey when it suited him. There are three notorious cases in which he reneged on his agreement when he discovered that he could get a mount with a better chance of winning the race.

Lord Derby had first claim on Donoghue's services in 1921, which required him to ride Glorioso in the Derby. Having been offered a ride on Humorist, who he regarded as a better prospect, he pleaded, begged and battled to get his way, eventually securing a release from his contract. He felt entirely vindicated when Humorist won. The following year he found himself embroiled in a row involving Lord Woolavington and Fred Darling, the owner and trainer of Derby hope Captain Cuttle. Darling decided to replace Captain Cuttle's usual jockey Victor Smyth, with another in the Derby because he believed that he did not get on well enough with the horse. Darling contacted the Irish-based Tommy Burns and asked him to come over to England specially to ride the horse in a private gallop. Burns understood that he was being booked as a replacement for Smyth, only to find on his arrival at Darling's stable that Donoghue was also there and claiming the ride. Darling put a stop to the heated arguments on the day by riding the horse himself in the gallop but in the end Burns lost out. Donoghue's reputation as the best big-race jockey around at the time ensured that he got his way. In due course he rode Captain Cuttle to victory at Epsom, while Burns was left to kick his heels in a temper.

Again in 1923 there was controversy, the victim this time being Captain Cuttle's owner Lord Woolavington. He had first claim on Donoghue that season and used the claim to get him to ride his second string, Knockando, trained by Peter Gilpin, in the Derby, insisting that the jockey honoured the agreement. Not only did Donoghue not fancy riding a second string but Basil Jarvis had offered him a mount on the third-favourite, Papyrus, a much more attractive prospect than Knockando. Insisting that his understanding of the retainer was that it only applied to horses owned by Lord Woolavington that were trained by Fred Darling and not to those trained by other trainers, Steve wriggled out of the commitment and found himself aboard yet another Derby winner.

Although his disloyalty lost him the support of many owners and trainers, he continued riding until the end of the 1937 season, going out in a blaze of glory by winning four classics: the 1,000 Guineas and the Oaks on Exhibitionist and the Irish 2,000 Guineas and the Irish Derby on Phideas.

Mr Paget O'Brien Butler (c.1880–1914)

Rider:

1907 Colonel T.Y.L. Kirkwood's APOLLO BELVEDERE – Galway Plate (J. Currid)

1909 Captain Mansfield's GABRIEL II – Ballyglunin Park Chase (J. Hunter)

Paget O'Brien Butler was one of the able young men whose life was snuffed out in the rat-infested trenches of the Great War. As bogged-down armies fought over a few hundred yards of no man's land, the cream of a generation was being wiped out. An all round athlete, 'Piery' O'Brien Butler played rugby for Monkstown as well as riding as an amateur and was capped for Ireland in 1900, playing at full back. He volunteered to serve in the Boer War and received special dispensation to play for Ireland, interrupting his studies, but he was able to qualify as a medical doctor in 1905.

One of the leading amateurs in Ireland, he was Ireland's Champion Amateur Jockey in 1906 and enjoyed success on horses owned by Colonel Tom Kirkwood, notably with Paddy Maher (Conyngham Cup) and Apollo Belvedere (Galway Plate). His four rides in the Aintree Grand National all ended in falls, but he enjoyed more luck in the Irish equivalent, winning on Civil War in 1914. Just called up by the army, he came to ride in the Galway Plate on the very day war was declared. Riding the favourite, Fast Brendan, in the Galway Plate, he was beaten by a head by Alice Rockthorn. After the race he joined his regiment and departed for France. He was killed in action two months later.

Mr Reginald H. Walker (1881–1951)

Rider:

1907 C. Taaffe's DERRAVARAGH – Renmore Corinthian 2m flat (Larry Hope)

1908 P.J. Byrne's ROSE MORION – County Handicap Chase (G.L. Walker)

1910 Baron de Tuyll's LOVE IN A MIST – Renmore Corinthian 2m flat (M. Arnott)

Trainer, Rathvale, Athboy, Co. Meath:

1914 T. Nolan's NEVER FEAR (F. Morgan) – County Handicap Chase £78

1916 T. Nolan's NEVER FEAR (F. Morgan) – Galway Plate Chase £44

1916 Frank Barbour's ELGON (Mr H.S. Harrison) – Galway Hurdle £171

1916 P. Cullinan's AUNT ANNA (Mr H.S. Harrison) – Ballybrit Chase £91

1918 T.D. McKeever's ADEQUATE (W. Barrett) – County 12f flat £46

1919 H.S. Harrison's FARICATE (W. Barrett) – Mervue 8f flat £90

1919 J.C. McKeever's JENNY JONES (Mr H.S. Harrison) – Galway Hurdle £201

1920 Frank Barbour's SIR HUON (F. Morgan) – Ballybrit Chase £83

1929 Mr Loughran's KILEAGER (Mr F.E. McKeever) – Corrib Hurdle £44

1932 Mrs A. Wall's IRISH KNIGHT II (T. Cullen) – Galway Blazers Chase £44

1933 Lady Nugent's LACATOI (Mr F.E. McKeever) – Ballybrit Chase £44

Reginald Walker, the son of George L. Walker, the Rathvale trainer, and grandson of E.K. Walker, came from a family steeped in racing. Actually born in England, he began riding as an amateur in 1900, firing his enthusiasm and making his name on Rose Graft and Kicks. He won ten races on the former. He went to England with Atty Persse but returned in 1907 to become Irish Champion Amateur Rider four times, from 1907 to 1910.

Reggie Walker did not win either of the Galway feature races, although he was placed three times in the Plate and once in the Hurdle, but he did win the Irish Grand National four times. His father, George L. Walker, used to ride as an amateur under the name of 'Mr Arthur' and trained Royston-Crow to win the 1896 Irish Grand National. His death in July 1914 at the age of fifty-four interrupted his son's riding career. Prematurely landed with the responsibilities of running a stable, Reggie continued riding for a couple of years, but on a reduced scale as he settled in as a trainer.

In 1916 Walker won the Irish Grand National with Punch, a horse he rode to victory himself, on Easter Monday, the day of the Easter Rising. Later that year he trained both winners of the big Galway double, winning the Plate with Never Fear and the Hurdle with Frank Barbour's Elgon, the first person to do so. Recently retired as the Master of the Westmeath Foxhounds, Barbour was going into racing in a big way but, unfortunately for Walker, he got so big that he opened his own private training stable instead of using public trainers.

The best horse Reggie trained was Royal Danieli, beaten by a head in a visual decision by Battleship in the 1938 Grand National. The finish was a judge's nightmare, the two horses racing on opposite sides of the course, running neck and neck, with the fast-finishing pint-sized stallion, Battleship, catching the judge's eye. Dan Moore was adamant that Royal Danieli had won. A photograph – not a photo-finish picture it has to be said – indicates that there was precious little between the two. Reggie Walker died in January 1951 and although his son, M.N. Walker, succeeded him at Rathvale, the stable was later sold to Clem Magnier.

Clyde Aylin (1887–1922)

Rider:

1906   J.W. Gregg's GREY FACE – His Majesty's Plate 2m flat (J.W. Gregg)

1915   E.J. Hope's PRUDENT MAN – Express Hurdle (R.E. Harrison)

1915   H.C. Bourke's NELLIE MAC – His Majesty's Plate 2m flat (Private)

1916   J. Meleady's SNOUT – Traders' Plate 1m flat (Private)

1917   H.C. Bourke's NELLIE MAC – Salthill Hurdle (Private)

1917   Mrs N.J. Kelly's TREPAM – Express Hurdle (Langan)

1919   F. Stanner's CARRA LASS – Stewards' Handicap 12f flat (J. Coghlan)

English-born Clyde Aylin was apprenticed to W.T. 'Jack' Robinson, the former jockey who was training at Foxhill. He came to Ireland in 1905, when he was still only eighteen, to join S.C. Jeffrey at Heath House, Maryborough. His introduction came via his brother Alfred, who had been with Jeffrey some years previously, but he did not stay at Heath House long, moving to the Curragh to join Michael Dawson's powerful yard. He rode Dawson's charge, Killeagh, to victory in the Irish Derby of 1906 and the following year partnered Lady Americus to win the Fifteen Hundred for trainer Jim Parkinson. He finished second in the list of leading Irish jockeys to John Thompson in 1906 and 1907, but found winners much harder to come by after that, as he was fighting a constant battle with his increasing weight. In 1910 he went to ride in Germany.

He returned to Ireland after one season there, married a sister of Shem Jeffrey's wife and began riding over jumps, teaming up with Reggie Walker. Slowly but surely he began his climb to the top again, riding over jumps but taking the occasional ride on the flat if the weights allowed. In 1921 he rode Soldennis to victory in the National Stakes and the following year won the Irish Cambridgeshire on Flower Vale. He had his seventieth winner of the season when he won the first race at Leopardstown on St Stephen's Day on Guinea Stamp, trained by Willie Rankin, in a maiden hurdle. That was the final winner of his career. The following afternoon he had a bad fall from Parkstown, trained by Reggie Walker, in the Bray Handicap Steeplechase, and died in hospital the following day. He ended the year as Champion Jockey but that was no consolation to his grieving wife and his six young children, one of whom was only two months old.

Clyde Aylin was a respected jockey, straight, honest and non-betting and had three brothers involved in racing. Alf, a talented jockey won an Irish Derby and an Irish Oaks for the Heath House stable, Arthur was Harry Ussher's head lad and another brother, Harry, was riding in Belgium.

Henry I. Ussher (1882–1957)

Rider:

1910 R.M. Liddell's ASHBROOKE – Galway Plate Handicap Chase (H.I. Ussher)

1911 James Ryan's STRANGEGATE – Galway Blazers Chase (H.I. Ussher)

1911 P. Fox's TORY HILL II – Ballybrit Chase (H.I. Ussher)

Trainer, Eastwell, Loughrea, Co. Galway:

1908 T.G. Fletcher's STONE WALL (A. Hogan) – Ballyglunin Park Chase £50

1910 R.M. Liddell's ASHBROOKE (Mr H.I. Ussher) – Galway Plate £181

1911 James Ryan's STRANGEGATE (Mr H.I. Ussher) – Galway Blazers Chase £52½

1911 P. Fox's TORY HILL II (Mr H.I. Ussher) – Ballybrit Chase £73

1916 Mrs Croft's CROVEDERG (F. Dainty) – Salthill Hurdle £64

1916 Mrs Croft's CROVEDERG (F. Dainty) – Express Hurdle £54

1918 Mrs Croft's MAROC (H. Harty) – Galway Handicap Hurdle £166

1919 Colonel R.P. Croft's PICTURE SAINT (M. Colbert) – Galway Plate £422

1920 Colonel R.P. Croft's MARLIAN (J. Hogan Jr) – Stewards' Handicap 8f flat £83

1920 Mrs Croft's KILMORAL (J. Hogan Jr) – Moyode Plate 20f flat £103

1920 A. Byrne's ONAGH (H.H. Beasley) – Mervue Plate 8f flat £83

1920 Mrs Croft's YOURS ONLY (J. Hogan Jr) – Express Hurdle £103

1920 Mrs Croft's SOLID GOLD (J. Hamilton) – Maiden Chase £201

1921 A.D. Comyn's MR VIGOROUS (F. Wootton) – Salthill Handicap Hurdle £83

1921 Mrs Croft's MAX (F. Wootton) – Galway Plate £592

1921 Colonel R.P. Croft's REGISTRATION (H.H. Beasley) – Mervue Plate 8f flat £83

1921 Colonel R.P. Croft's REGISTRATION (F. Wootton) – Traders' Plate 16f flat £88

Trainer, Brackenstown, Swords, Co. Dublin:

1923 R.J. Duggan's IONIAN (Joseph Canty) – Stewards' Handicap 8f flat £83

1923 J.E. Tyrrell's CLONSHEEVER (J. Hogan Jr) – Galway Plate £392

1923 Mrs Croft's GOLDEN STREET (F.B. Rees) – Ballybrit Chase £83

1923 H. McAlinden's FORT ELIZABETH (F.B. Rees) – Renmore Handicap Chase £83

1924 J.E. Tyrrell's CLONSHEEVER (F.B. Rees) – Galway Plate £442

1925 Mrs Croft's GOLDEN REBEL (J. Hogan Jr) – Ballybrit Chase £88

1925 Mrs Croft's GOFFEE (J. Hogan Jr) – Renmore Handicap Chase £83

1926 Mrs Croft's GOLDEN LIGHT (M. Doherty) – Galway Blazers Handicap Chase £84

1927 F.B. McDonogh's SANTHOME (J. Moylan) – Salthill Handicap Hurdle £83

1927 J.T. O'Ryan's TONY LAD (J. Maloney) – Galway Plate £492

1927 A.D. Comyn's GLENACLARA (J. Moylan) – Moyode Plate 20f flat £78

1927 Mrs Croft's GOLDEN REBEL (W. Beasley) – Ballybrit Chase £73

1927 Mrs Croft's GOLDEN REBEL (W. Beasley) – Galway Blazers Handicap Chase £74

1928 James McDonnell's FLEETING LOVE (J. Moylan) – Moyode Plate 20f flat £58½

1928 Richard Power's STRIPED SILK (J. Moylan) – His Majesty's Plate 2m flat £104

1931 A.D. Comyn's WANDERING WING (J. Moylan) – Stewards' Handicap 8f flat £44

1931 F. Burke's OLE MAN RIVER (J. Moylan) – Corrib Hurdle £44

1931 Miss K. Ussher's GALLANT PRINCE (J. Moylan) – His Majesty's Plate 2m flat £104

1932 Lord Milton's A.P. (W.T. O'Grady) – Ballybrit Chase £44

1933 Captain G.A. Boyd-Rochfort's BELIEVE ME (J. Moylan) – Mervue Plate 12f flat £44

1933 H.I. Ussher's DOPE KING (J. Moylan) – Stewards' Handicap 8f flat £44

1934 J.B. Magennis's GALLI GALLI (W.T. O'Grady) – Salthill Handicap Hurdle £44

1934 H.I. Ussher's ARMOURED PRINCE (W.T. O'Grady) – Corrib Hurdle £44

1934 P.D. Mathew's TOGA (J. Moylan) – His Majesty's Plate 2m flat £104

1935 R.J. Duggan's KYRAT (W.T. O'Grady) – Salthill Handicap Hurdle £49

1935 Joseph McGrath's STEP ASIDE BELLE (W.T. O'Grady) – Ballybrit Chase £49

1935 Joseph McGrath's BABY LEROY (W.T. O'Grady) – Corrib Hurdle £49

1936 P.J. Ruttledge's WILY GREEK (J. Moylan) – Mervue Plate 12f flat £49

1936 Mrs J.G. Fitzgerald's KINVARA (W.T. O'Grady) – Corrib Hurdle £49

1937 Captain D.W. Daly's BRIGHTER COTTAGE (W.T. O'Grady) Galway Plate £517

1940 Colonel D.W. Daly's RING OF GOLD (T. McNeill) – Galway Plate £740

1945 G. Chesney's GRECIAN VICTORY (D. Morgan) – Galway Plate £740

1945 H.I. Ussher's GOLDEN SOUVENIR (T. Molony) – Corrib Hurdle £89

1947 H.I. Ussher's SHINING GOLD (Mr J.R. Cox) – Moyode Bumper £111½

1947 G.F. Annesley's NO NIGHTY (J. Tyrrell) – Stewards' Handicap 8f flat £222

1948 Miss P. Magill's BRENNEVIN (G.H. Wells) – Corrib Maiden Hurdle £133½

1950 Sir Eric Ohlson's BARE MARGIN (Mr P.C. Heron) – Moyode Bumper £133½

1951 Lord Hemphill's CILLIE DOLLY (J. Tyrrell) – Mervue Maiden 12f flat £202

1955 Lord Hemphill's CILLIE DOLLY (J.V. Ahern) – Ballybrit Chase £133

1956 H.I. Ussher's GOLDEN REBEL (Mr B. Lenehan) – Moyode Bumper £133

1956 Lord Hemphill's ARCTIC PEARL (N. Brennan) – Renmore Maiden 8f flat £202

Trainer, W.A. Ussher:

1912 James Ryan's STRANGEGATE (E. Houlihan) – County Handicap Chase £69

1913 Martin McDonogh's DOUBLE MAC (R. Trudgill) – Galway Blazers Chase £59½

1914 P.J. Davy's ABNEGATE (R. Trudgill) – Salthill Handicap Hurdle £64

1914 H.F. Malcomson's LOUGH ERIN (John Doyle) – Mervue Plate 8f flat £44

Harry Ussher, the leading trainer at Galway until Dermot Weld raced past his total, was a son of Christopher Ussher, whose Luckpenny won the Forster Street Chase on the second day of the inaugural Galway Races in 1869. Christopher Ussher, who lived at Eastwell, Kilrickle, Co. Galway, was a subscriber to the Irish Racing Calendar and was a founder member of the Irish National Hunt Steeplechase Committee in 1870. Originally called Neville, the family came to Ireland with King John, changing their name to reflect their position as ushers to the King. One of the family, Henry Ussher, was the Royal Astromomer and was involved with the founding of the Dunsink observatory in northern Co. Dublin in 1783. At this period, time in Ireland was not accurate and differed from place to place. The observatory produced the accurate Dunsink Mean Time, which was twenty-five minutes behind Greenwich Mean Time, and this was adopted by the city of Dublin. The new railway network in Ireland used Dublin time in their timetables, which meant that at Galway railway station the clock was set to this time rather than local time, which was some minutes behind. Gradually all the railway towns began using 'railway time', which spread to the surrounding areas and eventually it became a standard time throughout Ireland.

Christopher Ussher died on 21 February 1884 and was buried in a private graveyard a few hundred yards from his home. His early death left his wife, Olivia, to cope with several young children alone. Their eldest son, William Arland, born in January 1878, was nearly five years older than his brother Harry. He inherited the racing bug and in 1902 first registered his racing colours. His father's colours of blue with white sleeves and hoop were dropped after his death, so probably were not available when Willie chose Cambridge blue with white sleeves and sash, and black cap, and began subscribing to the Irish Racing Calendar in 1903. He attended the Dublin Horse Show in August 1904 and returned with three horses, including The Accepted, which cost 50 guineas. He then purchased The Solicitor, winner of the 1902 Royal Hunt Cup at Royal Ascot, to stand as a stallion at Eastwell, installing his new acquisition in a specially constructed box, still called The Solicitor's box a hundred years later.

Willie took out a licence to ride as an amateur in 1905, although he took very few mounts, preferring to get professional riders for his runners. The Accepted won twice for him in 1905, a hurdle race at Mullingar and a flat handicap at Tubbercurry, but the following year the mare was registered as the property of Harry Ussher, who had just taken out a licence to ride and registered his colours as red, white hooped sleeves.

Harry took himself and The Accepted to England with the string of his erstwhile neighbour Atty Persse, who was in the process of moving his stable of jumpers there. The Accepted had already been placed twice, ridden on each occasion by Reggie Walker, before winning at Cheltenham in March with Captain Rasbotham in the saddle. The following day, with the same rider up, he finished second before travelling down for the Torquay meeting. In 1906 the Torquay Hunt races were run on a course situated at St Mary's Church, within a mile of the town centre. There was one National Hunt meeting each year on Easter Monday and Tuesday. It was a good galloping course with a run-in of 440 yards, but it raced for the last time in 1940, the year jump racing was suspended because of the Second World War. It was always a well-attended meeting and the race company intended to reopen the course when hostilities ended. However, a stray German bomb destroyed the grandstand in 1943. The cost of replacing it proved beyond the resources of the company and the racecourse never reopened.

It was at that old Torquay course that Harry Ussher unexpectedly rode his first winner, on Easter Tuesday 1906, when The Accepted won the Torre Handicap Hurdle, having won a handicap hurdle on the first day of the meeting with Mr W. Bulteel riding. That gentleman was expected to take the mount on the second day too, but he opted to ride St John's Wood instead, so The Accepted was left without a rider. Harry Ussher took the mount himself and finished alone.

The best amateur riders in Ireland in the years leading up to the outbreak of the Great War in 1914 were Leslie Brabazon and Reggie Walker, with Harry Ussher leading the others. Unlike those two, Harry rode a lot in England but never had much luck in the Grand National; the nearest he finished was a tenth place from four rides. He did have a couple of fancied mounts in the race; in 1912 he rode Glenside, winner of the race the previous year, and he was aboard the favourite Ballyhackle in 1913, but both horses failed to get round. He had only one ride in the Irish Grand National, finishing second on the hot favourite Dysart in 1911. However, he did win the Galway Plate on Ashbrooke in 1910, defeating the useful Noble Grecian, whom Jim Parkinson had purchased out of W.P. Hanly's yard after winning the National Hunt Cup at Punchestown. Noble Grecian was a really good chaser, subsequently winning the 1912 Galway Plate and the two feature races, the Prince of Wales's Plate and the Conyngham Cup, at successive Punchestown meetings. It was always said that Harry Ussher's greatest riding feat was when he was beaten on Dysart in the 1911 Conyngham Cup. There was only a short head in it at the post, the nod going to Victor Olympic, ridden by Count Stolberg, but the race was talked about for years after; apparently Harry Ussher's talent had never been seen to better effect.

He began training in 1908, while continuing to ride as an amateur, with Eastwell as his base. Eastwell house and stables are situated just off the main Ballinasloe to Loughrea road, between Aughrim and Kilreekle, but much nearer Kilreekle, which is only a couple of miles away. The big house is gone, except for its cellars, but the stables still stand, desolate and dilapidated, a lonely reminder of better times. As popular with his neighbours as he was within the racing fraternity, Harry Ussher liked to buy all his produce locally, even if it cost a little more, and his neighbours always had a friend to turn to long after he had departed for Dublin. He kept a couple of beds in a Dublin hospital for his jockeys, in case they were badly injured, and these were always available to a friend or neighbour in need. A jockey's life is a risky one today but a century ago it was infinitely more dangerous, with no crash helmets or back pads to protect them from injury. Fences were bigger, falls more frequent and proper medical attention at the races was non-existent. On the other hand, races were run at a much slower pace than they are today, ensuring that many falls did not result in a serious injury. Besides the hospital beds, Eastwell had its own infirmary for injured jockeys or lads, where they would receive the best medical attention available at the time.

Willie Ussher did not renew his gentleman rider's licence after 1910 but continued to run the Eastwell stud, while Harry was permanently away training in England between 1912 and 1914. Although Harry returned to Ireland occasionally to ride, Willie Ussher was living in Eastwell and ran the stable during this period. This is important because it affects the number of winners trained by Harry Ussher at the Galway Races down the years. I credit him as the trainer of fifty-eight winners at Galway between 1908 and 1956 but not the four that won when he was in England – one in 1912, one in 1913 and two in 1914 – which I have credited to W.A. Ussher. When the outbreak of the Great War in August 1914 sent Harry scuttling back to Galway with his string, he returned to Eastwell and assumed full control of the racehorses. Willie, now drinking like a fish and destined for an early grave, was in charge of the stud and the estate.

Harry Ussher was known as the Harry Lorrequer of the day, after a character in Charles Lever's humorous stage-Irish novel of the same name, which amused him. A ladies' man, he managed to avoid a marriage commitment, but his life was changed utterly by a decision of Maxie Arnott, his long-time rival for Galway training honours. Maxie decided to volunteer to fight in the war and to close his stable in 1915. Colonel and Mrs Croft declined to go to Joseph Maher, who was deputizing in Arnott's absence, and sent their horses to Eastwell instead. At the end of the war, Pansy Croft arranged for Harry Ussher to bring her horses over to a stable at Upavon, Wiltshire, for a winter campaign, returning to Eastwell in the spring. Pansy lived at Brackenstown, Swords, Co. Dublin. Her marriage to Colonel Croft had broken down and she was now close to the dashing trainer from Galway, being recognized in racing as Harry Ussher's girlfriend. She wanted Harry close at hand and persuaded him to move his stable to Brackenstown. One of the drawbacks of Eastwell was its distance from the railway – the nearest station, Woodlawn, was 8 miles away and the runners had to be walked that distance to and from the station when going to the races. Moving into Brackenstown in 1923,

The stewards' box gives a clear view of the race and the acting stewards enquired into thirteen separate incidents at the 2007 Festival

in his first full season there he trained sixty-seven winners and finished fifth in the list of leading trainers, clearly benefiting from the better facilities at his disposal, including his own private racecourse, with whitewashed rails and a miniature wooden stand to watch the horses gallop.

Harry Ussher loved to have winners at Galway and laid out horses for the meeting. Each year he would rent a large house in the area for race week, and invite old friends and acquaintances to stay with him; it was an annual holiday back in his home county. The leading trainer at the Galway Festival eleven times, he twice trained five winners at the meeting, in 1920 and 1927, and his nine victories in the Galway Plate – Ashbrooke (1910), Picture Saint (1919), Max (1921), Clonsheever (1922 and 1923), Tony Lad (1927), Brighter Cottage (1937), Ring of Gold (1940) and Grecian Victory (1945) – is a record for the race. He found the Galway Hurdle a harder nut to crack, only training one winner, Maroc (1918), owned by Pansy. In 1936 a brace of winners brought his Galway total to forty-six, one ahead of Maxie Arnott, to put him at the top of the table of all time winning trainers there. Maxie went back to the top of the table in 1941, and held the lead until 1947, when Harry regained the leadership and held on to it to the day he died. His total of fifty-eight Galway Festival winners remained the record until it was surpassed by Dermot Weld in 1988, and by Noel Meade ten years later. He is still in third place for the total number of winners at the Festival, but only just – Aidan O'Brien is breathing down his neck, being just one behind on fifty-seven winners.

Rotund, jolly and of medium height, Harry Ussher was an ailing 74-year-old in 1956, when he braved the bumper crowds and indifferent weather to saddle runners at Galway. He was rewarded with two winners, his last coming in the final race of that year's meeting when Arctic Pearl, ridden by Nicky Brennan, won the Renmore flat race. This last Galway winner came forty-eight years after his first, Stonewall, winner of the last race of the 1908 meeting, the Ballyglunin Park steeplechase. Arctic Pearl was a fitting last winner, being owned by Lord Hemphill, whose family had a long association with Galway and whose son would later become Chairman of the Galway Race Committee. Lord Hemphill, who died himself in 1957, was also the owner of Harry Ussher's last winner as a trainer, Silly Dorice, winner of the Barrow Maiden Hurdle at Naas on Saturday, 5 January 1957. When Harry Ussher died on 30 July, the eve of the Galway meeting and the news filtered through to Galway the following day, the jockeys marched down the course in single file as a mark of respect to a great and popular trainer.

Harry Ussher left all his property to his only niece Kathleen Browne (née Ussher), who had taken up residence at Brackenstown after her marriage broke up. Kathleen had tasted success as an owner at Galway when her horse Gallant Prince, trained of course by her uncle, won the King's Plate in 1931. Today Harry Ussher's training establishment at Brackenstown is buried under tons of concrete – condemned to become another housing estate in the greater Dublin area.

Pansy Croft (1888–1940)

Owner, purple, gold cap:

1911 SHOEBLACK (G. Brown) – County Handicap Chase £74 (M. Arnott)
1916 CROVEDERG (F. Dainty) – Salthill Hurdle £64 (H.I. Ussher)
1916 CROVEDERG (F. Dainty) – Express Hurdle £54 (H.I. Ussher)
1918 MAROC (H. Harty) – Galway Hurdle £166 (H.I. Ussher)
1920 KILMORAL (J. Hogan Jr) – Moyode Plate 20f flat £103 (H.I. Ussher)
1920 YOURS ONLY (J. Hogan Jr) – Express Hurdle £103 (H.I. Ussher)
1920 SOLID GOLD (J. Hamilton) – Maiden Chase £201 (H.I. Ussher)

1921   MAX (F. Wootton) – Galway Plate £592 (H.I. Ussher)
1923   GOLDEN STREET (F.B. Rees) – Ballybrit Chase £83 (H.I. Ussher)
1925   GOLDEN REBEL (J. Hogan Jr) – Ballybrit Chase £88 (H.I. Ussher)
1925   GOFFEE (J. Hogan Jr) – Renmore Handicap Chase £83 (H.I. Ussher)
1926   GOLDEN LIGHT (M. Doherty) – Galway Blazers Handicap Chase £84 (H.I. Ussher)
1927   GOLDEN REBEL (W. Beasley) – Ballybrit Chase £75 (H.I. Ussher)
1927   GOLDEN REBEL (W. Beasley) – Galway Blazers Handicap Chase £74 (H.I. Ussher)

Pansy Croft and her husband Colonel R.P. Croft had eighteen winners between them at the Galway races between 1911 and 1927, seventeen of them trained by Harry Ussher. Harry's liking for Galway winners meant that he would 'lay out' horses for the meeting, a policy that enabled Pansy Croft to be leading owner there on four occasions (1916, 1920, 1925 and 1927), and her husband once, in 1921. The Colonel and Pansy both won the Galway Plate, he with Picture Saint (1919) and she with Max (1921) and in addition Pansy won the Hurdle with Maroc (1918). Pansy's total of fourteen gave her the owner's record for the number of winners at Galway from 1926 to 1994 when Dr Michael Smurfit passed her total, having equalled it the previous year.

The Colonel and Pansy first registered their racing colours in 1910. Pansy's were purple jacket and gold cap and the colonel's royal blue, silver sleeves, braid and cap. Mrs Croft's first Irish winner was Shoeblack, trained by Maxie Arnott, winner of handicap chases at Dundalk and Galway. At Galway Shoeblack was ridden by Arnott's stable jockey George Brown, who succeeded Steve Donoghue as Irish Champion Jockey in 1909. In 1911 he won the Galway Plate on Noble Grecian, who was owned by Sir George Abercromby, an officer in the Scots Guards who was based in Ireland at the time. Following a very bad third to James Cowhy's Lincoln Green at Tuam, Shoeblack left the Arnott stable and was sent over to England with Harry Ussher's string. When he won a selling chase at Plumpton, with Leslie Brabazon up, he was claimed by Bob Gore for 70 guineas. Robert George Gore was born in Swords, Co. Dublin in 1865 and went to England as a young man, where he was a successful amateur rider. At this time he was training at Findon; later he trained two winners of the Grand National in successive years, Jerry M and Covertcoat in 1912 and 1913.

The upshot of this was that Maxie lost the patronage of the Crofts, who stayed with Harry Ussher. He was sent back to Ireland when the war broke out in 1914, and Colonel and Mrs Croft soon followed, settling at Brackenstown, Swords, Co. Dublin, where the Irish Derby winner Oppressor was bred. By the early 1920s the Croft marriage was in trouble, the couple separated and Pansy became increasingly attracted to the bachelor trainer from Co. Galway. Mrs Pansy Page Croft, as she now called herself, encouraged Harry Ussher to leave Eastwell and move to her in Brackenstown, which he duly did.

Pansy bred Ring of Gold, winner of the 1940 Galway Plate, who she leased to Colonel D.W. Daly, but he remained in Harry Ussher's stable. Colonel Daly had a great Galway that year, owning the winners of both the big races: Ring of Gold won the Plate on a very wet afternoon and Red Shaft, trained by Roderic More O'Ferrall, won the Hurdle.

Later that year Pansy took ill, and was rushed to St Vincent's Hospital, but she died there a week later on 17 December 1940 aged only fifty-two. The following day Wyndham Waithman (1887–1975) purchased a plot for his family at the cemetery in Galway city and allowed her body to be interred there. When Harry Ussher died in 1957, Mr Waithman agreed that he should be buried in his plot also, alongside his beloved Pansy, and the famous Galway trainer rested there in peace without a memorial.

It is curious how often similar names, of both people and horses, crop up in the same generation, causing endless confusion for those trying to research bygone times. In the 1920s Mrs R.P. Croft and Mrs E.M. Crofts were leading lady owners in Ireland. Because both tended to appear as 'Mrs Croft's' and 'Mrs Crofts' it is easy to confuse the pair – and to continue the coincidence both died within days of one another in December 1940.

Elizabeth Mary Crofts, from Buttevant, Co. Cork, was Mary Cowhy before she was married. Her brother James bred and raced horses on a small scale and travelled to Newmarket for the dispersal sale of John Musker on Monday and Tuesday, 2 and 3 July 1906. John Musker, one of the founders of the Home & Colonial Stores, retired in 1896 and began breeding horses on a lavish scale. The following year he repatriated the Derby winner Melton, who had been languishing in Italy, and was delighted by his success. However, ill health decided him to disband his stud and sell off all his bloodstock, except Melton and two of his sons. The prospect of buying into some of the best bloodlines brought buyers flocking to Newmarket and James Cowhy returned to Co. Cork with the broodmare Wild Betty and a yearling filly by Lord Melton, which had cost him 90 and 60 guineas respectively. The yearling filly traced back to Mirtherless Bairn, a half sister to Ben Battle, John Wardell's Irish Derby winner of 1874, which probably attracted Mr Cowhy to her. Named Mary Melton, she won two minor flat races as a five-year-old in 1910, the only season she was trained. In 1916 she bred a nice colt by Lomond, a leading two-year-old in 1911, who was duly sent to Michael Dawson on the Curragh to be trained.

Named Loch Lomond, this colt did not win at two years but showed potential and held an entry for the 1919 Irish Derby.

Unfortunately, James Cowhy died towards the end of the year and his sister Mary inherited his estate, including Loch Lomond. Having won at the Phoenix Park and at Leopardstown, Loch Lomond finished a well-beaten second to the useful Snow Maiden in the Baldoyle Derby, much to the dismay of his owner. Dawson was satisfied that the horse did not act on the sharp track but she blamed the jockey, Arthur Langford, a lightweight Australian who was Dawson's stable jockey that year. Miss Cowhy had become a fan of Jim Parkinson's up-and-coming apprentice jockey, Martin Quirke, and wanted him to ride Loch Lomond in the Irish Derby. Michael Dawson insisted that his stable jockey ride the horse but Mary Cowhy would not budge. Determined to get her man, she took Loch Lomond away from Dawson and sent it across the Curragh to Jim Parkinson's Maddenstown Lodge stable. With Martin Quirke in the saddle, Loch Lomond ran away with the race, winning easily by six lengths from Cheap Popularity and Snow Maiden. The bust-up did not sour relations between Mary Cowhy and Michael Dawson permanently, and when the time came for her to put Loch Lomond's own-brother Maynooth into training she gave it to Michael Dawson rather than Parkinson.

Not long after her success with Loch Lomond, Mary Cowhy married and from then on was known as Mrs E.M. Crofts. Her husband was Christopher George Crofts of Velvetstown, Buttevant, a man in his mid-fifties, about ten years her senior, who was a member of a well-known Protestant family which had been living in the area for three centuries. Difficulties surfaced immediately. Both were in middle age and set in their ways. She refused to leave her house and he would not leave his. The impasse was resolved by an agreement that each would continue to live in their own houses but every week Mary Crofts would visit Velvetstown House for Sunday lunch. The arrangement got off to a bad start when her motor-car could not fit through the avenue gate, but the gate was hastily widened and the couple enjoyed many years of happy Sunday lunches together.

The downside of marriage came home to Mary Crofts when she discovered that being a married woman was costing her money. The problem was income tax and the husband and wife allowance, which was lower than that of two people living together unmarried. Believing that this was discriminatory, she battled with the Revenue Commissioners and the courts for many years for the right to be assessed separately for tax. She continued to race and breed horses from her Churchtown Stud until her death in 1940, aged sixty-three.

Mr Cecil Brabazon (1884–1964)

Rider:

1911 P.D. Corry's LARAGEN – Express Hurdle (O'Malley)

1924 D. Kelly's MAY-EVE – Traders' 2m flat (Prendergast)

Trainer, Kilcumney House, Kildare:

1918 Sir R.M. Liddell's COMMANDER SMITH (Joseph Harty) – Committee 1m flat £46

1919 P.P. Gilpin's LIE LOW (N. Hayes) – Ballybrit Chase £90

1921 J.J. Moore's KING MICHAEL (Joseph Canty) – Galway Hurdle £246

Trainer, Trimblestown, Co. Meath:

1924 F. Barbour's RATH-LUIRE (T. Kelly Jr) – Renmore Chase £83

1925 Miss E.L.M. Barbour's BLANCONA (C. Donnelly) – Galway Plate £442

1925 Miss M.D. Barbour's ALROI (C. Donnelly) – Galway Hurdle £196

Trainer, Rangers Lodge, Curragh:

1932 R.S. Croker's CHIEFTAIN (T. Burns) – Mervue 12f flat £44

1938 Miss L. Brabazon's SPIRIT LEVEL (A. Brabazon) – Mervue 12f flat £49

1941 Miss M.O. Mathieson's ST MARTIN (A. Brabazon) – Galway Plate £740

1941 S.J. Parr's ALGER (John Power) – Stewards' 8f flat £49

1942 W.R. Ellis's FOAM CREST (G. Cooney) – His Majesty's Plate flat £104

1943 Sir T. Dixon's GLENGORMLEY (A. Brabazon) – Oranmore Handicap 12f flat £74

1944 J. Gorman's SEA-POINT (E. Newman) – Atlantic 8f flat £74

1945 T. Allen's LADY'S FIND (C. Fagan) – Mervue 12f flat £74

1945 Mrs E.J. King's ZARNA (C. Fagan) – Atlantic 8f flat £89

1950 H.E. Rawson's LADY'S FIND (F. McKenna) – Galway Hurdle £740

1950 Lord Fingall's SWEET SEVENTEEN (P. Canty) – His Majesty's Plate 2m flat £104

1958 A. Willis's BUT WHY (A. Brabazon) – Stewards' Handicap 8½f flat £202

Arthur Cecil Samuel Freeman Falkiner Brabazon, to give him his full name, was born on 1 July 1884 at Johnstown House, Mullingar. His father, William Thomas Brabazon, was prominent in Co. Westmeath racing and hunting circles and he provided Cecil with his first winner, Annie Symons in the Tally-Ho Hunt Flat race at Kilbeggan in May 1906. The Brabazons trained a couple of horses privately at Woodlands, Multifarnham, but in 1913 the two brothers took the historic Rossmore Lodge stable on the Curragh, with Cecil doing most of the training and Leslie most of the riding. The pair had a most successful season. Cecil won forty-one races with eighteen horses, compared to Michael Dawson, the Champion

Trainer that year, who won fifty-three races with thirty-seven horses; while Mr Leslie Brabazon finished the year as Ireland's Champion Jockey with thirty-seven wins. This success led to Cecil being offered a position he just could not refuse, that of private trainer to F. Ambrose Clark in America.

Mr and Mrs Clark were unknown in Europe at the time but were leading owners in America and would later become famous as the owners of the Grand National winner Kellsboro Jack and the Derby winner Never Say Die. Cecil began training at Belmont Park in 1914, calling his yard the Ward Union stable, a name that meant so much to American sportsmen who had hunted in Ireland. Intending to combine riding with training, Cecil put the licence in the name of his head lad Patrick Deegan, because he did not want to compromise his amateur status.

After a couple of years in America, he returned to Ireland to train at Kilcumney House, Co. Kildare. With Leslie's riding career over, Cecil began taking a lot more mounts, and in 1920 he became Champion Amateur Rider for the first and only time, sharing the honour with Mr Cyril Harty. His uncles, Robert Brabazon and Harry Nuttall, had been Champion Amateurs before him, so too was his brother Leslie, who is usually – and mistakenly – credited as being the better rider of the two brothers. Certainly Leslie was a fine horseman and his career was all too short, but he had the advantage of being light and took many more mounts. Cecil was a fine steeplechase rider and was quietly confident of winning the 1920 Grand National on Ballyboggan. A gallant runner-up to Poethlyn, ridden by Lester Piggott's grandfather Ernie, in the first post-war race at Aintree, Ballyboggan met that horse on 7-pound better terms the following year. Cecil Brabazon replaced Willie Head for his first and only ride in the great race. Unfortunately, neither horse got very far in 1920 – both crashed out of the rain-sodden race at the very first fence.

In 1921 Cecil Brabazon trained the one-eyed Bohernore to win the Irish Grand National and won the first of his three Galway Hurdles with King Michael, winner of ten races that year. When Frank Barbour came knocking in 1924 looking for a private trainer, Cecil eagerly accepted, moving into a magnificent yard at Trimblestown, Co. Meath, where every facility was at hand, including a miniature racecourse. Having completed a Galway Plate and Hurdle double and won the Irish Cesarewitch for the Misses Barbour in 1925, he moved out of Trimblestown to set up as a public trainer at Rangers Lodge, on the Curragh. At first he found life as a public trainer extremely difficult: racing was in crisis, stakes were very low and many of his traditional owners were either dead or had moved to England. Deprived of cash flow, Cecil and his family were desperate and struggling to survive when out of the blue Richard S. Croker invited him to be his private trainer. A son of the famous 'Boss' Croker, owner of Orby, the first Irish-trained Epsom Derby winner, he got Cecil Brabazon back on his feet.

Cecil was Champion Irish Trainer once, in 1940, due entirely to Jack Chaucer's victory in the Red Cross Chase at Leopardstown, the richest race run in Ireland that year and more valuable than the Irish Derby. However, he always maintained that St Martin was the best steeplechaser he ever trained. Easily the best flat horse he trained was Beau Sabreur, winner of the Irish 2,000 Guineas, the Irish St Leger and the Coronation Cup (Epsom).

Cecil Brabazon married Gladys, a daughter of Gussie Briscoe, the man who bought the estate of the late John Preston, the owner of the celebrated mare Brunette, at Bellinter, which included the famous Hill of Tara. Their son, Aubrey, continued the family tradition by becoming an Irish Champion Jockey and a very stylish one too.

Mr Leslie Brabazon (1885–1964)

Rider:

1908 C. Cole's BILLALI – Express Hurdle (C. Cole)
1913 T.J. Daly's MASSOL – Express Hurdle (C. Brabazon)

Born 8 October 1885, William Leslie Nuttall Brabazon was the younger brother of Cecil and rode his first winner when Wrong Age won a handicap flat race at the Skerries Strand meeting in August 1907. Leslie's first Galway winner, Billali in 1908, was a chance ride – he only got the mount because his brother turned up late. Lighter than Cecil, Leslie got a lot of mounts and consequently became more experienced than his elder brother, and it was said that no jockey was better at presenting a horse to a fence. Often referred to as 'LB', he really hit the headlines in 1913, when he ended the season as Champion Jockey, one of only three amateurs to do so in the twentieth century, when riding for Rossmore Lodge, where he ran the stable jointly with Cecil.

Mr Leslie Brabazon rode his last winner on 16 August 1916 on the Knight of Glin's Glencarbry in the Grace Dieu Handicap flat race at Tramore. The following day, in the last race of the meeting, he was seriously injured when Mrs Joseph Widger's Ballycadden fell during a 3-mile chase. Out cold, he was gently carried to the members' pavilion of an adjacent golf links and lay there unconscious for fourteen weeks. Too ill to be moved, he had to stay there, attended by a nurse, family and friends for ninety-eight days and nights. Then he suddenly woke up and was perfectly normal again.

When he had sufficiently recovered, he began training a few horses at Ballinter, Navan, but he never rode in races again. In 1923 he accepted a position as assistant trainer to Harry Ussher, who had recently come to Brackenstown from Galway. He was also involved in setting up the Proudstown Park racecourse, the current Navan venue, along with Major Thomas Collins Gerard, the owner of the Grand National winner Troytown, Albert Lowry, the local auctioneer, and Arthur McCann, a stockbroker.

Joseph Canty (1895–1971)

Rider:

1913 Captain F. Blacker's NILE VALLEY – Stewards' Handicap 12f flat (M. Dawson)

1913 T. O'K. White's TULLYLOST – Traders' Handicap 8f flat (M. Dawson)

1914 T.M. Carew's NELLA'S FAVOR – Stewards' Handicap 12f flat (M. Dawson)

1914 William Jackson's ROSA VISTA – Traders' Handicap 8f flat (M. Dawson)

1917 P.D. Coen's HAPPY MOMENTS – Galway Hurdle (P. Behan)

1919 A. McMahon's WALTZAWAY- Express Hurdle (M. Dawson)

1919 Joseph Whelan's ALWAYS – Maiden Chase (M. Dawson)

1920 Baron de Tuyll's SOUTHAMPTON – Traders' Plate 16f flat (H.M. Hartigan)

1921 J.J. Moore's KING MICHAEL – Galway Hurdle (J.J. Moore)

1923 R.J. Duggan's IONIAN – Stewards' Handicap 8f flat (H.I. Ussher)

1924 Florence Burke's HOLY FOOKS – Galway Hurdle (M. Dawson)

1925 Maxwell Arnott's PRIVIT'S PRIDE – Stewards' Handicap 8f flat (M. Arnott)

1926 Florence Burke's NOBLE PRINCE – Stewards' Handicap 8f flat (M.C. Collins)

1926 J.A. Coen's MARCUS SUPERBUS – Mervue Plate 8f flat (J.A. Coen)

1929 Mrs M. Dawson's MILENNIS – Stewards' Handicap 8f flat (Joseph Dawson)

1929 Hubert M. Hartigan's SHREWD KING – Galway Hurdle (H.M. Hartigan)

1930 P.J. Corbett's SAINT SENAN – Stewards' Handicap 8f flat (T. Nunan)

1930 Albert Lowry's A.P. – Mervue Plate 12f flat (Joseph Dawson)

1930 Hubert M. Hartigan's HO FANG – Corrib Hurdle (H.M. Hartigan)

1944 A. Fatah's HYDERABAD – Mervue Plate 12f flat (H.M. Hartigan)

1944 Miss V. O'Neill-Power's OOLA – His Majesty's Plate 2m flat (walk over) (H.M. Ryan)

1949 James Flahaven's MAITRE JINKS – Stewards' Handicap 8f flat (Michael Dawson)

1951 James Flahaven's MAITRE JINKS – Stewards' Handicap 8f flat (Michael Dawson)

Trainer, Ruanbeg, Curragh:

1961 Joseph Canty's CHARCOAL GREY (J.M. Canty) – Oranmore Handicap 7f flat £202

Limerick-born Joe Canty was one of the foremost jockeys riding in Ireland between the world wars, being Champion on seven occasions between 1919 and 1931, and riding 117 winners in 1925 – an all-time Irish record that stood until 1994, when Charlie Swan rode 123. Charlie set a new record with 147 wins the following year but his percentage of winners to rides was only 26.02 per cent against Canty's 34.51 per cent. Joe Canty was a brilliant jockey with a keen racing brain, and was regarded as the shrewdest of all Irish riders and a good judge of pace. He had the gift of good hands, was strong in a finish and without an equal at the starting gate, abilities that made him the perfect rider for gambling trainers. He also was a committed gambler himself, one of a number of jockeys who supplemented their income through successful betting at a time when prize money was pitifully small. He left nothing to chance when planning a bet, personally schooling the horse on the gallops beforehand and walking the course thoroughly before the race. A favourite trick of his was to get the groundsman to loosen the outside hurdle of the last two flights, so that when he came with his trademark rush on the outside in the closing stages, he knew that the hurdles would offer no resistance should his mount give them a clout. He was an expert at securing the rails berth at the start; the introduction of the draw for positions in flat races was only a temporary setback because he soon discovered that he could 'cooperate' with the official to secure the draw number he wanted.

Joe Canty rode four winners of the Galway Hurdle – Happy Moments (1917), King Michael (1921), Holy Fooks (1924) and Shrewd King (1929), a race record he shares with Pat Taaffe, but in 1931 he suffered two serious falls. During a layoff with a serious back injury, he actually lost some weight, which made it possible for him to ride more on the flat and convinced him to give up riding over jumps. During his career, he rode for two big gambling trainers Philie Behan, who excelled with two-year-olds, and later Hubert Hartigan, one of the great Irish trainers. At first Hartigan considered that he was fortunate indeed to have the top two jockeys riding for him, Joe Canty and Morny Wing, but became exasperated at Canty's tactic of keeping the odd gamble to himself by not revealing all on the gallops. After one particular upset, he publicly moaned: 'I have the two best jockeys in the country riding trials for me but I never have a clue because Wing never wants to lose a gallop whereas Canty never wants to win one.'

Joe Canty rode fifteen Irish classic winners, including the champion The Phoenix, winner of the Irish 2,000 Guineas and the Irish Derby in 1944. Starting an unbackable 8 to 1 on, The Phoenix was inexplicably trounced by Solferino in the Irish St Leger. Critics blamed Canty for making too much use of The Phoenix, but the jockey explained it away: 'The Phoenix was not at his best!' A rebel at heart, Canty upset the racing establishment when he spoiled the parade of Tulyar, the newly acquired champion racehorse, who was being shown off to Irish race-goers. The 1952 Epsom Derby winner had been purchased by the Irish Government for a world record price of £250,000 at the end of his three-year-old career with a view to racing at four years before retiring to the Irish National Stud. Sent to trainer Paddy Prendergast at Rossmore Lodge, Tulyar was to race in the colours of President Sean T. O'Kelly and the young Belfast jockey T.M. Burns was retained to ride it. However, there was a change of mind early in the 1953 flat season and Tulyar was abruptly retired without having contested a race, but too late to cover mares that season. In order to show Tulyar to Irish racegoers, after all the taxpayer had paid for the horse, it was arranged that the horse would parade at the Curragh during racing on both days of the Guinness Meeting. Joe Canty, the senior Irish flat jockey, was invited to ride Tulyar in the parade but he was told that he did not have to wear the St Patrick's blue, gold sleeves jacket of the President of Ireland. The organizers of the event were appalled when Canty turned out in scruffy, working clothes and an old black beret. The following day Aubrey Brabazon showed Tulyar off to the large crowd.

Joseph Canty retired in 1954 to take up training but was not successful in his new career, which lasted ten years. He died in 1971 and his jockey son, J.M. Canty, ran a small, but successful stable for many years.

Thomas Burns (1899–1991)

Rider:

1916 R.B. Dobell's DENIZULU – His Majesty's Plate 2m flat (J. Burns)

1920 Lord Lascelles's KING EBER – Galway Hurdle Handicap (M. Arnott)

1923 E. Bellaney's DESMOND DALE – Salthill Handicap Hurdle (J.J. Parkinson)

1923 Lt-Col O'Malley-Keyes's SMOKE CLOUD – Galway Hurdle Handicap (J.J. Parkinson)

1924 J.J. Parkinson's TEMPLEXYON – Salthill Handicap Hurdle (J.J. Parkinson)

1925 Major C. Mitchell's LITTLE CLIFTER – Moyode Plate 20f flat (R. Fetherstonhaugh)

1932 R.S. Croker's CHIEFTAIN – Mervue Plate 12f flat (C. Brabazon)

1933 J.A. Mangan's CASTLEBAGOT – His Majesty's Plate 2m flat (J.A. Mangan)

1934 H.T. de Vere Clifton's WOOLOGY – Mervue Plate 12f flat (T.J. Taaffe)

1936 Captain G.F. Dunne's LINDLEY – Stewards' Handicap 8f flat (Capt C.J. Clibborn)

1937 Joseph Maher's GOLDEN LANCER – His Majesty's Plate 2m flat (O.T.V. Slocock)

1941 Lord Glentoran's ROSE GARLAND – His Majesty's Plate 2m flat (H.G. Wellesley)

1942 Miss Dorothy Paget's ARTIST'S ISLAND – Mervue Plate 12f flat (C.A. Rogers)

1946 R. McIlhagga's CARBURY – Mervue Plate 12f flat (P. Nugent)

1946 R. McIlhagga's CLONGIFFIN – Oranmore Handicap 12f flat (P. Nugent)

1950 T. McCairns's COASTWARD – Mervue Maiden 12f flat (B. Gallivan)

1950 Miss Dorothy Paget's FAIR ACT – Stewards' Handicap 8f flat (C.A. Rogers)

Trainer (licence held by Bernard Gallivan):

1950 T. McCairns's COASTWARD (T. Burns) – Mervue Maiden 12f flat £202

1951 J.J. Roche's WATERFLOW (Mr J. Burns) – Moyode Bumper £133

1952 T. McCairns's COASTWARD (T.P. Burns) – Oranmore Handicap 12f flat £202

1953 J.J. Roche's WATERFLOW (T.P. Burns) – Stewards' Handicap 8f flat £202

1953 J.J. Roche's WATERFLOW (A. Duff) – Oranmore Handicap 12f flat £202

Trainer, Lumville, Curragh:

1957 Mrs T. Burns's TRUDEAU (T.P. Burns) – Renmore Maiden 8f flat £202

1966 T.P. McIvor's ON THE MAP (J. Hunter) – Spiddal Handicap 12f flat £567

1966 Thomas Burns's SCOTTISH KING (T.P. Burns) – Renmore Maiden 7f flat £438

Tommy Burns was apprenticed to his father, the Ayr trainer James Burns, and rode his first winner at Thirsk racecourse, North Yorkshire, in 1913. When Britain declared war on Germany on 3 August 1914 nobody was prepared for the carnage that would follow. By the spring of 1915 not only was there no end in sight, but the sinking of the Lusitania off the Old Head of Kinsale brought America into the fray and the world was engulfed in war. The UK Government used its emergency powers to centralize racing at Newmarket, forcing many trainers and jockeys who were not eligible for army service to seek employment in Ireland. Although it was part of the United Kingdom at the time, the Government agreed to allow racing to continue in Ireland 'for the present', so long as it did not hamper the war effort in any way. Having secured a position as trainer for Colonel William Hall Walker, owner of the Tully Stud, James Burns took his family to Ireland, settling on the Curragh. Father and son kicked off their Irish career with a winner at the Curragh on Derby Day 1915, Half Caste, a mare that they brought over from Scotland with them, winning a 5-furlong sprint by a head, from Single Stick, ridden by Dan McKenna.

Like the Burnses, James McKenna and his son Dan had come to Ireland because of the restrictions on racing in Britain. Although born in Salisbury in 1898, Dan Burke McKenna was a member of an Irish racing family that in previous generations had spent many years training on the Maze racecourse. James McKenna was warned off the turf in 1886, having been accused by the stewards of stopping his horse Wavelet in a race at his local course. Wavelet was a decent sort – Mr McKenna had ridden him to victory in two Queen's Plates at the

Curragh April meeting and two more at the June meeting – but there was not a shilling for the horse in the Thorn Cup at Down Royal. Hazelwood, ridden by the crack professional jockey Michael Dawson, and Wavelet, ridden by James McKenna, a relatively unknown amateur, went clear of the field, but the latter made a feeble attempt to ride out his mount. In the end Hazelwood, the 6-to-4 favourite, scrambled home by half a length but the stewards found James McKenna guilty of pulling his mount, suspended him for the rest of their meeting and referred the matter to the stewards of the Turf Club, who warned him off.

Moving to Park House, Cholderton, Salisbury, James McKenna became known as a horse-dealing trainer. His brother, H.E. McKenna the Epsom trainer, briefly had charge of Ballinode, usually trained in Ireland by Frank Morgan, winning a chase at Lingfield Park with the future Cheltenham Gold Cup winner in January 1923. McKenna was also reputed to have been involved in the notorious Trodmore Hunt betting coup in 1898. That coup involved backing The Reaper, a fictitious horse, at a meeting that never took place. Dan McKenna was apprenticed to Dick Wootton at Epsom before he came to Ireland. Rising weight restricted his career as a jockey, forcing him to relinquish his licence in 1917 and turn to training. He acquired patrons such as William Sanday, Mr Mansfield and Colonel C.H. Innes Hopkins, nice owners to have but insignificant players in the horseracing world. However, he had a big break when he was offered the opportunity to become Charles Frederick Kenyon's Irish trainer. This came about through his uncle, H.E. McKenna, who trained a horse or two for Kenyon, and obviously recommended Dan for the Irish job.

A wealthy Manchester businessman, Kenyon was reputed to have never won a race in his first twelve years as an owner. Determined to get out of that rut, he waited until the war was over before buying horses, hundreds of them. His enormous string required four trainers, three in England as well as McKenna in Ireland, and he was easily the largest owner on the turf at the time. A non-better, he raced for the sport and enjoyed his biggest win when Haine, trained by Captain Bob Davies, dead-heated in the 1924 Irish Derby with another English-trained runner, Zodiac. Three months later he was dead. His passing was a great shock to his trainers, particularly Dan McKenna; one can only speculate what they might have achieved had their munificent patron lived longer. His demise caused Haine to be withdrawn from the Irish St Leger, won in its absence by Zodiac, and the dispersal of his horses, one of which was Tipperary Tim. Bought by his younger brother Harold Kenyon, Tipperary Tim finished alone to win the 1928 Grand National at odds of 100 to 1.

Left stranded by the death of his patron, McKenna had no prospects training in an impoverished Irish Free State without at least one wealthy owner. Racing in

Ireland was in the middle of a slump; the newly independent state was desperately short of cash and even established trainers were struggling for survival. Cecil Brabazon admitted to not having a bean at this time; with his family virtually starving, his wife had to resort to making soup from nettles collected from the overgrown garden to survive. Returning to England, Daniel Burke McKenna began a new career as a playwright, his most successful play being on the life of the Dutch artist Van Gogh. He drowned tragically in Dun Leary while awaiting the mail boat in 1939. He was not related to the jockey Frankie McKenna, who carried off the big Galway double (the Plate and the Hurdle) in 1950 on Derrinstown and Lady's Find.

It did not take Tommy Burns long to make his mark on Irish racing; a double at Clonmel in August, on horses trained by his father, brought him to the attention of outside stables. Two days later James McKenna booked the young Scot to ride Symont at Laytown, which provided Burns with his first Irish winner for a trainer other than his father. James McKenna continued to use Tommy when Dan could not do the weight. The following year Tommy won the first of his twenty-one Irish classics, winning the Oaks and the Irish St Leger on Captive Princess, trained by 'Fairy' Dunne. He also rode the first of his Galway winners in 1916, on Denizulu, trained by his father, winner of the King's Plate, the third most valuable race at the meeting. In 1917 he won the Irish Oaks again, this time for Newmarket trainer S.G. 'Sam' Pickering, who had won the Cambridgeshire with the former Irish-trained Velocity.

James Burns had done well in Ireland, despite losing his principal patron, Colonel Hall Walker, before he could train a winner for him. Towards the end of 1915 Hall Walker decided to present his Tully Stud to the nation, together with all the bloodstock at the right price, to establish a national stud. The suddenness of the decision and its timing caused widespread surprise and it was said that it was based on his concern about the political stability of Ireland.

When the war finally ended in November 1918 and racing resumed in Britain the following year, James Burns did not hesitate, returning home to continue his career at Ayr. In 1920 he fulfilled a lifelong ambition when the giant Forest Guard won the Ayr Gold Cup, with Tommy in the saddle; the horse had finished second the previous year. While his father's decision to return home was a relatively easy one, Tommy was in a dilemma, because he had become one of the leading jockeys in Ireland but was completely unknown in England. He really had little option but to stay in Ireland, where he was always known as 'the Scotchman', retaining his thick Scottish accent throughout his life.

Tommy Burns retired from the saddle three times: firstly in 1928, to start a training career, but he was back riding in 1930; secondly, in 1938, to give his sons a chance; and finally in 1954. However, according to Guy St John Williams's official biography of his son, T.P. Burns, the real reason for 'the Scotchman's' second retirement was to maximize the damages he would receive from a libel action against Jack Jarvis. Burns was riding the Irish Derby winner Raeburn in the Ascot Gold Cup when the horse suddenly broke down in running; before Tommy Burns could pull up, he swerved, hampering Jack Jarvis's runner, Fearless Fox. In the heated aftermath of the race, Jarvis tackled 'the Scotchman' about his riding; an argument ensued during which the trainer called the jockey 'an Irish bastard'. Tommy decided to sue the English trainer for slander, and the case was eventually settled in his favour.

During his long career in the saddle, 'the Scotchman' rode twenty-one Irish classic winners, a total only exceeded by Morny Wing, and was Champion Jockey in 1932. While Wing was considered to be supreme in sprint races, Tommy Burns was said to be a better jockey over a distance. However, unlike Wing, Burns could not be depended upon to give his best, being particularly fond of a flutter himself and recognized in the business as the best stopping jockey in Ireland. He occasionally rode over hurdles. He was twice successful in the Galway Hurdle, on King Eber (1920) and Smoke Cloud (1923), and won the Gloucestershire Hurdle (Cheltenham) on Cobequid (1933). Although he rode many winners in England, he never won a classic race there but was second on Resplendent (Oaks) and Kingston Black (St Leger), and rode Thankerton into third place in both the 2,000 Guineas and the Derby in 1936.

Tommy Burns rode Beau Sabreur for his friend and neighbour Cecil Brabazon, who trained at Rangers Lodge next door. Beau Sabreur was a frisky individual with a habit of shaking off riders at work, but Cecil thought the world of the horse and depended on Tommy not to let him get loose on the gallops. Having won the Tetrarch Stakes, the Irish 2,000 Guineas and the Irish St Leger, Beau Sabreur was made favourite for the Aintree Derby in November but was beaten by a length by Marcel Boussac's Dernah II. Burns had ridden a shocking race, which Cecil thought very suspicious; others maintained the horse had been deliberately stopped. After the incident, Tommy lay low for a few months before arriving at Rangers Lodge with a bottle of whiskey. The pair sipped the drink, as Tommy joked and laughed himself back into favour, and when he left they were the best of friends again. Years later, long after both men had retired, the pair would often meet over a drink and talk about the old days. During these chats, Tommy would laugh and boast about the strokes he pulled and the horses he stopped, and he found the mention of Beau Sabreur particularly hilarious.

In 1947 Tommy Burns wanted to combine riding as a jockey with a career as a trainer but was frustrated by a Turf Club rule banning this practice. The top jump jockey of the time, Dan Moore, got round the rule by putting the licence in the name

Veteran Irish Jockey Tommy Burns gives the other European jockeys 'a bit of advice' prior to the 1953 Washington DC International at Laurel Park. (Left to right) Charlie Smirke, Manny Mercer, Tommy Burns, Tommy Gosling and Roger Poincelet

of his head lad but Tommy chose a friend of his named Barney Gallivan. Barney was a shopkeeper in Newbridge, who knew nothing about horses and did not work in the yard; he was a nominal licence holder. That he had no connection with the stable was well known on the Curragh and among the racing community. However, the records show that Bernard Gallivan trained a number of winners, including four minor races at Galway, and the farce was allowed to continue until June 1954, when the Royal Ascot stewards went looking for him. Upadee, ridden by Burns and ostensibly trained by Gallivan, displayed greatly improved form when winning the Queen Anne Stakes and the stewards wanted an explanation but Barney Gallivan could not be found. Repeated requests for Mr Gallivan to report to the Stewards' Room caused great mirth among the Irish, who knew he was at home running the shop. No longer able to turn a blind eye, the Irish stewards brought Gallivan and Burns before them, found that Gallivan had not gone to Ascot with the horse and withdrew his licence to train, on the grounds that he had not been exercising adequate supervision over the horses in his stable. With Gallivan gone, Tommy Burns decided to hang up his boots in order to put the licence in his own name.

Frank Wootton (1894–1940)

Rider:

1921   A. Daniel Comyn's MR VIGOROUS – Salthill Handicap Hurdle (H.I. Ussher)
1921   Mrs R.P. Croft's MAX – Galway Plate (H.I. Ussher)
1921   Colonel R.P. Croft's REGISTRATION – Traders' Plate 16f flat (H.I. Ussher)

The Australian boy-wonder jockey who rode 882 winners on the flat in Britain between 1906 and 1913, rode his first classic at the age of fifteen and was Champion Jockey at sixteen. The son of an Australian trainer, Dick Wootton, young Frank displayed such ability as a rider that attempts were made to get him a licence to ride at the age of nine. The Australian racing authorities refused to issue a jockey's licence to anyone under fourteen years of age, so Dick Wootton uprooted his family and moved to South Africa, where the regulations were less strict. There, at the age of nine, Frank began riding in races, winning the important Goldfields Handicap at Johannesburg, and had ridden seventeen winners by the time the family left for England in 1905.

With Frank and his younger brother Stanley, Dick Wootton settled in Treadwell House, Epsom, from where he began training in 1906. Starting out as a gambling trainer with a yard full of his own horses and with a brilliant stable jockey, he secured the patronage of Sir Edward Hulton, the owner of the *Sporting Chronicle*, which set him on the road to success. With decent horses in the yard and the services of one of the best jockeys of his time, who compared with the legendary Fred Archer, he won the Gimcrack Stakes three years running, with Lomond (1911), Flippant (1912) and Stornoway (1913). His charge Shogun was considered a very unlucky loser of the 1913 Epsom Derby, having been badly interfered with during a mêlée, which resulted in the winner, Craganour, controversially being disqualified. He also had the dubious distinction of being awarded a farthing in damages by a jury, having sued his erstwhile friend Bob Sievier, following a series of libellous attacks in his periodical *The Winning Post*. In court his case was hampered by his gambling activities and love of landing betting coups, which is why he was awarded the smallest coin in circulation.

The outbreak of the Great War in 1914 changed Dick Wootton's life. Frank and Stanley both enlisted in the forces, racing was drastically scaled down and Dick decided to retire and return home to Australia.

Stanley Wootton, two and a half years younger than Frank, was a competent jockey, although much less successful than his brother, but it must be remembered that he was only seventeen when the war forced his retirement. When it ended, he began training at Treadwell House, proving that had inherited his father's skills by becoming famous as a trainer who would pull off huge betting coups with moderate horses. Like his father, he also was a great tutor of young jockeys, notably Charlie Smirke, Staff Ingham, Joseph Marshall and Ken Gethin – Wootton apprentices who rose to the top of their profession. In 1927 he shrewdly purchased all the principal training gallops on the Epsom Downs. Forty-two years later he ensured the future of Epsom as a training centre by handing the gallops over to the British Horserace Betting Levy Board.

Born 14 December 1894, Frank rode his first winner in England when the five-year-old Retrieve won the Cinque Ports Handicap over 5 furlongs at Folkestone, by a length on 23 August 1906. The eleven-year-old went on to win fifteen more races that year, including a significant victory by half a length on Nero, trained by P.P. Gilpin, in the Portland Handicap at the Doncaster St Leger meeting, beating the great Danny Maher, who was riding the favourite. Just as George Fordham had problems with young Fred Archer and Sir Gordon Richards with Lester Piggott later in the century, the older jockey, in this case, the American Danny Maher, found it difficult to accept the under-age pretender, and a fierce rivalry grew up between them.

Frank Wootton rode 129 winners as a fourteen-year-old in 1908, to finish runner-up to Maher in the list of leading jockeys. He would have been Champion had he not missed a chunk of the season, first because of an injury and then a family bereavement which took him back to Australia. However, he put that right the following year, when he was only fifteen, heading the list with 165 winners, 49 in front of Danny Maher, who finished second. He held the title for the next three years but his three-year reign ended in 1913, when Maher regained his crown, pushing Frank Wootton into second place by 115 winners to 91. The young rider won his first classic race in 1909, the Oaks (Epsom) on Perola, owned by Sir William Cooper, who began racing in Australia and owned the runners-up in the Melbourne Cup in successive years, Trenton and Silvermine in 1886 and 1887.

The following year Frank got a job as stable jockey to Lord Derby, although still only sixteen, but ran into trouble with the stewards in a manner that was remarkably similar to Lester Piggott forty-four years later. At the Newbury spring meeting Wootton, riding St Elroy, beat Maher on Flower Saint, but the senior jockey objected. St Elroy was disqualified and his young jockey was suspended from riding for two months. Recovering from this setback, Wootton won his second classic, the St Leger, on Lord Derby's Swynford later that year, defeating the odds-on favourite

Lemberg, ridden by Maher, into third place. Many racegoers at the time were convinced that Maher gave Lemberg a bad ride, but George Lambton, Lord Derby's trainer, stated that Swynford outstayed the favourite in a fast-run race. Although friendly with Maher, who had ridden for the stable until he took a retainer from the Australian A.W. 'Fairy' Cox, Lambton blamed the quick-tempered Maher for his feud with Frank Wootton, although he accepted that the young jockey was sometimes over-keen to get to the running rail. This was because Dick Wootton had instilled in his son the need to go the shortest way round and Frank's fear of what his father might say caused him to sometimes be a little reckless in his anxiety to get there. Lambton believed that Frank was a great jockey, who kept a very cool head during a race and seldom came back with an excuse when a race was over.

By 1912 Frank, now eighteen, was beginning his losing battle with his weight and was unable to ride many of the stable runners. This led to Freddie Rickaby being appointed as George Lambton's first jockey, with Frank riding Lord Derby's horses when he could do the weight. He managed to retain his title as Champion Jockey that year, but his number of winners dropped from 187 to 118 as his opportunities became restricted. Although he was second in the list of winning jockeys in 1913, he knew his career was over and announced that he would retire at the end of the season. His last winning mount on the flat was Sir Edward Hulton's Fairy King at Warwick in November – the 'boy wonder' was finished before he was twenty years old. Like his brother Stanley, Frank Wootton volunteered for service when the war broke out, and was sent to the Middle East. There he developed a liking for jumping, raced when he was free and rode winners over jumps at Baghdad racecourse. On returning safely to England after the war, he decided to ride over jumps, having his first win over hurdles at Birmingham in 1920.

The following year he arrived at Galway to ride for Harry Ussher, taking seven mounts over the two days and riding three winners. On the Wednesday, the first day, he rode Dan Comyn's heavily backed favourite, Mr Vigorous, to win the opening race, which was over hurdles, to the delight of the big crowd. Superstar jockeys were not often seen at Galway, and Frank Wootton was a name well known among racegoers in Ireland, who followed English racing closely and cheered him loudly in appreciation. His next ride was in the Galway Plate, in which he partnered Pansy Croft's Max. Again his mount was supported, starting second-favourite at 4 to 1, and once again he triumphed. Having won over hurdles and over fences, his treble attempt was in a welter flat race, in which his mount Kyleclare, owned by Galway Chairman Martin McDonogh, was set to carry 11 stones 3 pounds. The favourite, Drinmond, with H.H. Beasley up, won the race easily; Kyleclare finished six lengths back in third.

Frank was back the following day, riding the 2-to-1 on favourite Sir Blare, owned by Colonel Croft, in the first race but could only dead-heat with Rockdaile. At the time the Rules permitted a run-off but Harry Ussher was reluctant, preferring to share the spoils. The other trainer refused, however, and Rockdaile was allowed a walkover. Unplaced in the Galway Hurdle, Wootton completed his fences, hurdle and flat race treble by winning the Traders' Plate, a 2-mile flat race, on Colonel Croft's Registration, another winning favourite. His final ride was on Long Lough, owned by the bookie Dick Power, in the Galway Blazers Handicap Steeplechase, and the four-times English Champion jockey finished third to yet another favourite, The Coiner, trained by J.P. Hogan and ridden by Jack Anthony.

That year Frank Wootton failed by only four wins to become the first flat Champion Jockey to be champion over jumps. After two more successful seasons, during which he rode ninety-four winners, he retired and returned home to his father in Australia. He came back to Epsom in 1927, where he trained jumpers for a few years before going back home for good in 1933. He predeceased his father by six years, dying in Sydney in 1940.

John R. Anthony (1890–1954)

Rider:

1921   J.P. Hogan's THE COINER – Galway Blazers Handicap Chase (J.P. Hogan)

In 1921 Galway racegoers were able to see two of the best jockeys of the time, Frank Wootton and 'Jack' Anthony, an outstanding amateur who had turned professional the previous year. They were not disappointed with what they saw: Frank Wootton rode three outright winners, one dead-heater and two thirds from seven rides and Jack Anthony rode a winner from his only ride at the meeting. One of the celebrated Anthony brothers from Carmarthenshire, Wales, Jack was not related to Algy Anthony, the well-known jockey and trainer associated with Ambush II and Troytown. Ivor, Owen, Jack and Gwynne all rode with success as amateurs, with Ivor and Jack becoming household names and eventually turning professional. Gwynne, the youngest, was merely a good point-to-point rider, well known in Wales but nowhere else. Ivor, the eldest of the brothers, was Champion Jockey in his first year as a professional. He became one of the few jockeys to ride every winner on a card, doing so at the Pembroke Hunt meeting, run over a course at Alleston, in 1906. Owen trained the 1923 Grand National winner Music Hall, succeeded Basil Briscoe as Dorothy Paget's trainer and trained the great Golden Miller to win the last of his five Cheltenham Gold Cups.

Jack Anthony was the best jockey of the four brothers. He was sixteen when he rode his first winner, at Ludlow in 1906. He rode as an amateur for fourteen years, being one of the few amateurs to become overall Champion Jockey in England, a feat he achieved in 1912. He rode three winners of the Grand National – Glenside (1911), Ally Sloper (1915) and Troytown (1920) – and apparently had no intention of turning professional. However, Troytown was sent over to France to contest a couple of big races there during the summer of 1920 and the French Jockey Club would not let Jack Anthony ride unless he turned professional. His hand forced, he did so there and then.

He was Champion Jockey again in 1922, but never succeeded in winning the Grand National as a professional, although he did finish runner-up twice on Old Tay Bridge and was third on Bright's Boy in 1927, the year he retired from race riding. Following a long holiday in America, he began training at Letcombe Regis and among the horses under his care was Easter Hero. Winner of the Cheltenham Gold Cup in 1929 and 1930, Easter Hero was unlucky in the Grand National, second to Gregalach, having spread a plate in running, and one of the best steeplechasers of his time. Jack also trained Brown Tony, winner of only two hurdle races before being killed one of which was the 1930 Champion Hurdle. It is one of those strange twists of fate that Anthony, who rode in races for twenty-one years without suffering a serious injury, broke his leg dismounting from a horse while on holiday in America in 1930. It turned out to be a serious break, and he spent months in hospital and then more months recuperating in a nursing home. He was left with a permanent limp, but he was able to return to training and had charge of the unfortunate Thomond II, who won seventeen steeplechases but was around at the same time as the brilliant Golden Miller.

F.B. 'Dick' Rees (1894–1951)

Rider:

1923   Mrs R.P. Croft's GOLDEN STREET – Ballybrit Chase (H.I. Ussher)
1923   H. McAlinden's FORT ELIZABETH – Renmore Handicap Chase (H.I. Ussher)
1924   J.E. Tyrrell's CLONSHEEVER – Galway Plate (H.I. Ussher)

The son of a South Welsh vet and younger brother of jockey Bilby Rees, Frederick Brychan Rees, known in racing as Dick, came into the sport via the hunting field, pony races and point-to-points. His father had ridden in point-to-points into his sixties and as a teenager young Dick Rees was riding winners as an amateur for David Harrison, who trained at Tenby. When the Great War broke out in 1914, he joined up and was one of the lucky few to serve throughout the hostilities and live to tell the tale. Resuming his career as an amateur, he turned professional in May 1920, having ridden a winner at Uttoxeter and enjoyed a dramatic rise to the top. Making an immediate impression, he became Champion Jockey in his first season as a professional, the British jump season corresponding with the calendar year until the 1925–6 season. A gifted horseman with a keen tactical brain, he was acclaimed as the best National Hunt rider of his era and won the Grand National in 1921 when the Roman-nosed Shaun Spadah, formerly owned by Frank Barbour, finished alone, with Mr Harry Brown (The Bore) and Robert Chadwick (All White) remounting to claim the minor money. Chadwick had previously remounted to claim a place in the famous race, hopping back on board Rathnally to finish second in 1911.

Dick Rees won the Cheltenham Gold Cup twice, on Patron Saint (1928) and Easter Hero (1929), and the Grand Steeplechase de Paris on Silvo (1925). In 1929 he won both the Gold Cup and the Champion Hurdle at Cheltenham, partnering Royal Falcon to victory in the latter event. Five times Champion Jockey, he rode 108 winners in 1924, breaking the previous record of 78, held jointly by the Anthony brothers, Ivor (1912) and Jack (1923). Rees lost his best years to the war but he may have continued race riding longer were it not for weight problems, which were brought on by his love of alcohol.

Daniel P. O'Brien (d. 1943)

Trainer, Churchtown, Co. Cork:
1931 D.P. O'Brien's TANSY (P. Fitzgerald) – Mervue Plate 12f flat £44

Dan O'Brien, was essentially a farmer who trained a few horses on the side at home. He was in racing for the sport and tasted success at Galway when Tansy won the Mervue flat race back in 1931.

William T. O'Grady (1913–72)

Rider:
1932 Lord Milton's A.P. – Ballybrit Chase (H.I. Ussher)
1933 M. Fogarty's GOLDEN GEORGE – Salthill Handicap Hurdle (M. Fogarty)
1933 Mrs C. O'Neill's REVIEWER – Galway Blazers Handicap Chase (L.T. Byrne)
1934 J.B. Magennis's GALLI GALLI – Salthill Handicap Hurdle (H.I. Ussher)

1934 H.I. Ussher's ARMOURED PRINCE – Corrib Hurdle (H.I. Ussher)

1935 R.J. Duggan's KYRAT – Salthill Handicap Hurdle (H.I. Ussher)

1935 Joseph McGrath's STEP ASIDE BELLE – Ballybrit Chase (H.I. Ussher)

1935 Joseph McGrath's BABY LEROY – Corrib Hurdle (H.I. Ussher)

1935 J. Browne's BLOODSHOT – Renmore Handicap Chase (J. Browne)

1936 Mrs J.G. Fitzgerald's KINVARA – Corrib Hurdle (H.I. Ussher)

1937 Captain D.W. Daly's BRIGHTER COTTAGE – Galway Plate (H.I. Ussher)

1938 E. Delany's MAGNUM II – Renmore Handicap Chase (E. Delany)

Trainer, Ballymonty, Thurles, Co. Tipperary:

1944 E.H. Johnson's CALLALY (D. Morgan) – Galway Blazers Handicap Chase £90½

1951 Mrs Adam Bell's ST KATHLEEN II (P.J. Doyle) – Galway Plate £1,110

1961 Mrs A.W. Riddell Martin's OLD MULL (Mr J.R. Cox) – Players' Amateur Handicap £955

Willie O'Grady is one of only eight men to have both ridden and trained a winner of the Galway Plate, the others being Willie Cullen, Harry Ussher, Algy Anthony, Frank Morgan, Gus Mangan, Harry Freeman Jackson and Jimmy Brogan. His riding career was relatively short. Starting off as an amateur, he turned professional in 1930 and was Irish Champion Jockey in 1934 and again in 1935. He won the Galway Plate on Brighter Cottage, trained by Harry Ussher, who also provided him with his best chance of winning the Aintree Grand National in 1932, with the brilliant mare Heartbreak Hill. She eventually finished sixth but was severely baulked in running. Willie O'Grady also had no luck in the Irish Grand National, never winning it as a jockey but being placed four times.

In 1940 he began training at Ballynonty, a small village between Kilanaule and Thurles in Co. Tipperary but continued to ride for another five years, retiring shortly before the stewards banned professional jockeys from training. As a trainer he won the Irish Grand National twice, with Blayney Hamilton's Hamstar and Paddy Grey's Icy Calm. The same year as Icy Calm's win, 1951, he sent out the coal black mare St Kathleen II, owned by Mrs Adam Bell from Shillelagh, Co. Wicklow, to win the Ladies' Cup (Punchestown) and the Galway Plate. A decade later he trained Old Mull, Bunny Cox up, to win the Players' Navy Cut Amateur Handicap holding off the challenges of Mr Alan Lillingston, on Hind, and Mr Francis Flood, on Don't Comment. He sent out Kinloch Brae and Solfen to win at Cheltenham – the latter was probably the best horse he trained. He died in January 1972; he was a heavy drinker, but socializing with owners was an important part of the job. After his death the stable was taken over by his son, Edward J., who was an infinitely more successful trainer than his father ever was.

Mr Patrick Sleator (1910–96)

Rider:

1934 Mrs C. O'Neill's REVIEWER – Galway Plate (M. Deegan)

1936 A. Morrow's UP SABRE – Moyode Bumper (J. Ruttle)

1937 Miss H. Bell's BAYBUSH – Moyode Bumper (J.W. Osborne)

Trainer, Grange Con, Co. Wicklow:

1948 A.J. Cope's SILENT PRAYER (T. Molony) – Galway Plate £1,110

1954 Mrs A.B. Biddle's AMBER POINT (C. Sleator) – Galway Plate £1,110

1956 Mrs R. More O'Ferrall's AMBER POINT (P.A. Farrell) – Galway Plate £1,160

1956 Clifford Nicholson's DEPRECIATION (N. Brennan) – Mervue Maiden 12f flat £202

1956 Mrs R. More O'Ferrall's KNIGHT ERRANT (P.A. Farrell) – Corrib Hurdle £133

1957 Mrs A.B. Biddle's KNIGHT ERRANT (H.R. Beasley) – Galway Plate £1,160

1957 Mrs P. Meehan's TYMON CASTLE (G.W. Robinson) – Galway Hurdle £775

1958 F.L. Vickerman's CLIPADOR (H.R. Beasley) – Ballybrit Chase £133

1958 G.B. Sanderson's HERN'S GIFT (H.R. Beasley) – Corrib Hurdle £133

1960 C. Balding's SPARKLING FLAME (H.R. Beasley) – Galway Plate £1,160

1961 Mrs K.L. Urquhart's CONNIVANCE (H.R. Beasley) – Claddagh Handicap Chase £133

1961 C. Balding's FIREAWAY (H.R. Beasley) – Ballindooly Maiden Hurdle £202

1961 F.L. Vickerman's CLIPADOR (H.R. Beasley) – Galway Plate £1,160

1961 Michael Purcell's SEYCHELLES (L. Ward) – Barna Handicap 16f flat £133

1961 Mrs K.L. Urquhart's CONNIVANCE (C. Finnegan) –Galway Blazers Handicap Chase £133

1962 Norman H. Wachman's VALAMINTHA (John Power) – Briarhill Handicap 8½f flat £203

1964 John Byrne's CHORUS (John Power) – Briarhill Handicap 8½f flat £203

1966 J. Veseloky's GENTLE BOY (L. Ward) – Menlo 16f flat £396¾

1967 P. Dunne Cullinan's ROYAL DAY (R. Coonan) – Galway Plate £1,900

1967 Mrs P. Meehan's TARQUIN CASTLE (Mr F. Flood) – Moyode Bumper £387

1969 P. Dunne Cullinan's ROYAL DAY (R. Coonan) – Galway Plate £2,380

1970 T.H. Moore's SWING LOW (Mr R. Barry) – Amateur Handicap 2m flat £1,545

1973 Mrs P. Leeman's DOCTOR DOMORE (J. Corr) – Spiddal Handicap 12f flat £548

1976 D. Jackson's O'LEARY (R. Coonan) – Galway Plate £3,450

Mr Patrick Joseph Sleator won the 1934 Galway Plate, and was Champion Irish Amateur Rider three times, in 1934, 1937 and 1938, but is remembered as one of the shrewdest and best of the Irish gambling trainers. An attack of rheumatic fever at the age of nine decided his career because the doctors advised horse riding to help his convalescence. Given a pony, young Paddy's riding career progressed from jogging to hunting, and when he was sixteen he purchased a horse named Slaney Boy for £12, later passing it on to Captain T.J. Wilson. The latter became his first client when he took out a trainer's licence in 1928, just to train Slaney Boy and West Wicklow. Slaney Boy provided the young man, riding as Mr P. Sleator Jr, with his first winner, both as a rider and a trainer, when he was victorious at the Meath Hunt meeting, run over the Boyerstown course near Navan, on 12 April 1928. From 1921 until 1933, there were two Navan racecourses: the Meath Hunt and Navan meeting at Boyerstown and the Proudstown Park meeting.

Eight days after that Boyerstown win, Paddy rode West Wicklow to victory in a bumper at Leopardstown, beating the gambled on favourite, Tiddley Baits, ridden by Eric McKeever. The furious owner of the favourite, the bookmaker Dan Leahy, insisted that McKeever lodge an objection for crossing, notwithstanding the fact that West Wickow had won the race by ten lengths. When his trainer, Bob Fetherstonhaugh, told his jockey to withdraw the objection, Dan Leahy himself marched into the weighing room to object – not for crossing but on the grounds that a horse in Paddy Sleator's stable (Slaney Boy) had run at an illegal meeting. The stewards overruled his objection, West Wicklow was declared 'all right', which meant that all bets had to be settled, and the bookie was stuck with a big financial loss on the race. Stung, and eager to exact revenge on the young upstart of a trainer, Leahy appealed to the stewards of the Irish National Hunt Committee, adding the extra allegation that Captain Wilson was not the true owner of the horse and Sleator had made a fraudulent and wilful misstatement. Only when the stewards dismissed all the objections did Leahy begin to think straight and realize that a horse that could beat Tiddley Baits by ten lengths must be a good one. When Paddy Sleator rode West Wicklow to victory in a hurdle race at the Curragh in May, Dan Leahy bought the horse and sent him over to L. Todd at Burbage, Wiltshire. His belated reasoning proved correct: West Wicklow won the 1929 Cesarewitch Handicap at Newmarket, with Cliff Richards, Gordon's brother, in the saddle.

Two amateur riders, Eric McKeever and Paddy Sleator, were both riding a lot of winners in the early 1930s, with the former becoming Irish Champion Jockey in 1933. Irritated by this cheap competition, the professional jockeys began to lobby the stewards that these two should be riding as professionals. The stewards agreed and asked the pair to turn professional. McKeever did so but Sleator refused. In response, the stewards put a limit on the number of rides he could take against professional jockeys, basically confining him to riding in races restricted to amateurs.

On his retirement from race riding in 1945, Paddy Sleator's training career quickly blossomed. The stable was turning out winners, farming handicaps and landing gambles. The first big winner he trained was Silent Prayer, ridden by Tim

Molony in the 1948 Galway Plate. Sleator went on to equal Harry Ussher's record of nine wins in that race, including the double winners Amber Point and Royal Day. In addition he trained two winners of the Galway Hurdle and was the leading Irish trainer, according to races won – seven in a row between 1955 and 1961. He won three Irish Cesarewitch Handicaps in a row between 1957 and 1959 with Sword Flash, Havasnack and Another Flash, and became Champion Irish Trainer in 1958. However, all these successes led to problems with the handicapper, who refused to drop a Sleator-trained horse, even when it was obviously past its best. This restricted opportunities for the older horses in Ireland, so the trainer looked to England.

Between 1961 and 1967 he had an arrangement with Arthur Thomas, a British licensed trainer with ample facilities at Guy's Cliffe, Warwick, to train his horses there. In reality Thomas had nothing to do with the training at all; the Irish horses were stabled in a separate yard, staffed by Irish lads, all getting their orders from Paddy Sleator by telephone. Sleator's jockey Bobby Beasley, now based in Warwick, was instructed to tell Arthur Thomas absolutely nothing, which exposed the charade because the licensed trainer could not tell the press anything about the horses or the future plans. When he did make a comment, it invariably turned out to be wrong. Warwick was a central location, convenient to many jumping race-courses and near Birmingham Airport, so that Paddy Sleator could easily fly in for the big races. This arrangement opened up a wide range of races to the Sleator-trained horses and proved very successful, despite the controversy. The first winner of this novel tie-up was Clipador, owned by Frank Vickerman.

Having won the 1961 Galway Plate, Clipador was among the first batch of Sleator horses to go over to Guy's Cliffe. Ridden by Bobby Beasley, Clipador won the Somerset Chase at Wincanton on 21 September 1961, the first of many winners nominally trained by Arthur Thomas. Suddenly Arthur Thomas was basking in a blaze of publicity as he was turning out winner after winner with ex-Sleator horses. One of them, Scottish Memories, winner of the 1961 Mackeson Gold Cup, won no fewer than twenty-three races from Arthur Thomas's yard. Then questions began to be asked about how Thomas was getting these horses, which were not changing hands and were being ridden by Paddy Sleator's jockey. A merchant who trained flat racers on the side, Arthur J. Thomas was born in 1902 and began training in 1956; the inconsistent Coronation Year, the winner of two big handicap races, the City & Surburban and the Victoria Cup, was the best horse he trained. Yet, overnight, he had become one of the hottest jumping trainers in England and the Sleator link was puzzling everyone. It did not take long for the truth to emerge; Thomas was merely a 'front' for Paddy Sleator. As the winners

*Snappers in action,
Pat Healy in pole
position on the right*

flowed, so did the howls of protest. Loudest in their condemnation were the English trainers, who demanded that the stewards take action. Their point was that horses purporting to be trained by Arthur Thomas were racing in England but were not trained by him at all and the real trainer was outside the jurisdiction of the English stewards. The press was concerned about the subterfuge, which was misleading members of the public as well as the stewards, and eventually the Jockey Club decided to close down the operation. At this point Paddy Sleator and Bobby Beasley went their separate ways; Bobby decided to stay in England to ride for Derick Ancil rather than return to Ireland, with Bobby Coonan coming to Grange Con as his replacement.

An outbreak of foot-and-mouth disease in Britain resulted in a government ban on horse racing there from 25 November 1967, which the Irish Government extended to Ireland as a precaution. Although racing closed down it had to be ready to resume at a moment's notice, so racing stables continued to train horses that were temporarily unable to race. Not content to pace impatiently around Grange Con, Paddy Sleator took seven horses to Cagnes-Sur-Mer, near Nice in the south of France, and campaigned them there with success.

While he was the leading jumping trainer of his time, it was for the quantity of his winners, rather than the quality of his horses. Another Flash, winner of an Irish Cesarewitch and a Champion Hurdle, is probably the best horse he trained but he also won races at Cheltenham with Sparkling Flame, Scottish Memories, Havago and Ballywilliam Boy. He never won an Irish Grand National, although Copp and Knight Errant were both placed in it, but won the Kerry National at Listowel three times, with Pass Friend (1958), Pearl of Montreal (1971), owned by the north Tipperary-based German, G.F.F. Fasenfeld, and O'Leary.

Bobby Coonan, Sleator's new stable jockey, got off to the best possible start by winning the Galway Plate on Royal Day in 1967. Just like Beasley before him, Coonan enjoyed a long spell with Sleator, the pair remaining together for the remainder of their careers. The last big winner trained by Paddy Sleator was O'Leary, winner of the Galway Plate and the Kerry National (Listowel) in 1976. At the end of 1977 he decided to retire and Bobby Coonan, leading jumping rider in Ireland six times in succession from 1967 to 1972, was earmarked to take over the Grange Con yard. Coonan also intended to retire but Sleator persuaded him to wait until Galway, and have his last ride on Lough Patrick in the 1978 Galway Plate. He thought that Lough Patrick was sure to win and wanted his jockey to go out in the limelight, which would help publicize his switch to training. Raced only once all year, Lough Patrick was laid out for the Plate in typical Sleator fashion, but disaster struck racing into the dip, when Coonan drove his mount up to challenge the leader, Amoristic, ridden by Liam O'Donnell. Amoristic veered suddenly and Lough Patrick was sent out over the running rail. Bobby Coonan was lucky he was not killed. He suffered three broken ribs, one of which punctured his lung, dislocated both shoulders and broke a collarbone as well.

Paddy Sleator probably retired too early. His continuing interest in the stable made it difficult for Bobby Coonan to be his own man, who also had the extra pressure of being watched. Despite an excellent start, Coonan did not stay long in Grange Con before moving on and drifting into obscurity. He died a lonely, forgotten man in March 2007.

Patrick Dunne Cullinan (d. 1978)

Owner, blue, gold sleeves, blue cap:
1938 WEST POINT (D.L. Moore) – Galway Blazers Handicap Chase £49 (M. Arnott)
1967 ROYAL DAY (R. Coonan) – Galway Plate Handicap Chase £1,900 (P. Sleator)
1969 ROYAL DAY (R. Coonan) – Galway Plate Handicap Chase £2,380 (P. Sleator)

Pat Cullinan, Paddy Dunne Cullinan's father, was a cattle dealer from the west of Ireland who married a daughter of P.J. Dunne of Carrollstown, Trim. His children all bore the surname Dunne Cullinan. A substantial owner and breeder of horses, including Flax Park, winner of the Irish Derby in 1905, P.J. Dunne was a consistent supporter of Irish racing, particularly jumping. A non-better, Mr Dunne raced purely for the sport and had a burning ambition to win the Grand National. He won the prestigious Conyngham Cup three times, twice with Foreman (1878 and 1880) and once with Oldtown (1896), and the Irish Grand National in 1904 with Ascetic's Silver, trained privately at Carrollstown by William Sperrin. He also lived to see that horse pass the post in front in the 1905 Aintree Grand National but unfortunately without its rider. In his later years P.J. Dunne began to take an interest in the flat and had horses with 'Fairy' Dunne at Osborne Lodge. Unfortunately, he was dying when his Flax Park beat the useful and unlucky Velocity in the 1905 Irish Derby, passing away the following September. On his death his executors instructed Joseph Lowry, the Navan auctioneer, to sell most of his bloodstock, including Ascetic's Silver, destined to win the 1906 Aintree Grand National, who realized 850 guineas, and the former Irish Grand National winner, Breemount's Pride, who made 300 guineas. Flax Park was sold to Sir Ernest Cochrane for just over 3,000 guineas but failed to pass the vet and the deal was cancelled. Sir Ernest then turned his attention to Velocity, second to Flax Park at the Curragh, but refused to pay the asking price of 5,000 guineas. He always regretted the decision because Velocity went on to win the Cambridgeshire and was rated by Dick Luckman of the *Daily Express* as 'one of the best horses which ever ran in handicap class'.

Pat Cullinan inherited the property at Carrollstown, Trim, together with the unsold Flax Park, from his father-in-law. At the 1906 Grand National meeting Flax Park caused an upset by winning the Liverpool Spring Cup but subsequently lost his form and never won afterwards. P.J. Dunne's vague blue and yellow colours were now registered to Patrick Cullinan as blue, gold sleeves and cap, while those of his son, Paddy Dunne Cullinan, were similar except for a blue cap. The inheritance, together with the new contacts his marriage had opened up, expanded Pat Cullinan's business greatly, and his increased income enabled him to indulge in his passion for racing. The leading owner in Ireland in 1912, when ten of his horses won twenty races and £3,658, he won a number of important races, such as the Irish Oaks with the half-bred May Eager (1914), the National Stakes with Royal Weaver (1912) and the Railway Stakes with Flax Meadow (1912), but his success was not in proportion to the number of mares he maintained at Carrollstown. He died following a stroke in December 1923.

His son, Paddy Dunne Cullinan, was an excellent amateur rider and was described by Joe Canty, arguably the best Irish jockey of all time, as being the best heavyweight amateur he had ever seen. His riding ability led to him being chosen to play a part in a film called *Irish Destiny* (1926), the brainchild of a Dublin doctor named Epples. Paddy played the part of Denis O'Hara in the film, the first feature-length film to be made in Ireland. Set during the War of Independence, the plot involved the hero being forced into the IRA after witnessing British aggression in the fictitious village of Clonmore. During the struggle that followed, the hero was wounded and captured but escaped to save his fiancée Moira, played by Frances MacNamara, from the clutch of evil illicit whiskey distillers. A commercial failure, *Irish Destiny* was considered lost until a copy was found recently in America and restored. A small amount of newsreel footage was used in the making of the film and it is a pity that a lot more was not included because, apart from that, the whole film is a bore, albeit an historical bore.

In 1926, the year the film was made, Paddy Dunne Cullinan rode his own horse, Wild Cast, to victory in the La Touche Memorial Cup at Punchestown. Riding at 12 stones 3 pounds, Paddy had to put up 1 pound overweight and his size prevented him from riding in the vast majority of the races open to amateur riders. His father had won six races at Galway, including three King's Plates with The Best (1911) and Royal Hackle (1912 and 1914), but Paddy managed only three. However, two of these were Galway Plates, with Royal Day, trained by Paddy Sleator. In 1938 he won the Galway Blazers Handicap Chase with West Point, trained by Maxie Arnott and ridden by Dan Moore. Nearly thirty years later, in 1967, he had his second Galway winner when Royal Day, with Bobby Coonan up, scraped home to beat Rack Venture, ridden by Macer Gifford, in the Plate by a neck. Macer's older brother Josh, the English Champion Jockey, finished third on the veteran Ross Sea, winner of the race in 1964 and 1965. Royal Day returned to Ballybrit in 1969 to win the Plate a second time, the Centenary Plate, much to Paddy Dunne Cullinan's delight because he was a steward at Galway for many years, and retained that position until his death in September 1978.

Daniel L. Moore (1910–80)

Rider:

1938 P. Dunne Cullinan's WEST POINT – Galway Blazers Handicap Chase (M. Arnott)

1940 Miss Dorothy Paget's ATCO – Ballybrit Chase (C.A. Rogers)

1941 Miss Dorothy Paget's GOLDEN JACK – Galway Blazers Handicap Chase (C.A. Rogers)

1942 T. McD. Kelly's MOUNT BROWN – Salthill Handicap Hurdle (T. McD. Kelly)

1942 Miss Dorothy Paget's GOLDEN JACK – Galway Plate (C.A. Rogers)

1942 Miss Dorothy Paget's GOLD RAINBOW – Renmore Chase (C.A. Rogers)

1944 Miss Dorothy Paget's CAPITAL STAR – Ballybrit Chase (C.A. Rogers)

1944 Miss Dorothy Paget's STEEL FLAME – Connaught Handicap Chase (C.A. Rogers)

1945 Miss Dorothy Paget's ROMAN HACKLE – Galway Blazers Handicap Chase (C.A. Rogers)

1946 Miss Dorothy Paget's HAMLET – Ballybrit Chase (C.A. Rogers)

Trainer, Richard O'Connell, Old Fairyhouse, Ratoath, Co. Meath:

1948 Miss E. Shortiss's ROYAL BRIDGE (M. Browne) – Galway Blazers Handicap Chase £202

Trainer, Daniel L. Moore, Old Fairyhouse, Ratoath, Co. Meath:

1951 Mrs A.W. Riddell Martin's TIMBER TOPPER (E.L. McKenzie) – Corrib Maiden Hurdle £158½

1954 D.L. Moore's MAGIC SLEIGH (D. Page) – Mervue Maiden 12f flat £202

1954 J.M. Raftery's BALLYMAC (P.J. Doyle) – Corrib Hurdle £133

1954 Major P. Dennis's SWINGING LIGHT (P.J. Doyle) – Dead-heated, Galway Blazers Handicap Chase £85½

1955 Leslie Brand's OUR VIEW (Mr B. Lenehan) – Moyode Bumper £133

1955 Thomas Doyle's ANTIGUE II (P. Powell Jr) – Galway Hurdle Handicap £740

1960 Major L. Gardner's COMMUTERING (G.W. Robinson) – Galway Hurdle Handicap £727

1961 Mrs D.R. Brand's YOURS ONLY (G.W. Robinson) – Salthill Handicap Hurdle £133

1962 Edward Sturman's BAHRAIN (Sir W. Pigott-Brown) – Amateur Handicap 16f flat £948

1962 Lady Honor Svejdar's TRIPACER (T. Carberry) – Galway Hurdle £905

1963 Lady Honor Svejdar's DIONYSUS III (T. Carberry) – Menlo 2m flat £203

1964 H.R. Catherwood's LITTLE CHAMP (T. Carberry) – Claddagh Handicap Chase £203

Trainer, Ballysax Manor, Curragh:

1966 A.L. Moore's HOT CONTACT (T. Carberry) – Galway Blazers Handicap Chase £351

1971 A. Stanley Robinson's PREGANDA (Mr A.S. Robinson) – Ballindooly Hurdle £450½

1974 Mrs J.L. White's COLONIAL PRINCE (T. Carberry) – Claddagh Chase £405

Willie Cullen stands alone as being the only Irish Champion Jockey to have also been a Champion Trainer in Ireland; Dan Moore was an outstanding Irish Champion Jockey and became a very successful trainer of jumpers, but did not head the list. Starting out as an amateur rider in 1932, Dan turned professional in 1937 and was the leading jump jockey in Ireland, winning the championship in 1940. He once rode four winners in a day at Cheltenham but was beaten by a head in the Aintree Grand National on Royal Danieli, trained by Reggie Walker, in a celebrated finish. It was a desperately close thing; Royal Danieli and Battleship raced on opposite sides of the course and the judge did not have the aid of a camera. Dan Moore rode two Irish Grand National winners, Golden Jack (1943) and Revelry (1947), and also won a Galway Plate on the former. Although he did not retire until 1948, Dick O'Connell his head lad was training on his behalf from 1937.

The best horse Dan Moore trained was L'Escargot, twice winner of the Cheltenham Gold Cup and the winner of the Grand National, beating the great Red Rum in 1975. He won a second Gold Cup with Tied Cottage in 1980, shortly before his death, but the horse was subsequently disqualified when a trace of a drug called Theobromide showed up in the post-race test. He trained three winners of the Galway Hurdle – Antigue II, Commutering and Tripacer – as well as the popular chasers Quita Que and Flying Wild. When he died on 16 June 1980, Joan his widow took over the stable and continued training for a few years. Their son Arthur was a good professional jockey and is now a leading trainer of jumpers, and their daughter Pamela married Tommy Carberry, the jockey-turned-trainer. Tommy and Pamela are the parents of the leading jockeys Paul and Nina (the best female amateur rider to have ridden in Ireland.

Bernard Nugent (d. 1971)

Trainer, The Naul, Co. Dublin:

1942 Miss A.E. Hall's POINT D'ATOUT (J. Lenehan) – Galway Hurdle £220

1945 R. McIlhagga's KING OF THE JUNGLE (D. Morgan) – Galway Hurdle £444

1946 Mrs M.J. Keogh's NORTHERN DANDY (T. Ellis) – Salthill Handicap Hurdle £111½

1946 Mrs S.J. Noble's EDNA'S COURAGE (Mr P.J. Lenehan) – Moyode 2m flat £111½

1946 Mrs S.J. Noble's EDNA'S COURAGE (J. Brogan) – Corrib Hurdle £111½

1946 R. McIlhagga's KING OF THE JUNGLE (D. Morgan) – Galway Hurdle £444

1947 W. Hide's CHARLES EDWARD (J. Brogan) – Galway Plate £1,110

1947 W. Noble's BELL BOY II (J. Brogan) – Galway Blazers Handicap Chase £222

1947 Miss A.E. Hall's POINT D'ATOUT (Mr A.O. Scannell) – Galway Hurdle £740

1947 W. Noble's EDNA'S COURAGE (M. Molony) – His Majesty's Plate 2m flat £104

1948 Mrs H. Carruthers's HURRI-BOMBER (B. Cooper) – Renmore Chase £133½

1949 Mrs C. Wilkinson's PALM HILL (T. Wallace) – Mervue Maiden 12f flat £202

1950 P. Rafter's CLONCAW (B. Cooper) – Salthill Handicap Hurdle £133½

1958 J.J. Ward's AND HOW (Herbert Holmes) – Renmore Maiden 8½f flat £202

1960 P. Rafter's PRINCESS PALM (Mr J. Nugent) – Menlo Novice Chase £202

Barney Nugent began training at The Naul, Co. Dublin, in 1941 and enjoyed a great run of success in the immediate post-war years, only to decline just as dramatically as he had risen. He trained four winners of the Galway Hurdle, a race record held jointly with Paddy Mullins and Clem Magnier, with Point d'Atout (1942 and 1947) and King of the Jungle (1945 and 1946). In 1945 he trained the Galway Hurdle winner and won the Phoenix 1,500 with Momentum, the latter being the second most valuable race run in Ireland that year. In 1947 he became the third trainer to win both the Plate and the Hurdle in the same year and also won the King's Plate with Edna's Courage, ridden by Martin Molony. His sister married Thomas J. Taaffe of Rathcoole, making him an uncle of the jockeys Pat and Toss Taaffe. Tony Scannell, who rode Point D'Atout to its second hurdle victory, later worked as a postman. Barney Nugent retired from training in 1968; The Hedger, the winner of two minor hurdles ridden by Ben Hannon, was one of his last winners.

John 'Jack' Cox (c. 1890–1980)

Trainer, Lisnawilly, Dundalk:

1950   J. Grew's SCOTTISH WELCOME (M. Molony) – Renmore Novice Chase £133½

1951   J. Grew's MONALEEN (T. Molony) – Renmore Novice Chase £133½

1961   John Cox's FOUR ACES (P. Taaffe) – Corrib Hurdle £202

1962   John Cox's FOUR ACES (John J. Rafferty) – Barna Handicap 2m flat £203

1962   Mrs J.A. McAllister's WILLIE WAGTAIL III (Mr J.R. Cox) – Moyode Bumper £203

1963   John Cox's SNOW TRIX (B. Hannon) – Galway Hurdle Handicap £1,308

1966   M.F. McCourt's GOLDNAGRENA (Mr C. Ronaldson) – Dangan Handicap Hurdle £401

1966   Mrs G. Pelan's VULNAGRENA (P. Black) – Corrib Hurdle £434

1967   Mrs R.G. Patton's GUESS WHO (P. Black) – Menlo 2m flat £404

1968   Mrs B.J. Eastwood's GOOD BREW (P. Black) – Corrib Hurdle £462

1968   Mrs B.J. Eastwood's ANNALONG (P. Black) – Galway Hurdle £1,980

1969   T.H. Moore's SWING LOW (T. Carberry) – Menlo 2m flat £432

1970   L.A. Kaitcer's THE REBBITZEN (R.F. Parnell) – Menlo 2m flat £446

1971   Charles Carr's HIGHWAY VIEW (P. Black) – Galway Hurdle £2,207½

John Cox went to the old Quaker school in Armagh but spent most of his time playing truant to go hunting, coursing or racing. He farmed and hunted all his life, first at Mount Bailie, just outside Dundalk on the Armagh road, and later at Blackrock farm, which he bought for £1,000. The price amazed the editor of the local paper, the *Dundalk Democrat*, who wrote a piece about the huge price given for very bad land. However, Jack Cox knew what he was doing and set about reclaiming the land from the sea, eventually turning it into good farming land. Always involved with hunters and point-to-points, he took out a trainer's licence in 1932 and held it until 1971, when the stable was officially handed over to his son 'Bunny'. He trained fourteen winners at the Galway Festival, including three winners of the Hurdle, Snow Trix, Annalong and Highway View.

Jockey Pat Black was associated with the Cox stable and rode two of its Galway Hurdle winners. Apprenticed to Kevin Prendergast, Pat was from Drogheda and when he became too heavy for the flat he joined Jack Cox's stable. Bunny always said that Pat 'rode too many winners early on' and he never really fulfilled his potential. Riding winners for gambling owners earned him easy money, which led to excessive drinking and the inevitable weight problems that ended his career. He trained under permit for a while, and did a bit of dealing in horses before his life ended tragically in August 1990.

John R. 'Bunny' Cox (1925–2006)

Rider:

1944 A.D. Comyn's MAJESTIC STAR – Moyode Bumper 2m (R. O'Connell)

1945 J.D. Wood's ROYAL BRIDGE – Moyode Bumper 2m (R. O'Connell)

1947 H.I. Ussher's SHINING GOLD – Moyode Bumper 2m (H.I. Ussher)

1961 Mrs A.W. Riddell Martin's OLD MULL – Amateur Handicap 1½m flat (W.T. O'Grady)

1961 J.P. Bourke's CASTLEGAR – Moyode Bumper 2m (J. Brogan)

1962 Mrs J.A. McAllister's WILLIE WAGTAIL III – Moyode Bumper 2m (John Cox)

1963 F. Leinder's MAIGRET – Amateur Handicap 2m flat (D. Brennan)

Trainer, Lisnawilly, Dundalk:

1973 F. Hillman's CHOTARANCE (J. Roe) – Menlo 2m flat £408

1977 P.W. McDowell's NATIVE TIME (T. McGivern) – Castlegar Maiden Hurdle £892

1979 C.F. Cronin's DUD CHEQUE (T. McGivern) – Ballindooley Hurdle £828

1985 Mrs J.C. Walsh's BAY TRIX (D. Parnell) – Barna Handicap flat £1,380

1989 Mrs M.C.L. Hughes's ORIEL LION (T.J. Taaffe) – Guinness Chase £3,450

Two sons of Jack Cox rode as amateurs, Mr J.R. Cox Jr and Mr R.D. 'Mickie' Cox, the former becoming one of the best in the country. He was a chubby baby, and somebody commented that he looked like a little bunny and the name stuck with him throughout his life. He began riding on a wonderful pony named Charlie, whose displays in the hunting field made him a celebrity in the locality. Riding as Mr J.R. Cox Jr, he rode his first winner in March 1938, having just turned fourteen. The venue was the Dundalk Harriers point-to-point at Rossmakea, the horse Marlfield, in the Open Farmers' Race. Marlfield fell during the race but young

'Bunny' held on, bounded back into the saddle unaided and got up to win the race by half a length. The victory was achieved despite his mount having to carry 5 stones of deadweight lead. On the same afternoon his sister Dobo Cox also rode a winner, giving the family a rare riding double.

A qualified vet, 'Bunny' became one of the best amateur riders of his time, was Champion Irish Amateur Rider on five occasions and won the big Galway Amateur Handicap on Old Mull (1961) and Maigret (1954). He rode his father's gelding, Drumbilla, to victory in the Troytown Chase at Navan in 1940, won the Conyngham Cup at Punchestown on Loyal Antrim and Little Trix, and finished third in an Irish Grand National on Copp, trained by Paddy Sleator. A combination of back trouble and age brought about his retirement from the saddle in 1971, and he officially took over his father's training licence the following year. While Jack Cox is officially the trainer of Highway View, winner of the 1971 Galway Hurdle, he was over eighty years of age at the time and 'Bunny' was actually doing the training.

He married Sally, a daughter of Aubrey Brabazon, in 1973. She served as a member of the Racing Board and, although she has not taken out a trainer's licence, she breeds and prepares point-to-pointers at Lisnawilly. This family of Cox is not related to Stephen Michael Cox, who trained Kohoutek to win a Maiden Hurdle at Galway in 1997.

Thomas Pascal Burns (b. 1924)

Rider:

1947 T. McCairns's TOMSHA – Mervue Plat 12f flat (M. Dawson)

1952 D.J. Duggan's WARRENSCOURT LAD – Galway Hurdle (D.J. Duggan)

1952 T. McCairns's COASTWARD – Oranmore Handicap 12f flat (B. Gallivan)

1953 J.J. Roche's WATERFLOW – Stewards' Handicap 8f flat (B. Gallivan)

1955 Captain W. Townsend's ROCINT – Salthill Handicap Hurdle (C.L. Weld)

1957 Mrs T. Burns's TRUDEAU – Renmore Maiden 8f flat (T. Burns)

1959 R. Liddle's HEDONIST – Corrib Hurdle (A.S. O'Brien)

1962 Walter Norris's ANTHOS – Stewards' Handicap 10f flat (D. Kinane)

1962 W. Freeman's PROUD BOY – Oranmore Handicap 7f flat (John Murphy)

1963 P.J. Kilmartin's GORM SLIPPER – Mervue Maiden 12f flat (K. Bell)

1966 Thomas Burns's SCOTTISH KING – Renmore Maiden 7f flat (T. Burns)

1971 G.M. Bell's GREEK WATERS – Thomas McDonogh Handicap 8½f flat (P.J. Prendergast)

1971 Michael McStay's SIMEAD – Spiddal Handicap 12f flat (M. Conolly)

1971 P.M. McCarthy's ARTOGAN – Mervue Maiden 12f flat (M. Conolly)

1972 Michael Cuddy's SENTHIA – Renmore Maiden 7f flat (John Murphy)
1973 C. Kennelly's ROBINCA – Oranmore Handicap 7f flat (P. Norris)
1974 R.D. Crossman's JACK DE LILO – Mervue Maiden 12f flat (P. Norris)

Thomas Burns, usually referred to as T.P. by Irish racegoers, was the second son of Tommy 'the Scotchman' and was apprenticed to his father, who had temporarily retired from riding in 1938. Young Thomas and his older brother James both rode their first winners on the same afternoon, at the Curragh Derby meeting in June 1938, T.P. winning the first race on Prudent Rose and J.G. the last on Kilglass. When Tommy resumed riding, T.P.'s indentures were transferred to Steve Donoghue in England, but the young jockey returned to Ireland in 1940 because of the Second World War. With weight problems restricting his opportunities on the flat, he was encouraged to ride over jumps as well but decided to give up riding in chases following a back injury sustained at Baldoyle on New Year's Day 1953.

Unlike his father, T.P. was straight and honest, but he was not in the same league as his father as a jockey, notwithstanding the fact that he was Champion Jockey in Ireland three times, in 1954, 1955 and 1957. His success in the championship was due to the fact that he was riding under both codes and he never headed the individual lists of leading flat jockeys or leading jump jockeys. Poor T.P. had the misfortune to be outridden by his father, then in his mid-fifties and in his last full season as a jockey, in the 1953 Irish 1,000 Guineas, when Tommy on Northern Gleam beat T.P. on Beau Co Co by a neck. Quiet, competent and a good judge of a horse, T.P. Burns was employed by the top trainers of the time, John Oxx and Vincent O'Brien, but could never establish himself as the undisputed stable jockey.

Although he gave up steeplechase riding, T.P. Burns continued to ride in hurdle races and enjoyed a successful run in that sphere on horses trained by Vincent O'Brien, including a second place in the Champion Hurdle on Stroller. Having established himself as Vincent's hurdle jockey, T.P. was in the right place at the right time when the great jumping trainer began to move into flat racing, which led to his association with Ballymoss. One of the best horses to have won the Irish Derby in its pre-Sweeps days, Ballymoss ran second to Crepello in the Epsom Derby before lifting Ireland's premier race, which was the first of T.P. Burns's six Irish classic wins. Ballymoss's next target was the St Leger at Doncaster, the oldest classic race and one that had never been won by an Irish-trained horse, although Russborough had dead-heated with Voltigeur in 1850 only to be beaten in the run-off. A shock defeat by Brioche in the Great Voltigeur Stakes at York, a race named after that St Leger winner of 1850, was a setback but Ballymoss bounced back, winning the 1957 St Leger from Court Harwell and Brioche. By winning an English classic race, T.P. had achieved something his father had failed to do and, with Ballymoss remaining in training for a four-year-old career, he must have expected exciting times ahead.

In the spring of 1958 Vincent O'Brien and T.P. Burns won both divisions of the Gloucestershire Hurdle, with Admiral Stuart and Prudent King, to the delight of the Irish contingent, who were having a very good time at that year's Cheltenham Festival meeting. Vincent had done that particular double three years before in a race that was completely dominated by the Irish in the 1950s. T.P. duly teamed up again with the O'Brien flat stars, Ballymoss and Gladness, but his season was left in tatters after a bad fall on the flat at Clonmel, which put him in hospital for ten weeks. Scobie Breasley deputized for him on Ballymoss, winning the Coronation Cup (Epsom), Eclipse Stakes (Sandown Park) and King George VI & Queen Elizabeth Stakes (Ascot), while Lester Piggott took over on Gladness, successful in the Gold Cup (Royal Ascot), the Goodwood Cup and the Ebor Handicap (York). Although T.P. Burns was fit and back riding well before the Prix de l'Arc de Triomphe, Ballymoss's next race, Vincent was not inclined to drop Breasley, who had enjoyed such a successful run on the colt. In 1959 Vincent O'Brien trained the last of his twenty-two Cheltenham Festival winners; he would in future be concentrating on the flat. But in a surprise move he dropped T.P. Burns and brought in the Australian rider Garnet Bougoure, who had been riding in Singapore and was recommended by Scobie Breasley.

Now riding as second jockey, T.P. unexpectedly won his second Irish classic on Vincent O'Brien's second-string El Toro in the Irish 2,000 Guineas, Bougoure having chosen Ross Sea in preference. Ross Sea could only finished fifth but would later make a mark as a steeplechaser, particularly at Galway, where he became only the fourth horse to win the Plate twice in succession. Two years later, in 1961, T.P. enjoyed one of the best moments of his career when partnering Vimadee, trained by his father Tommy, to victory in the Irish St Leger. He also had the distinction of riding Arkle to victory, in a flat race at Navan.

He held the prestigious position of retained jockey for the President of Ireland's horses, which were trained by John Oxx. His regular appearances at Currabeg got him many rides for that stable but on the big occasion Oxx preferred Bill Williamson. Consequently, T.P. Burns came to be regarded as a 'bread and butter' jockey – a good judge, ideal for the small trainer but doomed to be replaced on the big day. However, his calm nature and experience were put to good use by Kevin Prendergast, who was battling with his temperamental filly Pidget, winner of the Irish 1,000 Guineas, and turned to T.P. to see what he could do. This fortunate consultation resulted in T.P. winning the 1972 Irish St Leger on the filly, beating the hot favourite Our Mirage, runner-up in the St Leger at Doncaster. Making virtually all the running, Pidget appeared to deviate from a straight course, taking the ground of Our Mirage, ridden by Bill Williamson, at least twice in the closing stages. After a protracted stewards' enquiry, Pidget was allowed to keep the race, probably because the winning distance was two lengths and because the out-paced Our Mirage never really looked likely to pass her.

Soldiering on until 1975, T.P. retired after riding over a thousand winners and took up a position as one of Vincent O'Brien's work riders at Ballydoyle.

Martin Molony (b. 1926)

Rider:

1942   Captain C.B. Harty's KNIGHT OF VENOSAS – Ballybrit Chase (Captain C.B. Harty)

1946   F.W.E. Gradwell's YUNG-YAT – Renmore Chase (J.A. Farrell)

1947   P. King's TAVOY – Salthill Handicap Hurdle (P.J. Lenehan)

1947   W. Noble's EDNA'S COURAGE – His Majesty's Plate 2m flat (B. Nugent)

1949   Miss M.O. Mathieson's RATHENESKER – Renmore Chase (J.W. Osborne)

1950   J. Grew's SCOTTISH WELCOME – Renmore Chase (John Cox)

1950   R. McIlhagga's REDEMPTOR – Corrib Maiden Hurdle (R. Morrison)

1950   J.G. Duggan's GREEN DOLPHIN – Galway Blazers Handicap Chase (J.W. Osborne)

1950   Mrs E.J. Lewis's MR DIBS – Ballybrit Chase (M.V. O'Brien)

1951   Mrs E.J. Lewis's WYE FLY – Galway Hurdle Handicap (M.V. O'Brien)

People who saw Martin Molony ride seem to be in agreement that he was the greatest jockey of them all. Equally proficient on the flat and over jumps, he had an uncanny ability to keep a tired horse going and was brilliant at the last fence or hurdle, landing perfectly balanced to race for the line. He won three Irish classics, on Desert Drive (Oaks 1947), Princess Trudy (1,000 Guineas 1950) and Signal Box (2,000 Guineas 1951) as well as the Cheltenham Gold Cup (Silver Fame 1951), three Irish Grand Nationals (Knight's Crest, Golden View II and Dominick's Bar), and the Galway Hurdle. He was the son of Captain William Molony, who owned and trained Hill of Camas, winner of the 1915 Galway Plate. Although his elder brother, Tim, began his career as an amateur rider in 1936, Martin was sent over to Martin Hartigan's stable at Ogbourne, Wiltshire, when he was only thirteen. By working in a racing stable, Martin lost his amateur status and his route into racing was as an apprentice jockey.

Martin Hartigan originally came from Croom, Co. Limerick, and rode over fences before Jimmy White appointed him as his private trainer at Foxhill. His brother, Patrick F. Hartigan, trained successfully in Ireland, principally for J.C. Lyons, before moving to Ogbourne in 1909 to take over George Edwardes's stable, later marrying his daughter. In March 1921, Pat Hartigan, who lost an eye in the Great War, fell out of his hotel bedroom in Liverpool while opening the window during the night and was killed. After his death, Martin took control of his stable and later married his widow. A trainer of handicappers, such as The Pen and Pappageno II, he is notable as the master of an apprentice named Gordon Richards, who became Champion Jockey in Britain no less than twenty-six times.

On the outbreak of the Second World War, young Martin Molony was sent back home and joined George Harris's stable at Kilmallock. Within weeks Harris had provided him with his first winner, the rank-outsider Chitor in a three-year-old maiden at the Curragh at the end of October 1939.

Despite spending half his time travelling back and forth to England, Martin Molony was Irish Champion Jockey from 1946, when he shared the title with Aubrey Brabazon, until 1951, the last year he rode, a sequence of six in succession. At various times during his short career, he rode for Captain Cyril Harty, Joseph Osborne, Jimmy Rank and Lord Bicester, but if he was free he would accept the first ride offered to him. Offered a retainer by leading flat trainer Paddy Prendergast to ride for him in 1952, at twenty-six he was the top jockey with his best years ahead of him, but it all ended in a fall. He rode the last winner of his career at Thurles on Tuesday, 18 September 1951, winning the first race, a maiden hurdle, on External Relations, trained by Martin Quirke. Two hours later he was at death's door in the local hospital following a fall from Bursary, also trained by Quirke, in the Munster Steeplechase. He made a good recovery, but the doctors advised him to rest for a year. He never came back.

Tim Molony, Martin's brother, was not considered to be as good a jockey but he was Champion National Hunt Jockey in Britain five times running, from 1948 to 1952. He won the Cheltenham Gold Cup on Knock Hard, the Champion Hurdle on Hatton's Grace and three times on Sir Ken, and the Galway Plate on Silent Prayer. Like Martin, he had no luck in the Aintree Grand National and was never even placed in it.

Michael Vincent O'Brien (b. 1917)

Trainer, Churchtown, Co. Cork:
1950 Mrs E.J. Lewis's MR DIBS (M. Molony) – Ballybrit Chase £133½

Trainer, Ballydoyle House, Cashel, Co. Tipperary:
1951 Mrs E.J. Lewis's WYE FLY (M. Molony) – Galway Hurdle £740

1952 H.H.M. Stanley's ALBERONI (L. Stephens) – Galway Plate £1,110

1953 P.G. Lynch's KILBALLYOWEN (Mr A.S. O'Brien) – Moyode Bumper £133

1968 C.W. Engelhard's RIBOLLIRE (L. Ward) – Spiddal Handicap 12f flat £581

Vincent O'Brien, the eldest son of Dan O'Brien from his second marriage, won his first race at Galway when Mrs E.J. Lewis's Mr Dibs, ridden by the brilliant Martin Molony, won the Ballybrit Steeplechase. The following year (1950) the same combination won the Galway Hurdle with Wye Fly, the 8-to-1 joint-favourite, beating twenty-four opponents by eight lengths, and the following year Alberoni won both the Irish Grand National and the Galway Plate. Despite his dominance in the National Hunt sphere, winning four Cheltenham Gold Cups, three Champion Hurdles and three Grand Nationals, O'Brien only won the Irish Grand National and the two big Galway races once. The last of the four Galway Festival winners of his National Hunt career came in 1953, when Kilballyowen, ridden by his brother Phonsie O'Brien, won the bumper.

By the autumn of 1955 he was looking ambitiously at the flat, and by the time Ballymoss swept all before him in 1958, winning the Coronation Cup (Epsom), Eclipse Stakes (Sandown Park), King George VI & Queen Elizabeth Stakes (Ascot) and the Prix de l'Arc de Triomphe (Longchamp), and Gladness won the Ascot Gold Cup, the Goodwood Cup and the Ebor Handicap (York), he was established as a flat trainer. He only had one winner at the Galway Festival between then and his retirement at the end of the 1994 season: Charles Engelhard's Ribolliere, ridden by the stable jockey Liam Ward, in the Spiddal Flat Handicap in 1968.

Patrick Taaffe (1930–92)

Rider:

1949 J.M. Lawlor's TOO-RA-LOO – Corrib Maiden Hurdle (T.J. Taaffe)

1951 Mrs B.M. Webster's METROPOLITAN – Galway Blazers Handicap Chase (C.A. Rogers)

1952 Omer Vanlandeghem's SANTA LUCIA – Salthill Handicap Hurdle (T.W. Dreaper)

1952 I.E. Levy's DOVETAIL – Corrib Handicap Hurdle (J.W. Osborne)

1952 W.H. Corry's SEPTEMUM – Galway Blazers Handicap Chase (J.W. Osborne)

1953 R.B. Beaumont's SURGE – Salthill Handicap Hurdle (J.W. Osborne)

1953 Mrs B.M. Lawlor's NAS NA RIOGH – Ballybrit Chase (T.J. Taaffe)

1953 Mrs B.M. Lawlor's NAS NA RIOGH – Corrib Hurdle (T.J. Taaffe)

1954 J.G. Duggan's COLONIAL JACK – Dead-heated, Galway Blazers Handicap Chase (J.W. Osborne)

1955 Con Rooney's UMM – Galway Plate (G.H. Wells)

1956 J.G. Duggan's IVY GREEN – Galway Hurdle (J.W. Osborne)

1959 Duchess of Westminster's SUIRVALE – Ballybrit Chase (T.W. Dreaper)

1959 Duchess of Westminster's CASHEL VIEW – Galway Hurdle (T.W. Dreaper)

1961 John Cox's FOUR ACES – Corrib Hurdle (John Cox)

1961 M. Sayer's CYGNE NOIR – Dead-heated, Galway Hurdle (J. Lenehan)

1963 Mrs S.E. Gurry's GRANVILLE PETA – Ballindooly Maiden Hurdle (G.H. Wells)

1963 Colonel S.S. Hill-Dillon's HIGH PRIEST – Corrib Hurdle (J. Brogan)

1966 Mrs John Thomson's PRINCE TINO – Ballindooly Maiden Hurdle (T.W. Dreaper)

1969 S.P. Muldoon's BONNE – Guinness Galway Hurdle (P.D. McCreery)

1970 J.A.N. Glover's SAXON SLIPPER – Corrib Hurdle (A. Watson)

Trainer, Alasty, Straffan, Co. Kildare:

1972 F.J. Quinn's TRACKED (M. Ennis) – Salthill Handicap Hurdle £483

Forever associated with the mighty Arkle, Pat Taaffe was one of the great jump jockeys of his time. A natural horseman, he may have looked a little ungainly in a tight finish but it was always said that he won his races 'in the country', where he got his horses jumping properly. About 6-feet tall, he was a son of Thomas J. Taaffe, trainer of the Grand National hero Mr What, and was one of three brothers riding at the time, the other two being Toss, another professional, and Willie, who rode as an amateur. Pat started in the unpaid ranks, riding his first winner at Bray Harriers point-to-point at Cabinteely in 1946 and a few weeks later, at the Phoenix Park, he rode his first racecourse winner, Ballincorona. Turning professional on 1 January 1950, he took a job as Tom Dreaper's jockey, a position he held until his retirement twenty years later. He rode six winners of the Irish Grand National, a record. His four wins in the Galway Hurdle is another race record, held jointly with Bobby Beasley, and he won Aintree Grand Nationals on Quare Times (1955) and Gay Trip (1970), Cheltenham Gold Cups on Arkle (1964, 1965 and 1966) and Fort Leney (1968), and the Galway Plate on Umm (1955). The latter's victory was described thus in *The Irish Horse*: 'In the blazing heat and the swirling dust of one of the hottest Galway Plate days in history, before the greatest crowd to ever pack the vast stands at Ballybrit, Pat Taaffe completed an unique treble of the Grand National, Irish Grand National and Galway Plate. Umm snatched victory in the last few strides to beat Athenian.'

Seriously injured in fall off a horse named Ireland at Kilbeggan in 1956, Pat was unconscious for a week, but three months later he was back in the saddle riding winners, including a double at Manchester for Dreaper on Dizzy and Rose's Quarter. His partnership with the Duchess of Westminster's Arkle, trained by Tom Dreaper, is one of the most famous in horse racing, the only disappointment being that this three-times Gold Cup winner was never allowed to run in the Grand National. Dreaper and Pat Taaffe were adamant that he would win it but the Duchess refused to risk her wonder horse over the big fences, with a big weight in a big field. Pat picked up a winning spare ride on Gay Trip in the 1970 Grand National, when Terry Biddlecombe received a life-threatening fall from King's Dream in a hurdle race at Kempton Park.

Pat Taaffe retired at the end of 1970, his final winner being Straight Fort at Fairyhouse in December, having twice been the Irish Champion Jockey, in 1952 and 1953, and the top Jump Jockey in Ireland on nine occasions. On his retirement from the saddle, he began a new career as a trainer, at Straffan, Co. Kildare, getting off to a flying start with Captain Christy, winner of the Irish Sweeps Hurdle and the Cheltenham Gold Cup. His son Tom was a top professional rider in his day and is now training in Straffan. Pat had a heart transplant some years before his death in 1992, one of the first operations of this kind to be done in Ireland.

H. Robert Beasley (1936–2008)

Rider:

1956 Michael Connolly's KILBALLYOWEN – Galway Blazers Handicap Chase (M. Connolly)
1957 Mrs A.B. Biddle's KNIGHT ERRANT – Galway Plate (P. Sleator)
1958 F.L. Vickerman's CLIPADOR – Ballybrit Chase (P. Sleator)
1958 G.B. Sanderson's HERN'S GIFT – Corrib Hurdle (P. Sleator)
1958 Mrs A.B. Biddle's KNIGHT ERRANT – Galway Hurdle (P. Sleator)
1960 Charles Balding's SPARKLING FLAME – Galway Plate (P. Sleator)
1960 J.F. Cleary's HAZARDLESS – Corrib Hurdle (L.B. Keating)
1961 Mrs K.L. Urquhart's CONNIVANCE – Claddagh Handicap Chase (P. Sleator)
1961 Charles Balding's FIREAWAY – Ballindooly Maiden Hurdle (P. Sleator)
1961 F.L. Vickerman's CLIPADOR – Galway Plate (P. Sleator)
1963 Lord Fermoy's BLUNTS CROSS – Galway Plate (A.S. O'Brien)
1971 Miss G.B. Hand's TARQUIN BID – Galway Blazers Handicap Chase (P.D. McCreery)

Son of the classic-winning flat jockey Henry H. Beasley and grandson of the famous Mr Harry Beasley, Bobby Beasley was the third generation of the jockey family. His mother was a sister of the film star Valerie Hobson, who was married to John Profumo, the War Minister involved in a political scandal in the early 1960s. Bobby came into racing with an ambition to win the Grand National, which he did in 1961 when Nicolaus Silver became only the second grey horse to win the race.

Starting off as an amateur, Beasley was sixteen when he rode his first winner, Touareg, in a bumper at Leopardstown in May 1952 for Dorothy Paget and her Irish trainer Charlie Rogers, whom his father was assisting at the time. His father enjoyed a great season riding on the flat in Ireland in 1918, winning the Irish Derby on King John and finishing the year as Champion Jockey. He then accepted a position as stable jockey to Atty Persse in England, where he won the 2,000 Guineas on Mr Jinks, the Irish Derby on Zionist and the Irish 2,000 Guineas on Fourth Hand. Cool, calm and reserved, Harry Beasley was tall for a flat jockey and retired just before the Second World War, taking up the position of head lad with Charlie Rogers.

Bobby emulated him by becoming Irish Champion Jockey in 1960, unusual for a jump jockey, but then he was riding for the brilliant Paddy Sleator. Having won the Grand National on Nicolaus Silver (1961), the Cheltenham Gold Cup on Roddy Owen (1959) and the Champion Hurdle on Another Flash (1960), he was at the very top of his profession and had got used to having a few drinks to celebrate after the races following the death of his father in 1959. According to Bobby, his father had a 'horror of drink', which meant that so long as he was alive Bobby could never take so much as a drop. However, after he was gone the young man became immersed in the pub culture, particularly on those lonely evenings when he was away from home riding in England, and was idolized and treated to free drinks wherever he went.

Shortly after Bobby married a daughter of the former Grand National-winning jockey Arthur Thompson, Sleator opened up an English stable under the guise of Arthur Thomas. Bobby changed from being an Irish-based jockey riding for an Irish trainer, to being an Irish-based jockey riding for an English trainer, which meant that he was away from home for days on end. He was riding winner after winner but a dangerous world of alcohol, girls and bookies was opening up and sucking him into the abyss.

When the stewards broke up Sleator's association with Arthur Thomas, Bobby decided to stay in England to ride for Derek Ancil rather than return home. Deprived of the Paddy Sleator winner conveyor belt, he found winning rides more difficult to come by as Ancil had only a small string of horses and Bobby was not being offered outside rides. In addition, his increasing weight, caused by his drinking, restricted the mounts he could take, and the lack of patronage forced him to accept any mount that came along, which in turn led to falls and injuries. The bitter truth was that he was not as good a jockey as he used to be and everybody knew it. As Bobby Beasley was in England, slowly descending into the depths of alcoholism, Bobby Coonan was riding the Sleator-winners back home. The former Champion Jockey was about to realize that nobody is forgotten more quickly than an ex-jockey.

Then, after eighteen months out of the limelight, he was offered a job as stable

Moscow Express (Ruby Walsh) wins the 1999 Galway Plate from Lucky Town and Nicholls Cross

jockey to Fred Winter, one of the top jumping trainers in the country. It started well enough; Bobby rode a few winners for the stable and was riding regularly, despite his drinking, until matters got out of control following a fall at Newbury. A broken wrist put him out of action and during that period of enforced idleness he really hit the bottle. Now he was an abusive and aggressive drunk, and the boozers and hangers-on who had previously craved his company hastily disappeared; Bobby Beasley had become a chronic alcoholic. When he returned to the saddle, he was a shadow of his former self and was not riding well, but Winter stayed loyal, continuing to put him up when nobody else would touch him.

After he had a public association with another woman, Shirley, his wife, felt that she had no option but to leave him and take the children back to Ireland. Now struggling to make 11 stones 7 pounds, drinking heavily into the small hours, Bobby was unable to get up in the morning to ride work and he was no longer a hot-shot jockey who could be put up on a horse that he had never seen before. If Bobby Beasley wanted rides then he would have to ride work, but he was unable to ride work – it was a vicious circle and the easiest way out of it was to retire.

Bobby was offered a job selling life insurance, which occupied the hours when the pubs were shut. Initially he did well, with friends and acquaintances signing up just to get him started, but he soon ran out of friends and discovered that drinking buddies do not buy policies. When the business dried up the company fired him, leaving him desolate and stony broke. The former Champion Jockey had only one asset – his farm in Co. Wexford, which he was fortunate to have purchased at the peak of his career. Now he had no choice but to return there, although he did not have a clue what he would do.

Tom Conroy, who was training in a small way at the time in Co. Wexford and subsequently owned a good horse named Moscow Express, winner at the 1998 Galway Festival, helped him as much as he could. An opportunity arose when Stewart Barrett asked Bobby to train a few horses privately for him but unfortunately he was still drinking, and had found a new drinking partner, Nicky Rackard. Just like the former jockey, Rackard, a former Wexford hurling star and a vet by profession, had drunk himself to oblivion, but he was somehow prevailed upon to seek help from Alcoholics Anonymous. He stopped drinking and set about restoring his career, and this change of habit actually helped Bobby too. With his friend off the bottle, the latter was drinking less, which in turn meant that he had more time for his horses. Anxious to ride these horses in their work, Bobby sought professional help to lose weight in order to do so and further cut back on his drinking. Having shed 2½ stones regularly riding horses in their work and aware of his friend's new life without alcohol, he began thinking about resuming his riding career – if only to ride the Barrett horses in their races. He successfully reapplied for his licence from the Turf Club and H.R. Beasley began to appear on racecourse number boards once again.

On 'Little Christmas Day' on 6 January 1971 Beasley rode Stewart Barrett's Gordon into third place in a maiden hurdle at Thurles, reviving memories of his past brilliance. Paddy Murphy, who had been training since 1953 at Sunnyhill House, Kilcullen, witnessed the comeback and immediately thought of Bobby Beasley when his stable jockey, Francis Shortt, broke his leg in a fall. He approached Bobby, asking him to stand in while Shortt was out of action. Having agreed to do so, Bobby asked his friend, Nicky Rackard for an introduction to Alcoholics Anonymous. He had decided to give up the drink – his 'second start' was about to begin.

It did not take the reformed Bobby Beasley long to get off the mark, riding Mrs Paddy Murphy's Norwegian Flag to victory in a maiden hurdle at Naas on 20 February 1971. It was his first winning ride since partnering Rimmon, trained by Fred Winter, to victory in a novice hurdle at Fontwell Park on 7 May 1969. His second career in the saddle lasted until 1974 and saw him ride the brilliant enigma, Captain Christy, winner of the Cheltenham Gold Cup. It happened that Captain Christy played a part in his decision to retire for good. Initially offered a retainer of £1,000 to ride the horse for the 1974/5 season, this was subsequently reduced by half as the owner reflected on it and finally withdrawn on the grounds that she could not afford to pay it. Then came a frustrating fall from a horse in the 1974 Irish Grand National, followed by boos and abuse from a section of the crowd on the way to the start for the Power Gold Cup the following afternoon. Punters who had backed him to win the Irish Grand National vented their frustration at the jockey, who felt unfairly treated because he did not think the fall was his fault. His spirits were lifted by the easy win in the Power Gold Cup but retirement was now on his mind. After riding 800 winners, he felt lucky to be still in one piece, and he did not need the aggravation of an abusive crowd; he would call it a day at the end of the season.

Although his training career got off to a flying start with two winners, he was never cut out to be a trainer. Barely able to cope with the constant anxiety of a trainer's life he could not watch a race involving a horse he had trained; he emerged after it was over to find out the result. Living in close proximity to his estranged wife was another difficulty, which encouraged him to transfer his training operation to England. His training career lasted until June 1988, when he retired for good, commenting ruefully, 'The game has changed a lot. Unless you're a hustler or do the clubs, you just won't make the grade.' On his retirement, he took over a pub – of all things. The Baiting House at Upper Sapey in Worcestershire was the new venture for the 53-year-old, who would miss the horses but not the hassle a small trainer has to face.

He was the third generation of his family to ride a winner at Galway. His grandfather, Mr Harry Beasley (1852–1939) won four steeplechases there, including the famous Plate twice in succession, and his father Henry H. (1898–59) rode three flat winners at the meeting, one in 1920 and two the following year. Bobby's total of twelve included the Galway Plate a record four times, on Knight Errant, Sparkling Flame, Clipador and Blunts Cross, and the Galway Hurdle on Knight Errant. His talent can be gauged by the fact that ten of his twelve Galway winners started favourite, and the other two were second-favourites.

Patrick Mullins (b. 1919)

Trainer, Doninga, Goresbridge, Co. Kilkenny:

1959 A.J. Nicholson's WHAT EVER (Mr. F. Flood) – Moyode Bumper £133

1960 David A. Pim's LOVELY LEE (J. Conway) – Ballindooly Maiden Hurdle £202

1965 George Doran's DEVENISH ARTIST (G.W. Robinson) – Galway Blazers Handicap Chase £351¾

1966 Malcolm D. Thorp's COSY WRAP (G. McGrath) – Briarhill Handicap 8½f flat £366

1967 Mrs D. Archer Houston's SOME JEST (P. Powell Jr) – Oranmore Handicap 7f flat £377

1968   John P. Kennedy's COOLROBIN (J. Roe) – Oranmore Handicap 7f flat £388

1969   John P. Kennedy's COOLROBIN (R.F. Parnell) – Oranmore Handicap 7f flat £404

1973   Malcolm D. Thorp's ST MULLINS (R. Shortt) – Salthill Handicap Hurdle £451

1975   J.P.M. O'Connor's LARKVIEW (R.F. Parnell) – Menlo Race 9f flat £553

1975   Mrs P. Mullins's ANDY PANDY (Mr W.P. Mullins) – Ballindooley Hurdle £867

1975   E.G. Green's SILVER ROAD (J. Roe) – Barna Handicap 2m flat £552

1975   Lady Elizabeth Byng's VULCOTT (S. Treacy) – Galway Blazers Handicap Chase £552

1975   J.P.M. O'Connor's LARKVIEW (R.F. Parnell) – Oranmore Handicap 7f flat £552

1976   Captain Luke Mullins's NEGRADA (S. Treacy) – Guinness Galway Handicap Hurdle £3,775

1976   T.C. Vigors's SLAP UP (S. Treacy) – Stewards' Handicap £953

1976   John P. Kennedy's BUCCO REEF (Mr W.P. Mullins) – Moyode Bumper £552

1976   J.J. Murphy's RENVYLE (S. Treacy) – Kinvara Handicap Hurdle £552

1977   Mrs T.A. Connolly's VICTOR'S BARGE (Mr W.P. Mullins) – Lough Atalia Bumper £553

1977   Lady Elizabeth Byng's BILLY'S COTTAGE (Mr W.P. Mullins) – Moyode Bumper £552

1978   Kevin O'Donnell's PRINCE TAMMY (S. Treacy) – Guinness Galway Hurdle £6,062

1978   Lady Elizabeth Byng's BILLY'S COTTAGE (P. Daly) – Salthill Handicap Hurdle £690

1980   William W. Brainard Jr's PEARLSTONE (T.V. Finn) – Guinness Handicap Hurdle £10,865

1981   T. Ruane's REGAL SHOW (D. Parnell) – Sean Graham Handicap £1,658

1982   Mrs C.D. Hill's DAWN RUN (Mr T. Mullins) – Tonroe Bumper £1,380

1984   Oliver Freaney's STREET ANGEL (Mr J. Shortt) – GPT Amateur Handicap flat £10,341

1984   Paul Callan's ASH CREEK (C.F. Swan) – McDonogh Handicap 8½f flat £12,588

1984   David A. Pim's STERN SATURN (S. Craine) – Bushy Park Handicap 2m flat £1,382

1984   Commander H. Grenfell's GIGOLETTA (P.J. Cooney) Salthill Handicap Hurdle £1,242

1984   Charles D. Mansergh's CLANWILLIAM (A. Mullins) – Oranmore Handicap Hurdle £9,097

1985   Mrs P. Mullins's PARGAN (Mr W.P. Mullins) – GPT Amateur Handicap 2m flat £11,108

1985   W. Neville's BRIDESWELL DEW (Mr W.P. Mullins) – Salthill Handicap Hurdle £1,380

1985   Hugh McCann's CANINOT (Mr W.P. Mullins) – Tonroe Bumper £1,380

1986   Mrs C.D. Hill's BORO QUARTER (P. Kavanagh) – Digital Galway Plate £27,786

1986   J.M. Cusack's HAZY BIRD (S. Craine) – Fairhill Handicap 12f flat £1,380

1987   Patrick F. Keogh's PROMINENT RULER (Mr W.P. Mullins) – Moyode Bumper £1,380

1988   Mrs G. Robinson's PHEOPOTSTOWN (N. McCullagh) – McDonogh Handicap flat £14,802

1988   Thomas Mullins's LADY KAROLA (M.G. Cleary) – Smithwicks Handicap flat £2,960

1992   Thomas Mullins's WHEATSHEAF LADY (J.P. Murtagh) – McDonogh 2yo Maiden £5,522

1992   Thomas J. Farrell's FURRY STAR (Mr W.P. Mullins) – Digital Hurdle £3,795

1992   Mrs M. O'Leary's THE GOOSER (A. Maguire) – Digital Galway Plate £22,100

1993   Miss Carmel Byrne's CAMDEN BUZZ (C.F. Swan) – Guinness Galway Hurdle £21,700

1996   Mrs P.J. O'Meara's BEAKSTOWN (R. Dunwoody) – Jockeys' Association Chase £4,452

1999   Mrs P. Mullins's BOB WHAT (M.J. Kinane) – McDonogh Timber Handicap 2m flat £6,187

2002 Cabin Hill Syndicate's ULYSEES (M.J. Kinane) – McDonogh 3yo Maiden €11,385
2003 Michael J. McGinley's NEARLY A MOOSE (R.M. Power) HP Galway Plate €92,975
2003 Mrs Paul Duffin's EMPEROR'S GUEST (K.A. Kelly) – Tara Towers Chase €12,765

Paddy Mullins was one of Ireland's most versatile trainers, sending out top-class winners on the flat, over hurdles and over fences. He trained: Hurry Harriet to beat Allez France, the best filly in Europe at the time, to win the 1973 Champion Stakes at Newmarket; Dawn Run, the only horse to win the Champion Hurdle and the Cheltenham Gold Cup; Gabel, the highest-earning National Hunt horse to that time, successful in the $750,000 Dueling Grounds International Hurdle at Franklin, Kentucky, in 1990; and four winners of the Irish Grand National – Vulpine, Herring Gull, Dim Wit and Luska. Joint leading trainer with Barney Nugent in the Galway Hurdle, with four winners – Negrada, Prince Tammy, Pearlstone and Camden Buzz, he won the Plate twice, with The Gooser and Nearly A Moose, the Amateur Handicap with Street Angel and Pargan, and the McDonogh Handicap with Ash Creek and Pheopotstown.

Paddy Mullins, the shrewdest trainer of them all has trained major winners on the flat and over hurdles and fences

Riding as an amateur, mainly in point-to-points, he assisted his father, William, who trained in a small way, before taking out his own training licence in 1953. Mixing training and riding until he retired from the saddle in 1959, he did the best he could with moderate horses, but that changed in 1961 with the early death of local trainer Dan Kirwan. Dan's father John had trained a lot of winners, particularly in the south of Ireland, and won an Irish Grand National with Heirdom and a Galway Hurdle with Erinox, while Dan had been a successful jump jockey, riding Red Park to victory in the Irish Grand National and the Galway Plate in 1933. When John Kirwan died in 1950, Dan took over the established stable with its good owners and quality horses, winning the Kerry National with Hallie. He died suddenly in 1961, having taken ill while driving to Dublin, and the subsequent closure of his stable left his owners without a trainer. Many turned to the other trainer in the area, Paddy Mullins, upgrading the quality of the horses in his yard. One of the first good horses trained by Paddy was Height O'Fashion, famous later for her thrilling battles with the mighty Arkle, owned by local auctioneer John Donoghoe.

Still going strong at eight-four years of age in 2003, Paddy Mullins won his first classic race, the Irish Oaks, with Vintage Tipple, ridden by Frankie Dettori. It was the Italian-born English Champion's first ride for Paddy and he excitedly proclaimed to the veteran trainer after the race: 'I liked the instructions you gave me – none!' At the end of February 2005 Paddy Mullins decided to retire and handed the stable over to his son and long-time assistant Tom, a brother of Willie and Tony, former jockeys now training in their own right.

Alphonsus S. O'Brien (b. 1929)

Trainer, South Lodge, Carrick-on-Suir, Co. Tipperary:

1959 R. Liddle's HEDONIST (T.P. Burns) – Corrib Hurdle £133

1962 Mrs M. Valentine's CARRAROE (F.T. Winter) – Galway Plate £1,160

1963 Lord Fermoy's BLUNTS CROSS (H.R. Beasley) – Galway Plate £1,530

1964 Miss G. Buchanan's ROSS SEA (S. Mellor) – Galway Plate £1,530

1965 Miss G. Buchanan's ROSS SEA (S. Mellor) – Galway Plate £1,900

1966 H.T. McKnight Jr's BAXIER (Owner) – Claddagh Handicap Chase £332

1967 Mrs M. Valentine's BOLD FENCER (T.S. Murphy) – Corrib Hurdle £421

1970 Mrs D. Jackson's EBONY LAD (John Crowley) – Ballindooly Hurdle £448

Trainer, The Grove, Golden, Co. Tipperary:

1972 J. Jones's NEWMAN NOGGS (T.S. Murphy) – Claddagh Chase £384½

1972 Mrs A. Manning's FRESH DEAL (T.S. Murphy) – Corrib Hurdle £453

1976 Mrs M. Valentine's RATHNURE (F. Berry) – Corrib Hurdle £785

Trainer, Kilsheelan, Co. Tipperary:
1980 Mrs M. Valentine's ASKAMORE (Mr N. Madden) – Claddagh Chase £1,382

When Vincent O'Brien gave up jump training to train on the flat in the 1950s, his brother Phonsie carried the family flag at Galway. The first of his twelve winners came in 1959, when Hedonist (T.P. Burns) won the Corrib Hurdle. He trained Carraroe (1962), Blunts Cross (1963) and Ross Sea (1964 and 1965) to win the Galway Plate in four successive years, surpassing the successive trebles scored by H.E. Linde and H.I. Ussher. Carraroe was owned by the American, Mrs Miles Valentine, a long-standing patron of the stable who used the distinctive colours of pink, with cherry red hearts, and a pink cap. Mrs Valentine also owned Askamore, Phonsie's last (1980) and his daughter Gillian's first (1982) and only Galway Festival winner.

The unusual feature of Phonsie's Galway Plate winners was the jockeys: top English-based jockeys rarely seen riding on Irish racecourses at that time, enticed to Galway during the English National Hunt close season. Carraroe was ridden by Fred Winter, the brilliant and popular four-time Champion Jockey; Blunts Cross had the services of Irishman Bobby Beasley, who was riding for Paddy Sleator's Grange Con stable but was spending much of his time in England riding Sleator horses with Arthur Thomas nominally in charge; and two-time winner, Ross Sea, had Stan Mellor up on both occasions. Mellor, three times English Champion Jockey, later become the first jump jockey to ride over a thousand winners in Britain. The presence of these names greatly enhanced the reputation of the Galway races, which was rapidly completing its journey from a class three to a grade one racecourse.

John G. Duggan (d. 1967)

Owner, slate grey, scarlet spots and cap:
1950 GREEN DOLPHIN (M. Molony) – Galway Blazers Handicap Chase £202 (J.W. Osborne)
1953 COLONIAL JACK (P.J. Doyle) – Galway Blazers Handicap Chase £133 (J.W. Osborne)
1956 IVY GREEN (P. Taaffe) – Galway Hurdle £734½ (J.W. Osborne)

Jack Duggan was the driving force behind Gowran Park racecourse and was responsible for the introduction of its feature race, the Thyestes Chase. A former mayor of Kilkenny, he was appointed a member of the Racing Board in 1950 and was elected to the Irish National Hunt Steeplechase Committee in 1952, serving as a steward between 1955 and 1957. He was elected to the position again in 1966, but died during his term of office. He was also Chairman of Tramore Racecourse. In 1956 his horse Ivy Green won the Galway Hurdle, a race won by a few racecourse people down the years. Martin McDonogh (Kyleclare 1931) and Captain Luke Mullins (Negrada 1976) both involved in the Galway racecourse won the race as owners, and George Gradwell, later Clerk of the Course at Galway, owned the Galway Plate winner Drogheda.

Mrs Anne Bullitt Biddle (1924–2007)

Owner, navy blue, white hoop, navy blue cap with white hoop, Mrs A.M.B. Biddle:
1954 AMBER POINT (C. Sleator) – Galway Plate £1,110 (P. Sleator)

Mrs R. More O'Ferrall:
1956 AMBER POINT (P.A. Farrell) – Galway Plate £1,160 (P. Sleator)
1956 KNIGHT ERRANT (P.A. Farrell) – Corrib Hurdle £133 (P. Sleator)

Mrs A.B. Biddle:
1957 KNIGHT ERRANT (H.R. Beasley) – Galway Plate £1,160 (P. Sleator)
1958 KNIGHT ERRANT (H.R. Beasley) – Galway Hurdle £748 (P. Sleator)
1960 LIUVIA (M. Cournane) – Spiddal Handicap 7f flat £202 (T. Shaw)

Anne Bullitt Biddle, owner of two horses that won three Galway Plates and one Galway Hurdle between them in the mid-fifties, made a significant contribution to Irish racing as an owner, a breeder and later a trainer. She was the daughter of William C. Bullitt, an American diplomat and the first American Ambassador to the Soviet Union, and his wife Louise, whose relationship became the storyline for the Oscar-winning film *Reds*. Young, strikingly beautiful and with two failed marriages behind her, Anne Biddle arrived in Ireland and immersed herself in horse racing, employing two of the best trainers of the time; Paddy Sleator trained her jumpers and Paddy Prendergast was in charge of the flat racers. The new owner became instantly successful in both spheres; Sleator trained her first Galway winner, Amber Point, winner of the 1954 Plate, while Prendergast turned out Sarissa to win the Phoenix Stakes the following year, the sixth of the great trainer's sequence of seven in a row in that race.

She married Roderick More O'Ferrall, the former trainer, of the Kildangan Stud in Mexico, in December 1954, but the marriage lasted no time and its collapse caused havoc within a section of the Irish racing community. First to become embroiled in the mayhem was Paddy Prendergast. He was very close to Frankie More O'Ferrall, Roderick's brother, the founder and Chairman of the Anglo-Irish Bloodstock Agency, training for him and doing business with him. Forced to choose between his friend and one of his owners, Prendergast sided with the More O'Ferralls, and had an acrimonious split with Anne Biddle in October 1955. Out of Rossmore Lodge went the Biddle horses and into Rathbride Manor, where Michael Dawson trained. Tommy Shaw, Prendergast's travelling head lad, went with them. In due course Roderick and Anne More O'Ferrall's bitter separation battle spilled over into the Irish courts, pulling in big crowds. Some came to hear the gossip but many young men turned out just for a glimpse at the beauty in the middle of it all. The case caused a sensation and hit the headlines when Anne flummoxed the judge – and most of the Irish people as well – when she described her former husband as 'a fairy' in open court. The outcome of the case was the annulment of their marriage in 1956, upon which Mrs More O'Ferrall reverted to being called Mrs Anne Bullitt Biddle.

While all this was going on, Paddy Sleator won three Galway Plates and a Galway Hurdle with two horses, Amber Point and Knight Errant, between 1954 and 1958. In that latter year Anne Biddle's flat trainer Michael Dawson sent out the maiden Sindon to win the Irish Derby, beating the Epsom Derby runner-up Paddy's Point by a short head. She ended the year as the top owner in Ireland, only the second woman ever to head that list, her nine horses winning fourteen races. However, she was now about to get out of jumping and was in the process of taking her string away from Rathbride Manor.

After the split with Roderick More O'Ferrall, her father cheered her up by buying the Palmerstown Stud, a property of 700 acres adjacent to the Dublin–Naas main road at Kill, from W.J. Kelly, the trainer of Amor de Cuba, winner of the 1941 Galway Hurdle. Having settled in, Anne installed her sprinter, Milesian, winner of the Imperial Stakes at Kempton Park and the Rockingham Handicap at the Curragh, as the resident stallion and set about establishing a stud. Giving up jump racing, she concentrated on flat breeding extensively from Milesian and opening her own private stable at Palmerstown, under the control of Tommy Shaw. She retained the leading jockey Liam Ward, whom she greatly admired, to ride her horses. Having put all her eggs in one basket with her faith in Milesian, Anne Biddle was fortunate that he became an outstanding sire, producing a number of big winners for the stable from his early crops of foals. Unfortunately, this encouraged her to continue the policy with other stallions, such as Ionian and Le Prince, whose failure to sire winners helped bring down the whole operation.

However, the stable enjoyed five years of considerable success before things began to go wrong. Tommy Shaw's training career got off to a satisfactory start when Mrs Biddle's Bois Belleau finished second to Fidalgo in the Irish Derby in 1959. The following year Zenobia won the Irish 1,000 Guineas and March Wind, a half-brother to Bois Belleau, won the Irish Champion Stakes, then run at the Curragh. By this time the Milesian factor was beginning to kick in, as its stock hit the racecourse running, getting eleven individual winners from his first crop of foals. Over the next couple of years Mrs Biddle had a lot of success with Milesian horses. Satan won the Diadem Stakes at Ascot; Mystery and Partholon won successive runnings of the National Stakes, one of the top two-year-old races; and Scissors won the Beresford Stakes. Among the near misses was Ionian, pipped at the post by Only For Life in the 2,000 Guineas, having just failed to stay on the soft ground. Partholon trained on to win the Ebor Handicap at York, Atlantis won the Ulster Derby and L'Homme Arme and Marco Polo were good winners.

Her luck ran out spectacularly. It all began at Doncaster in October 1963 when Scissors was contesting the Timeform Gold Cup, sponsored by Phil Bull's company. Ridden as usual by Liam Ward, the horse was boxed in on the rails during the race. With his mount full of running Ward, in his haste to escape, pushed his way out, bumping the favourite, Con Brio, ridden Lester Piggott. However, once clear Scissors finished like a train to catch and beat Pushful by a neck, clearly winning the race on merit. Few expected an enquiry to be announced, and nobody anticipated that the stewards would reverse the placings of Scissors and Pushful, declaring Pushful the winner and relegating Scissors to second place. Scissors had been the best horse on the day, he had not interfered with Pushful at all and, although he had interfered with the chances of Con Brio, that horse was well beaten in the finish. The decision puzzled just about everyone, not least the sponsor, who commented:

> There is no doubt at all that Scissors was the best horse on the day, and if he had been able to get a clear run, he would have been a more decisive winner. The objection by the Stewards for interference came as a surprise, and their disqualification of Scissors a shock. It is true that strictly according to Rule 140 Scissors contravened the rules of racing by interfering with the chance of Con Brio, but Scissors in no way interfered with the chance of Pushful; the two horses were never racing close enough together for Scissors to have bumped Pushful.

He continued:

> As every racegoer knows, this sort of thing happens in racing nearly every day, and if the rule were to be interpreted rigidly, with a fine disregard for the attendant circumstances, racing would soon come to a dead stop.

This ridiculous decision was a bitter blow for Anne Biddle and Tommy Shaw, but worse was to follow within six months. Tragedy came over to Newmarket from Palmerstown strongly fancied to win the 1,000 Guineas, but the filly trailed in a hopeless last, having never got racing at all. The stewards ordered a dope test, which turned out to be positive. It turned out that she had been nobbled by a gang of dopers that were active in British racing at the time. Disillusioned, Anne Biddle closed down her private stable at the end of the 1964 season and sent her horses back to Michael Dawson, who won the Gladness Stakes with another Milesian colt, Western Wind, but within eighteen months the horses were back in Palmerstown again.

During the summer of 1966, the Turf Club and the Irish National Hunt Steeplechase Committee decided to lift a long-standing convention that only men could apply for a trainer's licence. Two ladies availed themselves of the opportunity to take out a licence: Anne Biddle, who was granted a licence to train on the flat, and Peggy St John Nolan, who received a licence to train on the flat and over jumps. Mrs Biddle won the race to become the first woman to officially train a winner in Ireland, when Flying Tiger, a three-year-old by Milesian whom she bred and owned herself, won the Cork Stakes at Naas on 31 August 1966, the 6-to-4 favourite being ridden to victory by Liam Ward.

Unfortunately, as she was about to become Mrs D.B. Brewster, her breeding policy was slowly going downhill. Too much use of inferior home stallions lowered the quality of the stock, the good mares were not breeding winners, stock was not culled and more and more of the fillies were not seeing the racecourse at all. Slowly but surely she faded from the racing scene and her speedy blood was diluted with mediocrity of the slowest sort – a tragic loss for Irish racing. Now even the Palmerstown Stud is gone; the first commercial stud farm in Ireland has been broken up and developed by speculators.

Tommy O'Brien (trainer's permit/licence 1958–62)

Rider White, red cross of Lorraine, red cap:

1956 Mrs P.J. Loughlin's JINGO – Salthill Handicap Hurdle (D. Kirwan)

This Tommy O'Brien was from Co. Kilkenny and rode mainly for trainer Dan Kirwan. His biggest win came in the 1956 Irish Grand National on Beatrice McClintock's Air Prince, trained by her husband Jimmy. Retiring to run a pub in Graiguenamanagh, he trained a horse or two under permit, but only as a hobby.

Tommy 'Coalminer' O'Brien (trainer's permit/licence 1958–62)

Trainer, white, red cross of Lorraine, red cap, Clonmel, Co. Tipperary:
1959 T. O'Brien's MISS MacDONALD (D. Page) – Spiddal Handicap 7f flat £133
1962 T. O'Brien's MR PHOENIX (M. Kennedy) – Spiddal Handicap 7f flat £534

Tommy O'Brien, from Ballingarry, Co. Limerick, was an extremely reckless gambler, who briefly took out a licence to train his own horses, employing Wille Treacy to do the work. On a fateful day in 1960, when Chamour's victory in the Ballysax Plate was to cost his namesake, Vincent O'Brien, his licence, 'the Coalminer' went for a touch, backing his horse Miss MacDonald to win over £20,000 in the second race on the card. The filly landed the spoils in a three-way photo finish, netting the Coalminer something in the region of £22,000. Incredibly, he came out of the course a loser to the tune of £10,000, having frittered away all his winnings, plus a lot more, on the remaining races. Miss MacDonald was his 'crowded hour of glorious life' and provided him with many highs, one of which was a victory in the Spiddal Handicap at Galway in 1959, ridden by Doug Page, bringing off another successful gamble.

Undoubtedly however, his biggest success was when Moss Bank, trained by him for Mary, his wife, won the Queen Alexandra Stakes at Royal Ascot in 1961, with Bill Williamson up, beating Agreement, owned by H.M. The Queen, and Farney Fox, trained in Ireland by Charlie Weld. Naturally, such a compulsive gambler could not last, but his philosophy was that he may have lost a lot of money playing the horses, but it was his own money and he was entitled to do what he liked with it.

Originally from County Mayo, Tommy O'Brien went to England, got work in a coalmine and returned to Ireland to buy the old Ballingarry Coal Mine in South Tipperary. Using the experience he had gained as a miner in England, he got that old mine going again, turning out anthracite. He lived in Clonmel until his spending spree on horses, a private training stable and uncontrolled gambling gobbled up all his ready cash. He could have welched – gaming debts are not recoverable at law – but he settled all his debts, although he had to sell up to do so. The house, stables, gallops, horses and the coalmine all went and the ex-coalminer retired to Cork and an early death, in a tractor accident, a few years later.

Noel Meade (b. 1951)

Trainer, Castletown, Co. Meath:

1972 Norman Allen's LARK'S VENTURE (T. Carberry) - Castlegar Maiden Hurdle £456

1980 P.J. Moran's AVOCAN (J.P. Byrne) – Kinvara Handicap Hurdle £832

1980 B. McGuckian's WHISPER GENTLY (S. Craine) – Sean Graham Handicap £1,658

1980 Denis F. Howard's LADY TIFFANY (S. Craine) – Claregalway Nursery £1,328

1980 Mrs R.A. Keogh's NATIONAL IMAGE (S. Craine) – Stewards' Handicap £1,104

1980 P.J. Moran's AVOCAN (P. Leech) – Salthill Handicap Hurdle £828

1981 B. Carolan's PINCH HITTER (S. Craine) – McDonogh Handicap £8,028

1981 N. Kavanagh's STEEL DUKE (Mr J. Queally) – Amateur Handicap £9,294

1981 Noel Meade's DUSKY FOX (Mr J. Halpin) – Moyode Bumper £828

1981 N. Kavanagh's STEEL DUKE (S. Craine) – Ashford Castle Handicap £4,991

1982 B. Carolan's PINCH HITTER (S. Craine) – McDonogh Handicap £10,110

1982 P.G. Carroll's WELSHWOOD (S. Craine) – Sean Grahan Handicap £1,244

1982 N. Kavanagh's STEEL DUKE (S. Craine) – Mervue Race £1,104

1982 B. Carolan's PINCH HITTER (J.J. O'Neill) – Galway Hurdle Handicap £15,250

1982 P.G. Carroll's WELSHWOOD (S. Craine) – Stewards' Handicap £1,104

1982 N. Kavanagh's STEEL DUKE (S. Craine) – Nilands Handicap £8,766

1983 Richard McCarthy's ACTION GIRL (S. Craine) – Claregalway 2yo Maiden £1,175

1983 Michael Magill's RED REALM (S. Craine) – Briar Hill Handicap £1,173

1983 B. Carolan's PINCH HITTER (J.J. O'Neill) – Galway Hurdle £14,646

1983 Mrs Carmel Meade's FRIGATE LADY (H. Rogers) – Salthill Handicap Hurdle £1,242

1983 Mrs E.M. Burke's SAINT CYNTHIA (S. Craine) – Menlo Race £966

1984 Noel Meade's TANBARK (J.P. Byrne) – Kinvara Handicap Hurdle £968

1984 Peter O'Gorman's GENTLE FAVOR (M. Duffy) – Loughrea Handicap £1,244

1984 Donal Kinsella's WHITERIVER GROVE (Mr D.H. O'Connor) – Lough Atalia Bumper £968

1984 Stephen Banville's DUSKY FOX (P. Leech) – Galway Blazers Handicap Chase £1,173

1984 Peter O'Gorman's GENTLE FAVOR (K. Moses) – Fairhill Handicap £1,104

1984 Donal Kinsella's WHITERIVER GROVE (Mr D.H. O'Connor) – Tonroe Bumper £1,380

1985 Mrs Catherine Howard's BALLYVAUGHAN BOY (P. Leech) – Kinvara Handicap Hurdle £1,382

1985 C.J. Milligan's BALLYWOODEN (Mr T.M. Walsh) – Lough Atalia Bumper £1,382

1986 Turform Ltd's RINNCOIR (P.V. Gilson) – Renmore Maiden £1,380

1986 Turform Ltd's RINNCOIR (P.V. Gilson) – Oranmore Handicap £1,380

1987 Mrs P.J. Carr's DROMOD HILL (S. Craine) – McDonogh Handicap £13,210

1987 John P. Moore's WELSH FLYER (S. Craine) – Renmore Maiden £1,380

1987 Fernando Jaconelli's CIAMPINO (D. Parnell) – Oranmore Handicap £1,380

1987 Ms C. Gannon's WESTERN WOLF (S. Craine) – County Nursery £2,760

1987   Fernando Jaconelli's CIAMPINO (S. Craine) – Oranmore Handicap £1,725

1988   Donal Kinsella's THE HYACE DRIVER (Mr J. Queally) – Moyode Bumper £2,070

1988   Patrick White's STRING QUARTET (S. Craine) – Tuam 2yo Race £2,072

1989   John P. Moore's FISH MERCHANT (S. Craine) – Musgrave Handicap £2,072

1990   P.G. Tierney's SELKIS (T. Carmody) – GPT Dublin Handicap Hurdle £2,762

1991   Mrs Rita Polly's LEAR FANTASTIQUE (R. Hughes) – McDonogh Timber Handicap £3,797

1991   Mrs Rita Polly's LEAR FANTASTIQUE (S. Craine) – Smithwicks Handicap £3,795

1992   Donal Kinsella's BEAU BEAUCHAMP (Mr S.R. Murphy) - Amateur Handicap £10,052

1992   John P. Moore's REFINED HEIR (Mr S.R. Murphy) – GPT Bumper £3,797

1992   Liam Keating's MUBADIR (C.F. Swan) – Albatross Maiden Hurdle £3,797

1992   Mrs Rita Polly's LEAR FANTASTIQUE (C.F. Swan) – Digital Handicap Hurdle £3,795

1992   Mrs M. Cahill's FANE BANKS (H. Rogers) – Oranmore Handicap Chase £4,140

1993   Mrs H.A. Hegarty's LIFE SAVER (P. Carberry) – Digital Hurdle £4,160

1993   Mrs Maureen Hunt's LE CENERENTOLA (P. Carberry) – Guinness Handicap £4,140

1993   Liam Doherty's SHIRLEY'S DELIGHT (P. Carberry) – Smithwicks Handicap £4,140

1995   Mrs G. Mathews's HEIST (Mr G.J. Harford) – Amateur Handicap £9,975

1995   N. Coburn's RANDOM PRINCE (Mr G.J. Harford) – Budweiser Handicap Hurdle £4,110

1996   Mrs A.S. O'Brien's LIFE SUPPORT (P. Carberry) – Digital Hurdle £4,110

1996   Mrs A. McAteer's WESPERADA (S. Craine) – Kerry Spring Handicap £4,110

1997   Mrs F. Towey's SAVING BOND (Mr Thomas Gibney) – Amateur Handicap £16,550

1997   N. Coburn's FANE PATH (Mr G.J. Harford) – Budweiser Handicap Hurdle £4,110

1998   Mrs Mary Doherty's MIDNIGHT LOVER (J.P. Murtagh) – Albatross Handicap £4,812

1988   P.R. Charles's RASHAY (E. Ahern) McDonogh Fertilizers Maiden £4,125

1999   A. Gannon's ADMIRAL WINGS (B.J. Geraghty) – Chatterbox Maiden Hurdle £5,550

2000   Mrs J. Hurley's SUN STRAND (P. Carberry) – Ready to Go Chase £8,970

2001   Clogher Stud's RIVER PILOT (N. Williamson) – Jockeys' Association Chase £8,625

2002   Vincent Dunne's LADY CORDUFF (W.M. Lordan) – Carlsberg 2yo Maiden €11,730

2002   D.P. Sharkey's SNOB WELLS (P. Carberry) – Jockeys' Association Chase €11,040

2004   M.J. Smith's ATHLUMNEY LAD (J.R. Barry) – GPT Dublin Handicap Hurdle €13,474

2005   Mrs P. Towey's CARLESIMO (F.M. Berry) – McDonogh Handicap €10,710

2005   Neighbours Syndicate's MORE RAINBOWS (N.P. Madden) – Galway Hurdle Handicap €115,200

2005   Kieran McGinn's NAPLES (Miss Nina Carberry) – Guinness Bumper €8,292

2005   P.R. Syndicate's PEPPERWOOD (F.M. Berry) – St James's Gate Race €14,322

2005   D.P. Sharkey's ALWAYS (B.J. Geraghty) – Tony O'Malley Handicap Chase €32,950

2005   Oyster Homes Syndicate's MY NATIVE LAD (P. Carberry) – Jockeys' Association Maiden Hurdle €11,056

2006   Mighty Macs Syndicate's ECOLE D'ART (D.F. O'Regan) – William Hill Hurdle €17,577

2006   J.P. McManus's MORATORIUM (F.M. Berry) – William Hill Handicap €11,401

Noel Meade left school at the age of sixteen to run the family farm at Castletown, Kilpatrick, Co. Meath, about 10 miles from Navan, for his ailing father. At first he wanted to be an amateur rider and rode out with Cyril Bryce-Smith, who trained at Kells, but in 1971 he decided to apply for a permit to train. He purchased Tu Va out of Captain Cyril Harty's stable and rode it himself in races during that summer. After four seconds and two thirds, he eventually found himself in the winner's enclosure at Wexford at the end of August, where Tu Va beat Stewart Barrett's Gordon, trained privately by Bobby Beasley and ridden by John Fowler. Having a difficult ride, not liking being in front, Tu Va was beaten by a neck at Galway by Wild Buck (Mr M.F. Morris) in the Dangan Amateur Handicap Hurdle, the first race on Plate day. Although a modest hurdler, Tu Va made Noel Meade and when his proper stable yard was built, he named it after that horse.

Although Noel had intended training jumpers, he did well with some of the flat horses that found their way into his stable and has probably become better known as a flat trainer. In 1978 he trained the top-class sprinter, Sweet Mint, a winner at Royal Ascot, and returned twenty years later to win the Cornwallis Stakes with Show Me The Money. Now firmly established as a dual-purpose trainer, perhaps he is not known for turning out chasers, although he has done so at the top level,

Noel Meade's horseboxes carry the slogan 'Keep the Faith' but the religion is a football team

winning the Ericsson Chase with Johnny Setaside. He headed the list of Irish trainers, according to races won, in 1980. He has a reputation of being sympathetic to his owners, which is part of his success story. Leading trainer six times, he has trained seventy-two winners at the Galway Festival, a total only surpassed by Dermot Weld's 192, and well ahead of Harry Ussher, in third place with fifty-eight. Cheltenham was the one meeting where he just could not get a winner; it became a bogey place, the hoodoo annually hyped by the press.

It may have started with Batista's short head defeat by Heighlin in the 1980 Triumph Hurdle, which landed jockey Joe Byrne with a three month suspension for misuse of the whip. Joe, who rode for Meade from 1975 to 1982, tended to be hard on horses and was liberal in his use of the whip, but his suspension, which was actually a warning off that was not recognized in Ireland, was a typical example of trial by television. Apparently adverse reaction by viewers to Joe's use of the whip on The Vintner at a previous meeting had been fed back to the stewards, who were waiting for him at Cheltenham. At the time there were no guidelines as to the use of whips but at Cheltenham that day the stewards, without warning, decided to declare war on the whip jockeys. Noel Meade may have thought the elusive winner would never come, but they always do for those who wait, and in 2000 Sausalito Bay broke the duck by winning the Supreme Novices Hurdle.

Dermot K. Weld (b. 1948)

Trainer, Rosewell House, Curragh:

1972 Mrs B.E. Allen Jones's KLAIRVIMY (J.V. Smith) – Athenry 2yo Stakes £526

1972 Mrs M.T. Jackson's SPANNER (Mr D.K. Weld) – Amateur Handicap £1,480

1973 E. Martin Smith's LORD OF THE MARK (R.F. Parnell) – Athenry 2yo Stakes £526

1973 Mrs M.T. Jackson's SPANNER (Mr D.K. Weld) – Amateur Handicap £1,380

1974 R.B. Bamber's WENTWORTH (M. Murphy) – Salthill Handicap Hurdle £572

1974 P.J. Thornton's MARTIAL CALL (C.K. McGarrity) – Renmore Maiden £620

1975 Lt-Comdr E.A. Collard's TOWER BIRD (J. Roe) – Bushy Park Stakes £793

1975 Mrs M.T. Jackson's SPANNER (Mr D.K. Weld) – Amateur Handicap £1,381

1975 Mrs M.T. Jackson's SPANNER (P. Russell) – Galway Hurdle Handicap £2,203

1975 G.M. Garrey's LANE COURT (J. Roe) – Stewards' Handicap £877

1976 Homer Scott's SLAVONIC (W. Swinburn) – Tuam 2yo Stakes £934

1977 Bertram R. Firestone's DIAMONDS ARE TRUMP (W. Swinburn) – Athenry 2yo Stakes £836

1977 Sir Hugh Fraser's LAVACHE (W. Swinburn) – Sean Graham Handicap £1,613

1977 Mrs Joseph O'Grady's NOZINE (W. Swinburn) – Renmore Maiden £906

1977 Lt-Comdr E.A.J. Collard's EDMUND TUDOR (W. Swinburn) – Mervue Stakes £813

1977 Bertram R. Firestone's RUNNING BROOK (W. Swinburn) – Tuam 2yo Stakes £839

1978 P. McGee's ADIRONDACK (W. Swinburn) – Renmore Maiden £830

1978 Mrs B. Kearney's BLACKWATER BRIDGE (Mr T.A. Jones) – Dangan Handicap Hurdle £552

1978 Mrs B. Kearney's FIXED PRICE (T. Carberry) – Ballindooley Hurdle £690

1978 Mrs B. Kearney's SMILING JIM (W. Swinburn) – Barna Handicap £552

1978 Bertram R. Firestone's VALLEY FORGE (W. Swinburn) – Mervue Plate £828

1978 S.M. Saud's PORTIMAO (W. Swinburn) – Parkmore Maiden £828

1978 Mrs B. Kearney's NEWRY HILL (W. Swinburn) – Menlo Plate £552

1979 Sir Christopher Soames's CLERICAL ERROR (W. Swinburn) – Briarhill Handicap £1,035

1979 J.L. Albritton's PARVA STELLA (W. Swinburn) – Mervue Plate £1,035

1981 Mrs B.R. Firestone's OVERPLAY (W. Swinburn) – Bushy Park Race £1,106

1981 M. Soudavar's BURRENDALE (J. Deegan) – Claregalway Nursery £1,382

1981 M. Soudavar's EPODE (W. Swinburn) – Renmore Maiden £1,037

1981 N.H. Phillips's LADOUCETTE (W. Swinburn) – Mervue Race £1,104

1981 M. Soudavar's EPODE (W. Swinburn) – Oranmore Handicap £828

1981 Morgan Sheehy's KIWI SLAVE (W. Swinburn) – Parkmore Maiden £1,035

1982 Walter Haefner's STRONG DOLLAR (W. Swinburn) – Athenry 2yo Maiden £1,106

1982 Torki M. Saud's NESREEN (J. Deegan) – Bushey Park Handicap £1,382

1982 Robert E. Sangster's COMMITTED (W. Swinburn) – Tuam 2yo Race £1,380

1982 James Francis Kelly's SEPT (J. Deegan) – County Nursery £1,380

1983 Frank L. Glusman's STRATHLINE (D. McHargue) – Bushy Park Handicap £1,382

1983 Mrs Elizabeth C. McLoughlin's WISCASSET (D. Manning) – Loughrea Handicap £1,244

1983 Michael B. Moore's CLERICAL ERROR (D. McHargue) – Barna Handicap £966

1983 Bertram R. Firestone's CLIFTON BAY (D. McHargue) – Parkmore Maiden £1,104

1983 Mrs Elizabeth C. McLoughlin's WISCASSET (D. Manning) – Fairhill Handicap £1,104

1984 Bertram R. Firestone's KAMAKURA (M.J. Kinane) – Athenry 2yo Maiden £1,727

1984 Moyglare Stud's SWEETENED OFFER (M.J. Kinane) – Claregalway Maiden £1,175

1984 Mrs B.R. Firestone's ALL A LARK (M.J. Kinane) – Briar Hill Handicap £1,173

1984 Bertram R. Firestone's SECURITY CLEARANCE (M.J. Kinane) – Mervue Race £1,173

1984 M.W.J. Smurfit's MARTIES LIGHT (M.J. Kinane) – Oranmore Handicap £966

1985 Bertram R. Firestone's INISHEER – Athenry 2yo Maiden £1,727

1985 Mrs Helen Smith's FRENCH CHAIN (M.J. Kinane) – Loughrea Handicap £1,382

1985 Mrs W. Whitehead's BONNIE BESS (M.J. Kinane)– McDonogh Handicap £11,623

1985 Thoroughbred Breeders Inc's GENTLE FAVOR (M.J. Kinane) – Mervue Race £1,382

1985 Bertram R. Firestone's WORLD TOUR (Mr M. Ahern) – Ballintemple Maiden £1,380

1985 M.W.J. Smurfit's STRATHLINE (T. Carmody) – Galway Hurdle Handicap £18,698

1985 Bertram R. Firestone's SWATCH (M.J. Kinane) – Stewards Handicap £1,380

1985 Allen E. Paulson's SON OF IVOR (M.J. Kinane) – Nilands Handicap £7,935

1985 Bertram R. Firestone's MOUNTAIN BROOK (F. Berry) – Bohermore Maiden Hurdle £1,380

1986 M.W.J. Smurfit's PERRIS VALLEY (Mr P.R. Lenehan) – Lough Atalia Bumper £1,382

1986 Mrs B.R. Firestone's BIG BREAK (M.J. Kinane) – Claregalway Maiden £1,382

1987 Allen E. Paulson's KIICHI (M.J. Kinane) – GPT Dublin 2yo Maiden £3,452

1987 Allen E. Paulson's ALLEN'S MISTAKE (M.J. Kinane) – Mervue Race £2,072

1988 Allen E. Paulson's KIRLA (M.J. Kinane) – GPT Dublin 2yo Maiden £3,702

1988 D.K. Weld's MIDSUMMER GAMBLE (M.J. Kinane) – Bushy Park Handicap £2,072

1988 Allen E. Paulson's ALLEN'S MISTAKE (M.J. Kinane) – Mervue Race £2,962

1989 Moyglare Stud's GO AND GO (M.J. Kinane) – GPT Dublin 2yo Maiden £3,452

1989 M.W.J. Smurfit's POPULAR GLEN (M.J. Kinane)–McDonogh Handicap £13,702

1989 F. Soudavar's MIDSUMMER GAMBLE (M.J. Kinane) – Bushy Park Handicap £2,072

1989 Moyglare Stud's RARE HOLIDAY (M.J. Kinane) – Mervue Race £2,762

1989 M.W.J. Smurfit's EMPEROR TO BE (M.J. Kinane) – Digital Handicap £4,140

1990 Yoshiki Akazawa's GOLDEN MINTAGE (M.J. Kinane) – GPT 2yo Maiden £3,452

1990 Moyglare Stud's WEEKEND BREAK (M.J. Kinane) – McDonogh Feeds 2yo Maiden £2,762

1990 Philip Fleming's INQUEST (M.J. Kinane) – McDonogh Timber Handicap £2,762

1990 Yoshiki Akazawa's ARABIAN NIGHTS (M.J. Kinane) – McDonogh Fertilizer Race £3,452

1990 M.W.J. Smurfit's KIICHI (B. Sheridan) – Galway Plate Handicap Chase £22,100

1990 Robert E. Sangster's SADLERS CONGRESS (M.J. Kinane) – Digital Handicap £4,140

1990 M.W.J. Smurfit's POPULAR GLEN (B. Sheridan) – Harp Lager Hurdle £3,280

1990 Moyglare Stud's STRONG DEMAND (M.J. Kinane) – O'Malley Group Maiden £2,762

1990 G. Olivero's NATURAL LAD (M.J. Kinane) – O'Malley Contractors Handicap £2,762

1991 Moyglare Stud's LEGAL PRESSURE (M.J. Kinane) – GPT 2yo Maiden £5,522

1991 Moyglare Stud's MARKET BOOSTER (M.J. Kinane) – McDonogh Feeds 2yo Maiden £5,522

1991 A.E. Paulson's COMMITTED DANCER (M.J. Kinane) – McDonogh Handicap £13,702

1991 M.W.J. Smurfit's CHEERING NEWS (B. Sheridan) – Digital Decsite Hurdle £3,795

1991 M. Benacerraf's ORVIETTO (P. Shanahan) – Digital Handicap £4,485

1991 Frank Stronach's GREEN MARINE (Mr A. Maguire) – Decwindows Maiden £3,795

1991 P. Brien's NOBLE PALOMA (B. Sheridan) – Harp Lager Novice Hurdle £4,140

1991 M.W.J. Smurfit's ARABIAN NIGHTS (B. Sheridan) – Bohermore Maiden Hurdle £3,795

1991 Moyglare Stud's POLITICAL FACT (M.J. Kinane) – Menlo 2yo Maiden £5,520

1992 Raymond J. Rooney's ARABIC TREASURE (M.J. Kinane) – GPT 2yo Maiden £5,522

1992 International Breeders's CLIVEDON GAIL (M.J. Kinane) – McDonogh Timber Handicap £3,797

1992 Moyglare Stud's OPEN MARKET (M.J. Kinane) – O'Malley Group Maiden £3,797

1992 Andrea Schiavi's ONESIXNINE (M.J. Kinane) – O'Malley Construction Handicap £7,202

1992 Allen E. Paulson's VINEY (M.J. Kinane) – Jockeys' Association 2yo Maiden £5,520

1993 M.W.J. Smurfit's PERSIAN TACTICS (B. Sheridan) – Albatross Maiden Hurdle £4,142

1993 Andrea Schiavi's GLACIAL ARCTIC (M.J. Kinane) – McDonogh Fertilizer Maiden £4,142

1993 Ovidstown Investment's RIENROE (M.J. Kinane) – Albatross Suregrass Handicap £3,797

1993 Andrea Schiavi's ASTRONAVE (M.J. Kinane) – McDonogh Feeds 2yo Maiden £5,522

1993 International Breeders's CLIVEDEN GAIL (M.J. Kinane)–McDonogh Timber Handicap £3,797

1993 M.W.J. Smurfit's GENERAL IDEA (A. Maguire) – Galway Plate Handicap Chase £22,100

1993 Michael Watt's LUSTRINO (Mr J.A. Nash) – Digital Decstation Maiden £4,140

1993 Raymond J. Rooney's GARBONI (M.J. Kinane) – Guinness Extra Stout Handicap £6,902

1993 M.W.J. Smurfit's PERSIAN TACTICS (M.J. Kinane) – Arthur's Race £4,142

1993 Moyglare Stud's BLAZING SPECTACLE (M.J. Kinane) – Oranmore Milk Handicap £3,795

1994 Moyglare Stud's UNION DECREE (M.J. Kinane) – GPT 2yo Maiden £5,480

1994 Moyglare Stud's SPRINT FOR GOLD (M.J. Kinane) – GPT Cork Maiden £4,110

1994 M.W.J. Smurfit's SKIPO (B. Sheridan) – Albatross Maiden Hurdle £4,110

1994 M.W.J. Smurfit's SAIBOT (J.F. Egan) – McDonogh Handicap £15,500

1994 Moyglare Stud's FEELING OF POWER (M.J. Kinane) – McDonogh 2yo Maiden £5,480

1994 S. Creaven's OPEN MARKET (A. Maguire) – Digital Handicap Hurdle £5,480

1994 M.W.J. Smurfit's TREBLE BOB (D.J. O'Donoghue) – Digital Unix Handicap £4,110

1994 M.W.J. Smurfit's POLITICAL DOMAIN (M.J. Kinane) – Arthur's Race £4,110

1994 Frank Stronach's KING LEON (M.J. Kinane) – Jockeys' Association 2yo Maiden £5,480

1994 Mrs J. Maxwell Moran's BRYN CLOVIS (M.J. Kinane) – Kerry Spring Handicap £4,110

1995 Moyglare Stud's DANCE DESIGN (M.J. Kinane) – McDonogh Feeds 2yo Maiden £1,240

1995 Mrs F. Sheridan's JUST AN ILLUSION (M.J. Kinane) – McDonogh Timber Handicap £4,110

1995 M.W.J. Smurfit's BLAZING SPECTACLE (R. Dunwoody) – Digital Euro Hurdle £4,110

1995 Moyglare Stud's ARCHIVE FOOTAGE (M.J. Kinane) – Smithwicks 3yo Maiden £4,110

1995 Mrs J. Maxwell Moran's FLAMING FEATHER (M.J. Kinane) – Dawn 2yo Maiden £5,480

1996 Michael Watt's CASEY TIBBS (M.J. Kinane) – GPT Industrial 2yo Maiden £5,480

1996 Jeremiah J. King's ZANKLE (M.J. Kinane) – GPT Cork 3yo Handicap £4,110

1996 M.W.J. Smurfit's CELTIC LORE (R. Dunwoody) – Albatross Maiden Hurdle £4,110

1996 J.D. Gunther's PRO TRADER (M.J. Kinane) – McDonogh Handicap £18,550

1996 Sheikh Mohammed's PECHORA (M.J. Kinane) – McDonogh Fertilizer 3yo Maiden £4,110

1996 Mrs Gaynor Watt's TRADE DISPUTE (M.J. Kinane) – McDonogh Timber Handicap £4,110

1996 Michael Watt's GATES (P. Shanahan) – Digital Services 3yo Maiden £4,110

1996 Moyglare Stud's STYLISH ALLURE (M.J. Kinane) – Guinness 3yo Handicap £4,110

1996 Jeremiah J. King's ZANKLE (M.J. Kinane) – Harp Lager Handicap £4,110

1997 Frank Stronach's WESTERN CHIEF (M.J. Kinane) – GPT Van & Trucks Handicap £4,110

1997 Moyglare Stud's SCREEN IDOL (M.J. Kinane) – McDonogh Feeds 2yo Maiden £5,480

1997 M.W.J. Smurfit's MUSICAL MAYHEM (Mr Edgar Byrne) – Digital Software Maiden £4,795

1997 Mount Juliet Club's SMILING BRAVE (M.J. Kinane) – Harp Lager Handicap £4,110

1998 Kak Yiu's SOCIAL GRACES (M.J. Kinane) – GPT Cork 3yo Handicap £4,125

1998 Moyglare Stud's FREE TO SPEAK (M.J. Kinane) – McDonogh Handicap £30,500

1998 M.W.J. Smurfit's MUSICAL MAYHEM (M.J. Kinane) – McDonogh Timber Handicap £5,550

1998 Anthony McManus's GOLD CHASER (P.J. Smullen) – Compaq Services Maiden £5,500

1998 Michael Watt's FRANCIS BAY (Mr Edgar Byrne) – Software Services Maiden £4,812

1998 Moyglare Stud's DUAL STAR (P.J. Smullen) – Business Support Maiden £4,125

1998 M.W.J. Smurfit's MUSICAL MAYHEM (R. Dunwoody) – Harp Lager Hurdle £4,125

1998 John G. Davis's ALEXIS (M.J. Kinane) – Carlsberg 2yo Race £4,125

1998 Anthony McManus's SUPPORT ACT (M.J. Kinane) – Arthur's Race £4,125

1998 M.W.J. Smurfit's TREBLE BOB (A. Maguire) – Galway Blazers Handicap Chase £5,500

1999 Kenneth L. Ramsey's UMPQUA EAGLE (P.J. Smullen) – GPT Cork 3yo Handicap £4,297

1999 Robert Sinclair's STAGE AFFAIR (D.T. Evans) – Albatross Maiden Hurdle £4,469

1999 M. Magowan's FRANCIS BAY (A.P. McCoy) – Compaq Alpha Hurdle £4,812

1999 Moyglare Stud's GRAND AMBITION (P.J. Smullen) – Compaq Services Maiden £4,469

1999 Moyglare Stud's SOUTH OF HEAVEN (P.J. Smullen) – Guinness 3yo Maiden £6,187

1999 Satish K. Sanan's PROSPECTOR JOHN (P.J. Smullen) – Smithwicks 3yo Maiden £4,469

1999 Moyglare Stud's SHARP FOCUS (P.J. Smullen) – Dawn 2yo Maiden £6,531

1999 S. Creaven's SOCIAL HARMONY (P.J. Smullen) – Eircell Handicap £19,425

2000 Michael Watt's ANSAR (N. Williamson) – Albatross Maiden Hurdle £5,520

2000 Oliver Murphy's CROWN CAPERS (P.J. Smullen) – McDonogh Feeds 2yo Maiden £8,280

2000 Henri Mastey's SAGE DANCER (Mr K.R. O'Ryan) – Compaq Ipaq Maiden £5,865

2000 Moyglare Stud's STEP WITH STYLE (P. Shanahan) – Compaq Non Stop Maiden £5,520

2000 Mrs Linda Tate's INITIAL FIGURE (P. Shanahan) – Compaq Storage 3yo Handicap £5,520

2000 Moyglare Stud's ROMANTIC VENTURE (P. Shanahan) – Guinness 2yo Maiden £8,510

2000 M. Magowen's FRANCIS BAY (P. Carberry) – Tony O'Malley Handicap Chase £10,700

2000 Michael Watt's ANSAR (P.J. Smullen) – Guinness Extra Cold Race £5,865

2000 Kenneth L. Ramsey's WORLDLY TREASURE (P.J. Smullen) – WAP 3yo Race £9,750

2001 Mrs K. Devlin's ANSAR (B.J. Geraghty) – GPT Dublin Handicap Hurdle £9,750

2001 Moyglare Stud's SIGHTS ON GOLD (P.J. Smullen) – GPT Access 2yo Maiden £11,050

2001 Bertram R. Firestone's SARANAL LAKE (P.J. Smullen) – McDonogh Feeds 2yo Maiden £11,050

2001 Moyglare Stud's WHISPER LIGHT (P.J. Smullen) – McDonogh Interiors 3yo Maiden £8,280

2001 M.W.J. Smurfit's ONE MORE ROUND (P.J. Smullen) – Compaq Software Maiden £7,590

2001 Mrs K. Devlin's ANSAR (P. Carberry) – Galway Hurdle Handicap £66,875

2001 M.W.J. Smurfit's CELTIC LORE (P.J. Smullen) – Smithwicks Handicap £8,625

2001 Hamden Al Maktoum's RAHN (P.J. Smullen) – Dawn 2yo Maiden £11,050

2001 Michael Watt's GOLD CHASER (G.D. Power) – Eircell Handicap £35,750

2001 Michael Hilary Burke's KILCREA SHYAN (Mr K.R. O'Ryan) – Vodafone Bumper £7,590

2002 M.W.J. Smurfit's MUTAKARRIM (B.J. Geraghty) – Albatross Feeds Maiden Hurdle €8,970

2002 Kenneth L. Ramsey's PARTY AIRS (P.J. Smullen) – H.P. Services Maiden €10,005

2002 Mrs K. Devlin's ANSAR (P. Carberry) – Guinness Novice Chase €13,000

2003 Mrs Rochelle Quinn's GREY SWALLOW (P.J. Smullen) – GPT Access 2yo Maiden €13,455

2003 M.W.J. Smurfit's DIRECT BEARING (P. Carberry) – H.P. Services Hurdle €12,420

2003 Hamden Al Maktoum's MANDHOOR (P.J. Smullen) – H.P. Imaging Maiden €10,695

2003 Moyglare Stud's STEEL LIGHT (P.J. Smullen) – Irish Stallion Farms Nursery €32,500

2004 Dr R. Lambe's ZEROBERTO (J. Culloty) – GPT Sligo Novice Hurdle €12,438

2004 Mrs K. Devlin's ANSAR (D.J. Casey) – Galway Plate Handicap Chase €103,725

2004 Moyglare Stud's RICH SENSE (P.J. Smullen) – H.P. Ireland Handicap €13,129

2004 J. Higgins's ORPINGTON (Mr N.P. Madden) – H.P. Software Maiden €13,129

2004 Moyglare Stud's SPIRIT OF AGE (P.J. Smullen) – H.P. Indigo Maiden €12,783

2004 Robert Sinclair's STAGE AFFAIR (D.J. Casey) – Tony O'Malley Handicap Chase €24,161

2005 Tamem Michael's KINGER ROCKS (R. Walsh) – GPT Sligo Novice Hurdle €12,438

2005 Mrs D.K. Weld's DASHER REILLY (Miss N. Carberry) – GPT Waterford Bumper €8,292

2005 Mrs K. Devlin's ANSAR (D.F. O'Regan) – Galway Plate Handicap Chase €121,800

2005 Geoffrey Bishop's NAVAJO CHIEFTAIN (Miss N. Carberry) – H.P. Software Maiden €10,365

2005 Moyglare Stud's SOCIETY HOSTESS (P.J. Smullen) – Guinness Handicap €19,530

2005 Moyglare Stud's CLEARING THE WATER (P.J. Smullen) – The 1759 3yo Maiden €13,020

2005 Dr M.W.J. Smurfit's STOLEN LIGHT (Miss N. Carberry) – Kerry Maid Bumper €9,674

2005 Hamden Al Maktoum's MOTAFARRED (P.J. Smullen) – Mercer Hotel Race €16,275

2006 Dr M.W.J. Smurfit's SUMMER SOUL (R. Walsh) – GPT Sligo Novice Hurdle €17,577

2006 Dr R. Lambe's ZEROBERTO (R. Walsh) – GPT Dublin Handicap Hurdle €13,020

2006 Dr R. Lambe's FLEETING SHADOW (P.J. Smullen) – GPT Access 2yo Maiden €13,020

2006 K. Abdullah's SUPPOSITION (P.J. Smullen) – Tote Exacta Maiden €13,020

2006 Hamdan Al Maktoum's TAJNEED (P.J. Smullen) – William Hill Maiden €12,092

2006 Dr R. Lambe's BLUE CORAL (P.J. Smullen) – Dawn Juice 2yo Maiden €13,020

2006 Kilboy Estate's BLING IT ON (P.J. Smullen) – Mercer Hotel Maiden €13,020

2007 Dr Michael Smurfit's LOYAL FOCUS (Mr M.M. O'Connor) – GPT Galway QR Handicap €65,500

2007 Dr R. Lambe's CAMPFIRE GLOW (P.J. Smullen) – Tote 2yo Fillies Maiden €13,020

2007 Dr R. Lambe's PRINCELY HERO (P.J. Smullen) – William Hill Maiden €12,092½

2007 Moyglare Stud's IN A RUSH (P.J. Smullen) – Guinness & Oysters Handicap €19,530

2007 Moyglare Stud's UNWRITTEN RULE (P.J. Smullen) – Dawn Juice 2yo Maiden €13,020

2007 Moyglare Stud's INSTANT SPARKLE (P.J. Smullen) – Mercer Hotel Fillies Maiden €13,020

Dermot Weld did for the Galway races what Vincent O'Brien did for Cheltenham; he greatly enhanced its prestige by running a higher class of horse there. His eagerness to win races there became infectious, and soon every owner and trainer in Ireland wanted a winner there, and the racing became more and more competitive on the flat as well as over jumps. The winning formula of good horses and competitive racing brought racegoers flocking to Galway; the betting market was strong and few owners could resist the special thrill of trying to win a race there, cheered on by all their friends and neighbours.

Charlie Weld, Dermot's father, trained the last of his ten Galway festival winners when Master Albert, with J.V. Smith up, won the Athenry Two-Year-Old Stakes in 1971. At the end of that season he handed the stable over to Dermot, who emulated his father by winning that same race in 1972 with Klairvimy, also ridden by J.V. Smith, to record his first Galway winner as a trainer. He may not be the most popular trainer in Ireland but he is certainly one of the best. He pioneered the sending of horses to obscure places to win big races on all four continents, and has been an outstanding ambassador for Ireland and Irish racing.

Tall, patrician and erudite, he was the youngest vet in the world when he qualified in 1971 and the youngest trainer in Ireland when he took control of his father's stable the following year. Most of the races he has won around the world were big ones in those particular places but irrelevant in terms of international

Dermot K. Weld, leading trainer at the Galway Festival on twenty-three occasions

racing, which is dominated by the United States, Ireland, Britain and France. However, in 1990 he sent Go and Go, winner at Galway the previous year, over to New York to contest the Belmont Stakes, one of the most important races in the world and a leg of the celebrated American Triple Crown. In my opinion that was his greatest feat of training, but others may point to his two Melbourne Cup wins, a handicap but the most important and sought-after prize in Australia, with Vintage Crop and Media Puzzle.

On his student travels Dermot had spent enough time in Australia to become acquainted with Banjo Patterson, Australia's Robert Service-type poet. At a press conference after his 1993 Melbourne Cup victory with Vintage Crop, Dermot recited 'The Man from Snowy River' to the impressed surprise of the Australian journalists. Every press conference has its cynic, and this was no exception. One journalist, suspecting that Dermot had learned the piece off especially for the occasion, challenged him to recite 'A Birth in the Outback', and was comprehensively floored when he did just that!

His father, Charlie Weld, grafted a living as a trainer in the 'hard times', when there was little money in Ireland. In those days a trainer's life was a constant battle with the weather and money, perhaps the hardest job in the world. Charlie did well enough out of training to be able to afford a decent education for his son. He turned out plenty of winners but comparatively few important ones – the best being Decies, the subsequent winner of the Irish 2,000 Guineas, which he trained at two years, and the Royal Ascot winner Wily Trout. In his career he trained ten winners at the Galway Festival, including big races with Highfield Lad (Plate), Ticonderoga (Amateur Handicap and the Hurdle) and Ballyflame (Amateur Handicap).

Predominantly a flat race trainer, Dermot Weld has nonetheless always kept a few jumpers; his record over jumps is phenomenal considering the small number of National Hunt horses in his stable: Allen's Mistake (Champion Four-Year-Old Hurdle), Archive Footage (Pierse Hurdle), Fortune and Fame (Irish Champion Hurdle), General Idea (Ericsson Chase and Power Gold Cup), Perris Valley (Irish Grand National), Pillar Brae (Heineken Gold Cup), Rare Holiday (Triumph Hurdle) and Treble Bob (Kerry National). In addition there are his four wins in the Galway Plate and three in the Galway Hurdle.

Since he began training in 1972, he has won 192 races at the Galway Festival meeting, has been leading trainer at the meeting no less than twenty-three times and on four occasions sent out ten winners at the meeting. Only once, in 1980, has he drawn a blank at the Festival during the thirty-five years of his training career. The leading trainer at the Festival for the first time in 1975, he ran up a sequence of nine in a row between 1988 and 1996. In 1986 he swept past Harry Ussher's record fifty-four winners at Galway – a record that had taken thirty-eight two-day meetings to accumulate. It was more than fitting that he saddled the 3,000th winner of his career at Galway, when Clearing the Water won at the Festival in 2005.

Edward O'Grady (b. 1949)

Trainer, Killeens, Ballynonty, Co. Tipperary:

1975 N. Griffin's BILLY DRUMMER (Mr T.A. Jones) – Lough Atalia Bumper £553

1978 A.G. Moylan's GLASSILAUN (T.J. Ryan) – Castlegar Maiden Hurdle £830

1978 J.P. McManus's SHINING FLAME (Mr N. Madden) – Galway Plate Handicap Chase £5,230

1979 D.L. O'Byrne's LARRY FAHY (Mr F. Codd) – Lough Atalia Bumper £692

1979 Mrs David Louthan's HINDHOPE (J.J. O'Neill) – Galway Plate Handicap Chase £14,572

1979 P. O'Sullivan's DON MOBILE (Mr F. Codd) – Galway Blazers Handicap Chase £1,035

1979 W.K. Hosford's HARD TARQUIN (J.J. O'Neill) – Galway Hurdle Handicap £10,559

1980 Mrs P. Quinn's GAY RETURN (Mr F. Codd) – Dangan Handicap Hurdle £828

1981 D.M. Brown's ISTIMEWA (Mr D.M. Brown) – Lough Atalia Bumper £830

1981 Jeremiah Dunne's RUGGED LUCY (T.J. Ryan) – Galway Plate Handicap Chase £15,286

1987 Mrs Anneke Thompson's GAELIC SONG (S. Craine) – Kilcolgan Handicap £1,382

1988 John G. O'Neill's CAPTAIN ANDY (T.J. Ryan) – Bohermore Maiden Hurdle £2,220

1990 J.P. McManus's ANY GOSSIP (T. Carmody) – GPT Maiden Hurdle £2,762

1990 John Horgan's DON LEONE (K.F. O'Brien) – Bohermore Maiden Hurdle £2,760

1991 J.M. O'Malley's EMPEROR GLEN (N.G. McCullagh) - GPT Handicap £3,797

1992 John C. Fitzgerald's JODI'S MONEY (N. Williamson) – Oranmore Handicap Hurdle £8,925

1994 Robert Butler's RUDI'S PRIDE (W.J. Smith) – Guinness Handicap £4,110

1995 Dr Jerome Torsney's LENNI LENAPE (J.P. Murtagh) – Guinness Handicap £4,110

1995 Cathal McCarthy's I AM (R. Dunwoody) – Dawn Milk Handicap Hurdle £9,675

1998 J.S. Gutkin's DANCE SO SUITE (N. Williamson) – Alpha Systems Hurdle £4,125

1999 J.P. McManus's GO ROGER GO (N. Williamson) – Guinness Novice Chase £6,875

2001 Edward Wallace's BEST GREY (N. Williamson) – Compaq Handicap Hurdle £8,970

2001 Wild Colonial Boy Syndicate's JACK DUGGAN (N. Williamson) - Eircell Maiden Hurdle £7,935

2002 Mrs Patricia Wallace's VATIRISK (B.J. Geraghty) – Dawn Milk Handicap Hurdle €32,500

2003 W.M. Roche's GOLDEN ROW (N. Williamson) – Carlsberg Novice Chase €19,500

2005 J.P. O'Shea's KENTUCKY CHARM (Mr K.E. Power) – Amateur Handicap €49,225

2005 J.P. McManus's MONJOYAU (A.P. McCoy) – Guinness Novice Chase €16,275

2005 J.P. O'Shea's KENTUCKY CHARM (B.J. Geraghty) –Dawn Milk Handicap Hurdle €27,667

Edward O'Grady took over the training stable at Killeens, Ballynonty, about 7 miles from Thurles, when his father died in January 1972. His father had been a top jump jockey, was Irish Champion Jockey on two occasions and ran a small but successful stable for many years, and his son rode winners as an amateur rider.

Thrown in at the deep end, Edward got off to a flying start, training his first winner when Vibrax, ridden by Timmy Hyde, won a handicap hurdle at Gowran Park on 27 January 1972, the race after Dim Wit won the Thyestes Chase. After that the winners began to flow. Hardishah, ridden by Michael 'Mouse' Morris, won a Fairyhouse bumper and a month after training his first winner Edward had a double at Gowran Park, with Happy Abbot and Esplanade. Then things became difficult, a virus hit the yard, all eighteen of his horses in training became sick, and many owners deserted him, but he survived and came back even stronger.

In 1974 he trained his first winner at the Cheltenham Festival when Mr Midland won the National Hunt Chase. However, in August of that year there was a big betting coup on a horse named Gay Future, trained in Scotland by Tony Collins. It was pulled off by backing Gay Future in a treble, with two other horses trained by Collins, and placing the bet in as many betting shops as possible. When Gay Future won at Cartmel at odds of 10 to 1, the other two horses were mysteriously withdrawn from their races and the treble bet became a single. The bookies cried foul, refused to pay and called Scotland Yard in to investigate. The police enquiries culminated in the dramatic arrest of Edward O'Grady, John Horgan, Brian Darrer and Tony Murphy at the Cheltenham races in 1975. They were charged with conspiracy to defraud the bookmakers. The charges against Edward O'Grady, John Horgan and Brian Darrer were subsequently dropped but Tony Murphy was later found guilty of the charge. Edward O'Grady's involvement was that he purchased Gay Future on behalf of Tony Collins and trained it for him secretly at Ballynonty. Not wishing it to be known that a young, up-and-coming professional Irish trainer had the horse, a Gay Future lookalike was sent over to Tony Collins, with Collins only being given the real Gay Future on the day of the race.

With the Gay Future uproar behind him, O'Grady became established as the leading National Hunt trainer in Ireland, with Golden Cygnet the stable star. Owned by Ray Rooney, Golden Cygnet won the Waterford Crystal Supreme Novice Hurdle at Cheltenham in 1978 by seventeen lengths, only to die following a fall in the Scottish Champion Hurdle the following month. Further tragedy was to hit the stable later that year when J.P. McManus's Shining Flame, bred by Nicky Rackard, winner of the Galway Plate, broke a leg at Tramore barely a fortnight after his big Galway success.

Leading trainer in the overall list in 1979, Edward O'Grady won three Galway

Plates in four years, with Shining Flame (1978), Hindhope (1979) and Rugged Lucy (1981). When he won the Galway Hurdle with Hard Tarquin (1979), he became only the fifth trainer to win both big races in the same year. Reggie Walker (1916), Cecil Brabazon (1925), Barney Nugent (1947) and Paddy Sleator (1957) all accomplished before him a feat that has not been done since. In 1983 he won the Whitbread Gold Cup with Drumlargan, and Bit of a Skite won the National Hunt Chase at Cheltenham and the Irish Grand National, with Northern Game winning the Triumph Hurdle the following year. However, Edward was starting to move into the flat and the jumpers had to make way.

In retrospect his decision to become a flat trainer was disastrous; he failed to make the transition and was forced back into jump racing. It was not that he was no good as a trainer on the flat – he has the particular honour of training a flat winner for the President of Ireland no less, turning out Dr Paddy Hilliary's Ballyvaskin (S. Craine) to win at Fairyhouse on 6 June 1987. But flat racing is a different game nowadays, with different owners, different punters and different racegoers, and not being on the Curragh was a distinct disadvantage. Having made the decision to go back to training jumpers, O'Grady had to start all over again, to find new owners and get his yard filled. Unfortunately for him, few people now remember his glory days; a young, suddenly-rich set have rushed into racehorse ownership on the back of the Celtic Tiger and to them a Golden Cygnet is a type of swan.

Jonjo O'Neill (b. 1952)

Rider:

1979 Mrs David Louthan's HINDHOPE – Galway Plate (E.J. O'Grady)

1979 W.K. Hosford's HARD TARQUIN – Galway Hurdle Handicap (E.J. O'Grady)

1982 Brendan Carolan's PINCH HITTER – Galway Hurdle Handicap (N. Meade)

1983 Brendan Carolan's PINCH HITTER – Galway Hurdle Handicap (N. Meade)

Jonjo O'Neill, from Co. Cork, started with Don Reid at Mallow before being apprenticed to Michael Connolly at Westenra. He rode his first winner when Lana, trained by Connolly, dead-heated with Cecil Ronaldson's Tomboy II, ridden by the ill-fated Michael Teelin, in an apprentice flat race at the Curragh in September 1970. Too heavy for flat racing, he joined Gordon W. Richards, who trained in north-western England, in 1972. He went on to ride over a hundred winners in a season three times and was twice the Champion National Hunt Jockey. Brimming with enthusiasm, despite having suffered a number of horrific injuries, he rode Sea

Pigeon to victory in the Champion Hurdle and the Ebor Handicap, Alverton in the Cheltenham Gold Cup, Ekbalco in the Welsh Champion Hurdle and Dawn Run in the Champion Hurdle and Cheltenham Gold Cup. He retired in 1986, fought a successful battle against cancer and is now training for John P. McManus at Jackdaw's Castle.

Gillian O'Brien (b. 1954)

Trainer, Kilsheelan, Co. Tipperary:
1982 Mrs M. Valentine's ASKAMORE (N. Madden) – Ardrahan Handicap Chase £2,072

Although women have been permitted to hold a trainer's licence since 1965 it was not until 1982 that a woman trainer won a race at the Galway festival. That honour went to Gillian O'Brien, granddaughter of Dan O'Brien, whose charge Askamore won the Ardrahan Handicap Chase with Niall Madden in the saddle. She had recently taken over the Co. Tipperary stable from her father, Phonsie, who had been the trainer of Askamore when it won the Claddagh Chase at the meeting two years earlier, also ridden by Madden, who was then still riding as an amateur. Niall Madden, nicknamed 'Boots', is now training and his promising jockey son, also named Niall but known to all and sundry as 'Slippers', won the 2006 Aintree Grand National on Numbersixvalverde.

Gillian won the Irish Cesarewitch twice with Five Nations, in 1982 and 1983. After a couple of years she moved her stable to Navan, at Painstown, Castletown, later winning the 1988 Power Gold Cup at Fairyhouse with Haepenny Well, ridden by Tommy Carmody. After becoming involved with Noel Meade, she decided to surrender her own licence.

David V. O'Brien (b. 1956)

Trainer, Rahinaghmore Cashel:
1983 R.E. Sangster's GOTAMA (C. Roche) – Renmore 3yo Maiden £1,106
1984 R.E. Sangster's COUVREUR (C. Roche) – Renmore 3yo Maiden £1,106

Vincent O'Brien's two sons, David and Charles, both followed in their famous father's footsteps, becoming trainers, although David's career was as brief as it was brilliant. An extremely talented trainer, apparently he could not handle the pressure and gave up after only seven years. Born in 1956, he began training in 1981, based at Rahinaghmore, Cashel, and trained completely independently of his father. D.V. O'Brien won the Railway Stakes in his first season with a horse called Anfield, owned by Jean Pierre Binet, and his runners brought a breath of fresh air to Irish racing, making flat racing infinitely more competitive. In 1982 he won the French and Irish Derbys with Assert, and two years later Secreto short-headed his father's El Gran Señor in a sensational Epsom Derby, after which a distressed and unbelieving Pat Eddery lodged an unsuccessful objection. Triptych and Authaal won Irish Classic races for him, the latter being the only classic winner to come from Shergar's single crop of foals. The young trainer did not ignore Galway, winning the Renmore Three-Year-Old Maiden two years in succession with Gotama and Couvreur, both ridden by his stable jockey, Christy Roche.

After 1986 racegoers began to notice that David O'Brien appeared to be training very few horses and then came the announcement in 1988 that he was giving up the business. He made a big contribution to Irish flat racing and now runs a vineyard in France.

Charles O'Brien is currently training at Straffan, Co. Kildare. He very nearly won the 1997 Irish Derby when Dr Johnson hit the front with 2 furlongs to race only to be collared by Desert King, a supposed non-stayer trained by Aidan O'Brien.

Thomas V. O'Brien (1923–85)

Trainer, Mountpargue, Grange, Athenry:
1976 T.V. O'Brien's COADY VI (P. Kiely) – Galway Blazers Handicap Chase £552
1978 T.V. O'Brien's JOSIE VI (P. Kiely) – Claddagh Chase £692
1981 T.V. O'Brien's DUALMOUNT (P. Kiely) – Kinvara Handicap Hurdle £830
1984 E.J. Scully's PENDOR LAWN (P.F. Kelly) – Ardrahan Handicap Chase £2,072

Thomas Valentine O'Brien trained at Mountpargue, Grange, Athenry, until his sudden death, which occurred in the stable yard at Roscommon in June 1985, at the age of sixty-two. He never had a large string of horses, nor had he fashionable owners, but he was never afraid to take on the 'big boys' of racing at his local meeting.

Stephen Craine (b. 1957)

Rider:

1976 D.W. Lufkin's VENTURE TO VICTORY – Barna Handicap 2m flat (M. Vance)

1976 J.B. Wilcox's LYLAH – Oranmore Handicap flat (M. Cunningham)

1977 R.E. Johnson's SCENERY – Barna Handicap flat (M. Neville)

1977 Mrs C. Magnier's ON YOU GO – Unidare Apprentice Handicap flat (C. Magnier)

1980 B. McGuckian's WHISPER GENTLY – Sean Graham Handicap flat (N. Meade)

1980 Denis F. Howard's LADY TIFFANY – Claregalway Nursery (N. Meade)

1980 Mrs R.A. Keogh's NATIONAL IMAGE – Stewards' Handicap flat (N. Meade)

1981 B. Carolan's PINCH HITTER – McDonogh Handicap flat (N. Meade)

1981 Michael Garrigan's ALWAYS SMILING – Barna Handicap flat (D.T. Hughes)

1981 N. Kavanagh's STEEL DUKE – Ashford Castle Handicap flat (N. Meade)

1982 B. Carolan's PINCH HITTER – McDonogh Handicap flat (N. Meade)

1982 P.G. Carroll's WELSHWOOD – Sean Graham Handicap flat (N. Meade)

1982 N. Kavanagh's STEEL DUKE – Mervue Race flat (N. Meade)

1982 P.G. Carroll's WELSHWOOD – Stewards' Handicap flat (N. Meade)

1982 N. Kavanagh's STEEL DUKE – Nilands Handicap flat (N. Meade)

1983 Richard McCarthy's ACTION GIRL – Claregalway 2yo Maiden (N. Meade)

1983 Michael Magill's RED REALM – Briar Hill Handicap flat (N. Meade)

1983 Mrs E.M. Burke's SAINT CYNTHIA – Menlo Race flat (N. Meade)

1984 David A. Pim's STERN SATURN – Bushy Park Handicap flat (P. Mullins)

1984 T. Harty's PAMPERED RUN – Menlo Race flat (P. Hughes)

1985 Mrs Christine O'Reilly's ROMMEL'S CHOICE – Tuam 2yo Race (L. Browne)

1985 Morgan Sheehy's SUPER MOVE – Parkmore Maiden flat (L. Browne)

1986 Mrs A. Forte's FLYING BARROW – Kilcolgan Handicap flat (W.M Durkan)

1986 J.M. Cusack's HAZY BIRD – Fairhill Handicap flat (P. Mullins)

1987 Mrs P.J. Carr's DROMOD HILL – McDonogh Handicap flat (N. Meade)

1987 Mrs Anneke Thompson's GAELIC SON – Kilcolgan Handicap flat (E.J. O'Grady)

1987 John P. Moore's WELSH FLYER – Renmore Maiden flat (N. Meade)

1987 Seamus McGrath's JATAAT – Tuam 2yo flat (B.V. Kelly)

1987 Ms C. Gannon's WESTERN WOLF – County Nursery (N. Meade)

1987 Fernando Jaconelli's CIAMPINO – Oranmore Handicap flat (N. Meade)

1988 Patrick White's STRING QUARTET – Tuam 2yo Race (N. Meade)

1989 Blackwater Racing's SWEET CHARMER – Digital Decnet Handicap flat (P.J. Flynn)

1989 Mrs T. Stack's MOLDAVIA – Musgrave Maiden flat (T. Stack)

1989 John P. Moore's FISH MERCHANT – Musgrave Handicap flat (N. Meade)

1989 Mrs M. O'Callaghan's SANDHURST GODDESS – Salthill Maiden flat (N. O'Callaghan)

1989 Albert M. Stall's SIMPLY TERRIFIC – County Nursery (T. Stack)

1990 M.J. Corbett's NATIVE HIGH-LINE – Guinness Handicap flat (M.J. Corbett)

1990 John P. O'Neill's BARNEY BUCHLYVIE – O'Malley Brothers Race flat (T. Stack)

1991 Mrs Rita Polly's LEAR FANTASTIQUE – Smithwicks Handicap flat (N. Meade)

1992 Yoshiki Akazawa's FOREST CONCERT – GPT Maiden flat (P. Prendergast)

1993 E.A. MacRedmond's FONTANAYS – GPT Handicap flat (B.V. Kelly)

1993 Mrs M. Cahill's MEJEVE – Digital Maiden flat (B.V. Kelly)

1995   B. Cunningham's WRAY – SMS Ireland Maiden flat (L. Browne)

1996 Mrs A. McAteer's WESPERADA – Kerry Spring Handicap flat (N. Meade)

1997 B. Cunningham's WRAY – McDonogh Handicap flat (L. Browne)

2000 A.D. Brennan's MONTY WOLLEY – Dawn 2yo Maiden (K. Prendergast)

2000 Hamdan Al Maktoum's SOORAH – Eircell Handicap flat (K. Prendergast)

Born in the Isle of Man, Craine was on the look-out for an introduction to a racing stable when he met an owner who had a horse with Liam Browne, the Curragh trainer. The owner had a word with Browne and Craine joined the stable in 1973. He was fortunate indeed because Liam Browne was a good trainer of horses but a better trainer of young jockeys and the young Manxman got a thorough grounding from his master.

He rode his first winner in 1976, with Carlow Rose at Dundalk, and his career immediately took off. In 1977, barely a year after riding his first winner, he had the honour of riding a winner for Robert Sangster at the new Manx racecourse, rode his first English winner, at Warwick, and ended the season as the Champion Irish Apprentice. Liam Browne's apprentices dominated that championship, holding the title seven years in succession: Tommy Carmody (1973–6), Stephen Craine (1977), Michael Kinane (1978), Pat Gilson (1979) and Mark Dwyer (1981) – a sequence only interrupted in 1980 by Dermot Weld's boy, Joe Deegan. The last of Stephen's forty-four Galway Festival winners came in 2000. Serious weight problems forced his retirement from the saddle in 2001 and he now holds a senior position in Kevin Prendergast's stable.

Michael 'Ironside' O'Brien (b. 1943)

Trainer, Rathbridge Manor, Curragh:

1981 R. Bomze's SPORTS REPORTER (G. Newman) – Claddagh Chase £1,382

1995 Miss G. Maher's MOUNTAIN BLOOM (T.P. Rudd) – Albatross Chase £5,512

Trainer, Beechcourt House, Naas, Co. Kildare:

1996 D.P. Sharkey's TAKLIF (E. Ahern) – Guinness Handicap £6,850

1999 J.W. Nawe's GREENHUE (T.P. Rudd) – Tony O'Malley Handicap Chase £9,712

2000 S. Mulryan's DOVALY (T.P. Rudd) – Galway Plate £61,250

2003 Newlands Syndicate's HIGH PRIESTESS (P.J. Smullen) – HP Maiden €11,040

2003 S. Mulryan's BANASAN (R. Walsh) – Guinness Beginners' Chase €13,000

2004 Dasun de Faoite's INDEMNITY (T.G.M. Ryan) – HP Hurdle €17,617

2004 S. Mulryan's SWORDPLAY (R. Walsh) – Budweiser Novice Chase €19,530

2004 Ardbraccan Syndicate's HIGH PRIESTESS (R.P. Cleary) – Guinness Handicap €45,507

2005 Mary Furlong's YOUNG ELODIE (T.G.M. Ryan) – HP Handicap Hurdle €17,577

Michael J.P. O'Brien and his brother Leo followed their father into Thomas J. Taaffe's stable at Rathcoole, Co. Dublin. Although both held jockeys' licences, they found it difficult to get rides. Leo decided to try his luck in America and Michael followed him. They got going in America, with Michael becoming one of the country's leading jump jockeys until his luck and his life changed abruptly. Seriously injured in a horrible fall, he was paralysed at the peak of his career and confined to a wheelchair for the rest of his life. Bravely facing the future, he returned to Ireland to pursue a training career, settling at Rathbride Manor, Curragh, with the support of several American owners, such as George Strawbridge Junior, and Rusty and Joy Carrier

Dubbed 'Ironside' after the television detective character confined to a wheelchair, it did not take Michael O'Brien long to make a mark in his new career. Bright Highway won the Mackeson and Hennessy Gold Cups, two of the biggest early-winter steeplechases in England, in 1980, Rusty Carrier's King Spruce was successful in the 1982 Irish Grand National and Sean Ogue won the Power Gold Cup at Fairyhouse the following day. In 1985 Michael O'Brien decided to return to America for personal reasons but it did not work out as he expected. Three years later he was back in Ireland trying to resurrect his training career at Beechcourt, Naas, Co. Kildare.

It took a bit of time for his training career to get going again; the first sign of a change in fortune was when his brother Leo, now a successful trainer in America, launched a historic and successful tilt at the Irish 2,000 Guineas in 1991 with Fourstars Allstar. A useful racer in America, Fourstars Allstar found suitable opportunities over a mile limited, which decided Leo to send the horse to the Curragh. The horse was an unlikely classic winner because its sire, Compliance, albeit an own-brother to Try My Best and El Gran Señor, failed to win a race of any kind. Beaten by a neck in a maiden race at the Phoenix Park by Millrock, trained by David O'Brien, Compliance was made favourite to win the Ballycorus Stakes at Leopardstown but could only finish a poor third to Tellurano.

Michael O'Brien's career came good again the following year when Vanton won the Irish Grand National, but once again the ups and downs of racing hit the stable. On his next outing, at the Punchestown meeting, Vanton fell, injuring his tendon and was out of racing for a year. Having been nursed back to fitness, he suffered another heavy fall, this time at Navan, where he broke a femur in December 1993. Although it was reported that he had been killed, Vanton survived to make a brief and fruitless comeback two years later, but he never won or was placed again. However, champion four-year-old hurdlers Shawiya and Shaihar kept the yard in the headlines during the mid-1990s, and in 1999 Glebe Lad was another Michael O'Brien-trained winner of the Irish Grand National.

Galway had not been a happy hunting ground for the stable. 'Ironside's' only winner at the Festival while at Rathbride was Sports Reporter, winner of the Claddagh Chase and third in the Galway Plate in 1981. He had to wait fifteen years for his second, when Mountain Bloom, ridden by Tom Rudd, won the Albatross Steeplechase. However, since Greehue's victory in 1999, the Galway winners have begun to flow. Sean Mulryan's Dovaly won the Plate in 2000 and finished third, beaten by two and a half lengths, to Grimes and Quinze the following year, Tom Rudd riding on both occasions. Indeed, the 2001 Galway Plate was unusual for an Irish steeplechase in that the first three home were all foaled in England. Since then High Priestess, Banasan, Indemnity, Swordplay and Young Elodie have been successful for the stable at Galway.

Francis M. O'Brien (1938–95)

Trainer, Piltown, Co. Kilkenny:
1983 J.P. Smyth's WOODNER (A.J. O'Brien) – Rosshill Chase £1,725

Francis M. O'Brien, of Gortrush, Piltown, Co. Kilkenny, trained for twenty-two years until his death in July 1995, aged only fifty-seven. His widow, Marie, continued the stable until her son David M. O'Brien was able to apply for a licence. Frank O'Brien's four sons became jockeys. Anthony J. and Kevin F. rode as professionals and John P. and David M. were amateurs.

Anthony J. O'Brien (b. 1961)

Rider:
1983 J.P. Smyth's WOODNER – Rosshill Chase (F.M. O'Brien)
1989 Noel Horgan's CLASSMATE VI – Galway Blazers Handicap Chase (J.E. Kiely)
1993 C.J. McCarthy's MACK A DAY – Guinness Chase (Michael Condon)

A.J. (Tony) O'Brien began his career as a apprentice jockey, attached to his father's stable, and began riding on the flat. However, his first winner came in a jumping race when Sing My Song, trained by his father, won a maiden hurdle in November 1977 at Limerick Junction, since renamed Tipperary. His biggest win on the flat was when winning the Hennessy Handicap on Mississippi, owned and trained by Mrs Brewster, formerly Anne B. Biddle, at Leopardstown in 1978. Tony O'Brien rode his father's only Galway Festival winner, Woodner, in the Rosshill Chase in 1983, but he had wins for other trainers, Classmate VI (Galway Blazers Handicap Chase) and Mack A Day (Guiness Steeplechase) and he was second on the outsider Knocklonogad Alley behind Double Wrapped in the 1981 Galway Hurdle. He retired from the saddle at the turn of the century and now, based near Cahir, Co. Tipperary, breaks horses and prepares them to go to the sales or into training.

Kevin F. O'Brien (b. 1963)

Rider:

1986 D.J. Reddan's WINNING NORA – Oranmore Dairies Handicap Hurdle (M. Hourigan)

1987 Mrs W. Costello's CANON CLASS – McDonogh Chase (E. Bolger)

1988 C. Rice's PARKEYS – Tony O'Malley Handicap Chase (D. O'Connell)

1990 E. Bolger's BUCK ME UP – Albatross Chase (E. Bolger)

1990 D.J. Reddan's DINNYS CORNER – Digital Novice Hurdle (D.J. Reddan)

1990 John Horgan's DON LEONE – Bohermore Maiden Hurdle (E.J. O'Grady)

1993 Mrs H.C. Taylor's TELL A TALE – GPT Maiden Hurdle (M. Hourigan)

1993 M.F. Murray's DANCINGCINDERELLA – Albatross Chase (M. Hourigan)

1994 Mrs J.J. Gordon's PARSONS BRIG – St James's Gate Handicap Hurdle (M. Hourigan)

Trainer, Milltown, Newbridge, Co. Kildare:

2003 PAFG Syndicate's MWALEY (C. O'Donoghue) – Guinness Handicap €18,850

Kevin was the most successful of the jockey O'Brien brothers, riding nine Galway Festival winners between 1986 and 1994, including a treble in 1990. He finished third in the Galway Plate on Winning Nora in 1886, behind Boro Quarter and Bold Agent; the mare reverted to hurdles on the Saturday of the meeting and lifted the Oranmore Handicap Hurdle. Apprenticed initially to Jim Bolger, Kevin rode his first winner when Tengello, trained by his father, won a maiden hurdle at Killarney in July 1980. The year 1994 stands out in his career, which lasted until October 1998, because having won the valuable Ladbroke Handicap Hurdle at

Leopardstown on Atone, owned by Robert Sinclair and trained by Bunny Cox, Kevin and the horse reappeared at the same venue a fortnight later to win the Arkle Chase. Another big winner followed at the Punchestown Festival when he partnered Merry Gale, owned by Herb Stanley and trained by Jim Dreaper, to victory in the Heineken Gold Cup. At the following year's big Punchestown meeting, Kevin rode Shaihar to win the Champion Four-year-old Hurdle for trainer M.J.P. O'Brien. Nowadays Kevin is training at The Swan, Co. Leix, having recently moved from Newbridge, where he had previously trained.

Aidan P. O'Brien (b. 1969)

Rider:

1989 J. Moynihan's MIDSUMMER FUN – Digital QR Maiden (J.S. Bolger)

1989 Mrs J.S. Bolger's BEDFORD RANGER – Bohermore Maiden Hurdle (J.S. Bolger)

1991 Joseph Crowley's SKY RANGE – GPT Sligo Maiden Hurdle (Miss A.M. Crowley)

1993 Thomas Conroy's BANNTOWN BILL – GPT Bumper (A.P. O'Brien)

1994 Seamus O'Farrell's KELLY'S PEARL – Digital Client QR Maiden (A.P. O'Brien)

Trainer, Carriganog, Owning Hill, Piltown, Co. Kilkenny:

1993 Thomas Conroy's BANNTOWN BILL (Mr A.P. O'Brien) – GPT Plant Bumper £3,797

1993 Mrs Anna Foxe's LOSHIAN (J.P. Murtagh) – Digital Decnet Handicap £4,140

1994 Mrs A.M. O'Brien's BOB BARNES (C. Roche) – McDonogh Timber Handicap £4,110

1994 Seamus O'Farrell's KELLY'S PEARL (Mr A.P. O'Brien) – Digital Client Bumper £4,795

1994 Mrs Anna Foxe's LOSHIAN (R. Dunwoody) – Guinness Chase £4,110

1994 Mrs Anna Foxe's BALLYHIRE LAD (R. Dunwoody) – Harp Lager Hurdle £4,110

1994 Mrs J.M. Ryan's PUTTY ROAD (Mr G.F. Ryan) – Kerry Maid Festival Bumper £4,110

1995 Aston Hotel Syndicate's ALLEGAN (C.F. Swan) – GPT Sligo Maiden Hurdle £4,110

1995 C. Munnelly's TEMPLEMARY BOY (C.F. Swan) – GPT Dublin Handicap Hurdle £4,110

1995 M.J. Clancy's LIFE OF A LORD (T. Horgan) – Galway Plate Handicap Chase £31,125

1995 Mrs G. Robinson's MOONBI RANGE (C. Roche) – Trinity Group Handicap £4,110

1995 M.G. Masterson's BALYARA (C. Roche) – Arthur's Race £4,110

1996 J.P. McManus's VICAR STREET (C.F. Swan) – GPT Sligo Maiden Hurdle £4,110

1996 J.P. McManus's LEWISHAM (Mr B.M. Cash) – GPT Contract Bumper £4,110

1996 M.J. Clancy's LIFE OF A LORD (C.F. Swan) – Galway Plate Handicap Chase £31,125

1996 R. Galvin's CLONAGAM (C.F. Swan) – Harp Lager Novice Hurdle £4,110

1996 Mrs Anne Campbell's DISTINCTLY WEST (M.J. Cullen) – Carlsberg 2yo Race £4,110

1996 Mrs John Magnier's MOUNT RUSHMORE (C. Roche) – Dawn 2yo Maiden £5,480

1996 Gaultier Syndicate's GAULTIER GALE (J.A. Heffernan) – E.B.F. Nursery £13,100

Trainer, Ballydoyle, Cashel, Co. Tipperary:

1997   Michael Tabor's GRASS ROOTS (C. Roche) – McDonogh Fertilizers 3yo Maiden £4,110

1997   Mrs A.M. O'Brien's LAFITTE THE PIRATE (C. Roche) – McDonogh Timber Handicap £4,110

1997   Golden Step Syndicate's TOAST THE SPREECE (A.P. McCoy) – Galway Hurdle Handicap £30,725

1997   Mrs John Magnier's CODE OF HONOUR (C. Roche) – Guinness 3yo Handicap £4,110

1997   Goldminers Syndicate's FEMALE LEAD (S.W. Kelly) – Smithwicks Handicap £4,110

1997   Blackwater Syndicate's IDIOTS VENTURE (C.F. Swan)–Tony O'Malley Handicap Chase £5,780

1997   Leonard Barrack's LIGHTNING STAR (C. Roche) – Dawn 2yo Maiden £5,480

1997   Mrs A.M. O'Brien's LAFITTE THE PIRATE (C. Roche) – Kerry Spring Handicap £4,110

1998   Michael Tabor's SUNSPANGLED (C. Roche) – McDonogh Feeds 2yo Maiden £6,187

1998   Chaparral Syndicate's CHAPARRAL LADY (P.J. Scallan) – Software Handicap £5,550

1998   Mrs John Magnier's MEMPARI (C. Roche) – Unix Clusters 3yo Race £5,500

1998   Michael Tabor's MATTIOCCO (C. Roche) – Guinness 3yo Maiden £5,500

1998   Mrs John Magnier's THEATRE WORLD (P.J. Scallan) – Guinness Handicap £13,000

1999   Mrs John Magnier's ARISTOTLE (M.J. Kinane) – GPT Industrial 2yo Maiden £6,531

1999   Mrs John Magnier's THEATRE WORLD (M.J. Kinane) – Guinness Handicap £16,250

1999   Michael Tabor's TWICKENHAM (M.J. Kinane) – Guinness Extra Cold Race £4,812

1999   Mrs John Magnier's KILCASH CASTLE (Mr T.V. Magnier) – Kerrymaid Bumper £4,469

1999   Mrs John Magnier's MOISEYEV (M.J. Kinane) – Up Front 3yo Race £8,250

2000   Michael Tabor's HEMINGWAY (M.J. Kinane) –GPT Industrial 2yo Maiden £8,280

2000   Michael Tabor's ROSTROPOVICH (M.J. Kinane) – Smithwicks 3yo Maiden £5,520

2001   J.P. McManus's DARAPOUR (C.F. Swan) – Compaq Hurdle £8,625

2002   Mrs John Magnier's THE GREAT GATSBY (J.A. Heffernan) – Dawn 2yo Maiden €13,975

2003   Mrs John Magnier's WOLFE TONE (M.J. Kinane) – Dawn 2yo Maiden €13,455

2004   Mrs John Magnier's KING OF SPADES (Mr M.V. Magnier) – GPT Waterford Bumper €8,637

2004   The Sangster Family's STARRYSTARRYNIGHT (J.P. Spencer) – Smirnoff 3yo Maiden €12,438

2004   Mrs John Magnier's SCANDINAVIA (J.P. Spencer) – Dawn 2yo Maiden €14,647

2004   Mrs John Magnier's BRONCO CHARLIE (Mr M.V. Magnier) – Kerrymaid Bumper €10,365

2004   Mrs John Magnier's THE ALAMO (Mr M.V. Magnier) – Tara Towers Bumper €11,747

2006   Mrs John Magnier's BORN FOR GLORY (Mr J.P. Magnier) – William Hill Maiden €10,365

2007   Mrs John Magnier's LUCIFER SAM (K. Fallon) – GPT Access 2yo Maiden €13,020

2007   Mrs John Magnier's THE ETHIOPIAN (Mr J.P. Magnier) – William Hill QR Maiden €10,365

Aidan O'Brien from Co. Wexford was born on 16 October 1969 and joined Jim Bolger's stable as a youth. Kevin Smith, in his Racing Club of Ireland days, was on a club visit to Bolger's yard and during the tour of the yard the trainer introduced a young man, who was not more than sixteen, to the group, 'This is Mr Aidan O'Brien; he will go far,' he said. That young man first made his mark as an amateur rider, becoming the Irish Champion twice, in 1989 and 1993, with twenty and nineteen winners respectively. His marriage to Anne-Marie Crowley changed his life completely. Anne-Marie was a daughter of trainer Joseph Crowley and her sister, Frances, was an up-and-coming rider who later would succeed Aidan as Ireland's Champion Amateur rider in 1994. Anne-Marie had successfully taken over her father's stable on his retirement, but she decided to relinquish her licence in 1993 and turn the yard over to her husband. Her last winner was Choisya, ridden by Joey Donnelly, in a handicap hurdle at Clonmel on 3 June.

It took Aidan only four days to get off the mark, his first winner being Wandering Thoughts, with Pat Gilson up, in the Ballybeggan Racegoers' Club Handicap at Tralee on 7 June 1993. An hour and a half later at Leopardstown, the other Irish meeting that Bank Holiday Monday, he made it a double when Tryarra, ridden by English jockey Kevin Darley, won a 10-furlong handicap. Darley was at Leopardstown to partner Peter Saville's Sea Gazer in its successful raid on the Ballyogan Stakes and Tryarra was the second leg of a 71-to-1 double.

The exploits of Wandering Thoughts during the remainder of 1993 ensured that Aidan O'Brien made an immediate impression on racing. The gelding recorded seven wins, three seconds, two thirds and a fourth in fourteen races on the flat that year. He was second twice at the Galway Festival, beaten by a neck both times, and among the races won by Wandering Thoughts was the Irish National Bookmakers' Association Handicap at Tralee and the Irish Cambridgeshire Handicap at the Curragh.

In 1994, his first full year as a trainer, Aidan won more races than any other trainer, his final total of 176 beating Dermot Weld's 1991 record of 150, and the following year he set a new record of 241 winners, winning over £1 million in stakes and was Champion Irish Trainer for the first time. In 1995 Aidan O'Brien came to the Galway meeting having trained a winner on each of the previous twenty-two Irish racing days. The victory of Allegan in the first race of the Festival was his twenty-third winner of consecutive racing days but the sequence ended on the Tuesday when he drew a blank. However, he set another record the following day by saddling the first three horses home in the Galway Plate, Life of a Lord, Kelly's Pearl and Loshian.

Unbelievably, it took Aidan just over five years to train his thousandth winner in Ireland. This milestone was set when Cupid won at Leopardstown on 24 October 1998, establishing a world record for the fastest thousand winners by a trainer on his home soil. He won his first group race in 1994, when Paddy Burns's Dancing Sunset won the Royal Whip at the Curragh. Snapped up by John Magnier to take over the Ballydoyle stable recently vacated when Vincent O'Brien, to whom he is not related, retired, Aidan trained his first Group One winner in his first season,

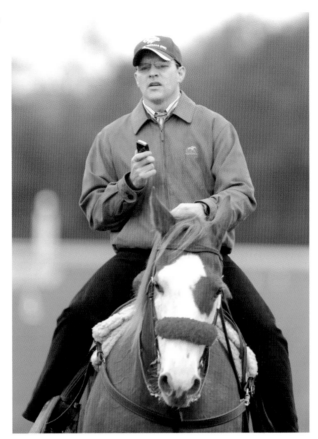

Aidan O'Brien won his first race at Galway in 1995, his twenty-third consecutive winner on Irish racing days

Michael Tabor's Desert King, winner of the National Stakes in 1996. The following season he trained his first Irish Classic winners when he won both the 2,000 and 1,000 Guineas, with the colt Desert King and the filly Classic Park. Desert King went on to win the Irish Derby, the first of Aidan's four winners to date in Ireland's premier race and only two behind Vincent O'Brien's race record of six. However, his total of fifteen Irish Classics is still a long way from Vincent's record total of twenty-seven, so there are still fields to be conquered.

The association with Ballydoyle and its powerful owners, John Magnier, Michael Tabor and Derrick Smith, has made the name Aidan O'Brien even more awesome than that of his predecessor, concentrating the minds of the best trainers of horses in Britain, France and America. The partners draw lots to decide in whose name each horse will race but they got caught out in 2007 when the colt Georgebernardshaw appeared in the first two-year-old race of the season. The draw had not yet taken place so Georgebernardshaw raced under the banner of the Ballydoyle Racing Partnership, sporting dark blue colours, with white stars on sleeves. The list of big race winners owned by the partnership include King of

Jamie Spencer, stable jockey at Ballydoyle in 2004

Kings, winner of the 1998 2,000 Guineas and Aidan's first English classic winner. Galileo won him his first Epsom Derby, winning the race in 2001, the year Aidan O'Brien established another world record, by winning twenty-three Group/Grade One races. That same year he also bettered Charles Semblat's 1950 record of six classics wins, in Ireland, England and France, training seven that year: Black Minnaloushe, Imagine and Galileo in Ireland, Galileo, Imagine and Milan in England and Rose Gypsy in France.

Stable jockey Christy Roche retired at the end of the 1998 season and was replaced by Michael Kinane, for many years stable jockey to Dermot Weld. When he left to join John Oxx after the 2003 season, John Magnier's godchild, Jamie Spencer, took over but the young jockey had a torrid year, being blamed for everything and was squeezed out after only one season. Certainly he made mistakes, but he was an easy target for the press, and the barrage of criticism affected his confidence in the big races. He wisely resigned the position, and has deservedly prospered outside the intense glare of publicity associated with Ballydoyle. Kieran

Fallon was brought in as the new stable jockey but in 2006 he was banned from riding in Britain when he was charged after an investigation into betting activities.

Besides his exploits on the flat, Aidan O'Brien continued to make a mark with his reduced string of jumpers, winning the Whitbread Gold Cup and Galway Plate with Life of a Lord. However, by far the best jumper he trained was John P. McManus's Istabraq, winner of three champion hurdles in a row in 1998, 1999 and 2000 and desperately unlucky not to have won a record fourth in 2001, when the outbreak of foot-and-mouth disease caused the meeting to be abandoned. When Istabraq was retired in 2002 Aidan O'Brien gave up training National Hunt horses.

Valentine T. O'Brien (b. 1949)

Trainer, Mountpargue, Grange, Athenry:

1989 P.J. O'Brien's ARCTIC TOUR (K. Morgan) – Digital Novice Hurdle £2,760

1998 V.T. O'Brien's HALF BARRELL (Mr D.J. Kelly) – Guinness Bumper £4,125

1999 K.C. Hill Syndicate's KILMORE LADY (Mr P. Moloney) – GPT Bumper £4,297

2001 Mrs K. Gillane's CLOONE RIVER (Mr A.K. Wise) – GPT Bumper £6,900

2001 V.T. O'Brien's HALF BARRELL (R. Walsh) – Tony O'Malley Handicap Chase £17,850

2001 Patrick J. Fahy's U JUMP I JUMP (C. O'Dwyer) – High Speed Handicap Hurdle £19,500

2002 John J. McGrath's GATSO (R. Walsh) – GPRS Handicap Hurdle €26,000

2003 V.T. O'Brien's HALF BARRELL (D.J. Casey) – Tony O'Malley Handicap Chase €24,125

2003 Galway to Boston Syndicate's BOSGAL NATIVE (Mr D.F. O'Regan) – Kerry Maid Bumper €10,350

2006 Mrs Bernadette O'Brien's GERANNJO (M.P. Fahy) – Jockeys' Association Maiden Hurdle €11,056

2006 V.T. O'Brien's HALF BARRELL (N.P. Madden) – Galway Blazers Handicap Chase €12,092

T.V. 'Tommy' O'Brien's son Val was born on his father's twenty-sixth birthday, St Valentine's Day. Christened like his father Thomas Valentine, the boy was called Val, and racing was in his blood. On leaving school he joined Tom Dreaper's stable. Starting out as an amateur, he turned professional in 1970 and, when Pat Taaffe retired, was given rides in the big races. The best horse he rode was Leap Frog, on whom he finished second to L'Escargot in the 1971 Cheltenham Gold Cup and won the Massey-Ferguson Gold Cup at Cheltenham on 11 December 1971. He gave Leap Frog a great ride at Cheltenham, keeping his mount going right to the line as The Dikler mounted a sustained challenge. Leap Frog held on to beat the future Cheltenham Gold Cup winner by a head, with quality jumpers like Titus Oates, winner of the Whitbread Gold Cup, Crisp, winner of the 2 Mile Champion Chase at the Cheltenham Festival and the Grand

National winner Gay Trip behind. Unfortunately for Val this victory was over-shadowed somewhat by Stan Mellor's quest for his thousandth winner and trainer Tom Dreaper's imminent retirement.

Stan Mellor had notched up 999 winners in Britain since his first visit to the winner's enclosure, on Straight Border at Wolverhampton in January 1954. Three times Champion Jockey, he had passed Fred Winter's record of 923 winners and was now on the brink of the magical thousandth. Urged on by the huge crowd, he had five rides, four of them for Fulke Walwyn, and the nation's press arrived in numbers, fully expecting him to make history that afternoon. Beaten into third place on a short-priced favourite in the first race, he was not expected to win the Massey-Ferguson on Orient War, but Charlie Potheen looked a likely winner of the novice chase. Jumping well, Charlie seemed a certainty until he made a bad mistake three fences from home, veered off the course to the right and went the wrong side of a marker doll. That put paid to the thousandth winner for that day and it took over a week to come as the media and the racing public waited. Stan eventually broke through the invisible barrier when Ouzo won at Nottingham on Monday, 18 December 1971. Stan retired at the end of that jump season, having ridden 1,035 winners, to embark on a training career. He is now only in third place in the list of all-time winning National Hunt jockeys, behind Peter Scudamore (1,678) and John Francome (1,138).

By winning the Massey-Ferguson, Connie Burrell's Leap Frog became the last British winner for Tom Dreaper, who retired and handed the stable over to his son Jim on New Year's Day 1972. His training career ended in style at the Leopardstown Christmas meeting in 1971, when he sent out four winners on the first day of the meeting and one on the second. On the first day Colebridge, Sea Brief and Good Review all won with Val O'Brien in the saddle and Jim Dreaper rode the future Cheltenham Gold Cup winner, Ten Up, to victory in the bumper. The final winner came on the second day of the meeting. Owned, fittingly, by Anne, Duchess of Westminster, Buca de Bacco won the Maiden Hurdle with Sean Barker up.

Tom had trained four really brilliant jumpers – Prince Regent, Royal Approach, Arkle and Flyingboat – and a host of important winners down the years, including seven successive Irish Grand National victors. Always noted for quality rather than quantity, he trained fourteen Festival winners at Galway, including the Galway Plate with Keep Faith and the Hurdle with Cashel View and Muir. Archie Willis, an estate agent from Belfast, whose black and white hoops were prominent on the Irish turf for over forty years, provided Tom Dreaper with his first and last Galway winner, Mulligatawny, winner of a bumper in 1942 and the front-running Muir, who with Ben Hannon aboard sprang a shock when winning the 1967 Galway

Jim Dreaper trained Leap Frog and Bold Flyer to win the Galway Plate

Hurdle. In between Tom Dreaper won two important Galway races for Jimmy Rank in 1946, the Plate with Keep Faith (Tim Hyde) and the Galway Blazers Handicap Chase with Brick Bat (Eddie Newman). For another long-standing patron of the stable, Anne, Duchess of Westminster, the owner of Arkle, he won the Galway Hurdle with Cashel View (Pat Taaffe) in 1959.

Jim Dreaper's first winner as a trainer was at Sandown Park on Friday, 7 January 1972, when Straight Fort, ridden by Eddie Wright, won the Express Chase. The following day he trained his first winner in Ireland, Geordie Hugh, owned by the Duchess of Westminster and ridden by Val O'Brien, in the Blackwater Steeplechase at Naas. Val O'Brien rode Jim's first big English winner, Good Review in the Schweppes Gold Trophy at Newbury the following month, but competition for rides within the stable was fierce. Eddie Wright, Peter McLoughlin and Sean Barker were all capable riders and Tommy Carberry was brought in to handle Leap Frog, winning the 1973 Galway Plate on him. Being one of the best riders at the time, he would ride for Jim Dreaper when he was available, and later

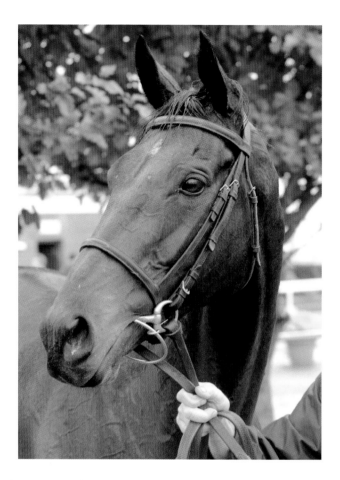

Kathleen Gillane's Cloone River won a bumper at Galway and went on to win the 2004 Galway Hurdle

partnered the Dreaper-trained Brown Lad in two of his three Irish Grand National victories. With Val O'Brien struggling to keep his weight under control, it was an opportune time for him to return home to ride his father's Tubs VI.

Tubs VI, a ten-year-old half-bred, won five decent handicap steeplechases in 1973, including the Ulster Grand National, and was placed second eight times and third once. His victories when winning at the Fairyhouse December meeting included Colebridge and Skymas, both high-class chasers. Val O'Brien rode Tubs VI in four of these victories and the exploits of this unlikely champion encouraged his father, who trained the horse privately, to apply for a trainer's licence. Although Tubs VI finished third to Brown Lad and Highway View in the 1975 Irish Grand National, Val O'Brien was no longer riding the high-profile Dreaper horses and it was a case of 'out of sight, out of mind'. He was not getting enough mounts and his name just disappeared. He actually retired from race riding in 1978 and went into business outside racing until his life was changed by the sudden death of his father. Then he made the decision to apply for a trainer's licence to keep the Mountpargue stable going.

Arctic Tour, ridden by Ken Morgan, provided him with his first winner on his local course, winning a novice hurdle in 1989. One of his well-known horses, Half Barrell, won a bumper at Galway in 1998, and three years later was one leg of a wonderful treble, winning the Tony O'Malley Memorial Handicap Chase, a race he won again in 2003. The other horses involved in that memorable Galway were Cloone River, bumper winner on the first day, and U Jump I Jump, winner of a handicap hurdle on the final day of the meeting. Unfortunately, Kathleen Gillane took Cloone River away from Val, and when it won the 2004 Galway Hurdle Paul Nolan was the trainer. Val O'Brien enjoyed a fine double at the 2006 Galway Festival, winning the Galway Blazers Handicap Chase with the veteran Half Barrell and a maiden hurdle with Gerannjo, both 16-to-1 shots, on the Saturday. His son Tommy is keen on riding and is likely to follow in his father's footsteps and try his luck as a jockey.

Michael J. Kinane (b. 1959)

Rider:

1976 Paul Magnier's BROCCOLI – Clare Galway Nursery (C. Magnier)

1978 Comte A. de Laubespin's MAGIC NORTH – Athenry 2yo Race (M. Kauntze)

1979 Mrs E.M. Burke's MINNIE TUDOR – Oranmore Handicap (M. Kauntze)

1980 C.S. Gainsford St Lawrence's COLLECTOR'S ITEM – Briar Hill Handicap (M. Kauntze)

1980 Simon Fraser's EMBRYO – Parkmore Maiden (M. Kauntze)

1981 J. Kane's BROTHER SLANEY – Briar Hill Handicap (L. Browne)

1981 Mrs M.M. Keogh's MOREDA – Tuam 2yo Race (L. Browne)

1984 Bertram R. Firestone's KAMAKURA – Athenry 2yo Maiden (D.K. Weld)

1984 Moyglare Stud's SWEETENED OFFER – Claregalway Maiden (D.K. Weld)

1984 Mrs B.R. Firestone's ALL A LARK – Briar Hill Handicap (D.K. Weld)

1984 Bertram R. Firestone's SECURITY CLEARANCE – Mervue Race (D.K. Weld)

1984 M.W.J. Smurfit's MARTIES LIGHT – Oranmore Handicap (D.K. Weld)

1984 Mrs C. Kinane's ANNETTES DELIGHT – Parkmore Maiden (C. Kinane)

1985 Bertram R. Firestone's INISHEER – Athenry 2yo Maiden (D.K. Weld)

1985 Mrs Helen Smith's FRENCH CHAIN – Loughrea Handicap (D.K. Weld)

1985 Mrs W. Whitehead's BONNIE BESS – McDonogh Handicap (D.K. Weld)

1985 Thoroughbred Breeders Inc's GENTLE FAVOR – Mervue Race (D.K. Weld)

1985 Bertram R. Firestone's SWATCH – Stewards' Handicap (D.K. Weld)

1985 Allen E. Paulson's SON OF IVOR – Nilands Handicap (D.K. Weld)

1986 Mrs B.R. Firestone's BIG BREAK – Claregalway Maiden (D.K. Weld)

1987 Allen E. Paulson's KIICHI – GPT Dublin 2yo Maiden (D.K. Weld)

1987 Allen E. Paulson's ALLEN'S MISTAKE – Mervue Race (D.K. Weld)

1988 Allen E. Paulson's KIRLA – GPT Dublin 2yo Maiden (D.K. Weld)

1988 D.K. Weld's MIDSUMMER GAMBLE – Bushy Park Handicap (D.K. Weld)

1988 Allen E. Paulson's ALLEN'S MISTAKE – Mervue Race (D.K. Weld)

1989 Moyglare Stud's GO AND GO – GPT Dublin 2yo Maiden (D.K. Weld)

1989 M.W.J. Smurfit's POPULAR GLEN –McDonogh Handicap (D.K. Weld)

1989 F. Soudavar's MIDSUMMER GAMBLE – Bushy Park Handicap (D.K. Weld)

1989 Moyglare Stud's RARE HOLIDAY – Mervue Race (D.K. Weld)

1989 M.W.J. Smurfit's EMPEROR TO BE (M.J. Kinane) – Digital Handicap (D.K. Weld)

1990 Yoshiki Akazawa's GOLDEN MINTAGE – GPT 2yo Maiden (D.K. Weld)

1990 Moyglare Stud's WEEKEND BREAK – McDonogh Feeds 2yo Maiden (D.K. Weld)

1990 Philip Fleming's INQUEST – McDonogh Timber Handicap (D.K. Weld)

1990 Yoshiki Akazawa's ARABIAN NIGHTS – McDonogh Fertilizer Race (D.K. Weld)

1990 Robert E. Sangster's SADLERS CONGRESS – Digital Handicap (D.K. Weld)

1990 Moyglare Stud's STRONG DEMAND – O'Malley Group Maiden (D.K. Weld)

1990 G. Olivero's NATURAL LAD – O'Malley Contractors Handicap (D.K. Weld)

1991 Moyglare Stud's LEGAL PRESSURE – GPT 2yo Maiden (D.K. Weld)

1991 Moyglare Stud's MARKET BOOSTER – McDonogh Feeds 2yo Maiden (D.K. Weld)

1991 A.E. Paulson's COMMITTED DANCER – McDonogh Handicap (D.K. Weld)

1991 M. Benacerraf's ORVIETTO – Digital All-in-1 Handicap (D.K. Weld)

1991 Moyglare Stud's POLITICAL FACT - Menlo 2yo Maiden (D.K. Weld)

1991 Mrs Michael Watt's MOHAWK TRAIL – County Nursery (M.A. O'Toole)

1992 Raymond J. Rooney's ARABIC TREASURE – GPT 2yo Maiden (D.K. Weld)

1992 International Breeders's CLIVEDON GAIL – McDonogh Timber Handicap (D.K. Weld)

1992 Moyglare Stud's OPEN MARKET – O'Malley Group Maiden (D.K. Weld)

1992 Andrea Schiavi's ONESIXNINE – O'Malley Construction Handicap (D.K. Weld)

1992 Allen E. Paulson's VINEY – Jockeys' Association 2yo Maiden (D.K. Weld)

1993 Andrea Schiavi's GLACIAL ARCTIC – McDonogh Fertilizer Maiden (D.K. Weld)

1993 Ovidstown Investment's RIENROE – Albatross Suregrass Handicap (D.K. Weld)

1993 Andrea Schiavi's ASTRONAVE – McDonogh Feeds 2yo Maiden (D.K. Weld)

1993 International Breeders' CLIVEDEN GAIL – McDonogh Timber Handicap (D.K. Weld)

1993 Raymond J. Rooney's GARBONI – Guinness Extra Stout Handicap (D.K. Weld)

1993 M.W.J. Smurfit's PERSIAN TACTICS – Arthur's Race (D.K. Weld)

1993 Mrs Helen Walsh's DOHERTY – Carlsberg 2yo Race (T.M. Walsh)

1993 Moyglare Stud's BLAZING SPECTACLE – Oranmore Milk Handicap (D.K. Weld)

1994 Moyglare Stud's UNION DECREE – GPT 2yo Maiden (D.K. Weld)

1994 Moyglare Stud's SPRINT FOR GOLD – GPT Cork Maiden (D.K. Weld)

1994 Moyglare Stud's FEELING OF POWER – McDonogh 2yo Maiden (D.K. Weld)

1994 M.W.J. Smurfit's POLITICAL DOMAIN – Arthur's Race (D.K. Weld)

1994 Frank Stronach's KING LEON – Jockeys' Association 2yo Maiden (D.K. Weld)

1994 Mrs J. Maxwell Moran's BRYN CLOVIS – Kerry Spring Handicap (D.K. Weld)

1995 Moyglare Stud's DANCE DESIGN – McDonogh Feeds 2yo Maiden (D.K. Weld)

1995 Mrs F. Sheridan's JUST AN ILLUSION – McDonogh Timber Handicap (D.K. Weld)

1995 Moyglare Stud's ARCHIVE FOOTAGE – Smithwicks 3yo Maiden (D.K. Weld)

1995 Mrs J. Maxwell Moran's FLAMING FEATHER – Dawn 2yo Maiden (D.K. Weld)

1996 Michael Watt's CASEY TIBBS – GPT Industrial 2yo Maiden (D.K. Weld)

1996 Jeremiah J. King's ZANKLE – GPT Cork 3yo Handicap (D.K. Weld)

1996 J.D. Gunther's PRO TRADER – McDonogh Handicap (D.K. Weld)

1996 Sheikh Mohammed's PECHORA – McDonogh Fertilizer 3yo Maiden (D.K. Weld)

1996 Mrs Gaynor Watt's TRADE DISPUTE – McDonogh Timber Handicap (D.K. Weld)

1996 Moyglare Stud's STYLISH ALLURE – Guinness 3yo Handicap (D.K. Weld)

1996 Jeremiah J. King's ZANKLE – Harp Lager Handicap (D.K. Weld)

1997 Frank Stronach's WESTERN CHIEF – GPT Van & Trucks Handicap (D.K. Weld)

1997 Moyglare Stud's SCREEN IDOL – McDonogh Feeds 2yo Maiden (D.K. Weld)

1997 Mount Juliet Club's SMILING BRAVE – Harp Lager Handicap (D.K. Weld)

1998 Kak Yiu's SOCIAL GRACES – GPT Cork 3yo Handicap (D.K. Weld)

1998 Moyglare Stud's FREE TO SPEAK – McDonogh Handicap (D.K. Weld)

1998 M.W.J. Smurfit's MUSICAL MAYHEM – McDonogh Timber Handicap (D.K. Weld)

1998 John G. Davis's ALEXIS – Carlsberg 2yo Race (D.K. Weld)

1998 Anthony McManus's SUPPORT ACT – Arthur's Race (D.K. Weld)

1999 Mrs John Magnier's ARISTOTLE – GPT 2yo Maiden (A.P. O'Brien)

1999 Albert Hausammann's CIEL D'OR – GPT 3yo Handicap (Martin Brassil)

1999 Mrs Patrick Mullins's BOB WHAT – McDonogh Timber Handicap (P. Mullins)

1999 Mrs John Magnier's THEATRE WORLD – Guinness Extra Stout Handicap (A.P. O'Brien)

1999 Michael Tabor's TWICKENHAM – Guinness Extra Cold Race (A.P. O'Brien)

1999 Mrs John Magnier's MOISEYEV – Up Front 3yo Race (A.P. O'Brien)

2000 Michael Tabor's HEMMINGWAY – GPT 2yo Maiden (A.P. O'Brien)

2000 Michael Tabor's ROSTROPOVICH – Smithwicks 3yo Maiden (A.P. O'Brien)

2002 Cabin Hill Syndicate's ULYSEES – McDonogh 3yo Maiden (P. Mullins)

2002 Michael N. Walsh's DISCERNING AIR – McDonogh Builders Handicap (M. Hourigan)

2003 Seamus Ross's PANTAREZ – GPT 3yo Handicap (David Wachman)

2003 EKJ Syndicate's HUXLEY – McDonogh DIY Handicap (Paul A. Roche)

2003 Dwyer, Finn & O'Rourke's LOVE TRIANGLE – Smithwicks 2yo Maiden (D.R.C. Elsworth)

2003 Mrs John Magnier's WOLFE TONE – Dawn 2yo Maiden (A.P. O'Brien)

2004 HH Aga Khan's CARADAK – McDonogh 3yo Maiden (J.M. Oxx)

2004 HH Aga Khan's ALAYAN – Irish Stallion Farms Nursery (J.M. Oxx)
2004 Brendan Smith's FIT THE COVE – Galway Fairgreen Hotel Handicap (H. Rogers)
2007 Mrs S. Crowley's PROSPECTOROUS – William Hill 3yo Handicap (Joseph Crowley)
2007 Mrs R. Jacobs's REALLY RANSOM – Guinness 2yo Auction Maiden (J.M. Oxx)

Born in Cashel, Co. Tipperary, Michael Kinane was the son of the well-known jockey Tommy Kinane, who had ridden his first winner the previous year. Born in 1933, Tommy took a long time to get established as a jockey. Starting with Tim Hyde at Cashel, he went to England, where he got a few rides but failed to partner a winner. His break came when his brother, Dan, began training in 1957. Tommy came back to Ireland to work with him, was given a ride and rode his first winner, at the age of twenty-four, on Trade Union in a handicap hurdle at Leopardstown. During the next decade he rode many winners but few of any importance until he teamed up with Pearl of Montreal in 1973, winning the Kerry National at Listowel and the Sean Graham Chase at Leopardstown. The following year he won the Kerry National again, this time on Irishman, but it was his association with the game hurdler Monksfield that made his name. Among his wins aboard that champion was the 1978 Champion Hurdle at Cheltenham, the pinnacle of his career as a jockey.

An injury sustained in the Irish Grand National only two weeks later meant that he was unable to ride Monksfield to victory at Aintree, being confined to bed for three months. Although he was now forty-four years old, a real veteran as far as jump jockeys are concerned, he battled his way back into the saddle but, following a poor run at Leopardstown, he was 'jocked off' Monksfield for the 1979 Champion Hurdle and Dessie Hughes got the ride. Devastated, he had some consolation when Dessie McDonogh, Monksfield's trainer, gave him a consolation ride on Stranfield in the Supreme Novice Hurdle. Although he won the race, the victory did little to erase the disappointment of missing out on Monksfield's second Champion Hurdle. At this time his sons were riding as jockeys, and he decided to hang up his boots in 1980 to start a new career as a trainer.

His eldest son, Thomas Kinane junior, was a good amateur rider before turning professional in 1979. It was he who was aboard Smoke Charger when he won the PZ Mower Chase at Thurles, the biggest winner of his father's training career. Paul P. Kinane was the tallest of the siblings, a very promising claiming rider who, like so many, found it difficult to get opportunities when he lost his claim. J.K. 'Jayo' Kinane was a talented rider but did not get the rub of the green and never became fashionable, although he did ride a lot of winners for Ken Oliver in England.

However, the cream of the crop was Michael, who was apprenticed to Curragh trainer Liam Browne. Liam Browne had been Champion Apprentice in Ireland three

Michael Kinane, thirteen times leading jockey at the Galway Festival

times in the mid-fifties but failed to become established as a fully fledged jockey, drifting in and out of racing until he made up his mind to train in 1971. Starting with very limited resources, he trained Tameric to win the Irish Lincolnshire Handicap at the Curragh in 1973 but quickly gained a reputation of being good with young jockeys. Unlike many trainers, he gave his apprentices tuition as well as opportunities and was the 'Irish Frenchie Nicholson' of his day, turning out a number of well-mannered and competent riders. A very strict disciplinarian, he was a formidable figure and took no nonsense at all, which was probably the secret of his success. He produced five Champion Apprentices – Tommy Carmody, Stephen Craine, Michael J. Kinane, Pat Gilson and Warren O'Connor – as well as the brilliant but ill-fated David Parnell, son of Buster, the former Irish Champion Jockey. Liam's son Dermot, was a talented amateur rider, but a scandal concerning his riding of Browne's Gazette, the odds-on favourite for the Champion Hurdle in 1985, led to him being banned from racing for ten years. The bad publicity rubbed off on his completely innocent father, whose training career suffered badly, eventually forcing his retirement.

With his cousin Martin Kinane riding, Michael was registered as M.J. to avoid confusion. Known familiarly throughout racing as 'Mick' and occasionally as 'Mickey Joe', he prefers to be called by his full name. However, he did not help his cause by calling his official biography *Mick Kinane – The Big Race King*. He rode his first winner when Muscari, trained by Larry Greene, won the Firmount Apprentice Handicap at Leopardstown on 19 March 1975, beating Quick Gift, ridden by Padge Gill. He would later be given the mount on the horse that made his father famous, winning an apprentice race at Naas on Monksfield. The first trainer to use the young apprentice regularly was Michael Kauntze, a former assistant to Vincent O'Brien and husband of Tom Dreaper's daughter Eva, who began training at Bullstown, Ashbourne, Co. Meath, in 1975. He provided the young jockey with his first big race winner, Reelin Jig, winner of the Group Three Ballyogan Stakes at Leopardstown.

However, it was his mentor Liam Brown who provided him with his first classic winner, Dara Monarch, the surprise winner of the 1982 Irish 2,000 Guineas. The following year they had a successful run with Judge Roe's Carlingford Castle, second to Teenoso and Lester Piggott in the Epsom Derby. In that same year, 1983, Dermot Weld's stable jockey Wally Swinburn retired and was replaced by the American Darrel McHargue, who had ridden over 2,000 winners in the United States, including Master Derby in the Preakness Stakes. It is believed that Dermot Weld wanted to give the job to Kinane but was talked out of it by some of his larger owners, who wanted a more experienced rider on their horses. The American jockey never really came to grips with race riding in Ireland and the public never warmed to him, but he did ride three winners at the 1983 Galway Festival for Dermot Weld. He only lasted a year with Weld before departing to England, and was replaced by Michael Kinane.

Kinane rode his first winner at the Galway Festival when Paul Magnier's Broccoli won the Claregalway Nursery for trainer Clem Magnier. In the seven seasons since that winner, he had only ridden seven winners at the meeting but now it was a different story. In the years that followed he was the leading jockey at the meeting nine times and shared that honour on four other occasions. His current tally of winners there is 100, more than any other rider. Riding well and with the backing of one of the biggest and most successful stables in Ireland, he ended the 1984 season as Irish Champion Jockey, the first of his nine titles. Not many jockeys ride every winner on the day's programme. The Liverpool-born jockey Frederick 'Tich' Mason rode all five winners at Cavan on 8 September 1900, Frank Morgan rode all five at Downpatrick on 12 March 1914, and Martin Molony won all five races open to professional jockeys (the sixth race was a bumper) at Navan in 1949. Michael Kinane nearly did it at the Phoenix Park on Saturday, 7 June 1986. Having ridden the first five winners on the six-race programme, all for Dermot Weld, he was beaten by half a length on Amplification by the favourite Hungry Giant, trained by John M. Oxx and ridden by Dermot Hogan. All six favourites won at the meeting.

Although nobody realized it at the time, Lester Piggott was responsible for a complete change in the relationship between trainers and jockeys. Forty years ago every trainer had a stable jockey, who was paid a retainer and was expected to ride every horse trained in that stable, whether it was likely to win or not. Steve Donoghue bent these rules but Lester was a law unto himself, ringing owners to suggest himself as the jockey to ride a fancied horse in a big race rather than its usual rider. He was the perfect big-race jockey, cool, collected and a brilliant judge, who started his career as a young and brilliant upstart who was treading on the toes of the senior jockeys, particularly Sir Gordon Richards, at whom he was alleged to have shouted during a race, 'Move over Grandad!' Having won the Derby on Never Say Die as a teenager in 1954, he was snapped up by Noel Murless to ride for his powerful stable, which provided him with seven classics in five seasons, including the Derby on Crepello and St Paddy. However, the purple patch passed, Murless did not train a single classic winner in the next five seasons and a frustrated Piggott accepted Vincent O'Brien's invitation to ride Valoris in the Oaks. This left Noel Murless without a rider for Varinia and he had to get Cecil Boyd-Rochfort's jockey, Stan Clayton, instead and then watch his stable jockey win the Oaks on Valoris, leaving Varinia trailing into third place. That was the beginning of the end of the Murless/Piggott partnership and Lester went freelance in 1967, with George Moore being imported from Australia to replace him.

Piggott's timing was dreadful. In 1967 Noel Murless had a marvellous season with the top-class Royal Palace, winner of the 2,000 Guineas and the Derby, in his yard that year as well as the 1,000 Guineas winner Fleet. However, Lester did have some consolation in winning the Irish Derby on Ribocco that year, beating the Murless hope Sucaryl, ridden by Moore, by three-quarters of a length. Although the initial verdict on Piggott's decision to go freelance was that it was a big mistake, his arrangement with Vincent O'Brien that he would ride his top horses in their races outside Ireland proved extremely lucrative. The memorable success of Sir Ivor in the Derby led to the making of a film *The Year of Sir Ivor* and two years later he was aboard the great Nijinsky, the last winner of the Triple Crown.

The availability of a top-class jockey like Piggott continually tempted owners to 'jock-off' their stable jockeys in big races. There were many victims: Bill Williamson lost the winning ride on Roberto in the Derby; Ernie Johnson was 'jocked-off' Rheingold after being beaten by Roberto and Lester Piggott, aided by giving his mount an almighty crack of the whip, in the same Derby; Wally Swinburn was replaced on Blue Wind in the Oaks; and Luca Cumani's stable jockey Darrel McHargue went fishing rather than watch Lester win the St Leger on Commanche Run. That latter victory enabled Lester to beat Frank Buckle's record of twenty-seven English classic wins.

Initially replacing a horse's regular rider in big races was regarded as unsporting, a case of commercial considerations overriding sportsmanship, but the very same opinions had been expressed twenty-five years earlier when a pacemaker was used in a race for the first time. Like the pacemaker issue, it came to be accepted that the top riders would be booked for the big races and the lesser riders would have to accept it. Trainers justified this by stating that the stable jockey is not necessarily the best rider for every horse in the yard; some horses go better for other riders and all horses perform better when ridden by the best jockey. This new system has led to a new breed coming into horse racing, the jockey's agent, who books rides on behalf of his jockey client. A form expert, the agent picks out the horses that have the best chance of winning and contacts the trainer, offering the services of the jockey he represents.

With the traditional role of the stable jockey now changed, it is normal for the less fashionable jockeys to be 'jocked-off' when a top jockey comes looking for the ride. It happens on the flat and it happens over jumps. With Michael Kinane now rated as one of the best jockeys around, trainers were looking for him to ride their horses in the major races when Dermot Weld did not have a fancied runner. One of the first such mounts was Alydaress, winner of the Irish Oaks, for Henry Cecil in 1989. Shortly afterwards Michael Jarvis booked him to ride Carroll House in the Champion Stakes at the Phoenix Park. Carroll House's usual rider, Walter Swinburn, son of Wally, was riding in England that day and Kinane came in for the winning ride. He retained the ride on Carroll House in the Prix de L'Arc de Triomphe and won another important race. In 1990 he won his first English classic, the 2,000 Guineas, on Tirol, trained by Richard Hannon, and owned by the Irishman John Horgan, a well-known cattle dealer.

In 1994 Michael Kinane was signed up to ride for Sheikh Mohammed but continued to ride for Dermot Weld, who was happy to release him for the big races or when his runners did not have a realistic chance of winning. However, that winter the Sheikh started up his Godolphin stable, which took his most promising horses to Dubai for the winter months. When they returned to

Britain in 1995 they did not return to their original trainers, nor did they race in the Sheikh's familiar maroon with white sleeves. Instead all the better horses were assembled together under the care of Saeed bin Suroor, raced in the royal blue jacket of Godolphin, and were ridden by Frankie Dettori. This restricted Kinane's opportunities in the big races but he was riding regularly in England when he was not required in Ireland.

One of the big Irish races to elude him was the Irish Derby and he was very disappointed when he missed Dermot Weld's first winner of the race, Zagreb. The press began calling the Irish Derby 'Mick Kinane's hoodoo race' because he had never won it; his fourteen rides had yielded three seconds but he had had few fancied mounts in the race. All but five of his rides had been on outsiders and he was only once beaten on a favourite, King's Theatre in 1994. He had finished second on Theatrical (1985) and Definite Article (1995) for Dermot Weld but he did not fancy Weld's 1996 runner, Zagreb, and with the trainer's permission switched to Dr Massini, the second-favourite for the race, trained by Michael Stoute. After the race he was kicking himself because Zagreb won by six lengths, with Weld's number two jockey, Pat Shanahan, in the saddle. After dismounting from Dr Massini, who had finished a disappointing seventh, a shattered Kinane could only offer the terse comment, 'He was never travelling.' He had to wait another five years before landing his bogey race, winning his first Irish Derby on Galileo in 2001. The following year he won the race again, this time on High Chaparral, both horses being trained by the brilliant Aidan O'Brien.

During the 1997 season rumours began to surface that Christy Roche, Aidan O'Brien's stable jockey, was contemplating retirement. Michael Kinane was indentified as a possible successor when he was given rides for the stable, winning the *Racing Post* Trophy on Saratoga Springs and the Grand Criterium in France on Second Empire. The following year he won the 2,000 Guineas at Newmarket on King of Kings for Aidan O'Brien. By now the racing world was waiting for Roche's retirement. It duly came in mid-season and Michael Kinane took over as the Ballydoyle number one jockey. In his five years at Ballydoyle, he rode fifty-eight Group One winners for the stable, including Giant's Causeway, Galileo, High Chaparral, Hawk Wing and Sir Alec Ferguson's Rock of Gibraltar, but at times he found it difficult to pick the right one when Aidan ran two or three horses in the same race. Then in November 2003 came, as the *Racing Post* dubbed it, 'The Big Reshuffle', when it was announced that Michael Kinane was relinquishing his post with Aidan O'Brien and would be riding for John Oxx in 2004. This move had a knock-on effect because Oxx's erstwhile

Johnny Murtagh, Ireland's Champion Jockey, rode ten Group One winners in 2007

stable jockey Johnny Murtagh was leaving to ride as a freelance and Jamie Spencer, who had been riding as a freelance in England, had been chosen to replace Kinane at Ballydoyle.

John P. McManus (b. 1951)

Owner, emerald green and orange hoops, white cap:

1978 SHINING FLAME (Mr N. Madden) – Galway Plate (E.J. O'Grady) £5,230

1990 ANY GOSSIP (T. Carmody) – GPT Maiden Hurdle (E.J. O'Grady) £2,762

1995 SHANKORAK (C. O'Dwyer) – Guinness Novice Chase (F. Berry) £4,110

1996 VICAR STREET (C.F. Swan) – GPT Maiden Hurdle (A.P. O'Brien) £4,110

1996 LEWISHAM (Mr B.M. Cash) – GPT Bumper (A.P. O'Brien) £4,110

1999 GO ROGER GO (N. Williamson) – Guinness Novice Chase (E.J. O'Grady) £6,875

1999 BLOW WIND BLOW (C. O'Dwyer) – Networker Handicap Hurdle (F. Berry) £19,425

2000 KHAIRABAR (Paul Moloney) – Jockeys' Association Beginners Chase (C. Roche) £6,210

2001 GET IT ON (Paul Moloney) – Albatross Maiden Hurdle (C. Roche) £6,900

2001 HARDIMAN (Paul Moloney) – Albatross Chase (C. Roche) £13,000

2001 DARAPOUR (C.F. Swan) – Compaq Hurdle (A.P. O'Brien) £8,625

2001 GRIMES (C. O'Dwyer) – Compaq Galway Plate (C. Roche) £61,250

2001 DECKIE (Mr A.P. Crowe) – Budweiser QR Handicap Hurdle (C. Roche) £8,280

2002 PUCK OUT (Paul Moloney) – GPT Maiden Hurdle (C. Roche) €8,790

2002 WOULDN'T YOU AGREE (Mr A.P. Crowe) – GPT Bumper (C. Roche) €8,970

2002 DONADINO (D.J. Casey) – Tony O'Malley Maiden (C.F. Swan) €23,800

2002 WOULDN'T YOU AGREE (Paul Moloney) – Maiden Hurdle (C. Roche) €11,040

2005 MONJOYAU (A.P. McCoy) – Budweiser Novice Chase (E.J. O'Grady) €16,275

2006 MORATORIUM (F.M. Berry) – William Hill Handicap (N. Meade) €11,401

2006 FAR FROM TROUBLE (R. Loughran) – Galway Plate (C. Roche) €121,800

2006 ON THE OTHER HAND (D.G. Hogan) – Cork Airport Handicap Hurdle (C.F. Swan) €26,040

John McManus, a former bookmaker and now an international financier, has horses with virtually every trainer in Ireland so it is surprising that only six different trainers have trained Galway winners for him. His twenty-one winners include

John P. McManus is the third most successful owner at the Festival but has yet to win the Galway Hurdle

Shining Flame, Grimes and Far From Trouble, winners of the Galway Plate, and three is a race record for an owner held jointly with T.B. Holmes, Gus Mangan and Anne Biddle. However, 'J.P'. is the only one of the trio to have won it with three different horses. His five winners at the 2001 meeting equalled the record established by Mrs Brendan Kearney in 1980 and he is now the third most winning owner at the Festival.

Born in Limerick in 1951, he started at the bottom of the bookmaking tree and worked his way to the top before leaving the business for the world financial stage. A man of enormous wealth, he himself is probably not exactly sure how many horses he actually has in training, but his ubiquitous colours will be seen at all the big jumping meetings throughout Ireland and the UK. He has his own private stable at Jackdaw's Castle in England, where Jonjo O'Neill is in charge, and also has a few jumpers in training in France. The king of National Hunt racing, owner of the brilliant Champion Hurdler Istabraq, J.P. hit the headlines of both the financial and the sports pages with his investment in Manchester United Football Club. He did it again when he decided to sell out to the Glazer family of America, which infuriated the many fans of that club. They should not have been surprised because McManus never claimed to be a football fan; he was an investor and investors always sell eventually.

Moyglare Stud Farm

Owners, black, white sleeves, red cap, black star:
(All Galway Winners trained by D.K. Weld)

1984 SWEETENED OFFER (M.J. Kinane) – Clare Galway 2yo Maiden £1,175

1989 GO AND GO (M.J. Kinane) – GPT 2yo Maiden £3,452

1989 RARE HOLIDAY (M.J. Kinane) – Mervue Race 3yo £2,762

1990 WEEKEND BREAK (M.J. Kinane) – McDonogh Feeds 2yo Maiden £2,762

1990 STRONG DEMAND (M.J. Kinane) – O'Malley Group Maiden £2,762

1991 LEGAL PRESSURE (M.J. Kinane) – GPT 2yo Maiden £5,522

1991 MARKET BOOSTER (M.J. Kinane) – McDonogh Feeds 2yo Maiden £5,522

1991 POLITICAL FACT (M.J. Kinane) – Menlo 2yo Maiden £5,520

1992 OPEN MARKET (M.J. Kinane) – O'Malley Group Maiden £3,797

1993 BLAZING SPECTACLE (M.J. Kinane) – Oranmore Handicap £3,795

1994 UNION DECREE (M.J. Kinane) – GPT 2yo Maiden £5,480

1994 SPRINT FOR GOLD (M.J. Kinane) – GPT Maiden £4,110

1994 FEELING OF POWER (M.J. Kinane) – McDonogh Feeds 2yo Maiden £5,480

1995 DANCE DESIGN (M.J. Kinane) – McDonogh Feeds 2yo Maiden £5,480

1995 ARCHIVE FOOTAGE (M.J. Kinane) – Smithwicks 3yo Maiden £4,110

1996 STYLISH ALLURE (M.J. Kinane) – Guinness 3yo Handicap £4,110

1997 SCREEN IDOL (M.J. Kinane) – McDonogh Feeds 2yo Maiden £5,480

1998 FREE TO SPEAK (M.J. Kinane) – McDonogh Handicap £30,500

1998 DUAL STAR (P.J. Smullen) – Compaq Maiden £4,125

1999 GRAND AMBITION (P.J. Smullen) – Compaq Maiden £4,469

1999 SOUTH OF HEAVEN (P.J. Smullen) – Guinness 3yo Maiden £6,187

1999 SHARP FOCUS (P.J. Smullen) – Dawn 2yo Maiden £6,531

2000 STEP WITH STYLE (P. Shanahan) – Compaq Maiden £5,520

2000 ROMANTIC VENTURE (P. Shanahan) – Guinness 2yo Maiden £8,510

2001 SIGHTS ON GOLD (P.J. Smullen) – GPT 2yo Maiden £11,050

2001 WHISPER LIGHT (P.J. Smullen) – McDonogh 3yo Maiden £8,280

2003 STEEL LIGHT (P.J. Smullen) – Nursery €32,500

2004 RICH SENSE (P.J. Smullen) – HP Handicap €13,129

2004 SPIRIT OF AGE (P.J. Smullen) – HP Maiden €12,783

2005 SOCIETY HOSTESS (P.J. Smullen) – Guinness Fillies Handicap €19,530

2005 CLEARING THE WATER (P.J. Smullen) – 3yo Maiden €13,020

2007 IN A RUSH (P.J. Smullen) – Guinness & Oysters Handicap €19,530

2007 UNWRITTEN RULE (P.J. Smullen) – Dawn Juice 2yo Maiden €13,020

2007 INSTANT SPARKLE (P.J. Smullen) – Mercer Hotel Fillies Maiden €13,020

Dermot Weld's liking for Galway winners has put two of his owners at the top of the all-time list of festival winners. The Moyglare Stud tops the table with thirty-four, just four ahead of Dr Michael Smurfit. Five times leading owner at Galway, the Moyglare Stud, Maynooth, Co. Kildare, was bought by the Swiss industrialist Walter Heafner in 1960, and the first foals were born there in 1962. The stud consists of about 450 acres and is managed by Stan Cosgrove, a vet with a squeaky voice, who is frequently asked to entertain guests at racing functions with his stand-up comic routine.

Walter Haefner paid US $450,000 for What A Treat, a brood mare in foal to Vaguely Noble in February 1972, at the time a world-record price for a brood mare. He sold the resulting filly, named Treat me Nobly, for a European record price. At Goffs in 1975, a yearling colt by Northern Dancer out of What A Treat was sold for 127,000 guineas, another European record, although one that only stood for a month. Mr Haefner may have regretted parting with the colt, named Be My Guest, because he won the Waterford Crystal Mile at Goodwood and was syndicated as a stallion for £800,000, but at least he got a good price. That was not the case with Assert. The Irish and French Derby winner bred by Moyglare made only £16,000 at the yearling sales, being knocked down to Robert Sangster.

Originally Mr and Mrs Walter Haefner bred for the sales ring rather than the race-course but they had a small number of horses in training. Walter Haefner was with Kevin Prendergast, who trained Areola (Phoenix Stakes 1970), and Mrs Haefner (who died in 1979) was with Vincent O'Brien; her most notable horses were Niebo (unbeaten at two years 1975) and Padroug. In 1980 Mr Haefner decided to breed to race rather than to sell, establishing the Moyglare Stud Farm Company Ltd to embrace the whole operation. Owned by him, his wife and family, the Moyglare Stud Farm registered its own colours of black, white sleeves, red cap, black star, and began racing horses in 1983. All the Moyglare yearlings, about thirty-five or so each year, go into training with Dermot Weld but the stud does not race jumpers, selling off potential jumping stock, such as Rare Holiday and Archive Footage, which were bought from the stud at the end of their flat careers by Michael Smurfit. Half a dozen of the better older horses are sent to Christophe Clement in America, where there are better opportunities for that type of horse; Society Hostess won three listed races there in 2006. The best of the current crop of two-year-olds is Capital Expense, winner of a Leopardstown maiden and runner-up in the Beresford Stakes.

Reports that heavy losses might curtail the Moyglare operation seem to have been overstated, and the stud clearly benefits from the substantial increase in Irish prize money. Among the best winners it has bred and raced are Trusted Partner (Irish 1,000 Guineas), Definite Article (touched off by a short head in the Irish Derby), Dance Design (Irish Oaks), Big Shuffle (Cork and Orrery Stakes) and Media Puzzle (Melbourne Cup).

Dr Michael W.J. Smurfit (b. 1936)

Owner, yellow, royal blue epaulettes, yellow cap, royal blue star:

1984 MARTIES LIGHT (M.J. Kinane) – Oranmore Handicap £966 (D.K. Weld)

1985 STRATHLINE (T. Carmody) – Galway Hurdle Handicap £18,698 (D.K. Weld)

1986 PERRIS VALLEY (Mr P.R. Lenehan) – Lough Atalia Bumper £1,382 (D.K. Weld)

1989 POPULAR GLEN (M.J. Kinane) – McDonogh Handicap £13,702 (D.K. Weld)

1989 EMPEROR TO BE (M.J. Kinane) – Digital Handicap £4,140 (D.K. Weld)

1990 KIICHI (B. Sheridan) – Digital Galway Plate Handicap Chase £22,100 (D.K. Weld)

1990 POPULAR GLEN (B. Sheridan) – Harp Lager Hurdle £3,280 (D.K. Weld)

1991 CHEERING NEWS (B. Sheridan) – Digital Hurdle £3,795 (D.K. Weld)

1991 ARABIAN NIGHTS (B. Sheridan) – Bohermore Maiden Hurdle £3,795 (D.K. Weld)

1992 APPEALING BUBBLES (K.J. Manning) – McDonogh Race £3,797 (J.S. Bolger)

1992 PERFECT IMPOSTER (K.J. Manning) – Tuam 2yo £7,402 (J.S. Bolger)

1993 PERSIAN TACTICS (B. Sheridan) – Albatross Maiden Hurdle £4,142 (D.K. Weld)

1993 GENERAL IDEA (A. Maguire) - Galway Plate Handicap Chase £22,100 (D.K. Weld)

1993 PERSIAN TACTICS (M.J. Kinane) – Arthur's Race £4,142 (D.K. Weld)

1994 SKIPO (B. Sheridan) – Albatross Maiden Hurdle £4,110 (D.K. Weld)

1994 SAIBOT (W.J. Smith) – McDonogh Handicap £15,500 (D.K. Weld)

1994 TREBLE BOB (D.J. O'Donohue) – Digital Handicap £4,110 (D.K. Weld)

1994 POLITICAL DOMAIN (M.J. Kinane) – Arthur's Race £4,110 (D.K. Weld)

1995 BLAZING SPECTACLE (R. Dunwoody) – Digital Hurdle £4,110 (D.K. Weld)

1996 CELTIC LORE (R. Dunwoody) – Albatross Maiden Hurdle £4,110 (D.K. Weld)

1997 MUSICAL MAYHEM (Mr Edgar Byrne) – Digital Maiden £4,795 (D.K. Weld)

1998 MUSICAL MAYHEM (M.J. Kinane) – McDonogh Timber Handicap £5,550 (D.K. Weld)

1998 MUSICAL MAYHEM (R. Dunwoody) – Harp Lager Novice Hurdle £4,125 (D.K. Weld)

1998 TREBLE BOB (A. Maguire) – Galway Blazers Handicap Chase £5,500 (D.K. Weld)

2001 ONE MORE ROUND (P.J. Smullen) – Compaq Maiden £7,590 (D.K. Weld)

2001 CELTIC LORE (P.J. Smullen) – Smithwicks Handicap £8,625 (D.K. Weld)

2002 MUTAKARRIM (B.J. Geraghty) – Albatross Maiden Hurdle €8,970 (D.K. Weld)

2003 DIRECT BEARING (P. Carberry) – HP Hurdle €12,420 (D.K. Weld)

2005 STOLEN LIGHT (Miss N. Carberry) – Kerry Maid Bumper €9,674 (D.K. Weld)

2006 SUMMER SOUL (R. Walsh) – GPT Novice Hurdle €17,577 (D.K. Weld)

2007 LOYAL FOCUS (Mr M.M. O'Connor) – GPT Galway QR Handicap €65,500 (D.K. Weld)

Dr Michael W.J. Smurfit, the Lancashire-born chairman of Jefferson Smurfit Ltd, Clonskeagh, is a prominent owner on the Irish turf. Sponsors of the Irish St Leger since 1982, Jefferson Smurfit Plc is an Irish paper and packaging firm that was founded by his father and his 7.3% stake in that company is worth about €50 million. Michael Smurfit also has extensive property interests, including the K Club, Straffan, where he has a residence, and a valuable art collection. Domiciled in Monaco, he is a long-standing patron of the Dermot Weld stable, but most of his horses are jumpers nowadays and he does not keep bad horses in training. Between 1984 and 2006, he has won thirty races at the Galway Festival, all bar two of them being trained by Dermot Weld. His policy of buying horses with good form off the flat as prospective jumpers has served him well and he has been leading owner at Galway five times. He has won two Galway Plates, with Kiichi and General Idea, and a Hurdle, with Strathline. Smurfit horses that have won big races apart from Galway include Perris Valley (Irish Grand National), Treble Bob (Kerry National) and the good hurdlers Fortune and Fame and Archive Footage. The outstanding horse he owned was Vintage Crop, twice winner of the Irish St Leger and the first European-trained horse to win the Melbourne Cup.

Dr Michael Smurfit and Ruby Walsh after Summer Soul's victory at the 2006 Galway Festival. It was their only success together at the Galway Festival, at which the owner has had thirty-one victories and the jockey has ridden twenty-five winners

Michael Smurfit was appointed Chairman of the Racing Board in 1984. He had a radical agenda for changes, which included a perspicacious proposal of getting a Levy on Off-Course Betting to fund Irish racing. However, he ran into problems with the Off-Course bookmakers, who feared that his demand would result in an extra 2 per cent tax on Off-Course bets. Having won a hard-fought battle to get the Government to reduce the ridiculously high 20 per cent rate down to a more manageable 10 per cent, they opposed Smurfit's plans because they feared that the tax would go up to 12 per cent. Although Michael Smurfit made an attempt to go along with the bookmakers' proposal that the 2 per cent should come out of the 10 per cent, rather than go on top of it, he was never convinced that the Government would agree to drop its share to 8 per cent and his scepticism showed.

He also did not endear himself to other sectors of the sport by appearing to suggest the closure of many of the smaller racecourses, in what appeared to be an attempt to centralize Irish horse racing. Although he also drew back from that position somewhat, those opposed to change lobbied against him and the Government did not appoint him for a second term. During his one-term tenure, the first Irish Sunday meeting was held, at Leopardstown in July 1985, the Racing Board's building in Merrion Square was sold off and the money used to build new offices at Leopardstown and he expressed his commitment to computerize the tote. Denis Brosnan replaced Michael Smurfit as Chairman of the Racing Board in 1989.

Kieran Fallon (b. 1965)

Rider:

1987 Hamdan Al Maktoum's ALKHAYYAM – Loughrea Handicap flat (K. Prendergast)
2006 Jaykayenn Syndicate's FLYING KNIGHT – William Hill Handicap flat (Noel Lawlor)
2006 Enda Hunston's BOLODENKA – Arthur Guinness Handicap flat (R.A. Fahey)
2007 Mrs John Magnier's LUCIFER SAM – GPT Access 2yo Maiden (A.P. O'Brien)

Described as 'a flawed genius', jockey Kieran Fallon has hogged the headlines, for both the right and the wrong reasons, for over a decade. Born in Crusheen, Co. Clare, in 1965, he began on the pony racing circuit before being apprenticed to Kevin Prendergast, riding his first winner when Piccadilly Lord won in Navan in 1984. When he finished his apprenticeship in 1987, Fallon went to England to ride for Jimmy Fitzgerald and few people put his name down as a future Champion Jockey. His first big win came in the 1993 Lincoln Handicap, in which he landed a huge gamble for Jack and Lynda Ramsden on High Forum. Bad headlines followed when he hit fellow jockey Chris Rutter with his whip, receiving a seven-day ban. Three months later he pulled Stuart Webster off his horse at Beverley. Rumours circulated of a brawl in the jockeys' room, in which Webster came off worst, which is not surprising because Fallon is an excellent boxer, and the stewards clamped down, suspending the Irishman for six months.

Bouncing back, Fallon got a job with Henry Cecil in 1997, won his first classic race, the 1,000 Guineas on Sleepytime, and ended the year as Champion Jockey, the first of his six titles. The following year he joined with Jack and Lynda Ramsden in a libel action against *Sporting Life*, known as the Top Cees case, in which allegations of stopping horses were openly debated in court. The jury found against *Sporting Life* and awarded Fallon £70,000 damages. The following year he won both the Derby and the Oaks at Epsom, on Oath and Ramrura, but soon the headlines turned bad again. First he was fined for using foul and abusive language at Yarmouth and then, out of the blue in July 1999, came the bombshell – Cecil sacked his jockey. He did not give a reason for his action, and Kieran Fallon filed a claim for unfair dismissal. The tabloid press reported gossip about the jockey and the trainer's wife.

In 2000 Fallon began riding for Sir Michael Stoute and immediately had to endure the highs and lows of life. The high was a win on King's Best in the 2,000 Guineas, with the low following six weeks later as he lay on the Ascot turf with a serious shoulder injury, which threatened his career. Out for the rest of the season, he recovered and was back riding for Stoute, but his contract was not renewed in 2002; apparently some of his biggest owners didn't want him.

Fallon continued to ride for Stoute, despite having to admit to an alcohol problem, and rewarded the trainer's faith in him by winning the 2003 Derby on Kris Kin, which was the medium of a huge betting-shop gamble. In March 2004 Fallon was in the news again, with Sky News showing a race on the all-weather track at Lingfield Park over and over again. His mount Ballinger Rouge went ten lengths clear, and was eased prematurely; the favourite, Rye, got up to win by a short head. Fallon admitted that he had been 'over-confident' but the situation was not helped by the on-going inquiry into allegeations of race fixing by Britain's Horseracing Regulatory Authority. Its investigation into possible breaches of the Rules of Racing was referred to the City of London Police and Operation Crypton got under way.

Michael Tabor, the cockney who sold his Arthur Prince betting shop chain to Corals in 1995 and went into bloodstock

Fallon's private life was in turmoil. He had to seek treatment for an alcohol-related problem, and was having marital difficulties which would lead to a separation, but he continued to ride the winners of important races, including an Epsom Derby Oaks double in 2004 on North Light and Ouija Board. In September of that year the balloon went up and British racing was in the dock, when sixteen people, including Fallon, were arrested in a dawn raid to answer allegations relating to the race-fixing enquiry. Released on police bail, he continued his career and was appointed first jockey to Aidan O'Brien at Ballydoyle in 2005, succeeding Jamie Spencer. Riding top-class horses owned by John Magnier, Derrick Smith and Michael Tabor, he had a sensational eighteen months, winning back-to-back Irish Derbies on Hurricane Run and Dylan Thomas and a Group One treble on Arc day 2005 at Longchamp, with Hurricane Run, Horatio Nelson and Rumplestiltskin.

After winning the Irish Derby on Dylan Thomas, Fallon returned to London to report to Bishopsgate Police Station the next day (Monday, 3 July 2006). There he was informed that he was being charged with 'conspiracy to defraud Betfair customers' and ordered to appear in court on 17 July. Charged with him were the trainer Alan Berry, son of Jack, the popular trainer who retired in 2000, and jockeys Fergal Lynch and Darren Williams. 'A complete joke' was Fallon's comment as he maintained his innocence of the charge, but he was in a serious predicament when the Horseracing Regulatory Authority banned him from riding in Britain. Although he could continue riding in Ireland and France, he would be unable to ride Aidan O'Brien's runners in their English races. The trainer and his owners stood by their jockey, and there was vague talk of a boycott of British races but this came to nothing as Fallon went through the appeal process. When the Appeal Board dismissed his appeal, he went to the High Court claiming, 'It's unfair that I am denied a living in Britain', but he lost there too. His case was not helped by the fact that he was an Irish-based jockey, licensed by the Turf Club, and only rode in Britain as a visitor. America and Hong Kong confirmed the ban on Fallon but the Australian authorities allowed him to ride Yeats in the Melbourne Cup.

Betfair is an on-line betting exchange that allows punters to bypass the bookmaker and the tote and lay bets to each other on the payment of a commission. Founded in 2000 by Ed Wray and Andrew Black, it opened up a new method of betting for punters, laying favourites rather than backing them. However, evidence began to surface that persons connected with fancied runners were laying them to lose on the exchange, which gave rise to suspicions that such horses might be deliberately stopped from winning. Betfair provided the records and the police analysed thousands of bets to establish a pattern of betting activity, which led to the charges; in other words they were accused of 'laying dead ones'.

At the end of November 2006 the news broke that Kieran Fallon had failed a drugs test in France and was banned from riding for six months. The positive test was taken when he rode the also-ran, Ivan Denisovich, trained by Aidan O'Brien, in the Prix Jean Prat at Chantilly on 9 July. He was selected for a random test and tiny traces of a prohibited substance, described as a 'metabolite of cocaine', was detected and a riding ban was automatic. Fallon's response to this ban, which prevented him from riding in Ireland too, is to deny wrongdoing. He also implied that he might retire and start up as a trainer. Often referred to as the best big-race jockey since Lester Piggott, Kieran Fallon is strong in the finish and keeps a cool head but his ability to position a horse in a race is not as good as that of Piggott or Pat Eddery.

Kieran Fallon and five other defendants were charged with conspiracy to defraud Betfair customers and the trial began on Monday 8 October 2006. After fifty-three days of evidence Mr Justice Forbes stopped the trial on Friday, 7 December, deciding that there was no case to answer. He instructed the jury to acquit all six defendants of the charges.

Unfortunately, Fallon was almost immediately in trouble again when the French Racing Authorities suspended him for 18 months after he failed another drug test. The sample was taken at Deauville on the day he won the Prix Morny aboard Myboycharlie, trained by Tommy Stack.

Sean F. Cleary (1981–2003)

Rider:

2003 Eamonn Griffin's ANIMAL LOVER – HP Handicap 3yo flat (T. Hogan)
2003 Michael C. Burke's SOPHIYAH–Kerry Spring Handicap flat (Joanna Morgan)

Jockey Sean Cleary only lived to ride two winners at the Galway Festival. He rode a double at the meeting in 2003 before his untimely death the following October, following a fall at Galway when his mount, All Heart, trained by Paddy Mullins, clipped the heels of a horse in front and fell. Sean was thrown into the path of the field, receiving serious head injuries. Rushed by ambulance to the University Hospital in Galway, he was then transferred by helicopter to the Beaumount Hospital in Dublin, where he died a week later. Despite wearing a crash helmet, severe head injuries resulted in his death. He was the twenty-first rider to be killed race riding in Ireland (point-to-points not included) since 1900 and the fifth to be killed riding in an Irish flat race during this period; Mr H.R. Poe (Listowel 1902), John H. Harty (Curragh 1929), Patrick F. 'Mutt' Conlon (Kilbeggan 1952) and

Michael Teelin (Leopardstown 1971) were the others. He was the first casualty at Ballybrit. Unfortunately, he was not the only jockey to be killed in 2003 – Kieran Kelly was fatally injured in a steeplechase at Kilbeggan three months earlier.

Only twenty-two years old and still an apprentice, Sean Cleary was a member of a well-known racing family from Athlone. His father, Tom, was Chairman and his mother, Kathleen, Joint Treasurer of the Midlands Pony Racing Association and Sean rode over a hundred winners under that code, including the biggest race, the Dingle Derby. Having spent some time with his uncle, Mattie O'Toole, who trains in Headford, Co. Galway, he joined Jim Bolger as an apprentice jockey, riding his first winner, Montana Lady, at Cork in June 2000. Having ridden nineteen winners, seven of whom were trained by Jim Bolger, his indentures were transferred to Pat Flynn; among his fourteen winners in 2003 was Traverse. A winner at Ballinrobe at the end of August, Traverse was the star of a documentary film being made by his owner, a TV personality named Hector, called *Only Fools Buy Horses*. With the cameras rolling, extraordinary scenes of delight unfolded after the race when Hector, and anybody else who was willing, made fools of themselves hopping and dancing around. The spectacle ended with Sean Cleary, wielding an open bottle of champagne instead of a whip, riding piggyback on Hector around the parade ring to the accompaniment of the loud cheers, jeers and catcalls from the bemused onlookers.

Sean Cleary rode his last winner when Church House Lady, trained by David Wachman, won at Roscommon on 7 September. His younger brother Rory is currently among the top apprentices riding in Ireland.

Declan P. McDonogh (b. 1980)

Rider:

1999 Celtic Tiger Syndicate's THE BOXER – Compaq Handicap (E. Lynam)

1999 Glassdrummon Syndicate's CHATEAU LINA – Carlsberg 2yo Race (F. Berry)

2002 Hamdan Al Maktoum's ABUNAWWAS – GPT 2yo Maiden (K.Prendergast)

2003 Hamdan Al Maktoum's TAKRICE – McDonogh 2yo Maiden (K.Prendergast)

2003 Hamdan Al Maktoum's ELKIM – McDonogh Handicap (K. Prendergast)

2003 F. Hinojosa's BLAVA – McDonogh 3yo Maiden (K. Prendergast)

2004 Lady O'Reilly's DEFI – GPT 2yo Maiden (K. Prendergast)

2004 Lady O'Reilly's RIGHT KEY – McDonogh 2yo Maiden (K. Prendergast)

2005 Joseph Joyce's NOEND – GPT 3yo Handicap (Miss F.M. Crowley)

2005 Sue Bramall's HEEMANELA – H.P. Handicap (Mrs S. Bramall)

2005 Helensburgh Syndicate's HELENSBURGH – Budweiser Handicap (P.Hughes)

2006 Clive Craig's DANI'S GIRL – Guinness Fillies Race (P.A. Fahy)

2006 Cheveley Park Stud's ELUSIVE DREAM – St James's Gate Race (Sir M. Prescott in Great Britain)

2006 R. Stokes's KEVKAT – Guinness Handicap (Eoin Griffin)

2006 Hamdan Al Maktoum's RAJEH – 1759 3yo Maiden (K. Prendergast)

2006 Enda Hunston's BOLODENKA – Michael McNamara Handicap (R.A. Fahey in Great Britain)

2007 Bernard Caldwell's MISS UNA – Parknasilla Hotel Handicap (Patrick Martin)

Declan McDonogh from Moynalty, Co. Meath, comes from a family steeped in racing. His father Des trained Monksfield to win the Champion Hurdle in successive years, 1978 and 1979, and in that latter year also won the Supreme Novices Hurdle with Stranfield, a former Galway winner. Declan's mother, the former Helen Bryce-Smith, was a leading point-to-point rider and a daughter of the Kells trainer Cyril Bryce-Smith. Although regarded as a jumping trainer, having won important races with Injunction, Cannobie Lee and Hunter's Breeze, Cyril trained three winners of the Naas October Handicap on the flat. His son (Declan's uncle) John Bryce-Smith, trained Poacher's Tale, Quick Result and Rathinree to win flat races at Galway and won the Galway Plate and the Kerry Grand National with Spittin Image. He also had charge of Mwanadike, the ill-fated champion four-year-old hurdler of 1976.

Declan McDonogh rode his first Festival winner on The Boxer in 1999 and became Irish Champion Jockey in 2006

Starting his career as an apprentice, Declan McDonogh rode his first winner, Aine's Pet, trained by his father, at Leopardstown in June 1995. His mount made all the running to win the Derrinstown Apprentice Handicap by a head over the old straight six-furlong course, which has since been gobbled up to make way for the M50 motorway. Although he was never Champion Apprentice, Declan was one of the leading young riders, scoring a double at the 1999 Galway Festival. The retirement of Stephen Craine gave Declan an opportunity to ride many of the Kevin Prendergast horses. Lady Chryss O'Reilly's Rebelline provided the young jockey with his first Group One winner when winning the 2002 Tattersalls Gold Cup at the Curragh. The following year Galway racegoers got a glimpse of the boy's talent when he rode a 615-to-1 treble for Kevin on the second day of the festival. Having established himself as the stable jockey, Declan rode brilliantly throughout 2006, had five winners at the Galway Festival to share the honour of leading rider with Ruby Walsh and Davy Condon, and rode his first winner at Royal Ascot. His final tally of 89 winners in 2006 ensured that he became Irish Champion Flat Jockey for the first time, thirteen winners ahead of the reigning flat champion Pat Smullen. Declan McDonogh's hero is Steve Cauthen, the brilliant young American jockey who came to Britain at the age of nineteen in 1979 and confounded the experts by becoming the first American-born Champion Jockey since Danny Maher in 1913.

Pat Smullen, leading jockey at the 2007 Galway Festival

Galway Plate and Galway Hurdle Placings

The Plate was first run in 1869 and the Hurdle in 1913. For each race the first three are given. The second bracketed name after the name of the winning horse is the horse's trainer.

GALWAY PLATE

1869
ABSENTEE (W. Bell) 3/1 (Richard Bell)
Quickstep (T. Ryan) 2/1f
Lady Clarendon (M. Broderick) 10/1
1½ lengths, 1 length.

1870
COMET (Mr J.D. Whyte) 5/1 (Michael Igoe)
Gamekeeper (Whelan) 33/1
Lazy Moll (McDonald) 33/1
1½ lengths, same.

1871
ASTER (Mr R. Exshaw) 9/1 (H.S. Croker)
Venison (M. Murphy) 8/1
Stella (late Lady of Kars) (M. Connolly) 10/1
3 lengths, 4 lengths.

1872
BELLE (W. Bell) 3/1f (Richard Bell)
Ishmael (Mr G. Moore) 12/1
Quickstep (Mr R. Exshaw) 20/1
6 lengths, 2 lengths.

1873
LANCET (late Blue Pill) (M. Connolly) 16/1
    (Thomas Ryan)
Gamebird (Mr T. Beasley) 16/1
Mickey Free (Burke) 25/1
4 lengths, same.

1874
REVOKE (T. Miller) 6/1 (John Hubert Moore)
Bashful (W. Ryan) 2/1f
Humble Bee (Mr Apleton) 100/8
5 lengths, wretched third.

1875
THE LIBERATOR (T. Ryan) 7/1 (John Hubert
    Moore)
Mimulus (P. Gavin) 8/1
Pride of Kildare (G. Gray) 4/1jf
1 length, same.

1876
MARTHA (Mr T. Beasley) 8/1 (Henry Eyre Linde)
Ilderim (W. Bell) 10/1
Kangaroo (W. Behan) 8/1
3 lengths, neck.

1877
TATTOO (W. Canavan) 5/1 (Joseph G. Blake)
Foxhound (W. Bell) 10/1
Martinet (P. Gavin) Unquoted
In a canter, head.

1878
JUPITER TONANS (Mr J.F. Lee Barber) 2/1f (Capt.
    George Joy)
Lottery (T. Miller) Unquoted
Emily (M. Behan) 5/1
The Inny (Byrne) won but disqualified for going
    the wrong side of a post.

1879
ROCKSAVAGE (Mr J.F. Lee Barber) 8/1 (Capt.
    George Joy)
Reveller (Mr P.P. Lynch) 6/1
Premium (P. Gavin) 5/1
In a canter by several lengths, a bad third.

1880
LADY NEWMAN (D. Meany) 7/1 (James Monahan)
Pinnace (W. Behan) 5/2f
Lobelia (Mr D. Russell) 8/1
1½ lengths, moderate third.

1881
NIGHTFALL (Mr T. Beasley) 6/1 (Henry Eyre Linde)
The Gift (T. Kelly) 10/1
Rose of Richmond (J. Walsh) 5/1
2 lengths, third well up.

1882
SUGAR PLUM (Mr H. Beasley) 6/1 (Henry Eyre
    Linde)
Wild Norah II (P. Keys) 6/1
Rhea (T. Kelly) 8/1
1 length, good third.

1883
VENTRILOQUIST (Mr H. Beasley) 5/6f (Henry Eyre
    Linde)
Lovelace (P. Gavin) 4/1
First Love (Mr Igoe Jr) 13/2
1½ lengths, bad third.

1884
NEW MEADOW (Mr R. Brabazon) 4/1 (George L.
    Walker)
Harkaway (P. Lynch Snr) 13/2
Duster (S. Burke) 4/1
10 lengths, bad third.

1885
ERIN'S STAR (Mr W.P. Cullen) 9/2 (F.F. & W.P.
    Cullen)
2= Rosa (J. Behan) 3/1f
2= Eva (P. Fiely) 10/1
Half a neck, dead heat.

1886
ZULU II (T. Kavanagh) 4/1 (Daniel Broderick)
Lord Chatham (Mr F.F. Cullen) 8/1
Eva (Coghlan) 5/1
3 lengths, 4 lengths.

1887
VICTRIX (Mr W.P. Cullen) 9/4 (Frederick F. Cullen)
Lord Chatham (Mr W. McAuliffe) 20/1
Sweetness (Mr H. Beasley) 6/4f
Neck, 4 lengths.

1888
FETHARD (J. Hoysted) 7/2 (Thomas Broderick)
Sir Hugh (Mr H. Beasley) 5/1
Zulu II (Mr W.P. Cullen) 5/1
2 lengths, same.

1889
ALEXANDER (T. Kavanagh) 4/1 (Henry Eyre Linde)
Zulu II (Mr W.P. Cullen) 3/1
J.P. (Mr G.W. Lushington) 4/1
1 length, same.

1890
LAKEFIELD (J. Walsh) 6/1 (Michael Dennehy)
Brown Eyes (L. Ryan) 4/1
Huron (J. Hoysted) 7/1
2 lengths, bad third.

1891
QUEEN OF THE MAY (Mr W. Beasley) 1/1f
    (Frederick F. Cullen)
Spring Daisy (L. Kelly) 8/1
The Drummer (N. Waterson) 8/1
8 lengths, bad third.

1892
SPRINGFIELD MAID (E. Reilly) 4/1 (S.A. Leonard)
May Night (T. Kavanagh) 5/1
Little Widow (J. Gourley) 3/1f
½ length, 7 lengths.

1893
LADY PAT (T. Bailey) 1/1f (William McAuliffe)
Specs (Mr M.J. Harty) 6/1
Happy Girl (Mr P. Purcell) 8/1
4 lengths, bad third.

1894
STAR ONE (E. Reilly) 8/1 (George L. Walker)
Specs (Mr M.J. Harty) 7/2f
Duchess of Fife (Mr J. Phelan) 10/1
1½ lengths, head.

1895
DOUBLE PRIMROSE (W. Hoysted) 5/2f (Henry
    Eyre Linde)
Valentine II (N. Waterson) 4/1
Miss Baron (Sherwin) 10/1
1½ lengths, neck.

1896
CASTLE WARDEN (Mr W.P. Cullen) 5/2f (William
    P. Cullen)
Sweet Charlotte (T. Kavanagh) 7/1
Oldtown (Mr L. Sheil) 10/1
6 lengths, 4 lengths.

1897
DROGHEDA (Dowdall) 4/1 (George F. Gradwell)
Castle Warden (C. Hogan) 7/2jf
Antelope (Dempsey) 10/1
3 lengths, 5 lengths.

1898
BOREENCHREEOGUE (J. Cheshire) 8/1 (James
    Cheshire)
Chevy Chase (C. Hogan) 11/2
Foremast (T. Lane) 5/2f
½ length, 6 lengths.

1899
TIPPERARY BOY (T. Moran) 8/1 (Frederick F.
    Cullen)
Carline (T. Lane) 33/1
Blue Guts (Mr H.S. Kenny) 33/1
6 lengths, 3 lengths.

1900
IVANOFF (J. O'Brien) 10/1 (F. Moran)
Springfield (T. Dowdall) 10/1
Honeymoon II (M. Walsh) 10/1
8 lengths, neck.

1901
TIPPERARY BOY (T. Moran) 5/2f (Frederick F.
    Cullen)
Astronomer II (T. Fiely) 5/1
Moral Mary (A. Anthony) 7/1
15 lengths, same.

1902
TIPPERARY BOY (T. Kavanagh) 6/1 (Frederick F.
    Cullen)
Shallon (T. Dent) 8/1
Benvenir (Mr M. Hayes) 10/1
5 lengths, 8 lengths.

1903
HAMPTON BOY (A. Anthony) 5/2f (Michael
    Dawson)
Lord of the Soil (R. Morgan) 8/1
Springfield (T. Fiely) 100/6
2 lengths, 10 lengths.

1904
STRATEGY (A. Magee) 4/1f (William P. Cullen)
Knocksouna (J. Scully) 10/1
Brown Study (Mr J.W. Widger) 10/1
Won in a canter, bad third.

1905
GOLDFIELD II (M. Walsh) 7/2f (Edward Malone)
Lord of the Soil (R. Morgan) 5/1
Miss Tessie (Mr T. Price) 4/1
¾ length, ½ length.

1906
ROYAL TARA (R. Morgan) 8/1 (Denis Shanahan)
Capitulate (Mr P. O'Brien Butler) 6/1
Flight (Mr R.H. Walker) 8/1
10 lengths, ¾ length.

1907
APOLLO BELVEDERE (Mr P. O'Brien Butler) 6/1
    (J. Currid)
Cowboy (Mr R.H. Walker) 5/1f
Prospect II (A. Anthony) 6/1
Neck, 10 lengths.

1908
SHADY GIRL (G. Brown) 5/1jf (Maxwell Arnott)
Rosy Symons (Hon R. Bruce) 7/1
Alice Delvin (F. Morgan) 20/1
4 lengths, 3 lengths.

1909
SCHWARMER (A. Anthony) 5/1 (Michael Dawson)
Rosy Symons (P. Cowley) 3/1f
Sore Toes (Mr R.H. Walker) 6/1
8 lengths, 1½ lengths.

1910
ASHBROOKE (Mr H. Ussher) 4/1 (W.A. Ussher)
Noble Grecian (A. Anthony) 4/1
Another Delight (G. Brown) 3/1f
3 lengths, 5 lengths.

1911
DEAR SONNY (E. Lawn) 5/2 (H.L. Fitzpatrick)
The Miner (H. Harty) 7/1
Gra ma Cree (W. Watkinson) 7/1
Head, same.

1912
NOBLE GRECIAN (G. Brown) 4/1f (Maxwell Arnott)
Koepinicker (Mr P. Nugent) 100/8
Spinning Queen (Mr J. Coghlan) 33/1
2 lengths, 5 lengths.

1913
GEORGE B (Mr G. Harty) 10/1 (John Ruttle)
Raida (Mr J.C. Kelly) 10/1
Prince Abercorn (T. Dowdall) 10/1
8 lengths, 2 lengths.

1914
ALICE ROCKTHORN (Mr P. Nugent) 8/1 (Algernon Anthony)
Fast Brendan (Capt. P. O'Brien Butler) 5/2f
Silver Dart (J. Lynn) 20/1
Head, 2 lengths.

1915
HILL OF CAMAS (G. Harty) 20/1 (Capt. W. Molony)
Lie Low (C.O. Hawkins) 6/1
Glenpatrick (Mr L. Brabazon) 7/2
¾ length, a bad third.

1916
NEVER FEAR (F. Morgan) 20/1 (Reginald H. Walker)
Alice Rockthorn (Mr P. Nugent) 16/1
Golden Fleece (Mr L.S. Ward) 8/1
Neck, 4 lengths.

1917
PRIVIT (W. Smith) 20/1 (Maxwell Arnott)
Golden Fleece (Mr L.S. Ward) 7/1
Awbeg (Mr T. O'Roarke) 100/8
3 lengths, 8 lengths.

1918
GOLDEN FLEECE (A. Stubbs) 7/1jf (John T. Rogers)
Semper Idem (Joseph Canty) 7/1jf
Hotcap (H. Harty) 100/8
Neck, a bad third.

1919
PICTURE SAINT (M. Colbert) 20/1 (Henry I. Ussher)
Templedowney (H. Harty) 10/1
Pacifist (Joseph Canty) 10/1
4 lengths, 1 length.

1920
CLONREE (F. Morgan) 3/1f (Francis Morgan)
Ganzey (Joseph Canty) 8/1
Pam Nut (M. Dillon) 25/1
20 lengths, 2 lengths.

1921
MAX (F. Wootton) 4/1 (Henry I. Ussher)
Sir Huon (C. Aylin) 5/2f
Pacifist (Joseph Canty) 6/1
3 lengths, ½ length.

1922 No Meeting

1923
CLONSHEEVER (J. Hogan jr) 10/1 (Henry I. Ussher)
Helmet (W. Horan) 7/1
Maureen Bawn (P. Lynch) 7/2
3 lengths, 2 lengths.

1924
CLONSHEEVER (F.B. Rees) 8/1 (Henry I. Ussher)
Fort Elizabeth (L.B. Rees) 100/8
Ballystockart (J. Meaney) 100/6
15 lengths, 6 lengths.

1925
BLANCONA (C. Donnelly) 6/1 (Cecil Brabazon)
Ingomar (M. Keogh) 6/1
Clonsheever (J. Hogan Jr) 2/1f
8 lengths, 3 lengths.

1926
FAIR RICHARD (D. Ward) 6/4f (Maxwell Arnott)
Tiranogue (Mr B. Masterson) 9/2
Silent Doon (J. McNeill) 100/8
15 lengths, 6 lengths.

1927
TONY LAD (J. Moloney) 6/4 (Henry I. Ussher)
Easter Hero (P. Powell) 1/1f
Rare Sort (Joseph Doyle) 50/1
3 lengths, 10 lengths.

1928
EAST GALWAY (D. Ward) 1/1f (Maxwell Arnott)
Tiranogue (T.B. Cullinan) 4/1
Odd Cat (J. McNeill) 20/1
3 lengths, 1½ lengths.

1929
GUIDING LIGHT (P. Powell) 6/1 (Joseph Dawson)
East Galway (D. Ward) 6/4f
Southern Prince (T. Morgan) 9/2
1½ lengths, 20 lengths.

1930
EAST GALWAY (J. McNeill) 5/4f (Maxwell Arnott)
Bayview (Mr F.E. McKeever) 4/1
Fanmond (T.B. Cullinan) 6/1
3 lengths, 10 lengths.

1931
PUCKA SHIKHARI (Mr J.A. Mangan) 100/8 (J.A. (Gus) Mangan)
Gold Heart (Mr F.E. McKeever) 3/1jf
Heartbreak Hill (Mr T.W. Dreaper) 100/14
2 lengths, same.

1932
SEAVIEW (Timothy Regan) 50/1 (Matt Cunningham)
Koscie's Star (Mr F.E. McKeever) 7/2f
Nell's Son (Mr R.H. Stern) 10/1
¾ length, 4 lengths.

1933
RED PARK (D. Kirwan) 3/1 (J.J. Barry)
Cushendall (J. Costello) 10/1
Brave Edna (E. Dempsey) 100/8
1½ lengths, 3 lengths.

1934
REVIEWER (Mr P. Sleator Jr) 5/1 (M. Deegan)
Avondale (Timothy Regan) 4/1
Cottage View (W.T. O'Grady) 5/2f
1 length, 6 lengths.

1935
SOUTHERNMORE (J. Hamey) 10/1 (Capt. E.A. Gargan)
Lucky Fool (Mr T. Hyde) 5/1
Flying Rose (W.T. O'Grady) 100/8
4 lengths, 3 lengths.

1936
YELLOW FURZE (J. McNeill) 4/1f (J.P. Loughran)
Cabin Fire (Timothy Regan) 5/1
Pucka Shikhari (W. Rea) 16/1
10 lengths, 20 lengths.

1937
BRIGHTER COTTAGE (W.T. O'Grady) 8/1jf (Henry I. Ussher)
Cabin Fire (R. Browne) 10/1
Rockquilla (Mr R.H. Stern) 100/8
4 lengths, 6 lengths.

1938
SYMAETHIS (D. Butchers) 20/1 (Robert Fetherstonhaugh)
Golden Star (T. McNeill) 8/1
Cabin Fire (T. Hide) 12/1
2½ lengths, 1 length.

1939
PULCHER (J. Costello) 100/8 (Robert
    Fetherstonhaugh)
Drumlargin (W.T. O'Grady) 4/1f
Bistro (J. Brogan) 100/8
1½ lengths, 2 lengths.

1940
RING OF GOLD (T. McNeill) 100/8 (Henry I.
    Ussher)
Sir Sen (S. Magee) 100/6
Swindon Glory (Mr P.P. Hogan) 40/1
1½ lengths, 2½ lengths.

1941
ST MARTIN (A. Brabazon) 6/4f (Cecil Brabazon)
General Chiang (S. Magee) 6/1
Cabin Fire (T. Hide) 14/1
15 lengths, 3 lengths.

1942
GOLDEN JACK (D.L. Moore) 7/4f (Charles A.
    Rogers)
The Gripper (J. Lenehan) 6/1
Drumlargin (J. Brogan) 10/1
1½ lengths, head.

1943
SWINDON GLORY (A. Brabazon) 5/1 (J.A. (Gus)
    Mangan)
Funny (T. Hyde) 11/4
Golden Jack (R. McCarthy) 2/1f
5 lengths, head.

1944
SWINDON GLORY (A. Brabazon) 7/2f (J.A. (Gus)
    Mangan)
Grecian Victory (J. Brogan) 20/1
Knight's Crest (M. Molony) 9/2
1½ lengths, 2 lengths.

1945
GRECIAN VICTORY (D. Morgan) 10/1 (Henry I.
    Ussher)
Sun Bird (T.V. Wyse) 100/8
Pongo (B. O'Neill) 7/2jf
½ length, 1½ length.

1946
KEEP FAITH (T. Hyde) 7/1jf (Thomas W. Dreaper)
Swindon Glory (A. Brabazon) 7/1jf
Shaun Ogue (M. Molony) 8/1
8 lengths, 2 lengths.

1947
CHARLES EDWARD (J. Brogan) 100/6 (Bernard
    Nugent)
New Pyjamas (M. Browne) 20/1
Lough Conn (D. McCann) 8/1
½ length, 6 lengths.

1948
SILENT PRAYER (T. Molony) 100/8 (Patrick Sleator)
Rockcorry (D. McCann) 50/1
Aaron's Rod (B. O'Neill) 100/8
¾ length, same.

1949
RESULT (Mr H. Freeman Jackson) 20/1 (Henry
    Freeman Jackson)
Sadlers Wells (T.P. Burns) 6/1jf
3= Colin Bell (R. McCarthy) 10/1
3= Green Dolphin (M. Molony) 10/1
½ length, 1 length.

1950
DERRINSTOWN (F. McKenna) 100/7 (Gerard
    Flood)
Whale Harbour (C. Grassick) 20/1
Homer Gray (James Power) 100/8
3 lengths, ½ length.

1951
ST KATHLEEN II (P.J. Doyle) 15/2 (William T.
    O'Grady)
Alberoni (C. Grassick) 100/8
Green Dolphin (M. Molony) 100/8
3 lengths, 6 lengths.

1952
ALBERONI (L. Stephens) 3/1jf (M. Vincent O'Brien)
Lucky Dome (P.J. Doyle) 7/1
Nice Work (P. Taaffe) 3/1jf
Short head, 2 lengths.

1953
GALLANT WOLF (T. Taaffe) 6/1jf (Thomas J. Taaffe)
Arctic Silver (B. Cooper) 10/1
Southern Coup (James Walshe) 6/1jf
5 lengths, ¾ length.

1954
AMBER POINT (C. Sleator) 6/1jf (Patrick Sleator)
Dovetail (C. Grassick) 100/6
Carey's Cottage (G.J. Coogan) 20/1
1½ lengths, 8 lengths.

1955
UMM (P. Taaffe) 11/4f (George H. Wells)
Athenian (T. O'Brien) 100/8
Skateaway (C. Sleator) 11/4jf
Head, 4 lengths.

1956
AMBER POINT (P.A. Farrell) 2/1f (Patrick Sleator)
New Hope (C. Kinane) 9/1
Brookling (H.R. Beasley) 8/1
10 lengths, 4 lengths.

1957
KNIGHT ERRANT (H.R. Beasley) 4/1f (Patrick Sleator)
New Hope (D. Kinane) 20/1
Nickleby (M. Scudamore) 100/8
3 lengths, ½ length.

1958
HOPEFUL COLLEEN (J.A. Mahony) 20/1 (James Brogan)
Amber Point (C. Finnegan) 7/1
Steel Friend (J. Morrissey) 100/7
3 lengths, same.

1959
HIGHFIELD LAD (J. Lehane) 100/9 (Charles L. Weld)
Mazzibell (P. Taaffe) 7/2f
Monsieur Trois Etoiles (F. Carroll) 100/7
8 lengths, same.

1960
SPARKLING FLAME (H.R. Beasley) 5/4f (Patrick Sleator)
Clipador (F. Shortt) 7/1
Knoxtown (F. Carroll) 100/7
12 lengths, 3 lengths.

1961
CLIPADOR (H.R. Beasley) 7/4f (Patrick Sleator)
Irish Coffee (J. Magee) 7/1
Roddy Owen (T. Taaffe) 20/1
¾ length, neck.

1962
CARRAROE (F.T. Winter) 4/1f (A.S. O'Brien)
Height o' Fashion (T.F. Lacy) 100/8
Trial Game (L. McLoughlin) 10/1
½ length, 5 lengths.

1963
BLUNTS CROSS (H.R. Beasley) 9/4f (A.S. O'Brien)
Baxier (Mr W.A. McLernon) 100/8
Maggie Gore (Mr G. Rooney) 33/1
2 lengths, 2½ lengths.

1964
ROSS SEA (S. Mellor) 9/2f (A.S. O'Brien)
Highfield Lad (B. Hannon) 100/8
Burton Brown II (F. Shortt) 20/1
1½ lengths, 8 lengths.

1965
ROSS SEA (S. Mellor) 8/1 (A.S. O'Brien)
Greek Lad (B. Hannon) 10/1
Carobin (A. Redmond) 5/1
3 lengths, 5 lengths.

1966
CAPPAWHITE (T. Finn) 20/1 (George Spencer)
Splash (P. Woods) 6/1
Arctic Sea (C. Finnegan) 100/8
Neck, 2 lengths. (Photo)

1967
ROYAL DAY (R. Coonan) 19/2 (Patrick Sleator)
Rock Venture (M.C. Gifford) 13/2
Ross Sea (J. Gifford) 100/8
Neck, 6 lengths. (Photo)

1968
TEROSSIAN (G.W. Robinson) 7/2f (George H. Wells)
Kilcoo (Mr A. Stanley Robinson) 10/1
Vulnagrena (P. Black) 10/1
2½ lengths, 1 length.

1969
ROYAL DAY (R. Coonan) 7/1 (Patrick Sleator)
Common Entrance (T. Carberry) 100/7
Nostra (F. Carroll) 100/7
2 lengths, ½ length.

1970
LISNAREE (F. Shortt) 20/1 (A. Watson)
Herring Gull (P. Taaffe) 2/1f
Twigairy (S. Barker) 7/1
6 lengths, 1½ lengths.

1971
SAREJAY DAY (S. Shields) 33/1 (Edward Farrell)
Larbawn (M.C. Gifford) 7/1
Storyville (J.P. Harty) 16/1
Short head, ¾ length. (Photo)

1972
PERSIAN LARK (J.P. Harty) 13/2 (Jeremy F.C. Maxwell)
Escari (P. Black) 6/1
Red Candle (D.T. Hughes) 11/2f
2 lengths, 1½ lengths.

1973
LEAP FROG (T. Carberry) 11/2 (J.T.R. Dreaper)
Vulforo (E. Wright) 8/1
Rossbracken (S. Shields) 14/1
2½ lengths, ½ length.

1974
BUNCLODY TIGER (T. Browne) 4/1 (Kevin Bell)
Spittin Image (J.P. Harty) 7/1
I'm Happy (J.J. O'Neill) 6/1
2 lengths, 8 lengths.

1975
OUR ALBERT (D.T. Hughes) 3/1 (Michael A. O'Toole)
Colonial Prince (L. O'Donnell) 25/1
I'm Happy (P. Kiely) 4/1
6 lengths, 2 lengths.

1976
O'LEARY (R. Coonan) 8/1 (Patrick Sleator)
Andy Pandy (Mr W.P. Mullins) 13/2
Kiltotan (F. Murphy) 5/1
1½ lengths, head.

1977
SPITTIN IMAGE (M. Cummins) 7/1 (John R. Bryce-Smith)
Maniwaki (G. Thorner) 25/1
Claddagh Boy (S. Treacy) 16/1
2½ lengths, same.

1978
SHINING FLAME (Mr N. Madden) 4/1jf (Edward J. O'Grady)
Kilkilwell (D.T. Hughes) 10/1
Bright and Well (G. Newman) 10/1
4 lengths, 1½ lengths.

1979
HINDHOPE (J.J. O'Neill) 6/1 (Edward J. O'Grady)
The Lady's Master (F. Berry) 9/2f
Appease (P.G. Murphy) 14/1
5 lengths, 1 length.

1980
SIR BARRY (P. Kiely) 10/1 (J.William Boyers)
Under Way (Mr N. Madden) 6/1jf
Corrib Chieftain (T. McGivern) 6/1jf
5 lengths, head.

1981
RUGGED LUCY (T.J. Ryan) 14/1 (Edward J. O'Grady)
Pillar Brae (Mr T.M. Walsh) 3/1f
*Sports Reporter (G. Newman) 10/1
1 length. * 4th promoted.

1982
THE LADY'S MASTER (N. Madden) 12/1 (Matt C.
    Duggan)
Duncreggan (G. McGlinchey) 25/1
Luska (T.V. Finn) 7/1
1 length, same.

1983
HAMERS FLAME (J. Brassil) 12/1 (Michael Neville)
Avocan (P. Leech) 14/1
Foggy Buoy (J.J. O'Neill) 12/1
3 lengths, ½ length.

1984
MASTER PLAYER (J.P. Byrne) 40/1 (Thomas
    Bergin)
Doubtful Venture (Mr W.P. Mullins) 10/1
Wheels (J.J. O'Neill) 9/2f
5 lengths, short head.

1985
CHOW MEIN (T. Morgan) 7/1 (Desmond T.
    Hughes)
Greasepaint (T. Carmody) 5/1
Pendor Lawn (P.F. Kiely) 33/1
1 length, 2½ lengths.

1986
BORO QUARTER (P. Kavanagh) 10/1 (Patrick
    Mullins)
Bold Agent (T.J. Taaffe) 12/1
Winning Nora (K.F. O'Brien) 10/1
4 lengths, 10 lengths.

1987
RANDOSS (K. Morgan) 6/1jf (Miss Anne Collen)
Super Furrow (M.M. Treacy) 10/1
Afford A King (Mr G.T. Lynch) 25/1
2 lengths, 6 lengths.

1988
AFFORD A KING (P. Gill) 10/1 (Anthony Mullins)
Kalamalka (T. Kinane Jr) 10/1
Belsir (B. Sheridan) 8/1
6 lengths, 5 lengths.

1989
BOLD FLYER (Miss S.G. Collen) 8/1 (James T.R.
    Dreaper)
Another Plano (C.F. Swan) 16/1
Vulgan's Pass (L.P. Cusack) 20/1
8 lengths, 6 lengths.

1990
KIICHI USA (B. Sheridan) 2/1f (Dermot K. Weld)
Amative (J.F. Titley) 20/1
Belsir (T. Carmody) 16/1
Head, 5 lengths. (Photo)

1991
FIRIONS LAW (M. Flynn) 9/1 (Victor Bowens)
Never Be Great (C. O'Dwyer) 14/1
Ace Of Spies (N. Williamson) 16/1
3 lengths, ¾ length.

1992
THE GOOSER (A. Maguire) 25/1 (Patrick Mullins)
Baptismal Fire (J.F. Titley) 33/1
Four Trix (R. Dunwoody) 12/1
10 lengths, 3 lengths.

1993
GENERAL IDEA (A. Maguire) 9/2f (Dermot K.
    Weld)
Harristown Lady (J.R. Kavanagh) 33/1
Galevilla Express (C.N. Bowens) 7/1
6 lengths, neck.

1994
FEATHERED GALE (F. Woods) 8/1 (Arthur L.T.
    Moore)
Minister For Fun (C.F. Swan) 11/2
Mubadir USA (P. Carberry) 10/1
Head, neck. (Photo)

1995
LIFE OF A LORD (T. Horgan) 12/1 (Aidan P.
    O'Brien)
Kelly's Pearl (J.F. Titley) 16/1
Loshian (C.F. Swan) 6/1
20 lengths, 3 ½ lengths.

1996
LIFE OF A LORD (C.F. Swan) 9/2 (Aidan P. O'Brien)
Bishops Hall (R. Dunwoody) 14/1
King Wah Glory (C. O'Dwyer) 9/4f
1½ lengths, 8 lengths.

1997
STROLL HOME (P. Carberry) 11/2 (James John
    Mangan)
Idiot's Venture (C.F. Swan) 14/1
Derrymoyle (Mr G. Elliott) 20/1
Neck, 10 lengths. (Photo)

1998
AMLAH USA (B.G. Powell) 16/1 (Philip J. Hobbs
    GB)
Lucky Town (D.J. Casey) 9/2f
Corket (A. Dobbin) 8/1
13 lengths, 10 lengths.

1999
MOSCOW EXPRESS (R. Walsh) 4/1 (Miss Frances
    M. Crowley)
Lucky Town (D.J. Casey) 10/1
Nicholls Cross (N. Williamson) 16/1
1 length, neck.

2000
DOVALY GB (T.P. Rudd) 20/1 (Michael J.P. O'Brien)
Monty's Pass (K. Whelan) 16/1
Palette (R. Walsh) 10/1
3 lengths, 2 lengths.

2001
GRIMES GB (C. O'Dwyer) 4/1jf (Christopher
    Roche)
Quinze GB (P.A. Carberry) 7/1
Dovaly GB (T.P. Rudd) 12/1
1½ lengths, 1 length.

2002
ROCKHOLM BOY (K. Hadnett) 20/1 (Michael
    Hourigan)
Wotsitooya (D.T. Hughes) 14/1
Ridgewood Water (Paul Moloney) 25/1
3½ lengths, 3 lengths.

2003
NEARLY A MOOSE (R.M. Power) 25/1 (Patrick
    Mullins)
Kadoun (Mr D.W. Cullen) 10/1
Glynn Dingle (G. Lee) 16/1
4 lengths, ½ length.

2004
ANSAR (D.J. Casey) 10/1 (Dermot K. Weld)
Risk Accessor (A.P. McCoy) 20/1
Manjoe (M.D. Grant) 14/1
1 length, ½ length.

2005
ANSAR (D.F. O'Regan) 10/1 (Dermot K. Weld)
Ursumman (N.P. Madden) 14/1
Light on the Broom (M.P. Walsh) 25/1
7 lengths, ¾ length.

2006
FAR FROM TROUBLE (R. Loughran) 8/1
    (Christopher Roche)
Ansar (R. Walsh) 4/1f
Dix Villez FR (P.J. Brennan) 16/1
3½ lengths, 1¼ lengths.

2007
SIR FREDERICK (K.T. Coleman) 12/1 (W.J. Burke)
Ballyagran (P. Carberry) 20/1
Cool Running (A.P. McCoy) 8/1
3 lengths, 4½ lengths.

Galway Hurdle

1913
RED DAMSEL (F. Morgan) 10/1 (Maxwell Arnott)
Shikaree (Mr R.H. Walker)100/8
Misdeed (R. Trudgill) 100/8
Short head, 2 lengths.

1914
CLONMEEN (F. Morgan) 3/1f (Maxwell Arnott)
Don't Worry II (M. Dowdall) 10/1
Land Agent (C. Aylin) 100/8
1 length, ¾ length.

1915
NAUGHTY EARL (C.O. Hawkins) 7/4f (Michael
    Dawson)
Mostrim (M. Colbert) 10/1
Bitter Cherry (Mr J.R. Anthony) 20/1
3 lengths, same.

1916
ELGON (Mr H.S. Harrison) 9/4 (Reginald H.
    Walker)
Lola (C. Aylin) 5/1
Simon Ashton (T. Burns) 6/4f
1 length, 2 lengths.

1917
HAPPY MOMENTS (Joseph Canty) 5/1 (Philip
    Behan)
Donnybrook (C. Aylin) 4/1jf
Last Draft (C.O. Hawkins) 4/1jf
2½ lengths, 1 length.

1918
MAROC (H. Harty) 100/8 (Henry I. Ussher)
Pacifist (Joseph Canty) 7/1
Light Division (Mr H.S. Harrison) 100/8
2 lengths, 5 lengths.

1919
JENNY JONES (Mr H.S. Harrison) 6/1 (Reginald H.
    Walker)
Maroc (H. Harty) 6/1
Catchim (E. Houlihan) 100/8
2 lengths, 4 lengths.

1920
KING EBER (T. Burns) 7/1 (Maxwell Arnott)
Happy Moments (J. Sinnott) 100/6
Just for Luck (W. Smith) 6/1
4 lengths, 1 length.

1921
KING MICHAEL (Joseph Canty) 2/1f (C. Brabazon)
Mount Prospect (C. Aylin) 6/1
Benediction (J. Hogan Jr) 5/1
3 lengths, ½ length.

1922 No Meeting

1923
SMOKE CLOUD (T. Burns) 2/1f (James J.
    Parkinson)
Silver Morsel (Joseph Canty) 4/1
Shotmaker (Joseph Doyle) 6/1
3 lengths, 10 lengths.

1924
HOLY FOOKS (Joseph Canty) 6/4f (Michael
    Dawson)
Quarry Boy (T. Kelly jr) 20/1
No Worry (P. Curran) 8/1
Neck, ½ length.

1925
ALROI (C. Donnelly) 2/1f (Cecil Brabazon)
Bolshevist (J. Hogan jr) 10/1
Holy Fooks (Joseph Canty) 5/1
½ length, 4 lengths.

1926
BLANCONA (E. Foster) 4/7f (G.P. Bracebridge)
Mischievous (J. Moylan) 7/1
Precept (J. Meaney) 100/6
3 lengths, 5 lengths.

1927
SOUTHERN PRINCE (J.H. Harty) 5/1 (Matt
    Cunningham)
Lady Lavender (D. Kirwan) 7/1
Bonnie Braes (C. McCarthy) 20/1
5 lengths, 1 length.

1928
PRUDENT PAT (J. Moloney) 5/4f (Joseph Dawson)
Good Thing (D. Kirwan) 16/1
Lady Lavender (J.H. Harty) 8/1
3 lengths, short head.

1929
SHREWD KING (Joseph Canty) 2/1f (Hubert M.
    Hartigan)
Gamefellow (Mr W.T. O'Grady) 100/8
Seaview (J.H. Harty) 5/1
¾ length, 12 lengths

1930
PUCKA RANEE (Mr J.A. Mangan) 100/8 (J.A. (Gus) Mangan)
Stranathro (W. Beasley) 20/1
Pucka Shikhari (Capt. D. Corry) 100/1
1 length, ¾ length.

1931
KYLECLARE (C. O'Connor) 8/1 (James J. Parkinson)
Sahabelle (Mr J.A. Mangan) 5/1
Lord Burdon (T. Whitehead) 100/6
5 lengths, 2 lengths.

1932
KNUCKLEDUSTER (Mr F.E. McKeever) 7/2 (Major H.D. Beamish)
Sir Johah (W.T. O'Grady) 5/2f
Peter III (P. Graham) 7/1
3 lengths, 5 lengths

1933
KNUCKLEDUSTER (Mr F.E. McKeever) 6/4f (Major H.D. Beamish)
Cottage View (Timothy Regan) 10/1
Gipsy Jane (T. Burns) 8/1
3 lengths, 1 length.

1934
RED HILLMAN (Timothy Regan) 8/1 (A. Percy Harris)
Golden Rock (W.T. O'Grady) 4/1
Farraboy (Mr H.J. Delmege) 8/1
4 lengths, 2 lengths.

1935
KATE CARLIN (Timothy Regan) 100/8 (Matt Cunningham)
Pride of Munster (A.P. Thompson) 20/1
D.M.S. (Mr J.C. Ferrall) 100/8
1½ lengths, ½ length.

1936
BACHELOR'S LANE (L.C. Keating) 8/1 (Edward T. O'Meara)
Swindle (W. Cummins) 20/1
Knight o' London (Timothy Regan) 8/1
1½ lengths, ½ length.

1937
GORGIA (L.C. Keating) 10/1 (Edward T. O'Meara)
Docket (T.V. Ryan) 100/8
Culleen's Actress (J. Hamey) 20/1
½ length, 3 lengths.

1938
SERPOLETTE (D. Butchers) 14/1 (Edward Delany)
Savota (J. Tiernan) 7/1
Kaor (W.T. O'Grady) 10/1
2 lengths, 1½ lengths.

1939
HONOR'S CHOICE (J. Barrett) 2/1f (James J. Parkinson)
Bourbon's Pride (Mr H. Harty Jr) 100/8
Chief Count (T. Hyde) 8/1
¾ length, 2 lengths.

1940
RED SHAFT (S. Magee) 6/1jf (Roderick More O'Ferrall)
Senville (J. Lenehan) 6/1jf
Camilla (T. McNeill) 33/1
2 lengths, 3 lengths.

1941
AMOR DE CUBA (T. Hyde) 20/1 (W.J. Kelly)
Swindon Beauty (A. Brabazon) 100/8
Antrim (J. Moloney) 6/4f
2 lengths, ¾ length.

1942
POINT D'ATOUT (J. Lenehan) 9/2 (Bernard Nugent)
Sweet Eileen (J.P. Maguire) 8/1
Persian Rose (W.T. O'Grady) 4/1
4 lengths, neck.

1943
ERINOX (J.P. Maguire) 10/1 (John Kirwan)
Smuts (T. McNeill) 100/7
Ballynure (A. Brabazon) 9/4f
1½ lengths, ½ length.

1944
COCKASNOOK (Jerry Fitzgerald) 20/1 (W. Barry)
African Collection (A. Brabazon) 5/1
Caughoo (B. O'Neill) 100/6
3 lengths, ¾ length.

1945
KING OF THE JUNGLE (D. Morgan)3/1f (Bernard
    Nugent)
Desdichado (A. Brabazon) 4/1
Belted Monarch (Mr J.R. Cox) 4/1
Head, 2½ lengths.

1946
(Fair Pearl (Mr M.J. Tully) 10/1 DISQ)
KING OF THE JUNGLE (D. Morgan)5/2f (Bernard
    Nugent)
Submarine (E.J. Kennedy) 10/1
Resolve (A. Brabazon) 7/1
Head, 1½ lengths.

1947
POINT D'ATOUT(Mr A.O.Scannell)10/1 (Bernard
    Nugent)
Lady's Find (A. Brabazon) 5/1f
3=Submarine (Pierce J. Murphy) 8/1
3=Knockaney (M.J. Murray) 20/1
5 lengths, 2 lengths.

1948
CARRANTRYLLA (T. Molony) 8/1 (Daniel Ruttle)
Strathfinn (M. Gordon) 100/7
Barberstown Prince (Mr P.C. Heron)100/6
¾ length, neck.

1949
BARBERSTOWN PRINCE (Mr P.C. Heron) 7/2f
    (Peter L. Heron)
Homer Gray (P.J. Murphy) 10/1
Tackler (A. Brabazon) 10/1
Neck, 1½ lengths.

1950
LADY'S FIND (F. McKenna) 50/1 (Cecil Brabazon)
Osberstown's Sister (P. Taaffe) 20/1
Mariner's Light (E. Newman) 100/7
8 lengths, 5 lengths.

1951
WYE FLY (M. Molony) 8/1jf (M. Vincent O'Brien)
Lonely Boy (Mr J.V. Ahern) 100/8
The Beetle (James Eddery) 8/1jf
8 lengths, 6 lengths.

1952
WARRENSCOURT LAD (T.P. Burns) 6/1 (D.J.
    Duggan)
Cloncaw (B. Cooper) 3/1
Cool Water (P.J. Doyle) 2/1f
¾ length, same.

1953
PRINCE OF DEVON (E. Newman) 6/1 (Clement
    Magnier)
Lucky Dome (P.J. Doyle) 9/2f
Rose o' Meath (T.P. Burns) 5/1
3 lengths, ½ length.

1954
CLOUDLESS DAYS (E. Newman) 100/8 (Michael
    Dawson)
Tantivvy Cottage (E.L. McKenzie) 20/1
In View (P.J. Doyle) 6/1
10 lengths, 4 lengths.

1955
ANTIGUE II (P. Powell Jr) 9/2 (Daniel L. Moore)
Quita Que (P.J. Doyle) 4/1f
Proud Dandy (M.R. Magee) 20/1
½ length, 6 lengths.

1956
IVY GREEN (P. Taaffe) 4/1 (Joseph W. Osborne)
Clonleason (W.J. Brennan) 7/1
Sporting Record (H.R. Beasley) 20/1
2½ lengths, 2 lengths.

1957
TYMON CASTLE (G.W. Robinson) 20/1 (Patrick
    Sleator)
Ballybrittas (T.P. Burns) 5/2
Amber Point (H.R. Beasley) 7/4f
Neck, same. (Photo)

1958
KNIGHT ERRANT (H.R Beasley) 5/2f (Patrick
    Sleator)
Sorrel (F. Carroll) 33/1
Regal Token (D. Page) 20/1
4 lengths, 3 lengths.

1959
CASHEL VIEW (P. Taaffe) 7/4f (Thomas W.
    Dreaper)
Malar (C. Kinane) 20/1
Grappa (G.W. Robinson) 100/8
1¼ lengths, ½ length.

1960
COMMUTERING (G.W. Robinson) 3/1 (Daniel L.
    Moore)
Cloncahir (P. Powell Jr) 100/7
Narcotic Nora (T. Regan) 10/1
1 length, head.

1961
1= CYGNE NOIR (P. Taaffe) 8/1 (James Lenehan)
1= NEWGROVE (C. Kinane) 33/1 (Vincent
    Leavy Jr)
Full Flight (T.P. Burns) 5/1
Dead-heat, 2½ lengths

1962
TRIPACER (T. Carberry) 9/1 (Daniel L. Moore)
Buckleto (P. Powell Jr) 7/1
Ben Stack (P. Taaffe) 4/5f
Neck, 7 lengths. (Photo)

1963
SNOW TRIX (B. Hannon) 20/1 (John Cox)
Some Slipper (A. Redmond) 8/1
Fiora (G.W. Robinson) 6/1
2½ lengths, 2 lengths.

1964
EXTRA STOUT (T. Taaffe) 10/1 (R.A. Hoey)
Breakers Hill (P. Powell jr) 10/1
Choni Star (F. Shortt) 22/1
2½ lengths, 4 lengths.

1965
TICONDEROGA (P. Powell Jr) 15/2 (Charles L.
    Weld)
Tinker's Hill (John Cullen) 40/1
Hunch (G.W. Robinson) 5/1
6 lengths, 4 lengths.

1966
WARKEY (F. Carroll) 10/1 (Kevin Prendergast)
Worsted Wizard (John Cullen) 10/1
Diritto (G.W. Robinson) 10/1
2 lengths, 2½ lengths.

1967
MUIR (B. Hannon) 25/1 (Thomas W. Dreaper)
Evilo (P. Woods) 100/8
Common Entrance (T. Carberry) 10/1
½ length, 6 lengths. (Photo)

1968
ANNALONG (P. Black) 11/2 (John Cox)
Interosian (G.W. Robinson) 7/1
Good Mop (F. Carroll) 20/1
1½ lengths, ½ length.

1969
BONNE (P. Taaffe) 9/2 (Peter D. McCreery)
Good Mop (J.P. Harty) 100/7
Esban (F. Shortt) 33/1
4 lengths, 2 lengths.

1970
DICTORA (Thomas Murphy) 10/1 (Clement
    Magnier)
Persian Lark (D.T. Hughes) 6/1
Park Avenue (L. Young) 33/1
Short-head, 2 lengths. (Photo)

1971
HIGHWAY VIEW (P. Black) 9/1 (John Cox)
Maltese Cross (M.C. Gifford) 12/1
I Zingari (Thomas Murphy) 9/1
2 lengths, 1 length.

1972
HARDBOY (Thomas Murphy) 16/1 (Richard
   McCormick)
William Love (T. McGee) 33/1
High Buckle (D.T. Hughes) 20/1
6 lengths, 1½ lengths.

1973
LESABELLE (L. O'Donnell) 25/1 (M.A. Scully)
Druid Hill (T. Carberry) 9/1
Patent Slipper (Mr John R. Fowler) 7/1
5 lengths, short head.

1974
JUST FO FUN (John Cullen) 10/1 (Thomas Bergin)
Not At All (J.P. Harty) 8/1
Gladstone Prince (D.T. Hughes) 16/1
½ length, 2½ lengths. (Photo)

1975
Div I: SPANNER (P. Russell) 10/1 (Dermot K. Weld)
Arctic Heir (J.J. O'Neill) 12/1
Taravic (John Cullen) 13/2
2½ lengths, neck.
Div II: DOUBLE DEFAULT (Mr C.P. Magnier) 6/4f
   (Clement Magnier)
Helenium (J. Brassil) 14/1
Guiscard (T. Carberry) 16/1
Neck, neck. (Photo)

1976
NEGRADA (S. Treacy) 16/1 (Patrick Mullins)
Taravic (G. Newman) 16/1
Prince Rudi (Mr R.S. Townend) 33/1
1½ lengths, same.

1977
PADDY BOULER (S. Lynch) 8/1 (Patrick Rooney)
Hard Tarquin (M.F. Morris) 8/1
Red Invader (J. McCutcheon) 4/1f
4 lengths, 1 length.

1978
PRINCE TAMMY (S. Treacy) 16/1 (Patrick Mullins)
Daletta (R.S. Townend) 16/1
Victor's Barge (P. Gill) 33/1
5 lengths, ½ length.

1979
HARD TARQUIN (J.J. O'Neill) 9/4f (Edward J.
   O'Grady)
Lylah (J.P. Byrne) 20/1
Accipiter (T. Carberry) 8/1
½ length, 3 lengths.

1980
PEARLSTONE (T.V. Finn) 14/1 (Patrick Mullins)
Rent-A-Row (P. Kiely) 10/1
Noble Star (D. O'Gorman) 25/1
2 lengths, 2½ lengths.

1981
DOUBLE WRAPPED (D.O'Gorman)14/1 (Clement
   Magnier)
Knocklonogad Alley (A.J. O'Brien) 20/1
Empoli (T. Morgan) 14/1
1½ lengths, 8 lengths.

1982
PINCH HITTER (J.J. O'Neill) 6/1 (Noel Meade)
Hi Harry (T. Carberry) 16/1
The Centaur FR (D. O'Gorman) 14/1
3 lengths, 2 lengths.

1983
PINCH HITTER (J.J. O'Neill) 7/2f (Noel Meade)
Northern Sky (F. Berry) 10/1
Track Scout FR (T. Morgan) 9/1
2½ lengths, 2 lengths.

1984
TARA LEE (J.P. Byrne) 8/1 (William Durkan)
Stern Saturn (T. Carmody) 8/1
Chammsky (Mr W.P. Mullins) 8/1
3 lengths, 1½ lengths.

1985
STRATHLINE (T. Carmody) 8/1 (Dermot K. Weld)
Derryvale (E. Tyrrell) 12/1
William Crump (S. Smith-Eccles) 7/2f
1½ lengths, same.

1986
RUSHMOOR (P. Scudamore) 4/1jf (Raymond E.
    Peacock GB)
Fane Ranger (P. Leech) 5/1
Four Trix (M. Flynn) 8/1
8 lengths, 5 lengths.

1987
BELSIR (P. Gill) 14/1 (Richard Nevin)
Swingsville (C.F. Swan) 10/1
Timber Creek (J.P. Byrne) 7/1
1½ lengths, 12 lengths.

1988
TRY A BRANDY (H. Rogers) 4/1jf (Martin Dunne)
Stormy Guy (B. Sheridan) 10/1
Lazy River (C. O'Dwyer) 20/1
4 lengths, 5 lengths.

1989
I'M CONFIDENT (Mr F.J. Flood) 33/1 (M.F.
    McDonagh)
Capa (A. Webb) 12/1
Derrynap (R. Byrne) 14/1
Head, 4 lengths. (Photo)

1990
ATHY SPIRIT (T.J. Taaffe) 9/4f (William Fennin)
Montefiore (T. Carmody) 5/2
Valtaki (P. Leech) 33/1
8 lengths, 1 length.

1991
SAGAMAN GER (Mr P. Fenton) 25/1 (Liam J.
    Codd GB)
Cheering News (N. Williamson) 8/1
Cock Cockburn (P. McWilliams) 15/2
5 lengths, 4 lengths.

1992
NATALIES FANCY (J.F. Titley) 33/1 (Patrick G. Kelly)
Natural Ability (C.F. Swan) 13/2
Mansion House (P. Scudamore) 16/1
2 lengths, 3½ lengths.

1993
CAMDEN BUZZ (C.F. Swan) 4/1 (Patrick Mullins)
Mubadir USA (P. Carberry) 12/1
Native Portrait (Mr P. Fenton) 20/1
2½ lengths, 6 lengths.

1994
OH SO GRUMPY GB (M.P. Dwyer) 7/1 (Mrs John
    (Jessica) Harrington)
Royal Print (M. Richards) 20/1
No Tag (J.F. Titley) 6/1
1½ lengths, 3 lengths.

1995
NO TAG (J.F. Titley) 11/2 (Patrick G. Kelly)
Saibot USA (R. Dunwoody) 14/1
Skipo USA (D.T. Evans) 20/1
Short head, 2 lengths. (Photo)

1996
MYSTICAL CITY (D.J. Casey) 20/1 (William P.
    Mullins)
Space Trucker (N. Williamson) 7/1
Just Little GB (C.F. Swan) 14/1
2½ lengths, neck.

1997
TOAST THE SPREECE (A.P. McCoy) 12/1 (Aidan P.
    O'Brien)
Kinnescash (N. Williamson) 20/1
Valley Erne (R. Dunwoody) 8/1
½ length, 3½ lengths.

1998
BLACK QUEEN (J.R. Barry) 10/1 (John E. Kiely)
Tidjani (F.M. Berry) 10/1
Shantarini (K.P. Gaule) 9/1
4½ lengths, 5½ lengths.

1999
QUINZE GB (R. Dunwoody) 11/1 (Patrick Hughes)
Dance So Suite GB (N. Williamson) 10/1
Vivo (C.F. Swan) 7/1
14 lengths, 3½ lengths.

2000
PERUGINO DIAMOND (J. Culloty) 14/1 (Seamus O'Farrell)
Darialann (J.R. Barry) 12/1
Barba Papa (C. Llewellyn) 5/1
1½ lengths, head.

2001
ANSAR (P. Carberry) 6/1 (Dermot K. Weld)
The Gatherer (D.J. Casey) 9/1
Vivo (K.A. Kelly) 14/1
3 lengths, same.

2002
SAY AGAIN (J.L. Cullen) 16/1 (Paul Nolan)
Mutakarrim GB (B.J. Geraghty) 12/1
Just Our Job (K.A. Kelly) 25/1
2 lengths, short head.

2003
SABADILLA USA (P.M. Verling) 14/1 (Patrick Michael Verling)
Cloone River (T.J. Murphy) 8/1
Lafayette (J.R. Barry) 20/1
¾ length, 1½ lengths.

2004
CLOONE RIVER (J.L. Cullen) 7/2f (Paul Nolan)
Gemini Guest (J. Culloty) 12/1
Mirpour (G. Lee) 16/1
2 lengths, 3½ lengths.

2005
MORE RAINBOWS (N.P. Madden) 33/1 (Niall Madden)
Tiger Cry (P.A. Carberry) 16/1
Callow Lake (M.D. Grant) 14/1
1 length, 1½ lengths.

2006
CUAN NA GRAI (P.W. Flood) 7/1 (Paul Nolan)
Shandon Star (R. Walsh) 6/1f
The Last Hurrah (A.D. Leigh) 10/1
4 lengths, ½ length.

2007
FARMER BROWN (D.N. Russell) 9/2f (Patrick Hughes)
Freeloader (P. Whelan) 16/1
Eagle's Pass (P.W. Flood) 20/1
2½ lengths, 1 length.

Galway Handicap Steeplechase Plate

Winner	Owner	Trainer	SP
1869 ABSENTEE (W. Bell)	Richard Bell	Richard Bell	3/1
1970 COMET (Mr J.D. Whyte)	James Moffat	M. Igoe	5/1
1871 ASTER (Mr R. Exshaw)	*Henry S. Croker	Private	9/1
1872 BELLE (W. Bell)	*Martin Kavanagh	Richard Bell	3/1f
1873 LANCET (M. Connolly)	J.E. George	T. Ryan	16/1
1874 REVOKE (T. Miller)	*Capt. Rupert Neville	J.H. Moore	6/1
1875 THE LIBERATOR (T. Ryan)	C. Hawkes	J.H. Moore	7/1
1876 MARTHA (Mr T. Beasley)	Thomas N. Wade	H.E. Linde	4/1
1877 TATTOO (W. Canavan)	Joseph G. Blake	Joseph G. Blake	5/1
1878 JUPITER TONANS (Capt. J.S. Lee-Barber)	Capt. J.S.F. Lee-Barber	Capt. George Joy	2/1f
1879 ROCK SAVAGE (Capt. J.S. Lee-Barber)	L. Wilsea	Capt. George Joy	8/1
1880 LADY NEWMAN (D. Meaney)	*Michael Sage	James Monahan	7/1
1881 NIGHTFALL (Mr T. Beasley)	Henry Eyre Linde	H.E. Linde	6/1
1882 SUGAR PLUM (Mr H. Beasley)	Capt. T.Y.L. Kirkwood	H.E. Linde	6/1
1883 VENTRILOQUIST (Mr H. Beasley)	Capt. Walker	H.E. Linde	5/6f
1884 NEW MEADOW (Mr R. Brabazon)	P.N. Fitzgerald	George L. Walker	10/3
1885 ERIN'S STAR (Mr W.P. Cullen)	Francis Fawcett	F.F. & W.P. Cullen	9/2
1886 ZULU II (T. Kavanagh)	Capt. St Lawrence	Daniel Broderick	4/1
1887 VICTRIX (Mr W.P. Cullen)	C.W. Bagge	F.F. Cullen	9/4
1888 FETHARD (J. Hoysted)	James A. Cassidy	Thomas Broderick	7/2
1889 ALEXANDER (T. Kavanagh)	E. Frazer	H.E. Linde	4/1
1890 LAKEFIELD (J. Walsh)	J. Brady	Michael Dennehy	6/1
1891 QUEEN OF THE MAY (Mr W. Beasley)	Col R. Thomson	F.F. Cullen	1/1f
1892 SPRINGFIELD MAID (E. Reilly)	S.A. Leonard	S.A. Leonard	4/1
1893 LADY PAT (T. Bailey)	Maj. R.G. Alexander	Wm McAuliffe	1/1f
1894 STAR ONE (E. Reilly)	Gustavus V. Briscoe	George L. Walker	8/1
1895 DOUBLE PRIMROSE (W. Hoysted)	Henry Eyre Linde	H.E. Linde	5/2f
1896 CASTLE WARDEN (Mr W.P. Cullen)	Richard C. Dawson	W.P. Cullen	5/2f
1897 DROGHEDA (T. Dowdall)	George F. Gradwell	G.F. Gradwell	4/1
1898 BOREENCHREEOGUE (J. Cheshire)	T. Cleary	James Cheshire	8/1
1899 TIPPERARY BOY (T. Moran)	T.B. Holmes	F.F. Cullen	8/1
1900 IVANOFF (James O'Brien)	L. Leybuck	F. Moran	10/1
1901 TIPPERARY BOY (T.Moran)	T.B. Holmes	F.F. Cullen	5/2f

Winner	Owner	Trainer	SP
1902 TIPPERARY BOY (T. Kavanagh)	T.B. Holmes	F.F. Cullen	6/1
1903 HAMPTON BOY (A. Anthony)	T. McMahon	Michael Dawson	5/2f
1904 STRATEGY (A. Magee)	C.E. Byrne	W.P. Cullen (GB)	4/1f
1905 GOLDFIELD II (M. Walsh)	Abel Buckley Jr	Edward Malone	7/2f
1906 ROYAL TARA (R. Morgan)	John Read	Denis Shanahan	8/1
1907 APOLLO BELVEDERE (Mr P. O'Brien Butler)	Col T.Y.L. Kirkwood	J. Currid	6/1
1908 SHADY GIRL (G. Brown)	Maxwell Arnott	Maxwell Arnott	5/1jf
1909 SCHWARMER (A. Anthony)	M. Farrell	Michael Dawson	5/1
1910 ASHBROOKE (Mr H.I. Ussher)	Robert M. Liddell	H.I. Ussher	4/1
1911 DEAR SONNY (E. Lawn)	H.L. Fitzpatrick	H.L. Fitzpatrick	5/2
1912 NOBLE GRECIAN (G. Brown)	Sir George Abercromby	Maxwell Arnott	4/1f
1913 GEORGE B (Mr G. Harty)	Sir Thomas Dixon	John Ruttle	10/1
1914 ALICE ROCKTHORN (Mr P. Nugent)	J. Nugent	Algernon Anthony	8/1
1915 HILL OF CAMAS (G. Harty)	Capt. William Molony	Capt. William Molony	20/1
1916 NEVER FEAR (F. Morgan)	T. Nolan	R.H. Walker	20/1
1917 PRIVIT (W. Smith)	Maj. Dermot McCalmont	Maxwell Arnott	20/1
1918 GOLDEN FLEECE (A. Stubbs)	William Parrish	John T. Rogers	7/1jf
1919 PICTURE SAINT (M. Colbert)	Col R.P. Croft	H.I. Ussher	20/1
1920 CLONREE (F. Morgan)	Mrs Owen Toole	Francis Morgan	3/1f
1921 MAX (F. Wootton)	Mrs R.P. Croft	H.I. Ussher	4/1
1922 No Meeting			
1923 CLONSHEEVER (J. Hogan Jr)	J.E. Tyrrell	H.I. Ussher	10/1
1924 CLONSHEEVER (F.B. Rees)	J.E. Tyrrell	H.I. Ussher	8/1
1925 BLANCONA (C. Donnelly)	Miss E.L.M. Barbour	Cecil Brabazon	6/1
1926 FAIR RICHARD (D. Ward)	Maxwell Arnott	Maxwell Arnott	6/4f
1927 TONY LAD (J. Moloney)	J.T. O'Ryan	H.I. Ussher	6/4
1928 EAST GALWAY (D. Ward)	J.S. Shepherd	Maxwell Arnott	1/1f
1929 GUIDING LIGHT (P. Powell)	J.B. D'Ardenne	Joseph Dawson	6/1
1930 EAST GALWAY (J. McNeill)	J.S. Shepherd	Maxwell Arnott	5/4f
1931 PUCKA SHIKHARI (Mr J.A. Mangan)	J.A. Mangan	J.A. Mangan	100/8
1932 SEAVIEW (T. Regan)	E. Cunningham	Matt Cunningham	50/1
1933 RED PARK (D. Kirwan)	Lady Helen McCalmont	J.J. Barry	3/1
1934 REVIEWER (Mr P. Sleator Jr)	Mrs C. O'Neill	M. Deegan	5/1
1935 SOUTHERNMORE (J. Hamey)	Capt. E.A. Gargan	Capt. E.A. Gargan	10/1
1936 YELLOW FURZE (J. McNeill)	Lt-Col S.S. Hill-Dillon	J.P. Loughran	4/1f
1937 BRIGHTER COTTAGE (W.T. O'Grady)	Capt. Denis W. Daly	H.I. Ussher	8/1jf
1938 SYMAETHIS (D. Butchers)	Lt-Col S.S. Hill-Dillon	R. Fetherstonhaugh	20/1
1939 PULCHER (J. Costello)	Colonel Scott Moore	R. Fetherstonhaugh	100/8
1940 RING OF GOLD (T. McNeill)	Col Denis W. Daly	H.I. Ussher	100/8
1941 ST MARTIN (A. Brabazon)	Miss M.O. Mathieson	Cecil Brabazon	6/4f
1942 GOLDEN JACK (D.L. Moore)	Miss Dorothy Paget	Charles A. Rogers	7/4f
1943 SWINDON GLORY (A. Brabazon)	J.A. Mangan	J.A. Mangan	5/1
1944 SWINDON GLORY (A. Brabazon)	J.A. Mangan	J.A. Mangan	7/2f
1945 GRECIAN VICTORY (D.J. Morgan)	G. Chesney	H.I. Ussher	10/1
1946 KEEP FAITH (T. Hyde)	James V. Rank	T.W. Dreaper	7/1jf

Winner	Owner	Trainer	SP
1947 CHARLES EDWARD (J. Brogan)	W. Hide	Bernard Nugent	100/6
1948 SILENT PRAYER (T. Molony)	A.J. Cope	Patrick Sleator	100/8
1949 RESULT (Mr H. Freeman Jackson)	H. Freeman Jackson	H. Freeman Jackson	20/1
1950 DERRINSTOWN (F.McKenna)	P. Digney	Gerard Flood	100/7
1951 ST KATHLEEN II (P.J. Doyle)	Mrs Adam Bell	W.T. O'Grady	15/2
1952 ALBERONI (L. Stephens)	H.H.M. Stanley	M.V. O'Brien	3/1jf
1953 GALLANT WOLF (T. Taaffe)	H.R.D. McCarrick	Thomas J. Taaffe	6/1jf
1954 AMBER POINT (C. Sleator)	Mrs Anne B. Biddle	Patrick Sleator	6/1jf
1955 UMM (P. Taaffe)	Con Rooney	G.H. Wells	11/4jf
1956 AMBER POINT (P.A. Farrell)	Mrs R. More O'Ferrall (Anne B. Biddle)	Patrick Sleator	2/1f
1957 KNIGHT ERRANT (H.R. Beasley)	Mrs Anne B. Biddle	Patrick Sleator	4/1f
1958 HOPEFUL COLLEEN (J.A. Mahony)	J. Graham	James Brogan	20/1
1959 HIGHFIELD LAD (J. Lehane)	Charles L. Weld	C.L. Weld	100/9
1960 SPARKLING FLAME (H.R. Beasley)	Charles Balding	Patrick Sleator	5/4f
1961 CLIPADOR (H.R. Beasley)	F.L. Vickerman	Patrick Sleator	7/4f
1962 CARRAROE (F.T. Winter)	Mrs Miles Valentine	A.S. O'Brien	4/1f
1963 BLUNTS CROSS (H.R. Beasley)	Lord Fermoy	A.S. O'Brien	9/4f
1964 ROSS SEA (S. Mellor)	Mrs Gillian Buchanan	A.S. O'Brien	9/2f
1965 ROSS SEA (S. Mellor)	Mrs Gillian Buchanan	A.S. O'Brien	8/1
1966 CAPPAWHITE (T. Finn)	Denis Murphy	George Spencer	20/1
1967 ROYAL DAY (R. Coonan)	P. Dunne-Cullinan	Patrick Sleator	19/2
1968 TEROSSIAN (G.W. Robinson)	Richard McIlhagga	G.H. Wells	7/2f
1969 ROYAL DAY (R. Coonan)	P. Dunne-Cullinan	Patrick Sleator	7/1
1970 LISNAREE (F. Shortt)	Thomas H. Moore	Archie Watson	20/1
1971 SAREJAY DAY (S. Shields)	Mrs E.R. Farrell	Eugene Farrell	33/1
1972 PERSIAN LARK (J.P. Harty)	J.F. Clifton	J.F. Maxwell	13/2
1973 LEAP FROG (T. Carberry)	Mrs Peter E. Burrell	J.T.R. Dreaper	11/2
1974 BUNCLODY TIGER (T. Browne)	Andrew Redmond	Kevin Bell	4/1
1975 O'LEARY (R. Coonan)	D. Jackson	Patrick Sleator	8/1
1977 SPITTIN IMAGE (M. Cummins)	Joseph Welsh Jr	J.R. Bryce-Smith	7/1
1978 SHINING FLAME (Mr N. Madden)	John P. McManus	E.J. O'Grady	4/1jf
1979 HINDHOPE (J.J. O'Neill)	Mrs David Louthan	E.J. O'Grady	6/1
1980 SIR BARRY (P. Kiely)	Paul Clarke	J.W. Boyers	10/1
1981 RUGGED LUCY (T.J. Ryan)	Jeremiah Dunne	E.J. O'Grady	14/1
1982 THE LADY'S MASTER (N. Madden)	Matt C. Duggan	M.C. Duggan	12/1
1983 HAMER'S FLAME (J. Brassil)	Edward Farrell	Michael Neville	12/1
1984 MASTER PLAYER (J.P. Byrne)	Mrs R. Eastwood	Thomas Bergin	40/1
1985 CHOW MEIN (T. Morgan)	Mrs Josephine Downey	D.T. Hughes	7/1
1986 BORO QUARTER (P. Kavanagh)	Mrs C.D. Hill	Patrick Mullins	10/1
1987 RANDOSS (K. Morgan)	S.W.N. Collen	Anne Collen	6/1jf
1988 AFFORD A KING (P. Gill)	Charles King	Anthony Mullins	10/1
1989 BOLD FLYER (Miss Sarah Collen)	S.W.N. Collen	J.T.R. Dreaper	8/1
1990 KIICHI USA (B. Sheridan)	Michael W.J. Smurfit	D.K. Weld	2/1f
1991 FIRION'S LAW (M. Flynn)	Mrs M.T. Quinn	Victor Bowens	9/1

	Winner	Owner	Trainer	SP
1992	THE GOOSER (A. Maguire)	Mrs M. O'Leary	Patrick Mullins	25/1
1993	GENERAL IDEA (A. Maguire)	Michael W.J. Smurfit	D.K. Weld	9/2f
1994	FEATHERED GALE (F. Woods)	Eamonn P. King	A.L.T. Moore	8/1
1995	LIFE OF A LORD (T. Horgan)	Michael J. Clancy	A.P. O'Brien	12/1
1996	LIFE OF A LORD (C.F. Swan)	Michael J. Clancy	A.P. O'Brien	9/2
1997	STROLL HOME (P. Carberry)	Mrs M. Mangan	James J. Mangan	11/2
1998	AMLAH USA (B.G. Powell)	Salvo Giannini	P.J. Hobbs (GB)	16/1
1999	MOSCOW EXPRESS (R. Walsh)	John Corr	Miss F.M. Crowley	4/1
2000	DOVALY GB (T.P. Rudd)	Sean Mulryan	M.J.P. O'Brien	20/1
2001	GRIMES GB (C. O'Dwyer)	John P. McManus	Christopher Roche	4/1jf
2002	ROCKHOLM BOY (K. Hadnett)	M.G.H. Syndicate	Michael Hourigan	20/1
2003	NEARLY A MOOSE (R.M. Power)	Michael J. McGinley	Patrick Mullins	25/1
2004	ANSAR (D.J. Casey)	Mrs K. Devlin	D.K. Weld	10/1
2005	ANSAR (D.F. O'Regan)	Mrs K. Devlin	D.K. Weld	10/1
2006	FAR FROM TROUBLE (R. Loughran)	John P. McManus	Christopher Roche	8/1
2007	SIR FREDERICK (K.T. Coleman)	Seven Heads Syndicate	W.J. Burke	12/1

* Used an assumed name.

Race Title: Galway Plate 1869–1968; Galway Centenary Plate 1969; Galway Plate 1970–8; Hygeia Galway Plate 1979–81; O'Malley Construction Galway Plate 1982–4; Digital Galway Galway Plate 1985–97; Compaq Galway Plate 1998-2001; Hewlett Packard Galway Plate 2002–05; William Hill Galway Plate 2006–07.

Leading Owner: T.B. Holmes, J.A. Mangan, Anne Biddle and J.P. McManus (3)

Leading Trainer: H.I. Ussher and P. Sleator (9)

Leading Rider: H.R. Beasley (4)

Galway Handicap Hurdle

Winner	Owner	Trainer	SP
1913 RED DAMSEL (F. Morgan)	Baron F. de Tuyll	Maxwell Arnott	10/1
1914 CLONMEEN (F. Morgan)	Stephen Grehan	Maxwell Arnott	3/1f
1915 NAUGHTY EARL (C.O. Hawkins)	George H. Dennehy	Michael Dawson	7/4f
1916 ELGON (Mr H.S. Harrison)	Frank Barbour	R.H. Walker	9/4
1917 HAPPY MOMENTS (Joseph Canty)	P.D. Coen	Philip Behan	5/1
1918 MAROC (H. Haty)	Mrs R.P. Croft	H.I. Ussher	100/8
1919 JENNY JONES (Mr H.S. Harrison)	J.C. McKeever	R.H. Walker	6/1
1920 KING EBER (T. Burns)	Lord Lascelles	Maxwell Arnott	7/1
1921 KING MICHAEL (Joseph Canty)	J.J. Moore	Cecil Brabazon	2/1f
1922 No Meeting			
1923 SMOKE CLOUD (T. Burns)	Lt-Col O'Malley Keyes	J.J. Parkinson	2/1f
1924 HOLY FOOKS (Joseph Canty)	Florence Burke	Michael Dawson	6/4f
1925 ALROI (C. Donnelly)	Miss M.D. Barbour	Cecil Brabazon	2/1f
1926 BLANCONA (E. Foster)	Miss E.L.M. Barbour	G.P. Bracebridge	4/7f
1927 SOUTHERN PRINCE (J.H. Harty)	Matt Cunningham	Matt Cunningham	5/1
1928 PRUDENT PAT (J. Moloney)	Wing-Cdr W.R. Read	Joseph Dawson	5/4f
1929 SHREWD KING (Joseph Canty)	Hubert M. Hartigan	H.M. Hartigan	2/1f
1930 PUCKA RANEE (Mr J.A. Mangan)	J.A. Mangan	J.A. Mangan	100/8
1931 KYLECLARE (C. O'Connor)	Martin McDonogh	J.J. Parkinson	8/1
1932 KNUCKLEDUSTER (Mr F.E. McKeever)	Maj. H.D. Beamish	Maj. H. Beamish	7/2
1933 KNUCKLEDUSTER (Mr F.E. McKeever)	Maj. H.D. Beamish	Maj. H. Beamish	6/4f
1934 RED HILLMAN (Timothy Regan)	E.T. O'Meara	A.P. Harris	8/1
1935 KATE CARLIN (Timothy Regan)	D.W.H. Garde	Matt Cunningham	100/8
1936 BACHELOR'S LANE (L.C. Keating)	E.T. O'Meara	E.T. O'Meara	8/1
1937 GORGIA (L.C. Keating)	E.T. O'Meara	E.T. O'Meara	10/1
1938 SERPOLETTE (D. Butchers)	Edward Delany	Edward Delany	14/1
1939 HONOR'S CHOICE (J. Barrett)	Michael McDonough	J.J. Parkinson	2/1f
1940 RED SHAFT (S. Magee)	Col Denis W. Daly	R. More O'Ferrall	6/1jf
1941 AMOR DE CUBA (T. Hyde)	Mrs M. Mitchell	W.J. Kelly	20/1
1942 POINT D'ATOUT (J. Lenehan)	Miss A.E. Hall	Bernard Nugent	9/2
1943 ERINOX (J.P. Maguire)	J.C. Landy	John Kirwan	10/1
1944 COCKASNOOK (J. Fitzgerald)	W. Barry	W. Barry	20/1
1945 KING OF THE JUNGLE (D.J. Morgan)	Richard McIlhagga	Bernard Nugent	3/1f

Winner	Owner	Trainer	SP
1946 *KING OF THE JUNGLE (D.J. Morgan)	Richard McIlhagga	Bernard Nugent	5/2f
1947 POINT D'ATOUT (Mr A.O. Scannell)	Miss A.E. Hall	Bernard Nugent	10/1
1948 CARRANTRYLLA (T. Molony)	M.J. Gleeson	Daniel Ruttle	8/1
1949 BARBERSTOWN PRINCE (Mr P.C. Heron)	Peter L. Heron	P.L. Heron	7/2f
1950 LADY'S FIND (F. McKenna)	H.E. Rawson	Cecil Brabazon	50/1
1951 WYE FLY (M. Molony)	Mrs E.J. Lewis	M.V. O'Brien	8/1jf
1952 WARRENSCOURT LAD (T.P. Burns)	D.J. Duggan	D.J. Duggan	6/1
1953 PRINCE OF DEVON (E. Newman)	Mrs C. Magnier	Clement Magnier	6/1
1954 CLOUDLESS DAYS (E. Newman)	Mrs F. Blacker	Michael Dawson	100/8
1955 ANTIGUE II (P. Powell Jr)	Thomas Doyle	D.L. Moore	9/2
1956 IVY GREEN (P. Taaffe)	John G. Duggan	J.W. Osborne	4/1
1957 TYMON CASTLE (G.W. Robinson)	Mrs Patrick Meehan	Patrick Sleator	20/1
1958 KNIGHT ERRANT (H.R. Beasley)	Mrs Anne B. Biddle	Patrick Sleator	5/2f
1959 CASHEL VIEW (P. Taaffe)	Duchess of Westminster	T. W. Dreaper	7/4f
1960 COMMUTERING (G.W. Robinson)	Major Laurie Gardner	D.L. Moore	3/1
1961 CYGNE NOIR (P. Taaffe)	M. Sayers	James Lenehan	8/1
Dead heat: NEWGROVE (C. Kinane)	J. Vincent Leavy	Vincent Leavy Jr	33/1
1962 TRIPACER (T. Carberry)	Lady Honor Svejdar	D.L. Moore	9/1
1963 SNOW TRIX (B. Hannon)	John Cox	John Cox	20/1
1964 EXTRA STOUT (T. Taaffe)	J. Frederick Hoey	R.A. Hoey	10/1
1965 TICONDEROGA (P. Powell Jr)	Colonel J. Reid	C.L. Weld	15/2
1966 WARKEY (F. Carroll)	Mrs P.J. Hume	Kevin Prendergast	10/1
1967 MUIR (B. Hannon)	Archie Willis	T.W. Dreaper	25/1
1968 ANNALONG (P. Black)	Mrs B.J. Eastwood	John Cox	11/2
1969 BONNE (P. Taaffe)	S.P. Muldoon	P.D. McCreery	9/2
1970 DICTORA (Thomas Murphy)	Mrs M. Egan	Clement Magnier	10/1
1971 HIGHWAY VIEW (P. Black)	Charles Carr	John Cox	9/1
1972 HARDBOY (Thomas Murphy)	Gene H. Kruger	R.J. McCormick	16/1
1973 LESABELLE (L. O'Donnell)	Christopher D. Lee	Mark Scully	25/1
1974 JUST FOR FUN (John Cullen)	Patrick Deere	Thomas Bergin	10/1
1975 Div 1 SPANNER (P. Russell)	Mrs M.T. Jackson	D.K. Weld	10/1
Div 2 DOUBLE DEFAULT (Mr C.P. Magnier)	Col Sir Douglas Clague	Clement Magnier	6/4f
1976 NEGRADA (S.J. Treacy)	Capt. Luke Mullins	Patrick Mullins	16/1
1977 PADDY BOULER (S. Lynch)	Patrick Rooney	Patrick Rooney	8/1
1978 PRINCE TAMMY (S.J. Treacy)	Kevin O'Donnell	Patrick Mullins	16/1
1979 HARD TARQUIN (J.J. O'Neill)	W.K. Hosford	E.J. O'Grady	9/4f
1980 PEARLSTONE (T.V. Finn)	William W. Brainard Jr	Patrick Mullins	14/1
1981 DOUBLE WRAPPED (D. O'Gorman)	Colin P. Magnier	Clement Magnier	14/1
1982 PINCH HITTER (J.J. O'Neill)	Brendan Carolan	Noel Meade	6/1
1983 PINCH HITTER (J.J. O'Neill)	Brendan Carolan	Noel Meade	7/2f
1984 TARA LEE (J.P. Byrne)	Patrick F. Durkan	William Durkan	8/1
1985 STRATHLINE (T. Carmody)	Michael W.J. Smurfit	D.K. Weld	8/1
1986 RUSHMOOR (P. Scudamore)	Jim Ennis	R.E. Peacock (GB)	4/1jf
1987 BELSIR (P. Gill)	Patrick Anglim	Richard Nevin	14/1
1988 TRY A BRANDY (H. Rogers)	Martin Dunne	Martin Dunne	4/1jf

Winner	Owner	Trainer	SP
1989 I'M CONFIDENT (Mr F.J. Flood)	M. McDonagh	Michael McDonagh	33/1
1990 ATHY SPIRIT (T.J. Taaffe)	William Fennin	William Fennin	9/4f
1991 SAGAMAN GER (Mr P. Fenton)	M. Doocey	L.J. Codd (GB)	25/1
1992 NATALIE'S FANCY (J.F. Titley)	Mrs Eileen Crowe	Patrick G. Kelly	33/1
1993 CAMDEN BUZZ (C.F. Swan)	Miss Carmel Byrne	Patrick Mullins	4/1
1994 OH SO GRUMPY GB (M.P. Dwyer)	Mrs E. Queally	Jessica Harrington	7/1
1995 NO TAG (J.F. Titley)	Mary Hayes	Patrick G. Kelly	8/1
1996 MYSTICAL CITY (D.J. Casey)	Phantom Syndicate	W.P. Mullins	20/1
1997 TOAST THE SPREECE (A.P. McCoy)	Golden Step Syndicate	A.P. O'Brien	12/1
1998 BLACK QUEEN (J.R. Barry)	Heinz Pollmeier	J.E. Kiely	10/1
1999 QUINZE GB (R. Dunwoody)	Patrick C. Byrne	Patrick Hughes	11/1
2000 PERUGINO DIAMOND (J. Culloty)	Seamus O'Farrell	Seamus O'Farrell	14/1
2001 ANSAR (P. Carberry)	Mrs K. Devlin	D.K. Weld	6/1
2002 SAY AGAIN (J.L. Cullen)	Sean Duggan	Paul Nolan	16/1
2003 SABADILLA USA (P.M. Verling)	W. Coleman	P.M. Verling	14/1
2004 CLOONE RIVER (J.L. Cullen)	Mrs Kathleen Gillane	Paul Nolan	7/2f
2005 MORE RAINBOWS (N.P. Madden)	Neighbours Racing Club	Noel Meade	33/1
2006 CUAN NA GRAI (P.W. Flood)	John J. Brennan	Paul Nolan	7/1
2007 FARMER BROWN (D.N. Russell)	Plantation Stud	Patrick Hughes	9/2f

* Awarded race when winner Fair Pearl (10/1) was subsequently disqualified by INHSC.

Race Title: Galway Hurdle 1913–64; Guinness Hurdle 1965–77; Guinness Handicap Hurdle 1978–80; Guinness Hurdle Handicap 1981–2; Guinness Handicap Hurdle 1983; Guinness Galway Quincentennial Handicap Hurdle 1984; Guinness Handicap Hurdle 1985–94; Guinness Galway Handicap Hurdle 1995-2007.

Leading Owner: Edward T. O'Meara (3)

Leading Trainer: B. Nugent, C. Magnier and P. Mullins (4)

Leading Rider: Joseph Canty and P. Taaffe (4)

H.M. Plate (Galway)

Winner	Owner	Trainer	SP
1879 TOM THUMB (J. Conolly)	M.B. Joyce	T. Connolly	100/8
1880 BARON FARNEY (F. Wynne)	Charles J. Blake	James Dunne	2/1
1881 BARON FARNEY (Callaghan)	Charles J. Blake	James Dunne	5/2
1882 THEORIST (Peploe)	Garrett Moore	Garrett Moore	1/3f
1883 SYLPH (T. Harris)	Charles J. Blake	James Dunne	5/2
1884 TELEPHONE (T. Broderick)	Joseph G. Blake	Private	WO
1885 ST KEVIN (H. Saunders)	Charles J. Blake	James Dunne	WO
1886 DRACO (H. Saunders)	Joseph Lyons	James Dunne	WO
1887 CLAN CHATTAN (T. Kavanagh)	J.W. Nuttall	J.W. Nuttall	8/1
1888 PERICLES (T. Harris)	Joseph Lyons	James Dunne	1/2f
1889 GAWSWORTH (J. Foster)	C.W. Bagge	F.F. Cullen	4/6f
1890 MERVYN (J. Foster)	Mr McCracken	F.F. Cullen	2/5f
1891 GOLDEN CRESCENT (John Doyle)	Richard N. Talbot	F.F. Cullen	1/3f
1892 GOLDMINER (T. Harris)	Charles J. Blake	Thomas Harris	2/1
1893 CLOGHRAN (A. Magee)	William P. Cullen	W.P. Cullen	6/1
1894 TRANBY CROFT (T. Kavanagh)	John James	Charles Ellison	2/1
1895 CALCHAS (J. Bresname)	R. Richards	W.P. Cullen	3/1
1896 CATCH THE WIND (J. Bresname)	R.J. Love	W.P. Cullen	WO
1897 SWEET CHARLOTTE (James O'Brien)	James Phelan	R.C. Dawson	7/4
1898 FRIARY (A. Anthony)	H. Walker	Denis Shanahan	2/5f
1899 LILLIAN NOEL (J. Westlake)	William P. Cullen	W.P. Cullen	1/1f
1900 YELLOW VIXEN (J. Behan Jr)	W. Jackson	Michael Dawson	8/11f
1901 GLENMALUR (Peter Hughes)	F. Frame	Denis Shanahan	4/1
1902 YELLOW VIXEN (D. Condon)	W. Jackson	Michael Dawson	5/2
1903 STRELMA (J. Thompson)	Capt. Harding	J.J. Parkinson	8/100f
1904 SLEEP (F. Morgan)	Michael Dawson	Michael Dawson	2/1
1905 YOUNG ABERCORN (J. Thompson)	Capt. William Scott	T. McGuire	4/5f
1906 GREY FACE (C. Aylin)	J.W. Gregg	J.W. Gregg	6/1
1907 JIGGINSTOWN (J. Thompson)	Patrick J. Brophy	J.J. Parkinson	2/5f
1908 BOUNCING BESS (J. Thompson)	W.W. Bailey	Maxwell Arnott	1/4f
1909 OCTOCIDE (J. Thompson)	R.A. Wilson	Richard Harrison	5/4
1910 HINEMOA (J. Foran)	Capt. William Scott	Capt. W. Scott	2/1
1911 THE BEST (F. Hunter)	Patrick Cullinan	James Dunne	4/6f

Winner	Owner	Trainer	SP
1912 ROYAL HACKLE II (John Doyle)	Patrick Cullinan	James Dunne	4/9f
1913 LAOGHAIRE (James Canty)	T. Leonard	Michael Dawson	4/6f
1914 ROYAL HACKLE II (John Doyle)	Patrick Cullinan	James Dunne	1/25f
1915 NELLIE MAC (C. Aylin)	H.C. Bourke	Private	25/1
1916 DENIZULU (T. Burns)	R.B. Dobell	James Burns	4/7f
1917 MOHACZ (W. Barrett)	Capt. Percy W. Bewicke	Capt. Percy W. Bewicke	4/6f
1918 KING FRUSQUIN (W. Barrett)	Sir William Nelson	P. Mullen	WO
1919 FRONT LINE (M. Beary)	H.J. Kirwan	Ronald Moss	4/6f
1920 STEADY SCOTCH (M. Beary)	Denis J. Cogan	Michael Rice	1/6f
1921 VAGABOND (John Beary)	W. Morrissey	C. Prendergast	1/6f
1922 No meeting			
1923 DOUBLE FIRST (D. Ward)	P. Rogers	Maxwell Arnott	1/2f
1924 BLUE FISH (D. Ward)	P. Rogers	Maxwell Arnott	1/2f
1925 FATHER TOM (P. Beasley)	J.J. Parkinson	J.J. Parkinson	5/2
1926 LOUVIXEN (E.M. Quirke)	T.P. O'Neill	J.J. Parkinson	1/20f
1927 O MAY (E.M. Quirke)	Archie Willis	J.J. Parkinson	2/5f
1928 STRIPED SILK (J. Moylan)	Richard Power	H.I. Ussher	6/4
1929 CRAFTY CAPTAIN (E.M. Quirke)	Sir Thomas Dixon	J.J. Parkinson	WO
1930 AGONDA (J. Moylan)	C. Odlum	Maxwell Arnott	5/4
1931 GALLANT PRINCE (J. Moylan)	Miss Kathleen Ussher	H.I. Ussher	2/5f
1932 ORANGE GIRL (John Doyle)	Edward J. Hope	John Ruttle	2/5f
1933 CASTLEBAGOT (T. Burns)	J.A. Mangan	J.A. Mangan	5/1
1934 TOGA (J. Moylan)	P.D. Mathews	H.I. Ussher	11/8
1935 PRUDENT TOI (Peter Maher)	Sir James Nelson	Maj. R.H. Scott	5/1
1936 CULLEEN'S ACTRESS (M. Wing)	Mrs E.A. Gargan	Capt. E.A. Gargan	4/6f
1937 GOLDEN LANCER (T. Burns)	Joseph Maher	Oliver Slocock	5/2
1938 COROFIN (M. Wing)	Michael O'Donough	J.J. Parkinson	1/4f
1939 COROFIN (M. Wing)	Michael O'Donough	J.J. Parkinson	4/5f
1940 AVATEA (M. Wing)	M.J. Fanning	M.J. Fanning	No SP (fav)
1941 ROSE GARLAND (T. Burns)	Lord Glentoran	H.G. Wellesley	1/1
1942 FOAM CREST (G. Cooney)	William R. Ellis	Cecil Brabazon	9/4
1943 MARITIME LAW (G. Wells)	J.P. Maher	T.W. Dreaper	5/2
1944 OOLA (Joseph Canty)	Miss V. O'Neill-Power	H.M. Ryan	WO
1945 EQUATOR (Herbert Holmes)	Lord Sefton	R. Fetherstonhaugh	10/11f
1946 INSPIRED (Herbert Holmes)	Maj. Dermot McCalmont	R. Fetherstonhaugh	10/1
1947 EDNA'S COURAGE (M. Molony)	W. Noble	Bernard Nugent	5/4f
1948 LADY QAIM (M. Gordon)	Mrs M. Ferns	Maxwell Arnott	3/1
1949 OWENS CUTS (P. Powell Jr)	Lord Glentoran	H.V.S. Murless	2/11f
1950 SWEET SEVENTEEN (P. Canty)	Lord Fingall	Cecil Brabazon	4/1
1951 OLLERTON HILLS (A. Brabazon)	M.J. Gleeson	P.J. Prendergast	2/5f
1952 EXCELSA (Herbert Holmes)	Capt. C. Boyd-Rochfort	R.N. Fetherstonhaugh	8/11f
1953 GAY MARCIA (Herbert Holmes)	Mrs M. McCall	R.N. Fetherstonhaugh	10/11f
1954 ITALASSU (L. Ward)	A.J. Piexoto de Castro	P.J. Prendergast	1/2f
1955 ITALASSU (L. Ward)	A.J. Piexoto de Castro	P.J. Prendergast	8/100f
1956 SHETLANDS (J. Mullane)	John Dunlop	M.C. Collins	5/2jf

1957 ST PHIDEAS (P. Canty)	A.O. Dietz	P.J. Prendergast	1/1f
1958 BY-PASSED (G.W. Robinson)	Charles McCarthy	George Robinson	6/4

Race Discontinued after 1958.

Distance:	2 miles (1879–1956)
	1½ miles (1957 and 1958)
Race title:	Her Majesty's Plate 1879–1900 and 1952–8
	His Majesty's Plate 1901–51
Leading Owner:	C.J. Blake (5)
Leading Trainer:	James Dunne (9)
Leading Rider:	J. Thompson (5)

Galway Blazers Steeplechase

Winner	Owner	Trainer	SP
1894 ALICE H (Mr M.J. Harty)	Michael J. Harty	Thomas Miller	2/1jf
1895 MANDRAKE (Henneberry)	M. Spain	William McCormick	8/1
1896 HOLLYHOCK (Dowdall)	George F. Gradwell	G.F. Gradwell	5/2
1897 SPITFIRE (A. Anthony)	E.S. Jackson	Denis Shanahan	5/4f
1898 GAY GIRL (C. Hogan)	Frederick F. Cullen	Robert Exshaw	5/2
1899 BIRD OF THE TEMPEST (J. Ruttle)	C.L. Davis	M.J. Harty	6/1
1900 CREAN (C. Hogan)	P.J. Hartigan	William McCormick	5/1
1901 SUNNY SHOWER (Mr H.S. Persse)	Mrs Joseph Widger	J.J. Parkinson	1/2f
1902 BALLISTA (T. Dent)	H.L. Fitzpatrick	Capt. R.H. Dewhurst	4/1
1903 OXHILL (Mr H.S. Persse)	J. Butler	Private	4/6f
1904 SPRINGFIELD (W. Dillon)	B.R. McCarrick	Blakestown Stable	5/2
1905 LAUREL VALE (A. Anthony)	Joseph Whelan	Michael Dawson	2/5f
1906 RYE VALE (Mr W.P. Cullen)	Mrs N.J. Kelly	N.J. Kelly	4/6f
1907 STOLEN BRIDE (M. Kelly)	V.J. Blake	Private	5/2jf
1908 BLACK NUN (J. Lynn)	J.B. Batten	Lawrence Hope	6/4f
1909 MASTER TIM (A. Hogan)	Leslie Brabazon	Cecil Brabazon	6/1
1910 DEAR SONNY (A. Anthony)	H.L. Fitzpatrick	H.L. Fitzpatrick	1/1f
1911 STRANGEGATE (Mr H. Ussher)	James Ryan	H.I. Ussher	4/5f
1912 BALLINCARROCNA (T. Regan)	D. Moloney	D. Moloney	10/1
1913 DOUBLE MAC (R. Trudgill)	M. McDonogh	W.A. Ussher	WO
1914 LOLLYPOP II (Mr J. Manley)	J. Comerford	R.G. Cleary	5/4f
1915 DUNDESERT (H. Harty)	Major Daniel Dixon	John Ruttle	7/1
1916 RATHRUE (E. Houlihan)	J.A. Kennedy	R.G. Cleary	2/1f
1917 TIRHUGH (Mr J. Coghlan)	J. Coghlan	J. Coghlan	4/6f
1918 FRANK ASH (J. Banahan)	G. Martyn	G. Martyn	20/1
1919 THREE X (J. Hogan Jr)	James Dwyer	J. Downes	4/1
1920 CATCHIM (M. Farragher)	J.S. Barrett	M.J. Harty	3/1
1921 THE COINER (J.R. Anthony)	J.P. Hogan	J.P. Hogan	1/1f
1922 No Meeting			
1923 HARRY HART (F. Morgan)	Charles A. Rogers	Maxwell Arnott	3/1
1924 PRIDE OF DELVIN (M. Doherty)	T. O'Roarke	T. O'Roarke	6/1
1925 SOLUS (K. Lenehan)	R. Wallace	R. Wallace	9/4
1926 GOLDEN LIGHT (M. Doherty)	Mrs R.P. Croft	H.I. Ussher	4/6f
1927 GOLDEN REBEL (W. Beasley)	Mrs R.P. Croft	H.I. Ussher	WO

Winner	Owner	Trainer	SP
1928 BALLY YARN (Mr T. Nugent)	M. Macabe	Maxwell Arnott	5/2
1929 ODD CAT (J. McNeill)	T. Ray	T. Ray	5/2
1930 SOME VIEW (Mr F.E. McKeever)	E. Cunningham	Matt Cunningham	6/1
1931 CARMENITA (M. Hynes)	John Brennan	F.W. Mitchell	2/1
1932 IRISH KNIGHT II (T. Cullen)	Mrs A. Wall	R.H. Walker	7/2
1933 REVIEWER (W.T. O'Grady)	Mrs C. O'Neill	L.T. Byrne	8/1
1934 GAULTIER (J. Grogan)	M. O'Regan	John Kirwan	4/1
1935 NORMAN GLORY (J. McCarthy)	C. Lawless	C. Lawless	6/1
1936 PUCKA SHIKHARI (W. Rea)	J.A. Mangan	J.A. Mangan	2/1
1937 NANCY'S COTTAGE (T.V. Ryan)	P. Walsh	John Kirwan	4/5f
1938 WEST POINT (D.L. Moore)	P. Dunne Cullinan	Maxwell Arnott	4/6f
1939 GRANGE CROSS (P. Cahalin)	P.J. O'Meara	E.T. O'Meara	4/1
1940 BROWN JOKER (Mr H. Harty Jr)	G. Carr Lett	John Ruttle	100/12
1941 GOLDEN JACK (D.L. Moore)	Miss Dorothy Paget	C.A. Rogers	5/1
1942 BROWN JOKER (P. Sherry)	G. Carr Lett	G. Carr Lett	100/8
1943 BLACK MASK (M. Gordon)	W.J. Purcell	W.J. Purcell	7/1
1944 CALLALY (D. Morgan)	E.H. Johnson	W.T. O'Grady	6/1
1945 ROMAN HACKLE (D.L. Moore)	Miss Dorothy Paget	C.A. Rogers	2/1
1946 BRICK BAT (E. Newman)	James V. Rank	T.W. Dreaper	10/1
1947 BELL BOY II (J. Brogan)	W. Noble	Bernard Nugent	8/1
1948 ROYAL BRIDGE (M. Browne)	Miss Elizabeth Shortiss	R. O'Connell	7/2
1949 LONELY BOY (B. O'Neill)	C. Lawless	C. Lawless	5/1
1950 GREEN DOLPHIN (M. Molony)	J.G. Duggan	J.W. Osborne	7/4f
1951 METROPOLITAN (P. Taaffe)	Mrs B.M. Webster	C.A. Rogers	100/6
1952 SEPTEMUM (P. Taaffe)	W.H. Corry	J.W. Osborne	6/4f
1953 COLONIAL JACK (P.J. Doyle)	John G. Duggan	J.W. Osborne	100/7
1954 SWINGING LIGHT (P.J. Doyle)	Major P. Dennis	D.L. Moore	11/10f
Dead heat: COLONIAL JACK (P. Taaffe)	J.G. Duggan	J.W. Osborne	3/1
1955 GREEK BATTLE (J. Lehane)	P. Rooney	P. Rooney	5/2
1956 KILBALLYOWEN (H.R. Beasley)	Michael Connolly	Michael Connolly	6/4f
1957 TRINCULO (T. Taaffe)	Mrs C.M. Malcomson	Thomas J. Taaffe	3/1
1958 KNIGHTSBROOK (T. Taaffe)	J.L. Young	Thomas J. Taaffe	2/1
1959 UNCLE WHISKERS (C. Finnegan)	J.A. Hale	C. McCartan Jr	1/1f
1960 BLUEBELL II (P. Woods)	Lord Suirdale	T.W. Dreaper	5/1
1961 CONNIVANCE (C. Finnegan)	Mrs K.L. Urquhart	Patrick Sleator	10/11f
1962 KILSKYRE (C. Kinane)	J.A. Wilson	J.A. Wilson	5/2jf
1963 BURTON BROWN II (F. Shortt)	P. Dunny	Patrick Murphy	2/1f
1964 CLONCAHIR (C. Kinane)	Mrs B. Farquhar	J. Cullen	6/1
1965 DEVENISH ARTIST (G.W. Robinson)	George Doran	Patrick Mullins	1/1f
1966 HOT CONTACT (T. Carberry)	A.L. Moore	D.L. Moore	7/2
1967 GOOD MOP (Mr B. Hanbury)	A. Watson	Archie Watson	9/2
1968 SKELLY'S CASSIUS (C. Finnegan)	Thomas Costello	Thomas Costello	7/1
1969 MISS ITA (J.B. Brogan)	Lord Fingall	Lord Fingall	7/1
1970 ALECTRYON (D.T. Hughes)	Mrs B.J. Eastwood	M.A. O'Toole	1/1f
1971 TARQUIN BID (H.R. Beasley)	Miss G.B. Hard	P.D. McCreery	11/10f

Winner	Owner	Trainer	SP
1972 RED ROHAN (B. Hannon)	Capt. J.A. Hornsby	Toss Taaffe	11/5
1973 NATIVE CLOVER (Patrick Mooney)	Mrs C.P. Smith	J.A. O'Connell	12/1
1974 IRISHMAN (D.T. Hughes)	David Cornwall	Archie Watson	14/1
1975 VULCOTT (S. Treacy)	Lady Elizabeth Byng	Patrick Mullins	12/1
1976 COADY VI (P. Kiely)	T.V. O'Brien	T.V. O'Brien	6/1
1977 HOPE'S CHOICE (J.P. Harty)	J.A.N. Glover	F. Fitzsimons	10/1
1978 LEVANKA (E. Murphy)	P.C. Heron	Robert Coonan	9/4jf
1979 DON MOBILE (Mr F. Codd)	P. O'Sullivan	E.J. O'Grady	9/4f
1980 SILVER MOUNT (J. Goodwin)	M. Hodgett	Francis Flood	8/1
1981 Div I SEGAHAN DAM (M.J. Byrne)	D. McParland	C. Kinane	3/1f
Div II CRAIGVIEW (J.P. Byrne)	P.W. McDowell	P.W. McDowell	6/1
1982 PEARSE SQUARE (M.M. Lynch)	Denis Fitzgerald	Denis Fitzgerald	5/2
1983 FLOWER MASTER (J.K. Kinane)	Martin O'Neill	J.W. Boyers	6/1
1984 DUSKY FOX (P. Leech)	Stephen Banville	Noel Meade	4/1
1985 RANDOSS (K. Morgan)	Executors of S.W.N. Collen	J.T.R. Dreaper	100/30f
1986 RICH HILL (T. Carmody)	C. Mitchell	E.P. Mitchell	5/2f
1987 ARCTIC GOSSIP (M.M. Lynch)	John A. Duffy	Patrick Griffin	2/1f
1988 HASTY PRINCE (C. O'Dwyer)	M.P. Farrell	Thomas Carberry	5/2f
1989 CLASSMATE VI (A.J. O'Brien)	Noel Horgan	J.E. Kiely	7/1
1990 ARCTIC GOSSIP (Mr C.T.G. Kinane)	Matthew Cahill	C. Kinane	9/4
1991 BLACK MONEY (C.F. Swan)	Mrs J. Harrington	Jessica Harrington	7/1
1992 FANE BANKS (H. Rogers)	Mrs M. Cahill	Noel Meade	9/2
1993 JOEY KELLY (C. O'Dwyer)	Stephen A. O'Hara	William Rock	8/1
1994 BOBBY SOCKS (P.J. McLoughlin)	Risk Factor Partnership	R. Lee (GB)	7/1
1995 VITAL TRIX (C. O'Dwyer)	Thomas Matthews	Thomas Matthews	5/1
1996 BEET STATEMENT (T.J. Mitchell)	W.M. Sheehy	W.T. Murphy	16/1
1997 BROWNRATH KING (G. Cotter)	P.J. Lohan	Owen Weldon	20/1
1998 TREBLE BOB (A. Maguire)	Michael W.J. Smurfit	D.K. Weld	11/2
1999 MARTY'S STEP (G. Cotter)	Joseph Kinsella	Michael McCullagh	20/1
2000 COLM'S ROCK (R. Walsh)	R. Finnegan	Miss F.M. Crowley	11/1
2001 PRINCE OF PLEASURE (B.M. Cash)	Home & Dry Syndicate	D. Broad	10/1
2002 RIGHT 'N' ROYAL (G.T. Hutchinson)	Mrs Fiona O'Connor	M.J. O'Connor	16/1
2003 BLITZY BOY (D.J. Casey)	G.T. Lynch	G.T. Lynch	12/1
2004 ALEXANDER FOURBALL (D.J. Howard)	Mrs A.L.T. Moore	A.L.T. Moore	10/1
2005 MON OISEAU (P.A. Carberry)	Mrs A. Dunlop	A.L.T. Moore	8/1
2006 HALF BARRELL (N.P. Madden)	V.T. O'Brien	V.T. O'Brien	16/1
2007 BARREGARROW (D.J. Condon)	Mrs S. Neville	Seamus Neville	14/1

Distance:	3 miles (1894–1939)
	2 miles 5 furlongs (1940–91)
	2 miles 6 furlongs (1992–2007)
Conditions:	Chase 1894–1917
	Handicap Chase 1918–2007
Race Title:	Oranmore Dairies Freshmilk 1992 and 1993
	Low Low Galway Blazers 1994–2007

Leading Owner: J.G. Duggan (3)
Leading Trainer: J.W. Osborne (4)
Leading Rider: A. Anthony, D.L. Moore, P. Taaffe, C. Finnegan and C. O'Dwyer (3)

Tote Galway Mile Handicap (Listed Race)

Winner	Owner	Trainer	SP
1971 GREEK WATERS (T.P. Burns)	G.M. Bell	P.J. Prendergast	11/5f
1972 RYKER (G. Curran)	B. White	Kevin Prendergast	5/2f
1973 SUPER ANNA (Thomas Murphy)	E. Thornton	C. Grassick	25/1
1974 SWING-A-DING (T. Carmody)	J.J. Maher	John Murphy	8/1
1975 DUNSTAN (C. Roche)	Mrs J. Bingham	P.J. Prendergast	5/2f
1976 PAROLE (R.M. Connolly)	Michael McStay	Michael Connolly	6/1
1977 MOVE ON WAG (Joanna Morgan)	William Fennin	Philip Canty	10/1
1978 READJUST USA (R. Hogan)	R.N. Webster	P. Prendergast Jr	7/1
1979 MAJESTIC NURSE (C. Roche)	G.F. Freyne	C.R. Nelson (GB)	10/1
1980 RARE DUKE (M.P. Dwyer)	J.F. O'Malley	P. Prendergast Jr	12/1
1981 PINCH HITTER (S. Craine)	Brendan Carolan	Noel Meade	20/1
1982 PINCH HITTER (S. Craine)	Brendan Carolan	Noel Meade	6/1
1983 SILVER HEART (P. Braiden)	M.H. Keogh	Francis Dunne	8/1
1984 ASH CREEK (C.F. Swan)	P. Callan	Patrick Mullins	11/2
1985 BONNIE BESS (M.J. Kinane)	Mrs W. Whitehead	D.K. Weld	6/4f
1986 ALDER ROSE (D. Gillespie)	G. Cotter	M.J. Grassick	20/1
1987 DROMOD HILL (S. Craine)	Mrs P.J. Carr	Noel Meade	3/1f
1988 PHEOPOTSTOWN (N.G. McCullagh)	Mrs G. Robinson	Patrick Mullins	12/1
1989 POPULAR GLEN (M.J. Kinane)	Michael W.J. Smurfit	D.K. Weld	6/1
1990 MUDARRIS USA (R.M. Burke)	Hamdan Al Maktoum	Kevin Prendergast	14/1
1991 COMMITTED DANCER USA (M.J. Kinane)	Allen E. Paulson	D.K. Weld	14/1
1992 SALMON EILE (J.P. Murtagh)	Mrs M.C. O'Connor	P.J. Flynn	10/1
1993 BE MY HOPE (N.G. McCullagh)	K.M. Griffin	David Hanley	16/1
1994 SAIBOT USA (J.F. Egan)	Michael W.J. Smurfit	D.K. Weld	9/4f
1995 TIMARIDA (C. Roche)	HH Aga Khan IV	J.M. Oxx	11/4f
1996 PRO TRADER USA (M.J. Kinane)	J.D. Gunther	D.K. Weld	7/1
1997 WRAY (S. Craine)	B. Cunningham	Liam Browne	8/1
1998 FREE TO SPEAK (M.J. Kinane)	Moyglare Stud Farm	D.K. Weld	14/1
1999 TIGER SHARK USA (K.J. Manning)	Henryk de Kwiatkowski	J.S. Bolger	6/1f
2000 TUSHNA (T.P. Queally)	D.H.W. Dobson	J.S. Bolger	16/1
2001 SHEER TENBY (C. O'Donoghue)	Halfway House Syndicate	P.A. Roche	20/1
2002 VINTHEA (T.M. Houlihan)	Colman O'Flynn	J.G. Burns	8/1
2003 ELKIM (D.P. McDonogh)	Hamdan Al Maktoum	Kevin Prendergast	10/1

Winner	Owner	Trainer	SP
2004 PALACE STAR (R.P. Cleary)	Seamus Murphy	Peter Casey	7/1
2005 LATINO MAGIC (R.M. Burke)	Mrs P.D. Osborne	R.S. Osborne	9/1
2006 QUINMASTER (J.P. Murtagh)	William Durkan	Michael Halford	8/1
2007 INCLINE (D.J. Moran)	Paul Crossan	R. McGlinchey	25/1

Distance: 1 mile 100 yards
Conditions: Three-year-old and upwards
Race Title: Thomas McDonogh & Sons Ltd Handicap (1971–9)
                  McDonogh Handicap (1980–2005)
                  The Tote Galway Mile Handicap 2006–07
Leading Owner: Brendan Carolan (2)
Leading Trainer: D.K. Weld (5)
Leading Rider: M.J. Kinane (5)

GPT Access Equipment EBF

Winner	Owner	Trainer	SP
1971 MASTER ALBERT (J.V. Smith)	Gordon McGarrey	C.L. Weld	7/4
1972 KLAIRVIMY (J.V. Smith)	Mrs B.E. Allen-Jones	D.K. Weld	3/1
1973 LORD OF THE MARK (R.F. Parnell)	E. Martin-Smith	D.K. Weld	11/8f
1974 Race abandoned			
1975 PADDY BOULER (J. Corr)	P. Rooney	Michael Kauntze	5/1
1976 Div I INDEPENDENT MISS (J.V. Smith)	Mrs T.R. Davies	P.V. Doyle	5/2
Div II WELSH STEEL (W. Swinburn)	Mrs Cyril Parke	Michael Kauntze	25/1
1977 DIAMONDS ARE TRUMP (W. Swinburn)	Bertram R. Firestone	D.K. Weld	1/1f
1978 MAGIC NORTH (M.J. Kinane)	Comte A. de Laubespin	Michael Kauntze	7/1
1979 LORD GREEN (D. Gillespie)	Robert J. Downes	J.S. Bolger	6/1
1980 WHAT A RIOT (C. Roche)	James Comerford	Liam Browne	9/1
1981 GREAT IMAGE (D. Hogan)	Arthur L. Suite	C. Grassick	25/1
1982 STRONG DOLLAR (W. Swinburn)	Walter Haefner	D.K. Weld	7/4f
1983 HEAVENLY PLAIN (G. McGrath)	Lady Clague	Patrick Prendergast	5/1
1984 KAMAKURA (M.J. Kinane)	Bertram R. Firestone	D.K. Weld	4/6f
1985 INISHEER (M.J. Kinane)	Bertram R. Firestone	D.K. Weld	5/4f
1986 DERBY KELLY (S. Martinez)	Edwin K. Cleveland	P.V. Doyle	5/1
1987 KIICHI (M.J. Kinane)	Allen E. Paulson	D.K. Weld	1/1f
1988 KIRLA (M.J. Kinane)	Allen E. Paulson	D.K. Weld	7/4f
1989 GO AND GO (M.J. Kinane)	Moyglare Stud Farm	D.K. Weld	1/1f
1990 GOLDEN MINTAGE (M.J. Kinane)	Yoshiki Akazawa	D.K. Weld	1/1f
1991 LEGAL PRESSURE (M.J. Kinane)	Moyglare Stud Farm	D.K. Weld	4/6f
1992 ARABIC TREASURE (M.J. Kinane)	Raymond J. Rooney	D.K. Weld	1/2f
1993 MUSICAL INSIGHT (J.P. Murtagh)	Lady Clague	J.M. Oxx	9/4
1994 UNION DECREE (M.J. Kinane)	Moyglare Stud Farm	D.K. Weld	3/1
1995 APACHE TWIST (J.A. Heffernan)	J. Monaghan	J.S. Bolger	9/2
1996 CASEY TIBBS (M.J. Kinane)	Michael Watt	D.K. Weld	8/15f
1997 PELAGIUS (J.P. Murtagh)	Lady Clague	J.M. Oxx	9/1
1998 WINDWARD ROCK (J.P. Murtagh)	Sheikh Mohammed	J.M. Oxx	5/2
1999 ARISTOTLE (M.J. Kinane)	Mrs John Magnier	A.P. O'Brien	4/5f
2000 HEMINGWAY (M.J. Kinane)	Michael Tabor	A.P. O'Brien	2/7f
2001 SIGHTS ON GOLD (P.J. Smullen)	Moyglare Stud Farm	D.K. Weld	1/1f
2002 ABUNAWWAS (D.P. McDonogh)	Hamdan Al Maktoum	Kevin Prendergast	13/2
2003 GREY SWALLOW (P.J. Smullen)	Mrs Rochelle Quinn	D.K. Weld	11/8

2004 DEFI (D.P. McDonogh)	Lady O'Reilly	Kevin Prendergast	5/1
2005 SANDTON CITY (J.P. Murtagh)	Mrs Mary J. Walshe	Francis Ennis	5/2f
2006 FLEETING SHADOW (P.J. Smullen)	Dr R. Lambe	D.K. Weld	11/8f
2007 LUCIFER SAM (K. Fallon)	Mrs John Magnier	A.P. O'Brien	3/1

Distance: 7 furlongs
Conditions: Two-year-old maiden
Race Title: Athenry (1971–86)
              GPT Dublin (1987–9)
              GPT Industrial Properties (1990–2000)
              GPT Access Equipment (2001–07)
Leading Owner: Moyglare Stud Farm (4)
Leading Trainer: D.K. Weld (17)
Leading Rider: M. J. Kinane (13)

Leading Owners, Trainers and Riders at the Galway Festival

Contenders must have more than one winner at the meeting to qualify. Non-festival meetings do not count.

Year (Races)	Owner	Trainer	Rider
1869 (8)	John Ussher (3)		Richard Bell (2)
1870 (10)	Garrett Moore (2)		Mr G. Moore (4)
1871 (11)	H. Blake (2)		James Murphy (2)
1872 (11)	R. Newcomen (2)		'Mr St James' (2)
			Robert Murphy (2)
1873 (11)	Lord Howth (2)		Mr G. Moore (2)
1874 (10)	R.H. Long (2)		Mr T. Beasley (2)
	J.D. Whyte (2)		George Gray (2)
1875 (9)	Mr Apleton (2)		Thomas Ryan (2)
1876 (9)	P.J. Russell (2)		Mr T. Beasley (3)
1877 (10)	Mr Thornhill (2)	J. Monaghan (2)	
		R. Murphy (2)	
1878 (10)			Mr T. Beasley (2)
1879 (10)	Mr Hartigan (2)	T. Connolly (2)	Mr J. Beasley (2)
	M.B. Joyce (2)		
1880 (10)	Charles J. Blake (3)	James Dunne (3)	
1881 (10)	Henry E. Linde (2)	H.E. Linde (2)	Mr T. Beasley (2)
	Charles J. Blake (2)	James Dunne (2)	J. Callaghan (2)
1882 (10)	P. Wall (2)	Michael Dennehy (3)	Mr W. Beasley (2)
1883 (10)	Capt. Boycott (2)	James Dunne (3)	Thomas Harris (2)
1884 (11)	T. Andrews (3)	F.F. and W.P. Cullen (2)	
1885 (10)	Charles J. Blake (2)	F.F. and W.P. Cullen (2)	Mr W.P. Cullen (3)
		M.A. Maher (2)	
1886 (10)	Capt. St Lawrence (2)	D. Broderick (2)	Saunders (2)
		James Dunne (2)	
1887 (10)	J. Brabazon (2)		Mr R. Brabazon (3)
1888 (11)	J.A. Cassidy (2)	H. Beasley (2)	Terence Kavanagh (3)
	John Gubbins (2)	T. Broderick (2)	
		H.E. Linde (2)	

Year (Races)	Owner	Trainer	Rider
1889 (10)	Andrew Tiernan (2) Colonel Thomson (2)	Frederick F. Cullen (6)	J. Foster (3)
1890 (10)		Frederick F. Cullen (4)	Lawrence Ryan (1½)
1891 (10)	Andrew Tiernan (2)	Frederick F. Cullen (3)	Mr William Beasley (2) J. Doyle (2)
1892 (10)	Charles J. Blake (2)	Thomas Harris (2)	Thomas Harris (2) J. Dunne (2)
1893 (10)			William Taylor (2) Mr Leonard Sheil (2)
1894 (10)	Mr Williams (2) E. Shaw (2)	C. Perkins (2) Michael Dawson (2)	
1895 (11)	M. Spain (2) R. Richards (2)		
1896 (10)	R.C. Dawson (2)	Brian O'Donnell (2) William P. Cullen (2)	
1897 (10)		Leonard Sheil (2) William P. Cullen (2)	Thomas Fiely (2)
1898 (10)	Frederick F. Cullen (2) W. Jackson (2) O. Mosley (2)	Robert Exshaw (2) Michael Dawson (2) William P. Cullen (2)	Charles Hogan (2) Mr O. Mosley (2)
1899 (10)	William P. Cullen (2)	Frederick F. Cullen (3)	Thomas Moran (3)
1900 (10)	William P. Cullen (2)	William P. Cullen (2)	
1901 (10)	Mrs Joseph Widger (2)	Frederick F. Cullen (3) Denis Shanahan (3) J.J. Parkinson (3)	Mr H. Nuttall (2)
1902 (10)	John Doyle (2)	Denis Shanahan (4)	Mr H. Nuttall (2)
1903 (11)	Michael Dawson (2)	Mr H.S. Persse (2) Denis Shanahan (2)	
1904 (10)	W.A. Byrne (2)	J.J. Parkinson (2) Michael Dawson (2) Capt. R.H. Dewhurst (2)	John Thompson (2) Patrick Cowley (2)
1905 (10)		Michael Dawson (2)	John Thompson (2)
1906 (10)		J.J. Parkinson (3)	John Thompson (2)
1907 (10)		Lawrence Hope (2) J.J. Parkinson (2)	John Thompson (3)
1908 (10)	J.C. Lyons (2)	P.F. Hartigan (2) Maxwell Arnott (2)	M. Colbert (2)
1909 (11)		Michael Dawson (3)	Mr J. Manley (2) John Thompson (2)
1910 (12)	Baron F. de Tuyll (2)	Maxwell Arnott (4)	George Brown (3)
1911 (12)		Henry I. Ussher (2) Maxwell Arnott (2)	Edward Lawn (2) Mr H.I. Ussher (2) George Brown (2)
1912 (12)	Patrick Cullinan (2)	Maxwell Arnott (2) James Dunne (2) Batt Kirby (2)	E. Houlihan (2) John Doyle (2)

Year (Races)	Owner	Trainer	Rider
1913 (12)		Michael Dawson (3)	Joseph Canty (2)
			Francis Morgan (2)
1914 (12)		W.A. Ussher (2)	Joseph Canty (2)
		Michael Dawson (2)	John Doyle (2)
			Francis Morgan (2)
1915 (12)	Hubert M. Hartigan (2)	Ronald Moss (3)	Mr W.J. Parkinson (3)
1916 (12)	Mrs R.P. Croft (2)	R.H. Walker (3)	F. Dainty (2)
		R.G. Cleary (3)	Mr H.S. Harrison (2)
			E. Houlihan (2)
1917 (13)		Maxwell Arnott (2)	Clyde Aylin (2)
		Philip Behan (2)	Mr L.L. Firth (2)
1918 (14)	Lord Savile (2)	Maxwell Arnott (2)	Francis Morgan (2)
			W. Barrett (2)
1919 (12)		R.H. Walker (2)	Joseph Canty (2)
		Michael Dawson (2)	Michael Beary (2)
1920 (12)	Mrs R.P. Croft (3)	H.I. Ussher (5)	J. Hogan Jr (4)
1921 (12)	Colonel R.P. Croft (2)	H.I. Ussher (4)	F. Wootton (3)
1922	Meeting Abandoned		
1923 (12)		H.I. Ussher (4)	J. Moylan (2)
			J. Hogan Jr (2)
			T. Burns (2)
			F.B. Rees (2)
1924 (12)		Maxwell Arnott (3)	D. Ward (3)
1925 (12)	Mrs R.P. Croft (2)	Cecil Brabazon (2)	C. Donnelly (2)
		H.I. Ussher (2)	J. Hogan Jr (2)
		J.J. Parkinson (2)	K. Lenehan (2)
1926 (12)	Maxwell Arnott (2)	Maxwell Arnott (2)	Joseph Canty (2)
		Alfred Bickley (2)	E. Foster (2)
1927 (12)	Mrs R.P. Croft (2)	H.I. Ussher (5)	J. Moylan (2)
			D. Ward (2)
			W. Beasley (2)
1928 (10)	J.S. Shepherd (2)	Maxwell Arnott (3)	D. Ward (2)
			J. Moylan (2)
1929 (12)	M. Maccabe (2)	Joseph Dawson (2)	Joseph Canty (2)
		Maxwell Arnott (2)	E.M. Quirke (2)
		J.J. Parkinson (2)	
1930 (12)		Maxwell Arnott (5)	Joseph Canty (3)
1931 (12)		H.I. Ussher (3)	J. Moylan (3)
1932 (12)	N. Kelly (2)	J.A. Mangan (2)	Mr F.E. McKeever (2)
			Mr R.H. Stern (2)
1933 (12)	E.M. O'Meara (2)	H.I. Ussher (2)	Mr F.W. McKeever (3)
		E.T. O'Meara (2)	
1934 (12)		H.I. Ussher (3)	W.T. O'Grady (2)
1935 (12)	Joseph McGrath (2)	H.I. Ussher (3)	W.T. O'Grady (4)
1936 (12)	J.A. Mangan (2)	E.T. O'Meara (3)	L.C. Keating (2)
	Mrs L. Carroll (2)		

Year (Races)	Owner	Trainer	Rider
1937 (12)	J.A. Mangan (2)	J.A. Mangan (2)	
1938 (12)	Miss M. Wallace (2)	P. Molony (2)	D. Butchers (2)
		J.J. Parkinson (2)	W. Howard (2)
		Edward Delany (2)	
		R. Wallace (2)	
1939 (12)	Mrs E. McGrath (2)	J.J. Parkinson (5)	M. Wing (2)
	Michael McDonough (2)		T. Hyde (2)
1940 (12)	Mrs E. McGrath (3)	J.J. Parkinson (4)	M. Wing (3)
1941 (12)		Cecil Brabazon (2)	J. Brogan (2)
1942 (14)	Miss Dorothy Paget (3)	C.A. Rogers (3)	D.L. Moore (3)
1943 (14)		W.J. Byrne (2)	G.H. Wells (3)
		C.A. Rogers (2)	
		John Kirwan (2)	
1944 (14)	Miss Dorothy Paget (3)	C.A. Rogers (4)	D.L. Moore (2)
	W. Barry (3)		Joseph Canty (2)
1945 (14)		R. O'Connell (2)	D. Morgan (3)
		H.I. Ussher (2)	
		R. Fetherstonhaugh (2)	
		C. Brabazon (2)	
1946 (12)	Richard McIlhagga (3)	Bernard Nugent (4)	T. Burns (2)
1947 (12)	W. Noble (2)	Bernard Nugent (4)	J. Brogan (2)
	P. King (2)		M. Molony (2)
1948 (12)		George Robinson (2)	T. Molony (2)
			M. Gordon (2)
			James Eddery (2)
1949 (12)	C. Lawless (2)	C. Lawless (2)	
1950 (12)		Cecil Brabazon (2)	M. Molony (4)
1951 (12)			
1952 (12)		Joseph W. Osborne (2)	P. Taaffe (3)
1953 (12)	Mrs B.M. Lawlor (2)	Thomas J. Taaffe (3)	P. Taaffe (3)
	J.J. Roche (2)		
1954 (12)		Daniel L. Moore (2½)	P.J. Doyle (2)
			L. Ward (2)
1955 (12)		George H. Wells (2)	L. Ward (2)
		Daniel L. Moore (2)	
1956 (12)	Mrs R. More O'Ferrall (2)	Patrick Sleator (3)	N. Brennan (4)
1957 (12)	Mrs E.F. Carroll (2)	Patrick Sleator (2)	G.W. Robinson (3)
		Clement Magnier (2)	
1958 (12)	Charles MCarthy (2)	Patrick Sleator (3)	H.R. Beasley (3)
1959 (18)	A.F. McNeill (2)	C. McCartan Jr (3)	C. Finnegan (3)
	J.A. Hale (2)		
	Duchess of Westminster (2)		
1960 (18)		Michael Connolly (2)	G.W. Robinson (3)
1961 (18)	Mrs K.L. Urquhart (2)	Patrick Sleator (5)	H.R. Beasley (3)

Year (Races)	Owner	Trainer	Rider
1962 (18)		Daniel L. Moore (2)	L. McLoughlin (2)
		John Cox (2)	P. Powell Jr (2)
			John J. Rafferty (2)
			T.P. Burns (2)
1963 (18)	Mrs S.E. Gurry (2)	G.H. Wells (3)	L. Ward (2)
	H.S. Rubin (2)	Con Collins (3)	P. Taaffe (2)
1964 (18)	Mrs M.E. Whitney-Tippett (2)		
	Mrs M. Egan (2)	Clement Magnier (3)	G. Griffin (2)
1965 (18)		Kevin Bell (2)	P. Powell Jr (2)
1966 (18)		Thomas Burns (2)	Mr C. Ronaldson (2)
		Thomas W. Dreaper (2)	
		John Cox (2)	
1967 (18)		Clement Magnier (2)	T.S. Murphy (2)
		Patrick Sleator (2)	
1968 (18)	Mrs B.J. Eastwood (2)	Edward Mahon (2)	J. Roe (3)
		Thomas Costello (2)	
		John Cox (2)	
1969 (18)	Joseph Crowley (2)	Michael Connolly (3)	
1970 (18)	T.H. Moore (2)	A. Watson (3)	Thomas Murphy (2)
1971 (24)	Lady Honor Svejdar (2)	Kevin Prendergast (3)	T.P. Burns (3)
1972 (24)		Michael A. O'Toole (3)	P. Sullivan (3)
			Thomas Murphy (3)
1973 (24)	Arthur McCashin (2)	Michael A. O'Toole (3)	Mr D.K. Weld (2)
			D.T. Hughes (2)
			P. Black (2)
			J. Corr (2)
1974 (21)		John Murphy (3)	T. Carmody (5)
1975 (30)	Colonel Sir Douglas Clague (4)	Patrick Mullins (5)	J. Roe (3)
		Clement Magnier (5)	R. Carroll (3)
			R.F. Parnell (3)
1976 (31)		Patrick Mullins (4)	S. Treacy (3)
1977 (30)	P. Rooney (2)	Dermot K. Weld (5)	W. Swinburn (5)
1978 (30)	Mrs Brian Kearney (5)	Dermot K. Weld (7)	W. Swinburn (5)
1979 (30)	C.A.B. St George (2)	Edward J. O'Grady (4)	C. Roche (3)
	William Fennin (2)		
1980 (30)	Mrs Brian Kearney (2)	Noel Meade (5)	S. Craine (3)
	P.J. Moran (2)		C. Roche (3)
	Dr Herbert Schnapka (2)		
	J.F. O'Malley (2)		
1981 (32)	M. Soudavar (3)	Dermot K. Weld (6)	W. Swinburn (5)
1982 (36)	Denis Fitzgerald (2)	Noel Meade (6)	S. Craine (5)
	Brendan Carolan (2)		
	P.G. Carroll (2)		
	Dan McCaffrey (2)		
	N. Kavanagh (2)		
	Austin Delaney (2)		

Year (Races)	Owner	Trainer	Rider
1983 (36)	Robert E. Sangster (2)	Dermot K. Weld (5)	D. Manning (4)
	Lady Clague (2)	Noel Meade (5)	
	Anthony N. Durkan (2)		
1984 (36)	Bertram R. Firestone (3)	Noel Meade (6)	M.J. Kinane (6)
1985 (39)	Bertram R. Firestone (3)	Dermot K. Weld (9)	M.J. Kinane (6)
1986 (40)	Maurice Bergl (2)	Michael Connolly (4)	C. Roche (5)
	Turform Ltd (2)		T. Carmody (5)
	C. Mitchell (2)		
1987 (40)	Allen E. Paulson (2)	Noel Meade (5)	S. Craine (6)
	Mrs M.A. O'Toole (2)		
	Miss Una Bolger (2)		
	Robert Burke (2)		
	Fernando Jaconelli (2)		
1988 (40)	Allen E. Paulson (2)	Dermot K. Weld (3)	M.J. Kinane (3)
	Mrs J.B. McGowan (2)	Frank Dunne (3)	C. O'Dwyer (3)
	Frank Dunne (2)		
	Martin Dunne (2)		
	T. Donohue (2)		
1989 (41)	Moyglare Stud Farm (2)	Dermot K. Weld (5)	S. Craine (5)
	Michael W.J. Smurfit (2)		
	Mrs A. Keane (2)		
	Mrs Patrick Prendergast (2)		
1990 (42)	John J. McLoughlin (3)	Dermot K. Weld (9)	M.J. Kinane (7)
1991 (42)	Moyglare Stud Farm (3)	Dermot K. Weld (9)	M.J. Kinane (6)
	Joseph Crowley (3)		
1992 (42)	Michael W.J. Smurfit (2)	Noel Meade (5)	M.J. Kinane (5)
		Dermot K. Weld (5)	
1993 (42)	Michael W.J. Smurfit (3)	Dermot K. Weld (10)	M.J. Kinane (8)
1994 (42)	Michael W.J. Smurfit (4)	Dermot K. Weld (10)	M.J. Kinane (6)
1995 (42)	Moyglare Stud Farm (2)	Aidan P. O'Brien (5)	J.P. Murtagh (5)
	Maktoum Al Maktoum (2)	Dermot K. Weld (5)	
	Mrs Theresa McCoubrey (2)		
1996 (42)	John P. McManus (2)	Dermot K. Weld (9)	M.J. Kinane (7)
	Michael Watt (2)		
	Sheikh Mohammed (2)		
	Mrs M. Mangan (2)		
	Yoshiki Akazawa (2)		
	Jeremiah J. King (2)		
1997 (42)	Mrs A.M. O'Brien (2)	Aidan P. O'Brien (8)	C. Roche (5)
1998 (44)	Michael W.J. Smurfit (3)	Dermot K. Weld (10)	M.J. Kinane (5)
1999 (52)	Mrs John Magnier (4)	Dermot K. Weld (8)	P.J. Smullen (6)
			M.J. Kinane (6)

Year (Races)	Owner	Trainer	Rider
2000 (51)	Moyglare Stud Farm (2) Michael Tabor (2) Mark Barrett (2) Michael Watt (2) Mrs Paul Shanahan (2) Anne Backer Synd (2)	Dermot K. Weld (9)	N. Williamson (4)
2001 (52)	John P. McManus (5)	Dermot K. Weld (10)	P.J. Smullen (6)
2002 (51)	John P. McManus (4)	Michael Hourigan (4)	Paul Carberry (4)
2003 (51)	Hamdan Al Maktoum (3)	Kevin Prendergast (4) Dermot K. Weld (4)	M.J. Kinane (4) P.J. Smullen (4)
2004 (51)	Mrs John Magnier (4)	Dermot K. Weld (6)	R.P. Cleary (3) J.P. Spencer (3) R. Walsh (3) J. Culloty (3) M.J. Kinane (3) Mr M.V. Magnier (3)
2005 (51)	Moyglare Stud Farm (2) J.P. O'Shea (2) Patrick Tallis (2)	Dermot K. Weld (8)	F.M. Berry (5)
2006 (51)	John P. McManus (3)	Dermot K. Weld (7)	R. Walsh (5) D.P. McDonogh (5) D.J. Condon (5)
2007 (51)	Moyglare Stud Farm (3)	Dermot K. Weld (6)	P.J. Smullen (6)

Number of Festival Titles

* denotes a share of the honour.

Owners

6	Mrs R.P. Croft	1911, 1916, 1920, 1923*, 1925 & 1927.
6	J.A. Mangan	1930*, 1931*, 1934*, 1936*, 1937 & 1943.
6	Dorothy Paget	1941*, 1942, 1944*, 1945*, 1950* & 1952*.
5	Charles J. Blake	1873*, 1880, 1881*, 1885 & 1892.
5	Michael W.J. Smurfit	1989*, 1992, 1993, 1994 & 1998.
6	Moyglare Stud Farm	1989*, 1991*, 1995*, 2000*, 2005* & 2007.

Trainers

23	Dermot K. Weld	1977, 1978, 1981, 1983*, 1985, 1988*, 1989, 1990, 1991, 1992*, 1993, 1994, 1995*, 1996, 1998, 1999, 2000, 2001, 2003*, 2004, 2005, 2006 & 2007.
12	Maxwell Arnott	1904*, 1908*, 1910, 1911*, 1912*, 1917*, 1918, 1924, 1926*, 1928, 1929* & 1930.
11	Henry I. Ussher	1911*, 1920, 1921, 1923, 1925*, 1927, 1931, 1933*, 1934, 1935 & 1945*.
9	Michael Dawson	1894*, 1898*, 1903*, 1904*, 1905, 1909, 1913, 1914* & 1919*.
9	James J. Parkinson	1901*, 1904*, 1906, 1907*, 1925*, 1929*, 1938*, 1939 & 1940.
9	Frederick F. Cullen	1884*, 1885, 1887*, 1889, 1890, 1891, 1893*, 1899 & 1901*.
8	William P. Cullen	1884, 1885, 1893*, 1895, 1896*, 1897*, 1898* & 1900.
6	Noel Meade	1980, 1982, 1983*, 1984, 1987 & 1992*.

Riders

13	Michael J. Kinane	1984, 1985, 1988*, 1990, 1991, 1992, 1993, 1994, 1996, 1998, 1999*, 2003* & 2004*.
8	Joseph Canty	1913*, 1914*, 1919*, 1926*, 1929*, 1930, 1944* & 1949*.
5	John Thompson	1904*, 1905, 1906, 1907 & 1909*.
4	Mr Thomas Beasley	1874*, 1876, 1878 & 1881*.
4	John Moylan	1923*, 1927*, 1928* & 1931.
4	Stephen Craine	1980*, 1982, 1987 & 1989.
4	Christopher Roche	1979, 1980*, 1986* & 1997.
4	Patrick J. Smullen	1999*, 2001, 2003* & 2007.

Office Holders and Members of the Galway Race Committee

Chairmen

Martin McDonogh 1907–34
Joseph S. Young 1935–58
Joseph Costello 1959
Thomas McDermott Kelly 1960–69
Lord Killanin 1970–85
Patrick D. Ryan 1986– 91
Lord Hemphill 1992– 96
Thomas McDonogh 1997–2000
John D. Coyle 2001–04
Raymond J. Rooney 2005 –

Secretaries/Managers

George Mack to 1917
Martin Thomas Donnellan 1918–38
Joseph Gavin 1939– c.1949
Comdt. Patrick Canavan c.1950–70
Capt. Luke Mullins 1971–88
John Moloney 1989–

Members of the Committee
(Elected since 1945)

Peter Allen 1999–
W.B. Allen 1980–99
J. Brennan 1975–87   Died 6 November 1987
Gerald I. Corbett 1952–75
John D. Coyle 1975–
T.J. Cunningham 1990–
Colm Gavin 1990–
Lord Hemphill 1959–2004
Joseph Higgins 2005–
Dr Conal Kavanagh 2005–
R. Kelly 1967–99   Died 16 November 2005

Lord Killanin 1947–99   Died 25 April 1999
Thomas McDonogh 1959–2004
Tom A. McDonogh 2004–
Brigadier E.R. Mahony 1952–78
Jerome Mahony 1980–2001   Died 25 January 2001
Gerald D. Naughton 1945–80
Timothy I. Naughton 1980–
Colm O'Flaherty 2001–
P. O'Flaherty 1967–89   Died 11 March 1989
Raymond J. Rooney 1975–
Anthony Ryan 1999–
Patrick D. Ryan 1959–99   Died 12 April 2004

Significant Dates

1869 Inaugural meeting held at Ballybrit over two days (Monday and Tuesday, 17 and 18 August).

1870 Last time a race run in heats: Renmore Plate (10 furlongs flat) Fontenoy won both heats.

1871 Meeting run on Wednesday and Thursday for the first time.
First handicap run at the meeting – the Galway Handicap Steeplechase Plate.
Last time a race was restricted to half-breds: Renmore Plate (10f Flat) won by Fanny.
First dead-heat: Queen Scotia and Banshee in the Western Hunt Chase.

1872 First disqualification: The Lad (George Gray) in the Forster Street Chase.

1873 First race run over 5 furlongs: Flying Plate won by Crust (Francis Wynne)

1876 Meeting run first week in August for the first time.

1877 The first hurdle race run: Bushy Park Handicap Hurdle (12 furlongs) won by Thirsk.

1878 The Inny disqualified after finishing first past the post in the Galway Hurdle.

1879 A Royal Plate is run at Galway for the first time.

1881 Mr Tommy Beasley is the leading rider at the meeting for the fourth time.

1882 The English crack gentleman rider, Roddy Owen, rides at the meeting.

1883 Captain Boycott's Butte des Morts wins twice at the meeting.

1884 Meeting held four week earlier than usual (1 and 2 July)

1885 Meeting held 30 June and 1 July. The Irish Derby winner St Kevin wins on successive days – the Renmore Handcap (1 mile flat) and walked over for the King's Plate.

1886 Meeting held 7 and 8 July.

1887 After three years the meeting moves back to the first week in August.
The last time a 5-furlong race is run at Galway.

1889 Frederick F. Cullen trained the winner of all five races (second day – 8 August)

1890 New stand built.

1892 Charles Blake is the leading owner at the meeting for the fifth time.

1895 Last race for ponies run: The Ladies' Flat Race won by W.P. Odlum's Meelick.

1897 Last run-off after a dead-heat: Red Ray beat Trueno.

1900 Ashstick, owned by Bertha Dewhurst, wife of Bob the trainer, is the first winner owned by a woman.

1902 Tipperary Boy wins the Galway Plate for a record third time.
The last time a 6-furlong race is run at Galway.

1904 The Inspector of Courses issues a warning to all racecourses.

1907 The future English Champion Jockey, Steve Donoghue, rides a winner.

1909 Nine furlong shoot course used for the first and only time.
John Thompson is the leading rider at the meeting for the fifth time and wins his fifth, and last, King's Plate.

1913   Galway Handicap Hurdle first run: won by Red Damsel.

1914   Patrick Cullinan's Royal Hackle II wins the King's Plate at odds of 25 to 1 on. It is trainer 'Fairy' Dunne's record ninth winner of the race.

1916   Reggie Walker trains the winners of both the Plate and the Hurdle.

1917   A seven-race programme is run for first time.

1918   Seven races run on both days.

1922   Meeting abandoned.

1923   The Tuam meeting moves to the Friday of Galway Race week.

1925   The jockey and trainer, Charlie Donnelly and Cecil Brabazon, win both the Plate and the Hurdle.

1926   Blancona wins the Hurdle, having won the Plate the previous year.

1927   Pansy Croft is the leading owner at the meeting for the sixth time.

1928   The Mervue Plate has to be declared void because there are no runners.

1929   The first modern-style bumper is run at Galway: Moyode Plate over 2½ miles.
       Joe Canty wins his fourth Galway Hurdle, a record for a jockey.

1930   The tote is in operation at Galway for the first time.
       Maxie Arnott is the leading trainer at the meeting for the twelfth time.

1937   Owner Edward T. O'Meara has his third Galway Hurdle winner – a race record.

1938   Jockey Don Butchers wins the Plate and the Hurdle.

1940   Owner Colonel Denis Daly wins both the Plate and the Hurdle – the only one to do so in the same year.

1945   Danny Morgan rides the winners of the Plate and the Hurdle.
       Harry Ussher trains his ninth Galway Plate winner, a race record.

1946   The Galway Hurdle winner, Fair Pearl, is subsequently disqualified on a technicality.

1947   Barney Nugent trains the winner of both the Plate and the Hurdle. It is his fourth Galway Hurdle win, a race record, and his third winner in succession.

1948   Tim Molony rides the winners of the Plate and the Hurdle.

1949   Joe Canty is the leading rider at the meeting for the eighth time.

1950   Frankie McKenna rides the winners of the Plate and the Hurdle.

1954   The Quick Snack building is built.

1956   The photo finish operates at Galway for the first time.

1957   Paddy Sleator trains the winners of the Plate and the Hurdle.

1958   Knight Errant emulates Blancona by winning the Hurdle, having won the Plate the previous year.

1959   Meeting extended to three days with the Galway Corinthian the new feature race.

1961   The Player's Navy Cut Amateur Handicap is first run, sponsored by John Player, Dublin.

1963   The meeting is given live television coverage for the first time.
       Bobby Beasley rides his fourth Galway Plate winner – a race record.

1965   The Galway Handicap Hurdle is sponsored for the first time, by Arthur Guinness.

1969   Professional riders threaten to boycott Thursday's card.
       Pat Taaffe rides his fourth winner of the Galway Hurdle to equal Joe Canty's record.
       Galway runs a one-day meeting on 8 September.

1970   The September meeting is extended to two days.

1971   The Festival meeting extended to four days. The Thomas McDonogh Handicap is the feature race on the first day of the meeting.
       The Athenry Stakes, the first race for two-year-olds, is introduced.
       A January fixture is held for the one and only time.
       A one-day meeting in October is held, bringing Galway's fixtures for the year to eight.

1972   Mrs S.R. Morshead rides Top Up into third place in the Galway Blazers Handicap Chase.
The October meeting is extended to two days.
The West Stand is built.

1973   Tuam racecourse is closed. The Galway Festival meeting is extended to five days.
Waterlogging forces the abandonment of the first evening's card after the third race.
Wednesday's card is washed out – run instead of the Friday programme. The Galway Plate is run that day.

1974   All five days of the meeting are run for the first time.

1975   Paddy Sleator trains his ninth Galway Plate winner to equal Harry Ussher's record.

1977   Joanna Morgan becomes the first woman to ride a winner, being successful on Move On Wag.

1979   Edward O'Grady wins both the Plate and the Hurdle – the fifth and last trainer to do so.
Pope John Paul II says mass at Ballybrit attended by a crowd of 250,000.

1979   English-based jockey Jonjo O'Neill wins the Plate and the Hurdle.
The September meeting is extended to three days.

1981   Clem Magnier equals Barney Nugent's record by training his fourth Galway Hurdle winner.

1982   Gillian O'Brien becomes the first woman to train a winner – Askamore.

1984   Joe Byrne is the seventh and last jockey to win the Plate and the Hurdle in the same year.

1991   The restaurant is built.

1993   Dermot Weld trains ten winners at the meeting, including the Galway Plate.
Paddy Mullins trains his fourth winner of the Galway Hurdle, equalling the record.

1994   Big Screen used for the first time at Galway.

1995   Aidan O'Brien wins the first race of the meeting with Allegan. It is his twenty-third consecutive winner on Irish racing days.
Dermot Weld is the leading trainer at the meeting for the thirteenth time.

1999   The New Stand is built.

2004   Ansar wins the Plate, having won the Hurdle in 2001 – only the third horse to win both races.
Michael Kinane in the leading jockey at the meeting for the thirteenth time.
The new weigh room and administration building are built.

2006   Dermot Weld is the leading trainer at the meeting for the twenty-second time.
Construction work on the new West Stand begins.

2007   New Killanin Stand opened.

Notable Records

Galway Plate and Hurdle Double

Owner
1940   Colonel Denis W. Daly – Ring of Gold and Red Shaft

Trainers
1916   Reggie Walker – Never Fear and Elgon
1925   Cecil Brabazon – Blancona and Alroi
1947   Barney Nugent – Charles Edward and Point D'Atout
1957   Paddy Sleator – Knight Errant and Tymon Castle
1979   Edward O'Grady – Hindhope and Hard Tarquin

Riders
1925   Charlie Donnelly – Blancona and Alroi
1938   Don Butchers – Symaethis and Serpolette
1945   Danny Morgan – Grecian Victory and King of the Jungle
1948   Tim Molony – Silent Prayer and Carrantrylla
1950   Frankie McKenna – Derrinstown and Lady's Find
1979   Jonjo O'Neill – Hindhope and Hard Tarquin
1984   Joe Byrne – Master Player and Tara Lee

Horses Winning Both Races
Blancona   Plate 1925 and Hurdle 1926
Knight Errant   Plate 1957 and Hurdle 1958
Ansar   Plate 2004 and 2005 and Hurdle 2001

Galway Plate
Tipperary Boy   1899, 1901 and 1902
Clonsheever   1923 and 1924
East Galway   1928 and 1930
Swindon Glory   1943 and 1944
Amber Point   1954 and 1956
Ross Sea   1964 and 1965
Royal Day   1967 and 1969

Life of a Lord   1995 and 1996
Ansar   2004 and 2005

Galway Hurdle
Knuckleduster   1932 and 1933
King of the Jungle   1945 and 1946
Point D'Atout   1942 and 1947
Pinch Hitter   1982 and 1983

Bibliography

Abelson, Edward and Tyrrel, John, *The Breedon Book of Horse Racing Records* (Breedon, 1993)

Beasley, Bobby, *Second Start* (W.H. Allen, 1976)

Bird, T.H., *A Hundred Grand Nationals* (Country Life, 1937)

Brabazon, Aubrey, *Racing Through My Mind* (Voto, 1998)

Bull, Phil, *Racehorses of 1951 to Date* (Timeform Annuals)

Clower, Michael, *Mick Kinane: Big Race King* (Mainstream, 1996)

D'Arcy, Fergus A., *Horses, Lords and Racing Men* (Turf Club, 1991)

Darling, Sam, *Reminiscences* (Mills & Boon, 1914)

Donoghue, Steve, *Donoghue Up!* (Collins, 1938)

Green, Reg, *A Race Apart: The History of the Grand National* (Hodder & Stoughton, 1988)

Fairfax-Blakeborough, J., *The Turf Who's Who* (May Fair Press, 1932)

Hyland, Francis P.M., *Taken For A Ride* (Gill & Macmillan, 2006)

Lambton, Hon George, *Men and Horses I Have Known* (Thornton Butterworth, 1924)

Mahon, Jack, *The Galway Races* (Blackwater, 1995)

Mortimer, Roger, Onslow, Richard and Willett, Peter, *Biographical Encyclopaedia of British Flat Racing* (Macdonald & Jane's, 1978)

Mortimer, Richard, *The History of the Derby Stakes* (Michael Joseph, 1973)

O'Leary, Con, *Grand National* (Rockliff, 1945)

O'Neill, Jonjo, *Jonjo: An Autobiography* (Stanley Paul, 1985)

O'Neill, Peter and Boyne, Sean, *Paddy Mullins: The Master of Doninga* (Mainstream, 1995)

Pitt, Chris, *A Long Time Gone* (Portway Press, 1966)

Ramsden, Caroline, *Farewell Manchester* (J.A. Allen, 1966)

Sargent, Harry R., *Thoughts Upon Sport* (Simpkin, Marshall, 1895)

Sloan, Tod, *Tod Sloan by Himself* (Grant Richards, 1915)

Smith, Raymond, *The High Rollers of the Turf* (Sporting Books, 1992)

Smith, Vian, *The Grand National* (Stanley Paul, 1969)

Smyly, Patricia, *Encyclopaedia of Steeplechasing* (Robert Hale, 1979)

Sweeney, Tony and Annie, *The Sweeney Guide to the Irish Turf from 1501 to 2001* (Burke, 2002)

Watson S.J., *Between the Flags* (Allen Figgis, 1969)

Williams, Guy St John and Hyland, Francis P.M., *The Irish Derby, 1866-1979* (J.A. Allen, 1980)

Williams, Guy St John and Hyland, Francis P.M., *Jameson Irish Grand National* (Daletta Press, 1995)

Williams, Guy St John, *The Racing Lodges of the Curragh* (Daletta, 1997)

Williams, Guy St John, *T.P. Burns: A Racing Life* (Hillgate, 2006)